Medieval Art and Architecture after the Middle Ages

Medieval Art and Architecture after the Middle Ages

Edited by

Janet T. Marquardt and Alyce A. Jordan

CAMBRIDGE SCHOLARS
PUBLISHING

Medieval Art and Architecture after the Middle Ages,
Edited by Janet T. Marquardt and Alyce A. Jordan

This book first published 2009. The present binding first published 2011.

Cambridge Scholars Publishing

12 Back Chapman Street, Newcastle upon Tyne, NE6 2XX, UK

British Library Cataloguing in Publication Data
A catalogue record for this book is available from the British Library

ISBN (10): 1-4438-2888-2, ISBN (13): 978-1-4438-2888-8

TABLE OF CONTENTS

PREFACE

While art history usually concentrates its interpretive energies on a work of art's original function and context, most works find the majority of their viewers after the death of their original audience. This anthology looks at the reception of medieval works of art and architecture in the centuries after their creation.

The volume begins with studies of the afterlife of medieval architectural sites. Since the rise of the Picturesque movement in England during the eighteenth century and the creation of a French national patrimony of medieval architecture in the nineteenth, buildings from the Middle Ages have inspired designs steeped in nostalgia for a past time. The Middle Ages came to represent an idyllic notion of pure faith, social order, and rich pageantry to generations of people negotiating the effects of the Enlightenment and continuous bloody revolutions. Unlike the ever popular classical styles associated with Rome and the ancient world, the Romanesque and Gothic styles were associated with the amazing growth of structural technology in Europe. These buildings were also originally designed to market Church power and ideals. Their lofty height conjured equally soaring spiritual effects, and their unabashedly elaborate decoration, complete with gem-like stained glass, offered a sense of luxury and "heavenly" beauty. It should come as no surprise, therefore, that the deterioration of medieval edifices sparked interest in their preservation, renovation, and replication among enthusiasts. Collectors and historians worked to have English and French church structures, which had been damaged as a result of the Dissolution and Revolution, recognized as valuable cultural treasures. Architects were drawn to sketch these medieval buildings, copy them into new designs, and even excavate their remains in order to better reconstruct their original appearances. Numerous papers in this collection chronicle and analyze the ongoing history of medieval architecture through imaginary literary and artistic evocations of their initial usage, practical conservation measures on their physical fabric, and/or referential allusions to them in plans for new buildings evocative of historical design.

Other essays consider medieval objects that survived into the modern period. They look at how works of medieval art have been interpreted since their making, or how particular periods understood, appropriated, and reinvented these works relative to the religious, political, and aesthetic agendas of their own age. These historiographical studies engage multiple disciplines and a variety of methodological approaches from scholars in all fields of medieval studies. Through them, the reader is given a view of the layered levels of meaning medieval objects have accrued and, with it, insight to a culture that has been inaccurately perceived as uniformly Christian and rigidly hierarchical. Probing deeper than commonly understood symbolism, consideration of a medieval work's later adaptation or use allows the reader to follow the changing valorization of medieval art and see how it served public and private interests in the centuries after its original function was ended.

The idea for this collection came from papers presented at two conference sessions held under sponsorship of the International Center of Medieval Art (ICMA). The first, entitled "Debates in the Historiography of Medieval Architecture," Janet Marquardt organized for the annual International Medieval Congress at Leeds University in England, July 2004. Meredith Cohen and Mary Shepard presented early versions of the topics included in this volume, and David Walsh spoke on a related subject. Marquardt and Alyce Jordan organized the second session for the 2006 conference of the Medieval Academy of America in Boston, when the ICMA was invited to prepare a special session in commemoration of its fiftieth anniversary. This latter, entitled "Medieval Art and Architecture after the Middle Ages," included an introduction by Janet Marquardt chronicling art study during the early history of the Medieval Academy, early versions of three essays in this volume by Elizabeth Emery, Laura Morowitz, and Nancy Thompson, as well as one by Peter Fergusson on John Chessel Buckler. Other essays derive from the proposals we received in the phenomenal response to our calls for papers, which we could not accommodate in the above-named sessions, but are delighted to be able to include in this volume.

We are grateful to the ICMA, the Medieval Academy, and the Leeds Congress for the opportunity to organize the interchange of ideas between colleagues with interests similar to ours. We would also like to thank all the authors who contributed to this volume with their essays and by reading each other's work as internal reviewers. In particular, everyone is indebted to the outside readers who so graciously gave their time and expertise to evaluate the submissions and offer wonderful constructive suggestions for improvement. Although remaining anonymous, they will see what an important impact their efforts made in the final versions printed here. Finally, Joe Boles's assistance with editing was priceless.

Janet Marquardt
Alyce Jordan
Fall, 2008

INTRODUCTION

JANET T. MARQUARDT

Of all historical periods, the European Middle Ages must be one of the most imagined and romanticized. Contemporary documentation was prolific, but it was shaped so carefully to reference Antique works or present politically-correct panegyrics, that reading between the lines has left much open to modern reconstruction. It is that process of "making history" out of the memories and monuments that survived which informs these essays. How we understand and appreciate medieval art has been filtered through the lens of time. Our authors attempt to unpack the layers of evidence, theories, and opinions that form each work's provenance. A great deal has been written over the past twenty years deconstructing the scholarship of previous generations in order to show how it has been shaped out of imagination and re-presentation. This process has revealed the extent to which we have hung our notions of history upon objects and monuments which evoke people, motivations, or events, firing our creative interpretations of extant signs in order to form images of a lost world.[1] At the same time, much has been forgotten that did not fit prevailing notions of the past and only the artifacts and monuments which contributed to those notions were preserved.[2] The essays in this anthology address many different ways of understanding the invocation of memory to fashion what we call the Middle Ages. As each successive contribution to art-historical literature adds new information to the imagined medieval past, scholarship creates a multi-dimensional grid of differing viewpoints, attitudes, and motivations for studying historical topics. The result has been termed "cultural memory" since there is no one set of collective memories, but rather, successive stages of history formation that have created layers of mediated cultural memories.[3] We partake in a process of "working memory," the active and constantly shifting practice that we call "remembering."[4]

After the Middle Ages, many chronicles continued to be shaped according to political needs, as **Kerry Boeye** explores in "**Re-Framing Saint-Denis for The Sun King: A Spectacular History**." Designed to encourage Louis XIV's patronage of the famous monastery and royal necropolis, Michel Félibien's lavish *Histoire de l'abbaye royale de Saint-Denys en France*, published in 1706, visually emphasizes how Saint-Denis figured within the history of royal ceremony and the construction of monarchy. Here we also learn that illustrations of medieval objects held in the abbey's treasury later served as the only visual documents of their existence.

Since medieval documents began to be treated as archival sources only during the eighteenth century, their early readers were already well removed from original circumstances.[5] Most of the historical material consists of monastic charters and the religious treatises written by learned medieval scholars. Like objects and monuments, many texts were modified or even destroyed as ideas about religion changed. Thus what we glean from these surviving records towards the understanding of the art and architecture of their day is both biased and meager. We are lucky that some medieval manuscripts were later chosen by powerful figures for their personal collections, thus often giving them a better chance of survival than those stored in religious libraries. A fourteenth-century psalter that was presented to Mary Tudor and thereafter kept in the royal collection is studied by **Anne Stanton** in her essay, "**Queen Mary and her Psalter: A Gothic Manuscript in Tudor England**." Stanton finds that the illustrations of the manuscript, which were tailored to the interests of a medieval owner, remained quite personally relevant to Mary in the sixteenth century.

Human fantasy loves to people the unknown, and the Middle Ages has proven a rich source for imagining colorful characters and dramatic ceremonies. Fanciful kings and queens, knights and armor, wars and processions, are drawn from slim descriptions contained in legal documents, surviving architectural spaces, and the imagery of medieval artists. The reality of that period has been nearly entirely lost, but that has not kept novelists, playwrights, historians, and filmmakers from recreating a romantic world of chivalrous culture, firing spectacular histories of nations and serving as both the foundation and the foil for modern revolutions. Those who write the stories of artistic monuments have decided which would be remembered and how they would figure in importance. They have also chosen which manuscripts would be recopied, thus privileging some over others and letting their own preparation affect the result. **Andrea Worm** studies, for instance, which books were reproduced during the nineteenth century in Germany ("**The Study of Medieval Illuminated Manuscripts in German Scholarship ca. 1750–1850**"). She finds that vernacular texts were of most interest, along with elaborate reproductions of their illustrations.

Another example of how much our imaginations can obscure the past can be found in the treatment of the Bayeux Tapestry. Not a tapestry at all, but rather a long embroidered linen strip, this work got its popular name from first references to it as "La Tapisserie de la Reine Mathilde." Although most likely made in Canterbury, England, it has consistently been considered a French artwork associated with Bayeux Cathedral, in whose city it still resides. **Elizabeth Pastan** investigates the earliest presentations of the scenes from this work of art in "**Montfaucon as Reader of the Bayeux Tapestry**." Bernard de Montfaucon, having seen classicizing drawings of a portion of the story, was led to commission a full set of sketches in the original "primitive" medieval style, much as it was deplored in his day, and in a publication of 1729-1730 tried to reconcile written chronicles of the event with what he saw pictured there.

The power of historians to shape taste cannot be underestimated. Take, for instance, the large number of essays in this very collection that concern medieval French art or architecture. The overwhelming dominance of French topics relative to those engaging other cultures in the proposals that we received for this anthology is reflective of our field. Yet the centrality of French art in historical studies of the European Middle Ages is a fact which brings into question the entire way Western history has, for so long, privileged France. Our awareness of this corresponds to some of the issues recently highlighted in another anthology entitled *Why France?*[6] In that book, Americans who have made their careers studying French history write about what drew them to the plethora of subjects ranging from Capetian historiography to the Vichy army, from the role of bread in the *ancien régime* to religion during the Revolution of 1848, from eighteenth-century explorers charting the meridian across France to a modern communist suburb of Paris, from France's aviation industry during World War II to the Algerian war for independence. Reading these testimonies led me to ask the question of my own field of medieval art history: "Why French Art?"[7] Clearly a dominant choice among art history dissertations and publications, French art has outshone most other areas of medieval cultural studies in status and accessibility. Introductions to medieval art in survey classes would be wholly incomplete without the widely-reproduced images of Carolingian manuscripts, Romanesque sculpture, or Gothic cathedrals. But investigating *why* French art is so essential, so extensively studied, and so well known helps us see the way art has also served the cultural needs of other lands in Europe and the British Isles.

Traditional explanations about French art's centrality would naturally point to France's superior artistic achievements, which have been molded and highlighted into legendary status by collectors and scholars. Yet one could also credit: 1) France's geographic location at the heart of Europe (a crossroads for many during the Middle Ages on their way to Rome or the Holy Land, as well as the political power center of modern Europe); 2) the easy access to monuments during the early days of art-historical scholarship; and 3) the various myths about the nation and its past that have been put forth since the early nineteenth century. All of this went together into forming the reputation of France's "superior artistic achievement."

In other words, although many of France's medieval accomplishments are real enough, plenty of other regions in Europe could have put forth similar claims. It is primarily historical circumstances that have placed France front and center in our memories of medieval art and in our desire to study French topics. The result has been an unbroken construction of France's past, since at least the so-called "generation of 1820" (those scholars who came of age around 1820), which rewrote French history after the Revolution.[8] These men (exclusively), trained to become the intellectuals of their day, were the children of the Revolution. They did not experience it personally, but everything in their lives was shaped by their parents' sense of "before" and "after," much the way contemporary Europeans regard World War II. This sense was carried directly into the work of historians such as Augustin Thierry, who tried to reform notions of the past by recounting the complex antecedents to self-rule found in the French Middle Ages, or François Guizot, who shaped all French history before the Revolution into a prefiguration of, and preparation for, the "modern" country he was helping administer in various government positions.[9] For these men, key cultural developments occurred during the Middle Ages, and they claimed for France the origin of many artistic achievements, such as the fusion of Classical and Celtic/Germanic traditions during the fifth to eighth centuries. French historians took Charles the Great for their own under the now more familiar French name used in the English language, Charlemagne, and called his support for learning and artistic production at his court a "renaissance," the *first* European renaissance—from which subsequent revivals would follow. Of course these claims were not universally acknowledged, for instance by German scholars, who, after 1870, claimed Charles the Great for Germany ("Karl der Grosse") as a Germanic predecessor of the Ottonian emperors and leader of the first reich.[10] During the Second World War, German leaders again looked to the medieval past to reinforce nationalistic pride. Medieval art, in particular, represented powerful symbols of wealth and power. In **"The Early Middle Ages in the Exhibition *Deutsche Größe***

(1940-1942)," **William Diebold** examines conflicting interpretations of early medieval art objects in a presentation designed to shape an understanding of the nascent German empire and counter France's claim to sole artistic achievement.

One of the most influential figures shaping the reception of medieval art during the 1789 Revolution in France was Alexandre Lenoir, who took on the care of monuments removed from their places of origin and brought to a depot in Paris because their messages were considered either too religious or aristocratic. There he gathered examples into rooms by the centuries they were made, effecting atmospheric reconstructions of imaginary pasts that were designed to elicit sympathetic responses from a hostile public. **Mary Shepard** traces Lenoir's early appreciation of the Gothic style and his attempt to determine the source of the pointed arch ("***L'Oeuf Sacré*: Alexandre Lenoir's *Cour Arabe* and the Pointed Arch**"). As she shows, Lenoir drew upon the travels of Louis IX and his architect to the Middle East, positing that the origin of the pointed arch could be found in Arab building forms seen in Syria, as well as in the shape of the primal sacred egg.

The engineering of the first seriously monumental buildings since Antiquity acquired a special stylistic name in Europe over the course of the nineteenth century—a style that had previously been described as "pre-Gothic" or defined by elements that pointed to foreign models like "Byzantine" or "Lombard"—as a way of claiming the broad variation of architectural features growing in France. The term "Romanesque" put Western Europe back into the Roman Empire, which Charlemagne had claimed to reunite in the ninth century. For a country like France, then in the process of recovering her medieval heritage, the name avoided ceding innovations to foreigners and suggested that there had been a local continuum of ancient Roman artistic practice of exceptional quality. The Roman models underlying medieval architecture were important in many of the Romantic prints that documented extant monuments during the nineteenth century, particularly those in ruins. Drawings made by artists like Emile Sagot were printed in the new graphic medium of lithography and distributed both singly and in books. **David Walsh** analyzes a multi-layered view of the ruined abbey of Cluny by Sagot, showing how the artist called upon his familiarity with both medieval remains in Cluny, and Roman monuments in nearby Autun, to imaginatively reconstruct an ideal view of the church and abbey precinct gateway ("**An Image of Cluny by Emile Sagot**").

Nineteenth-century French medievalists were not alone in their appropriation of the medieval past. Georges Petrie, for example, was also collecting "ancient" artifacts and conducting surveys of early documents, including measurements of buildings and drawings of ruins, only he was working in Ireland. Petrie was devoted to recording as much of medieval Irish culture as possible before it faded from view. The compilation of disparate items made by the Topographical Department of the Ordnance Survey, under his direction, served Petrie's vision of an idealized Middle Ages for Ireland. His story, as told by **Marion Bleeke** in "**George Petrie, the Ordnance Survey, and Nineteenth-Century Constructions of the Irish Past,**" offers us a glimpse into work comparable to that of more famous restoration theorists such as Viollet-le-Duc.

In Italy, we learn from **Nancy Thompson** that similar ideas were being propagated by a man named Giuseppe Martelli, whose plans for the restoration of the Bargello in Florence from a Medici prison back to a medieval palace served as a source of civic pride during that city's fledgling struggle to form a Republic, much as Greco-Roman antiquity had been appropriated during the reign of the Medici as a source of Italian pride during their Renaissance ("**Reviving 'the past greatness of the Florentine people': Restoring Medieval Florence in the Nineteenth Century**").

When we put together examples of medieval art for teaching, as art historians in the United States have done since about 1920, we pull from those scholars who pioneered descriptive analyses and comparisons, photographic documentation, and important exhibitions. The photographs of French buildings collected by Henry Hobson Richardson, who brought the Romanesque revival style to architecture with works such as his 1872 Trinity Church in Boston, and those of Lucy and Arthur Kingsley Porter, who scoured central and southern France and northern Spain for examples of Romanesque church sculpture, formed the basis of the visual resources available to early professors. The latter of course, led to Porter's massive ten-volume work, *Romanesque Sculpture of the Pilgrimage Roads*.[11] Efforts such as these provided a base for further scholarship and thus advanced the place of France in art-historical studies.

Porter had been influenced by the important work of scholars at European universities from the late nineteenth century through the 1920s.[12] Wilhelm Vöge, one of the first "official" German art historians, traveled extensively in France and was particularly drawn to the cathedral of Chartres. He published a book on the origins of monumental Gothic sculpture, which included a revision of Viollet-le-Duc's evaluation of Chartres' west portal as "leftover Byzantinism," by showing how the statues intimately related architectural and figurative form.[13] Certainly these scholars also studied German medieval art; Vöge's dissertation on

Ottonian manuscripts is an obvious example, but many seemed more drawn to study architectural sites in France rather than their own country. Did Chartres represent a transition between Speyer and Cologne not available at home?

Or perhaps it was merely a matter of finding a reason to spend time in a country where the superiority of the cuisine and wine was undisputed! One of the contributors to *Why France?* quotes the German adage: "To live like a king in France."[14] There is certainly a charm exerted by the French culture upon visitors, particularly those who are not from Romance language countries. One has only to conjure the cliché of "an American in Paris," which suggests both the arty musical film and Hemingway's bohemian café life. Art history survey texts tend to wait until the Renaissance to showcase Italy, and Spain has become a footnote in medieval art-historical studies, mentioned either in regard to its Islamic period or to the northern strip of its French-influenced pilgrimage sites, in other words always with respect to a powerful presence that is perceived (wrongly) as foreign and temporary. American appreciation, as well as that of British and French scholars, for German monuments has also surely been affected by sympathies with our allies in two catastrophic wars with that country.

Emile Mâle, a French scholar, was another great influence on early American art historians. He published his first book, on thirteenth-century French art, only four years after that of Vöge.[15] Mâle was to become the great expert on the theological meanings of French sculptural iconography. Mâle came from a background in the Classics, and thus could determine the Greek and Roman sources of many scenes, and his intense religious convictions, along with his mastery of Latin, led him to apply medieval theories, such as Vincent of Beauvais' *Speculum Majus*, as organizing principles.[16] He admired the work of nineteenth-century restorers of medieval monuments, such as Viollet-le-Duc, Merimée, and Vitet, all of whom worked for the *Monuments historiques,* the national conservation institute founded by François Guizot. Their attempts to establish the restored French Gothic as a national architecture resonated with him, and, as a professor at the Sorbonne, he claimed France to be the originator of the Gothic style, specifically refuting an older German claim, and showing through his lectures how the style spread across Europe. He was the first to trace the influence of the monastic orders of Cluny and Cîteaux on Spain and England and to suggest that French medieval mystery plays were the models for Petrarch and Dante, just as French architecture lay at the root of the Renaissance. Mâle taught the reading public, both inside France and beyond, to appreciate the French religious art of the Middle Ages in the artistic sense, not just as documents of Church history.

The development of art history in the United States first centered on women's colleges such as Vassar and Smith, since it was believed that mothers formed the cultural character of citizens.[17] Incorporating art history as a professional discipline within graduate programs on the more scientific model of German universities occurred at male-dominated institutions, however, initially Harvard University in Cambridge, Massachusetts and Princeton University in New Jersey. Cambridge lies across the river from Boston, the center of the medieval revival in the United States. Harvard benefited from its proximity to this intellectual and artistic movement to draw faculty and acquire works for the Fogg Museum, including cloister capitals from a French medieval abbey, secured through Porter's connections. This story is told by **Kathryn Brush** in "**The Capitals from Moutiers-Saint-Jean (Harvard University Art Museums) and the Carving of Medieval Art Study in America after World War I.**" Studies coming out of this circle quickly engaged a larger public interest in French medieval art. Henry Adams's account of *Mont-Saint-Michel and Chartres*, published in 1904, has been a non-stop success for over a century, and so many different presses have published it that one cannot even determine how many editions it has gone through except to say that the latest is from 2006. People who have never read any other book on medieval art often have just this one on their shelves. Adams's exposition was compelling because he tried to bring back to life buildings that were considered "dead" to his contemporaries. He wondered about the actual people who built these monuments and how they would have been perceived by their first audiences—a rather rare example of early contextual interest. He wrote as if he were directing the reader on a tour, using his niece as a device, and had a chatty style full of exclamation points. His sympathy for these works, especially his religious fervor in depicting Chartres as a shrine to the Virgin, was apparently irresistible.

Kingsley Porter's most enthusiastic student of the French Romanesque was Kenneth Conant, who studied and went on to teach at Harvard, while simultaneously carrying out excavations at the former abbey of Cluny, beginning with measurements taken on a Guggenheim grant in 1927 and ending around 1950, as he ran out of reasons to keep funding work there. My own publications have chronicled Conant's devotion to France, his efforts towards resurrecting interest in Cluny, and the romantic methodology he employed in order to recreate, on paper, the lost abbey buildings.[18] Conant's work also contributed to the construction of the medieval past and the central place of France in the development of the Romanesque style in Europe. It became part of a layering process of memory construction by many scholars who, like Conant himself, moved our understanding forward, as evidence was brought to light through excavations and textual analysis, even as it simultaneously offered erroneous reconstructions and romantic theories based upon personal beliefs or faulty methodology.

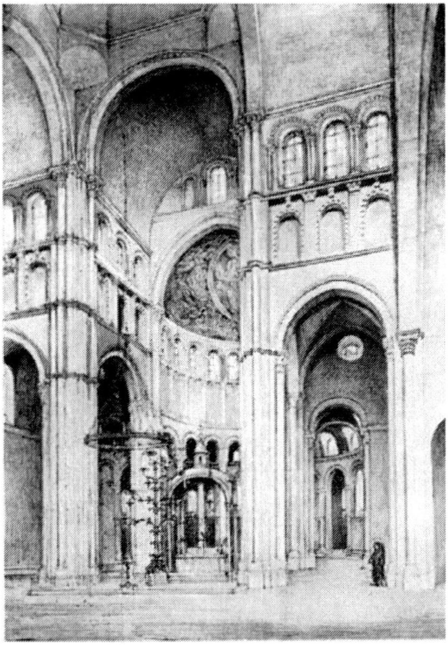

Fig. 1 Kenneth J. Conant, "Cluny III. Le sanctuaire. Vue perspective, restaurée," drawing, from *Cluny: Les Eglises et la maison du chef d'ordre* (Mâcon: Protat Frères, 1968). Pl. 45 (Photo: Cluny Collection, Loeb Library, Harvard University)

The effect of Conant's persuasive reconstructive drawings on Cluny's "working memory" was similar to that of dozens of equally convincing scholars whose work created images in our minds for lost or damaged medieval monuments [Fig. 1]. The way that many of these models and restorations have since been challenged by younger colleagues should also lead us to reconsider the similarly seductive reconstructions we can now devise with access to digital technology. These images satisfy comparable desires to allow viewers a virtual experience of the space in and around an historical monument. Yet in order to realize the dimensions, it is necessary to input every measurement, even extrapolating ones inaccessible today, thus holding the hard data of "science" together with the glue of guesswork. By the time the project is complete, the lines between the two are blurred, and we want to believe in what we have so painstakingly configured. Thus we all follow a certain romantic methodology as we imagine buildings back to life, just as we can only imagine the past in the framework of our own present, adding to the layers of working memory.[19]

Conant's acquaintance from Harvard undergraduate study, John Nicholas Brown (of Brown University, the institution he later founded), bankrolled the entire Cluny project from the first dig to the final monograph, often anonymously contributing his personal funds to the Medieval Academy for that purpose. Like Porter, he was a wealthy American who considered French culture the epitome of taste and hoped to help Cluny's renown, in a way comparable to John Simon Guggenheim's highly-publicized support for the restoration of the palace at Versailles and the cathedral of Reims.

The very way that repairs were realized on surviving monuments could change how contemporaries believed they looked in their original medieval form. Work on the interior and exterior of the west façade of Reims Cathedral is a good example of how easy it was to change appearances, and potentially meanings, of sculptural ensembles. **Donna Sadler** reviews the successive restoration programs carried out at Reims during the seventeenth, eighteenth, and nineteenth centuries in her essay, "**The Persistence of the Royal Past on the West Façade of Reims Cathedral**." She shows that, in spite of multiple stylistic interpretations and revisions of its architectural sculpture, the cathedral's role as the royal French coronation church was never lost from its iconographic programs.

The case of Reims suggests another way French art has dominated American consciousness since at least the First World War. **Elizabeth Emery** traces the role of Reims Cathedral in garnering American pro-war sentiment, suddenly bringing Reims front and center in American minds as a quintessential Gothic cathedral and war martyr ("**The Martyred Cathedral: American Attitudes toward Notre-Dame de Reims during the First World War**"). Other French cathedrals, including Amiens and Senlis, were also hit by bombs. In fact, an entire series of woven silk postcards, produced by Neyret Frères and published by E. Deffrene, were devoted to images of French and Flemish sites in flames.[20] Each card was captioned with the name of the location and the date it was burned from 1914-1918. The fact that such a series was seen as marketable suggests the intense interest people took in these events.

In 1915, that is, during the second year of the war, Ralph Adams Cram, a Boston medieval revival architect like Richardson, who later supported Conant's project, published a book entitled *Heart of Europe*.[21] The "heart" to which the title refers was by Cram described as the "beautiful land" "between the Seine and the Rhine," in other words Paris to Cologne and the Alps to the North Sea, where war had laid waste "a sanctuary." He characterized France in the medieval tradition as a Christian society, a "crowning civilization" illustrated by its "impossible romance" with rational yet wholly original masterpieces. Many of the sites covered in the Neyret Frères postcards are key subjects of his narrative: Louvain, Amiens, Reims. British and American readers were primed for this cry of outrage and rallied around the cathedral as a symbol of the victimization of Marianne. Emery argues that such attention weighed heavily on the decision of the United States to finally come in on the French side in 1917, a decision delayed not just because there were those who resisted any military involvement in a European war, but because there was initially strong support for the German cause. Thus the proponents of medieval art and the romantic view of its unfortunate demise again played a role in bringing France to the forefront.

By the late 1920s and early 1930s, **Laura Morowitz** shows us that Reims was one of the most evocative representatives of romantic medievalism in the United States, as evidenced by the lavish holiday displays mounted at Wanamaker's department stores in Philadelphia and New York City ("**The Cathedral of Commerce: French Gothic Architecture and Wanamaker's Department Store**"). There, French artistic styles were mixed with other well-known elements from British medieval art to create glowing interiors suggestive of ethical consumption and Old World quality craftsmanship. The pseudo-medieval objects rendered by Wanamaker's art department and outside fabricating companies fed stereotypical ideas not just about the forms, but also the meanings of medieval imagery. Stained glass, for instance, appeared in a style more reminiscent of Pre-Raphaelite works than authentic thirteenth-century glass. Yet even as these installations were being created, art historians were shaping interpretations of Gothic monuments that would affect the public's appreciation. The Sainte-Chapelle, Louis IX's small model of a complete French Gothic assemblage, has served as the focus of much scholarship defining such "modern" medieval engineering.[22] A key proponent in explaining the original form of this building was the art historian Robert Branner, who published an influential book in 1965 that defined a "Court Style" for the architecture built under Louis IX. **Meredith Cohen** traces the powerful effect of the theories Branner articulated in this book, and the methods employed by his followers to accept, reject, or adapt them, by applying Harold Bloom's theory of literary criticism in her essay "**Branner's 'Court Style' and the Anxiety of Influence.**" Many of the elements found in the Sainte-Chapelle today are, in fact, not original, much of the sculpture and stained glass having been not only restored but redesigned in the nineteenth century. In "**Restoration Politics: Recrafting Monarchy in the Windows of the Sainte-Chapelle**," **Alyce Jordan** shows how ideological messages regarding French kingship were revised and how the restorers' work intersected with contemporary religious concerns.

Many medieval objects left in churches had to be modified or reinterpreted according to changing religious tenets. Here we find a great difference between France and the countries that embraced Protestantism. **Grażyna Jurkowlaniec** studies medieval crucifixes still found in German and Swiss sites in her essay, "**Remnants of a Shared Past: Medieval Monumental Crucifixes after the Reformation**." She follows the additions and adjustments made to these artworks as they were newly interpreted by both Lutherans and Catholics alike.

Efforts have also been made to identify and catalogue art from the Romanesque period all over Europe, much of which was nearly lost to art-historical awareness. The success of over 300 books and a half century periodical run, under the rubric *Zodiaque*, has helped maintain general public knowledge of medieval artistic patrimony. From 1951 to 2001, the monastery of la Pierre-qui-Vire in Burgundy compiled multiple series of books on medieval art, primarily that from the period 1000-1200 CE usually called "Romanesque."[23] Predominantly picture books filled with rich and strikingly beautiful black-and-white photogravures, these collections were not assembled by art historians or administrative agencies for patrimony and tourism, but by a small group of Catholic monks who determined the sites for each volume, traveled to photograph them, chose texts to accompany the images, and selected the views and details that were included. In order to organize the examples into volumes, as well as find authors who could write authoritatively on groups of works, the first two series, *Les Travaux des Mois* ("Labors of the Months," which eventually ran to thirty-four volumes) and *La Nuit des Temps* (the "Dark Ages," which grew to eighty-eight volumes), were divided into significant individual monuments or arranged by region. The inaugural volume of the latter, *Bourgogne romane,* sold over 40,000 copies in its first edition and subsequently stretched to nine more, adding sites and changing authors in the process. Like Burgundy, other areas of France were designated by traditional regional names, while the monks' geographic scope expanded to include Spain, Italy, Germany, England, and beyond—eventually reaching from Scandinavia to Ethiopia, from Portugal to Russia, and from Ireland to the Holy Land. There were so many photographs, and the books were so popular, that new series were added regularly, many organized by iconographic themes. The La Pierre-qui-Vire team eventually stretched their chronological coverage forward to the Gothic and back into Early Christian, but always keeping Romanesque as the powerful central core.

As with other grand documentary projects, we must ask what the motivation for the Zodiaque series could have been. Here it is compelling to realize that not only did all this come out of a monastery, masterminded by a handful of monks who built much of the labor into a monastic printing atelier—like a latter-day medieval scriptorium—but that it grew from love of *l'esprit nouveau*, the modernist movement in the visual arts beginning around 1920. It is striking how the Romanesque aesthetic answered the new taste for clean, sharp, and orderly compositions while at the same time providing the content for a new sacred art, *l'art sacré*, so elusive but so much on the minds of everyone from Kandinsky to the Catholic Church.

One of the originators, Dom Angelico Surchamp, was allowed to study with Albert Gleizes, a cubist painter who wrote about the connection between modern art and spiritual content. Surchamp returned to the monastery to work with other young monks there on fresco murals executed in the new style, but also heavily dependent upon the figural form of their beloved Burgundian Romanesque. The sharply outlined, elongated figures of the Romanesque style, coupled with a flexible perspectival system predicated on how objects could best be understood in every scene (tables and beds turned up so we might see what lies on their surfaces; façades, interiors, and elevations of buildings merged in single images; exaggerated drapery or gestures employed to indicate movement), must have seemed refreshing after centuries of Renaissance inspired naturalism and resonated with the work of contemporary artists, for whom the play of pattern and line was as important as illusion. Surchamp composed the photographs that fill the Zodiaque series to exaggerate this modernist sensibility through the use of side lighting and steep angles.

The popularity of the Zodiaque books, both in France and the United States, points to a number of intersecting interests in the second half of the twentieth century. On the one hand, the quality of the photogravure process draws us in with its profound beauty; the monochromic format elegantly echoes the contrasts of the linear Romanesque style that these photographs document better than anything previously published. On the other hand, there is the issue of the growing awareness of the equal stature of the Romanesque next to the highly popular Gothic style. The attractive dust jackets with bright color photographs also served well to market the books. Descriptions of the series identify their function as "guides for educated travelers" and translations of the text into English and German appeared at the end of each volume. Their focus on regions and religious themes made them ideal personalized gifts for religious occasions in France, such as the sacraments of first Holy Communion and Confirmation, driving up sales among non-academics, and bringing the Zodiaque books into regular exchange among the general public.[24] The small format, bright cloth covers (forming a counterpoint to the black-and-white photographs inside) and the ribbon bookmarks also suggested associations with religious books. Finally, as with any series, buyers were driven to complete their sets, encouraging a visible display of cultural and artistic awareness.

France had already claimed the Romanesque style, most famously by Pierre Francastel during the Second World War,[25] but now there was a new impetus to its appreciation; it could reflect a fresh aesthetic even while standing as a cultural tradition. The way Zodiaque editors arranged the monuments by region, beginning in France but quickly expanding beyond its borders, reinforced the way art historians tend to see styles associated with geographical areas and appropriated the non-French examples as mere extensions of the ur-Romanesque of the primary fourteen volumes of *Les Travaux des Mois* and central thirty-nine volumes of *La Nuit des Temps* devoted to French sites. The French word for each region, along with the very repetition of the term "roman(e)" in the titles, helped draw an association between the style and France. The huge number of books and their publication of many previously obscure sites carried an authority and contributed to the breadth of further study in Romanesque topics.

So the answer to "Why French Art?" and the predominance of French examples in historiographic studies such as those contained in this anthology has a lot to do with how French medieval art has been re-presented in the modern era. From historical nationalism to Romantic regret, the proliferation of published analyses and photographs has made the accessibility of French examples easy to employ as prototypes by which objects and monuments from other places might be measured. Both French and foreigners have contributed to this imbalance, furthering the scholarship on their favorite arts and encouraging others to go study them—and spend time living "like a king in France."

It is the goal of this anthology, through the collection of essays on the interpretation of medieval art and architecture from various countries in

Europe, to introduce some of the best work being done on French subjects today, but also to reach beyond the French bias to increase the medieval works familiar to readers and expand our understanding of how medieval art has served other European cultures. We hope to show how modern understandings of the Middle Ages have been driven by contemporary public and private perspectives. The stories are fascinating, not the least because they remind us that we too are shaped by our environment and that no history is ever truly objective.

We, the editors, were very happy to find the chronological and geographical breadth represented by the proposals for this anthology, along with serendipitous interrelations between the various threads within the essays. We tried hard not only to incorporate articles which treated medieval art outside of France, but also to vary the foci from architecture to manuscripts, glass, textiles, sculpture, and entire exhibitions, in order to encourage scholarship in new directions. We hope that the resulting compilation offers a better appreciation for the multiple appropriations to which medieval art has been subjected and inspires further re-examinations of motivation and method.

Notes

[1] Recent interest in the role of memory has brought back Maurice Halbwachs's notion of collective memory and the popularity of history "from the bottom up" as practiced by Georges Lefebvre and the *Annales* school, as well as the famous series of anthologies on "lieux de mémoire" (memory sites) compiled by Pierre Nora. Maurice Halbwachs and Lewis A. Coser, *On Collective Memory*, *The Heritage of Sociology* (Chicago: University of Chicago Press, 1992); Pierre Nora, *Les Lieux de mémoire*, 3 vols. (Paris: Gallimard, 1984-1986); Pierre Nora, *Rethinking France = Les Lieux de mémoire*, trans. Mary Trouille (Chicago: University of Chicago Press, 2001); Pierre Nora and Lawrence D. Kritzman, *Realms of Memory: Rethinking the French Past*, *European Perspectives,* 3 vols. (New York: Columbia University Press, 1996).

[2] Paul Ricoeur, *Memory, History, Forgetting* (Chicago: University of Chicago Press, 2004).

[3] This is a term used by Jan and Aleida Assmann in various publications. See, for instance, Jan Assmann and Rodney Livingstone, *Religion and Cultural Memory: Ten Studies* (Stanford, CA: Stanford University Press, 2006).

[4] This is Aleida Assmann, *Erinnerungsräume: Formen und Wandlungen des kulturellen Gedächtnisses* (Munich: C.H. Beck, 1999).

[5] I refer here to the age of Jean Mabillon and the first archivists of France under the Benedictine monks of the Order of Saint-Maur at Saint-Germain-des-Prés in Paris from approximately 1640 to 1789, skipping over the work of the Bollandists

whose purpose was more literary and religious than historical. See David Knowles, *Great Historical Enterprises* (London: Nelson, 1964). 35-62

[6] Laura Lee Downs and Stéphane Gerson, *Why France?: American Historians Reflect on an Enduring Fascination* (Ithaca: Cornell University Press, 2007).

[7] I presented a portion of this discussion in a keynote address: Janet Marquardt, "Why French Art?" (paper presented at "Medieval Places: Geographical Approaches to Medieval Culture," University of North Texas Medieval Graduate Student Symposium, Denton, TX, 8-9 November 2007). I wish to thank Mickey Abel for the invitation.

[8] Alan B. Spitzer, *The French Generation of 1820* (Princeton: Princeton University Press, 1987).

[9] Ceri Crossley, *French Historians and Romanticism: Thierry, Guizot, the Saint-Simonians, Quinet, Michelet* (London: Routledge, 1993).

[10] The unification of 1871 represents the beginning of the second reich and Hitler's rule that of the third.

[11] Arthur Kingsley Porter, *Romanesque Sculpture of the Pilgrimage Roads* (Boston: Marshall Jones Company, 1923).

[12] Kathryn Brush, *The Shaping of Art History: Wilhelm Vöge, Adolph Goldschmidt, and the Study of Medieval Art* (Cambridge, MA: Cambridge University Press, 1996).

[13] Wilhelm Vöge, *Die Anfänge des monumentalen Stiles im Mittelalter* (Strassburg,: J. H. E. Heitz, 1894).

[14] Herman Lebovics, "Tough Love for France," in *Why France*. 52

[15] Emile Mâle, *L'Art religieux du XIIIe siècle en France. Etude sur l'iconographie du moyen âge et sur ses sources d'inspiration* (Paris: E. Leroux, 1898).

[16] Joseph F. Byrnes, *Catholic and French Forever: Religious and National Identity in Modern France* (University Park, PA: Pennsylvania State University Press, 2005). 179-208

[17] Craig Hugh Smyth and Peter M. Lukehart, eds., *The Early Years of Art History in the United States: Notes and Essays on Departments, Teaching, and Scholars* (Princeton: Department of Art and Archaeology, Princeton University, 1993).

[18] Janet T. Marquardt, "'Cluny in all its perfection': Ur-Basilica or Romantic Reconstruction?" *Scholion/Kongressakten der Stiftung Bibliothek Werner Oechslin* (Zurich: GTA Verlag). (forthcoming)

[19] I am grateful to Michael Davis for the apt expression "romantic methodology."

[20] Chris Radley, *The Woven Silk Postcard* (Barking, Essex: Radley, 1978). 55-56, 69-71; http://www.stevengraphs.com/neyretfreres.html

[21] Ralph Adams Cram, *Heart of Europe* (New York: Scribner's, 1915).

[22] I am referring to Marvin Trachtenberg's convincing call for renaming the Gothic style in "Suger's Miracles, Branner's Bourges: Reflections on 'Gothic Architecture' as Medieval Modernism," *Gesta* 39 (2000). 183-205

[23] This is the subject of my current research, on which two articles are forthcoming: Janet T. Marquardt, "La Pierre-qui-Vire and Zodiaque: A Monastic Pilgrimage of Medieval Dimensions," *Peregrinations* 3 (2009), 118-129; and Janet T. Marquardt, "Defining French 'Romanesque': The Zodiaque series,"

Journal of Art Historiography 1 (December 2009), 1-JTM/1. I do not introduce the issues raised by the liberal use of the term "Romanesque" in this essay, however, it is addressed in the latter reference and is a central point for the series. All of these matters will be further studied in my monograph on the Zodiaque project to be entitled *Making Medieval Modern: The Zodiaque Publications 1951-2001.*

[24] I am grateful to Ilene Forsyth for sharing this observation about the way Zodiaque books entered into French culture.

[25] Pierre Francastel, *L'Histoire de l'art, instrument de la propagande germanique* (Paris: Librairie de Médicis, 1945).

QUEEN MARY AND HER PSALTER: A GOTHIC MANUSCRIPT IN TUDOR ENGLAND[1]

ANNE RUDLOFF STANTON

The manuscript now known as "Queen Mary's Psalter" (London, British Library, MS Royal 2B.vii) was written and illuminated in early fourteenth-century England.[2] It is one of the most luxuriously illuminated manuscripts from that period, yet neither inscriptions nor coats of arms survive to identify its original owner. Its current name stems from an inscription on its last folio that connects it with the first queen regnant of Renaissance England: Mary I, often remembered as "Bloody Mary," the daughter of Henry VIII. According to this inscription, in October 1553 the customs official Baldwin Smith confiscated the manuscript from an unknown party, who was on the point of leaving the country, and then presented it to Queen Mary.[3] In 1757, the library holdings of Saint James Palace, which included the Psalter, were donated to the nascent British Museum as the Royal Collection, and the manuscript was catalogued as Royal 2B.vii.[4] In 1854 Gustav Waagen noted the Baldwin Smith inscription and its connection to Queen Mary, and in 1865 Nat Westlake and William Purdue cemented the association by publishing engravings from the manuscript under the title *The Illustrations of Old Testament History in Queen Mary's Psalter*.[5]

Despite its connection with the Tudor queen, the sixteenth-century context of Royal 2B.vii has not been explored beyond a few paragraphs in George Warner's 1912 *Queen Mary's Psalter*. Warner lays out the slender evidence from the manuscript itself, which comprises three items. These include the 1553 Baldwin Smith inscription noted above, and another inscription, on fol. 84, that speaks to its ownership earlier in the sixteenth century: "This boke was sume tyme the Erle of Rutelands, and it was his wil that it shulde by successioun all way go to the lande of Ruteland or to him that linyally succedis by reson of inheritaunce in the seide lande." As Warner notes, this most likely refers either to Thomas Manners, the first Earl of Rutland of that family (d. 1543), or to his son Henry Manners, who was imprisoned in July of 1553 when Mary Tudor came to power.[6] The third piece of evidence that may help us reconstruct this part of the Psalter's life is its sixteenth-century velvet binding, which was placed on new boards when the manuscript was rebound early in the twentieth century. The original crimson of the velvet has faded, but it retains its embellishments: an embroidered appliqué of Mary's personal emblem—the pomegranate of Aragon, in honor of her mother—and metal fastenings engraved with the Tudor badges of a portcullis, fleur-de-lys, lion and dragon [Fig. 1].[7] According to Warner, the use of the pomegranate emblem suggested that Mary "regarded [the Psalter] rather as a cherished personal possession than as an ordinary addition to the royal library."[8]

This essay both examines and looks beyond the binding of Royal 2B.vii to explore the relevance of a medieval manuscript to a Renaissance queen. After a brief discussion of Mary's life, intellectual milieu, and library, I will turn to the iconography of the Psalter's exceptionally rich illustration program. I have argued elsewhere that this program was originally intended to suit the needs of a medieval queen, part of a broader tradition in which biblical figures provided behavioral and spiritual role models.[9] Here I will examine how the Psalter could also have engaged the interest of the Renaissance Mary, whose personal and dynastic concerns might well have seemed almost prophetically reflected in its pages.

Queen Mary I

The broad outlines of Queen Mary's biography are well-known. Born in 1516 to Henry VIII and his first wife, Catherine of Aragon, Mary was repudiated along with her mother when Henry's hopes for a male successor turned to Anne Boleyn.[10] Mary was the eldest of the three legitimate offspring of the king; Elizabeth, the daughter of Anne Boleyn, was sixteen years younger, and Edward was born to Jane Seymour when Mary was twenty-one. As the only son, Edward came to the throne on Henry's death in 1547, and an even briefer reign followed his death in July 1553 when Lady Jane Grey, the Protestant granddaughter of Henry's sister Mary, was put forward as the next ruler. The reign of Lady Jane, the "Nine Days Queen," was quickly suppressed when Mary and her supporters entered London.

Mary was crowned queen in London on October 1, 1553. She had remained faithful to the church of her mother and reinstated Catholicism with policies for which she would be remembered as "Bloody Mary."[11] Mary remains best known for this fierce loyalty to the Catholic faith, but she is also remembered as a disappointed wife and mother. Earlier marriage plans having fallen through or been abandoned, she began to negotiate her marriage with Philip II of Spain almost immediately on her accession to the throne.[12] They married in July of 1554, but for the remainder of Mary's brief reign, Philip was away from her court as often as he was in it. Mary's chronic ill health caught up with her in November of 1558, leaving the English throne to her younger sister Elizabeth I.

Popular evaluations of Mary have been overwhelmingly negative, but, as Judith Richards notes, even Renaissance scholars have remained underwhelmed by Mary's character. Mary is seen as her mother's daughter, so much so that she inherited the scholarly "bad press" devoted to Catherine of Aragon.[13] But Richards is not alone in observing that Mary was extremely well-educated in the humanist tradition, and that the Catholicism to which she subscribed so fiercely was of a distinctly Renaissance character.[14] She cannot be dismissed simply as a ruler who insisted on a return to a traditional medieval faith. Mary was one of the best-educated princesses in early sixteenth-century Europe, both during her early years at the royal court and later, during her exile with her mother.[15] She was a well-read collector of books, and was conversant with works in several languages. In this she was indeed her mother's daughter, for Catherine had been raised in the progressive court of Aragon, and her patronage was instrumental in humanist developments at the English court.[16]

In the context of this essay, Catherine's relationship with Juan de Vives, a Spanish humanist heavily influenced by Erasmus, is particularly interesting. Vives dedicated his *De Institutione Feminae Christianae* (*The Education of a Christian Woman*) to Catherine in 1523 and then came to England under her patronage. Later that year, while employed by Thomas Wolsey, Vives wrote *De Ratione Studii Puerilis* (*A Plan of Study for Children*) for Princess Mary.[17] While Mary was not, in the end, able to commission such pedagogical treatises for her own children, Richards suggests that she was very much interested in the production of religious manuals, primers imbued with the humanist teachings that had begun to change Catholicism in the decades before both the continental and the English reformations.[18]

Mary was also heir to her father's interest in books. During Henry's reign the number of books under royal control grew exponentially, fed both by an explosion in printed book production and by the monarch's own interests. Many of Henry's volumes are full of notations, scribbles, arguments, comments, and other relics of his interactions with their ideas, leaving rare personal witnesses to a king's reading habits.[19] While Mary's books do not display the copious annotations found in those of her father,

T. A. Birrell noted that their bindings look unusually scuffed and worn at the corners, giving the impression of regular use.[20]

Mary's personal library primarily contained contemporary philosophical and devotional texts that were bound in black or dark brown leather and stamped with either her name or the letter M, but she also owned books that were bound in velvet, a material often used for biblical texts or devotional books like the Psalter that now bears her name. The use of fine textiles for bindings was not limited to devotional books, but appears to have been more often used for such texts even into the Elizabethan period.[21] Velvet was also a material frequently used for the binding of books from monastic contexts, a flood of which entered the royal collections during the English Reformation.[22] The rebinding of Royal 2B.vii in velvet thus may have indicated not only its devotional function, but may also have drawn attention to its medieval, and Catholic, provenance.

As I noted above, the incorporation of the pomegranate badge of Aragon led Warner to assert that Mary felt some personal connection to this manuscript [Fig. 1].[23] More recently, John King used the Psalter's binding as an example of Mary's adoption of her mother's badge, noting that "the queen apparently kept [the book] as a private possession rather than as part of the royal library."[24] Bibliographic research indeed implies that the display of a private motto or emblem may indicate a personal

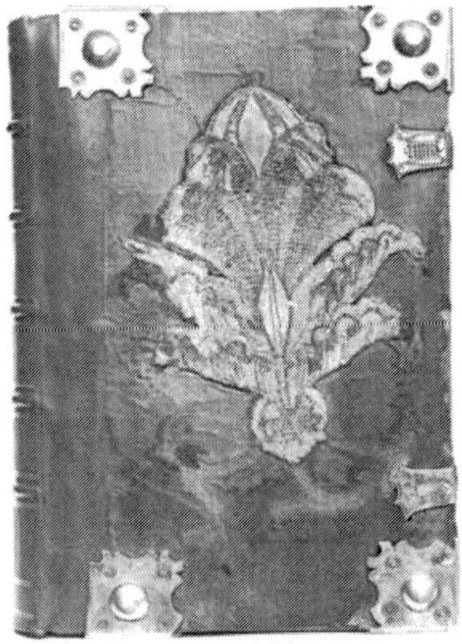

Fig. 1 Cover, "Queen Mary's Psalter," MS Royal 2B.vii, ca. 1310-1320, British Library, London (Photo: © The British Library Board)

relationship with a book.[25] On the other hand, Peter Kidd and Mirjam Foot have proposed that the rebinding might have been done before Mary received the book, perhaps by the order of Baldwin Smith.[26] This is a strong possibility whether one assumes that when he confiscated the manuscript, it was in its original early fourteenth-century binding—which must have been worn by that point—or that it had been rebound by a subsequent owner. Alternatively, the rebinding could have been ordered by the Royal Librarian, who also might have been eager to remove any indication of ownership by the Manners family.

While we cannot know who made the decisions about the current binding of the Queen Mary Psalter, the use of velvet may indicate that the Psalter was seen as a devotional book with a strong connection to the monastic culture of the past, and the embroidered pomegranate draws connections between the queen, the Psalter, and the queen's Spanish Catholic heritage. A look at the Psalter's iconography suggests that if Mary ever looked beyond its cover, these connections would have been sealed by the unusual trajectory of its visual narratives, which would have seemed to reflect the concerns of Queen Mary as much as those of its fourteenth-century audience.

Queen Mary's Psalter

The Psalter is a large manuscript and, at over 300 parchment folios, thicker and heavier than the printed volumes in Mary's library would have been. In addition to the psalms and other texts typical of medieval psalters, Mary's Psalter was decorated with over 800 tinted drawings and fully-illuminated miniatures.[27] The majority of these images tell stories that range from the beginnings of Christian history in the book of Genesis to events from the end of time. Along the way, the paintings and tinted drawings often present rarely-depicted episodes from Old Testament books, New Testament apocrypha and related literature, as well as scenes from the bestiary and the lives of the martyred saints. The entire first portion of the manuscript is devoted to scenes from the Old Testament, told in delicately-tinted, elegant drawings, with captions in the Anglo-Norman dialect of the fourteenth-century English court. The captions tend toward the descriptive, usually beginning with the words "Icy" or "Coment" to draw the attention of the viewer to the action in the drawings.[28] Like the drawings, they reflected a typical Gothic interest in the romantic and adventurous aspects of the biblical narrative that, even today, make for enjoyable reading.[29]

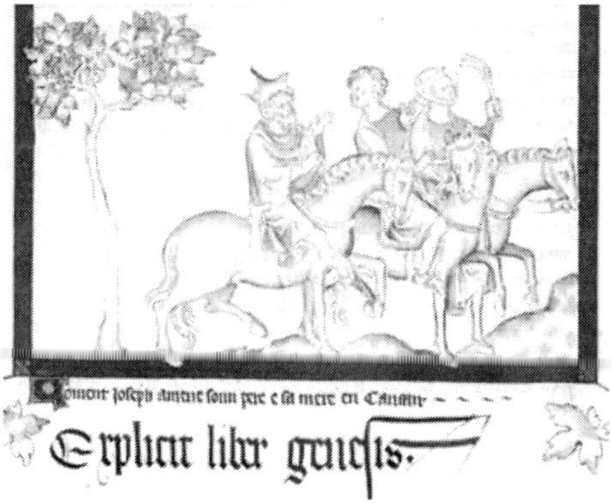

Fig. 2 Rachel, Joseph, and Jacob returning to Canaan, "Queen Mary's Psalter," MS Royal 2B.vii, fol. 20, detail, ca. 1310-1320, British Library, London (Photo: © The British Library Board)

While the Old Testament stories told by the elegant drawings and brief captions emphasize a variety of themes, the most prominent revolves around the importance of mothers—particularly mothers of sons. For example, in the Genesis text and its usual depictions, Rachel, the wife of Jacob and mother of Joseph, dies after giving birth to Benjamin; here, on the other hand, she not only survives Benjamin's birth but lives to visit Joseph in Egypt and is depicted leading the family back to Canaan [Fig. 2].[30] The way the histories of the major Old Testament patriarchs and heroes are presented is even richer. The Psalter's version of the story of Abraham is unusually long and focuses more on his need for a son than his role as a leader; accordingly, this narrative is well-populated by female characters.[31] Not only is Sarah a prominent figure—she and Abraham are shown together praying for a son, for example—but three very unusual scenes depict the story of Sarah's handmaid Hagar, who becomes Abraham's concubine and the mother of Ishmael. The designer drew attention to the legality of Sarah's marriage, representing Abraham espousing Sarah "par ley" ("by law"), and emphasized the irregularity of Hagar's status by showing her as a very small figure embraced by a tall Abraham [Figs. 3-4].

A reader in the 1550s, having opened a cover emblazoned with Catherine of Aragon's pomegranate emblem, might well have seen the focus on legal marriage in the Hagar story as a biblical retort to Henry's repudiation of Catherine and legitimation of his relationship with Anne

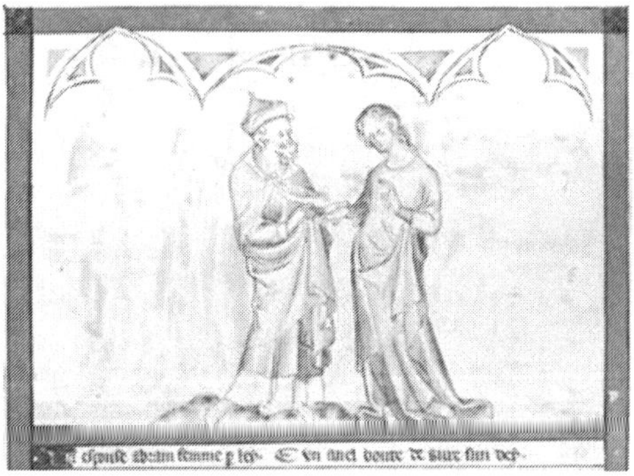

Fig. 3 Abraham marries Sarah "par ley," "Queen Mary's Psalter," MS Royal 2B.vii, fol. 8v, detail, ca. 1310-1320, British Library, London (Photo: © The British Library Board)

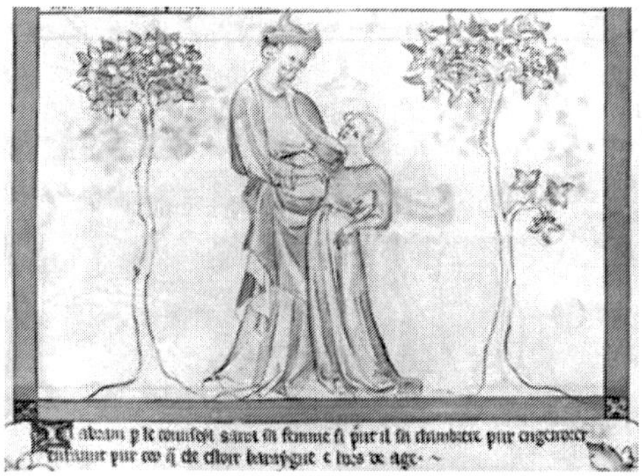

Fig. 4 Abraham embraces Hagar, "Queen Mary's Psalter," MS Royal 2B.vii, fol. 9v, detail, ca. 1310-1320, British Library, London (Photo: © The British Library Board)

Boleyn. A contemporary moral also could have been drawn from the story of King Solomon that ends the Old Testament sequence. Here, our conventional picture of the wise Solomon is almost overborne by his folly, as he marries several wives from other faiths and actually starts to practice their religions, which leads to the disintegration of the kingdom built by King David [Fig. 5]. Solomon is in fact the only polygamist left in the Psalter's version of the Old Testament, and his multiple marriages are disastrous for the people of Israel. If Mary read this sequence, the parallels between Solomon and her father would have been hard to miss, for Anne

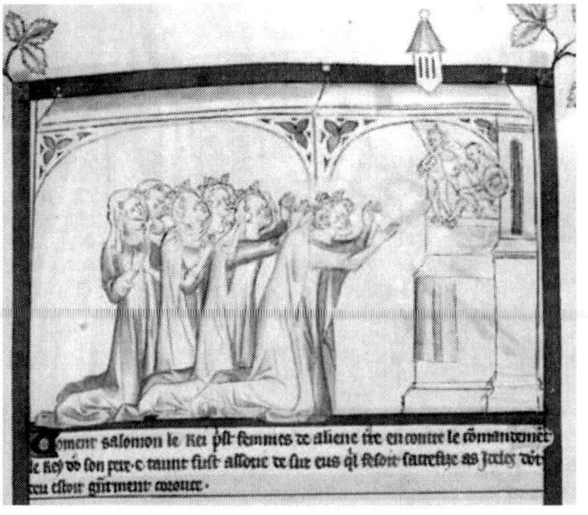

Fig. 5 Solomon worshipping with his wives, "Queen Mary's Psalter," MS Royal 2B.vii, fol. 66v, detail, ca. 1310-1320, British Library, London (Photo: © The British Library Board)

Boleyn's Protestant faith was an important element in the developments of the 1530s, when Henry formally declared himself head of the Church in England and began the dissolution of the monasteries.[32]

I have not yet found a sixteenth-century source that compared Anne Boleyn's influence on Henry with the story of Hagar, or with the influence of the pagan wives on Solomon, but images of Henry frequently drew on the iconography of David and Solomon.[33] In the Coverdale Bible (1535), the Psalter of Henry VIII (1530s), and other works with court connections, these Old Testament rulers are represented in the guise of Henry [Fig. 6]; they also appeared frequently in contemporary literature as models of wise kings.[34] Like Henry, medieval rulers were constantly directed to their Old Testament predecessors as role models, an approach reflected in the imagery of the Queen Mary Psalter.[35]

Biblical imagery intended for royal audiences in the Middle Ages also addressed the need for a male heir, particularly with material aimed specifically at royal and noble women.[36] Juan de Vives' pedagogical texts followed this tradition as well. In his chapter on the care of children in the *Education of a Christian Woman*, he directs the infertile woman to ask God for a child, citing as role models such Old Testament exemplars as Sarah and Rachel—as well as Elizabeth (the mother of John the Baptist), Anne (the mother of the biblical Mary), and of course the Queen of

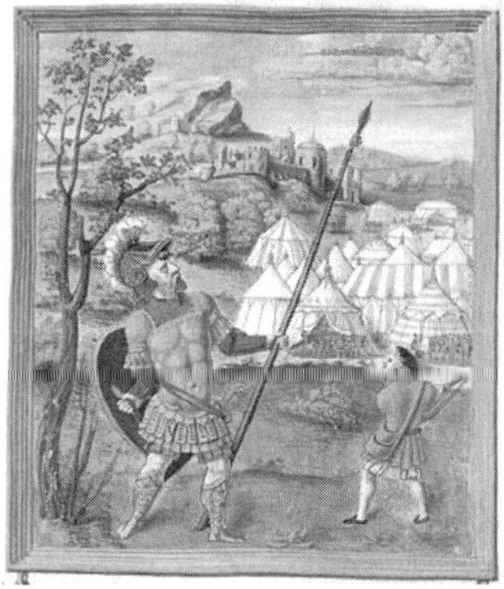

Fig. 6 Henry VIII as David fighting Goliath, Psalter of Henry VIII, MS Royal 2A.xvi, fol. 30, 1530s, British Library, London (Photo: © The British Library Board)

Heaven herself.[37] The Psalter's imagery, with its reiterated images of prayer followed by childbirth, would have seemed to illustrate directly the efficacy of Vives' advice.

The prophesied pregnancy of Sarah, which occurs after the exile of Hagar, announces the importance of motherhood in the Psalter's biblical narrative. Beginning with Sarah's role in the story of Abraham, the designer of the Psalter included scenes depicting the Old Testament mothers whose miraculous pregnancies were seen as prefigurations of the conception of Jesus. For example, we are shown Samson's parents praying for a son [Fig. 7], followed by a depiction of the hero's birth; the same pattern is repeated with the birth of Samuel.[38] These images of miraculous births paralleled Queen Mary's own desires. Having borne the burden of her father's struggles to provide an heir, she was clear about her own duty and endured at least two false pregnancies, the first of which lasted some two months after the supposed due date.[39]

The prefatory sequence ends, as noted above, with the story of Solomon. The next set of full-page paintings is essentially charts that represent the relationships between the Old and New Testaments.[40] The first image, a Tree of Jesse miniature, depicts one of the most popular didactic images in Gothic art, which presents the genealogical links between the Old and New Testaments in an easily-understood format.[41]

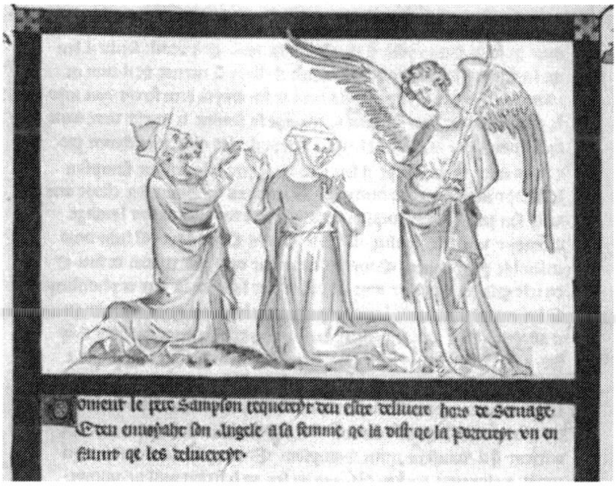

Fig. 7 The prayers of Samson's parents are answered by an angel, "Queen Mary's Psalter," MS Royal 2B.vii, fol. 42v, detail, ca. 1310-1320, British Library, London (Photo: © The British Library Board)

Jesse, the father of David, lies supine while a great vine grows up from his hips and creates roundels in which Old Testament kings and prophets sit or stand. This miniature, however, is unique among Jesse Tree images, for it depicts only the male descendants of Jesse, rather than culminating, as is customary, with an image of the Virgin and Child, or Jesus. Instead, the matrilineal ancestry and extended family of Jesus is depicted on the facing page, in a chart that depicts how Saint Anne, the mother of Mary, married three times [Fig. 8].[42] The daughters from each marriage, all of whom are named Mary, in turn produced six children: Jesus and his five cousins.

In the fourteenth century this image was less well-known than the Tree of Jesse—and thus merited its own Anglo-Norman caption—but, by the sixteenth-century, depictions of the Holy Kinship appeared widely in a variety of forms.[43] The composition and placement of these two images make the unmistakable point that mothers were vital figures in the genesis of the new Christian world that would be built on the foundations of the Jewish past. Queen Mary might have taken comfort in the legend of Saint Anne, which emphasized Anne's great age and infertility and the miraculousness of her pregnancy; in fact, Anne was included in the list of Old Testament mothers emphasized by Vives. That she went on to widowhood, and to marry twice more and bear two more daughters, may also have seemed to be at once a reminder of the brief widowhood and remarriage of Catherine of Aragon and a good omen for Mary herself.[44]

Again, the prominence of Catherine's pomegranate emblem, itself a symbol of fertility and renewal, may have insured that the memory of Mary's mother pervaded the Psalter.

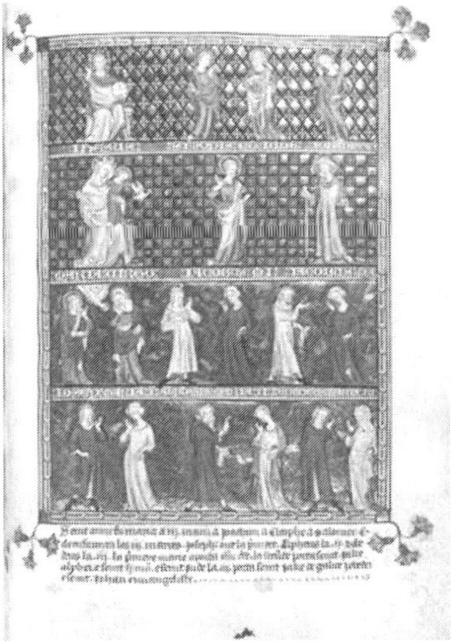

Fig. 8 The Holy Kinship, "Queen Mary's Psalter," MS Royal 2B.vii, fol. 68, ca. 1310-1320, British Library, London (Photo: © The British Library Board)

Saint Anne was also important as a model of the mother's role in education. Although the popular image of Anne teaching the Virgin to read is not included in Queen Mary's Psalter, it was frequently represented in texts and images throughout England and, in fact, was the subject of an early sixteenth-century sculptural group in the Chapel of Henry VII at Westminster Abbey.[45] Despite the absence of this image in the Psalter, the chart depicting Anne as a serial widow, mother, and grandmother, so closely connected to the idea of the mother's role in educating her children, would have resonated with Mary's own history. Not only did her own mother ensure her superb education, but some of her stepmothers, particularly Catherine Parr, were supportive of and, indeed, contributed to the literary culture of the court and the education of the royal offspring.[46] The centrality of Saint Anne in the Psalter's images would have been well suited to the educational culture of Mary's court.[47]

The rest of Queen Mary's Psalter contains narrative or episodic imagery on every folio, which splits into two levels. The most vivid images, which show scenes from the life of Christ, are the framed full-color illuminations that mark the divisions of the psalms into readable segments. Motherhood continues to play a strong role, now embodied in the queen's patron saint, the Virgin Mary, who often appears with more prominence than is typical in contemporary cycles.[48] For example, the famous episode in which the young Jesus disappears and is later found lecturing to the scholars in the temple is here depicted in two scenes. While the second scene is a typical illumination of the tiny Jesus lecturing to the massed scholars, the first is a unique image that appears to show Mary actually introducing her son to the scholars; this image shifts the responsibility for the confrontation from Jesus to his mother [Fig. 9]. She

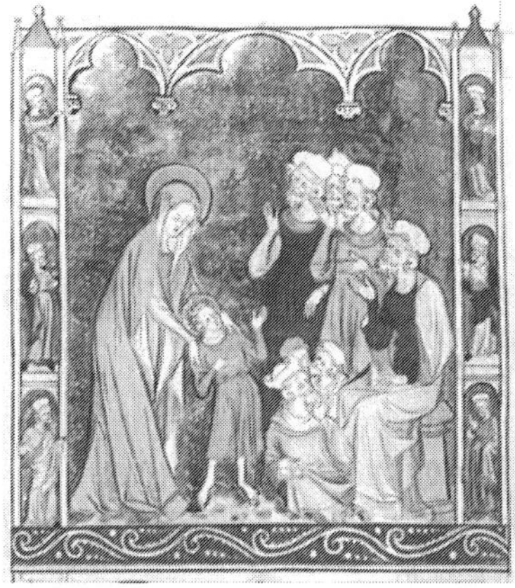

Fig. 9 Mary presents Jesus to the Hebrew Scholars, "Queen Mary's Psalter," MS Royal 2B.vii, fol. 150v, detail, ca. 1310-1320, British Library, London (Photo: © The British Library Board)

almost appears to push him toward them, like a Judaean stage mother. Mary's active assistance carries on through to the end of the Infancy cycle; the Passion sequence in the Psalter includes a scene in which Mary helps her son carry the cross through the streets of Jerusalem, a detail found in only a few other Gothic sequences [Fig. 10].[49]

In addition to these illuminations, every folio in the Psalter proper includes *bas-de-page* images presented in the same tinted drawing style as the prefatory narratives. These images fall into well-organized sequences, including scenes from the bestiary, the miracles of the Virgin, and the martyrdoms of the saints, in the latter case helpfully identified with rubrics. The fifty-six scenes devoted to the miracles of the Virgin make this series one of the longest of its type. Significantly, these images appear along a stretch of psalms that is otherwise decorated with scenes from the Ministry of Christ in framed illuminations. Mary thus appears to be continuing this ministry into the present day [Fig. 11].[50] Certainly they continue the theme of the active mother, familiar from the prefatory narrative and the main psalm illuminations, with the added attraction that, here, Mary is always represented, in typical Gothic fashion, as a crowned queen. Her salvific activities may have seemed to parallel the Renaissance Mary's labors in the service of her revived Catholic Church.

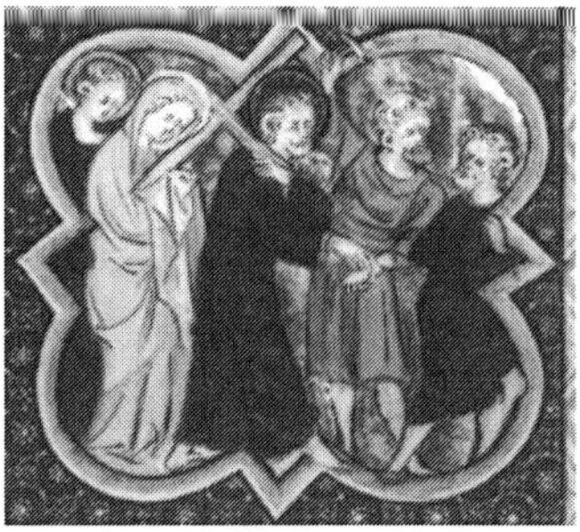

Fig. 10 Christ carrying the Cross, "Queen Mary's Psalter," MS Royal 2B.vii, fol. 253, detail, ca. 1310-1320, British Library, London (Photo: © The British Library Board)

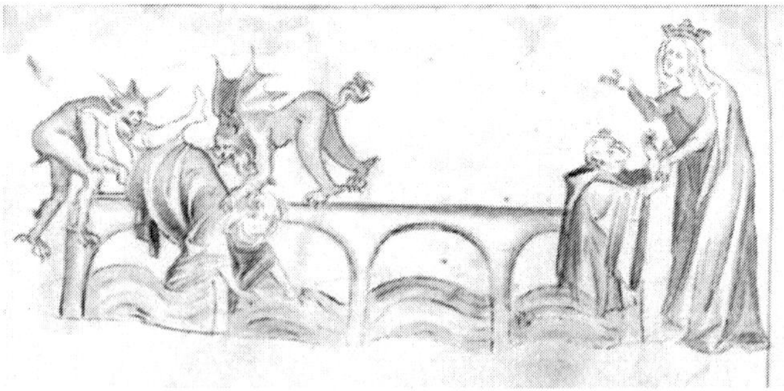

Fig. 11 The Virgin saves a drowning monk, "Queen Mary's Psalter," MS Royal 2B.vii, fol. 213v, detail, ca. 1310-1320, British Library, London (Photo: © The British Library Board)

Other saints emphasized in the martyrdom sequence also could have been valued in the context of motherhood.[51] Margaret of Antioch, the patron saint of women in childbirth, is given fourteen scenes; the martyrdom of Catherine of Alexandria, who shared a name with Mary's mother, is prominently chronicled in eight images. The sequence of twenty-two images that relates the life of Thomas Becket begins with a completely fictitious story that casts Becket's mother as a Saracen maiden who falls in love with Gilbert Becket, helps him escape, and then makes her way to London to be baptized as a Christian [Fig. 12], marry, and bear a son.[52] In this version, the entire history of Becket, a saint whose cult Mary was keen to revive, is made possible by the initiative of his mother.

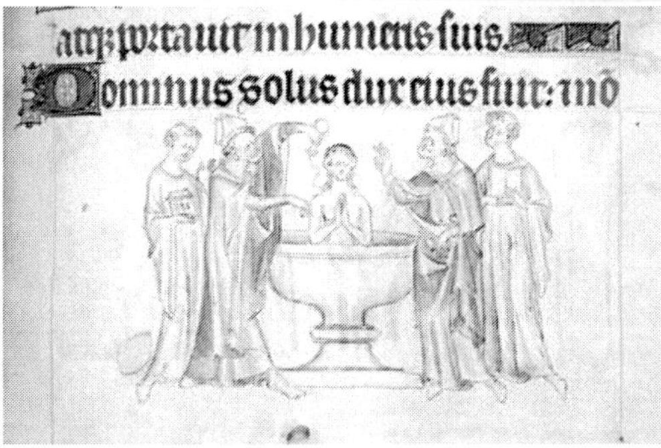

Fig. 12 Baptism of Saint Thomas Becket's mother, "Queen Mary's Psalter," MS Royal 2B.vii, fol. 289, detail, ca. 1310-1320, British Library, London (Photo: © The British Library Board)

These figures, along with the powerful mothers of the Old Testament sequence, form a constellation of strong women around the central figure of Mary, the queen of heaven. Mary, the queen of England, was often described and addressed in Marian terms, to the extent that "Ave Maria" formed the basis for texts ranging from an address by Cardinal Pole, to a wedding song sung by schoolboys in 1554.[53] While it was not unusual for a woman to be directed to Mary as a role model, such connections were particularly powerful during this brief revival of English Catholic rule under a queen of the same name.

Conclusion

Whether or not we take the appearance of Mary's emblem or the velvet binding as evidence of her personal use, we can see many reasons why the queen would have found this particular prayerbook to be appealing and in fact comforting. The Psalter is a stunning manuscript, full of a wide range of colors both soft and brilliant; for readers accustomed to the textures of paper, even the thick, creamy paper of the printed books of Mary's time, its parchment is a wonder to touch. Women, as I have noted, are strong actors throughout the narratives, from the Old Testament to the New, and among the saints who inhabit the margins. Mothers are particularly emphasized, and their actions go beyond childbearing as they support their children into adulthood. The fact that the most prominent of these mothers was the name-saint of the queen—and very often represented as a crowned queen—would not have gone unnoticed.

It may be significant in this context that the Queen Mary Psalter was not the only medieval psalter given to Mary. According to Carley, medieval manuscripts were only rarely given as gifts in the Tudor court. In the example he cites, a courtier presenting a fifteenth-century copy of Richard Rolle's Latin psalter to the Princess Mary apologized "for offering 'suche an olde boke', explaining that its contents alone redeemed the gift."[54] This evidence that Mary had already been directed to the contents of an old manuscript psalter strengthens the possibility that she might have looked beyond the velvet cover of Royal 2B.vii. Further, among the wedding gifts brought to her by Philip of Spain in 1554 was an even older illuminated psalter with royal connections, which has been identified with the Psalter of Ingeborg of Denmark (MS 66, Musée Condée, Chantilly).[55] Ingeborg married Philip Augustus of France in 1193, only to be cast off after their wedding night. She fought his divorce proceedings, despite his marriage to another woman who bore his children, and twenty years later was restored to her title as queen of France.[56] The prefatory illuminations in this earlier prayerbook also emphasize the role played by a crowned Virgin Mary [Fig. 13]; its suitability as a marriage gift and its ability to interest Queen Mary—if she opened it—would be worth another essay.

Queen Mary's Psalter may also have been owned by a medieval queen. As noted above, neither inscriptions nor heraldry mark the original owner of Royal 2B.vii. Nevertheless, the Psalter's iconography has suggested to several scholars that it was intended for the use of one of the most notorious medieval queens of England: Isabelle of France, the queen of Edward II, who is often remembered as the "She-Wolf of France."[57] Isabelle, the daughter of Philip the IV of France and sister of the last rulers of the Capetian dynasty, was instrumental in the downfall of Edward in 1326-1327, after which she ruled England in the name of their minor son, Edward III, until he gained enough power to oust her and her lover, Roger Mortimer. If the psalter presented by Philip was in fact the Ingeborg Psalter, and if the Queen Mary Psalter itself indeed belonged to Isabelle of France, the ownership of both manuscripts by Mary—daughter to a repudiated queen and frustrated mother—is a stunning coincidence. The

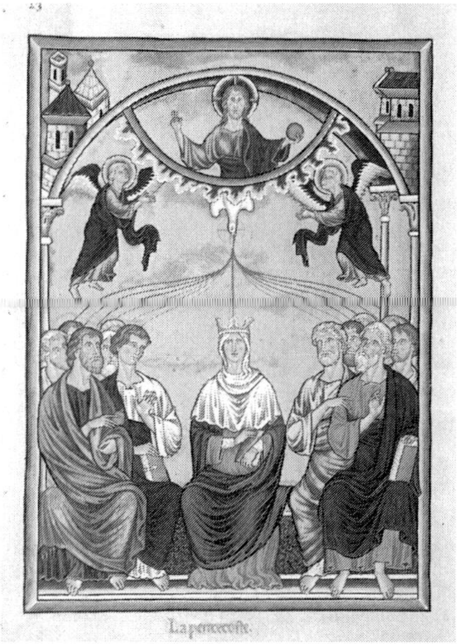

Fig. 13 Pentecost, Ingeborg Psalter, MS 66, fol. 32v, ca. 1200, Musée Condée, Chantilly (Photo: Réunion des musées nationaux/Art Resource, NY)

royal provenance of the Ingeborg Psalter was apparently known at the time, but it is not clear whether it was linked to Ingeborg herself. As for the Queen Mary Psalter, the link to Isabelle is based largely on its iconography, as well as its relationships with other manuscripts in the orbit of this controversial queen. There is however, on folio 83v, evidence of a paste-down that is now missing.[58] There is no mention of anything on that folio in the original description of the book, which suggests that whatever was there was removed before the manuscript entered the British Museum's collections. The chroniclers of the Tudor period treated Isabelle as one of the worst queens of England, a "She-Wolf" indeed, whose usurpation of her husband's power was only mitigated by his weakness.[59] It is tempting to suggest that the missing paste-down held some evidence of her ownership, removed by a subsequent Tudor owner; the connection of this luxurious psalter with a queen who had taken royal power into her own hands and used it unwisely would have been troubling.

Whether or not either of these two illuminated psalters was connected with a medieval queen, the one now known as Queen Mary's Psalter would have provided its Renaissance audience with a full panoply of biblical and saintly role models. If the Queen did indeed look at this manuscript, she would have found many reasons to pore over its folios, to keep it nearby, and to see in its 200-year-old images a mirror of her own concerns.

Notes

[1] Acknowledgments: A note of gratitude is due David Loades and James Carley, who provided considerable aid to this medievalist's research into Renaissance history and book culture, and to Kathleen Schowalter for her help with the Ingeborg Psalter. As I was unable to visit the Queen Mary Psalter while writing this essay, I relied on the help of Karen Limper, Peter Kidd, and Mirjam Foot in London, who contributed their time and energy to address several questions regarding the binding. A final tip of the hat for lucid criticism and commentary goes to our editors, Alyce Jordan and Janet Marquardt, as well as this essay's anonymous readers.

[2] George Warner, *Queen Mary's Psalter* (London: Trustees of The British Museum, 1912); and Lucy Freeman Sandler, *Gothic Manuscripts 1285-1385*, Survey of Manuscripts Illuminated in the British Isles, ed. J. J. G. Alexander, vol. 2 (London: Harvey Miller, 1985). cat. no. 56; see most recently Anne Rudloff Stanton, *The Queen Mary Psalter: a Study of Affect and Audience*, Transactions of the American Philosophical Society 91, 6 (Philadelphia: American Philosophical Society, 2001).

[3] Warner, *Queen Mary's Psalter*. 1-2; James P. Carley, *The Books of King Henry VIII and his Wives* (London: The British Library, 2004). 144 notes that in 1551 even the royal library was to be purged of all "superstitiouse bookes, as masse bookes, legendes, and such like…" according to a Council order, and that many other manuscripts were taken abroad on the death of Edward VI, when Mary came to power.

[4] George Warner and Julius Gilson, *Catalogue of Western Manuscripts in the Old Royal and King's Collection*, vol. 1 (London: Trustees of the British Museum, 1921). xvi - xvii singled out the Queen Mary Psalter as one of the most beautiful manuscripts in the whole collection.

[5] Gustav Waagen, *Treasures of Art in Great Britain*, vol. 1 (London: John Murray, 1854). 173; Nat Westlake and William Purdue, *Illustrations of Old Testament History* (London: Joseph Masters, 1865).

[6] Warner, *Queen Mary's Psalter*. 1

[7] Cyril Davenport, *English Embroidered Bookbindings* (London: Kegan Paul, Trench, Trubner and Company, Ltd., 1899). 57; Warner, *Queen Mary's Psalter*. 2; on Mary's use of the pomegranate see also John N. King, *Tudor Royal Iconography: Literature and Art in an Age of Religious Crisis* (Princeton: Princeton University Press, 1989). 185-186

[8] Warner, *Queen Mary's Psalter*. 2

[9] Stanton, *Queen Mary Psalter*. Studies of iconographic programs in which biblical figures provided types or antitypes for medieval queens include Madeline

Caviness, "Patron or Matron?: a Capetian Bride and a 'Vade Mecum' for her Marriage Bed," *Speculum* 68 (1993). 333-362; Joan A. Holladay, "The Education of Jeanne d'Evreux: Personal Piety and Dynastic Salvation in her Book of Hours," *Art History* 17 (1994). 585-611; Alyce A. Jordan, "Material Girls: Judith, Esther, Narrative Modes and Models of Queenship in the Windows of the Sainte-Chapelle in Paris," *Word and Image* 15 (1999). 337-350; Anne Rudloff Stanton, "The Psalter of Isabelle, Queen of England: Isabelle as the Audience," *Word and Image* 18 (2002). 1-27

[10] A standard reference for Mary's biography is David Loades, *Mary Tudor: a Life* (Oxford: Basil Blackwell, Ltd., 1989). Historical material in this essay is taken from Loades unless otherwise attributed. I was unable to consult Judith Richards' more recent *Mary Tudor* (London: Routledge Press, 2008) before the publication of this study.

[11] "Bloody Mary" was a phrase distilled from John Foxe's enormously popular treatise, known as *The Book of Martyrs*, first published in 1563. Judith M. Richards, "Mary Tudor: Renaissance Queen of England," in *"High and Mighty Queens" of Early Modern England: Realities and Representations*, ed. Carole Levin, Jo Eldridge Carney, and Debra Barrett-Graves (New York: Palgrave Macmillan, 2003). 27; see also the CD-Rom *Facsimile of John Foxe's Book of Martyrs*, ed. David G. Newcombe and Michael Pidd (Oxford: Oxford University Press, 2001).

[12] Richards, "Renaissance Queen of England." 33

[13] Ibid. 28

[14] Loades, *Mary Tudor*. 330. This point is taken up in several subsequent studies, such as Lucy E. C. Wooding, *Rethinking Catholicism in Reformation England* (Oxford: Clarendon Press, 2000); and the essays in *The Church of Mary Tudor*, ed. Eamon Duffy and David Loades (London: Ashgate Press, 2006).

[15] Timothy G. Elston, "Transformation or Continuity? Sixteenth-Century Education and the Legacy of Catherine of Aragon, Mary I, and Juan Luis Vives," in *"High and Mighty Queens" of Early Modern England: Realities and Representations*, ed. Carole Levin, Jo Eldridge Carney, and Debra Barrett-Graves (New York: Palgrave Macmillan, 2003). 11-26

[16] Wooding, *Rethinking Catholicism*. 38; Elston, "Transformation or Continuity?" discusses the Spanish tradition of commissioning pedagogical treatises. For more on Catherine and Tudor book culture see James P. Carley, *The Libraries of King Henry VIII,* Corpus of British Medieval Library Catalogues 7 (London: The British Library, 2000). xxix-xxx; and on treatises dedicated to her Carley, *Books of King Henry VIII and his Wives*. 109-123

[17] For more on Vives' life and works see the introduction to Juan Luis Vives, *The Education of a Christian Woman: A Sixteenth-Century Manual*, ed. and trans. Charles Fantazzi (Chicago: University of Chicago Press, 2000).

[18] Richards, "Renaissance Queen." 39

[19] Carley, *Books of King Henry VIII and his Wives*. 100-105

[20] T. A. Birrell, *English Monarchs and their Books: from Henry VII to Charles II*, The Panizzi Lectures, 1986 (London: The British Library, 1987). 21-23; and

Mirjam Foot, *Studies in the History of Bookbinding* (Brookfield, VT: Ashgate Press, 1993). 303

[21] Mirjam Foot, *The History of Bookbinding as a Mirror of Society*, The Panizzi Lectures, 1997 (London: The British Library, 1998). 62-64 and Fig. 45 for a red velvet binding, on a printed copy of the *Meditationes Christianarum libellus*, that is remarkably similar in many respects to the binding of Queen Mary's Psalter.

[22] See Jane Eagan and Maria Hayward, "A Textile Binding Once in the Library of Henry VIII—Technical Examination and Conservation," in *Care and Conservation of Manuscripts 8*, ed. Gillian Fellows-Jensen and Peter Springborg (Copenhagen: Museum Tusculanum Press, 2005). 124-125, no. 13. I thank Peter Kidd for directing me to this reference.

[23] Warner, *Queen Mary's Psalter*. 2

[24] King, *Tudor Royal Iconography*. 185-186

[25] Foot, *Studies in the History of Bookbinding*. 303

[26] Peter Kidd, e-mails to author 29 September 2006 and 27 October 2006; Mirjam Foot, e-mail to author 13 November 2006; I am grateful to both for examining the binding of the Psalter for me and to Karen Limper for contacting Professor Foot on my behalf. There is no indication that Smith saw any reward for his presentation in terms of preferments or positions, as he was still a customs official in March of 1555. See *Acts of the Privy Council of England: New Series* V (London: Eyre and Spottiswoode, 1890). 254

[27] See the preface in Warner, *Queen Mary's Psalter*, for a detailed listing of every scene and the Anglo-Norman texts that accompanied the preface; and Anne Rudloff Stanton, "The 'Queen Mary Psalter': Narrative and Devotion in Gothic England" (Ph.D. diss., University of Texas at Austin, 1992). 44-155, for a more extensive discussion of the stories and transcriptions of additional texts. For a chart that summarizes the complex relationships between all the image cycles see Stanton, "Notes on the Codicology of the Queen Mary Psalter," *Scriptorium* 49 (1995). 252

[28] The Anglo-Norman renderings of "Ici" (Here) and "Comment" (How) would easily have been intelligible to Mary, whose French apparently was serviceable. Richards, "Renaissance Queen." 30-31

[29] Nigel Morgan, "Old Testament Illustration in Thirteenth-Century England," in *The Bible in the Middle Ages: Its Influence on Literature and Art*, ed. Bernard S. Levy (Binghamton, NY: Medieval and Renaissance Texts and Studies, 1992). 172-174. Morgan cites the Queen Mary Psalter as a fully-developed example of this romantic approach.

[30] Anne Rudloff Stanton, "From Eve to Bathsheba and Beyond: Motherhood in the Queen Mary Psalter," in *Women and the Book: Assessing the Visual Evidence*, ed. Jane H. M. Taylor and Lesley Smith (London and Toronto: The British Library and the University of Toronto Press, 1997). 172-188. For the French Old Testament tradition see Harvey Stahl, *Picturing Kingship: History and Painting in the Psalter of St. Louis* (University Park, PA: Pennsylvania State University Press, 2008), particularly chap. 4, "Psalters and the Old Testament." Contemporary English manuscripts with significant Genesis material include the Psalter of Isabella of

France (cod. gall. 16, Bayerische Staatsbibliothek, Munich, ca. 1303-1308; see Stanton, "The Psalter of Isabelle, Queen of England.") and the Egerton Genesis (MS Egerton 1894, British Library, London, ca. 1360; see Mary Coker Joslin and Carolyn Coker Joslin Watson, *The Egerton Genesis* [London and Toronto: British Library and the University of Toronto Press, 2001]).

[31] Stanton, *Queen Mary Psalter*. 90-103

[32] E. W. Ives, *Anne Boleyn* (Oxford: Blackwell Press, 1986). 155-156

[33] Michael Hattaway, "Paradoxes of Solomon: Learning in the English Renaissance," *Journal of the History of Ideas* 29 (1968). 499-530

[34] King, *Tudor Royal Iconography*. 70-88

[35] For kingly role models in the Psalter, see Stanton, *Queen Mary Psalter*. 178-189; studies of other programs include Paul Binski, *Westminster Abbey and the Plantagenets: Kingship and the Representation of Power 1200-1400* (London: Yale University Press, 1995); Alyce A. Jordan, *Visualizing Kingship in the Windows of the Sainte-Chapelle*, Publications of the International Center of Medieval Art 5 (Turnhout: Brepols, 2002); William Chester Jordan, "The 'People' in the Psalter of Saint Louis and the Leadership of Moses," in *Medieval Paradigms: Essays in Honor of Jeremy duQuesnay Adams*, ed. Stephanie Hayes-Healey (New York: Palgrave Macmillan, 2005); and, in this volume, Donna Sadler, "The Persistence of the Royal Past on the West Façade of Reims Cathedral." For sixteenth-century examples see King, *Tudor Royal Iconography*. 70-88

[36] Caviness, "Patron or Matron"; Jordan, *Visualizing Kingship*. 18-21

[37] Vives, *Education of a Christian Woman*. 267-268

[38] For Samson see fols. 42v-43; for Samuel see fol. 48. Stanton, *Queen Mary Psalter*. 112, 120

[39] Loades, *Mary Tudor*. 248-250 (in 1554), 301-302 (in 1557)

[40] Anne Rudloff Stanton, "'*La genealogye comence*': Kinship and Difference in the Queen Mary Psalter," *Studies in Iconography* 17 (1996). 177-214

[41] The standard resource for the development of the Tree of Jesse iconography remains Arthur Watson, *The Early Iconography of the Tree of Jesse* (Oxford: Oxford University Press, 1934).

[42] See the editors' useful introductory chapter in *Interpreting Cultural Symbols: Saint Anne in Late Medieval Society*, ed. Kathleen Ashley and Pamela Sheingorn (Athens, GA: University of Georgia Press, 1990). 1-68. For the images in the Queen Mary Psalter see Stanton, *Queen Mary Psalter*. 149-152

[43] Werner Esser, "Die heilige Sippe: Studien zu einem spätmittelalterlichen Bildthema in Deutchschland und den Niederlanden" (Ph. D. diss., University of Bonn, 1986).

[44] Vives, *Education of a Christian Woman*. 312 also cites Anne in his chapter on widows.

[45] Pamela Sheingorn, "'The Wise Mother': The Image of St. Anne Teaching the Virgin Mary," *Gesta* 32 (1993). 69-80, Fig. 30. For more on late-medieval textual representations see Gail McMurray Gibson, *The Theater of Devotion: East Anglian*

Drama and Society in the Late Middle Ages (Chicago: University of Chicago Press, 1989). 82-84

[46] Carley, *Books of King Henry VIII and his Wives*. 138-139 notes that one of Mary's first acts on coming to the throne was to appropriate Catherine's library.

[47] For a study of the use of Saint Anne's iconography in contemporary French courtly culture see Myra Orth, "'Madame Sainte Anne': The Holy Kinship, the Royal Trinity, and Louis of Savoy," in *Interpreting Cultural Symbols: Saint Anne in Late Medieval Society*, ed. Kathleen Ashley and Pamela Sheingorn (Athens, GA: University of Georgia Press, 1990). 199-228

[48] Stanton, *Queen Mary Psalter*. 126-142

[49] Ibid. 132

[50] Stanton, *Queen Mary Psalter*. 139-142

[51] Ibid. 139-146

[52] Ibid. 142. For more on the legend of Thomas's Saracen mother see Paul A. Brown, *The Development of the Legend of Thomas Becket* (Philadelphia: no publisher, 1930).

[53] King, *Tudor Royal Iconography*. 197-199

[54] Carley, *Libraries of King Henry VIII*. xlviii n. 91. He does, however, discuss the influx of medieval manuscripts from the disbanded monastic libraries under Henry VIII.

[55] Carley, *Libraries of King Henry VIII*. lxxxvii; Carley, *Books of King Henry VIII and his Wives*. 149. The classic study is Florens Deuchler, *Der Ingeborgspsalter* (Berlin: de Gruyter, 1967). Carley's evidence comes from the records of the Royal Librarian Patrick Young, who reported in 1650 that in his inventory of the king's books he found "one of speciall note wanting, for antiquity and richnes of lyneing invaluable, to witt St Lewis king of France his Psalter in Latine…." Quoted in *Libraries of King Henry VIII*. lxxxvii n. 188. Two provenance notes in the Psalter mention its presence in England and complete the link to Young's inventory, but Deuchler, *Ingeborgspsalter*. 7 n. 21, sees them as misleading.

[56] Kathleen Schowalter, "The Ingeborg Psalter: Queenship, Legitimacy, and the Appropriation of Byzantine Art in the West," in *Capetian Women*, ed. Kathleen Nolan (New York: Palgrave MacMillan, 2003). 99-136. I am grateful to Professor Schowalter for directing me to the work of Allison Anne Merrill, "A Study of the Ingeborg Psalter Atelier" (Ph.D. diss., Columbia University, 1994).

[57] Kathryn A. Smith, "History, Typology and Homily: The Joseph Cycle in the Queen Mary Psalter," *Gesta* 32 (1993). 154-156; Stanton, *Queen Mary Psalter*. 231-241; Stanton, "Isabelle of France and her Manuscripts," in *Capetian Women*. 234-237. For Isabelle, see Alison Weir, *Queen Isabella: Treachery, Adultery, and Murder in Medieval England* (New York: Ballantine Books, 2005); and Paul Doherty, *Isabella and the Strange Death of Edward II* (New York: Caroll and Graf Publishers, 2003).

[58] Stanton, "Notes on the Codicology." 261

[59] Joan Parks, "History, Tragedy, and Truth in Christopher Marlowe's *Edward II*," *Studies in English Literature* 39 (1999). 275-290 examines the chronicle background of Marlowe's drama.

REFRAMING SAINT-DENIS FOR THE SUN KING: A SPECTACULAR HISTORY[1]

KERRY PAUL BOEYE

Dramatic alterations to works of medieval art and architecture have sometimes occurred without a hand being laid upon them. Literary or scholarly works, ceremonies, or historical events, to name only a few potential catalysts of change, can profoundly shift the perception of an artwork or building and thereby fundamentally transform them in the eyes of their audiences. The medieval abbey church of Saint-Denis, situated on the northern outskirts of Paris, is widely known today as the birthplace of Gothic architecture. This fame rests, however, upon the work of generations of scholars who, beginning in the nineteenth century, reframed the church within a modern discourse on the development of Gothic as an architectural style.[2] Other efforts to reframe Saint-Denis often arose in direct response to political circumstances. One of the most ambitious of such attempts was made by Michel Félibien (1664–1719), a resident monk, who sought to alter the perception of the abbey through his book, the *Histoire de l'abbaye royale de Saint-Denys en France*, published in 1706. In this large, sumptuously illustrated work Félibien recounted the abbey's history, documented its privileges, and described its treasures while simultaneously seeking to position Saint-Denis within the visual regimes of royal spectacle developed under Louis XIV (reigned 1643–1715). The book's extensive illustrations were critical to Félibien's effort to shift the perception of the abbey, and they provide insight into the representational strategies used by Félibien to accomplish his task.[3]

Félibien's ultimate goal for the *Histoire* was to restore Saint-Denis to the favor of Louis XIV.[4] The king had last visited the abbey as a young monarch in 1654, more than fifty years before Félibien personally presented the book to the king at Versailles in 1706. Such apparent disregard for the abbey veered toward virtual hostility when, in 1691, Louis XIV went so far as to obtain a papal bull that allowed him to suppress the office of abbot of Saint-Denis. He then re-allocated the resources dedicated to maintaining the abbacy to his own project, the

Maison de Saint-Louis at Saint-Cyr, which the king had founded in 1686 to house and educate impoverished girls of noble blood. Saint-Denis, as a result, was reduced to a priory, and it was the first prior of the once-proud abbey who encouraged Félibien, in 1697, to take up his pen and write the *Histoire*.

Illustration as Persuasion

Anne Lombard-Jourdan first drew attention to the political motivations behind Félibien's *Histoire* in an important study of the book's production and illustration. She argued that the rich program of imagery was vital to the conception of the *Histoire*, and that, by beautifying the book, the illustrations heightened its appeal and contributed enormously to its success.[5] The illustrations were indeed critical in helping the *Histoire* strike the register of address appropriate to Louis XIV and his court, but the illustrations were also designed to persuade as much as to decorate. An exploration of the visual rhetoric of the illustrations reveals how Félibien tried to convince the Sun King to bestow his goodwill and patronage upon Saint-Denis. Persuading the elderly autocrat demanded delicacy, however, and neither outright flattery nor addressing the king's neglect of Saint-Denis directly would have succeeded. Instead, Félibien sought to reframe Saint-Denis through the *Histoire* by using representational strategies that had been developed by ministers of Louis XIV to promote the king's glory.[6] By imposing such an interpretive framework upon Saint-Denis, Félibien hoped to transform the abbey from a neglected institution disdained by the king into a royal monument that would reflect the Sun King's grandeur.

While the visual strategies deployed by Félibien in the *Histoire* have gone largely unexamined, some of the illustrations from the book have received intense scrutiny, since they provide valuable documentation of medieval Saint-Denis. Most notable among these illustrations are the five large engravings of reliquaries, royal regalia, precious manuscripts, and other objects in the abbey's treasury [Fig. 1]. A large portion of these objects were collected over the centuries by the abbey in its traditional capacities as the burial place of the French kings and the repository of the regalia worn by the kings during their coronation.[7] The treasury engravings have become fundamental sources for studying these important objects, many of which were destroyed or dispersed during the French Revolution.[8] Comparisons with extant works from the treasury have allowed scholars to confirm the descriptive accuracy of the engravings, which have served, in turn, as documents for reconstructing the more numerous lost or damaged works.[9] As a result of their archaeological value, the engravings have been frequently reproduced in modern scholarship, which has conferred upon them the familiarity and status of academic icons.

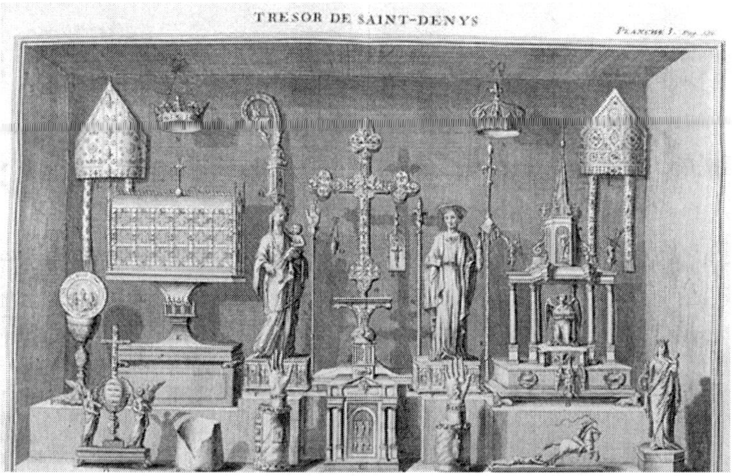

Fig. 1 Philippe Simonneau, *Trésor de Saint-Denys,* engraving, from Michel Félibien, *Histoire de l'abbaye royale de Saint-Denys en France* (Paris: Frédéric Léonard, 1706). Pl. I (fold-out plate opposite 536)

The use of these engravings as archaeological documents is emblematic of the valuation of Félibien's *Histoire* as a whole by scholars, who praise the book as a great advance in the critical historical study of the abbey.[10] For Félibien, exacting description and historical accuracy were critical aspects of his project that assured the dissemination, and, to some degree, preservation of the treasury objects. But the treasury engravings do more than open a window onto medieval Saint-Denis, they also mirror the circumstances in which the *Histoire* was created; the archaeological exactitude of these illustrations, in other words, might also have had a political purpose.

Many other illustrations that embellish Félibien's *Histoire* lack the painstaking, descriptive character of the treasury engravings. For the most part these other illustrations depict scenes from the abbey's history and contribute substantially to the book's impact and meaning. To take the most prominent example, the full-page frontispiece of the *Histoire* depicts King Phillip III (reigned 1270–1285) carrying the remains of his father, Saint Louis (reigned 1226–1270), as part of the funeral cortege that moves toward Saint-Denis, seen in the distance [Fig. 2]. The bearded archbishop of Sens, standing on the left, calls a halt to the procession with his outstretched left hand so that an ailing man, supported by his wife in the foreground, can touch the casket and be healed miraculously by the saintly bones within.

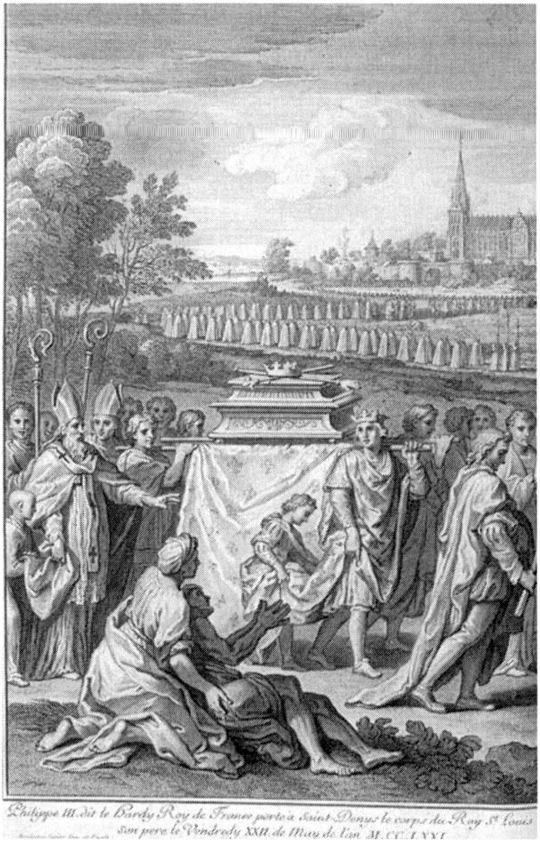

Fig. 2 Louis Boulogne the Younger and Sébastien Leclerc, design; Jean-Baptiste Poilly, engraving, *Philippe III dit le Hardy, Roy de France porte à Saint-Denys le corps du Roy St. Louis son pere le Vendredy XXII. de May de l'an M. CC. LXXI*, from Michel Félibien, *Histoire de l'abbaye royale de Saint-Denys en France* (Paris: Frédéric Léonard, 1706). frontispiece

The royal casket appears near the center of the picture, simultaneously anchoring the composition and demanding our attention as the most significant object in the crowded scene. Unlike the reliquaries and regalia recorded in the treasury engravings, however, the rendering of the casket and the royal implements on its lid is anachronistic and inexact. Although the caption below the image specifies the date as "Friday, 22 May 1271," the casket, with its pyramidal form, broad proportions, and chaste curves, is drawn from a late seventeenth-century neoclassical—not a Gothic—stylistic vocabulary. This anachronism may be excused by the fact that the artist had no authentic model to draw upon, because the actual casket had been lost. But this was not the case for the crown and two scepters on the lid of the casket, for which potential models lay in the abbey's treasury. While the crown is too generic to be identified, the two scepters are recognizable as those created in 1594 for the coronation of Henry IV (reigned 1589–1610), which are also reproduced in the first treasury

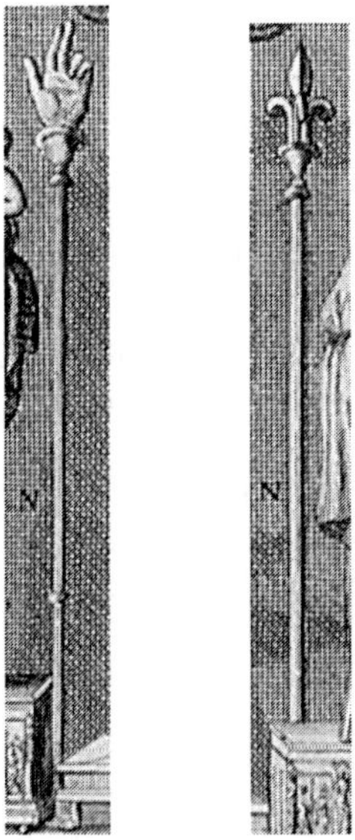

Fig. 3 *Main de justice* and scepter of Henry IV, detail of Fig. 1

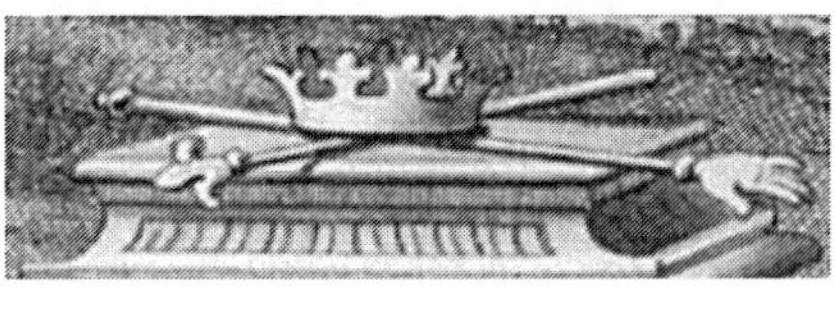

Fig. 4 *Main de justice* and scepter of Henry IV, detail of Fig. 2

engraving [Fig. 3]. Aside from the obvious anachronism of placing these scepters in a scene that transpired three hundred years before they were made, the depiction of the scepters in the frontispiece is surprisingly less precise than their reproduction in the treasury engraving. One of the scepters on the casket is represented accurately with a fleur-de-lys on the terminus, while the other—known as a *main de justice* ("hand of justice")—ends in a gesturing hand that makes the wrong gesture.[11] In the treasury engraving the hand of the *main de justice* makes the proper gesture with thumb and two fingers extended, but the one on the casket in the frontispiece extends all five fingers, giving it an unfortunate resemblance to a backscratcher [Fig. 4].

The imprecision of the frontispiece and other historical illustrations has rendered them far less valuable in recovering the medieval history of Saint-Denis, with the consequence that these illustrations, unlike the treasury engravings, are rarely reproduced and virtually unknown today. Yet the images of past events were as important as the treasury engravings in achieving Félibien's larger objective of reversing the abbey's declining fortunes through the *Histoire*. As we will see, Félibien was very deliberate in planning the illustration of the book, and he supervised the production of the illustrations closely. The *Histoire* displays the influence of several different genres of history writing, but the most consequential influence, especially where the illustrations were concerned, came from royal histories and descriptions of royal monuments written in praise of Louis XIV. Although Félibien clearly attempted to emulate such works, they have never, to my knowledge, been compared to the *Histoire* by scholars. Yet pursuing precisely this kind of comparison below promises both to illuminate some of the visual and rhetorical strategies used by Félibien and to change our perceptions of how the illustrations—both archaeological and historical—operated as persuasion.

The Making of the *Histoire*

Félibien appears to have been intimately involved in every aspect of the production of the *Histoire de l'abbaye royale de Saint-Denys en France*, judging from the contracts and correspondence found among his papers.[12] Félibien began working on the *Histoire* in 1697, at the urging of the prior of Saint-Denis, and completed a draft in 1703. He clearly envisioned an elaborate set of illustrations as an essential feature of the book, for in March 1703 he obtained funds from Saint-Denis to provide the *Histoire* with engravings. The necessary arrangements for publishing the book were made rapidly over the next few months: in May of that year

Félibien completed a contract with the royal printer, Frédéric Léonard; in June he received the approval to publish the book from the royal censors; and in July he secured a royal copyright.[13]

Three more years would pass, however, before the book was finally published. Much of that time appears to have been spent on the illustration of the *Histoire*. The earliest payments to artists recorded in a list drawn up by Félibien date to December 1703, which suggests that he was busy contracting artists during that year.[14] Félibien seems to have exercised great care in selecting established draftsmen and engravers, most notably the famous and prolific Sébastien Leclerc, who was appointed the King's Engraver [*Graveur ordinaire du Roi*] from 1693 to 1705.[15] The majority of payments to artists date to 1704 and 1705, indicating that the illustrations were produced primarily during these years.

Félibien certainly selected the subject matter for the illustrations, and circumstantial evidence intimates that he closely supervised their production.[16] His hand may be detected, for example, in a subtle modification that was made to the frontispiece [Fig. 2]. The long line of waiting monks that snakes through the middle ground of the illustration was much shorter in the original design, executed by Louis Boulogne the Younger. Leclerc later lengthened this procession, perhaps, as Lombard-Jourdan suggests, at the behest of Félibien, who wanted to emphasize the important role played by the monks in royal funeral ceremonies.[17] That Félibien immersed himself in such fine points is revealed by the stipulation in the printer's contract that the paper chosen for the book was subject to Félibien's approval. The evidence, therefore, suggests that Félibien was as exacting with the production of the illustrations and the material quality of the *Histoire* as he was meticulous in researching and writing its text.

Finally, almost nine years after Félibien began the project, around eight hundred copies of the *Histoire* were printed, a typical number for such a large and expensive book during this period.[18] Nearly all of the expenses were underwritten by the abbey.[19] Printed in folio and numbering over 810 pages, the *Histoire* is divided into three principal parts: 1) the historical narrative proper, entitled the "Histoire de l'abbaye royale de Saint-Denys en France," itself divided into eight books and encompassing 524 pages; 2) the "Description de l'église de Saint-Denys en France," a painstaking description of the church and its contents in sixty-seven pages; and 3) the "Recueil de pièces justificatives," a collection of transcribed documents that runs to 223 pages.[20]

The illustrations are concentrated in the first two parts of the book, and begin with the large frontispiece [Fig. 2]. The book quickly establishes a visual rhythm that begins with the preface and continues at the opening of each major text division throughout the remainder of the book. The first page of the "Dissertation préliminaire," a prefatory section that discusses the site of Saint Denis' martyrdom, furnishes an example of the standard page layout used for each of these openings [Fig. 5]. A narrative vignette

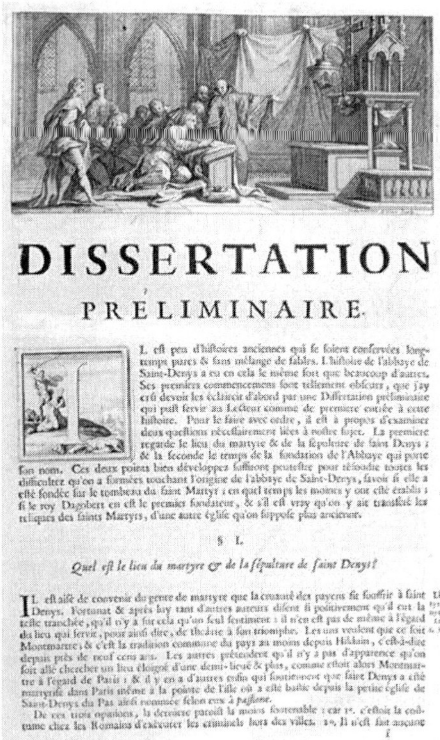

DISSERTATION

PRELIMINAIRE.

§ I.

Fig. 5 Claude-Guy Hallé, design; Philippe Simonneau, engraving, King kneeling before an altar in Saint-Denis. Nicholas Guérard, design and engraving (attributed), Martyrdom of Saint Denis, historiated initial, from Michel Félibien, *Histoire de l'abbaye royale de Saint-Denys en France* (Paris: Frédéric Léonard, 1706). unpaginated

of a historical scene, positioned at the head of the page, marks the beginning of the section, and a smaller framed initial with another historical scene opens the text. This layout, typical of illustrated seventeenth-century French books, is followed on the first page of each of the eight books of the "Histoire," as well as the opening of the

"Description" and "Recueil."[21] In punctuating the volume with these images, Félibien enlivened the lengthy text and established a measured visual pace for the reader of the book's first 540 pages.

With the "Description" that comprises the second part of the book, this regular rhythm accelerates into a more concentrated and dramatic pace. Rather than a series of smaller engravings printed directly on the text pages, the reader encounters eleven large engravings, each printed on a fold-out of heavier stock tipped into the book. These interrupt the flow of the text every few pages. Along with the five treasury plates [Figs. 1, 10–11], the eleven engravings include detailed views of the prized "Cup of the Ptolemies," a plan of the church, and views of the elaborate tombs of Louis XII, Francis I, Henry II, and the Viscount of Turenne. Except for a map of the town of Saint-Denis inserted opposite the "Dissertation préliminaire" near the beginning of the book, the fold-out format is reserved for engravings in the "Description." Compared to the vignettes and historiated intials, these fold-out engravings demand a more tactile engagement. The simple drama of opening them yields a pleasure of discovery that the smaller engravings cannot approach and that the static reproductions in this essay cannot capture.

Sight and Spectacle in the Works of André Félibien

Historians working for Louis XIV did not write monographic histories of religious institutions. Books such as Félibien's *Histoire* that focused solely on the history of a particular church or monastery were instead typically the work of monks and clergymen.[22] The challenge of reframing Saint-Denis for the Sun King, therefore, required that Félibien merge two distinct genres of historical writing: monographs of religious foundations and royal histories written to glorify the king.[23] The illustrations of the *Histoire* were instrumental in helping Félibien overcome this challenge, since many of the monographic histories were unpublished and even the few published histories were humble in format and featured minimal decoration.[24] The rich illustration that Félibien chose for the *Histoire* was instead typical of books produced under the extensive network of royal patronage, for the exuberant and copious illustration of books in France during the reign of Louis XIV was "reserved for celebrating the king's glory."[25] The sumptuous illustration of the *Histoire*, consequently, fundamentally distinguished the book from the visually ascetic, cloistered histories written by other ecclesiastics during this period. We may see why Félibien invested two years in producing the illustrations for the *Histoire*, as the imagery, more than any other aspect of the book, ensured that his monograph of Saint-Denis would address a royal rather than monastic audience.

Of all the works on history, art, and science dedicated to the glory of the Sun King, Félibien chose to invoke the writings of one author in particular: his father, André Félibien (1619–1695). Upon presenting the *Histoire* to Louis XIV in February or March 1706, Félibien reportedly asked that the king receive the *Histoire* "with the same goodwill that he had in the past shown to the various works Mr. Félibien his father had composed in the king's service."[26] Michel Félibien here artfully alluded to his father, who had served in a number of important posts within the arts administration under Louis XIV, most notably as the Historian of the King's Works [*Historiographe des Bâtiments du Roi*] and the secretary of the royal architecture academy.[27] In these capacities, André Félibien authored numerous books, including the *Entretiens sur les vies et sur les ouvrages des plus excellens peintres anciens et modernes* (1666–1688), written on the model of Vasari's *Lives*, for which he is best known among art historians today.[28] The majority of his written work, however, was dedicated more explicitly to glorifying Louis XIV through descriptions of the king's palaces and gardens, his art collections, and royal festivities. During his long career André Félibien produced a number of books that indirectly praised the king by praising the buildings and artworks produced under royal patronage. These books ranged from the sumptuous folio volume, *Tapisseries du Roi, où sont representez les Quatre Elemens et les Quatre Saisons* (1670), to the *Description sommaire du Chasteau de Versailles* (1674), a plain pocket-sized book meant to circulate among a wider public.[29]

With the exception of the *Description sommaire*, for which affordability was a primary concern, his publications were often provided with lavish engravings. Illustrations, as Félibien explained in the introduction to *Tapisseries du Roi*, were indispensable to disseminating the king's majesty:

> One of the great advantages that we have today over the ancients regarding the arts is that of printing and engraving. These are two marvelous means for multiplying the same discourse to infinity and displaying the same thing in many places.…As there is nothing in all the arts that the King does not render to the utility of his people and the glory of his reign, he is not content with raising magnificent edifices, adorning his palaces with paintings and inimitable statues…he also desires that distant peoples should find pleasure in them in some way, and that through descriptions and images of his superb buildings and his royal enterprises they will know something of their excellence. It is with this thought that His Majesty, having set his eyes upon persons capable of executing his intentions,

> created collections such as this one here, in which the beauty of the characters, joined to that of the images, leaves nothing to be desired, so that they [the collections as reproduced in books] will one day be precious monuments of all that is done in our days and that those who come after us will be, in some way, spectators of the marvels of which we are witnesses.[30]

The desire articulated by André Félibien to replicate an artwork through engraving and thereby display "the same thing in many places" clearly motivated the precise depictions of the reliquaries and regalia in the treasury engravings from his son's *Histoire* [Figs. 1, 10–11]. Since the king had not visited Saint-Denis for decades, the illustrations brought the precious objects in the abbey's treasury to him.

Reproductive engravings of artworks had long served to circulate images to wider European audiences.[31] What distinguished André Félibien's use of reproductive engravings, however, was how he placed them in a book with an accompanying descriptive text that also served as an interpretive apparatus. Although Félibien ostensibly described the artwork reproduced, he was simultaneously circumscribing the field of potential interpretations to which the artwork could be subjected. He could thus insistently direct a reader's attention toward the patronage of the king, so that praise of the artwork would be tantamount to praise of the monarch.[32] In this way André Félibien created a dialectic between objects and the royal person in which the magnificence of the Sun King was heightened by the works that he had commanded to be created and collected around him.

Events, as well as objects, could be manipulated through this strategy in order to glorify the king. Between 4 July and 31 August 1674, for example, the king staged six grand *fêtes* for his court at Versailles in celebration of his military conquest of the Franche-Comté earlier that year.[33] In 1676, André Félibien published *Les Divertissemens de Versailles donnez par le roy à toute sa cour au retour de la conqueste de la Franche-Comté en l'année M. DC. LXXIV*, a slender folio volume that describes the six *fêtes* in six chapters. Each chapter contains a closely observed description of the events, and opens with a large fold-out engraving of a climactic moment in the celebratory spectacle. Perhaps the most dazzling of these is the *Fifth Day: Fireworks Display above the Canal of Versailles* [Fig. 6], which depicts the blazing trails of fireworks streaking across an inky black sky and their reflections in the Apollo Basin below. On the far side of the basin stands a row of monuments, temporarily erected for the event, centered on an obelisk, all densely decorated with royal insignia, instruments of warfare, and mythological figures. On the near side sit

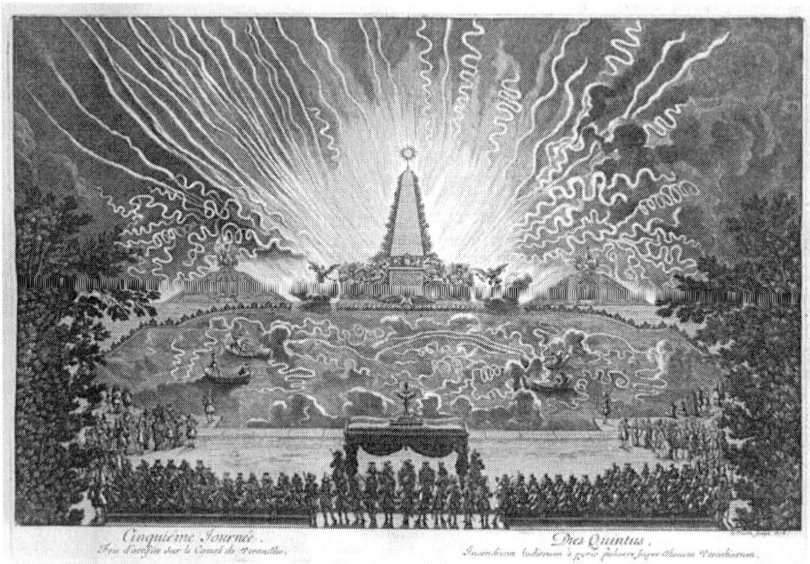

Fig. 6 *Cinquième journée: feu d'artifice sur le Canal de Versailles*, engraving, from André Félibien, *Les Divertissemens de Versailles* (Paris: Imprimerie Royale, 1676). opposite 19 (Photo: Courtesy of the John M. Wing Foundation, the Newberry Library, Chicago)

members of the court ranged on rows of benches, in the center of which a prominent baldachin announces the presence of the king beneath it.

The splendid qualities of light in this engraving, and its unexpected, awe-inspiring brilliance, or *éclat*, index the glory of the Sun King. His privileged position is understated, overwhelmed as he is by the complexity of the fireworks display. Yet his presence cannot be overlooked because of his placement on the central axis of the illustration. The king's centrality, moreover, gives him the most commanding view of the display and suggests his role as the patron of the spectacle. Félibien *père* structured the written description of the event around the king in a similar way. The display begins only "when the king was seated beneath a large tent that had been pitched between the Basin of Apollo and the Canal."[34] The temporal priority assumed by Louis XIV over the spectacle in the narrative complements his centrality in the illustration; both signal that it is the king's presence—and by extension his patronage and magnificence—that authorizes and structures the performance. [35]

André Félibien's strategy rests upon objectifying the *fêtes* both as illustrations and as narrative descriptions seen from the king's normative point-of-view. *Les Divertissemens* may be termed a "spectacular" history not only because of the grand spectacles that it documents, but because Félibien constructed the king's transcendent glory through insistently visual means—particularly in the way in which the narrative descriptions and the engravings open out from the king's person as if he were the vanishing point from which they arose.[36] As a result, Félibien could present the celebrations according to the same interpretive logic used in his publications of royal artworks and buildings. Not only did he document the *fêtes* in *Les Divertissemens* to make them accessible to a larger audience, he structured the visual and written representations of the spectacles upon a model of carefully controlled spectatorship designed to glorify the king.

When Michel Félibien explicitly invoked his father's literary production upon presenting the *Histoire* to Louis XIV, he demonstrated his determination to locate his own work within the genre of royal history exemplified by books like *Les Divertissemens*. Formal resemblances between Félibien's *Histoire* and his father's works, such as the use of the large fold-out illustrations [Figs. 1, 6, 10–11], reinforced this comparison. Indeed, Michel Félibien's effort to calibrate the illustration of the *Histoire* with the visual splendor of his father's books is indicated by the two years he invested in producing the engravings.[37] Félibien's concern to encourage such comparisons implies that he believed the ultimate success of his project to rest upon the king's recognition of the *Histoire* as a work of "spectacular" history.

The Spectacular History of Saint-Denis

Michel Félibien confronted an immense difficulty in trying to assimilate the *Histoire* to the works of his father. Whereas Félibien *père* structured the objects and events he described around the person of the king, Félibien *fils*, ironically, had undertaken the *Histoire* to rectify the king's absence. Compounding the problem was the fact he had to write about the many significant events in the abbey's history that took place centuries before Louis XIV was born. How could Félibien reframe the history of Saint-Denis within a genre of royal history writing, writing whose point of departure was the glorious presence of the Sun King? His solution, it appears, was to reconcile the visual devices used by his father with another strategy of royal historiography that had its roots in the Middle Ages. Through this latter strategy, which relied upon a rhetoric of reiteration and similitude, Félibien asserted the existence of an archetypal relationship between the kings of France and Saint-Denis that dated back to the abbey's founding in the seventh century.

Repetitive elements appear in most of the illustrations of historical events in the *Histoire*, but no repetition is as striking as the repeated use of the same vignette to illustrate both the *Dissertation préliminaire* and book six of the *Histoire* [Figs. 5, 7]. The vignette depicts a king kneeling before

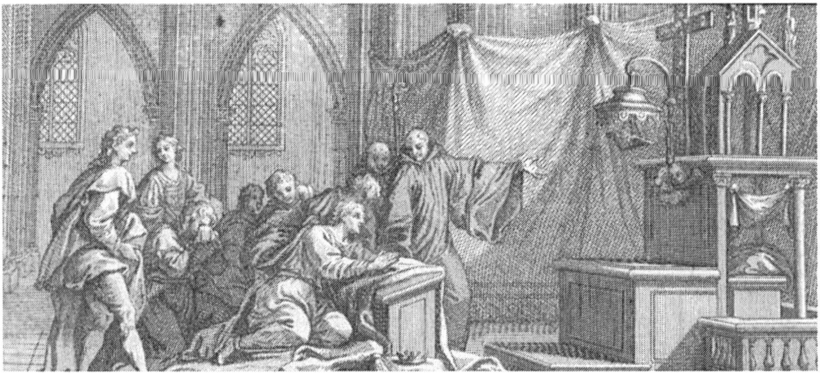

Fig. 7 Claude-Guy Hallé, design; Philippe Simonneau, engraving, King kneeling before an altar in Saint-Denis, from Michel Félibien, *Histoire de l'abbaye royale de Saint-Denys en France* (Paris: Frédéric Léonard,1706). unpaginated

an altar-shrine in the abbey church with his crown placed on a pillow at his side in a gesture of deference [Fig. 7]. Among the crowd of figures surrounding the king stands the abbot of Saint-Denis, identified by his tonsure and the crosier, carried by an attendant monk, who directs the attention of the prostrate king toward the altar-shrine. The king fixes the altar-shrine with an intense stare, and the angular lean of his body conveys the intensity of his contemplation. In the notes discovered among his papers, Félibien identified the praying figure as the abbey's founding patron, King Dagobert, who died in 638.[38] Félibien was presumably referring to this vignette in its position at the head of the *Dissertation préliminaire* [Fig. 5], but his identification of the king is complicated by the fact that the same engraving is used in book six to represent not Dagobert, but Charles VI, who ascended the throne in 1380.

Nothing in this repeated vignette indicates that it portrays royal homage six hundred years apart, nor does it faithfully represent the time and place of either king. Gothic architecture did not exist in Dagobert's age, and while the setting would be more appropriate for Charles VI, the depicted space does not replicate any recognizable part of the abbey church. We have already learned from the frontispiece, however, that archaeological accuracy was not a criterion of authenticity for representing history in Félibien's book. Louis XIV, for instance, accepted the scene of Philip III carrying his father's casket as historical fact when, upon leafing through the book for the first time, he "registered some surprise to see in the frontispiece that the body of Saint Louis was carried by his own son, Philip the Bold."[39] The expectation that an historical representation include an accurate depiction of a period's material culture is rather a late eighteenth- and nineteenth-century development.[40] The pictorial vocabulary of the frontispiece, the repeated vignette, and the other historical images in Félibien's *Histoire* draws from the idealized and dramatic style known as *la grande manière* ("the grand manner") that was used during the seventeenth and eighteenth centuries to depict elevated subjects from history and mythology.[41] In accord with these conventions, Félibien and the artists he commissioned focused not upon carefully depicting Dagobert or Charles VI in the dress or setting appropriate to their time, but employed instead an arsenal of theatrical techniques that dramatized the actions of the historical actors through pose, gesture, and staging; a theatrical rhetoric exemplified in the vignette by the exaggerated sweep of the abbot's stupendously billowing sleeve.

The repetition of the same engraving for two kings exemplifies a view of the past in which historical authenticity inheres not in particulars—reproducing the vagaries and superficial details of costumes and places—but in asserting continuity across history. Félibien and his audience recognized, of course, that Dagobert and Charles VI were different people living in very different times, but the relative positions of the vignette within the book adequately conveyed this historical distinction. Through the repetition of the vignette, however, the kings' shared identity as holders of the royal office trumped the lesser accent placed on their individuality. In deciding to stamp the book twice with the same plate Félibien forged between these rulers a powerful resemblance that two *different* images could never match. Like a mirror reflection, this repetition created a perfect visual similitude between the two kings that asserts that they were essentially identical and that royal tradition was unbroken. By dramatically emphasizing action, moreover, the vignette posits the similitude of Dagobert and Charles VI not upon physical likeness, but upon their deeds as kings. Indeed, the repetition of the vignette establishes the act of devotion pictured in the image as an archetype that holders of the royal office should follow, and the profound sameness of these kings resides precisely in their faithful adherence to this archetypal act throughout the abbey's history.[42]

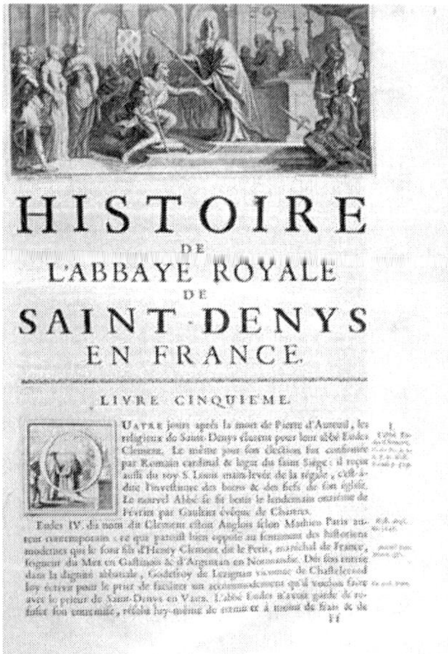

Fig. 8 Louis Boulogne the Younger, design; Philippe Simonneau, engraving, Saint Louis before the papal legate. Nicolas Guérard, design and engraving (attributed), Two monks preparing to board a ship, historiated initial, from Michel Félibien, *Histoire de l'abbaye royale de Saint-Denys en France* (Paris: Frédéric Léonard, 1706). 239

The vignette of Dagobert and Charles VI stands as an extreme example of a rhetoric of reiteration that fundamentally shaped Félibien's narrative and the engravings of historical events. We read again and again of kings' donations and visits to the abbey, their devotion to Saint Denis, and their funerals, which were held in the abbey church. These events unfold repeatedly in the frontispiece, vignettes, and historiated initials, as well as in the written narrative. Dagobert, for example, appears in another vignette at the opening of book one of the *Histoire* handing a charter to the abbot of Saint-Denis, and Saint Louis appears in the beginning of the fifth book [Fig. 8] receiving emblems of pilgrimage from the papal legate as he prepares to embark on crusade in 1270. Félibien even incorporated Louis XIV into the parade of kings that march through the illustrations of the *Histoire* in the historiated initial of book eight [Fig. 9], which depicts the boy-king's entry into the church in 1652, during one of his few visits to the abbey.[43] By repeating a fixed set of themes, Félibien forcefully articulated an archetypal relationship between the kings and Saint-Denis; the relationship was one of mutual benefit and support in which the kings' patronage of the abbey and devotion to Saint Denis himself, whose remains the abbey enshrined, were reciprocated by the powerful blessings and protection of the saint and the monks.

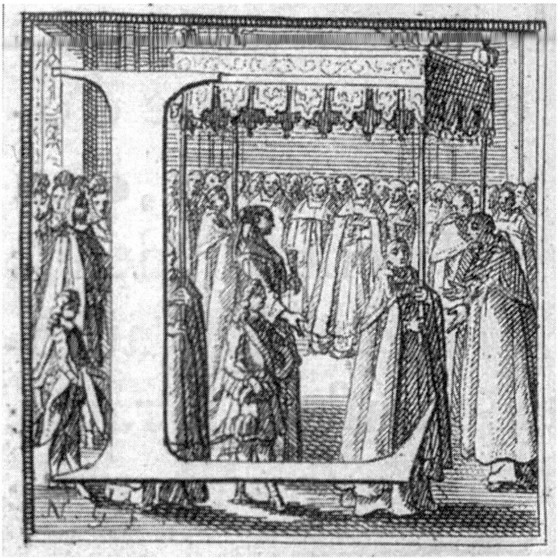

Fig. 9 Nicolas Guérard, Louis XIV entering Saint-Denis in 1652, engraving, historiated initial, from Michel Félibien, *Histoire de l'abbaye royale de Saint-Denys en France* (Paris: Frédéric Léonard,1706). 459

The rhetoric of reiteration used by Félibien had a deep historical association with Saint-Denis that extended back to the Middle Ages. The strategy was founded upon the belief that ideal models or types from the past were repeated in, and even explained, the present. The types thus transcended time and served as a basis for viewing history as a continuum united by their repetition. Beginning in the twelfth century, the monks of Saint-Denis applied this strategy to the writing of royal history; comparable techniques were also adapted to numerous artworks of the thirteenth and fourteenth centuries, such as the lavishly illustrated *Grandes Chroniques de France*, which undoubtedly served as one of Félibien's sources.[44] The influence of medieval histories and artworks upon

Félibien's use of types in the *Histoire* cannot be explored in detail here, but types continued to feature in the histories of many seventeenth-century French authors as well.[45] Regardless of his particular sources for this rhetoric of reiteration, Félibien employed the strategy to circumscribe the potential interpretations of the abbey's past, much as his father had used the description of artworks and spectacles to orient his readers.

No absolute monarch, however, reigns over the entire *Histoire* as the figure of Louis XIV had done in André Félibien's *Les Divertissemens*. Michel Félibien substituted the archetypal relationship between kings and the abbey in the place of the Sun King, whose presence had provided the organizing principle in the works of his father, André Félibien. Whereas Félibien *père*'s books were designed to glorify Louis XIV, Félibien *fils*' book was dedicated to revealing an archetypal relationship of mutual support between the kings and Saint-Denis. The authority of this archetype, moreover, derived primarily from its status as a venerable tradition, but the authority present in André Félibien's works emanated entirely from Louis XIV.

Given these critical differences between his work and that of his father, Michel Félibien evidently attempted to integrate Louis XIV into the archetypal relationship between the French kings and the royal abbey of Saint-Denis whenever he could. Consequently, Louis XIV appears in the historiated initial for book eight of the "Histoire" mentioned above [Fig. 9], and the preface of the *Histoire* features a vignette with the face of Apollo surrounded by sunrays—a signature motif of the Sun King. More effective than the representations of Louis XIV himself, however, were the frequent depictions of historical figures within the *Histoire* upon whom the Sun King deliberately modeled himself. With these models, who served almost as avatars of the Sun King, Félibien *fils* could project the person of Louis XIV into the far earlier history of the abbey and thereby more persuasively present the archetypal king as a reflection of Louis XIV. Foremost among these esteemed predecessors of the Sun King was Louis IX, canonized in 1297 as Saint Louis, whose remains lie in the casket depicted so prominently on the frontispiece of the *Histoire* [Fig. 2].

Saint Louis and Saint-Denis

It may seem odd that in a history book about Saint-Denis, the saint himself does not figure in the frontispiece and that the abbey dedicated to him appears only on the horizon. But Félibien's choice of subject appears to have been driven by the political calculus of the *Histoire*, not by a desire to summarize the history of the abbey through the person of its patron saint. By deciding to depict the funeral procession of Saint Louis in the frontispiece, Félibien undoubtedly sought to appeal to Louis XIV, who was earnestly devoted to his name saint and assiduously tried to promote associations between himself and his holy ancestor.[46] Félibien gave the relics of Saint Louis prominence in the frontispiece because they encouraged the identification of the royal saint with the abbey.[47]

This strategy for reframing Saint-Denis rested, on the one hand, upon a pragmatic recognition—one is tempted to say resignation—that Louis XIV venerated Saint Louis far more than he ever would Saint Denis.[48] On the other hand, the strategy was also an ingenious response to the most egregious example of the king's disregard for the abbey: namely, his decision in 1691 to eliminate the position of the abbot of Saint-Denis. This liberated the funds dedicated to maintaining the abbatial office, and Louis XIV subsequently diverted them to the school of Saint-Cyr, which he had founded and dedicated to Saint Louis.[49] Félibien responded precisely to these circumstances in choosing a scene for the frontispiece that linked Saint-Denis both to the miraculous power of Saint Louis' remains and the familial devotion shown by his successors. Saint-Denis, not the school of Saint-Cyr—so the illustration seems to claim—was the proper site for venerating Saint Louis.

Another important layer of association is added to the frontispiece by the scepter and *main de justice* of Henry IV that rest on the lid of the casket. Although these regalia were used only for the coronation of Henry IV in 1594, they appear to have been more closely connected to his descendants, the Bourbon kings, than the older scepter and *main de justice* traditionally used for coronations.[50] Louis XIV, for instance, rests his right hand on the inverted scepter with Henry IV's *main de justice* sitting on the stool at his side in Hyacinthe Rigaud's famous portrait of 1701 in the Louvre.[51] The identification of this particular scepter and *main de justice* with the Bourbon kings suggests that the anachronism of depicting these regalia in the frontispiece was a deliberate effort to associate Louis XIV with Saint Louis.

Such interweaving of the present and past through the regalia of Henry IV carries with it a mingling of the descriptive style of the treasury engravings and *la grande manière* of the history engravings. Despite the inaccuracy of the rendition of the *main de justice* in the frontispiece, the regalia still remain recognizable as particular historical objects rather than theatrical confections such as the reliquary casket created for staging the historical scene. The coexistence of the veristic and theatrical modes of representation suggests that these modes were not antithetical, but could instead be strategically combined. In this case, the relative realism of the regalia links their portrayal in the frontispiece to their even more exacting image in the treasury engraving. The object depicted in a past event thereby becomes identified as the same object displayed in the abbey's treasury. Within the theatrical mode of representation that predominates in the frontispiece, in other words, the more descriptive rendering of the regalia indexes their physical existence in the present. The detailed view of the abbey church in the distance similarly points to the actual building as it stood in Félibien's day.

The relics of Saint Louis in the frontispiece initiate a similar visual itinerary that begins in the past, with their arrival at Saint-Denis in 1271, and culminates in their display in the abbey's treasury in 1706. Every treasury engraving contains relics and royal regalia of interest to Louis XIV, but the third engraving in the series [Fig. 10] addresses him directly through the selection and arrangement of objects. Next to a reliquary holding the head of Saint Denis at the center of the cabinet are gathered a number of relics of Saint Louis: a reliquary holding his mandible; the clasp of his mantle; the sword that he took on crusade; his *main de justice*; and his crown. Resting strategically beside Saint Louis' crown, moreover, sits the coronation crown of Louis XIV. These juxtapositions of objects reinforce the associations between Saint Louis, Saint Denis, and the Sun King asserted in the frontispiece. The visual, almost diagrammatic relationship created between kings and saints through these objects, furthermore, echoes the spectacular framework deployed by André Félibien in his publications and recalls how he structured the presentation of objects and events as reflections of the king himself.

Meaning arises not only in the arrangement of objects within each engraving, moreover, but also through the arrangement of the cabinets themselves, in a manner similar to the increasing grandeur of each subsequent *fête* described in *Les Divertissemens*.[52] The appeal to Louis XIV begun on the frontispiece reaches a climax in the fifth and final treasury engraving [Fig. 11], which is the least visually cluttered of the group, enabling it to link Saint Louis, Saint Denis, and Louis XIV in the most direct terms. The church-shaped reliquary holding Saint Louis' body rises magnificently in the place of privilege at the center of the illustration. To the right sits another church-shaped reliquary with the remains of Saint Denis, and on the left the reliquary of Saint Peter the Exorcist. Draped on the walls of the cabinet, finally, are the garments worn by Louis XIV during his coronation of 1654. His ermine-trimmed mantle provides a resplendent backdrop for the reliquaries, while his camisole, shirt, dalmatic, and boots hang from the sidewalls. Félibien's effort to integrate Saint Louis into the institutional identity of Saint-Denis is realized fully in

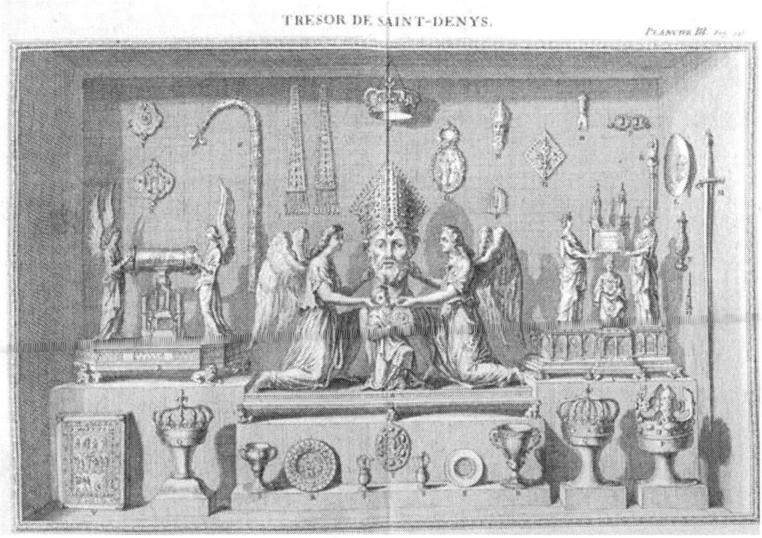

Fig. 10 Nicolas Guérard, *Trésor de Saint-Denys,* engraving, from Michel Félibien, *Histoire de l'abbaye royale de Saint-Denys en France* (Paris: Frédéric Léonard, 1706). Pl. III (fold-out plate opposite 540)

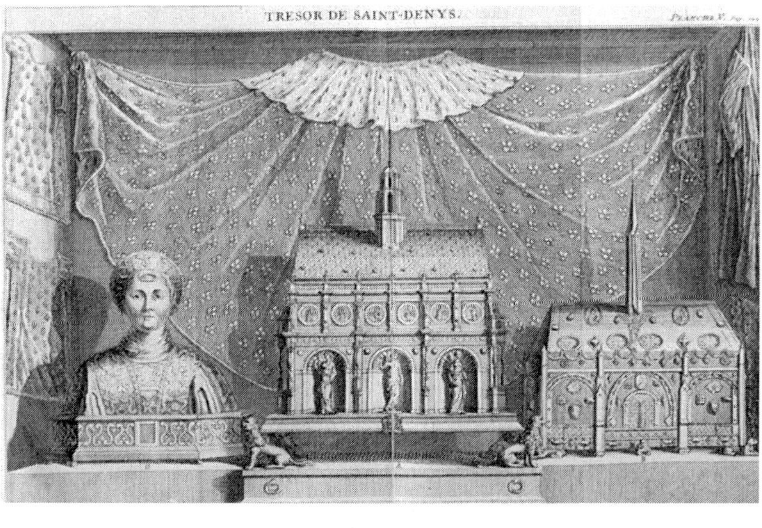

Fig. 11 Nicolas Guérard, *Trésor de Saint-Denys*, engraving, from Michel Félibien, *Histoire de l'abbaye royale de Saint-Denys en France* (Paris: Frédéric Léonard, 1706). Pl. V (fold-out plate opposite 544)

this illustration by the fact that the body of the royal saint, rather than the abbey's patron saint, occupies the position of superiority. The arrangement of the relics and regalia also seemingly document the continuity of the archetypal relationship between the French kings and Saint-Denis into the present. The coronation regalia of Louis XIV, moreover, implicate the king in this relationship even though he had neglected the abbey for most of his life: his mantle, in other words, suggests the Sun King's presence despite his absence. The mantle even implies his protection of the abbey in the way it "embraces" the reliquaries like an image of the Virgin *misericordia* sheltering with her cloak a group of figures huddled around her feet.[53] This illustration, like the *Histoire* as a whole, reframes Saint-Denis as a royal monument dedicated to the cult of Saint Louis and the glory of Louis XIV, in the hope of persuading the king to restore the neglected abbey to the position of favor to which it was entitled by history.[54]

Notes

[1] I wish to thank the librarians and staff of the following libraries for graciously allowing me to consult materials in their collections: the Fine Arts Library at the University of Michigan; Special Collections, Regenstein Library, University of Chicago; the Newberry Library, Chicago; and the Charles Deering McCormick Library of Special Collections, Northwestern University. I also want to express my gratitude to Maribeth Graybill, Janet Marquardt, Alyce Jordan, Elizabeth Sears, and two anonymous readers for the insightful comments and suggestions they provided on an earlier version of this essay.

[2] See Paul Frankl, *The Gothic: Literary Sources and Interpretations through Eight Centuries* (Princeton: Princeton University Press, 1960). 491–538, esp. 531–534

[3] Scholars have analyzed such phenomena through a number of theoretical rubrics, and readers may find other concepts and terminology more appropriate than the ones I use here. One could, for example, describe such profound changes in perception as a "paradigm shift." I have elected to use the concept of "frame" to signal how Félibien attempted to place his book and, by extension Saint-Denis, within established categories of discourse. By ensconcing Saint-Denis within certain categorical frames, Félibien hoped to make the assumptions and *a priori* distinctions that helped constitute the frame apply to Saint-Denis. In order to emphasize the fact that Félibien was trying to move Saint-Denis into a frame in which it did not previously belong, I have added a prefix: hence, the term "reframe." The concept of "framing" was developed by Jacques Derrida in *The Truth in Painting* as part of a critique of Kant's aesthetics. For useful analyses of Derrida's argument and the broader application of "framing" within discourse I have relied upon Jonathan Culler, *On Deconstruction: Theory and Criticism after*

Structuralism (Ithaca: Cornell University Press, 1982). 193–199; and Mieke Bal and Norman Bryson, "Semiotics and Art History," *Art Bulletin* 73 (1991). 174–208

[4] Anne Lombard-Jourdan, "Archéologie d'un '*bel ouvrage*': *Histoire de l'abbaye royale de Saint-Denis en France* par Michel Félibien," in *Saint-Denis, lieu de mémoire* (Paris: Fédération des Sociétés historiques et archéologiques de Paris et de l'Ile-de-France, 2000). 287–356, esp. 293–300

[5] Upon receiving the *Histoire* from Félibien and leafing through it the king is reported to have praised the book as a "beautiful work" [*un bel ouvrage*]. The anecdote was first published by René Prosper Tassin, *Histoire littéraire de la Congrégation de Saint-Maur* (1770; reprint, Ridgewood, NJ: Gregg Press, 1965). 414 and quoted by Lombard-Jourdan, "Archéologie d'un '*bel ouvrage*'." 298, who uses the king's words in the title of her article. The extensive illustration also had the practical consequence of making the *Histoire* prohibitively expensive for all but the wealthy. Lombard-Jourdan, "Archéologie d'un '*bel ouvrage*'." 308–309

[6] On the extensive propaganda system erected to glorify Louis XIV see Peter Burke, *The Fabrication of Louis XIV* (New Haven: Yale University Press, 1992). 49–69

[7] For an overview of Saint-Denis' role as the French royal necropolis see Elizabeth A. R. Brown, *Saint-Denis, la basilique*, trans. Divina Cabo (Saint-Léger-Vauban: Zodiaque, 2001). 347–438; on Saint-Denis as the repository of the French coronation regalia see Danielle Gaborit-Chopin, *Regalia: Les instruments du sacre des rois de France, les "honneurs de Charlemagne"* (Paris: Réunion des musées nationaux, 1987). 22–33. Both of these privileges were firmly established in the thirteenth century.

[8] On the fate of the treasury of Saint-Denis during the Revolution see Danielle Gaborit-Chopin, *Le Trésor de Saint-Denis* (Paris: Réunion des musées nationaux, 1991). 345–351

[9] See, for example, Sumner McKnight Crosby et al., *The Royal Abbey of Saint-Denis in the Time of Abbot Suger (1122–1151)* (New York: Metropolitan Museum of Art, 1981). 102–103; the essays by Danielle Gaborit-Chopin, "Suger's Liturgical Vessels," and William Wixom, "Traditional Forms in Suger's Contributions to the Treasury of Saint-Denis," in *Abbot Suger and Saint-Denis, A Symposium*, ed. Paula Gerson (New York: Metropolitan Museum of Art, 1986), 282 and 294; and Gaborit-Chopin, *Le Trésor de Saint-Denis*. 26–38, 56–338

[10] Sumner McKnight Crosby, *The Abbey of St.-Denis, 475–1122*, vol. 1 (New Haven: Yale University Press, 1942). 18: "The study of St.-Denis, however, received serious attention at an early date, and Dom Michel Félibien deserves a place apart among the historians of the Abbey."

[11] Gaborit-Chopin, *Regalia*. 77, Fig. 8 misidentifies the *main de justice* in the first treasury engraving of Félibien's *Histoire* as the *main de justice de licorne*, which was a *main de justice* with an ivory hand that was used in royal coronations beginning in the fourteenth century. The scepter and *main de justice* in this engraving are properly identified in the same book on 16, Fig. 9. On the different *mains de justice* and scepters, see Gaborit-Chopin, *Regalia*. 73–83

[12] Many of these documents were published by Lombard-Jourdan, "Archéologie d'un '*bel ouvrage*'." 343–352, who uses them to provide an indispensable account of the production of the *Histoire*.
[13] Lombard-Jourdan, "Archéologie d'un '*bel ouvrage*'." 294–296
[14] The list is published by Lombard-Jourdan, "Archéologie d'un '*bel ouvrage*'." 348–350
[15] Maxime Préaud, "Leclerc," *Grove Art Online*: http://www.groveart.com
[16] Lombard-Jourdan, "Archéologie d'un '*bel ouvrage*'." 333–338 suggests that Félibien also decided that some of the decorative engravings at the end of each chapter, known as *culs-de-lampe*, should depict objects associated with Saint-Denis.
[17] Lombard-Jourdan, "Archéologie d'un '*bel ouvrage*'." 314. The drawing is reproduced in Jean Guiffrey and Pierre Marcel, *Inventaire général des dessins du Musée du Louvre: Ecole française*, vol. 2 (Paris: Librairie centrale d'art et d'architecture, 1908). 81, no. 1509
[18] Lombard-Jourdan, "Archéologie d'un '*bel ouvrage*'." 297; on the print-runs of books from this era see Henri-Jean Martin, *The French Book: Religion, Absolutism, and Readership, 1585–1715*, trans. Paul and Nadine Saenger (Baltimore: Johns Hopkins University Press, 1996). 3
[19] Funds were allotted for the production of the book by Félibien's superiors on 30 March 1703 and in April 1705. Lombard-Jourdan, "Archéologie d'un '*bel ouvrage*'." 294–297, 315–317
[20] Each page measures approximately 39.5 x 26.5 cm. The pagination begins with the text of the "Histoire de l'abbaye royale" and continues through the "Description" (592 pages). The "Recueil," the third part of Félibien's book, is paginated separately with Roman numerals (i–ccxxiii). The prefatory material, title page and frontispiece, the fold-out folios inserted into the book, and the twenty-one-page index at the end of the book are unpaginated.
[21] Roger Laufer, "L'Espace visuel du livre ancien," in *Histoire de l'édition française*, vol. 1, *Le Livre conquérant: du moyen âge au milieu du XVII*[e] *siècle*, ed. Henri-Jean Martin and Roger Chartier (Paris: Promodis, 1982). 479–499; David Pottinger, *The French Book Trade in the Ancien Régime, 1500–1791* (Cambridge: Harvard University Press, 1958). 310–324; Martin, *The French Book*. 77–96
[22] The relationship between Félibien's *Histoire* and these other histories cannot be examined in detail here. An important precedent for Félibien's book was the *Histoire de l'abbaye de S. Denys en France* published in 1625 by Jacques Doublet, a monk at Saint-Denis. Scholars usually view Doublet's book as a work full of legends and false documents in comparison with Félibien's more critical history (e.g. Lombard-Jourdan, "Archéologie d'un '*bel ouvrage*'." 293; more sympathetic critiques are given by Gaborit-Chopin, *Le Trésor de Saint-Denis*. 28; and Sumner Crosby, *The Abbey of St.-Denis*. 1:17).
[23] "Genre" could serve as another theoretical perspective from which one could usefully analyze the *Histoire*. Culler, *On Deconstruction*. 196, for instance, points to the identification of a text with a certain genre as an example of framing. On genre as a "conventionalized orienting framework for the production and reception

of discourse" see Richard Bauman, "Genre," *Journal of Linguistic Anthropology* 9 (2000). 84–87. Many of Félibien's contemporaries were acutely aware of different genres as categories or certain types of cultural production. Burke, *Fabrication.* 18–23

[24] Only seventeen of the sixty-three monographs cited in the list published by Damien Blanchard, "A propos d'un texte de Dom Racine (1699–1777): les monographies d'abbayes, de dom Mabillon aux éditeurs du XIXe siècle," in *Erudition et commerce épistolaire: Jean Mabillon et la tradition monastique*, ed. Daniel-Odon Hurel (Paris: J. Vrin, 2003). 226–232, or twenty-seven percent, were published before the French Revolution. Of these seventeen, only five, including Félibien's *Histoire*, were printed in folio, and of these five, only Félibien's book and the *Histoire de l'abbaye royale de Saint-Germain-des-prez*, written by the monk Jacques Bouillart, feature any illustration other than an insignia on the title page. Bouillart's book, published in 1724, was clearly modeled on Félibien's *Histoire.*

[25] Martin, *The French Book.* 92; see also Henri-Jean Martin, *Print, Power, and People in Seventeenth-Century France*, trans. David Gerard (Metuchen, NJ: Scarecrow Press, 1993). 565

[26] "L'auteur présenta son livre suppliant le Roi de l'agréer avec la même bonté qu'il avoit autrefois agréé divers ouvrages que M. Félibien son père avoit composés pour son service." Quoted in Tassin, *Histoire littéraire.* 414; see also Lombard-Jourdan, "Archéologie d'un '*bel ouvrage*'." 298

[27] See the introduction by René Démoris in André Félibien, *Entretiens sur les vies et sur les ouvrages des plus excellents peintres anciens et modernes (Entretiens I et II)* (Paris: Société d'Édition "Les Belles Lettres," 1987). 9–73; and Alexandre Skliar-Piguet, "Félibien, André, Sieur des Avaux et de Jàvercy," *Grove Art Online.*

[28] Jacques Thuillier, "Les Debuts de l'histoire de l'art en France et Vasari," in *Il Vasari storiografo e artista: atti del Congresso internazionale nel IV centenario della morte, Arezzo-Firenze, 2–8 settembre 1974* (Florence: Istituto Nazionale di Studi sul Rinascimento, 1976). 667–684

[29] On the *Tapisseries* see Christa C. Mayer Thurman and Koenraad Brosens, "*Autumn* and *Winter*: Two Gobelins Tapestries after Charles Le Brun," in *Old Masters at the Art Institute of Chicago, Art Institute of Chicago Museum Studies* 32, 2 (2006). 61–71

[30] "Un des plus grands avantages que nous ayons aujourd'huy sur les Anciens, en ce qui regarde les Arts, est celuy de l'Imprimerie & de la Graveure. Ce sont deux moyens merveilleux pour multiplier à l'infini un mesme discourse, & faire voir l'image d'une mesme chose en divers lieux. . . . Comme il n'y a rien dans tous les Arts que le Roy ne fasse servir à l'utilité de ses Peuples, & à la gloire de son Regne, il ne se contente pas d'élever de magnifiques Edifices, d'orner ses Palais de Peintures, & de Statuës inimitables....il veut encore que les Peuples éloignez en jouïssent en quelque sorte, & que par les Descriptions & les Figures de ses superbes Bastimens, & de ses Royales entreprises, ils en connoissent l'excellence. C'est dans cette pensée que Sa Majesté ayant jetté les yeux sur des Personnes capables d'exécuter ses intentions, fait mettre au jour des Recueïls pareils à celuy-

cy, où la beauté des Caractères, jointe à celle des Figures, ne laisse rien à desirer, afin qu'ils soient un jour de précieux Monumens de tout ce qui se fait aujourd'hui, & que ceux qui viendront après nous soient en quelque sorte spectateurs des merveilles dont nous sommes témoins." André Félibien, *Tapisseries du Roi, ou sont representez les Quatre Elemens et les Quatre Saisons* (Paris: Imprimerie Royale, 1670). unpaginated [5]

[31] See Rebecca Zorach, "On Imitation and Invention: An Introduction to the Reproductive Print," in *Paper Museums: The Reproductive Print in Europe, 1500–1800*, ed. Rebecca Zorach and Elizabeth Rodini (Chicago: David and Alfred Smart Museum of Art, 2005). 1–29

[32] Louis Marin, *Portrait of the King*, trans. Martha Houle (Minneapolis: University of Minnesota Press, 1988). 180–192 provides a semiotic analysis of this process at work in André Félibien's *Description sommaire du Chasteau de Versailles*, Stefan Germer, "The Royal Phantasm: (Re-)Presenting Louis XIV and Imagining Versailles," Tomás Harris Lectures in the History of Art, University College, London, 6 March 1997 emphasized the controlling aspect of André Félibien's descriptions in an analysis of Félibien's account of the royal entry into Paris in 1660.

[33] For a summary of the *fêtes* see Emile Magne, *Les Plaisirs et le fêtes en France au XVIIe siècle* (Geneva: Editions de la frégate, 1944). 135–149

[34] "Quand le Roy fut placé sous une grande tente qu'on avoit dressée entre le basin d'Apollon & le Canal." André Félibien, *Les Divertissemens de Versailles donnez par le roy à toute sa cour au retour de la conqueste de la Franche-Comté en l'année M. DC. LXXIV* (Paris: Imprimerie Royale, 1676). 24

[35] Marin, *Portrait of the King*. 196–205; for another perspective on similar questions, see Clifford Geertz, "Centers, Kings and Charisma: Reflections on the Symbolics of Power," in *Rites of Power: Symbolism, Ritual, and Politics since the Middle Ages*, ed. Sean Wilentz (Philadelphia: University of Pennsylvania Press, 1985). 13–38

[36] Marin, *Portrait of the King*. 199–203 uses the term "spectacular framework" to describe the narrative strategy that Félibien employs in *Les Divertissemens*.

[37] Lombard-Jourdan, "Archéologie d'un '*bel ouvrage*'." 294–296

[38] Lombard-Jourdan, "Archéologie d'un '*bel ouvrage*'." 322

[39] "Le Roi…témoigna quelque surprise de voir dans l'estampe du frontispice que le corps de S. Louis fût porté par son propre fils, Philippe le Hardi." Quoted in Tassin, *Histoire littéraire*. 414

[40] Stephen Bann, *The Clothing of Clio: A Study of the Representation of History in Nineteenth-Century Britain and France* (Cambridge: Cambridge University Press, 1984).

[41] On the use of *la grande manière* during the reign of Louis XIV, see Burke, *Fabrication*. 23–26; on the theatrical sources for historical representations in the late seventeenth and eighteenth centuries see Stephen Bann, *Romanticism and the Rise of History* (New York: Twayne, 1995). 45–59

[42] On Saint Denis and the abbey as royal protector, see Sumner McKnight Crosby, *The Royal Abbey of Saint-Denis from Its Beginnings to the Death of Suger, 475–1151* (New Haven: Yale University Press, 1987). 3–12

[43] Lombard-Jourdan, "Archéologie d'un '*bel ouvrage*'." 330–331 identified the scene.

[44] On this typological model of history and royal historiography at Saint-Denis see Gabrielle Spiegel, "Political Utility in Medieval Historiography: A Sketch," *History and Theory* 14 (1975). 314–325; and Gabrielle Spiegel, "The Cult of Saint Denis and Capetian Kingship," *Journal of Medieval History* 1 (1975). 43–69; for the *Grandes Chroniques de France* see Anne Hedeman, *The Royal Image: Illustrations of the* Grandes Chroniques de France (Berkeley: University of California Press, 1991). Other examples of artworks in which this strategy is used include the stained glass of the Sainte-Chapelle in Paris, which dates between 1239 and 1248, the first series of royal tombs made for Saint-Denis in the 1260s, and the sculptures on the verso of the west façade of Reims cathedral from the 1250s or 1260s. For these works see Alyce A. Jordan, *Visualizing Kingship in the Windows of the Sainte-Chapelle*, Publications of the International Center of Medieval Art, 5 (Turnhout: Brepols, 2002); Georgia Sommers Wright, "A Royal Tomb Program in the Reign of St. Louis," *Art Bulletin* 56 (1974). 224–243; Georgia Sommers Wright, "The Tomb of St. Louis," *Journal of the Warburg and Courtauld Institutes* 34 (1971). 65–82; and Donna Sadler, "Lessons Fit for a King: The Sculptural Program of the Verso of the West Façade of Reims Cathedral," *Arte medievale*, ser. 2, 9 (1995). 49–68. Michel Félibien's strategy of repetition is similar to the rhetorical device of *expolitio*, which Jordan, *Visualizing Kingship*. 13 describes as "saying the same thing, repeating the same thought, restating the same theme, in as many different ways as possible." I wish to thank Elizabeth Sears and an anonymous reader for the suggested comparisons between Félibien's *Histoire* and these medieval artworks. The emphasis upon similitude as the basis of identity in relation to the use of seals in the twelfth and thirteenth centuries has been the subject of work by Brigitte Bedos-Rezak, "Medieval Identity: A Sign and a Concept," *American Historical Review* 105 (2000). 1489–1533; and Brigitte Bedos-Rezak, "Replica: Images of Identity and the Identity of Images in Medieval France," in *The Mind's Eye: Art and Theological Argument in the Middle Ages*, ed. Jeffrey Hamburger and Anne-Marie Bouché (Princeton: Department of Art and Archaeology, Princeton University in association with Princeton University Press, 2006). 46–64

[45] Orest Ranum, *Artisans of Glory: Writers and Historical Thought in Seventeenth-Century France* (Chapel Hill: University of North Carolina Press, 1980). 17–21

[46] Louis had founded the Order of Saint Louis in 1693 and was sometimes identified as the *rex christianissimus*, a motto typically applied to Saint Louis. See Burke, *Fabrication*. 113–115

[47] Saint Louis' grandson, Philip IV, known as Philip the Fair, had the skull of Saint Louis transferred from the abbey to the Sainte-Chapelle in Paris in 1306. See Brown, *Saint-Denis, la basilique*. 402–403

[48] In this regard the motivations behind Félibien's *Histoire* appear strikingly similar to those that appear to have driven the production of an illuminated manuscript at Saint-Denis between 1314 and 1322 known as the *Vie de Saint Denis* (MS fr. 2090-2092, Bibliothèque nationale de France, Paris). See Charlotte Lacaze, *The "Vie de St. Denis" Manuscript (Paris, Bibliothèque Nationale, Ms. fr. 2090–2092)* (New York: Garland Publishing, 1979), 65: "The gift of the St.-Denis manuscript [to the French king] was probably designed…to counterbalance the growing cult of St. Louis, since the abbey had much to lose if future kings…were to neglect their devotion to St. Denis." The manuscript was given to Louis XIV in 1662 (Lacaze, *The "Vie de St. Denis" Manuscript*. 83–84), but it is unknown whether Michel Félibien was acquainted with it.

[49] On Saint-Louis at Saint-Cyr see Bruno Neveu, "Du Culte de Saint Louis à la glorification de Louis XIV: La Maison royale de Saint-Cyr," *Journal des Savants* (July–December 1988). 277–290

[50] Gaborit-Chopin, *Regalia*. 79

[51] Gaborit-Chopin, *Regalia*. 79. A high quality image of the painting with further information is readily accessible on the website of the Louvre: http://www.louvre.fr; Burke, *Fabrication*. 192 points out that Louis XIV showed less interest in appearing with the regalia or other traditional trappings of his office later in his reign.

[52] Marin, *Portrait of the King*. 202–205 highlights this aspect of the *fêtes*.

[53] I wish to thank the editors for this insightful comment and comparison.

[54] According to Lombard-Jourdan, "Archéologie d'un '*bel ouvrage*'." 291, 300–302, the *Histoire* was well received by Louis XIV and his court. One measure of the book's success was the fact that, in 1710, the provost of Paris commissioned Félibien to write a history of the city. Jacques Brouillart's *Histoire de Saint-Germaine-des-Prez* was also clearly inspired by Félibien's *Histoire*. The book also persuaded the king to sponsor reconstruction work on the cloister of Saint-Denis that was directed by Robert de Cotte, the king's architect (Chaussy, *Les Bénédictins de Saint-Maur*. 102). The king himself, however, never returned to the abbey.

REMNANTS OF A SHARED PAST: MEDIEVAL MONUMENTAL CRUCIFIXES AFTER THE REFORMATION

GRAŻYNA JURKOWLANIEC

Early Modern Disputes over Images and History

The likeness of the crucified Savior, seemingly the most elemental image in a church's interior, has repeatedly proved a concern among Christians. A crucifix was reportedly the first image to have been insulted by non-Christians: according to a legend attributed to Athanasius of Alexandria (d. 373), the likeness of the crucified Christ in Beirut was allegedly "crucified anew" by the Jews, who hammered nails into the icon and pierced its side, upon which, as the legend has it, blood and water emerged from the wounded panel.[1] During the Second Council of Nicea, convened after the first period of iconoclasm in Byzantium (730-787), the story of the crucifix of Beirut was presented among arguments put forward to affirm the worship of images. The propriety of Christian imagery and thus also the issue of the cross and crucifix, returned in the Europe of the sixteenth century.

This article will examine the place of medieval crucifixes in churches north of the Alps after the Reformation. I will elucidate a variety of attitudes towards the presence of medieval church furnishings, which stemmed from the way in which not only images, such as the crucifix, but also historical figures of rulers and saints were regarded by specific denominations. Scholars have noted that Protestant attitudes were not monolithic; Calvinists were harsh critics of both religious imagery and the history of the Church, while Lutherans proved to be much more tolerant. Yet, my point is not to show how much Lutherans differed from Calvinists, but rather that the attitudes of Lutherans and Catholics were often surprisingly close. Lutherans tended to reconsider, rather than eliminate, religious imagery in churches, and they reinterpreted Church history instead of erasing it. Catholics were also constantly revising their understanding of the past but they particularly valued the medieval Church and the artistic remains of that period. In order to explain the reasons for removing, preserving, or displaying medieval crucifixes in early modern churches, I will emphasize historical factors alongside the more commonly documented theological ones.

At the outset of the Reformation movement, images were only a marginal problem in Saxony (central-eastern Germany), where Martin Luther (1483-1546) first attacked the corruption of the Roman Church.[2] In his ninety-five theses (1517), Luther condemned the Church's program of indulgences, not its images. After having refused to renounce his theses at the Diet of Worms (1521), Luther took refuge in Wartburg Castle. Meanwhile, his close associate, Andreas Karlstadt (1486-1541) performed the first reformed communion service in Wittenberg on Christmas Day of that year, and it was under his influence that the city council authorized removal of imagery from the churches in January 1522. Alarmed by acts of violence, Luther returned to Wittenberg and, in March 1522, preached his series of "Invocavit" sermons, in which he argued that images, as such, are neither good nor bad, but essentially neutral. Karlstadt pointed out that they were forbidden in the Ten Commandments, but Luther countered with Saint Paul's doctrine of Christian freedom and concluded that images could be neither imposed nor prohibited. In subsequent discussion Karlstadt insisted that "idols" should be removed even by force because their superstitious worship would lead the faithful to damnation. Luther, however, considered the social unrest that often accompanied such removal of religious imagery a much more serious danger than the theoretical risk of idolatry.

The progress of the Reformation in Switzerland and southern Germany differed from that of Saxony.[3] On 1 September 1523, Leo Jud (1482-1542) preached a sermon in Saint Peter's church in Zurich, which initiated the removal of images. Key Swiss and South German reformers, including Huldrych Zwingli (1484-1531), Martin Bucer (1491-1551), Ludwig Hätzer (ca. 1500-1529), and John Calvin (1509-1564), confirmed this stance, each proclaiming that images should be both eliminated from churches and erased from people's memory. However, they insisted that these "vestiges of superstitions" be only peacefully and legally removed.

The controversy among the advocates of the Reformation continued throughout the sixteenth century. Meanwhile, Catholic writers, Johann Eck (1486–1543) and Jerome Emser (1477-1527), argued that images were not only allowed, but recommended, and their lead was followed by innumerable writers.[4] In this discussion, authors not only invoked theological and historical statements (e.g. documents of the Second Council of Nicaea and writings of the Church Fathers), but also referred directly to the images themselves. Whereas Calvinists claimed that Early Christian churches had contained no images, Roman Catholics believed many to have been found—among them the crucifix of Beirut—which testified to the existence of images from the very beginning of Christianity.[5]

Negative pronouncements on "idols" were made by Protestants in Swiss and south German catechisms and creeds,[6] while the Roman Church proffered an apology for the sacred image in its early modern doctrine.[7] The Lutherans, however, were initially reluctant to incorporate their attitude into the growing body of doctrine, thus remaining consistent with Luther's opinion that images were free and indifferent things that should be neither recommended nor prohibited.[8] Only occasionally were "idols" mentioned in Lutheran Church ordinances, especially in the second half of the sixteenth century during the controversy over the "indifferent things" (*adiaphora* in Greek), that broke out after Luther's death. Luther's close collaborator Philipp Melanchton (1497-1560) numbered images among *adiaphora*,[9] a position rejected by Melanchton's former student, Matthias Flacius Illyricus (1520-1575), famous as the founder of Lutheran historiography and author of the declaration "History is the foundation of doctrine."[10]

The past of the Church was, *nolens volens*, shared by all Christian denominations, but its evaluation differentiated adherents of the Reformation from Catholics, even while both assumed similar methodological approaches to historical evidence. Flacius tended to reinterpret the past in order to demonstrate that the "papists" had always led the Church into decline, while simultaneously presenting Lutherans as the legitimate heirs of an original, true Christianity.[11] Together with a group of scholars, he outlined the whole history of the Church in a book known as "Magdeburg Centuries."[12] Flacius insisted that not only writings, but all ancient monuments bearing imprints of the Church's past should be studied by historians.[13] Some Catholic authors shared this attitude, among them Cardinal Caesar Baronius (1538-1607), who formulated a response to "Magdeburg Centuries" in his *Annales ecclesiastici*[14] in order to demonstrate the historical continuity of the Roman Church through "living witnesses of the Christian antiquity" (i.e. not only writings, but also inscriptions, medals, buildings, and the earliest images of Christ, Mary, and the saints).[15] This was not a discussion between two authors, but rather, between two monumental historiographic, apologetic works which presented two competitive visions of the history of the Church. Seen in this context, medieval decorations preserved in churches after the Reformation can be regarded as remnants of the past.

A special importance was attached to crosses and crucifixes. Although no explicit proscriptions concerning them were put forward,[16] some meaningful opinions were expressed. Zwingli categorically declared that he had "never seen a cross displayed in church without someone making it into an idol."[17] On the other hand, the Catholic Stanislaus Hosius (1504-1579) insisted that a crucifix should be displayed in the middle of every church.[18] Between these two extremes we again find the Lutherans. Luther himself had said, "…when I hear the word Christ, there delineates itself in my heart the picture of a man who hangs on the cross."[19] Subsequently, the Lutherans disapproved iconoclastic acts and accused the Calvinists of not *re*forming but *de*forming churches. In 1597, a Lutheran writer, Abraham Teurer, even declared that to attack crucifixes was "to tear open again the holy wounds of Christ our Lord and to crucify him anew."[20] Moreover, the Lutherans insisted that they were neither idolaters nor iconoclasts, as Daniel Rücker, a theologian from Rothenburg ob der Tauber, wrote in 1646, "…we do not abolish the figure of the Cross from our churches, but allow it to remain inside, as a commemorative adornment or decoration."[21]

A spectrum of opinions regarding the nature and (im)propriety of religious imagery thus circulated in Northern Europe after the Reformation. These attitudes were realized in the variant ways that medieval crucifixes were alternately suppressed, preserved, or adapted in religious spaces.[22]

Destruction and Preservation

In Switzerland and Upper Germany, "Protestant iconoclasts took a special relish in breaking crucifixes."[23] A variety of violent rites were observed, among them old customs of "punishing" images, which would be broken, defaced, hung upside down, mocked, "forced" to drink, and otherwise abused.[24] Iconoclasts destroyed not only images displayed in churches, but also statues standing in public places, and Catholics sometimes provoked such iconoclastic reactions by erecting crucifixes in villages belonging to Dissidents.[25] One of the earliest Protestant iconoclasts was Klaus Hottinger, who, in 1523, broke a crucifix into pieces in Stadelhofen near Zürich. Hottinger was subsequently tried for blasphemy in the Catholic city of Lucerne and burnt at the stake. Thus, paradoxically, he suffered a Passion and was presented as the first evangelical martyr.[26] Heinrich Bullinger admitted in his *Chronicle of the Reformation* (1564) that the crucifix in Stadelhofen was "beautifully carved," notwithstanding it having to be destroyed.[27]

Occasionally, even iconophobes, such as English Puritans, acknowledged a possibility that a "reformed" cross could be allowed to remain, as evidenced by opinions on the Coventry Cross quoted by Thomas Fuller in *The Worthies of England* (1662). He characterized it as "a reformed cross … without any cross thereon, being a master-piece, all for ornament, nothing for superstition; so that the most curious hath just cause to commend, the most conscientious to allow, none to condemn it."[28] However, this cross was "reformed" in a very special sense. It was actually erected between 1541 and 1544, presumably to replace a medieval cross which had stood there since the thirteenth century to denote a market-place. Although called a "cross," it was rather an architectonical structure decorated with many statues of kings and saints, but did not actually include a crucifix or a cross.

Needless to say, many medieval crucifixes were preserved in Catholic churches. This was also the case in Lutheran churches, despite theologians' fear of idolatry. In fact, Lutherans often justified their continued use of medieval crucifixes with the same arguments employed since the Middle Ages, as is evident from the example of the altar of the Holy Cross in the Cistercian church of Doberan.

When the monastery at Doberan was secularized in 1552, the altarpiece was still crowned with a wooden beam forming the base of a large Gothic crucifix (ca. 1360)[29] bearing the inscription: *Effigiem Christi qui transis pronus adora. Sed non effigiem sed quem designat adora*[30] ("What time thou passest by the rood, bow humbly evermore. Yet not the rood, but Him which there was crucified, adore") [Fig. 1].[31] This inscription, containing a verse universally known since the Middle Ages,[32] was preserved by the Lutherans, who, finding it appropriate to their own agenda, also employed it in other regions, such as Scandinavia, in their campaign against idolatry.[33]

Theological Reinterpretations

Nevertheless, for the Lutherans, especially after the iconoclastic events of the early 1520s, "the image of the crucifix would never be the same again."[34] Crucifixes painted or carved after the Reformation presented a new theology of the cross and of Christ's sacrifice,[35] while historical representations of the crucified Savior were reinterpreted.

A new theological interpretation of the medieval crucifix was presented in the church of Saint John in Danzig (Gdańsk) where the Reformation was implemented in 1557.[36] Here a late-Gothic rood (ca. 1482) remained on a beam with a quotation from Saint Paul's epistle to the

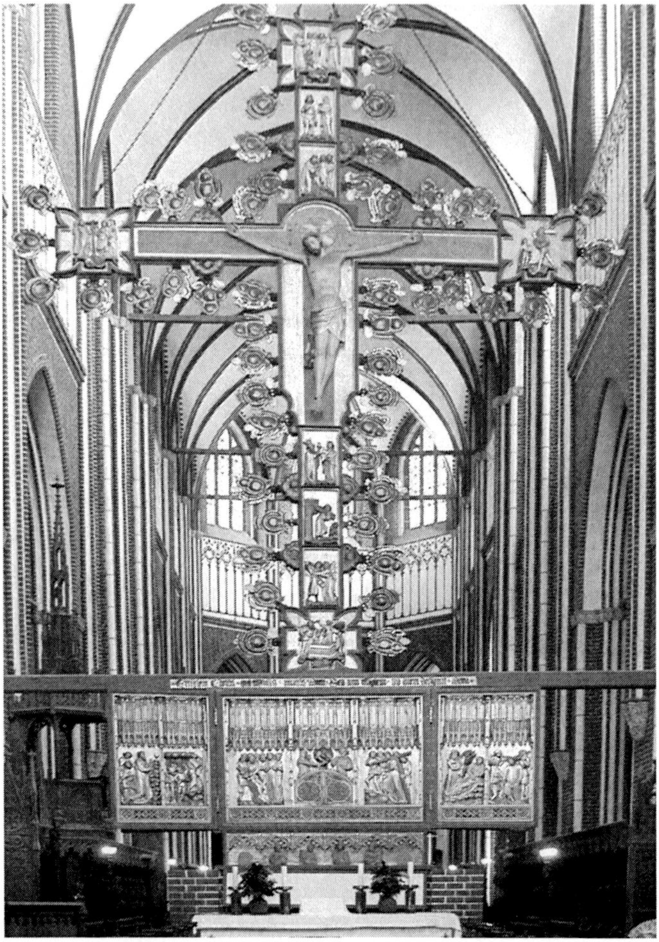

Fig. 1 Altar of the Holy Cross, ex-Cistercian church, Doberan (Photo: Author)

Philippians 2:8 added in the late seventeenth or early eighteenth century that reads: *Er erniedrigte sich selbst und ward gehorsam bis zum Tode, ja zum Tode am Kreuz* ("He humbled himself, and became obedient unto death, even the death of the cross"). On the reverse of the cross there appeared a depiction of the Brazen Serpent and the inscription *Num[eri] 21* (Numbers 21), recalling the story of the serpent of brass made by Moses and put upon a pole.[37] The writer of Saint John's gospel concluded that Christ's humiliation on the cross was an exaltation comparable to the

Brazen Serpent exalted by Moses, since they both promised eternal life to the faithful.[38] This idea was subsequently developed in the Lutheran *Formula of Concord* (1577) where Saint Paul's text also appeared:

> This majesty He [Christ] always had according to the personal union, and yet He abstained from it in the state of His humiliation…; therefore He exercised this majesty, not always, but when [as often as] it pleased Him, until after His resurrection He entirely laid aside the form of a servant, but not the [human] nature, and was established in the full use, manifestation, and declaration of the divine majesty, and thus entered into His glory, Phil. 2:6 ff.… Hence He also is able and it is very easy for Him to impart, as one who is present, His true body and blood in the Holy Supper, not according to the mode or property of the human nature, but according to the mode and property of the right hand of God, as Dr. Luther says in accordance with our Christian faith for children.[39]

Thus Christ, who took the form of a servant,[40] was tormented and humiliated in order to become the Savior. This motif recurred in Lutheran devotional literature of the seventeenth century. Johann Arndt, in *Vier Bücher vom wahren Christentum* (1605-1610),[41] described the crucified Christ as the Book of Life and recommended contemplation of his five wounds.[42] Such contemplation of the Passion was inspired by, and closely related to, medieval mysticism. This connection facilitated the adaptation of some medieval crucifixes as visual aids for Lutheran devotional practices.

Monumental crucifixes could be specifically adapted to Lutheran doctrine. The Christology outlined in the *Formula of Concord*, for example, was also closely connected with the Lutheran doctrine of Redemption and Eucharist: both applied to the image of a crucified Savior. A triptych from 1462 by Friedrich Herlin was kept on the main altar of Saint George's church in Nördlingen.[43] In 1683 the shrine was enclosed in a new architectural setting [Fig. 2]. After restoration, the painted wings were displayed on the back of the shrine,[44] while five carved figures were returned to their original place. The crucified Christ, Mary, and Saint John appeared within the shrine, Saints George and Mary Magdalene on the outside, as the so-called "Schreinwächter" (shrine watchers). The new inscription in the predella elaborates on a verse from the Epistle to the Hebrews 10:14 "For by one offering he hath perfected for ever them that are sanctified."[45] The Epistle to the Hebrews was often cited in Lutheran Eucharistic doctrine. It appears, for example, in the *Augsburg Confession*,[46] and in local church ordinances, such as those of Nördlingen.[47]

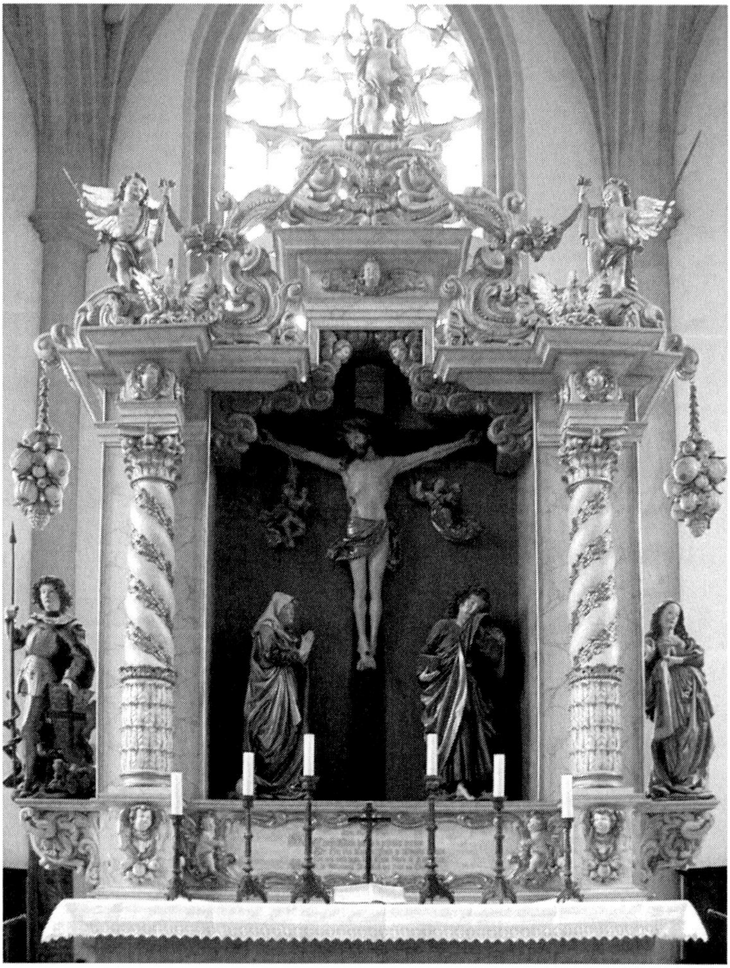

Fig. 2 Main altar, Saint George's church, Nördlingen (Photo: Author)

Further changes were made to the Nördlingen altarpiece beyond those already described. Three *putti* personifying virtues were added at the top: Faith appeared in the center with cross and chalice, while on the sides Righteousness held a sword and Peace an olive branch, along with garlands of fruit.[48] The sculpted figures of a Phoenix and Pelican (above the columns) emphasized Christ's resurrection and sacrifice. This old, established, Christian iconography was based on the interpretation of

Psalms 91:12 and 101:7 in the *Physiologus*.[49] Interestingly, neither the phoenix nor pelican appear in Luther's translation of the Bible, since the quoted phrases read as follows: "The righteous will become green like a palm tree," and "I am like a Great Bittern [a relative of the heron] in the desert" (Psalm 102:6).[50] Nonetheless, the earlier references evidently retained their validity in Lutheran perception as figures of the crucified and resurrected Christ, and the medieval crucifix in Nördlingen came to embody a new evangelical doctrine, shaped mainly from old motifs.

In 1683 not only the crucifix in the Lutheran church of Nördlingen, but also the so-called Gero Crucifix in Catholic Cologne Cathedral were displayed in a new altarpiece [Fig. 3]. The latter ranks among the earliest preserved monumental carved crucifixes (ca. 970) and the oldest representations of the dead Christ on the cross, in contrast to most earlier images of the crucified Savior, which presented him alive and triumphant over death.[51] The glory of the cross was proclaimed by Saint Paul and preached by later theologians,[52] among them Leo the Great (400-461) who was quoted twice in inscriptions on the marble altarpiece where the "Gero Crucifix" was displayed. The bottom-most sentence ("Let our understandings, illumined by the Spirit of Truth, foster with pure and free heart the glory of the cross which irradiates heaven and earth.") emphasized the original, triumphal sense of the cross.[53] The "Gero Crucifix" was displayed surrounded by golden rays, as if visualizing the triumphal second coming of the Messiah.[54]

By the seventeenth century, the "Gero Crucifix" was believed to have been commissioned by Gero, the archbishop of Cologne (d. 976), and to have figured in a legend about Saint Irmgardis (d. ca. 1080) who was allegedly told by a crucifix in the Early Christian basilica of Saint Paul-outside-the-Walls in Rome to pass on his regards to the crucifix in Cologne cathedral.[55] Displaying an old crucifix in a new setting was, therefore, also closely connected with the revival of interest in remote rulers and saints. In this way medieval images could become embedded in local history.

Historical Reinterpretations

It was not only Catholics but also Lutherans, who, to a perhaps surprising degree, emphasized their respect for Christian tradition through their interest in medieval saints. The city where "the preserving power of Lutheranism"[56] manifested itself exceptionally powerfully was Nuremberg.[57] In the Lutheran parish church of Saint Sebald, the majority

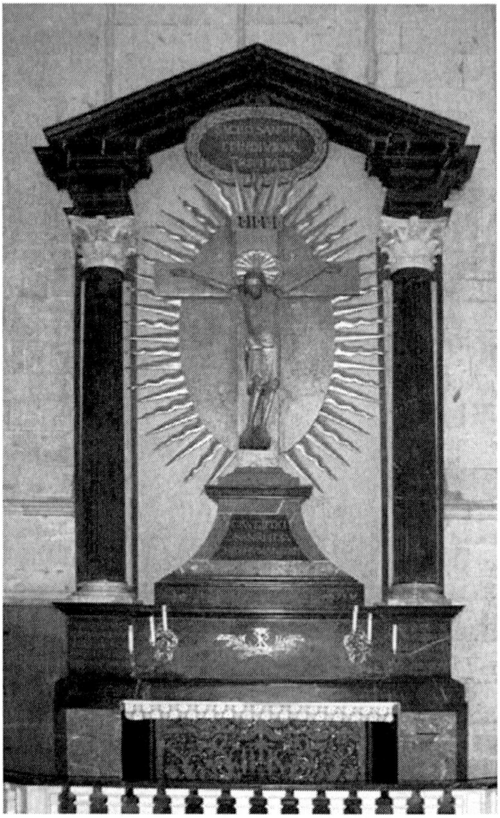

Fig. 3 "Gero Crucifix," Cologne Cathedral (Photo: Author)

of medieval furnishings were retained. Early in July 1542, however, the city council decided to make some changes. Three altarpieces were removed to facilitate the congregation's visual and acoustic access to the preacher and the Word of God. The panels from two side altarpieces were removed (but preserved), and the main altar was totally dismantled, together with the choir seats. Finally, a crucifix which stood in front of the pulpit—probably a sculpture commissioned by Nicklos Wickel and Augustin Tichtel and carved by Veit Stoss around 1520—was also removed.[58]

After 1542, the "Wickel Crucifix" stood in front of the grave of Saint Sebald.[59] This saint was believed to have been a Danish prince who broke his engagement to a French princess in order to become a missionary in

Franconia. He died and was buried in Saint Peter's church in Nuremberg before 1070, when the first pilgrimages to his grave are recorded. Between 1361 and 1372, the present church was built over the site. Sebald was canonized in 1425 and became a holy patron of Nuremberg. During the sixteenth and seventeenth centuries, appreciation for Saint Sebald by Lutheran and Catholic chroniclers varied.[60] The "Magdeburg Centuries" presented him as a missionary sent to Franconia in order to spread "pontifical superstitions."[61] Contemporary Bavarian (Catholic) authors regarded him as a symbol of the Catholic traditions of Nuremberg, while Lutheran interest in Saint Sebald revived after the Thirty Years' War (1618-1648) when he was reclaimed as a symbol of Nuremberg's flourishing past.

The "Wickel Crucifix" continued to stand in front of Saint Sebald's grave even after the church's interior was restored in 1657-1660. In 1663, another Stoss crucifix, along with figures of Mary and Saint John, was brought to Saint Sebald's from the church of Our Lady and displayed in a newly commissioned Baroque altarpiece over the main altar. Thus, in the mid-seventeenth century, two crucifixes by Veit Stoss were displayed along the main axis of Saint Sebald's church.[62] Seventeenth-century Lutheran preachers praised the splendor of Nuremberg's Gothic churches and occasionally called those who had built them "dear forefathers in the papacy."[63]

Catholics, naturally, were more likely to link medieval images with historic local rulers or saints and thus to glorify the local past identified with the origins of Christianity, seen as an equivalent to Roman Catholicism. In the Lutheran city of Regensburg, there remained a Catholic bishopric and some monasteries, among them Saint Emmeram's Abbey. This Benedictine abbey, founded around 729 at the grave of Emmeram (d. 652), houses a carved crucifix dating to the twelfth century, which is now displayed on an altar in the choir within a retable made in 1736 [Fig. 4].[64] In front of the altar lies the Gothic tombstone of Saint Emmeram, executed in 1340-1350, identified by an inscription in the ceiling above the entrance to the choir that reads: "S. EMMERAMUS THAUMATURGUS." Born into a noble family in Aquitane, Emmeram was a missionary active some time after the year 649 at the court of Theodo I (ca. 630-680), Duke of Bavaria. Theodo was the first to draw up plans for the Bavarian church, aiming at a greater independence from the Frankish Kingdom through closer association with the Pope.[65] The cult of Saint Emmeram revived in the mid-seventeenth century after the rediscovery of his relics in 1645.[66] A description of the monastery in the *Consuetudines* of 1744 speaks to the importance of the cross-altar and the "old grave" ("sepulchrum antiquum") of Saint Emmeram.[67] Theodo and Emmeram, the two founders of the Bavarian Church, both appear in the eighteenth-century fresco located on the ceiling above the crucifix and tombstone.

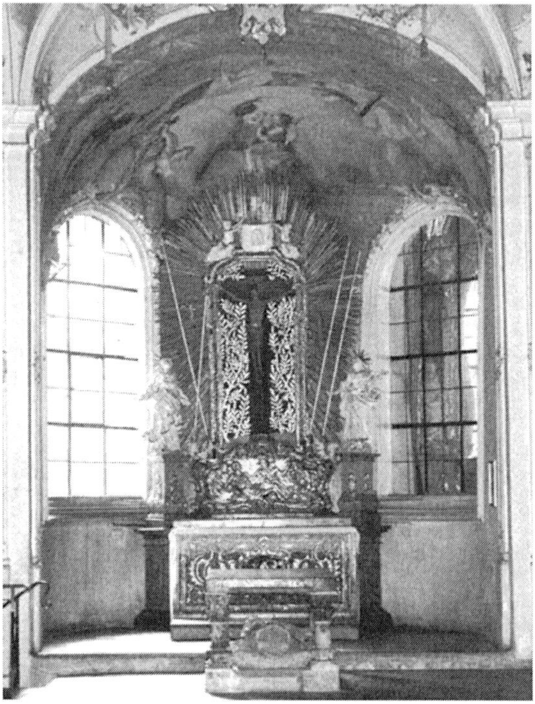

Fig. 4 Saint George's choir, Saint Emmeram's abbey church, Regensburg (Photo: Author)

Many other examples of medieval crucifixes being connected with medieval rulers or saints could be cited.[68] A common narrative device to encourage the association of an old crucifix with an historic person was the occurrence of a conversation between the historic personage and the crucified Christ. Such miraculous conversations were extraordinarily popular in Cracow, famous for its richness in holy relics and described at one time as the Polish Rome.[69] According to one legend, the crucifix in Cracow Cathedral (ca. 1380) spoke to queen Hedwig of Anjou (1374-1399).[70] From the late fifteenth or early sixteenth century it stood, along with the figures of the Virgin and Saint John. During the renovation of

1634, a silver repoussé sheet with ornamental motifs was added in the background, and, in 1745, the crucifix was displayed in the present altarpiece (the figures of Mary and Saint John were removed in the nineteenth century) [Fig. 5]. Among many other crucifixes in Cracow related to medieval saints and adapted into early modern altarpieces was the crucifix by Veit Stoss in the city's main parish church of Saint Mary's (ca. 1495). In the early modern era this crucifix was famous not as a work of art carved by an eminent sculptor, but as a miraculous figure that had spoken to a sacristan named Świętosław several years earlier.[71]

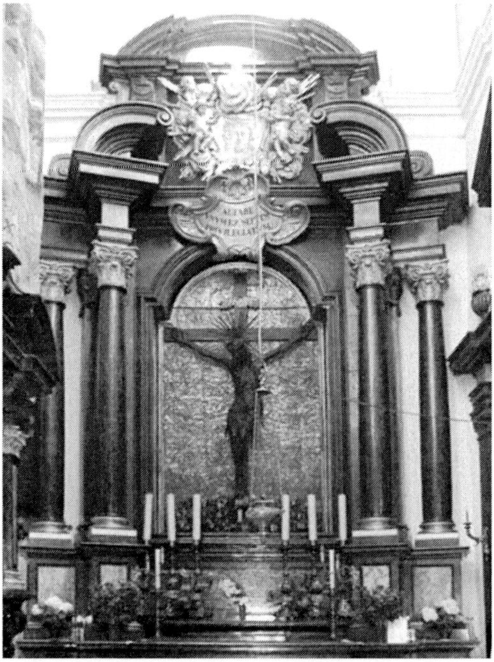

Fig. 5 "Crucifix of Queen Hedwig," Cracow Cathedral (Photo: Author)

Conclusions

This essay examines the reuse of medieval crucifixes after the Reformation from religious and historical perspectives. While the religious issues have, in general, received far greater attention in the scholarly literature, these analyses tend to focus on theory (i.e. doctrine) rather than practice. It is in practice, however, that one can find more specific, compelling reasons for the preservation and display of medieval crucifixes in early modern settings.

Lutherans, like Catholics, related medieval crucifixes to remote, regional histories and displayed them in new settings. Clearly the Lutherans' attitude stemmed not only from their tolerance towards images and from a conviction about the commemorative function of images, but also from a genuine respect for the past. The Lutherans did attempt a theological reinterpretation of late-medieval crucifixes emphasizing, for example, the unique nature of Christ's sacrifice and its Eucharistic consequences, as in Saint George's church in Nördlingen. Equal, or perhaps even more important, however, was the role medieval crucifixes played in the establishment of local or regional history. Although some of the legends concerning medieval crucifixes were cited only in the mid-seventeenth century, they testify to the cult of a given image in the early modern era, even if they do not explain its genesis. More importantly, although a medieval crucifix incorporated into a new setting was not always regarded as a holy image, its historical significance was such that the crucifix was preserved and continued to be displayed.

While the utility of medieval religious imagery in the construction of history has been acknowledged by some scholars, such utilization tends to be identified specifically with Catholicism. The past of the Church, however, was shared by all Christians, and it was scrutinized in order to legitimize particular denominations. Lutherans and Catholics clearly differed in their historical conclusions, but they had similar aims and adopted similar methodological approaches to history, just as they often adopted similar strategies vis-à-vis the preservation of medieval images in churches. Displaying medieval crucifixes in Baroque altarpieces and relating them to remote, regional histories thus constituted a conscious reinterpretation of the past on the part of both the Catholic Church and the new Lutheran denomination.

Finally, an important reservation must be stated. Neither the religious nor historical value of medieval crucifixes answers all questions. Even iconophobes sometimes noticed the artistic quality of images which were to be removed. Among reasons for preserving and reinterpreting medieval crucifixes in post-Reformation churches, aesthetic factors should be considered together with religious and historical ones. It is well known that Veit Stoss's crucifixes were appreciated and emulated in the early modern era, both in Lutheran Nuremberg and Catholic Cracow.[72] Although the complex problem of retrospective tendencies in the fine arts of the seventeenth and eighteenth centuries cannot be thoroughly discussed here, such an attitude, widespread both in Lutheran and Catholic regions, provides strong evidence of the richly nuanced reception of medieval art in the early modern era.

Notes

[1] I should like to express my thanks to Barbara Arciszewska, Peter Martyn, and Jacqueline Jung, as well as the editors of the present volume, who all helped in the preparation of this essay. I am often citing the Bible in this essay, using various translations depending on confessional context. When writing about Lutherans I am quoting Luther's translation: *Dr. Martin Luther's Bibelübersetzung nach der letzten Original-Ausgabe, kritisch bearbeitet*, ed. Heinrich Ernst Bindseil and Hermann Agathon Niemeyer, 7 vols. (Halle: Verlag der Canstein'schen Bibel-Anstalt, 1845-1855); and, as its English equivalent I chose (albeit with hesitation) the King James Version: *The Authorised Version of the English Bible, 1611*, ed. William Aldis Wright, 5 vols. (Cambridge: University Press, 1909). When writing about Catholics I am quoting the Clementine Vulgate (*Biblia Sacra juxta Vulgatam Clementinam*, ed. Michael Tweedale, [London: Editio Electronica, 2005]: http://vulsearch.sourceforge.ner/html/index/); and the English translation of the Vulgate, *Douay Reims-The Holy Bible* (Rockford, IL: Tan Books and Publishers, 1989). On the desecration of crosses see Jean-Marie Sansterre, "L'Image blessée, l'image souffrante: quelques récits de miracles entre Orient et Occident (VIe-XIIe siècle)," in *Les Images dans les sociétés médiévales. Pour une histoire comparée*, ed. Jean-Marie Sansterre and Jean-Claude Schmitt (Brussels and Rome:Institut historique belge de Rome, 1999). 113-130; Michele Bacci, "Quel bello miracolo onde si fa la festa del santo Salvatore: studio sulle metamorfosi di una leggenda," in *Santa Croce e Santo Volto. Contributi allo studio dell'origine e della fortuna del culto del Salvatore (secoli IX-XV)*, ed. Gabriella Rossetti (Pisa: GISEM Edizioni ETS, 2002). 7-86

[2] Margarete Stirm, *Die Bilderfrage in der Reformation* (Gütersloh: Gerd Mohn, 1977); Giuseppe Scavizzi, *Arte e architettura sacra. Cronache e documenti sulla controversia tra riformati e cattolici (1500-1550)* (Reggio Calabria: Gangemi, 1981); Helmut Feld, *Der Ikonoklasmus des Westens* (Leiden: E. J. Brill, 1990); Sergiusz Michalski, *The Reformation and the Visual Arts: The Protestant Image Question in Western and Eastern Europe* (London: Routledge, 1993); Joseph Leo Koerner, *The Reformation of the Image* (London: Reaktion Books, 2004).

[3] Charles Garside Jr., *Zwingli and the Arts* (New Haven: Yale University Press, 1966); Hans-Dietrich Altendorf and Peter Jezler, eds., *Bilderstreit: Kulturwandel in Zwinglis Reformation* (Zurich: Theologischer Verlag, 1984); Carlos M. N. Eire, *War Against Idols: The Reformation of Worship from Erasmus to Calvin* (Cambridge: Cambridge University Press, 1986); Giuseppe Scavizzi, *The Controversy on Images: From Calvin to Baronius* (New York: Peter Lang, 1992); Lee Palmer Wandel, *Voracious Idols and Violent Hands: Iconoclasm in Reformation Zurich, Strasbourg, and Basel* (Cambridge: Cambridge University Press, 1994).

[4] Christian Hecht, *Katholische Bildertheologie im Zeitalter von Gegenreformation und Barock. Studien zu Traktaten von Johannes Molanus, Gabriele Paleotti und anderen Autoren* (Berlin: Gebr. Mann, 1997).

[5] Occasionally the crucifix of Beirut was identified with the *Volto Santo* in Lucca, allegedly carved by Nicodemus. Scavizzi, *Controversy on Images*. 162, 170. The Lutheran "Magdeburg Centuries" included the story of the crucifix of Beirut among a selection of false miracles. *Ecclesiastica historia, integram Ecclesiae Christi…secundum singulas centurias, perspicuo ordine complectens: singulari diligentia et fide ex vetustissimis et optimis historicis, et aliis scriptoribus congesta per alioquot studiosos et pios viros ex urbe Magdeburgica*, vol. 2 (Basel, 1559). 1445

[6] See, for example, Martin Bucer, "Confessio Tetrapolitana und die Schriften des Jahres 1531," vol. 3 of *Deutsche Schriften*, ed. Robert Stupperich (Gütersloh: Gerd Mohn, 1969). 151-161, 299-314; Iohannes Calvinus [John Calvin], *Opera quae supersunt omnia*, ed. Guglielmus Baum, Eduard Cunitz, Eduard Reuss, vol. 1 (Braunschweig: Schwetschke, 1863). 32-34, 384-397; Heinrich Bullinger, "Confessio et expositio simplex orthodoxae fidei," in *Bekenntnis-schriften und Kirchenordnungen der nach Gottes Wort reformierten Kirche*, ed. Wilhelm Niesel (Zurich: Evangelischer Verlag, 1938). cap. 4; Heinrich Bullinger, *Catechismus. Darinn die fürnembsten Haubtpuncten Christlicher Religion gründtlich erklärt werden, von Weyland H. Heinrich Bullingern inn Latein beschrieben: Jetzt aber dem gemeinen Mann zum besten jhn das Teutsch gebracht* (Zürich, 1597). cap. 5

[7] Stanislaus Hosius, *Confessio fidei catholicae Christiana….* (Cracow, 1553). cap. XI, XIII, and LXXVII; the 1563 decree of the Council of Trent affirming the validity of religious imagery: "*De invocatione, veneratione et reliquiis sanctorum et sacris imaginibus*," in *Concilium Tridentinum. Diariorum, Actorum, Epistularum, tractatuum nova collectio*, ed. Societas Goerresiana, vol. 9 (Freiburg im Breisgau: Herder, 1976). 1077-1079. The impact of the Council of Trent's decree on contemporary discussions of religious imagery has been analyzed by Hubert Jedin, "Entstehung und Tragweite des Trienter Dekrets über die Bilderverehrung," *Theologische Quartalschrift* 116 (1935). 143-188, 404-429

[8] Images were mentioned neither in Luther's *Catechisms*, nor in the *Augsburg Confession* (1530) written by Melanchton who, however, forewarned against superstitious images in the *Apology of the Augsburg Confession* (article XXI, 34). All quoted texts appear in *Die Bekenntnisschriften der evangelisch–lutherischen Kirche*, 10th ed. (Göttingen: Vandenhoeck & Ruprecht, 1986). Martin Chemnitz, in his 1578 response to the decree of the Council of Trent, concluded that images in churches could be tolerated, provided they were not worshipped or venerated. Martin Chemnitz, *Examen Concilii Tridentini*, ed. Eduard Preuss (Berlin: G. Schlawitz, 1861). 761-797

[9] Melanchton defined the category of *adiaphora* in the *Leipzig interim* of 1548. Philipp Melanchton, *Opera quae supersunt omnia*, ed. Cardus G. Bretschneider, vol. 7 (Halle: Schwetschke, 1840). 263. The problem was discussed again in the *Formula of Concord* (1577) in which, however, images were not explicitly mentioned: *The Formula of Concord*, in *Triglot Concordia: The Symbolical Books*

of the Ev. Lutheran Church, trans. Friedrich Bente and William Hermann Theodore Dau (St. Louis: Concordia Publishing House, 1921). 503-529

[10] Quoted in Ermanno Nacinovich, *Flacio. Studio biografico-storico* (Fiume: Mohovich, 1886). chap. 4, n. 4; on Flacius' historiography see Martina Hartmann, *Humanismus und Kirchenkritik: Matthias Flacius Illyricus als Erforscher des Mittelalters* (Stuttgart: Thorbecke, 2001).

[11] Such was the agenda of his first book, *Catalogue of Witnesses to the Truth*. Matthias Flacius Illyricus, *Catalogus testium veritatis, qui ante nostram aetatem reclamarunt Papaei* (Basel, 1556); see also Bruce Gordon, "The Changing Face of Protestant History and Identity in the Sixteenth Century," in *Protestant History and Identity in Sixteenth-Century Europe*, vol. 1 of *The Medieval Inheritance*, ed. Bruce Gordon (Aldershot: Scolar Press, 1996). 1-22

[12] *Ecclesiastica historia*. (see n. 5)

[13] "Omnia vetera monumenta, quae qualiacunque vestigia historiae Ecclesiae commonstrare possent, praesertim autem, quae veritatis aliqua vestigia puriorisque doctrinae ostendere possent." Quoted in Nacinovich, *Flacio*. chap. 4

[14] Caesar Baronius, *Annales ecclesiastici a Christi nato ad annum 1198*, 12 vols. (Rome, 1587-1607). On Baronius see Stefano Zen, *Baronio storico. Controriforma e crisi del metodo umanistico* (Naples: Vivarium, 1994).

[15] Baronius, *Annales ecclesiastici*. 2:323. On Baronius's approach to Early Christian monuments see Romeo de Maio et al., eds., *Baronio e l'arte. Atti del convegno internationale di studi, Sora 10-13 ottobre 1984* (Sora: Centro studi Vincenzo Patriarca, 1985). On the development of this idea in the seventeenth century see Francis Haskell, *History and Its Images: Art and the Interpretation of the Past* (New Haven: Yale University Press, 1993); Gabriele Bickendorf, *Die Historisierung der italienischen Kunstbetrachtung im 17. und 18. Jahrhundert* (Berlin: Gebr. Mann, 1998); Peter Burke, "Image as Evidence in Seventeenth-Century Europe," *Journal of the History of Ideas* 64 (2003). 273-296

[16] Giuseppe Scavizzi, "The Cross: a Sixteenth-Century Controversy," *Storia dell'arte* 65 (1989). 27-43; Margaret Aston, "Cross and Crucifix in the English Reformation," in *Macht und Ohnmacht der Bilder. Reformatorischer Bildersturm im Kontext der europäischen Geschichte*, ed. Peter Blicke et al. (Munich: Oldenbourg, 2002). 253-272

[17] Quoted in Aston, "Cross and Crucifix." 258; Huldrych Zwingli, *Sämtliche Werke*, ed. Emil Egli, vol. 4 (Berlin: M. Heinsius, 1905). 120

[18] Hosius, *Confessio*. cap. 11

[19] *D. Martin Luthers Werke: Kritische Gesamtausgabe*, *Schriften*, vol. 18 (Weimar: Böhlau, 1908). 83

[20] Quoted in Koerner, *Reformation of the Image*. 161

[21] "Also verwerffen wir zwar die Creutzfigur in unsern Kirchen nicht, sondern lassen sie darinnen, als einen Erinnerungsschmuck oder einen Gedenckzierath passieren." Quoted in Hermann Hipp, "Studien zur 'Nachgotik' des 16. und 17. Jahrhunderts in Deutschland, Böhmen, Österreich und der Schweiz" (Ph. D. diss., Tübingen University, 1979). 473

[22] On displaying medieval images, figures, and altarpieces in early modern settings see Wolfgang Götz, "Gotische Plastik in barockem Gehäuse," in *Festschrift Johannes Jahn zum XXII. November MCMLVII* (Leipzig: Seemann, 1958). 187-193; Herbert Beck, "Mittelalterliche Skulpturen in Barockaltären," *Mitteilungen der Gesellschaft für Salzburger Landeskunde* 108 (1968). 209-293; Marcin Wisłocki, "Ort und Rolle vorreformatorischer Tradition im protestantischen Pommern im 16. und 17. Jahrhundert am Beispiel von Adaptationen mittelalterlicher Altäre," *Zeitschrift für Ostmitteleuropa-Forschung* 47, 3 (1998). 347-370; Werner Ziems, "Vorreformatorische Bildwerke in nachreformatorischen Altaraufsätzen. Vom Erhalt durch Nutzung," in *Dorfkirchen. Beiträge zu Architektur, Ausstattung und Denkmalpflege*, ed. Bernd Janowski and Dirk Schumann (Berlin: Lukas, 2004). 380-388; Tobias Kunz, "Inszenierte Vergangenheit. Mittelalterliche Bildwerke im Kontext barocker Klöster," in *Barocke Klöster in Mitteleuropa. Visualisierung monastischer Vergangenheit in Wissenschaft und Kunst, Tagungsband der Schwaben Akademie Irsee, 6.-8. Oktober 2006*, ed. Markwart Herzog and Huberta Weigl (Konstanz: UVK Verlagsgesellschaft, 2008). (in press)

[23] Koerner, *Reformation of the Image*. 127; see also Michalski, *Reformation and the Visual Arts*; Aston, "Cross and Crucifix." 253-272

[24] Michalski, *Reformation and the Visual Arts*. 129; Koerner, *Reformation of the Image*. 127-134

[25] Michalski, *Reformation and the Visual Arts*. 81

[26] Peter Jezler, "Tempelreinigung oder Barbarei? Eine Geschichte vom Bild des Bilderstürmers," in *Bilderstreit: Kulturwandel in Zwinglis Reformation*, ed. Hans-Dietrich Altendorf and Peter Jezler (Zurich: Theologischer Verlag, 1984). 78-79; Koerner, *Reformation of the Image*. 129-131

[27] "Ein groß und schoen geschnitzt und offgericht Crucifix." Heinrich Bullinger, *Reformationsgeschichte*, ed. Johann Jakob Hottinger and Hans Heinrich Vögeli, vol. 1 (Frauenfeld: Beyel, 1838). 127

[28] Thomas Fuller, *The Worthies of England*, ed. John Freeman (London: George Allen and Unwin, 1952). 579

[29] Johannes Voss, "Anmerkungen zur Geschichte des Kreuzaltars und seines Retabels im Doberaner Münster. Konzeption und Ergebnisse der Restaurierung 1975-1984," in *Figur und Raum. Mittelalterliche Holzbildwerke im historischen und kunstgeographischen Kontext*, ed. Uwe Albrecht and Jan von Bonsdorf (Berlin: Reimer, 1994). 112-123; Annegret Laabs, *Malerei und Plastik im Zisterzienserorden: Zum Bildgebrauch zwischen sakralem Zeremoniell und Stiftermemoria 1250-1430* (Petersberg: Imhof, 2000). 14, 74-84

[30] Laabs, *Malerei und Plastik im Zisterzienserorden*. 66-70

[31] Quoted in William Durandus, *The Symbolism of Churches and Church Ornaments. A translation of the first book of the Rationale Divinorum Officiorum*, ed. and trans. John Mason Neale and Benjamin Webb (London: Gibbings, 1893). 43

[32] Ulysse Chevalier, *Repertorium Hymnologicum*, vol. 3 (Louvain: Lefever, 1904). 190; Gulielmi Durandi, *Rationale Divinorum Officiorum, I-IV*, ed. Anselmus Davril and Timothy M. Thibodeau (Turnhout: Brepols, 1995). 35

[33] Ragne Bugge, "Effigiem Christi, qui transis, semper honora: Verses condemning the cult of sacred images in art and literature," *Acta ad Archeologiam et artium historiam pertinentia* 6 (1975). 127-139; Such measures, however, did not eradicate the cult of many crucifixes to which pilgrims still prayed as late as the eighteenth century. See Martin Blindheim, "The Cult of Medieval Wooden Sculptures in Post-Reformation Norway," in *Images of Cult and Devotion: Function and Reception of Christian Images in Medieval and Post-Medieval Europe*, ed. Søren Kaspersen (Copenhagen: Museum Tusculanum, 2004). 47-59

[34] Koerner, *Reformation of the Image*. 168

[35] Graham S. Tomlin, "The Medieval Origins of Luther's Theology of the Cross," *Archiv für Reformationsgeschichte* 89 (1998). 22-40; Robert Kolb, "Luther on the Theology of the Cross," *Lutheran Quarterly* 16 (2002). 443-466; Timothy J. Wengert, "'Peace, Peace Cross, Cross': Reflections on How Martin Luther Relates the Theology of the Cross to Suffering," *Theology Today* 59 (2002). 190-205

[36] Katarzyna Cieślak, *Między Rzymem, Wittenbergą a Genewą. Sztuka Gdańska jako miasta podzielonego wyznaniowo* (Wrocław: Fundacja na Rzecz Nauki Polskiej, 2000). 78-79

[37] Numbers 21: 8-9

[38] John 3:14-15; Hosius, *Confessio fidei catholicae Christiana*. cap. 11

[39] The Person of Christ, Affirmative Theses: Pure Doctrine of the Christian Church concerning the Person of Christ, in The Formula of Concord (above, n. 9). chap. VIII, 512

[40] Isaiah 52:13 - 53:12

[41] Johann Arndt, *True Christianity*, trans. Peter Erb (New York: Paulist Press, 1979). 57, 207-208; Johannes Wallmann, "Johann Arndt und die protestantische Frömmigkeit. Zur Rezeption der mittelalterlichen Mystik im Luthertum," *Chloe* 2 (1984). 50-74

[42] Arndt, *True Christianity*. 227

[43] Elmar D. Schmid, *Nördlingen-die Georgskirche und St. Salvator* (Stuttgart: Theiss, 1977). 97-123, 136-137; *Friedrich Herlin: Eine spätgotische Bilderwelt*, ed. Andrea Kugler and Monika Nebel (Nördlingen: Steinmaier, 2000). The figures were carved by an anonymous sculptor sometimes identified with Niklaus Gerhaerts van Leyden. See Robert Suckale, "Der Meister der Nördlingen Hochaltarfigurem und Till Riemenschneider. Exemplarische Beiträge zum Verständnis ihrer Kunst," in *Opus Tessellatum. Modi und Grenzgänge der Kunstwissenschaft. Festschrift für Peter Cornelius Claussen,* ed. Katharina Corsepius et al. (Hildesheim: Olms, 2004). 327-340

[44] Today they are situated against the north wall of the aisle.

[45] "Mit Einem Opfer hat die so geheiligt werden/Der Herr ans Creutzes Stam(m) in Ewigkeit vollendt/Und weil noch gegen uns Sein Herz in Liebe brennt/Gibt er im Abendmahl Sein Leib und Blut auf Erden." See Luther's translation of Hebrews 10:14, "Denn mit Opfer hat er für immer die vollendet, die geheiligt werden."

[46] *Augsburg Confession*, chap. XXIV, *Of the Mass*. See *The Confession of Faith Which Was Submitted to His Imperial Majesty Charles V At the Diet of Augsburg in the Year 1530*, in *Triglot Concordia* (above, n. 9). 37-95

[47] *Renovatio Ecclesiae Nordlingiacensis*, 1525, in *Die evangelischen Kirchenordnungen des XVI. Jahrhunderts*, Bd. 12, *Bayern*, T. 2, *Schwaben. Reichsstädte Augsburg, Dinkelsbühl, Donauwörth, Kaufbeuren, Kempten, Lindau, Memmingen, Nördlingen, Grafschaft Oettlingen-Oettingen*, ed. Emil Sehling, Institut für Evangelisches Kirchenrecht der Evangelischen Kirche in Deutschland zu Göttingen (Tübingen: Mohr, 1963). 289-306, esp. 297-302

[48] Epistle of James 3:18, "And the fruit of righteousness is sown in peace of them that make peace"; see also Second Epistle to Timothy 2:22.

[49] In the Late Middle Ages the *Physiologus* was commonly known in the Latin and German (as well as English and French) translations. For the original Greek version of the *Physiologus* attributed to Epiphanius (ca. 310-403) see *Patrologiae Cursus Completus, Series Graeca*, ed. Jacques-Paul Migne, vol. 43 (Paris: Garnier, 1864). 517-534; for the Latin translation see http://bestiary.ca/etexts/migne/epiphanius_physiologus. The author of *Physiologus* wrote in Greek, also he quoted the Psalms after the Greek *Septuaginta*. The respective verses read: *δίκαιος ὡς φοῖνιξ ἀνθήσει* (Psalm 91:13) and *ὡμοιώθην πελεκᾶνι ἐρημικῷ* (Psalm 101:7). (*φοῖνιξ* was translated as "palm" already in the Vulgate).

[50] "Der Gerechte wird grünen wie ein Palmbaum;" and "Ich bin wie eine Rohrdommel in der Wüste." (Psalm 102:6).

[51] Reiner Haussherr, "Der tote Christus am Kreuz. Zur Ikonographie des Gerokreuzes" (Ph.D. diss., University of Bonn, 1963); Reiner Haussherr "Kruzifixus," in *Lexikon der christlichen Ikonographie*, Bd. 2, *Allgemeine Ikonographie*, ed. Engelbert Kirschbaum (Rome: Herder, 1970). col. 677-695; Erich Dinkler and Erika Dinkler-von Schubert, "Kreuz," in *Lexikon der christlichen Ikonographie*, Bd. 2, *Allgemeine Ikonographie*, ed. Engelbert Kirschbaum (Rome: Herder, 1970). col. 574-588

[52] See especially First Epistle to Corinthians 1-2; Piotr Skubiszewski, *Le Croix dans le premier art chrétien* (Paris: Geuthner, 2002).

[53] "Noster intellectus quem spiritus veritatis illuminat/Gloriam Crucis coelo terraque radiantem/Puro ac libero corde suscupiat. Leo papa." See Sancti Leonis Magni, "Sermones in praecipuis totius anni festivitatibus ad romanam plebem habiti," in *Patrologiae Cursus Completus, Series Latina*, ed. Jacques-Paul Migne, vol. 54 (Turnholt: Brepols, 1846). 340

[54] Mathew 24:30; Renate Kroos, "Liturgische Quellen zum Kölner Domchor," *Kölner Domblatt* 44-45 (1979-1980). 96

[55] *Acta sanctorum septembris ex latinis et graecis, aliarumque gentium monumentis, servata promigenia veterum scriptorum phrasi*, ed. Société des Bollandistes, vol. 2 (Antwerp: B.-A. van der Plassche, 1748). 277. These beliefs were based on medieval accounts quoted by Kroos, "Liturgische Quellen," 46-47, 92-96. The crucifix in San Paolo was believed to have spoken to Saint Bridget of Sweden. See, for example, Giorgio Vasari, *Le Vite de' più eccelenti pittori scultori e architettori nelle redazioni del 1550 e 1568*, ed. Paola Barocchi, vol. 2 (Florence: Sansoni, 1967). 188; Gabriele Paleotti, *Discorso intorno alle imagini sacre e*

profane, in *Trattati d'arte del cinquecento fra manierismo e controriforma*, ed. Paola Barocchi, vol. 2 (Bari: Laterza, 1961). 166

[56] *Die bewahrende Kraft des Luthertums. Mittelalterliche Kunstwerke in evangelichen Kirchen*, ed. Johann Michael Fritz (Regensburg: Schnell and Steiner, 1997).

[57] Carl C. Christensen, "Iconoclasm and the Preservation of Ecclesiastical Art in Reformation Nuernberg," *Archiv für Reformationsgeschicht* 61 (1970). 205-221; Gudrun Litz, "Nürnberg und das Ausbleiben des 'Bildersturms'," in *Bildersturm. Wahnsinn oder Gottes Wille?* exh. cat., Bern Historical Museum and Strasburg, Notre-Dame Cathedral Museum, ed. Cécile Dupeux et al. (Munich: Fink, 2000). 90-96; Frank Schmidt, "Die Fülle der erhaltenen Denkmäler. Ein kürzer Überblick," in *Die bewahrende Kraft des Luthertums*. 71-78

[58] *Nürnberger Ratsverlässe über Kunst und Künstler im Zeitalter der Spätgotik und Renaissance*, Bd. 1, *(1449) 1474–1570*, ed. Theodor Hampe (Vienna: Graeser, 1904). nos. 2664-2665

[59] Rainer Kahsnitz, "Trauernde Maria und Johannes aus einer Kreuzigungsgruppe, 1506-1507," in *Veit Stoss in Nürnberg. Werke des Meisters und seiner Schule in Nürnberg und Umgebung*, ed. Rainer Kahsnitz (Munich: Deutscher Kunstverlag, 1983). 269-276; Ulrich Schneider, "Wickelscher Kruzifix, 1520," in *Veit Stoss in Nürnberg. Werke des Meisters und seiner Schule in Nürnberg und Umgebung*, ed. Rainer Kahsnitz (Munich: Deutscher Kunstverlag, 1983). 277-282

[60] Fritz Schnellbögl, "Sankt Sebald in Nürnberg nach der Reformation," *Zeitschrift für bayerische Kirchengeschichte* 32 (1963). 155-172

[61] *Ecclesiastica historia*, vol. 8 (Basel, 1564). 844

[62] This Baroque altarpiece is known only from descriptions and iconographic sources. In 1823, during a Gothic revival remodeling of the church, the "Wickel Crucifix," together with the figures of Mary and Saint John from the church of Our Lady, were displayed in a neo-Gothic altarpiece designed by Carl Alexander Heideloff. The Stoss crucifix from Our Lady was probably taken to another parish church devoted to Saint Laurence (where it was put into another Heideloff neo-Gothic altarpiece, destroyed in 1944). Ulrich Schneider, "Kruzifix auf dem Hochaltar," in *Veit Stoss in Nürnberg. Werke des Meisters und seiner Schule in Nürnberg und Umgebung*, ed. Rainer Kahsnitz (Munich: Deutscher Kunstverlag, 1983). 191. Today the "Wickel Crucifix" stands on the roodscreen, along with Veit Stoss' figures of the Virgin Mary and Saint John the Evangelist from Our Lady's church. Kahsnitz, "Trauernde Maria und Johannes."

[63] "Liebe Vorfahren in dem Papsttum." Quoted in Hipp, "Studien zur 'Nachgotik' des 16. und 17. Jahrhunderts." 467-475

[64] On the Baroque remodeling of Saint Emmeram's Abbey see Meinrad von Engelberg, *Renovatio Ecclesiae. Die "Barockisierung" mittelalterlicher Kirchen* (Petersberg: Imhoff, 2005). 596-598

[65] Ernst Klebel, "Zur Geschichte des Herzogs Theodo," *Verhandlungen des Historischen Vereins für Oberpfalz und Regensburg* 99 (1958). 188-205

[66] Karl Babl, "Emmeram von Regensburg. Legende und Kult," *Thurn-und-Taxis-Studien* 8 (1973). 186-203

[67] Quoted in Babl, "Emmeram." 194

[68] See, for example, Eva Ortner, "Das Pollinger Kruzifix," in *Das Aschaffenburger Tafelbild. Studien zur Tafelmalerei des 13. Jahrhunderts*, ed. Erwin Emmerling and Cornelia Ringer (Munich: Lipp, 1997). 87-98; Cristina Thieme, "Das Heilige Kreuz von Polling," in *Das Aschaffenburger Tafelbild. Studien zur Tafelmalerei des 13. Jahrhunderts*, ed. Erwin Emmerling and Cornelia Ringer (Munich: Lipp, 1997). 99-112; Rudolf Steiger, "Da reit Tessilo an daz gayt, ain her von Bayren. Zur Frage der Glaubwürdigkeit der Gründungstradition des Augustinerchorherrenstifts Polling," *Lech-Isar-Land* (2003). 3-26. Three other examples have been thoroughly scrutinized by Kunz, "Inszenierte Vergangenheit."

[69] Jan Władysław Woś, *Itinerario in Polonia del 1596 di Giovanni Paolo Mucante Cerimoniere Pontificio. Parte prima: Cracovia* (Rome: Il centro di ricerca, 1981). 39

[70] Presumably the legend originated in the late Middle Ages, but its earliest preserved record occurs in 1602. See Andrzej Sachetnik, "Ołtarz z Krucyfiksem królowej Jadwigi w katedrze wawelskiej," *Analecta Cracoviensia* 20 (1988). 341-351; Grażyna Jurkowlaniec, "Kult obrazów a kult świętych w nowożytnym Krakowie," *Barok. Historia-Literatura-Sztuka* 22 (2004). 73-76

[71] About ten medieval crucifixes in Cracow were linked with comparable legends. A crucifix in Saint Mark's church was believed to have conducted conversations with Michał Giedroyć (ca. 1420-1485). Between 1732 and 1735, it was displayed in a new altarpiece housing the relics of Saint Theodor. In 1782, the sculpture was set into the main altar, against a silver sheet presenting a panorama of Jerusalem. See Jurkowlaniec, "Kult." 69-87; Grażyna Jurkowlaniec, "The Slacker Crucifix in St. Mary's Church in Cracow: Cult and Craft," in *Wokół Wita Stwosza. Materiały z międzynarodowej konferencji naukowej w Muzeum Narodowym w Krakowie, 19-22 maja 2005*, ed. Dobrosława Horzela and Adam Organisty (Cracow: Muzeum Narodowe w Krakowie, 2006). 348-357

[72] The name of the sculptor was not mentioned in Cracow until as late as the nineteenth century. C. Theodor Müller, "Veit Stoss. zur Geltung seiner Werke im 17. Jahrhundert," *Zeitschrift des deutschen Vereins für Kunstwissenschaft* 9 (1942). 191-202; Jan Samek, "Życie sztuki Wita Stwosza," in *Tradycja i innowacja. Materiały Sesji Stowarzyszenia Historyków Sztuki, Łódź, listopad 1979* (Warsaw: PWN, 1981). 49-53; Adam Organisty and Marek Walczak, "'Życie po życiu' sztuki Wita Stwosza," in *Wokół Wita Stwosza*, exh. cat., National Museum in Cracow, ed. Krystyna Stefaniak et al. (Cracow: Muzeum Narodowe w Krakowie, 2005). 267-269

MONTFAUCON AS READER OF THE BAYEUX TAPESTRY[1]

ELIZABETH CARSON PASTAN

The publication of the Bayeux Tapestry by Abbé Bernard de Montfaucon (1655-1741) in his multi-volume work, *Les Monumens de la Monarchie Françoise, qui comprennent l'Histoire de France: avec les figures de chaque regne, que l'injure des tems a épargnées*,[2] brought a recently rediscovered medieval monument before a wider public. In 1724, the scholar Antoine Lancelot had found a drawing corresponding to about one-seventh of the medieval textile known as the Bayeux Tapestry in the papers of Nicolas-Joseph Foucault, an administrator in Normandy with a deep commitment to the history of the region.[3] That same year Lancelot presented this discovery to the *Académie royale des Inscriptions et Belles-Lettres* in Paris.[4] But it was Montfaucon who, in 1729, first published the partial images that Lancelot had found and had drawn to his attention.[5] Montfaucon was subsequently able to track down the actual textile that lay behind the incomplete drawing through Benedictine colleagues in Normandy.[6] In 1730, Montfaucon had the rest of the medieval embroidery illustrated in the second volume of his *Les Monumens de la Monarchie Françoise*.[7] The present study is devoted to an investigation of how Montfaucon analyzes the Tapestry.

This brief history of his discovery and publication of the Bayeux Tapestry only partially explains why Montfaucon is such an important figure.[8] For the last forty years of his life Montfaucon was scholar and cleric at the Benedictine abbey of Saint-Germain-des-Prés in Paris, a center of erudition. He assisted in preparing the edition of the Greek fathers produced there, and studied Greek, Hebrew, Chaldean, Syriac, and Coptic to do so. He published definitive editions of Saint Athanasius, Saint John Chrysostom, and Greek paleography, among others and, in 1719, began his influential ten-volume work on the monuments of antiquity, *L'Antiquité expliquée et representée en figures*.[9] This was a novel study because it presented ancient civilization through thematic groupings of works of art. It proved to be an enormous success, was translated almost immediately into English,[10] and followed by a supplement of five additional volumes,[11] as well as a second edition. The concept was similar to the one he developed for the work that concerns us, *Les Monumens de la Monarchie Françoise*, which he envisioned would be an entire history of France.

The magnitude of the task Montfaucon had realized with *L'Antiquité expliquée,* made him aware of what he faced in assembling *Les Monumens de la Monarchie Françoise*, however, and led him to suggest in the preface to the former volume that others might oversee the French history.[12] In the end it was Montfaucon himself who, in 1729-1733, published five volumes of the larger projected history of France.[13] It was also a labor that he undertook, astonishingly, only in the afternoons, devoting his mornings to works on the Church fathers.[14] Since these five volumes of his history of France essentially corresponded to the medieval period, they presented another difficulty. Medieval stylistic characteristics challenged artists charged with transcribing what was termed the "délicatesse" of medieval art.[15] Montfaucon acknowledged that many of the works of medieval art would shock his readers by their crudity.[16]

To date, Montfaucon has been credited with four key accomplishments regarding the Bayeux Tapestry: 1) His archeological investigations,[17] which led him to discover the Tapestry itself. 2) His incorporation of visual material chronologically within the text of *Les Monumens de la Monarchie Françoise* for ease of consultation by the reader.[18] 3) His "footnoting" of the images, meaning that he documented the provenance of each work, and thereby set a new standard for the information provided about the works of art.[19] And 4) his charge to the artist he sent to copy the embroidery to record the style of the medieval work faithfully, however "vulgar and barbarous" it might appear.[20] The ramifications of this latter decision may be appreciated by contrasting the images in Foucault's files [Figs. 1, 4-5] to the ones made for Montfaucon [Figs. 2, 3, 6-7].

Montfaucon's acknowledged accomplishments speak to his discovery of the Bayeux Tapestry and to issues of presentation, but how exactly does he engage the images he illustrates? Is it true, as Francis Haskell has claimed, that Montfaucon never succeeded in integrating medieval art into history?[21] And what implications, if any, does Montfaucon's study hold for scholarship of the embroidery today? In short, what can we learn from Montfaucon's reading of the images of the Bayeux Tapestry? First we will consider Montfaucon's general working methods, before proceeding to read a few episodes from the Tapestry over his shoulder. We will then turn with him to several of the more politically charged scenes, the interpretation of which has proved elusive. Finally we will endeavor to evaluate what kind of reader Montfaucon is and what he offers the modern scholar.

Montfaucon's working methods

The variety of materials Montfaucon brought together in *Les Monumens de la Monarchie Françoise* is strikingly demonstrated by the two volumes now in the department of manuscripts of the Bibliothèque nationale de France entitled, "Dessins et Gravures pour les *Monuments de la Monarchie Française.*"[22] These volumes, his version of a "paper museum,"[23] allow the modern viewer to behold the range of visual materials that he would draw upon. Indications in his correspondence suggest that he had begun collecting materials for this new project as early as 1710, and it is small wonder.[24] Intermingled here are cuttings from publications, marked up engravings, original red crayon drawings, and all kinds of disparate lists, clippings, and notations pasted in together, but, due to the variety of sources, the works are presented without any regard for relative scale. Two parchment folios from a thirteenth-century liturgical manuscript were even discovered in one of Montfaucon's compilations.[25] André Rostand, who sought to reveal Montfaucon's working method through consultation of his unpublished correspondence, pithily characterized Montfaucon's visual source materials as "tant de pièces hétèroclites."[26]

For *Les Monumens de la Monarchie Françoise*, Montfaucon had at his disposal engravings assembled by the antiquarian Roger de Gaignières, which ended up constituting three-quarters of his material.[27] However, given the different goals of their scholarly projects, Montfaucon had to be discriminating. The images made for Gaignières had as their principal end the documentation of costumes, customs, and lineage from the past. Not infrequently, Montfaucon found himself faced with an engraving from Gaignières said to be copied from a stained glass window that turned out to come from a tomb, or a pair of images, one of which was a copy from the original and thc other a free interpretation, and he had to determine which was nearer the medieval work.[28] The discrimination and research he needed to apply to the Gaignières material was needed even more for contributions from his other correspondents, who included an entire network of Benedictines and their family members. Because of the range of erudition and attention to detail among his various contributors, Montfaucon was required to undertake a considerable "travail d'élimination."[29]

It was just such a process of research and investigation that led to Montfaucon's role in the publication of the Bayeux Tapestry. The partial images of the embroidery that Lancelot had discovered in Foucault's files were published in the penultimate section of the first volume of *Les Monumens de la Monarchie Françoise* in 1729.[30] As noted above, these images illustrate only about thirty feet, or less than one-seventh, of the extant embroidery. Both Lancelot and Montfaucon recognized that what we'll call the "Foucault images" were only part of the whole: Lancelot because the Latin inscription ended with the dangling preposition "HIC" (a frequently recurring word meaning "here" that serves to introduce new scenes in the Tapestry);[31] and Montfaucon because he had been told that the work was actually hung in the nave of Bayeux Cathedral, and he reasoned that it therefore would have to be considerably longer.[32]

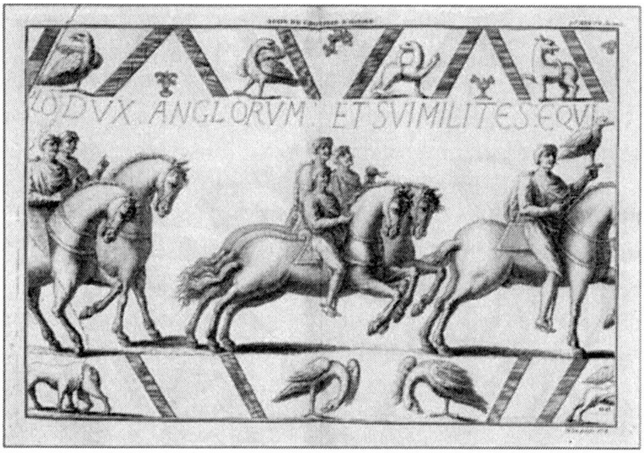

Fig. 1 Harold and his Men Riding to Bosham, Bayeux Tapestry, detail, engraving after drawing made before 1724, from Bernard de Montfaucon, *Les Monumens de la Monarchie Françoise*, vol. 1 (Paris: Julien-Michel Gandouin and Pierre-François Giffart, 1729). Pl. XXXVII

Besides the sheer variety of materials Montfaucon brought together and the investigations he undertook on them, it is useful to consider how he used the images themselves. The Foucault images he had first encountered are executed in a not unappealing classicizing style [Fig. 1].[33] When Montfaucon refers to the "bonnets uniformes" worn by the figures, he is actually referring to the artist's convention for representing the locks of hair as a dashing beret, locks which are often depicted in the embroidery itself as a kind of comb-over.[34] In addition, the horizontal line that separates the lower border is sometimes omitted, the better to plant the figures in cast shadow and to suggest an illusionistic spatial environment. Partly because of these representational strategies in the Foucault images, it is difficult to know in what medium they were executed, and Lancelot, who was the first to report on the images, guessed at a tomb relief, a fresco cycle, or stained glass, in addition to mentioning a tapestry.[35] Some of this uncertainty is still present in the first volume of *Les Monumens de la Monarchie Françoise*, where Montfaucon refers to the embroidery as "the monument," and "la peinture [painting] dans la copie de M. Foucaut [sic]," despite his acknowledgement that his colleagues in Normandy had led him to believe it "une bande de tapisserie."[36] Nonetheless, even in the second volume, while referring to the work explicitly and assuredly as a textile, he persists in calling it "cette peinture."[37] These continuing references recall the fact that Montfaucon may never have actually seen the original.[38] Indeed, as we shall see, his working method did not require it.

Volume two of *Les Monumens de la Monarchie Françoise* takes up where the previous volume left off, with Montfaucon stating that his diligence paid off and that he had discovered the rest of the medieval embroidery known as the Bayeux Tapestry.[39] The finding of the actual textile impacted the character of the illustrations. At the beginning of 1729 he sent his most able artist, Antoine Benoît, to copy the work in Bayeux Cathedral, with strict instructions to transcribe its style faithfully.[40] Montfaucon's decisions to record the style of the original and to reproduce the images within the text, underscore his respect for the evidentiary value of the images. The jarring difference between the diligently medievalizing images made by Benoît and the classicizing rendering of the scenes in the Foucault drawings [Figs. 3, 5] speaks to the newness of what Montfaucon was doing. However, Montfaucon does not dwell on the stylistic disparity between the two sets of depictions. Although he wanted an accurate documentation of the style, his analysis of the Tapestry depended instead on a close reading of text and pictorial action.

Montfaucon's use of images did not come entirely out of the blue, as Peter Burke and others have emphasized. In many ways, Montfaucon's enterprise synthesized developments taking place in his day. *Settecento* medievalists were inspired to regard artifacts increasingly seriously in part because of the excitement of archeological discoveries like the finding, in 1653, of the tomb of the Frankish ruler Childeric at Tournai.[41] In addition, scholars in the fields of law, natural philosophy, and medicine employed terms such as "clues" and "testimony," and drew upon empirical observations with new specificity and descriptive intent.[42] Although trained in the humanist tradition of philology that put "text before trowel,"[43] Montfaucon and others began to venture beyond the inscriptions. Yet, as Burke noted, these new interests should not be exaggerated, summarizing succinctly, "Neither Montfaucon or anyone else formulated general rules for interpreting visual evidence."[44]

Few of the questions that might establish when or where the work was undertaken engaged Montfaucon.[45] Haskell emphasizes that Montfaucon operated largely under the assumption that a work of art was contemporary with the subjects represented.[46] In the case of the sculptures on the portals of Gothic churches, this led him to conclude that the buildings were founded in the period of the Merovingian royalty, whom he believed the carvings represented.[47] The chronology of these sculptures, now dated in the twelfth and thirteenth centuries, raised delicate questions, such as the interpretive authority of the Benedictine scholars who preceded Montfaucon, as well as the early date of foundation of Benedictine institutions including his own at Saint-Germain-des-Prés. Others had broken ranks to look at the evidence in a more rigorous fashion, but Montfaucon declined to do so.[48] For him, the dating of the Bayeux Tapestry was established by the historical figures, such as Duke William of Normandy and King Edward of England, named in the inscriptions. For patronage, he cites without apology the local tradition that it was commissioned by William of Normandy's wife Matilda, adding that this was highly likely.[49] A royal commission of such simplicity gave Montfaucon pause, since the spaces between the colored wool embroidery on the bleached linen ground comprised "nothing but a simple sail cloth." He assumed however, that, had time permitted, the hanging would have been finished off in a more ornate fashion or "mise en sa perfection."[50]

Nonetheless, despite his assumptions about dating and patronage, Montfaucon does take some care to refer to the work as a physical object. This is evident not only in his occasional precise references to materials, but also in the fact that he gives the dimensions of the embroidery and records that the end of the work was damaged.[51] Moreover, a number of Montfaucon's comments are visually astute, such as his original observation that trees serve to mark off different scenes within the larger narrative, just as he had observed on the Column of Trajan.[52] In addition, Montfaucon's detailed analyses, though clearly indebted to Lancelot's in the opening scenes where their observations overlap, suggest fresh, independent observations.[53]

Reading the Tapestry

Montfaucon's method of reading the Tapestry involves discussing the story of the Conquest, as revealed in the embroidered inscription and pictorial narrative, and comparing these to written accounts by contemporaneous medieval authors. As might be expected, he reproduces the entire inscription in each of his volumes.[54] In fact, as I will demonstrate, Montfaucon goes far beyond what the words say or what the images show to speculate on what he thinks likely to have occurred, to fill in the context or background stories not explicitly evoked by the images, to address the motivations of characters, and to consider other narratives of the Conquest. It is these four characteristics of his analyses that I will develop in order to examine exactly how Montfaucon works through the images.

An example of one of Montfaucon's speculative inquiries is his discussion of whether or not Duke William burned the ships once the Normans landed in England so that his men would fight harder, because they knew there was no return.[55] Montfaucon quotes this poignant detail from the verse history of the dukes of Normandy in Old French, the *Roman de Rou* (ca. 1160-1174) by Wace.[56] This discussion is not motivated by the imagery or by the inscriptions in the Tapestry, as Montfaucon concedes: "There is not the least trace of this memorable deed."[57] And Montfaucon's solution accordingly comes from his own sense of probability: Wace is wrong because Duke William could have accomplished the same end by simply returning the ships to Normandy without destroying them. Montfaucon's interpolations here bring the formidable tradition of scholarship on the textual accounts of the Conquest to bear on the Bayeux Tapestry, but they also, admittedly, display his knowledge of the texts at the expense of understanding the story the embroidery recounts.

Among the background stories Montfaucon alludes to is the invasion of the north of England to which Harold had responded in the month before the Battle of Hastings.[58] The invading force included a dangerous combination of King Harold's own embittered brother, Tostig, Norwegians led by Harald Hardrada, and Flemish mercenaries. The battle culminated in Harold's decisive victory at Stamford Bridge on 25 September 1066. Montfaucon enlivens his narrative of this event by paraphrasing the later English historian Henry of Huntington, who recounts the tale of a brave Norwegian soldier who alone held off the English on the bridge, killing forty of them single handedly with his axe, before he was himself slain.[59]

Nonetheless, there are no images in the Tapestry that refer indisputably to this invasion and thus invite this account. There are images in the Tapestry that might hint obliquely at this history, such as the scene of King Harold seated askew on the throne as Haley's Comet passes above and empty ships crowd the waterfront in the border below [Fig. 2]. These ships might allude to the earlier invasion in the north,[60] although they are more persuasively glossed as the ships of William's fleet,[61] the images of which would thus foreshadow the Norman Conquest. But, as Montfaucon confirms, there is no explicit allusion: "L'inscription n'a que ce mot HAROLD."[62] And Montfaucon does not consider the strategic or propagandistic implications of leaving the victory at Stamford Bridge out of the Tapestry. In fact he rarely considers the editorial perspective driving the textual or pictorial narrative, even when choosing among alternative versions. On the other hand, it is important to note that his scrupulous references to the inscriptions, as in the above example, where he states "there's only this word Harold," do continuously remind the reader of what a laconic account the text on the Tapestry provides.[63]

Montfaucon frequently seeks to "round out" the story of the Norman Conquest by discussing the characters' motivations. One example is his portrayal of the Norman army's fear upon landing in England. His description of the emotions of the troops in the face of "the valor of Harold, the large numbers of his army, and the gold and silver they saw in abundance,"[64] draws from William of Poitiers' near-contemporary account,[65] and serves to build dramatic tension and impel the narrative forward. The problem, as Montfaucon wryly observes, is that the Tapestry does not actually portray the landing of the army, but features instead the debarkation of the horses, along with the terse accompanying inscription, "Here the horses come out of the boats" [Fig. 3].[66] In this instance, Montfaucon becomes an interlocutor, determined to tell a good story with or without prompting from the embroidery itself. Nevertheless, Montfaucon repeatedly insists that he is strictly adhering to what the Tapestry itself shows and says: "We must stick to our pictorial account and to the inscription."[67]

In the examples cited above, Montfaucon's interventions do not appear to be in the service of a particular approach or interpretation. We have had cause to cite his erudition, the historical context he supplies, and his enhancements of the narrative. His primary approach to the Bayeux Tapestry is as a work of living history. And this underscores Haskell's point that, because Montfaucon believed the Bayeux Tapestry to be an eyewitness account contemporary with the events, it was "therefore" true.[68] When faced with varieties of medieval sources about key scenes, he

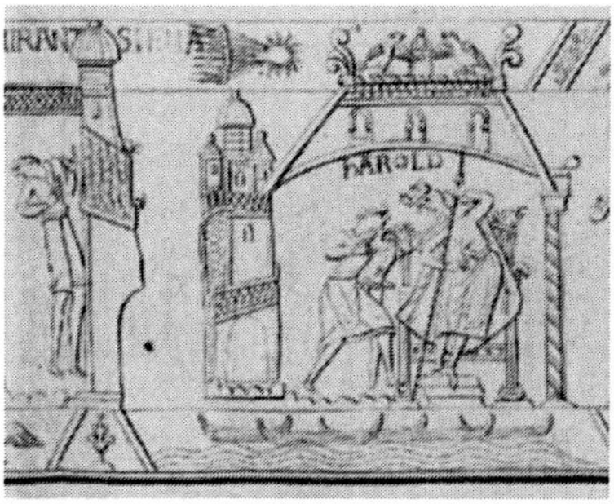

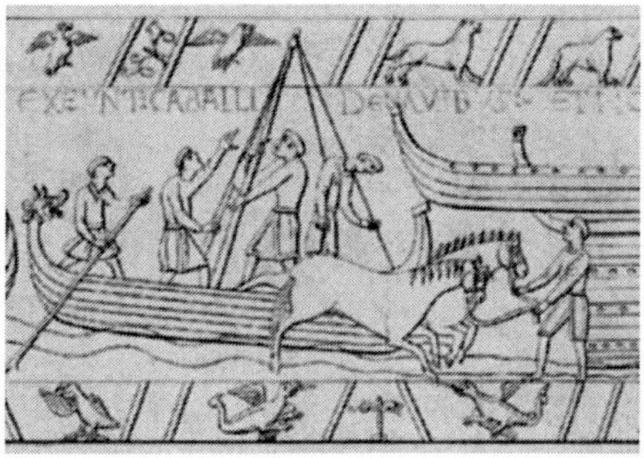

Fig. 2 (L) Antoine Benoît, Haley's Comet appears above King Harold, Bayeux Tapestry, detail, engraving, from Bernard de Montfaucon, *Les Monumens de la Monarchie Françoise*, vol. 2 (Paris: Julien-Michel Gandouin and Pierre-François Giffart, 1730). Pl. III

Fig. 3 (R) Antoine Benoît, Debarkation of the Horses after the Norman landing in England, Bayeux Tapestry, detail, engraving, from Bernard de Montfaucon, *Les Monumens de la Monarchie Françoise*, vol. 2 (Paris: Julien-Michel Gandouin and Pierre-François Giffart, 1730). Pl. V

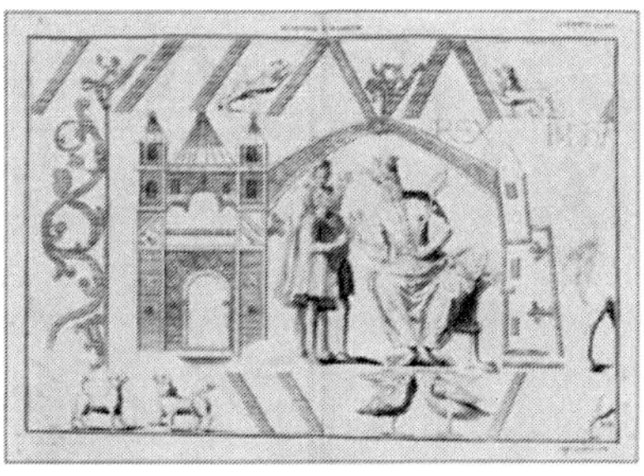

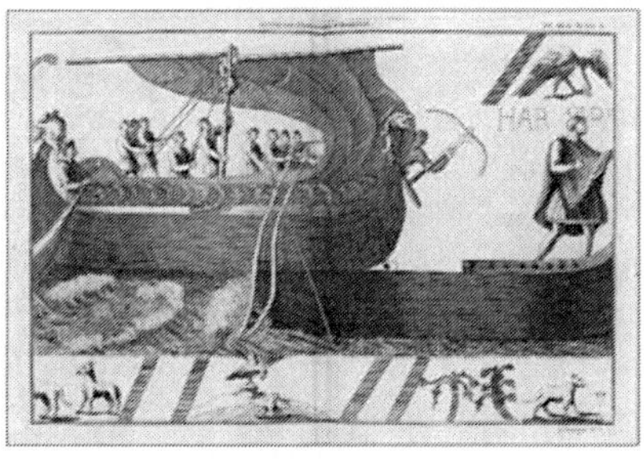

Fig. 4 (L) King Edward and Harold conversing, Bayeux Tapestry, detail, engraving after drawing made before 1724, from Bernard de Montfaucon, *Les Monumens de la Monarchie Françoise*, vol. 1 (Paris: Julien-Michel Gandouin and Pierre-François Giffart 1729). Pl. XXXVI

Fig 5 (R) Harold's ship journeying to the continent, Bayeux Tapestry, detail, engraving after drawing made before 1724, from Bernard de Montfaucon, *Les Monumens de la Monarchie Françoise*, vol. 1 (Paris: Julien-Michel Gandouin and Pierre-François Giffart, 1729). Pl. XLII

tends to judge as the best historian the one who is most detailed, and, for this reason, he generally prefers William of Poitiers, whose text was written ca. 1071-1077.[69] One also suspects that the Norman sources are more compatible with the nationalist sensibilities articulated in the title of his book, although he would occasionally forego citing Norman/French historians in favor of using a more colorful report. In portraying Duke William's exhortation to his troops before battle, for example, which is also not represented in the Tapestry, Montfaucon bypasses William of Poitiers, who offers only a *précis* of the speech,[70] and turns to an English historian, Henry of Huntington. Although later in date than William's text, Henry's *Historia Anglorum* of 1139 offers the most fulsome, first person, Shakespearean version of Duke William's harangue before the battle.[71] Montfaucon does not quote him directly, but one can imagine why he would be drawn to Henry's stirring account: "Raise your standards, men, and let there be no measure or moderation to your righteous anger. Let the lightning of your glory be seen from the east to the west, let the thunder of your charge be heard, and may you be the avengers of most noble blood."[72]

When faced with conflicting accounts, Montfaucon sometimes tries to weave them together into a single, fuller version. Various medieval texts, for example, name different places where Harold's oath to William took place. To explain these discrepancies, Montfaucon pursues a multi-pronged approach. Following his own sense of logic, he suggests that many oaths might have been made at a variety of places.[73] Then, observing that the Tapestry itself shows the oath taking place at Bayeux, he again enunciates the point "that this source is to be preferred to all others."[74] But he cannot resist quoting Wace, who says the oath took place at Bayeux, despite the fact that he sets Wace aside elsewhere.[75] Finally, he turns for further elaboration to William of Poitiers, who, although he had placed the oath swearing at Bonneville, adds the detail that Duke William made a parting gift to Harold of one of the hostages, a figure identified in other sources as Hakon, Harold's nephew.[76] Hostages are not explicitly shown in the Tapestry,[77] but are full of significance from a Norman perspective since, according to William of Poitiers, they had been sent to Normandy about fifteen years previously to serve as pledges for Duke William's succession to the English throne.[78] Clearly, a hostage of this kind would have been released only if succession were assured. In fact, just after remarking on the release of this hostage, William of Poitiers turns in a stinging direct address to Harold, "With what intent dared you *after this* take William's inheritance from him...when you had with both voice and hand subjected yourself and your people to him by a sacrosanct oath?"[79]

By adding William of Poitiers to the many alternative textual accounts of the Conquest, Montfaucon here overwhelms the story that the Tapestry itself is unfolding and adopts a perspective not present in the medieval embroidery.

Reading In

A partisan "reading in" is also evident when Montfaucon discusses two other strategic moments of particular political significance in the story of the Norman Conquest. The first is King Edward's conversation with Harold at the very beginning of the embroidery [Fig. 4], which raises the question of whether or not the king sent Harold on a diplomatic mission to the continent to confirm Duke William's succession to the throne, as the Normans claimed. The second is the scene at Edward's deathbed, when the king may have overturned the choice of Duke William as his successor in favor of Harold [Fig. 7].[80] Both events are depicted in the Bayeux Tapestry, but not from an overtly partisan perspective. In discussing the enigmatic opening scene [Fig. 4], Montfaucon reviews the nature of Harold's voyage to the continent,[81] stating that one should trust the "best historians of Normandy," namely Ingulf,[82] William of Poitiers,[83] William of Jumièges, and Orderic Vitalis,[84] all of whom say that Harold was on a diplomatic mission for King Edward to notify Duke William of his imminent succession, over English sources such as William of Malmesbury and Matthew Paris, who generally emphasize that Harold was on a fishing expedition and blown off course.[85] For good measure, he also cites his colleague Lancelot,[86] although he ignores Lancelot's observation that Harold's ship, which is decked out with shields and mastheads and therefore quite official looking [Fig. 5], does not resemble the simple fishing vessel that English sources claim landed by accident on the continent.[87] In fact, concerning the nature of Harold's journey, Lancelot judiciously concludes, "It is not easy to divine [which point of view] was followed."[88]

Montfaucon's partisan modus operandi is further revealed in his discussion of the scenes surrounding King Edward's death. These scenes have been much discussed because of their unusual presentation. Edward's actual death is presented chronologically, in the left to right sequence of the narrative, as occurring *after* his burial [Fig. 6]. Montfaucon draws attention to this inversion, and describes it as resulting from "who knows what kind of accident."[89] The deathbed scenes are shown in a unique "double-decker" composition that compels attention [Fig. 7]. In the upper tier of the two-part scene, King Edward addresses his faithful followers from his deathbed. Below, the king has died, as the inscription confirms: "ET HIC DEFUNCTUS EST."[90] Montfaucon, evidently sensing that these scenes did not make clear whether or not Edward made a last minute bequest to Harold, which would override previous designations, opines:

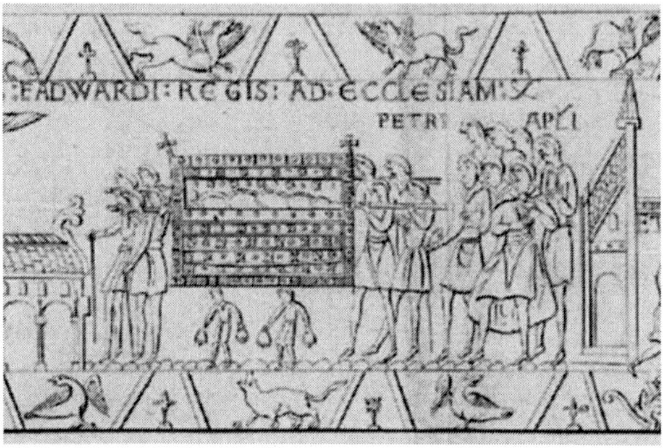

Fig. 6 Antoine Benoît, Burial of King Edward, Bayeux Tapestry, detail, engraving, from Bernard de Montfaucon, *Les Monumens de la Monarchie Françoise*, vol. 2 (Paris: Julien-Michel Gandouin and Pierre-François Giffart, 1730). Pl. III

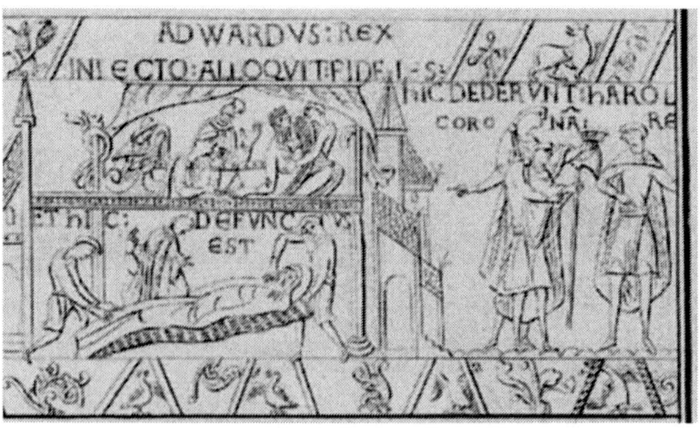

Fig. 7 Antoine Benoît, Deathbed scenes of King Edward (with left turret corresponding to right turret of Fig. 6), and Harold being offered crown, Bayeux Tapestry, detail, engraving, from Bernard de Montfaucon, *Les Monumens de la Monarchie Françoise*, vol. 2 (Paris: Julien-Michel Gandouin and Pierre-François Giffart, 1730). Pl. III

> Some English authors, among them Hoveden, say that before he died [the king] declared Harold his successor. But others are certain that he stuck to his first disposition in favor of William. It would seem that Harold, who could do anything at court, took pains to spread the story that Edward had declared him his successor before dying. He and his partisans published that everywhere and it was on this unsubstantiated declaration of Edward's that they crowned [Harold] king of England.[91]

In this instance, the longest passage cited here from *Les Monumens de la Monarchie Françoise,* Montfaucon reveals himself to be both disingenuous and partisan in selecting the authors he cites. While the Angevin historian Roger de Hoveden (d. ca. 1201) does refer to Edward appointing Harold his successor before his decease,[92] his account follows earlier authors like Eadmer (d. ca. 1124), who was nearer to the time of the events and therefore potentially a more reliable source.[93] It would have been an easy matter for Montfaucon to cite Eadmer, who is one of the medieval sources frequently quoted by Lancelot. Moreover, William of Poitiers (d. ca. 1087), one of Montfaucon's key Norman sources, also refers to the story that Edward named Harold as his successor from his deathbed, though William makes this reference long after his description of Edward's death and in a quotation attributed to Harold.[94] Whether or not Montfaucon deliberately ignored William of Poitiers and other early authors who refer to a deathbed bequest, it is clear that, in this passage, Montfaucon leaves both the Tapestry and his favorite authors behind in order to personally decry Harold's "unsubstantiated claim."

Precisely because of its political implications, the way in which Edward's death is depicted in the Bayeux Tapestry has been much discussed since Montfaucon [Fig. 7]. There are those who view the Tapestry as a Norman triumphal monument and claim that it portrays Edward's burial before the deathbed scenes in order to highlight Harold's unseemly haste in usurping the kingdom. Others, finding evidence of a pro-English subtext, believe the burial is portrayed earlier to show that Harold's coronation, which immediately follows it, was a consequence of a deathbed bequest.[95] As H. E. J. Cowdrey, one of the most recent scholars to analyze the scene, explained: "It must be conceded that the death bed scene in the Tapestry will bear either interpretation—either that Edward gave the kingdom to Harold…or that Edward charged Harold to protect the kingdom…and to bring about William's succession."[96] In short, by insisting only on Harold's usurpation, Montfaucon fails to adequately acknowledge the narrative perspective of the Tapestry itself. It is the ambiguous way in which the Tapestry depicts scenes like Edward's death that lies behind Richard Gameson's conclusion that the Tapestry, despite the fact that it resolutely depicts the Norman victory at the Battle of Hastings, is "not relentlessly, jingoistically pro-Norman."[97]

Montfaucon as Reader

The question may now be posed with particular emphasis: what should we learn from reading Montfaucon? How should a "post-medievalism" scholar regard his working method, which not only brings in anecdotes from disparate sources and cites events and speeches not treated in the embroidery itself, but also offers a Norman triumphalist reading of key scenes?

In closing, we may point to three ways of thinking about Montfaucon's work in current scholarly terms. The first is to recognize the importance of attending to the very aspects of art historical approach that he sets aside, namely the study of its dating, place of production, patronage, and choice of medium. The two great Bayeux Tapestry anthologies of our era, the volume edited by Frank Stenton in 1957, and the one overseen by Pierre Bouet, Brian Levy, and François Neveu in 2004, amply demonstrate that work on all of these issues will continue to be fruitful.[98] However, a second point to be learned from Montfaucon's method is the value of carrying on with the process he himself initiated of actively studying as many accounts of the Conquest as possible and inquiring into their authors' goals in writing them. I therefore disagree with Haskell's dismissal of Montfaucon's art historical method. Art historians must surely also attempt to assimilate "the irrecoverable mental and visual baggage of an eleventh-century beholder" by delving into external textual accounts, as Montfaucon does.[99] No single text should be scrutinized myopically to decode a particular scene or to bolster a partisan perspective but, rather, used to assay the character and variety of responses to the Norman Conquest. Jean Blacker's effort to understand the selection of material and shaping of narrative in Anglo-Norman textual accounts is instructive in this regard.[100]

Finally, a third way of thinking about Montfaucon is to observe how he actually highlights the narrative reticence of the embroidery in unfolding the story of the Conquest. No modern scholar has, to my knowledge, credited Montfaucon with this insight, although the unique perspective of the Tapestry's pictorial language has been much commented upon. N.P. Brooks and H.E. Walker, among others, have remarked on how "studiously non-committal" it is.[101] Moreover, the efforts of scholars who have sought to move from an acknowledgement of the Tapestry's open-ended narrative language to a new conceptualization of how to understand it should be commended. Richard Brilliant, for example, imagines a narrator/performer who uses the embroidery's laconic inscriptions as cues for "ad libs" that would complete the story.[102] In acknowledging that the story needed to be animated by a jongleur's narration, he is, in many ways, assigning to a medieval narrator the process that scholars have undertaken with the Bayeux Tapestry since Montfaucon. But he is also implicitly suggesting that the Tapestry is incomplete without an interlocutor's performance to explain and elaborate upon it. Another scholar who has struggled with the problem of teasing out the implications of the Tapestry's cryptic story is Suzanne Lewis, who theorizes that what she understands as the "erasures" in the story pressure the viewer into an active and complicit role in the unfolding drama.[103]

For all of Montfaucon's importance in the discovery and presentation of the Bayeux Tapestry, the most forward-looking features of his work are his close observations, even the ones he himself seems to slip in dismissively, of how the embroidered images and inscriptions overturn the expectations of a beholder who anticipates a clear-cut story of Norman triumph. His narratological insights derive from his rigorous analysis of both the pictorial vignettes and the inscriptions in the Tapestry, along with texts external to it. Unfortunately, by imposing a pro-Norman bias on his reading of several key scenes, he inadvertently demonstrates that reading the Bayeux Tapestry on its own terms—which is what he repeatedly says he wants to do—is extraordinarily difficult. And this, surely, is one of the most important things to be learned from his example.

Notes

[1] I gratefully acknowledge the interest and assistance of Frank Jackson, Danielle Johnson, Alyce Jordan, Janet Marquardt, my students in "Monastery and Cathedral," Margarete Tigges, Steve White, and curator Philippe Rouillard of the Cabinet des estampes of the Bibliothèque nationale de France in Paris.

[2] Bernard de Montfaucon, *Les Monumens de la Monarchie Françoise*, 5 vols. (Paris: Julien-Michel Gandouin and Pierre-François Giffart, 1729-1733). The full title translates as: "The Monuments of the French Monarchy, which comprise the History of France: with images from each reign that the ravages of time have spared." All translations, including this one, are my own. Besides the volumes themselves, available at the Bibliothèque nationale in Paris and elsewhere, scholars now have several resources for the consultation of Montfaucon. The Institut national d'histoire de l'art in Paris (INHA) has made available a complete electronic version on its website: http://bibliotheque-numerique.inha.fr/searchresults.cfm?cfid=23147&cftoken=94140013&isp=1&ism

=0&isv=0&ispdf=3&str=montfaucon. I thank Robert Maxwell and Karine Boulanger for their gracious assistance. In addition, images are available in Martin K. Foys, *The Bayeux Tapestry: Digital Edition* (Leicester: Scholarly Digital Editions, 2003). "Facsimiles: Montfaucon"

3 Shirley Ann Brown, *The Bayeux Tapestry: History and Bibliography* (Woodbridge, Suffolk: Boydell Press, 1988). 152, no. 447 notes that a roll of colored drawings entitled, "Première Partie de la Tenture de Bayeux dite la Toilette du Duc Guillaume," now Rés. Ad-102 fol. in the Cabinet des estampes of the Bibliothèque nationale de France, may correspond to the original drawing in the Foucault papers. The roll is approximately the same dimensions as the first seventh of the Bayeux Tapestry. Moreover, this roll extends to the same point in the narrative, and largely compares in details of mending and wear, as the exemplar Montfaucon published in volume 1, but the style of execution is entirely different and lacks the classicizing élan of the work associated with Foucault's files (and illustrated here in Figs. 1, 4-5). See the large color detail of Ad-102 in François Avril, *La France romane au temps des premiers Capétiens (987-1152)*, exh. cat., Paris, Musée du Louvre, 10 mars-6 Juin 2005 (Paris: Musée du Louvre). 334-335, cat. no. 256. Four smaller rolls, also subsumed under the same call number in the Cabinet des estampes, are ink on tracing paper with a penciled grid and correspond to the images Benoît produced for Montfaucon's publication (illustrated here in Figs. 2, 3, 6-7).

4 Lancelot's presentation ended up being published concurrently with Montfaucon's publication: Antoine Lancelot, "Explication d'un monument de Guillaume le Conquérant," *Mémoires de Litterature* 6 (1729). 739-755. See the resumé in Brown, *The Bayeux Tapestry: History and Bibliography*. 3-8; Francis Haskell, *History and Its Images: Art and the Interpretation of the Past* (New Haven: Yale University Press, 1993). 137-142 credits Lancelot with groundbreaking analyses that "use images to solve historical problems," but he focuses on Montfaucon as the one to popularize the Bayeux Tapestry. Note that Lancelot's publication of 1729 only discusses the images of the portion of the Tapestry of which he was aware (up through Harold's landing on the continent), and thus Montfaucon's remarks on the later parts of the Tapestry, which are the main focus of my analyses here, may be considered largely original. Lancelot did expand his approach considerably in his later publication, "(Suite de) Explication d'un monument de Guillaume le Conquérant," *Mémoires de Litterature* 8 (1733). 602-668, by which time Montfaucon had become a source for him.

5 Bernard de Montfaucon, *Les Monumens de la Monarchie Françoise*, vol. 1 (Paris: Julien-Michel Gandouin and Pierre-François Giffart, 1729). 371-379 with images interspersed.

6 Georges Huard, "Quelques lettres de Bénédictins Normands à Dom Bernard de Montfaucon pour la documentation des *Monumens de la Monarchie Françoise*," *Société des antiquaires de Normandie* 28 (1913). 343-375

7 Bernard de Montfaucon, *Les Monumens de la Monarchie Françoise*, vol. 2 (Paris: Julien-Michel Gandouin and Pierre-François Giffart, 1730). 1-32 with images interspersed.

[8] Louis Bréhier, "Bernard de Montfaucon," *The Catholic Encyclopedia*: http://www.newadvent.org/cathen/10539b; André Rostand, "La Documentation iconographique des *Monumens de la Monarchie Françoise* de Bernard de Montfaucon," *Bulletin de la Société de l'Histore de l'Art Français* (1932). 104-149; James Westfall Thompson, "The Age of Mabillon and Montfaucon," *The American Historical Review* 47 (1942). 237-340; Haskell, *History and Its Images*. 131-163

[9] Bernard de Montfaucon, *L'Antiquité expliquée et représentée en figures*, 10 vols. (Paris: F. Delaulne, 1719).

[10] Bernard de Montfaucon, *Antiquity Explained, and Represented in Sculptures*, trans. David Humphreys, 10 vols. (London: J. Tonson and J. Watts, 1721-1722).

[11] Bernard de Montfaucon, *Supplement au livre de l'Antiquité expliquée et représentée en figures*, 5 vols. (Paris: F. Delaulne, 1724); and Bernard de Montfaucon, *The Supplement to Antiquity Explained, and Represented in Sculptures*, trans. David Humphreys, 5 vols. (London: J. Tonson and J. Watts, 1725).

[12] Montfaucon, *L'Antiquité expliquée*. 1:xvi-xvii

[13] Rostand, "La Documentation iconographique des *Monumens*." 147-148 discusses the projected works.

[14] Ibid. 106

[15] Ibid. 149

[16] Montfaucon, *Monumens de la Monarchie Françoise*. 1:ii; Rostand, "La Documentation iconographique des *Monumens*." 105

[17] Thompson, "The Age of Mabillon and Montfaucon." 238-239, although he is referring to Montfaucon's *L'Antiquité expliquée* and does not mention *Les Monumens de la Monarchie Françoise*.

[18] Montfaucon, *Monumens de la Monarchie Françoise*. 1:i-ii

[19] Peter Burke, "Images as Evidence in Seventeenth-Century Europe," *Journal of the History of Ideas* 64 (2003). 295

[20] Montfaucon, *Monumens de la Monarchie Françoise*. 2:2

[21] Haskell, *History and its Images*. 137

[22] MS fr. 15634-15635, Bibliothèque nationale de France, Paris.

[23] This term was coined in reference to the sixteenth-century Roman collector, Cassiano del Pozzo. Burke, "Images as Evidence." 279

[24] Rostand, "La Documentation iconographique des *Monumens*."105

[25] Ibid.

[26] "So many disparate items." Rostand, "La Documentation iconographique des *Monumens*." 109

[27] On Gaignières see Jean Adhémar, "Les Tombeaux de la Collection Gaignières: dessins d'archéologie du XVIIe siècle," *Gazette des beaux-arts* 84 (1974); Jean Adhémar, "Les Tombeaux de la Collection Gaignières: dessins d'archéologie du XVIIe siècle," *Gazette des beaux-arts* 88 (1976); and Jean Adhémar, "Les Tombeaux de la Collection Gaignières: dessins d'archéologie du XVIIe siècle," *Gazette des beaux-arts* 90 (1977). Elizabeth A. R. Brown, *The Oxford Collection of the Drawings of Roger de Gaignières and the Royal Tombs of Saint-Denis,*

Transactions of the American Philosophical Society 78 (Philadelphia: American Philosophical Society, 1988).

[28] Rostand, "La Documentation iconographique des *Monumens*." 113-114; an example is illustrated in Haskell, *History and Its Images*. Figs. 93-94

[29] Rostand, "La Documentation iconographique des *Monumens*." 126

[30] Montfaucon, *Monumens de la Monarchie Françoise*. 1:371; it is also one of the clippings in Montfaucon's "Dessins et Gravures." fol. 157

[31] Lancelot, "Explication d'un monument de Guillaume le Conquérant." 754

[32] Montfaucon, *Monumens de la Monarchie Françoise*. 2:2. Huard, "Quelques lettres de Bénédictins Normands." 359-361 reproduces the letter of 22 September 1728 from the prior of Saint-Vigor of Bayeux to the prior of Saint-Etienne of Caen that first reported that the Bayeux Tapestry was hung in the nave of Bayeux "from the feast of Saint John the Baptist through the end of July." This letter, the contents of which were forwarded to Montfaucon, is also the earliest reference to the tradition that Queen Matilda herself sewed it. Father Mathurin Larcher, the prior of Saint-Vigor who wrote the letter, personally recalled seeing the work hung in the nave of Bayeux Cathedral. Abbé E. Deslandes, "Le Trésor de l'église Notre-Dame de Bayeux d'après les inventaires manuscrits de 1476, 1480, et 1498 conservés à la bibliothèque du chapitre de Bayeux," *Bulletin archéologique du comité des travaux historiques et scientifiques* (1896). 394, no. 262 publishes the earliest inventory of Bayeux Cathedral from 1476 (MS 199, Manuscrits du Chapitre de la cathédrale de Bayeux, Archives Départementales-Calvados, Caen) with the notice that the Tapestry was hung in the cathedral nave "the day and eight days following of the [Feast of the] Relics." Since the Feast of John the Baptist is June 24 and the Feast of the Relics is July 1, it suggests that this fifteenth-century tradition regarding the hanging of the Bayeux Tapestry was still loosely adhered to in the early eighteenth century.

[33] Note that when Lancelot published his own analyses, he did not use these images he himself had discovered. Lancelot, "Explication d'un monument de Guillaume le Conquérant." 738; Huard, "Quelques Lettres de Bénédictins Normands." 348 n. 1 attributes the images, more akin to Benoît's, to Louis Rustaing de Saint-Jory, an attaché to the Bishop of Bayeux.

[34] Montfaucon, *Monumens de la Monarchie Françoise*. 1:374

[35] Lancelot, "Explication d'un monument de Guillaume le Conquérant." 739

[36] Montfaucon, *Monumens de la Monarchie Françoise*. 1:374

[37] Two authors known to me keep the medium of the work foremost: Madeline H. Caviness, in the second chapter of her on-line book, *Reframing Medieval Art: Difference, Margins, Boundaries* (e-book, 2001): http://nils.lib.tufts.edu/Caviness, who refuses to refer to the textile as anything other than the embroidery it is; and Andrew Bridgeford, *1066: The Hidden History in the Bayeux Tapestry* (London: Fourth Estate, 2004). 48-154, where his adroit descriptions ("woolen actors," "threaded drama," "embroidered ships," "eyes narrowed to the width of a stitch,") constantly recall the nature of work.

[38] Brown, *The Bayeux Tapestry: History and Bibliography*. 7

[39] Montfaucon, *Monumens de la Monarchie Françoise*. 2:1

[40] Montfaucon, *Monumens de la Monarchie Françoise*. 1:2; Haskell, *History and Its Images*. 138
[41] "*Settecento* Medievalists" is a term coined by Eric Cochrane for scholars of the early eighteenth century interested in the Middle Ages. "*Settecento* Medievalists," *Journal of the History of Ideas* 19 (1958). 35-61, although his examples focus exclusively on Italy.
[42] Burke, "Images as Evidence." 273-296
[43] Ibid. 282, citing Simon Ditchfield, "Text before Trowel: Antonio Bosio's *Roma Sotterranea* Revisited," *Studies in Church History* 33 (1997). 343-360
[44] Burke, "Images as Evidence." 295
[45] For comparison, see N. P. Brooks and H.E. Walker, "The Authority and Interpretation of the Bayeux Tapestry," in *Proceedings of the Battle Conference on Anglo-Norman Studies*, ed. R. Allen Brown, 1 (1978). 1-34, 191-199; reprinted in Richard Gameson, ed., *The Study of the Bayeux Tapestry* (Woodbridge, Suffolk: Boydell Press, 1997). 63-92. Subsequent citations to Brooks and Walker will refer to the Gameson reprint.
[46] Haskell, *History and Its Images*. 142-143
[47] Jacques Vanuxem, "The Theories of Mabillon and Montfaucon on French Sculpture of the Twelfth Century," *Journal of the Warburg and Courtauld Institutes* 20 (1957). 45-58
[48] Ibid. 48-53. Note Vanuxem's indexing of the success of Montfaucon's analyses: in 1800, Lenoir quotes him without hesitation, but by 1821 he distances himself and characterizes Montfaucon's work as "not entirely acceptable." Ibid. 58
[49] Montfaucon, *Monumens de la Monarchie Françoise*. 2:2
[50] "ne sont qu'un simple cannevas." Ibid; "completed in its perfection." Ibid.
[51] Montfaucon, *Monumens de la Monarchie Françoise*. 2:2-3
[52] Montfaucon, *Monumens de la Monarchie Françoise*. 1:375 (although the page says 735); Montfaucon, *Monumens de la Monarchie Françoise*. 2:8
[53] Both authors refer to the scenes in the borders of the textile, though without engaging them. Montfacuon, *Monumens de la Monarchie Françoise*. 1:373; Lancelot, "Explication d'un monument de Guillaume le Conquérant." 747. On page 755, however, Lancelot comes close to dismissing the borders "as coming from the imagination of the workers and therefore hardly instructive." Works by modern scholars have focused on the interpretive possibilities of the borders. See J. Bard McNulty, *The Narrative Art of the Bayeux Tapestry Master* (New York: The Edwin Mellen Press, 1989); J. Bard McNulty, *Visual Meaning in the Bayeux Tapestry: Problems and Solutions in Picturing History* (Lewiston, NY: The Edwin Mellen Press, 2004); Carola Hicks, "The Borders of the Bayeux Tapestry," in *England in the Eleventh Century: Proceedings of the 1990 Harlaxton Symposium*, ed. J. Bard McNulty (Stamford: Paul Watkins, 1992). 251-265; Daniel Terkla, "Cut on the Norman Bias: Fabulous Borders and Visual Glosses on the Bayeux Tapestry," *Word and Image* 11 (1995). 264-290; and Gail Ivy Berlin, "The Fables of the Bayeux Tapestry: An Anglo-Saxon Perspective," in *Unlocking the Wordhold: Anglo-Saxon Studies in Memory of Edward B. Irving, Jr.*, ed. Mark C.

Amodio and Katherine O'Brien O'Keeffe (Toronto: University of Toronto Press, 2003). 191-216

[54] Montfaucon, *Monumens de la Monarchie Françoise*. 1:374; Montfaucon, *Monumens de la Monarchie Françoise*. 2:6

[55] Montfaucon, *Monumens de la Monarchie Françoise*. 2:24-25

[56] See the prose translation of the incident in *The History of the Norman People: Wace's "Roman de Rou,"* trans. Glyn S. Burgess, with notes by Glyn S. Burgess and Elisabeth van Houts (Woodbridge, Suffolk: Boydell Press, 2004). 165. All subsequent references to Wace will cite this edition.

[57] "*il n'y a pas la moindre trace d'un fait si mémorable*." Montfaucon, *Monumens de la Monarchie Françoise*. 2:24

[58] Montfaucon, *Monumens de la Monarchie Françoise*. 2:15-16, 21

[59] Ibid. 21. Henry of Huntington is credited only in the Latin text at the bottom of the page. See Henry of Huntingdon, *Henry, Archdeacon of Huntingdon, Historia Anglorum (History of the English People)*, ed. and trans. Diana Greenway (Oxford: Clarendon Press; New York: Oxford University Press, 1996). *vi*, *27*, 386-389. Here, as in all subsequent citations, the Roman and Arabic numbers in italics are standard references to section divisions within the text, while the final Arabic numbers are the pages of this particular edition. All subsequent references to Henry will cite this edition.

[60] Lucien Musset, *The Bayeux Tapestry*, trans. Richard Rex (Woodbridge, Suffolk: Boydell Press, 2005). 176-178

[61] Daniel J. Bernstein, *The Mystery of the Bayeux Tapestry* (London: Weidenfeld and Nicolson, 1986). 21

[62] "The inscription has only this word HAROLD." Montfaucon, *Monumens de la Monarchie Françoise*. 2:15

[63] For the latest discussion of the inscription see Elizabeth Coatsworth, "Inscriptions on Textiles Associated with Anglo-Saxon England," in *Writing and Texts in Anglo-Saxon England*, ed. Alexander R. Rumble (Cambridge: D. S. Brewer, 2006). 71-95. I am indebted to my colleague Stephen D. White for this reference.

[64] Montfaucon, *Monumens de la Monarchie Françoise*. 2:18

[65] Although not credited in Montfaucon, and not a verbatim citation, see *The Gesta Gvillelmi of William of Poitiers*, ed. and trans. R.H.C. Davis and Marjorie Chibnall (Oxford: Clarendon Press; New York: Oxford University Press, 1998). *ii*, *4-5*, 107-109. All subsequent references to William of Poitiers will cite this edition.

[66] Montfaucon, *Monumens de la Monarchie Françoise*. 2:18

[67] "Il faut s'en tenir à notre peintre et à l'inscription." Ibid. 2:15. This phrase is uttered when Montfaucon is discussing which archbishop presided at Harold's coronation. A similar phrasing is repeated in Ibid. 2:28 after Montfaucon's report that Orderic Vitalis said Harold's brothers were killed after him, which is not what is shown in the embroidery.

[68] Haskell, *History and Its Images*. 142

[69] On the dating of William of Poitiers, see the introduction by Davis and Chibnall to *The Gesta Gvillelmi*. xv-xvi, xx; Montfaucon, *Monumens de la Monarchie*

Françoise. 2:15 describes William of Poitiers as "le plus exact des historiens de la vie et des action du Roi Guillaume."

[70] William of Poitiers, *The Gesta Gvillelmi. ii, 15*, 124-127. William of Poitiers' account, adapted from Sallust, is relayed in the third person and in the past tense.

[71] Montfaucon, *Monumens de la Monarchie Françoise*. 2:26-27; Henry of Huntingdon, *Historia Anglorum. vi, 29*, 389-393

[72] Henry of Huntingdon, *Historia Anglorum. vi, 29*, 393

[73] Montfaucon, *Monumens de la Monarchie Françoise*. 2:12. This kind of analysis is still found. See Musset, *Bayeux Tapestry*. 148

[74] Montfaucon, *Monumens de la Monarchie Françoise*. 2:12

[75] Ibid. 2:13; Wace, *Roman de Rou*. 154-155

[76] Montfaucon, *Monumens de la Monarchie Françoise*. 2:13; William of Poitiers, *The Gesta Gvillelmi. i, 42*, 70-71 on the Oath; Ibid. *i, 46*, 76-78 for Harold's journey home after the Breton campaign.

[77] Although see Richard Wissolik, "The Saxon Statement: Code in the Bayeux Tapestry," *Annuale mediaevale* 19 (1979). 69-97

[78] William of Poitiers, *Gesta Gvillelmi. i, 41*, 68

[79] Ibid. *i, 46*, 76-77 (emphasis mine)

[80] These two events are underscored by Bernstein, *Mystery of the Bayeux Tapestry*. 114-123

[81] Montfaucon, *Monumens de la Monarchie Françoise*. 1:373

[82] *Ingulph's Chronicle of the Abbey of Croyland*, ed. and trans. Henry T. Riley (London: Henry G. Bohn, 1854). 137. As Riley explains in the Introduction (x-xiv), the work is now generally thought to be a fourteenth-century forgery.

[83] William of Poitiers, *The Gesta Gvillelmi. i, 41*, 69

[84] William of Jumièges, *The Gesta Normannorum Ducum of William of Jumièges, Orderic Vitalis, and Robert of Torigni*, ed. and trans. Elisabeth M.C. van Houts (Oxford: Clarendon Press, 1992). 158-161

[85] William of Malmesbury, *Gesta regum Anglorum: The history of the English kings*, ed. and trans. by R.A.B. Mynors, completed by R.M. Thomson and M. Winterbottom, vol. 1 (Oxford: Clarendon Press, 1998). *ii, 228, 3*, 416-417; Matthew Paris, *Historia Anglorum*, ed. Frederic Madden, Rolls Series, vol. 1 (London: Longmans, Green, Reader and Dyer, 1866). 5; also see Suzanne Lewis, *The Art of Matthew Paris in the Chronica Majora* (Berkeley: University of California Press, 1987). 176 for Matthew's use of shields to emphasize Harold's "epic treachery" in his *Chronica Majora*, which was then the starting point for his later *Historia Anglorum*. Matthew Paris, who is a rather curious citation in this context, also appears in Lancelot, "Explication d'un monument de Guillaume le Conquérant." 746

[86] Lancelot, "Explication d'un monument de Guillaume le Conquérant." 740-742

[87] Ibid. 746; Haskell, *History and Its Images*. 140-142 draws attention to Lancelot's observations. Montfaucon, *Monumens de la Monarchie Françoise*. 1:376 notes the shields on the vessel that took Harold to the continent, but he does not make an argument based on this visual evidence.

[88] Lancelot, "Explication d'un monument de Guillaume le Conquérant." 742

[89] Montfaucon, *Monumens de la Monarchie Françoise*. 2:14

[90] "And here he has died." See the transcription in Coatsworth, "Inscriptions on Textiles." 93

[91] Montfaucon, *Monumens de la Monarchie Françoise*. 2:14

[92] *The Annals of Roger de Hoveden comprising The History of England and of Other Countries of Europe*, trans. Henry T. Riley, 4 vols. (London: G. Bohn, 1853; reprinted in 2 vols., Felinfach: Llanerch Publishers, 1997). 2:130-131

[93] *Eadmer of Canterbury's History of Recent Events in England: Historia Novorum in Anglia,* trans. Geoffrey Bosanquet (London: Cresset Press, 1964). 8

[94] William of Poitiers, *The Gesta Gvillelmi, ii, 12*, 119

[95] Brooks and Walker, "The Authority and Interpretation of the Bayeux Tapestry." 73, 80; Richard Gameson, "The Origin, Art, and Message of the Bayeux Tapestry," in *The Study of the Bayeux Tapestry*, ed. Richard Gameson (Woodbridge, Suffolk: Boydell Press, 1997). 192-195. The account of this event in the *Vita AEdwardi Regis*, written before 1075, closely resembles the deathbed scene portrayed in the tapestry and describes it in comparably ambiguous terms. See *The Life of King Edward who rests at Westminster, attributed to a monk of Saint-Bertin*, ed. and trans. Frank Barlow (Oxford: Clarendon Press; New York: Oxford University Press, 1992). *ii, 11*, 24

[96] H.E.J. Cowdrey, "King Harold II and the Bayeux Tapestry: a Critical Introduction," in *King Harold II and the Bayeux Tapestry*, ed. Gale R. Owen-Crocker (Woodbridge, Suffolk: Boydell Press, 2005). 8. A point also made in Musset, *Bayeux Tapestry*. 166

[97] Gameson, "The Origin, Art, and Message of the Bayeux Tapestry." 202

[98] Frank M. Stenton, ed., *The Bayeux Tapestry: A Comprehensive Survey*, 2nd ed. (London: Phaidon Press, 1965); Pierre Bouet, Brian Levy, and François Neveu, *The Bayeux Tapestry: Embroidering the Facts of History* (Caen: Presses universitaires de Caen, 2004). Stephen D. White and I are currently preparing a study entitled, "Picturing the Norman Conquest: An Interdisciplinary Investigation into the Context and Meaning of the Bayeux Tapestry."

[99] Gameson, "The Origin, Art, and Message of the Bayeux Tapestry." 159-161

[100] Jean Blacker, *The Faces of Time: Portrayal of the Past in Old French and Latin Historical Narrative of the Anglo-Norman Regnum* (Austin: University of Texas Press, 1994). esp. 191-200

[101] Brooks and Walker, "The Authority and Interpretation of the Bayeux Tapestry." 73

[102] Richard Brilliant, "The Bayeux Tapestry: a Stripped Narrative for Their Eyes and Ears," *Word and Image* 7 (1991). 98-126

[103] Suzanne Lewis, *The Rhetoric of Power in the Bayeux Tapestry* (Cambridge: Cambridge University Press, 1999).

AN IMAGE OF CLUNY BY EMILE SAGOT

DAVID WALSH

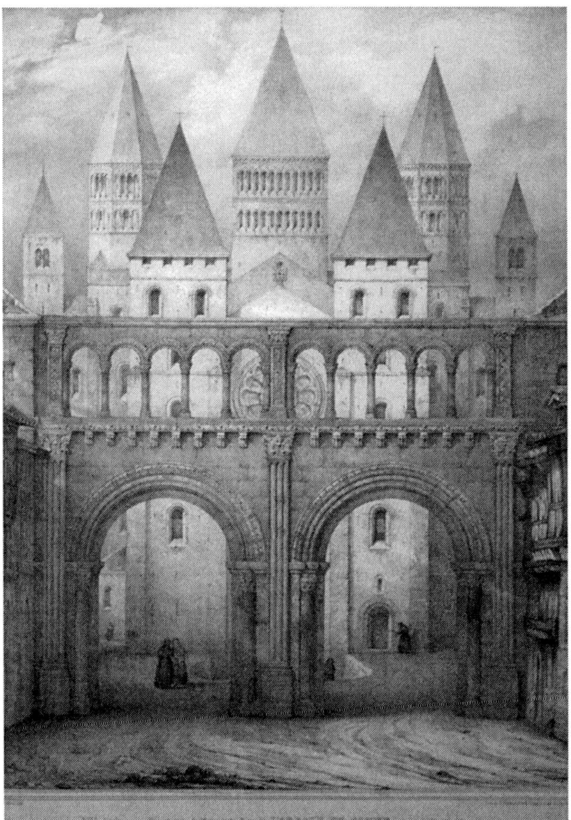

Fig. 1 Emile Sagot, West façade through the west precinct gateway, abbey church of Cluny, lithograph, 1838 (Photo: Author)

A lithograph by Emile Sagot depicting the west façade of the abbey church of Cluny, seen through a double-arched gateway in the precinct wall, appeared in Alexandre du Sommerard's *Les Arts du Moyen Age* in 1838 [Fig. 1].[1] This arresting image shows the church in its pre-Revolutionary state before its nearly complete reduction to ruins,[2] necessitating an imaginative reconstruction by the artist. Du Sommerard was a collector who created the museum of the Hôtel de Cluny in Paris, also a site of printmaking and publication. In du Sommerard's publication, medieval Cluny is illustrated by Sagot not only by this depiction of the abbey, but with images of some of the medieval houses in the Place Notre-Dame, thus including both the secular and ecclesiastical patrimony of the Middle Ages.[3] Sagot contributed to a number of other collections celebrating France's landscape and monuments. *Voyages pittoresques et romantiques dans l'ancienne France*, by Nodier, Taylor, and de Cailleux, for instance, was a vast undertaking comprising thousands of images presented in multiple volumes produced over more than half of the nineteenth century.[4] More specific collections, concentrating on regions or specific kinds of monuments, such as P. Lorain's *Essai historique sur l'abbaye de Cluny*,[5] where Sagot was the principal artist represented, could have substantial accompanying text, but all such publications shared abundant praise of the French Middle Ages, as effusive in pictorial expression as in language and giving visual form to national and cultural pride.

Emile Sagot was the ideal artist to create images for such publications. His career began some two decades before the lithograph of Cluny was made. His earliest training was in Dijon, his home town, where he became proficient not only in drawing and printmaking, but in architecture as well.[6] These two areas, illustration and architecture, made for his superior understanding of buildings and their depiction, resulting in his eye for both structure and aesthetic effect. Sagot's graphic works for publication show a mastery of the new medium of lithography. He exploited lithography's ability to depict the most subtle tonal transitions or the drama of contrasting values and, equally, to create fine linear detail, reproducing the characteristics of his own drawings.[7] This was the perfect medium for antiquarians who wanted evocative images that would inspire the interest of a wide audience. Tina Bizzarro points out the process itself "...not only stimulated the imaginations of viewers, artists, and writers, but also contributed to the autonomy of medieval architecture by facilitating its diffusion through images of these ruined monuments." Important to our sense of Sagot's contribution through multiple fields, she suggests that the texts and images actually "prompted the restoration of medieval buildings…."[8]

Sagot not only produced inspirational images, but, in his architectural activities, participated in their preservation. His career came to include overseeing the restoration of ancient monuments and creating architectural designs, leading him to become an inspector of the newly-formed *Monuments historiques*. Such an appointment meant that Sagot was in a position to be current in the most advanced thinking about medieval monuments and could himself be a major contributor to the burgeoning fields of study and preservation of France's medieval past.[9]

Sagot's image of Cluny is worthy of our close examination. In its reproduction in scholarly works, analysis has been focused mainly on its inaccuracies and the amount of reconstruction that does not seem to have a substantial basis.[10] While I intend to touch upon the sources for this image and the generation of its forms in Sagot's own work that led to this reconstruction, this paper will investigate the print more as a document of its time and audience. A close analysis of the work itself will, I believe, show a number of subtleties that may help us understand some of the ways in which Sagot's interpretation could satisfy the expectations of his patrons. By viewing these against the background of Sagot's career and his other work at this time, more may be understood about its impact and importance for his contemporaries.

Sagot's print was intended, we may be sure, to dramatize the monumentality and complexity of Cluny's abbey church. Both the area of the precinct gate and the church behind are emphasized, the former in a dark half-light and the church in a strong but suffused illumination. West of the gateway, the foreground shows a rutted street flanked by half-timbered houses with jettied second stories. The portal of the precinct gate is depicted as having two stories, two richly molded arches below, with pilasters between, visually supporting a cornice, which forms a base for a second story arcade. The arcade is composed of ten arches supported by colonettes; small pilasters, corresponding to the large members below, divide the arcade into two groups of five arches. The church is shown frontally, its parts obeying a strict symmetry. Seven towers are shown, forming a multi-pointed silhouette against a cloudy sky.

The composition is carefully constructed. The symmetry of the forms is striking and gives the composition a certain rigidity and static quality. The vertical axis of church and gate is exactly centered in the field, extending from the central pilaster of the gateway to the crossing tower of the church. The arcade of the gateway divides the field horizontally and the center of the Gothic rose window in the west wall of the narthex is positioned precisely in the middle of the composition. The rendition of forms of the church is simple with little texture indicated, a treatment that seems bland, emphasizing the simplicity of the architecture's geometry. Equally artificial is the treatment of space in the area east of the gateway. It is clear that the perspective through the gateway was not based on reality; the actual gate and church are, in fact, not aligned at all, something that Sagot was well aware of, having drawn the gateway on the site [Fig. 7]. He all but eliminated the diminution of perspective, so that the forms of the church appear much larger in comparison to the gateway, contributing to the effect of monumentality. The result is a compression of space seen in the planes of the architecture and even in the relation of the gateway to the west façade of the church. A limited aerial perspective in the eastern parts of the church does alleviate somewhat this crowding of forms, but the result is a silent, almost airless space.

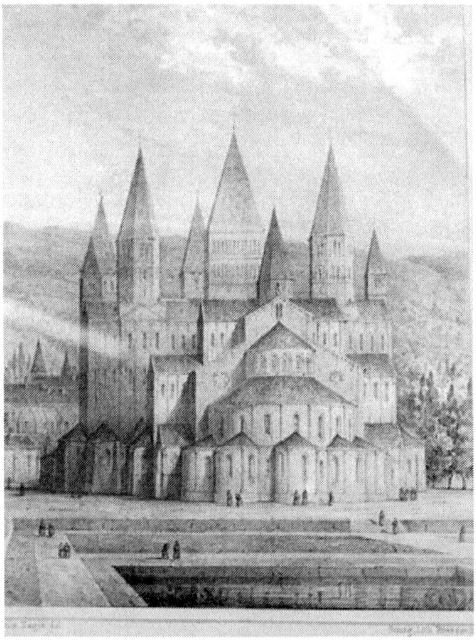

Fig. 2 Emile Sagot, east end, abbey church of Cluny as it might have appeared in the sixteenth century, lithograph, 1840 (Photo: Author)

A comparison of this print with other works by Sagot and his contemporaries emphasizes its uniqueness and suggests that we are seeing a specific kind of presentation of the monument. As a ruin, the abbey church invited reconstructed versions, and Sagot himself produced a number of views of it in a restored state. These differ from our image in significant ways. The closest representation in terms of combining extant and reconstructed parts is his 1839 print of the so-called "Gelasius" façade, the western entrance to eighteenth-century cloister buildings, with the towers of the abbey church behind, clearly based on the artist's 1835 drawing of the same view of the remaining parts.[11] This work lacks the centrality of the motif of the church and symmetrical distribution of forms in ours; the perspective is more convincing and the atmosphere seems to function to unify the architectural forms. The east end of the abbey church in a print of 1840 is of necessity a more total reconstruction, but simpler in treatment and more generalized, a very different kind of illustration [Fig. 2].[12] It may be helpful to make further comparisons of a similar motif in another illustration by Sagot, the view of the façade of the nearby church of Tournus as seen through the main gateway of the town defenses [Fig. 3],[13] and by Adrien Dauzats of the portal in the town wall of Vannes of 1845 [Fig. 4].[14] Both of these works show the monumental medieval features in the present day, animated, in the case of the Dauzats, with the bustle of contemporary life.

There were a number of sources available to Sagot for his views of pre-Revolutionary Cluny, the most important of which were the prints after Jean-Baptiste Lallemand.[15] Distant views drawn by Lallemand, such as that of the east end, engraved by Masquelier, or, more relevant for our print, that of the west façade, engraved by Claude Niquet [Fig. 5], both appeared with many others in Benjamin de la Bord's widely-known *Voyage pittoresque de France* of 1784.[16]

Although much of the façade of Cluny, save the bases of the west towers, had disappeared before his time, Sagot must have consulted the kinds of sources mentioned above for the church; however, part of the precinct gateway and houses to either side survived, as they still do today [Fig. 6]. Indeed, the principal source for the foreground of the composition of the lithograph, including the gateway and houses, is the site itself. We have Sagot's drawing of the gateway as it was in his time [Fig. 7], a work which was the basis for a lithograph published in 1835, only three years before the lithograph [Figs. 1, 8].[17] This drawing, and the lithograph after it, are likely to be the sources for parts of his print, and give us a view of Sagot's process of creating an image. Particularly interesting is the transformation of the foreground buildings, those to the left and right of the double portal. The older buildings on the right were preserved and are close to those depicted in the Sagot print, but we can see that he replaced the more recent houses on the left with half-timbered structures reminiscent of the extant medieval dwellings elsewhere in Cluny [Figs. 1,

6-8]. The gateway is another matter, for only the large double arches were preserved.

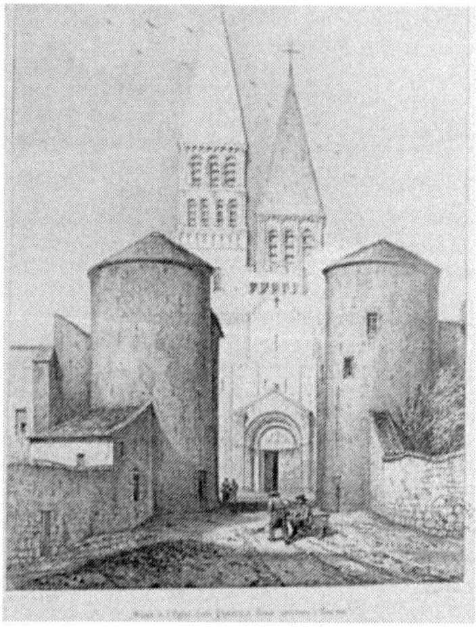

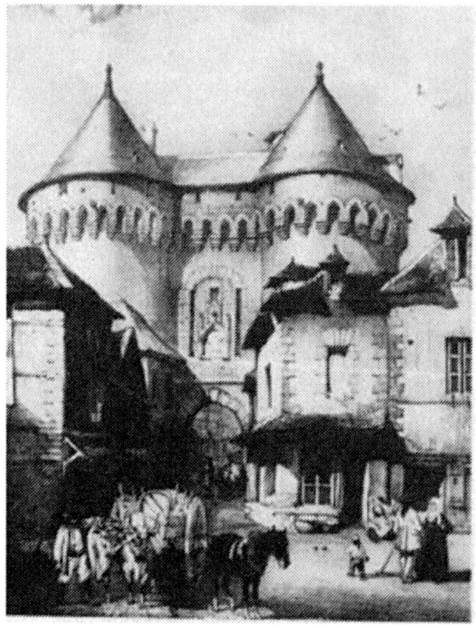

Fig. 3 (L) Emile Sagot, west façade through the gateway of the city wall, Abbey of Saint-Philibert, Tournus, lithograph, undated (Photo: Author)

Fig. 4 (R) Adrien Dauzats, west façade, Saint- Pol-de-Léon Cathedral, lithograph, 1845 (Photo: Author)

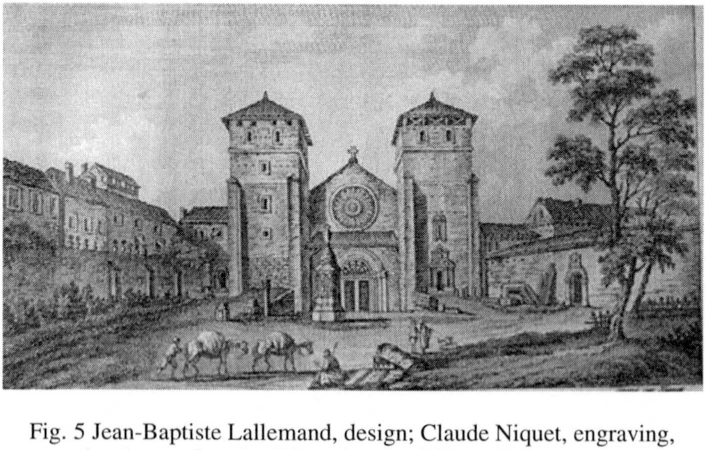

Fig. 5 Jean-Baptiste Lallemand, design; Claude Niquet, engraving, undated, west façade, abbey church of Cluny (Photo: Author)

The arcade above the double arches is, as a consequence, an invention, and the details of it are a remarkable testament to the knowledge and skill of the artist. Sagot copied the architectural detailing of the upper story arcade from the "clerestories" (second-story loggias) of the Romanesque houses in Cluny, reflecting their proportions, subdivision of arch sequences, and even the designs of the moldings and pilasters.[18] The town provided a remarkable number of these works, and Sagot himself executed numerous drawings of them. The decoration of these houses was itself derived from the decoration of the abbey church, and he may have been conscious of how appropriate it might be that the precinct wall between the church and town should share a common style. However, it is just possible that this design was also based on the composition of the western entrance to the church from its narthex, engraved after Jean-François Garnerey's drawing of 1825; on the church, the arched portal to the nave is under a blind arcade in a composition similar to the one he gave to the gateway in the precinct wall [Fig. 9].[19]

It should be pointed out that Sagot was basing his arcaded upper story on very slim evidence. Whatever the Romanesque composition of an upper story of the gateway may have been, it was in all likelihood destroyed by the rebuilding of that structure by Abbot Claude de Guise, the forty-eighth abbot of Cluny (1575-1612). Evidence of the appearance of this structure can be seen in an engraving done after a drawing by Louis Prévost executed between 1668 and 1672; the gateway was at least two bays deep and surmounted by a two story "tower." [20]

The Cluny houses and portal of the abbey church inside the narthex could have provided material for Sagot's reconstruction. Another possible inspiration was ancient Roman architecture, a source totally appropriate to the classicizing Romanesque of the abbey.[21] While Cluny itself had no Roman monuments, nearby Autun did. Sagot was intimately familiar with the actual remains of two of the extant portals in the ancient circuit walls of Autun, the Porte d'Arroux and the Porte Saint André, having made drawings of both and a lithograph of the latter [Fig. 10].[22] What distinguishes these monuments in Autun, and makes them relevant for our discussion, is their double-story compositions: arches across the roadway at street level and a second story with a smaller arcade. Sagot would have been familiar with illustrations of them made in the eighteenth and earlier nineteenth centuries, the compositions of which vary considerably: a rather diagrammatic version appears in Bernard de Montfaucon's *L'Antiquité expliquée et représentée en figures* [Fig. 11], but more romanticized versions are usual in the eighteenth century, sometimes showing the Roman monuments of Autun clustered in a landscape with no

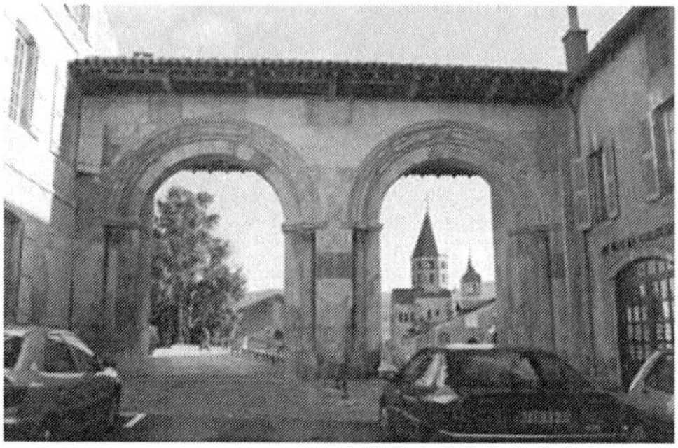

Fig. 6 West precinct gateway toward west end, abbey church of Cluny, 2006 (Photo: Author)

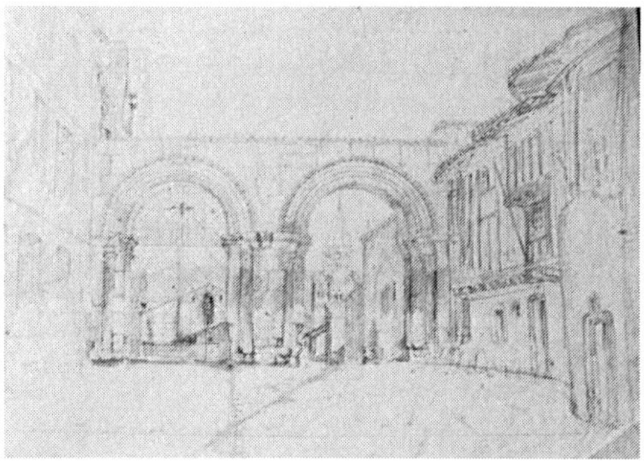

Fig. 7 Emile Sagot, west precinct gateway toward west end, abbey church of Cluny, drawing, before 1835 (Photo: Author)

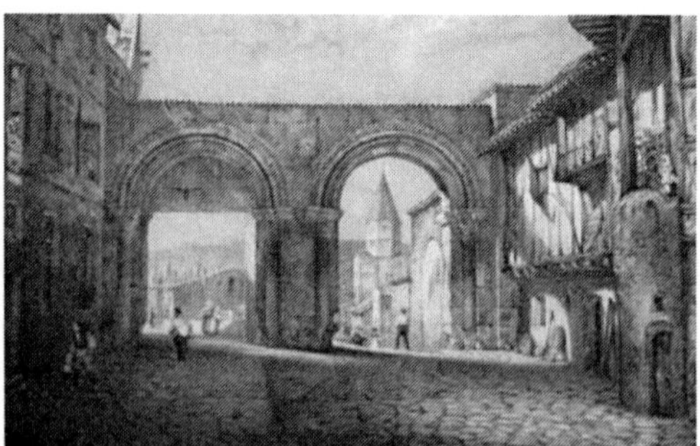

Fig. 8 Emile Sagot, west precinct gateway toward west end, abbey church of Cluny, lithograph, 1835 (Photo: Author)

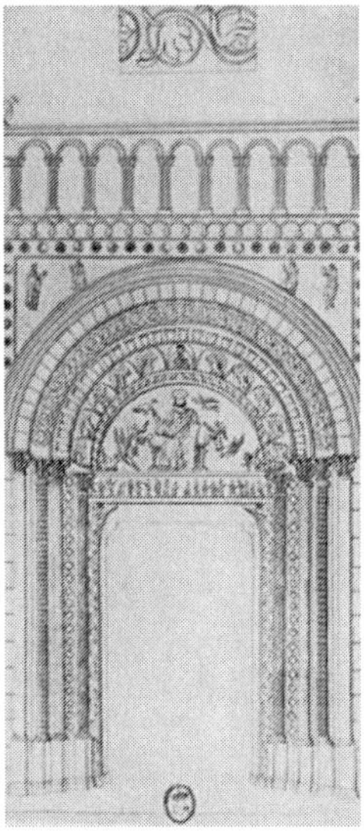

Fig. 9 Interior west portal, abbey church of Cluny, engraving after 1825 drawing by Jean-François Garneray (Photo: Author)

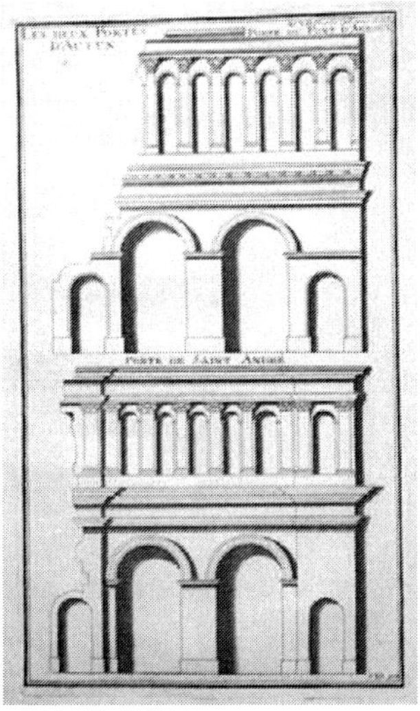

Fig. 11 Porte d'André and Porte d'Arroux, Autun, engraving, from Bernard de Montfaucon, *L'Antiquité expliquée et représentée en figures,* vol. 3 (Paris: F. Delaulne, 1719). Pl. 97

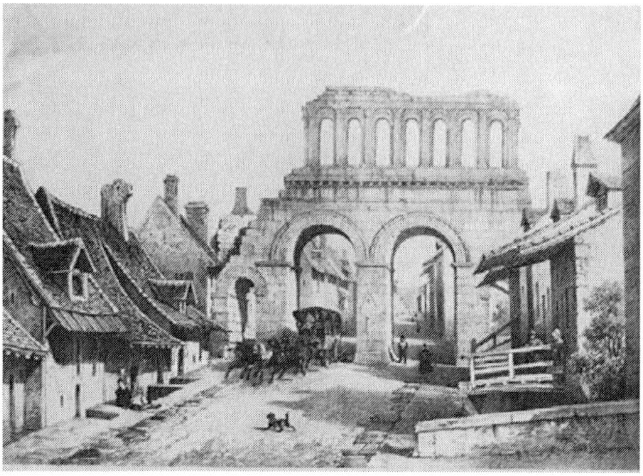

Fig. 10 Emile Sagot, Porte d'Arroux, Autun, lithograph, undated (Photo: Author)

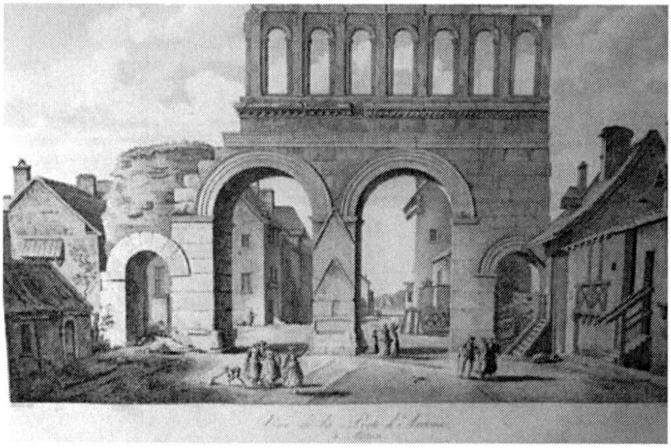

Fig. 12 Dormier, *Vue de la Porte d'Arroux à Autun*, engraving after ca.1775-1800 drawing by Charles (?) Dance (Photo: Author)

hint of their actual environment.[23] A remarkable image of the Porte d'Arroux of the late eighteenth century by Charles (?) Dance, engraved by Dormier [Fig. 12] is of particular interest, for it shows the monument in its contemporary setting with people going about their everyday lives around the impressive vestige of a Roman past, a theme that would become particularly popular with Sagot and his contemporaries and well illustrated by Sagot's own print [Fig. 10].

In order to suggest some of the possible interpretations of Sagot's print [Fig. 1], both the choices made in the subject and the treatment of it, I shall approach it by considering Sagot's expertise based on his training and activities, particularly his experience in the field of architecture. While Sagot's intentions cannot be precisely known, his patrons and their publications do articulate values that are likely to be in harmony with the images they admired and commissioned.

Sagot's image of Cluny is to some extent a reconstruction, and it is important to recall that overseeing repair and reconstruction were major parts of his profession. In 1833, he had become member of the *Commission des antiquités de la Côte d'Or*. He would thus have been aware of the discourse on the treatment of national heritage monuments. Soon after our print was made, Prosper Mérimée would be appointed *inspecteur générale* of the newly-founded *Monuments historiques*, and Viollet-le-Duc was beginning his restoration of Vézelay. Sagot became *inspecteur correspondant de la Commission des monuments historiques* in 1842.[24] The decades around the middle of the nineteenth century witnessed a revival of medieval building styles, as well as debate about historical buildings and their restoration. Among the most important issues was what should be restored and, if restored, to what state and "finish." Regularization was the rule of the day, and, in Western Europe, there seems to have been a widespread concept of producing restoration that was "resolved," consistent, and, above all, complete. Perhaps we could add the term "idealized," for behind the practice of restoration was the confidence that the restorer could know the architect or mason's intent or could confidently design and craft even better work to replace or extend it. Viollet-le-Duc, in his *Dictionnaire raisonné de l'architecture*, held that the purpose of restoration was "…to establish in a complete condition that which may never have existed at any given moment."[25] That the results of this philosophy should, in actual practice, lack the character of medieval building is not surprising given the training of the modern masons who executed it, and it is this attitude which, I believe, is related to the look of the architecture on paper. The negative reaction to the results of such attitudes and practices, and evidence of their pervasiveness, is exemplified most famously by John Ruskin in England, who cherished not only the irregular work of the hand of the medieval craftsman, but saw aspects of the decayed state of buildings as representing their changing appearance over time, deploring, as a consequence, most architectural practice of his own day. Nicholas Pevsner has written most tellingly of the contrast between Viollet-le-Duc and Ruskin on this issue.[26]

In Sagot's print, the treatment of buildings varies, particularly as seen in contrasts of texture. As an architect and member of an architectural commission to oversee restoration, it may be that such differentiation in the print was intended to express a difference between what was extant and what was the restoration—what was known and what was conjecture. The gateway and the houses are more exactingly depicted and precisely textured than the starkly rendered church. This differentiation is not wholly consistent, however, since some of the parts of the church, such as the south arm of the great transept and its towers, remained in Sagot's (and our) time. In any case, there appears to be a difference of treatment—a difference of mode even—between elements in the foreground and the church beyond the gateway.

We may consider that this contrast is due to Sagot's own awareness of the problems of restoration; perhaps he may be viewed as straddling both sides of the debate. On one side, his drawings and most of his prints display an emphasis on irregularity, contrasting surface textures, and asymmetrical albeit balanced compositions, exemplifying the idea of picturesque. But his attention to the quality of surfaces, especially showing the action of aging, is accompanied by architectural specificity and understanding of the structure. These are the qualities seen, in fact, in Sagot's drawings of the houses in Cluny, many of which can still be compared to extant buildings.[27] Little is restored in these structures or the images of them; they retain the features of post-medieval usage or replaced elements, such as roof timbers showing in the eaves. The ancient character of the works is expressed in their sagging rooflines and the weathered texture of their walls. Sagot's approach to these houses is very much in harmony with most of his larger images of Cluny's monastic ruins. The drama of backlighting or, more often, light fitfully falling across the time-worn surfaces, does not really alter the faithfulness of the rendering which, after all, might be compared by the owner of the print to the monument itself. But there is another Sagot who desired clarity foremost, who designed and built architectural elements, either in restoration campaigns or the invention of new structures, and who was aware of contemporary building and restoration aesthetics. Sagot's images of this class are not measured drawings which might be a plan for work; yet they do convey a related visual discipline and understanding.[28] So, with this experience in mind, we can appreciate that Sagot might well have imagined the abbey church as not only whole again, but in the pristine state that we see in the print.

It is possible to suggest iconographical reasons for the contrasts mentioned above; these are attached to the varied meanings of the classes of buildings and the relation of the spaces that they occupy. The entryway—the precinct gate—is important both as access to the church beyond and as a divider. It is the threshold between the two worlds, articulated here in the graphics of the print and expressing a medieval reality of the sacred and the secular. The gateway is the outermost precinct of the church's space and, as I have suggested, might have reflected the composition of its façade within the narthex. In any case, its decoration relates to that of the monastic architecture. Its form and the spires of the church towers, which could be seen from outside through and over the gateway, were visible signals of the monastic complex. The foreground is a darker space, enclosed by the medieval houses to left and right, and these houses are picturesque in their texture, irregularity, and lived-in look. The gate is modestly illuminated, while the whole space of the monastery beyond is lit brightly, and the forms of the architecture clear and regular; the towers signal aspiring vertical forms, contrasting with the foreground horizontality.

The arched gate is also an important image in itself, quite separate from its original function.[29] It has an obvious use as a frame within a picture where ruined monuments as elements of standing masonry were not only picturesque details but might function as markers for orienting the viewer, whether contemplating the monument on the basis of descriptions, plans, or views, or being present at the site, and so providing visual guides. Arches, of course, are among the most distinctive markers, as they can provide a precisely defined view beyond. Such elements could themselves become monuments, and, through their repeated occurrence in illustration, might stand for the whole site or ideas about its former distinction and eventual demise. In this print the portal arches could have a series of associations with medieval monuments in general, especially ecclesiastical ones, as well as the more ancient past of Roman Gaul. As in the case of the Porte d'Arroux at Autun, there is a resonance between ancient and medieval that had led, after all, to the invention of the term "Romanesque" to characterize medieval monumental vaulted architecture.[30]

This image of Cluny is part of a repertoire of pictorial representations of regional antiquities. Clearly designed for an audience interested in local history and monuments, Sagot aimed to satisfy the curiosity of his potential clients as well as encouraging their pride in the region. He also provided them with a variety of ways of looking at their past, including, as here, a reconstruction of a great medieval work, arguably the most famous monument in Burgundy.

In order to appreciate some of the feelings that he might have evoked in a contemporary audience, we need to search for evidence of the reception of such imagery. We do have an opportunity to see something of how this lithograph was viewed and used. There is a copy edition of *Le Nivernais. Album Historique et Pittoresque* in the Bibliothèque Municipale at Nevers (MS 2, N.382), published by a retired Commandant

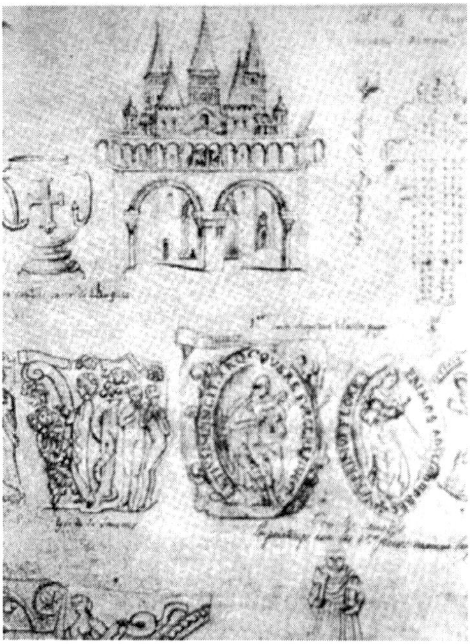

Fig. 13 Jean-Claude Barat, Sketches of Cluny, drawing, 1835-1855, MS 2, N.382, fol. 74r, Bibliothèque municipale, Nevers (Photo: from Neil Stratford, "A Cluny Capital in Hartford [Connecticut]," *Gesta* 27 [1988]. Fig. 5)

of the Army, Jean-Claude Barat between 1838 and 1840. Among the pages are drawings by Barat which show the site of Cluny. One drawing illustrates a credible view of the abbey from the northwest, featuring the remaining south arm of the great transept and the national stable buildings which replaced the church after 1822; significantly, Barat imposed a line drawing reconstructing the lost parts of the church. Another page illustrates numerous subjects, often in no apparent order, including the hemicycle capitals stored for a time in the Chapel of Jean de Bourbon (and so easily accessible) after the destruction of the eastern parts of the church, sculptures from the houses, and tiny views of the town and outer precinct wall. That showing the Tour de Fabry, part of the original abbey precinct wall, must have been based on an earlier image, as the gateway next to it had been destroyed by his time; some of the other views could have been done on site, but this cannot be verified. However, and most important to this discussion, is an image of Cluny at the top of the page, which can only have been taken from the Sagot print of the west façade and double portal gateway [Figs. 1, 13].[31] Thus, on a single page, one sees a mélange of little vignettes representing monuments, some drawn from life, others copied from illustrated antiquarian volumes, such as those of Lorain or du Sommerard, a testament to the eclectic collection of materials of interest that Barat had at hand. Stratford informs us that Barat had in mind to publish an additional collection of monuments, and one supposes that these leaves relate to the projected third volume.[32] Most of the drawings reflect, if anything, a very preliminary exploration of this material, although his attempt to reconstruct the abbey church might be the basis of a grand illustration. We may suppose that he compared graphic images with existing material, or felt the need to seek out monuments known from illustrations. Although such an enterprise never materialized, these images comprised a serious attempt to record great monuments, and suggest Barat contemplating, with educated contemporaries, the losses of the past, and participating in discourses on the meanings of history and the nature of the visual arts that were, in part, fueled by images of the kind Sagot provided.

Notes

[1] I am grateful to Janet Marquardt and Alyce Jordan for asking me to contribute to this collection of papers, for their valuable suggestions, and for their hard work and patience bringing this to publication. Research for this article was in part done in the archives of Cluny and Autun, and I thank Mary Sainsous at the Centre des monuments nationaux, Abbaye de Cluny, Brigitte Chabard and her staff at the Musée Rolin, and the archive staff of the Société Eduenne in Autun. I became interested in the post-medieval and post-Revolution record of Cluny as evidence for its remains during and after the destruction of the monastic complex as part of a larger study of the medieval monument with Neil Stratford and Brigitte Chabard (Stratford et al., *Corpus de la sculpture de Cluny,* forthcoming through Picard, Paris). The illustrations of Sagot seemed to me at first to be too late, romanticized, and idealized to have much value in the study; this print in particular, with its generalized and inaccurate depiction of the church and pastiche of the western gateway, did not appear to help in the project of reconstruction. But an edition of the print was kindly given to me as a wedding present by Neil and Jenny Stratford, and its presence on the wall of my home induced me to look at it more closely and

---

to ask the basic questions that led me to write this paper. The print appears in Alexandre du Sommerard, *Les Arts au moyen âge, en ce qui concerne principalement le Palais romain de Paris, l'Hôtel de Cluny, issu de ses ruines, et les objects d'art de la collection classée dans cet hôtel*, album 1 (Paris: Techener, 1838-1846). Pl. II

[2] See Bruno Marguery-Melin, *La Destruction de l'abbaye de Cluny 1789-1823* (Cluny: Centre d'Etudes Clunisiennes, 1985). The author gives an extensive account of the dismantling of the monastery in the late eighteenth and early nineteenth century.

[3] The print illustrated here has the following inscriptions above the field of the illustration: center, *Les Arts du Moyen Âge. (Chap. 4)*; left, *Album. 1er Sèrie.*; right, Planche III; and below the field of the illustration: centered title, *XII*[e] *Siècle - Vue générale de l'église et des Portes de L'ABBAYE DE CLUNY, prise de la Façade (Ouest.);* left, Emile Sagot del et lith.; right, *Lith. de A. Godard, Hotel Cluny, rue des Maturins SJ.*; and under the title*: le Clocher du sud de la tour carrée attenant, subsistent seulement aujourd'hui. (1838.)*

[4] See Xavier Dectot, *Sculptures des XI*[e]*-XII*[e] *siècles roman et premier art gothique. Catalogue Musée national du Moyen Âge Thermes de Cluny* (Paris: Editions de la Réunion des musées nationaux, 2005). 7-10, for a brief account of du Sommerard's enterprise. A number of Sagot's illustrations for such publications are discussed by Janet Marquardt, *From Martyr to Monument: The Abbey Church of Cluny as Cultural Patrimony* (Newcastle-upon-Tyne: Cambridge Scholars Publishing, 2007). 33-38

[5] P. Lorain, *Essai historique sur l'abbaye de Cluny* (Dijon: Popelain, 1839). Sagot's lithograph of the Cluny gateway in this publication is titled *Entrée de l'Abbaye au 17*[e] *siècle.*

[6] Anne de Thoisy, *Sagot mémoire de Bourgogne: dessins et lithographies du XIX*[e] *siècle* (Cluny: Musée Ochier, 1994). The essays in this catalogue are organized around Sagot's multiple careers as an architect, draftsman, lithographer, archaeologist, and Inspector of Monuments. See 5-8 for his early training in the Ecole des Beaux Arts, Dijon, 8-17 for his training in architecture, and 21-26 for his career as Inspector.

[7] For the early history of lithography see Wilhelm Webber, *A History of Lithography* (London: Thames and Hudson, 1966). For material more specific and relevant to Sagot and his contemporaries, Michael Twyman, *Lithography 1800-1850: The Techniques of Drawing on Stone in England and France and their Application in Works of Topography* (London: Oxford University Press, 1970); de Thoisy, *Sagot mémoire de Bourgogne*. 36-37 discusses lithography in Burgundy during Sagot's time.

[8] Tina Waldeier Bizzarro, *Romanesque Architectural Criticism: A Prehistory* (Cambridge: Cambridge University Press, 1992). 123; Marquardt, *From Martyr to Monument*. 37 sees Sagot's brand of picturesque as tuned to make the monuments' forms attractive, harmonious, and accessible as souvenirs of the past.

[9] de Thoisy, *Sagot mémoire de Bourgogne*. 22-26; for the creation of the *Monuments historiques* and the early legislation to protect ancient monuments see

Françoise Choay, *The Invention of the Historic Monument* (Cambridge: Cambridge University Press, 2001). 96-101

[10] Kenneth John Conant, *Cluny: les églises et la maison du chef d'ordre* (Mâcon: Imprimerie Protat Frères, 1968). Pl. XLI, Fig. 76. According to Conant, 115, "Si le dessin romantique de Sagot represénte un souvenir, ou si l'architecte était très traditioniste, il a dû exister au-dessus des grande arcs un étage avec de petits arcs faisant une sorte d'attique."

[11] *Cluny III La Maior Ecclesia*, exh. cat., Ecuries de Saint-Hugues, Cluny, 4 June-30 September, 1988, ed. Brigitte Maurice Chabard (Cluny: Musée Ochier, 1988). 55, cat. no. 44; the lithograph appeared in Lorain, *Essaye historique sur l'abbaye de Cluny*. 96-97, cat. no. 37

[12] Ibid. 56, cat. no. 46

[13] de Thoisy, *Sagot mémoire de Bourgogne*. 58, cat. no. 91

[14] Twyman, *Lithography 1800-1850*. 238-239

[15] Lallemand is discussed in relation to other post-medieval sources by Benoît Decron, "De la 'Maior Ecclesia' au bon usage des ruines: artistes, voyageurs et dictionnaires," in *Cluny III La Maior Ecclesia*. 11-22. The catalogue illustrates a large number of Lallemand's images of Cluny. *Cluny III La Maior Ecclesia*. cat. nos. 6-9, 11-17, 19

[16] *Cluny III La Maior Ecclesia*. 48-49, cat. no. 36

[17] Ibid. 53, cat. no. 41. This print appeared in Charles Maillard de Chambure, *Voyage pittoresque en Bourgogne: 2^e^ Partie Saône-et-Loire* (Dijon: Jobard, 1835).

[18] In Sagot's gateway, the pilasters of the arcade above are decorated with small medallions, *rinceaux*, and a zigzag. These motifs are paralleled in the houses. A house on the rue de la Barre, for instance, has a double *rinceau* of similar character. See Pierre Garrigou Grandchamp et al., *La Ville de Cluny et ses maisons XIe–XVe siècles* (Paris: Picard Editeur, 1997). 202 Fig. 219; Garrigou Grandchamp, *La Ville de Cluny*. 75 Fig. 105 illustrates a lithograph by Sagot of the Place Notre-Dame in which this house appears on the west side of the Place.

[19] *Cluny III La Maior Ecclesia*. 39, cat. no. 26

[20] Conant, *Cluny: les églises et la maison*. 24 n. 15

[21] Linda Seidel, *Legends in Limestone: Lazarus, Gislebertus, and the Cathedral of Autun* (Chicago: University of Chicago Press, 1999). 79-106 discusses the relation between medieval and Roman Autun, arguing convincingly that there was a self-consciousness in the medieval adoption of elements of the Roman past and suggesting specific reasons for attempting to create identification with local antiquities.

[22] These are housed in the Musée Rolin, Autun, and catalogued as nos. inv. 981.14.7 and 981.14.9 respectively.

[23] A fine example is the painting of Claude-Marie Repoux, *Le Temps Contemplant les Ruines d'Autun*, 1823, Musée Rolin, Autun, illustrated in Autun, Musée Rolin, *Autun, Augustodunu: Capitale des Eduens: ouvrage réalisé à partir de l'exposition qui s'est tenue à l'Hôtel de ville d'Autun du 16 mars au 27 octobre 1985* (Autun: l'Imprimerie PELUX, 1987). 6

[24] de Thoisy, *Sagot mémoire de Bourgogne*. 22-26

[25] M. F. Hearn, ed., *The Architectural Theory of Viollet-le-Duc: Readings and Commentary* (Cambridge, MA: MIT Press, 1990). 6
[26] Nicholas Pevsner, *Ruskin and Viollet-le-Duc: Englishness and Frenchness in the Appreciation of Gothic Architecture* (London: Thames and Hudson, 1969). 38-42; see also Choay, *The Invention of the Historic Monument*. 102-108
[27] Garrigou Grandchamp, *La Ville de Cluny*. 116-177
[28] Ibid. Pls. I-VI, for example, illustrate the house façades recorded by Aymer Verdier in the middle of the nineteenth century.
[29] Arches were a central element in the theories of architecture as related to culture, especially those of Pierre Leroux who saw two lines of architectural development, rectilinear and curvilinear. The later, expressed in the invention of the arch, attributed to the Etruscans and developed by the Romans, would, for him, be related to religious expression in the Middle Ages. See Robin Middleton, "The Rationalist Interpretations of Classicism of Leonce Reynaud and Viollet-le-Duc," *AA Files; Annals of the Architectural Association School of Architecture* 11 (1986). 41. I would like to thank Alyce Jordan for suggesting this reference.
[30] Bizzarro, *Romanesque Architectural Criticism*. 133 examines closely the use of the term "Romanesque" by de Gerville and his contemporaries. Bizzarro suggests that de Gerville's terminology was "ambiguous and unsteady," although in the 1820s, visual distinctions were becoming more precise as used, for instance, by Arcisse de Caumont, founder of the *Société française pour la description et la conservation des monuments historiques*. By this time there was recognition of the classical aspects of Romanesque. See also Middleton, "The Rationalist Interpretations of Classicism." 40 for the refinements of stylistic analysis of medieval monuments by Lenoir, Leroux and others; and Jean Nayrolles, *L'Invention de l'art roman à l'époque moderne (XVIIIe–XIXe siècles)* (Rennes: Presses Universitaires de Rennes, 2005).
[31] These drawings are identified as MS 3 N.5178, fol. 5 and MS 2 N.382, fol. 74 respectively. Barat's drawings are discussed by Neil Stratford, "A Cluny Capital in Hartford (Connecticut)," *Gesta* 27 (1988). 9-21. The drawings are also published in Stratford, "Balthazar Augustin Hubert de Saint-Didier," *Cluny III La Maior Ecclesia*. 60-63
[32] Ibid. 9

GEORGE PETRIE, THE ORDNANCE SURVEY, AND NINETEENTH-CENTURY CONSTRUCTIONS OF THE IRISH PAST

MARIAN BLEEKE

George du Noyer's drawing of Dungiven Old Church [Fig. 1], produced as part of his work for the Topographical Department of the Irish Ordnance Survey, includes one key detail; a figure in the left foreground, in a top hat and frock coat, with a pad and pencil. The inclusion of this figure transforms the image from a drawing by du Noyer of Dungiven Old Church into a drawing by du Noyer of du Noyer drawing Dungiven Old Church. Through this figure, du Noyer claims for himself and his drawing the authenticity and authority of having-been-there and having-seen-for-himself.

That claim was central to the work of the Topographical Department for it was supposed to set its work apart from that of other antiquarians also active in Ireland in the 1830s and 1840s. John O'Donovan, a leading member of the Department's staff, attributed their emphasis on fieldwork to the influence of their supervisor, George Petrie, writing:

> No one can have any claim to the name of an original investigator in antiquities or history but he who examines original manuscripts, inscriptions, tombs, styles of architecture, etc....In this sense of the word Mr. Petrie is the only original antiquarian that Ireland ever produced, and any skill I have in making discoveries of this kind has been derived from my contact with him.[1]

This valorization of Petrie's work, and in particular his methods, has outlived O'Donovan, the Topographical Department, and Petrie himself, as he is still celebrated as the "father" of scientific archeology in Ireland.[2]

On further reflection, however, du Noyer's drawing undermines the claim it makes to authenticity and authority, and it does so through the same figure of du Noyer drawing within the drawing: for du Noyer cannot have seen himself drawing. Either the figure is someone else (though he typically worked alone), or the drawing is something other than an

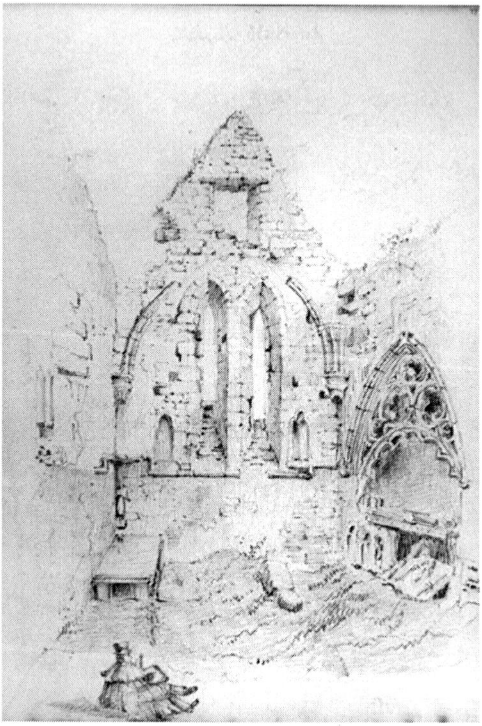

Fig. 1. George du Noyer, *Dungiven Old Church, Co. Londonderry*, ca. 1835-1838, Ordnance Survey Sketches, 12.T.7/77, Royal Irish Academy, Dublin (Photo: By permission of the Royal Irish Academy © RIA)

immediate record of what he saw. A journal that du Noyer kept during a portion of his time with the Topographical Department provides an alternative vocabulary for understanding this image. In this text, he repeatedly refers to "making" and "finishing" his drawings.[3] Drawing for du Noyer was not a process of seeing but a product to be made and finished, fabricated, or constructed. His drawing of Dungiven Old Church is a construction of the Irish countryside and his place in it.

The written records of the Topographical Department's work should likewise, I argue, be understood as constructions and not simple reportage. The letters that the members of the Department wrote also construct the Irish countryside and, as the Department's work increasingly became an historical undertaking, these letters likewise shape the Irish past. In this article I examine the letters against George Petrie's antiquarianism as a parallel, though differently realized, form of construction. My goal is to move beyond the celebration of Petrie's work as "science" and to ask new questions about it: Of what did his "science" consist? How did it work to construct the past? What kind of a past did it create for Ireland? These questions are important for the historiography of medieval art as Petrie's construction of the Irish past continues to shape both popular and scholarly presentations of medieval Ireland and its artistic remains.

My approach to these questions is grounded in the critical historiographical work of Hayden White and Stephen Bann. White challenges the notion that science provides an appropriate paradigm for historical work because the products of that work—historical texts—have much more in common with literature: like a novel, for example, an historical text must represent the world using the resources of language.[4] On the most fundamental level those resources consist of four poetic tropes: metaphor, metonymy, synecdoche, and irony. According to White, the dominant trope within an historical text generates its larger forms including the plot of its narrative, the form of its argument, and its ideological implications.[5] As all histories are shaped by tropes, so they all have ideological implications, and there is no real reason for choosing one historical account over another, as no account is more "realistic" than any other. White thus objects to "scientism" in the rhetoric of history, to the mimicking of scientific language as a way of appropriating science's authority to privilege certain historical texts over others.[6]

Bann builds on White's work by expanding the analysis to a range of forms of historical representation including images, collections, museums, and architectural environments. Bann writes of the contrast between metonymy, in which a part substitutes for a whole, and synecdoche, in which a part symbolizes the whole, as shaping the differences between the museums established by Alexandre Lenoir and Alexandre du Sommerard in late eighteenth- and early nineteenth-century France, as well as the differences between the Gothic Revival homes built by Lord Byron and Sir Walter Scott in England during approximately the same period.[7] Bann's work provides a model for my own as I come to focus on the differing presentations of collections and architectural monuments in the Ordnance Survey letters and George Petrie's projects as a contrast between metonymy and synecdoche.

George Petrie and the Irish Ordnance Survey

The Office of the Ordnance Survey makes maps, and in the 1820s-1840s, it was engaged in mapping all of Ireland.[8] From the beginning, the

Irish Survey had problems with place names: a single place often had multiple names, some in Irish and others in English, and yet the Survey's maps were to show only a single name for each place. Thomas Larcom, who oversaw the printing of the finished maps, was responsible for selecting the names to appear on them. His basic principle was to select contemporary names that came closest to the original Irish forms. This principle defined the problem of the place names as the need to determine their original Irish forms and, so, produced a need for knowledge of the Irish language.[9] Larcom had originally intended to learn Irish himself, but then he decided to hire an Irish scholar as "names expert." His first hire for this position, Edward O'Reilley, died in 1830 and O'Donovan was hired to replace him.

The Topographical Department grew from there, beginning in 1834 with the addition of Eugene Curry. Eventually the staff also included Patrick O'Keefe, Thomas O'Conor, and James Mangan, as well as the artists George Wakeman and George du Noyer. The Department's expansion was not limited to personnel, however; it grew in order to take on an expanded mission, the production of memoirs to accompany the maps. The Memoir was an unofficial undertaking until 1833, when Larcom suggested its publication to the government and received permission to produce one county's Memoir as an experiment. The parish of Templemore in County Londonderry was selected for the first experimental publication, and an initial version of the volume was circulated at the Dublin meeting of the British Association in 1835. Its final publication was delayed until November 1837, however, and, in the interim, it expanded exponentially. By the time the volume was published, the delay, along with the obvious time and expense that had been lavished on it, called the Memoir's future into question. The Topographical Department continued its work as the fate of the Memoir was debated by government agencies, special commissions, learned bodies, and the press. Finally, the project was brought to an end and the Department disbanded in 1842.

The letters written by members of the Department during their work in the field mirror the development of the Memoir project. Initially, O'Donovan considered his letters personal correspondence, rather than part of his official duties, and he experimented in these early texts with a variety of literary forms.[10] As the Memoir project took off, however, and other Department members went into the field, they too began to write letters, suggesting that letter writing was now a regular part of the fieldworkers' job. They soon adopted a standard form. The letters were divided into sections by parish, with the name of the parish used as a title for each section. This title was followed by two subheadings, SITUATION and NAME, and these were typically followed by accounts of local architectural antiquities. These later letters are particularly interesting because of the indications they give concerning the Department's working methods. The SITUATION and NAME portions were frequently left blank, to be filled in later by another writer.[11] Likewise, architectural remains would sometimes be visited and documented by one man and his notes then "put into form" for the letter by another.[12] These practices of joint authorship and piecemeal production demonstrate that the letters were not straightforward reports but rather deliberate constructions.

The final demise of the Memoir project and the Topographical Department has been attributed to a number of different causes. At the time, those critical of the project argued that such work ought to be left to local and private initiatives, while those sympathetic to it claimed that the project was disbanded because it was stirring up unwanted nationalist sentiments.[13] In retrospect, the controversy that surrounded the Department and the Memoir appears as part of a larger storm in antiquarian circles that centered on George Petrie. Trained as an artist, Petrie began his career by producing landscapes to be used as illustrations in a newly popular guidebook literature on Ireland. In the early 1820s, he devised a plan to write his own guidebook with enhanced antiquarian contents.[14] Although he never completed that project, in working on it he demonstrated sufficient knowledge of Irish antiquities to be elected to the Royal Irish Academy in 1828 and to join its governing council as a member of the Antiquities Committee in 1830. Soon after he was named head of the Topographical Department; its Dublin staff worked out of his back parlor and the fieldworkers' letters were often addressed to him.[15]

By the time he joined the Department, however, controversy was already brewing around Petrie over the topic of Ireland's round towers.[16] In 1829, Petrie proposed that the Academy sponsor a prize essay competition on the towers in order to finally settle questions surrounding their origins and significance. The competition produced a split decision. First prize was awarded to Petrie's own essay, which argued that the towers were Christian constructions used primarily as bell towers. A special second prize was created for an essay by Henry O'Brien, which argued that the towers were temples in the shape of an erect penis built by Buddhists from Persia who settled in Ireland in the remote past and became the legendary Tuatha-De-Danaan. O'Brien's essay represented an influential tradition in the understanding of Irish antiquities that argued for their extreme antiquity and close ties to the East. This tradition was part of the "diffusionist" account of the ancient past that was influential throughout Europe in the eighteenth and early nineteenth centuries.[17]

Reacting to the Academy's split decision, O'Brien concluded that the fix had been in for Petrie who, unlike himself, was an influential member of the Academy and that the second prize had been created because the Academy just could not ignore the obvious superiority of his own work. He published this interpretation of the situation as the preface to his essay, which appeared in 1834.[18] Soon after its publication, O'Brien went mad and died in 1835. His end made him a highly sympathetic figure, as a little guy destroyed by the weight of the Academy's authority. Petrie, on the other hand, took a long time in preparing his work on the towers for publication: it finally appeared in 1845 as part of his massive volume on the ecclesiastical architecture of Ireland before the Norman invasions. This delay allowed time for suspicions of his work to flourish.[19]

As Petrie prepared his round towers publication, he presented additional papers at the Academy and won additional prizes for them, including one for his 1837 paper on the antiquities of Tara hill. This paper was, admittedly, a part of the Memoir project, and it was intended to demonstrate the value of that project as its future was called into question. Instead of generating support for the Memoir, however, this paper too created controversy at the Academy. Sir William Betham questioned the relationship between the paper and the Memoir and challenged the accuracy of the translations of ancient Irish texts used in the paper, translations that conflicted with Betham's own.[20] Betham's work was closer in content to Henry O'Brien's, and his ire against Petrie seems to have been raised as Petrie's increasing influence at the Academy made it increasingly difficult for Betham to publish his work there.[21]

These conflicts over Petrie's round towers and Tara hill papers form the context in which his supporters defended his work as "scientific." For example, in his biography of Petrie, his friend William Stokes extols the Tara paper in particular as a model of Petrie's method in order to praise that method as "severe" and "scientific." In context, that claim to "scientific" status appears to be White's "scientism"—the appropriation of science's authority in order to promote one version of the past over others. As White writes, that kind of claim is only necessary in a situation of real conflict between multiple possible versions of the past.[22] Only because views similar to O'Brien's were seriously and strongly held by contemporary scholars did Petrie's work need the extra authority provided by the claim to "scientific" status. In retrospect, O'Brien's version of the past seems so outlandish that the value of Petrie's work is obvious in comparison, and the genuine controversy between them seems impossible.

In order to examine Petrie's "scientific" work more closely, the remainder of this paper pursues a comparison between Petrie's work and that of the Topographical Department. As the staff worked for Petrie, one might expect their work to be very similar to his, and yet a close examination reveals significant differences between them.

Collecting and the Construction of the Past

In addition to being an artist and a scholar, George Petrie was a dedicated collector. He collected inscriptions, songs and ballads, coins, medieval manuscripts, and other objects, primarily metalwork, both for himself and the Royal Irish Academy.[23] His work as an artist can be considered an extension of these collecting activities: he concentrated on historical sites and ruins as a way of collecting the uncollectible—buildings and places—through representation. Petrie's charge to the staff of the Topographical Department, finally, reveals the full extent of his ambitions as a collector: in a letter to John O'Donovan he writes, "do not hurry, but try to get as much of everything as you can, manners, customs, traditions, legends, songs, etc. The opportunities afforded at present may never occur again."[24] To Petrie, it seems, the work of the Ordnance Survey was an opportunity to collect *everything* or at least come as close as possible to that goal.

Topographical Department fieldwork was sometimes used as a scouting expedition for Petrie's collecting activities. He occasionally asked O'Donovan to acquire things for him, and O'Donovan's letters, likewise, suggested items for his attention, particularly crosiers, which he actively collected.[25] Known as *bachalls* in Irish, these objects were originally carried by bishops as signs of their office. Many of them had been passed down in families for generations. Some of these had been put to a new use in oath-taking ceremonies. John O'Donovan wrote to Petrie about Saint Grellan's crosier that it was:

> used in the country to be sworn upon when people wish to clear themselves of theft, on which occasion if the deponent takes a false oath, the violated *bachall* turns blue and green and the deponent's mouth turns to his ear, or his neck turns the face to look westward.[26]

He claimed that this particular crosier would be difficult to acquire because they would have to "storm Crannelly's belief [its hereditary owner] before it can be got from him for love or money."[27] Others were already losing their "belief," however, and these objects were beginning to lose their place in Irish local culture: the owner of Saint Barry's crosier was trying to trade or sell it in exchange for a job, and Saint Griollan's crosier had been thrown into a river after a priest objected to its use in an oath-taking ceremony.[28] When such objects entered Petrie's collections—instead of rivers—their meanings changed; rather than continuing to function as socially active objects in an on-going local culture, they became vestiges of the past.

Petrie intended to put the parts of the past together into a coherent whole by writing chronologically organized catalogues for his own collection and that of the Royal Irish Academy.[29] According to Petrie, the chronological organization was necessary if the collections were to serve their purpose, which was "to help, by an inductive process, the antiquarian investigator in his attempts to trace and, if possible, illustrate the origin and progress of a people from its earliest and rudest state to its final achievement of civilization and refinement."[30] Laid out in chronological order, the objects in a collection would tell a story of art that was also the story of a people, of their "origin and progress" towards "civilization and refinement." This story would compose the past into a unified whole and each object in the collection would function as a part of that whole, as "illustrating" the "progress of a people." In other words, the narrative created by the chronological ordering of the collection would compose the past through the trope of synecdoche, a trope that establishes an integrative relationship between discrete elements of an organic whole.[31] Unfortunately, neither of Petrie's catalogues was ever finished.

The work of the Topographical Department's staff was served by a different kind of collecting, the collection of "historical extracts" that men working in Dublin copied from manuscripts and printed books and sent to the fieldworkers who then incorporated them into their letters. This collecting activity differed from Petrie's on three key points. Where Petrie's planned chronological catalogues would have drawn the parts of the past together into a new whole, a story of the past, the preparation of the extracts took apart already existing wholes, the books and manuscripts from which they were drawn, and reduced them to parts. These parts, the individual extracts, were arranged according to the places to which they referred, so that space rather than time served as the primary organizing strategy for the collection. Finally, this dispersal of the extracts over space did not allow for the construction of any story about the past, or the past as any sort of whole. Even when incorporated into the letters, the extracts were rarely if ever used to such an end. In the letters as well, parts of the past were put together because they referred to the same place, but no effort was made to pull these parts together into a whole. The extract collections and the letters were shaped, not by the integrative trope of synecdoche, but by the reductive trope of metonymy, which deconstructs wholes into parts and juxtaposes those parts to one another.[32]

A section from one of Thomas O'Conor's letters on a place called Kilfeakle parish can exemplify the letters' metonymic structure. First a passage from a manuscript known as the Book of Lismore that tells a story to account for the name "Kilfeakle" is quoted in Irish and then translated. Its usefulness is immediately undercut, however; it does not contain the information that O'Conor desires, and the passage that does has apparently been left out of the extract collection.[33] Next, a passage on Kill-Fheacla from a printed source, Lanigan's *Ecclesiastical History*, is literally inserted into the letter; the actual pages having been ripped from the book and sent out from Dublin as part of the extract collection are physically incorporated into the letter. These pages, already severed from Lanigan's text, are pulled further apart as O'Conor inserts numbers between individual passages in order to refer the reader to comments of his own where he questions all of the information it contains. Next, notices of the place from two other manuscript sources, the "Annals of the Four Masters" and the "Annals of Innisfallen," are inserted, and these are followed immediately by measurements of Kilfeakle castle.[34] This section of the letter ends here with no conclusions drawn, no synthesis made, no story told.

Also notable in this letter is O'Connor's questioning of the historical extracts; the collection is incomplete, the bit of text he needs has been left out, and the information in the extracts is open to debate. These comments fit into a larger pattern of doubt that marks the letters, for the fieldworkers also doubted the information they collected from both oral informants and physical monuments. Collecting this information was the point of their work in the field: it was supposed to set them apart from other antiquarians and guarantee the worth of their work to their employers.[35] Nevertheless, the fieldworkers repeatedly undermined the value of this information for understanding the past. Their letters are thus also shaped by the trope of irony, which negates everything that it asserts.[36]

For example, passages in several of John O'Donovan's letters critique oral tradition as a source of information about the past. He writes in one letter:

> I have argued with a Doctor of Salamanca about oral tradition; he produced logic and ingenious subtlety; I produced facts that had fallen under my own eye; he adduced the accuracy of the Antediluvian pedigrees and other traditions; I produced the inaccuracy of what Oral tradition has preserved in Donegal in 1835, a more tangible epoch (era) [*sic*]. He urged the perfection of human memory: I urged the imperfection of my own...He

> argued from the immutability of the traditions of the Church; I from the forgeries of the Middle Ages...from the fact that no six persons will (or can) [*sic*] separately relate the same story in the same words, order, or detail and from the difficulty with which a case of open robbery can be proved to the satisfaction of men of wisdom and acquaintance with the laws of nature and society.[37]

In this passage, a back-and-forth pattern replicating oral exchange is finally overcome as O'Donovan's voice overwhelms that of his interlocutor. He then cites legal proceedings as a model for oral practices of producing the truth, but ironically as a model of their inadequacies.

Similar doubts likewise undercut the fieldworkers' accounts of physical monuments. Much of this doubt centered on Ogham stones, large stones inscribed with an early script made up of lines that they were unable to read. Eugene Curry wrote of one stone that it:

> has so many Ogham lines engraved upon it by the action of a neighboring thorn branch, that it would afford a fine field for the Oghamatical investigations of those erudite interpreters and fortunate discoverers of unborn languages and self-born druidical inscriptions, viz., Sir W. Betham and Father Matt Horgan.[38]

The natural action of a thorn branch is here producing false historical evidence and feeding the work of other antiquarians for whom the Department's staff have only scorn. As this pattern of doubt continues throughout the letters and escalates with the accumulation of written, oral, and physical sources, it reinforces the metonymic structure of these texts. These parts of the past cannot be drawn together into a coherent whole, since each individual part remains open to critique.

Architectural Antiquities and the Restoration of the Past

The largest group of physical monuments that the fieldworkers encountered was made up of architectural antiquities, old churches, and castles. Over time they developed a standard way of accounting for such structures in their letters: they measured them. Note, for example, that O'Connor's account of Kilfeakle ended with measurements of its castle. This practice of measuring buildings recalls the collection and use of the historical extracts in two ways. First, much as the production of the extracts pulled apart existing texts, so measuring a building has the effect of taking it apart as its walls, doors, windows, and even its individual stones are independently measured. Secondly, such measurements do not allow the fieldworkers to say anything about the history or significance of these structures. The numbers enter into their letter texts, along with the historical extracts and other kinds of collected information, but all of that information does not add up to anything. Once again, the letters are shaped by the trope of metonymy as they reduce wholes into parts and juxtapose those parts with one another.

Doing more with architectural antiquities, in particular dating them based on their features, was denied to the fieldworkers by Petrie himself. In a letter written from County Galway, John O'Donovan proposed a way of dating churches based primarily on the shapes of their windows. He drew a basic distinction between a "primitive" and a "curvilinearly pointed" or "Gothic Style," which was basically a division between early and late Medieval, before and after the twelfth-century Anglo-Norman invasions of Ireland.[39] In a letter dated two days later, however, Petrie harshly criticized O'Donovan's proposal, writing:

> I am by no means satisfied that these conclusions are always right, I mean particularly those that are new, for there are several which are undoubtedly true, but these are not new, at least they are not new to me, nor to anyone who has heard me converse on the topic.[40]

In other words, most of O'Donovan's conclusions were wrong and any that might have been right, were actually Petrie's. Petrie's words were so strong here that he followed this letter with another in which he made repeated assurances of his friendly feelings for O'Donovan—although he repeated his criticism of O'Donovan's proposal as well.[41]

O'Donovan, however, had already ironically distanced himself from his own undertaking. Striking a particularly sour note, he wrote:

> I am just sick to death of churchyards, skulls, and the mouldering [*sic*] walls of churches, and the misery of it is that I have not reaped the proper benefit from them as the great philosopher James Harvey has done. I have visited churches in order to ascertain their ages by examining their characteristic features and measured skulls for their animal and intellectual bumps, not to draw any moral lesson from them, but for this I will be sorry hereafter, when cold old age comes upon me.[42]

Soon after this exchange, O'Donovan suggested that the fieldworkers give up dealing with old buildings, given their apparent lack of skill in this particular area.[43] That did not happen; instead, measuring the buildings became standard procedure.

To date the buildings would have required that the fieldworkers understand them within a history of Irish architecture, understand them through the trope of synecdoche as parts of a whole, which was a privilege that Petrie seems to have claimed for himself alone. He presented a synthesis of Irish architectural history in writing, particularly in his *Ecclesiastical Architecture of Ireland Anterior to the Anglo-Norman Invasion* (the expanded version of his round towers essay), in his paintings of the *Last Circuit of Pilgrims at Clonmacnoise* [Fig. 2], and in his plan for a memorial complex for the Irish leader Daniel O'Connell. He produced two versions of the *Last Circuit of Pilgrims at Clonmacnoise*, one in 1828 and the other in 1838. Both show the façade of a church, a sculpted stone cross, a round tower along with a scattering of gravestones in the foreground, and a ruined building towards the back. Petrie selected the same three major monuments—a church, a stone cross, and a round tower—to make up the monument for O'Connell, although only the tower was ever built.[44]

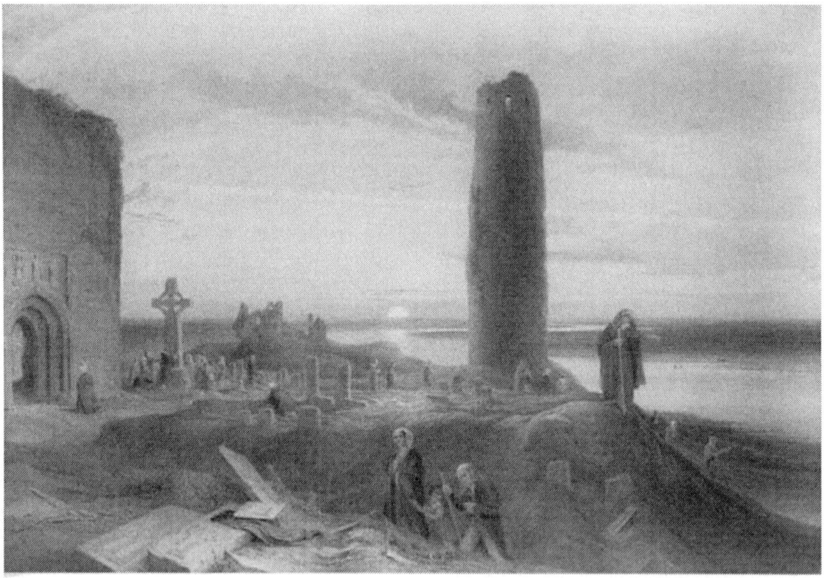

Fig. 2 George Petrie, *The Last Circuit of Pilgrims at Clonmacnoise*, ca. 1838 (Photo: National Gallery of Ireland)

Petrie wrote of the later version of the *Last Circuit of Pilgrims* that:

> It was my wish to produce an Irish picture somewhat historical in its object, and poetical in its sentiment—a landscape composed of several of

> the monuments characteristic of the past history of our country, and which will soon cease to exist, and to connect with them the expression of human feelings equally belonging to our history and which are destined to a similar extinction.[45]

This passage makes important claims about Petrie's artistic and antiquarian enterprise; that certain monuments and emotions are "characteristic" of the Irish past, are integral parts of that past, and that it is in Petrie's power to "connect" them together, to compose those parts into a coherent whole. Petrie described his plan for the O'Connell monument in similarly synecdochal terms. According to his report on the plan, he had again selected the church, cross, and round tower as being representative of early Christianity in Ireland: the church was to be "characteristic" in its style and was to have its two "characteristic" adjuncts, the cross and the tower.[46]

This "characteristic" church was to have served two functions: it was to be O'Connell's tomb, and, like the *Last Circuit of Pilgrims,* it was to be a representation of the past. As Petrie wrote:

> when every vestige shall have disappeared of those ancient ecclesiastical structures, in the possession of which any other nation would feel the highest national pride, but in which we take so little interest...it would secure to us for those better and more enlightened times to which the good look forward with hope, the forms and features of that simple ancient architecture, and be a typical monument to endure for ever, of that pure and ardent Christianity which gave it birth.[47]

Petrie's new ancient church was meant to guard against a future when the ancient churches themselves will have disappeared. Its status as "characteristic" would then allow it to function as a "typical" monument and thus represent all that had been lost. The fieldworkers' practice of measuring buildings was also meant to guard against a future when the ancient structures will have disappeared. O'Donovan wrote that "no description is worth the attention of the antiquarian unless it be so perfect that, by its assistance in case the building were destroyed, a similar one could be erected."[48] The difference is that where Petrie would have built a "characteristic" and "typical" ancient church, the measurements would allow for the detailed reconstruction of specific structures. Such a rebuilt structure would not represent some larger whole, whether "ancient architecture" or "pure and ardent Christianity," but would instead simply reproduce itself.

Conclusion: Clibborn's Celt

To visually summarize the differences between the Irish past as constructed by Petrie and the Ordnance Survey letters, I introduce a drawing that appears in a scrapbook assembled by yet another Irish antiquary, Edward Clibborn [Fig. 3]. This drawing is the work of an unnamed correspondent of Clibborn, who was apparently responding to a request for a drawing of a "celt."[49] The drawing plays with an ambiguity in that request arising from the double meaning of the word "celt." That word can, of course, refer to a type of person: in an Irish context, "Celt" used in this way would serve to distinguish the native Irish population from the English community also resident on the island. But "celt" is also the name of a type of prehistoric axe-head with a distinctive, double-curved shape. Clibborn's correspondent combined these two senses of the word to construct a Celt, a person, out of celts or axes.

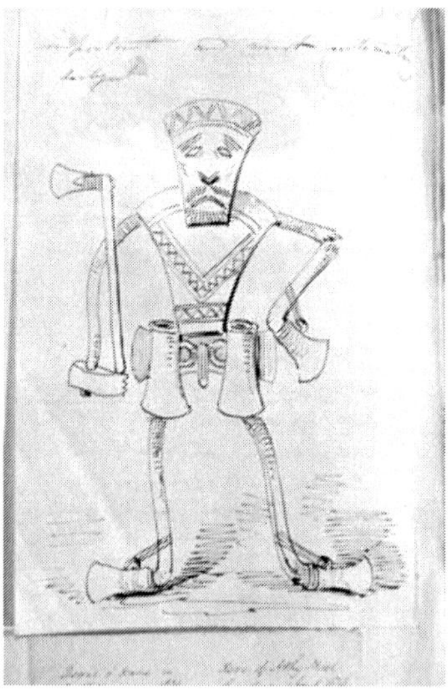

Fig. 3 Edward Clibborn, Drawing of a "Celt," ca. 1845-1850, Clibborn's Scrapbook or Specimen Book, MS 24. E. 34. fol. 107, Royal Irish Academy, Dublin (Photo: By permission of the Royal Irish Academy © RIA)

On first glance, this drawing recalls Petrie's use of synecdochal strategies to compose the parts of the Irish past into a coherent whole. Where Petrie intended to use chronology as the foundation for a narrative that would tie together the objects in his collections, and to use a single "characteristic" church to represent Irish architectural and religious history, this drawing uses the shape of the human body to suggest that all of the individual celts naturally go together to make up an organic whole, the Celt. But closer analysis of the body reveals an unconvincing whole: its joints seem particularly unstable and the lines that run from its feet to its legs suggest that it is held together by threads. The Celt's body could collapse at any moment, it seems, and scatter its component celts across the page. Disintegrated in this way, the celts instead recall the past as presented in the Ordnance Survey letters, as a metonymic assemblage of parts—historical extracts, oral traditions, measurements of buildings—all coexisting in the absence of any whole.

Just as the body in the drawing is not simply *any* body but very specifically that of a "Celt," so Petrie's *Last Circuit of Pilgrims* was to be an "Irish" picture composed of monuments and of feelings equally characteristic "of our country." Stokes, in his biography of Petrie, likewise identifies him as the "sole historian of our national art" and describes the plot that Petrie identified for that history: progress impelled by the coming of Christianity followed by a decline marked by the loss of "celtic" and "national" qualities, with the turning point fixed on the late eleventh or early twelfth century—the moment of the Anglo-Norman invasions.[50] The monuments that Petrie selects as "characteristic" conform to this plot: the round tower, the ancient church, and the stone cross are all Christian, and they are all pre-Norman. Assembled in the painting or the planned O'Connell monument, these three structures represent the idea of an autonomous Irish civilization that was also a deeply Christian culture.

Petrie's work fits into an overall pattern in Irish cultural nationalism as that discourse was constructed during the 1830s and 1840s. According to John Hutchinson, this discourse presented Ireland in stark contrast to England's "mass culture," secularizing society, and will to power. Ireland's medieval past presented a model of an authentic Irish civilization that stood in opposition to the modern world. Furthermore, this medieval past presented a vision of a harmonious Christian past that formed a clear contrast to contemporary sectarian conflicts.[51] This past presented an Ireland that Petrie could identify as "our country" despite the fact that he was Protestant and of Scottish descent.[52] In the *Last Circuit of Pilgrims*, a painting appears within the painting, lying on one of the tombstones in the center-left foreground, the just-visible form of the round tower identifying it with the painting itself. This doubling of the painted scene recalls my opening image of du Noyer inscribing himself within his drawing, except that Petrie does not accompany his painting within the painting. Instead, the painting lies upon a cloak, suggesting Petrie's former presence at the scene. As Tom Dunne suggests, Petrie seems to have disappeared into his painting and so become part of his picture of Ireland's past.[53]

Petrie's picture of pre-Norman Ireland as a golden age in Irish history, as the moment of an autonomous and authentic Irish and Christian civilization, finally, has continued to shape presentations of the Irish past in both popular history and scholarly art history. This was the moment when the Irish "saved civilization."[54] Likewise, this was the moment in Irish history that caught the attention of the American scholar of medieval art, Arthur Kingsley Porter. Like Petrie, Porter looked to Ireland's early medieval past to provide an alternative to the modern world, and he focused his scholarly attention on one of Petrie's "characteristic" monuments, the stone crosses.[55] Little attention has been given in art history to medieval Ireland's post-Norman period and its more complicated quasi-colonial situation.[56] The Ordnance Survey materials present an alternative model for approaching this understudied part of the Irish past. These materials are broader in their interests—looking once more at du Noyer's drawing of Dungiven Old Church, one can see the building is not really so old; its window is Gothic in form and thus post-Norman in date. The Survey materials' metonymic structure allows such a building to stand alongside an ancient church, a round tower, a stone cross, a crozier, an Ogham stone, as equally Irish, without having to become part of a single picture, or story, of Ireland's past.

Notes

[1] The records of the Topographical Department are now housed in the library of the Royal Irish Academy. My work with these records and other archival materials in Dublin was made possible by a Travel Fellowship in Art History from the Samuel Kress Foundation. The Ordnance Survey Letters are also available in a typescript copy reproduced under the directions of Rev. M.O. Flanagan in 1933. Ordnance Survey Letters, Co. Westmeath, vol. 1. 6

[2] See, for example, Joep Leerson's claim that Petrie redeemed historical and antiquarian studies in Ireland from "amateurish speculation" for the "precise, critical spirit of new scientific scholarship." Joep Leerson, *Remembrance and Imagination: Patterns in the Historical and Literary Representation of Ireland in the Nineteenth Century* (Cork: Cork University Press, 1996). 107

[3] George du Noyer, "Journal," MS 1441, National Library of Ireland, Dublin, Ireland.

[4] Hayden White, *Metahistory: The Historical Imagination in Nineteenth-Century Europe* (Baltimore: Johns Hopkins University Press, 1973). x-xi, 2-3; Hayden

White, "The Historical Text as Literary Artifact," in *Tropics of Discourse: Essays in Cultural Criticism* (Baltimore: Johns Hopkins University Press, 1978). 82-98

[5] White, *Metahistory*. x, 8-9, 30-37, 426-427; Hayden White, "Interpretation in History," in *Tropics of Discourse: Essays in Cultural Criticism* (Baltimore: Johns Hopkins University Press, 1978). 72-74; on narrative in the historical text see White, "The Historical Text as Literary Artifact." 82-84, 88; and Hayden White, *The Content of the Form: Narrative Discourse and Historical Representation* (Baltimore: Johns Hopkins University Press, 1987).

[6] White, *Metahistory*. xii, 20-21, 26-27, 432-433

[7] For Lenoir and du Sommerard see Stephen Bann, *The Clothing of Clio: A Study of the Representation of History in Nineteenth-century Britain and France* (Cambridge: Cambridge University Press, 1984). 77-92; for more on du Sommerard see Stephen Bann, *Romanticism and the Rise of History* (New York: Twayne Publishers, 1995). 144-150; for Ruskin and Scott see Bann, *The Clothing of Clio*. 93-111

[8] For a thorough history of the Ordnance Survey in Ireland see J.H. Andrews, *A Paper Landscape: The Ordnance Survey in Nineteenth-Century Ireland* (Oxford: Clarendon Press, 1975); for a fictionalized account of the Survey's work in Co. Donegal see Brian Friel's play *Translations* (London: Faber and Faber, 1981) along with John Paddy Brown, "Wonderful Knowledge: The Ordnance Survey of Ireland," *Eire-Ireland* 20, 1 (1985). 15-27; finally, for a critique of the Survey as a colonizing effort see Mary Hammer, "Putting Ireland on the Map," *Textual Practice* 3, 2 (1989). 184-201

[9] Andrews, *A Paper Landscape*. 122; Brown, "Wonderful Knowledge." 24-25

[10] Ordnance Survey Letters, Co. Down, 56. One letter from Armagh and Monaghan was written in imitation of the style of "Irish Romances" in order to make George Petrie laugh, others contain snatches of O'Donovan's original poetry, and still others contain passages in dialogue form that present O'Donovan engaged with a variety of interlocutors: Ordnance Survey Letters, Co. Armagh and Monaghan. 145-147; for poetry see Co. Londonderry. 9-10, 249-254; and Co. Donegal. 184-186; for dialogues Co. Down. 69-71, 76-77; and Co. Mayo, vol. 2. 31-46, 106

[11] See, for example, the "Name" sections for Templenoe, Emly, and Morrstownkirk, all in Co. Tipperary, which are all followed by O'Donovan's initials but within letters by Thomas O'Conor and Eugene Curry. Ordnance Survey Letters, Co. Tipperrary, vol. 3. 116, 118, 248

[12] See, for example, Emly, Kilmucklin, Ballymakey, and Ballygibbon, all examined by Anthony Curry but with notes arranged by Patrick O'Keeke. Ordnance Survey Letters, Co. Tipperary, vol. 3. 447

[13] On the controversy surrounding the Memoir see Andrews, *A Paper Landscape*. 157, 167, 172-174

[14] On these images and the guidebook project see William Stokes, *The Life and Labours in Art and Archeology of George Petrie* (London: Longmans, Green, and Co., 1868). 22-25; and Peter Murray, *George Petrie (1790-1866): The Rediscovery*

of Ireland's Past, with essays by Joep Leerson and Tom Dunne (Kinsale: Gandon Editions, 2004). 52-81

[15] The exact date of Petrie's appointment as head of the Department is not clear. On his involvement with the Department see Stokes, *Life and Labours*. 86-109; Murray, *George Petrie*. 90-102

[16] On the round towers controversy in general see Stokes, *Life and Labours*. 140-147; and Leerson, *Remembrance and Imagination*. 112-143

[17] On diffusionism see Partha Mitter, *Much Maligned Monsters: A History of European Reactions to Indian Art* (Oxford: Clarendon Press, 1977); George Stocking, *Victorian Anthropology* (New York: Free Press, 1987).

[18] Henry O'Brien, *The Round Towers of Ireland or the Mysteries of Freemasonry, of Sabaism, and of Budhism, for the First Time Unveiled. "Prize Essay" of the Royal Irish Academy, Enlarged and Embellished with Numerous Illustrations* (London: Whittaker and Co.; Dublin: J. Cumming, 1834).

[19] Leerson, *Remembrance and Imagination*. 132-133; George Petrie, "The Ecclesiastical Architecture of Ireland, anterior to the Anglo-Norman Invasion, comprising an Essay on the Origin and Use of the Round Towers of Ireland, which obtained a Gold Medal and Prize of the Royal Irish Academy," *Transactions of the Royal Irish Academy* 20 (1845).

[20] Stokes, *Life and Labours*. 109-119; Leerson, *Remembrance and Imagination*. 130-131; Murray, *George Petrie (1790-1866)*. 103

[21] Leerson, *Remembrance and Imagination*. 127

[22] White, *Metahistory*. 20-21, 26-27; and Hayden White, "The Value of Narrativity in the Representation of Reality," in White, *The Content of the Form*. 19-20

[23] On Petrie's collecting activities see Stokes, *Life and Labours*. vii, 80-82, 269-290; Jeanne Sheehy, *The Rediscovery of Ireland's Past: The Celtic Revival, 1830-1930* (London: Thames and Hudson, 1980). 17; Charles Graves, *Eloge on the Late George Petrie* (Dublin: University Press, 1866). 8-9; Patrick MacSweeney, *A Group of Nation Builders: O'Donovan - O'Curry - Petrie* (Dublin: Catholic Truth Society, 1913). 84-87; Joseph Raferty, "Aspects of George Petrie I: George Petrie, 1789-1866: A Re-Assessment," *Proceedings of the Royal Irish Academy* 72, sec. C, 6 (1972). 153-156

[24] Ordnance Survey Letters, Co. Roscommon, vol. 1. 273

[25] Ordnance Survey Letters, Co. Mayo, vol. 1. 218; Co. Armagh and Monaghan. 69-70; Co. Roscommon, vol. 2. 148-150, 266; Co. Westmeath. 264-266

[26] Ordnance Survey Letters, Co. Roscommon, vol. 1. 60-62

[27] Ibid.

[28] Ordnance Survey Letters, Co. Roscommon, vol. 2. 266; Co. Galway, vol. 1. 122

[29] Raferty, "Aspects of George Petrie." 155; Stokes, *Life and Labours*. 84-85

[30] Stokes, *Life and Labours*. 83

[31] White, *Metahistory*. 34-35; Bann, *The Clothing of Clio*. 84-85, 100-101

[32] White, *Metahistory*. 34-35; Bann, *The Clothing of Clio*. 84-85, 100-101

[33] Ordnance Survey Letters, Co. Tipperary, vol. 2. 271

[34] Ordnance Survey Letters, Co. Tipperary, vol. 2. 278-292

[35] See, for example, Ordnance Survey Letters, Co. Fermanagh. 15; Co. Londonderry. 217; Co. Cavan. 111-112; Co. Meath. 170; Co. Westmeath, vol. 1. 11, 51, 213; Co. Galway, vol. 2. 242, 253-254; Co. Clare, vol. 2. 148, 229, 254-255

[36] White, *Metahistory*. 34-35, 37, 231-232; Bann, *The Clothing of Clio*. 120-128

[37] Ordnance Survey Letters, Co. Donegal. 241-242

[38] Ordnance Survey Letters, Co. Wicklow. 188-189

[39] Ibid. 514-524

[40] Ibid. 569

[41] Ibid. 590-592

[42] Ibid. 610

[43] Ordnance Survey Letters, Co. Galway, vol. 2. 586-587

[44] Stokes, *Life and Labours*. 369-372; Leerson, *Remembrance and Imagination*. 141-143

[45] George Petrie to the Royal Irish Art Union, which had purchased the painting. Quoted in Stokes, *Life and Labours*. 15

[46] Ibid. 433

[47] Ibid. 434

[48] Ordnance Survey Letters, Co.Wicklow. 471

[49] The text above the drawing reads, in part, "In your last amusing note my dear Ed. C. you call upon me to supply the antiquarian and aesthetic world with a drawing of 'a celt'." Edward Clibborn, "Scrapbook," or "Specimen Book," MS 24.E.34., Royal Irish Academy, Dublin. fol. 107

[50] Stokes, *Life and Labours*. 264-266, 268-271, 300-301

[51] John Hutchinson's "mass culture" encompasses both mass production and the idea of a mass audience for/of culture. *The Dynamics of Cultural Nationalism: The Gaelic Revival and the Creation of the Irish Nation-State* (London: Allen and Unwin, 1987). 48-49, 79-86, 133-137, 197-199, 220-221

[52] Petrie's religion and ethnicity became an issue in the controversy surrounding his work. Some hostile antiquarians attacked him as not-Irish and therefore anti-Irish. See letters written from Richard Donovan to John Windele, 18 November 1845, MS 4B5, fol. 1160, Royal Irish Academy, Dublin; and from Thomas O'Flaherty to John Windele, 22 January 1846, MS 4B6, fol. 160, Royal Irish Academy, Dublin. At the same time, however, those hostile to the Memoir project attacked him as a closet Catholic and described the Topographical Department as a hotbed for Catholics and rebels. See an anonymous letter to Thomas Larcom, 2 May 1842, Larcom Letters (Private) Memoir, vol. 4, MS 7553, National Library of Ireland, Dublin.

[53] Tom Dunn, "Towards a National Art? George Petrie's Two Versions of *The Last Circuit of Pilgrims at Clonmacnoise*," in Murray, *George Petrie*. 134

[54] See Thomas Cahill, *How the Irish Saved Civilization: The Untold Story of Ireland's Heroic Role from the Fall of Rome to the Rise of Medieval Europe* (New York: Doubleday, 1995).

[55]Arthur Kingsley Porter, *The Crosses and Culture of Ireland* (New Haven: Yale University Press, 1931); on Porter see Nora Nercessian, "In Desperate Defiance: A

Modern Predicament for Medieval Art," *RES* 7, 8 (1984). 136-146; Kathryn Brush, "The Capitals from Moutiers-Saint-Jean (Harvard University Art Museums) and the Carving of Medieval Art Study in America after World War I," in this volume; on the historiography of Irish stone crosses see Maggie McEnroe Williams, "Constructing the Market Cross at Tuam: The Role of Cultural Patriotism in the Study of Irish High Crosses," in *From Ireland Coming: Irish Art from the Early Christian to the Late Gothic Period and Its European Context* (Princeton: Index of Christian Art and Princeton University Press, 2001). 141-160

[56] Some of the essays in *From Ireland Coming*, provide the exception to this rule. See, for example, Peter Harbison, "The Otherness of Irish Art in the Twelfth Century." 103-120; Tessa Garton, "Masks and Monsters: Some Recurring Themes in Irish Romanesque Sculpture." 121-140; and Raghnall O. Floinn, "Goldsmiths' Work in Ireland, 1200-1400." 289-312

L'OEUF SACRÉ: ALEXANDRE LENOIR'S *COUR ARABE* AND THE POINTED ARCH[1]

MARY B. SHEPARD

For Alexandre Lenoir, the seeds of French glory lay in the Middle East. History painter and museum impresario, Lenoir (1761-1839) was the guiding force behind the creation of the Musée des monuments français (1790-1816), a Parisian museum that exhibited works of art displaced during the French Revolution. With the nationalization of church property and attendant destruction of ecclesiastical monuments and aristocratic chateaux, Lenoir played a singular role not only in saving medieval works of art, but in re-shaping French sensibilities towards the medieval past. Eschewing his official mandate to simply warehouse seized works of art, Lenoir boldly transformed the provisional art depot under his command—the former monastery of the Petits Augustins sited on the city's left bank—into a museum chronicling the development of French art. In so doing, Lenoir looked to politically neutralize those works of art which had been sanctioned in 1792 by legislation authorizing the eradication of buildings and symbols of the *ancien régime* built in "pride, prejudice, and tyranny."[2] One ingenious solution was to break with the tradition of categorizing art within the reigns of kings and organize the museum as a series of chronological installations dedicated to individual centuries, beginning with the Gallery of the Thirteenth Century. Lenoir's intent was to trumpet the triumph of French art from "its origin up to its perfection."[3]

While scholars have outlined this chronological approach within the museum itself,[4] a series of analogously century-themed courtyards located to the southwest of the museum building have been mentioned only in passing [Fig. 1].[5] Indeed, the *Cour Arabe* (labeled as no. IV in the center of the plan), the smallest of the three courtyards, has been overlooked completely. This two-pronged essay addresses Lenoir's contention that the pointed arch originated in the area along the eastern shore of the Mediterranean Sea (the Levant)[6] and that, during the thirteenth century, French crusaders had been so inspired by its form that they recreated it at home, thereby stimulating the rise of French art. The *Cour Arabe* was Lenoir's artistic testimonial to this connection—in his view, the linchpin for the development of French art.

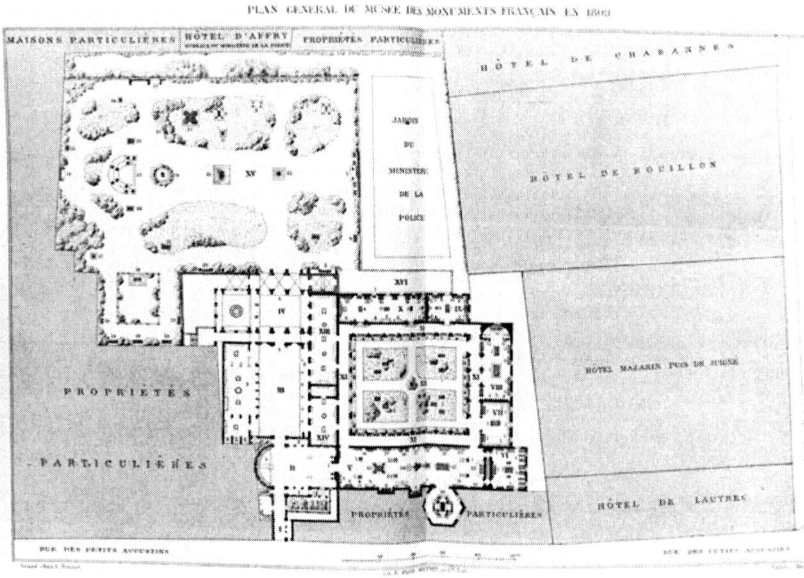

Fig. 1 Plan of the Musée des monuments français in 1809, from *Inventaire général des richesses d'art de la France: Archives du Musée des monuments français*, 3 vols. (Paris: Plon, 1883-1897). unpaginated

The Origin of the Pointed Arch: "Architecture called Gothic is truly Arab or Saracen architecture" –Alexander Lenoir, 1809

The origin of the pointed arch was a subject of intense scholarly debate at the turn of the nineteenth century.[7] Nationalism fueled the rhetoric of many of Lenoir's contemporaries, ranging from the British archbishop John Milner, who favored the idea of the pointed arch as an indigenously English form derived from the "happy effect of those intersecting semicircular arches" characteristic of Norman ornament, to critics like the French architect J.-C. Huet, who reiterated a long-standing belief that the interlocking branches of trees had inspired the first architects of Gothic buildings.[8] "Observe the position of the first branches," urged Huet, "you see them extending out from the trunk, appearing to the eye like as so many stone ribs of ogive arches…."[9] In Huet's mind, there was a literal (and positivist) link between Gothic architecture and the Goths as ancient inhabitants of Gaul; he argued, thus, that the foundation of Gothic art was to be found in France. "Why deny our ancestors their part of the glory?" Huet protested.[10] He likened the builders of French Gothic cathedrals to masters of the Italian Renaissance like Filippo Brunelleschi: as Italian architects of the fourteenth and fifteenth century had "purged" their buildings of the "vices" inherent in the "barbarian" architecture constructed in the years following the Fall of Rome, so French medieval architects adopted the best aspects of ancient "Gaulois" buildings in order to create works of "unique boldness" that towered to "inconceivable heights."[11]

Lenoir stubbornly dismissed any claim other than one that placed the origin of the pointed arch squarely in the Levant. He specifically singled out Huet and the British scientist, Sir James Hall (who had endeavored to prove an arboreal origin for the pointed arch by growing a Gothic "willow cathedral" in his own garden[12]) for rebuttal, asserting that physical evidence did not support the idea of such woodland structures in Gaul. The architectural legacy of the "Gaulois," Lenoir maintained, consisted solely of megaliths and grottos.[13] Instead, he contended, the pointed arch found its beginning in the eastern Mediterranean region he referred to as Syria.[14] And while Lenoir was far from the only proponent of such an origin for the pointed arch (without explanation, he essentially side-stepped the possibility it had traveled to Europe via Islamic Spain), his unique reasoning stands as an extraordinary (and willfully eclectic) mélange of French historiography, Johann Joachim Winckelmann's theories of artistic progress and decline, mythography, and Freemasonry.[15]

On the one hand, Lenoir argued that much of the confusion regarding the origin of the pointed arch lay in its mistaken association with the term Gothic.[16] Like Diderot's *Encyclopédie* before him, Lenoir claimed that the label Gothic, properly applied, was just that; it referred to the architecture of the migrating pagan tribes following the Fall of Rome.[17] Whereas Huet saw soaring forest structures created by the Goths, Lenoir maintained that the Goths remained ignorant of the fine arts, precluded by their continual state of warfare and barbarism. He felt their style of building, notably of megaliths and grottos, constituted what should be considered Gothic architecture. Under Charlemagne, a resurgence of the building style favored by the ancient Romans (which Lenoir sometimes called "Lombard") followed, with its "perfect curves of an arch" and "pilasters and columns."[18] This Roman or Lombard style, he contended, was abandoned during the epoch of the crusades. It was at this time, in

Lenoir's view, that a new style of architecture, one in which the "ogive arch replaces the arch," was introduced into France by artists who had traveled with the crusaders in order to reclaim Jerusalem from its Muslim rulers.[19] To call this style Gothic, in Lenoir's view, was a gross misnomer. Instead, he advocated that architecture featuring the ogive (or pointed) arch be called "syrien" after its place of origin.[20]

Citing the seventeenth-century historian François Eudes de Mézeray, Lenoir stated that the transmission of the "style syrien" to France was advanced by the many artists who, in 1248, accompanied Louis IX on the Seventh Crusade.[21] Lenoir specifically recalled the tradition that the architect Eudes de Montreuil (d. 1287; also spelled "Montreau" by Lenoir) had been a member of the king's retinue.[22] This convention went back to the late sixteenth century and the Franciscan monk André Thévet, who purported that Eudes, who was buried in the monastery of the Cordeliers in Paris, journeyed with Louis and, while encamped in Syria, was responsible for building the fortifications at Jaffa (now a suburb of modern Tel Aviv).[23] Lenoir cautioned his readers not to confuse Eudes with Pierre de Montreuil (also spelled Montreau, who died in 1267 and was buried in the Grande Chapelle de la Vierge at Saint-Germain-des-Prés). Yet, Lenoir himself appears to have fallen victim to the same conflation, asserting that his "celebrated Montreau" was the architect who built both the Sainte-Chapelle and the refectory of Saint-Germain-des-Prés in the "style of [buildings] which he had seen and copied in Jerusalem."[24]

Lenoir, building upon this implicit link between Louis IX and "his personal architect," posited that the influence of a Syrian sojourn on the architect he called "Montreau" could be proven through visual comparison of the cathedral of Paris with the Sainte-Chapelle.[25] While acknowledging the admirable plan of Notre-Dame, Lenoir pejoratively contrasted the cathedral's massiveness and lack of interior ornamentation to the "lightness" as well as bold and forward-thinking design of Louis IX's royal chapel. In his view, the Sainte-Chapelle offered "a perfect imitation of Arab monuments."[26] In order to create the latter, Lenoir believed the architect "Montreau" must have studied what he called the "primitive beauty" of Syrian "temples" in the field, insisting that the "bold style of architecture [practiced by Montreau] was copied from the Arabs."[27] This included not only the adoption of the pointed arch, but the signature effect of stained glass windows. "One admires the magical effect of stained glass," Lenoir observed, "which when struck by sunlight reflects its vibrant and varied colors upon the paintings and the gilding ornamenting the columns and vaults [of the building]."[28] It was this impression of the "mystical colors" produced by stained glass that Lenoir saw as something completely new in French art—a "foreign physiognomy" that distinguished buildings created following the king's return from crusade.[29] And here, one must bear in mind that Lenoir's knowledge of building chronology (e.g. that the Sainte-Chapelle was dedicated before Louis IX left on crusade rather than constructed upon the king's return) was at best in error. Lenoir had an enormous capacity to construct and collapse time to suit his artistic theories.[30]

While in his later years, Lenoir (incorrectly) conceded that Eudes and Pierre were likely one in the same (thus attempting to resolve the discrepancy he himself had perpetuated), he never veered from his fundamental belief that Louis IX's architect was responsible for bringing the pointed arch to France from Syria.[31] To an artist like Lenoir, well-educated in the merits of the *Prix de Rome*, this kind of design migration was a time-honored process in the development of style. In returning from travels abroad, artists would have absorbed the "focus, the style, the forms, and the taste of ancient monuments which they had studied…." It mirrored the practice, he observed, that was followed by artists in his own day.[32] The evidence lay in what Lenoir believed was a complete change of style following the king's homecoming.[33] Moreover, he vigorously denied that any one European nation could lay claim to Gothic architecture, signaling out in particular the pretensions of the English and Germans. Even Richard the Lionheart (1157-1199), Lenoir surmised, could not have brought the idea of the pointed arch from the East since artists were not allowed to remain with him during his detention in Germany at the end of the Third Crusade. Lenoir concluded: "In a word, the English are not the inventors of Gothic architecture." In a similar vein, Lenoir responded to a claim that the industrious Germans were the originators of the pointed arch by asserting that the people of each nation interpreted what they saw in Syria in their own way, modifying it according to their own national preferences.[34]

There was a certain political advantage in emphasizing this link with Syria. As Lenoir himself recounts, in 1800 Napoleon Bonaparte, then First Counsel, stood beneath the luminous blue vaults of the Gallery of the Thirteenth Century in the Musée des monuments français [Fig. 2] and exclaimed: "Lenoir, you transport me to Syria."[35] Lenoir likely highlighted this encounter not so much for political expediency (especially in light of Bonaparte's disastrous Syrian Campaign of 1799), but because he wished to imply official validation of his connection between the pointed arch and Syria.[36]

Indeed, Lenoir's zealous resolve to position the beginnings of the pointed arch in Syria was rooted in his own philosophical sympathies with

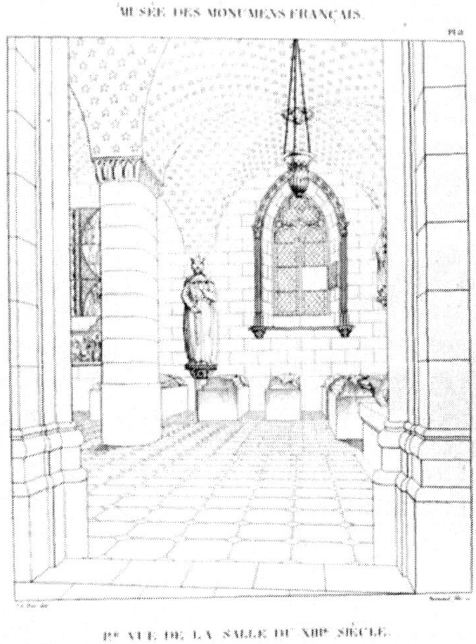

Fig. 2 Gallery of the Thirteenth Century, Musée des monuments français, from J.E. Biet and J.P. Brès, *Souvenirs du Musée des monumens français* (Paris: l'auteur et al., 1821). Pl. 13

mythography and Freemasonry. These convictions revealed themselves in his eccentric belief that the structural form of the pointed arch had ultimately derived from the egg (*oeuf*): "In cutting an egg in two equal parts, one has precisely an ogive arch."[37] In truth, Lenoir's surprising coupling of the pointed arch and the egg was part of a wider intellectual phenomenon that sought to elucidate a broad-reaching system of religious syncretism. This reductive and comparative approach had the effect of both diminishing the primacy of Christianity and elevating the moral authority of natural law. These principles were fundamental to Lenoir's way of thinking and Dominique Poulot is absolutely correct in observing that such late eighteenth-century ideals guided Lenoir throughout his adult life.[38]

Lenoir was specifically influenced by the mythographer Charles-François Dupuis (1742-1809), a member of the Institute de France and the subject of a portrait painting by Lenoir's wife Adélaïde.[39] In his multi-volume work, *Abrégé de l'origine de tous les cultes*, Dupuis argued that all religious traditions were ultimately extrapolated from nature. Accordingly, the ancient veneration of primal forms and elements was interpreted as having established the very basis of religious expression and practice among all peoples. For example, the sun, the moon, and stars were exemplified as having been worshiped from the very beginnings of history.[40] For Dupuis and other like-minded writers, such as Constantin-François Volney (1757-1820), the egg served as a collective symbol for the world. Both emphasized creation myths in which the egg/world was born through oral ejection.[41] Dupuis recognized the construct of its opposing identical halves as leading in later cultures to the egg's interpretation as an ancient emblem of the dual nature of good and evil, light and darkness, attributes that would find a place within Lenoir's theories as well.[42]

Lenoir took the singular approach of applying Dupuis' model to Gothic architecture.[43] In claiming the ogive arch to be a "representation of the sacred egg (*oeuf sacré*)," Lenoir reiterated that it had long been revered by the people of Asia as a symbol of the world and universal harmony. Like Dupuis, he traced the egg back to creation myths of the ancient Egyptians. The Persians, for whom he believed the egg represented unsullied light, were additionally singled out, as were the Greeks, for whom Lenoir claimed it symbolized the earth, and the followers of Bacchus, who found in the egg the principle of regeneration.[44] Given the ancients' proclivity to reuse forms from nature and to infuse them with symbolic meaning, Lenoir credited the holiness of the egg as the inspiration for its use in the decoration of their temples (e.g. the egg-and-dart motif), thus initiating an association between it and religious architecture, an association later codified in the shape of the ogive arch.[45] To Lenoir, ancient Syria (the Levant) was a kind of primal stew in which mythic associations and artistic developments mixed in a fluid and non-determinate manner. It was exactly this ancient heritage that influenced the "Saracens," who, he contended, had migrated from their native Arabia to Syria around the seventh century CE, a view that clearly informed his interchangeable use of the terms "Arabe" and "syrien."[46]

Unbuffeted by arguments like those of François-René de Chateaubriand (1768-1848), who interpreted Gothic architecture in terms of its inexorable bond with Christianity, Lenoir embraced the ancient universality of the *oeuf sacré*, its origin in Syria, and its role as the underpinning of the pointed arch with such unwavering certainty because of his fervent belief in the tenants of Freemasonry. Lenoir strongly embraced the philosophic foundations of this fraternal organization, particularly its notion of a spiritual quest for understanding supported by Masonic guardianship of "knowledge [believed to have been] passed down from Ancient Egypt itself."[47] Moreover, he found Freemasonry's moral emphasis on brotherhood to offer "a perfect picture of active causes in the Universe…a book in which is written the ethics of all people."[48] His commitment to its codes of belief was ardent and resolute.

For Lenoir, who had been introduced by his father and, in 1788, was formally inducted at the age of seventeen,[49] Freemasonry presented a philosophic underpinning for an ethical society in which the precedents of history could govern both the present and future, encompassing, as Lenoir put it, the "three ages of nature."[50] The idea articulated by James Stevens Curl that "architectural history [could be] equated with the development of society, and [that] architecture was seen as a means of establishing a just and ordered system," closely dovetailed with Lenoir's own assessment of historic building types.[51] For although Lenoir personally preferred the symmetry and order of sixteenth-century architecture, he embraced the Gothic, because, by virtue of its origin in Syria, the latter system was born in the same region as the prototypical and metaphorical Masonic building—the divinely inspired Temple of Solomon, whose original builders Freemasons claimed as their forbearers. This connection (however vague) allowed Lenoir to couple the transfer of the pointed arch *to* France with the realization of Masonic principles *in* France.

Lenoir was, thus, committed to tracing the origin of French Masonic rites within the practices of the inhabitants of what he understood to be ancient Syria, the Egyptians and Hebrews. The essential belief that architecture was the very foundation of Freemasonry (indeed, that *le Grand Architecte* was the binding spirit among men) and that the construction of the Temple of Solomon in Jerusalem was the archetypal Masonic building, undoubtedly informed and enforced Lenoir's conviction that the pointed arch had found its genesis in ancient Syria.[52] As a Freemason, Lenoir passionately believed that shapes and forms represented primeval values: "The building of temples by the Ancients, everything religiously ceremonial as well as sacred ornament…was symbolic and spread to join man with nature by the likeness between the appearance of religion and its worship."[53] Such an association is evocatively portrayed in an engraving included in Lenoir's book on the origins of French Freemasonry, published in 1814 [Fig. 3].[54] Ostensibly the engraving shows induction rituals, with initiates passing through fire, water, and air.[55] The architectural setting is rich in meaning. Evocative Egyptian-style columns and capitals commanding the darkened foreground are juxtaposed across a pool of water with a pointed archway bathed in light at the engraving's center. The juxtaposition of these two architectural styles within this context is clear: while the Egyptian orders denote the very beginnings of Masonic rites and ideals, the ogive arch represents their transference to France.

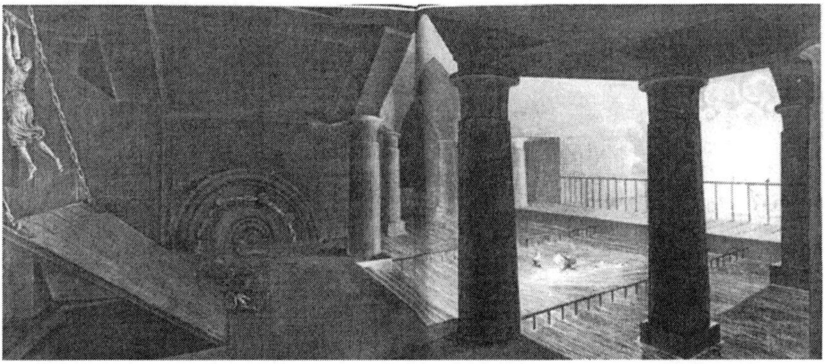

Fig. 3 *Trials by Fire, Water, and Air*, engraving, from Alexandre Lenoir, *Franche-maconnerie rendu a sa veritable origine* (Paris: Fournier, 1814). Pl. 10 (Photo: Trustees of Sir John Soane's Museum, London)

This Syrian link was crucial to Lenoir's belief in France as the inheritor of ancient greatness. From the adoption of the ogive arch (through the form of the egg) by the Saracens, who later populated Syria after "the ancients," Lenoir felt he could securely trace the route of the pointed arch from its origin to its "reinvigoration" and "perfection" in France. Indeed, Lenoir declared that the French had received the ogive from the Saracens.[56] Drawing from Edward Said's pioneering discussion of the idea of the Orient as a European construction, one can see in Lenoir's interpretation of architectural hegemony a variant on Said's "Orientalist stage": a self-interested Western assemblage of Eastern figures and ideas which, in turn, is fed by its own "system of moral and epistemological rigor."[57] For Lenoir, the concept of seminal buildings from ancient Syria, like the Temple of Solomon and the Saracens' adoption of pointed arches, provided a foundation for French art in the origins of civilization. But it also reflected, in a broader sense, the widespread French belief in the superiority of their culture.[58] This view, both linear and unfolding, embraced history and national identity in an extraordinary way. The adoption of the pointed arch through the aegis of Louis IX established this era as the inception of French art; just as French Freemasonry had its origins in Syria (the premise of Lenoir's book on Masonry), so too the pointed arch, with its Eastern beginnings, transferred the signification of the *œuf sacré*, with its associations of light, harmony, and regeneration, to France, and thus, provided the nourishing landscape from which French art could develop.

By advancing a theory based on the Arab origin of the pointed arch, and his increasing use of the term "l'architecture syrienne," paired with the French adoption and perfection of the form, Lenoir could establish (and validate) a foundation for his vision of the progress of French art.[59] In this way and in response to his critics, Lenoir furthered his aim of bestowing legitimacy upon the French historical past, demonstrating the value, in his words, of the "usefulness" of the Middle Ages within the continuum of French civilization. Thus, with its arrival in France and its "reinvigoration" upon French soil, the pointed arch functioned to designate a breaking point with the old and the initiation of true French artistic accomplishment.[60]

The *Cour Arabe*: "The Saracens' type of decoration, adopted in France following our crusades" —Alexandre Lenoir, 1809

Lenoir's theory of the *oeuf sacré* and the transfer of the pointed arch from Syria to France directly informed his design for the *Cour Arabe* [Fig. 1]. It was one of three courtyards unfolding from the Museum's entryway off the old Rue des Petits Augustins (now the Rue Bonaparte) that led to an English-style Elysium garden filled with tombs of great French *savants* like Descartres, Molière, La Fontaine, and Montfaucon.[61] Like the secluded and private "Elysium" described in Jean-Jacques Rousseau's celebrated epistolary novel *Julie, ou La Nouvelle Héloïse* (1761), Lenoir's *Jardin Elysée* was intended to function as an enclosed and self-contained environment, walled on four sides. Just as Julie's Elysium was noted to be "quite close to the house, [but] so well hidden…that it cannot be seen from anywhere," so Lenoir's garden was intended to be obscured by this succession of three courtyards between the Museum's entrance and that of the *Elysée*.[62] These spaces not only served to screen the garden from the immediate view of visitors entering the Museum complex, but also sequentially prepared the visitor to experience the garden and its redolence of the past.[63] Lenoir sought to adapt each courtyard to its respective time period by providing a signature façade which would serve to represent the three most notable epochs in French architecture: "The artist and art lover will enjoy seeing the three different styles [of architecture] that were successively used in France."[64] The first, dubbed the Courtyard of the Sixteenth Century, was composed of architectural elements taken from Diane de Poitiers' Chateau at Anet (ninety-five kilometers west of Paris) and was located directly outside the Museum's entrance.[65] The Courtyard of the Fifteenth Century, which followed, was installed with sections from the Chateau Gaillon of Cardinal d'Amboise (ninety-two kilometers northwest of Paris).[66]

Unlike the other two courtyards, with their representative façades composed of architectural elements removed from chateaux at Anet and Gaillon, there was no immediately recognizable structure for what Lenoir called the *Cour Arabe*. Rather, Lenoir envisioned this courtyard to occupy what had originally been the Petits Augustins' "small cloister."[67] The pointed arch was its intended focus. Lenoir designed an expansive gateway for the western end of the courtyard which, in turn, served as the entrance to the *Jardin Elysée* [Fig. 4]. Lenoir projected the structure to be "decorated with ogive arches forming arcades" gleaned from the "debris of ancient monuments."[68] Indeed, the projected structure was laid out in the manner of a church choir screen and articulated with original fragments from the Grande Chapelle de la Vierge (1244-1247) from the nearby abbey of Saint-Germain-des-Prés. This method of *bricolage* lay at the very heart of Lenoir's efforts of historical presentation. As with his tomb for Abelard and Heloise and numerous other monuments created for the Museum, Lenoir was not only proficient, but fearless, in removing objects from their original contexts and transforming them into polemical attributes to bolster his passionately held beliefs.[69]

Like a choir screen, Lenoir's "Arab" façade was intended both as an entrance and a partition. Recalling the basic organization of the Sainte-Madeleine jubé in Troyes, a triplet of cusped dado elements signaled the opening [Fig. 5].[70] Lenoir also added colonnettes to the gateway's dado heads, creating an open arcade. Access to the *Jardin Elysée* was possible, but the colonnettes also provided a kind of visual stop. It was not an open thruway (as at Troyes). Flanking this central ensemble were classical-style porticos that bring to mind the similar configuration (lacking the famous spiral staircases) at Saint-Etienne-du-Mont, a church in the vicinity of the Musée des monuments français and one with which Lenoir was familiar, having removed works of art from its enclosure [Fig. 6].[71] Certainly the Saint-Etienne-du-Mont jubé cannot be interpreted as more than general inspiration for Lenoir, but it is entirely possible that he saw in its general disposition a broadly conceived design solution for his "Arab" façade.

If he kept the idea of the porticos, he replaced the classical entablatures used in the Saint-Etienne jubé doorways with cusped trefoil moldings to echo the similarly shaped lancet heads used in the *Cour Arabe* gateway. Lenoir's choice of angels in the outer doorway spandrels recalls the angels carved in relief within the interior dado and reliquary platform spandrels of Louis IX's Sainte-Chapelle (designed, according to Lenoir, by the

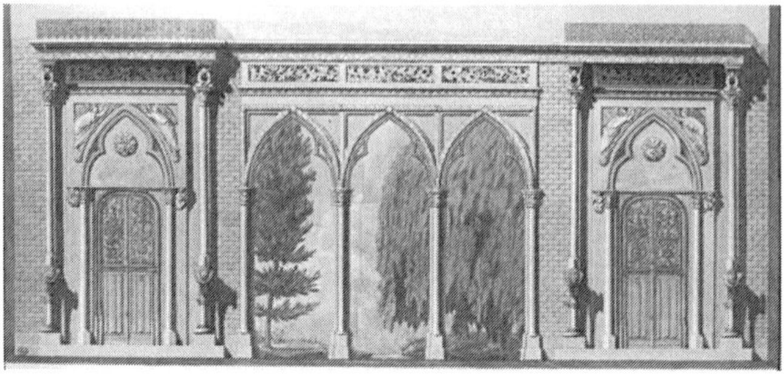

Fig. 4 Alexandre Lenoir, Design for the gateway of the *Cour Arabe*, drawing, undated, Arts graphiques, RF5279/37r, Musée du Louvre, Paris (Photo: Réunion des musées nationaux/Art Resource, NY)

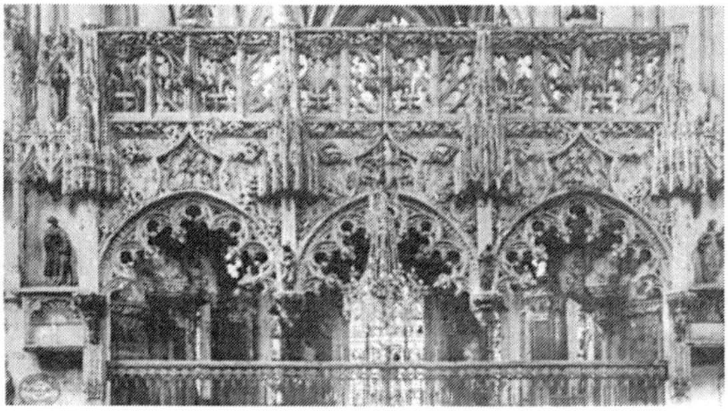

Fig. 5 Jubé, Sainte-Madeleine, Troyes, 1508-1515, postcard (Photo: Collection of the Author)

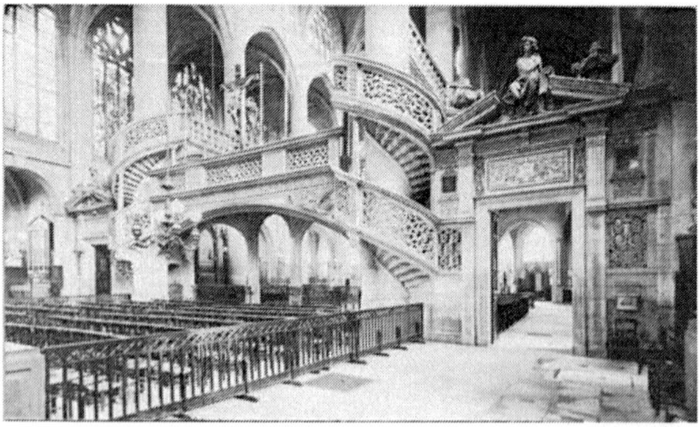

Fig. 6 Jubé, Saint-Etienne-du-Mont, Paris, ca. 1545 (Photo: Northwestern University, Special Collections)

king's architect "Montreau" in imitation of Arab monuments), as well as the angels depicted in the spandrels flanking the entryway of the Saint-Etienne-du-Mont jubé. Lenoir also called for foliate-head bosses to be installed at the apex of each trefoil;[72] one such *masque feuillu* likely survives at the Musée national du Moyen Age in Paris. While not octagonal in shape (like the Musée national example), the bosses shown in Lenoir's drawing strongly parallel the extant mask in the interpretation of the oak leaves, gaping mouth, and distinctively up-turned nose.[73] This attention to detail was important. In addition to the signature feature of the pointed arch, such grotesques and lush floral ornament (evoking Eastern textiles "brought to France by the crusaders") and other "arabesques," were essential features of Lenoir's definition of "Arab" or "Syrian-style" architecture.[74]

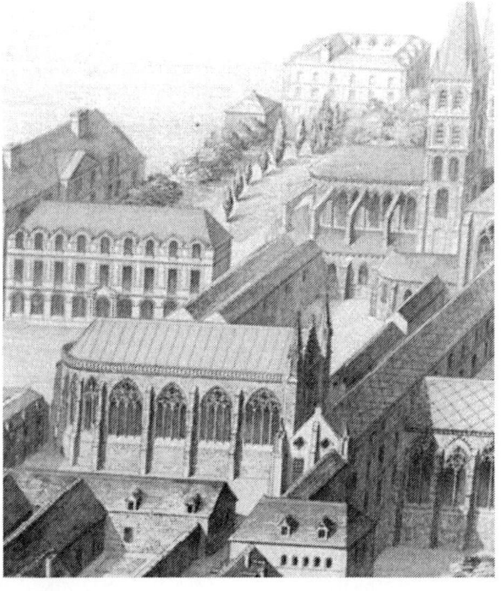

Fig. 7 Grande Chapelle de la Vierge, 1244-1247, Saint-Germain-des-Prés, from Albert Lenoir, *Statistique monumentale de Paris*, vol. 1 (Paris: Imprimerie impériale, 1867). Pl. XII

In this way, the gateway exhibited Lenoir's belief in the fundamental connection between the pointed arch and the "style Arabe." His strategic use of original architectural dado heads as emblematic "ogives" provided an authentic voice in making this correlation. Lenoir was not being pragmatic in deciding which architectural debris to salvage: he specifically chose fragments from the nearby Grande Chapelle de la Vierge at Saint-Germain-des-Prés [Fig. 7]. This sublime building, a free-standing chapel built by Pierre de Montreuil and comparable in date and design to the Sainte-Chapelle, had been sold and demolished by 1802.[75] By 1805, Lenoir was touting "ogives" from the razed chapel having been installed in the *Cour Arabe*.[76] He made explicit the connection between these style elements and their origin in Syria by singling out the celebrated "Montreau" as the architect of the Saint-Germain-des-Prés chapel, which he stated had been made for Louis IX.[77] In principle, this architectural *spolia* was not so much a metonymic shorthand standing in for its provenance, as suggested by Stephen Bann.[78] Rather, Lenoir intended the literal presence of pointed arches designed by "Montreau" himself—the agent of the ogive's transfer from Syria to France—to make his theory manifest. As such, the gateway, as the entrance to the *Jardin Elysée*, with its tombs of illustrious French writers and philosophers, was not a commemoration of the past or a *lieu de mémoire*, in the sense Pierre Nora has framed constructions of social memory, it was, at its core, an artistic proof utilizing material evidence to demonstrate the validity of the Arab (or "syrienne") origin of the pointed arch.[79]

Lenoir's design for the gateway was never fully realized. A colored drawing now in the Bibliothèque nationale de France shows the appliqué of the Saint-Germain-des-Prés dado triplet above the barrel-vaulted walkway, probably one reused from the original Petits Augustins complex [Fig. 8]. The doorway portico drawn at the left is much less sumptuous than in the earlier design, yet the distinctive foliate head is visible within the cusped trefoil. Despite such a desultory realization—especially given the prominence of the massive rounded archway within a structure meant to evoke the perfection of the ogive arch—one can still understand the courtyard having been intended both as a destination ("the third courtyard of the Museum of French Monuments," "the last courtyard of the Museum"), as well as the entrance to the *Jardin Elysée*.[80] These indications of directional focus are significant, as they reiterate the Winckelmannian emphasis on artistic progression of which Lenoir was an eager proponent. But while the courtyard was labeled as the "third" and the "last," it was by no means considered an end. Following Winckelmann's developmental schema, the gateway—with its direct tie to Louis IX's architect "Montreau"—signaled both the invention of the pointed arch in Syria and demonstrated its manifestation on French soil.[81] The gateway of the *Cour Arabe* functioned as Lenoir's corollary validation of this theory, both metaphorically and literally serving as the threshold for French artistic greatness.

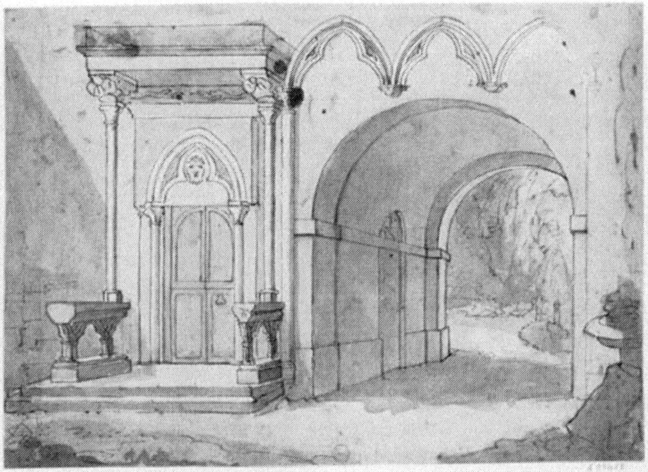

Fig. 8 Anonymous, *Entrée du jardin des Petits Augustins* (Lenoir's gateway of the *Cour Arabe)*, drawing, 1818, Estampes, Rés Ve-53g fol., Collection M. Hippolyte Destailleur, Paris, t. 5, no. 943, Bibliothèque nationale de France, Paris (Photo: Bibliothèque nationale de France)

Notes

[1] My investigation of Lenoir's theories on the origin of the pointed arch as deriving from the "oeuf sacré" (the sacred egg), his belief that medieval crusaders from France first encountered this architectural form in Syria, and his creation of a courtyard at the Musée des monuments français—dubbed the "Cour Arabe" (the Arab Courtyard)—to artistically confirm these convictions is part of a larger study on Lenoir's interpretation of medieval art. These ideas have been aired in a variety of forums, including the International Congress of Medieval Studies, Western Michigan University, Kalamazoo, MI (2003); the Mid-America Medieval Association, University of Missouri, Columbia, MO (2004); and the International Medieval Congress, University of Leeds, UK (2004). I am grateful to Elisabeth Antoine, Elizabeth Childs, Michael W. Cothren, Elizabeth Emery, Claudine Lautier, and Janet Marquardt who all provided valuable help at junctures along the way, together with Susan Palmer, archivist at Sir John Soane's Museum and Russell Maylone, Curator of Special Collections at Northwestern University. I am also indebted to the American Council of Learned Societies for funding my work on Lenoir. Unless otherwise indicated, translations from the original French are my own. It is with heartfelt gratitude and affection that I dedicate this essay in honor of

my first graduate advisor, Prof. Marion E. Roberts, upon her retirement from the University of Virginia.

[2] Louis Réau, *Histoire du vandalisme: Les Monuments détruits de l'art français*, ed. Michel Fleury and Guy-Michel Leproux (Paris: Editions Robert Laffont, 1994). 297

[3] J. E. Biet and J. P. Brès, *Souvenirs du Musée des monumens français* (Paris: l'auteur et al., 1821). no pagination

[4] Recent studies include Alain Erlande-Brandenburg, "Alexandre Lenoir et le Musée des monuments français," in *Le "Gothique" retrouvé avant Viollet-le-Duc*, exh. cat., Paris, Hôtel de Sully 1979-1980 (Paris: Caisse Nationale des Monuments Historiques et des Sites, 1979). 75-84; Stephen Bann, *The Clothing of Clio: A Study of the Representation of History in Nineteenth-Century Britain and France* (Cambridge: Cambridge University Press, 1984). 77-92; Francis Haskell, *History and its Images: Art and the Interpretation of the Past* (New Haven: Yale University Press, 1993). 236-252; Andrew McClellan, *Inventing the Louvre: Art, Politics, and the Origins of the Modern Museum in Eighteenth-Century Paris* (Berkeley: University of California Press, 1999). 155-197; and Dominique Poulot, "Alexandre Lenoir et les Musées des monuments français," in *Les Lieux de mémoire*, ed. Pierre Nora, vol. 2 (Paris: Gallimard, 1984). 497-531; and Dominique Poulot, *Musée, nation, patrimoine 1789-1815* (Paris: Gallimard, 1997).

[5] Anthony Vidler should be singled out for his brief, but considered, discussion of the courtyards in *The Writing on the Walls: Architectural Theory in the Late Enlightenment* (Princeton: Princeton Architectural Press, 1987). 172-173; McClellan, *Inventing the Louvre*. 118

[6] Jacques Vanuxem, "Aperçus sur quelques tableaux représentant le Musée des monuments français de Lenoir," *Bulletin de la Société de l'Histoire de l'Art Français* 1971 (1972). 145-151. Vanuxem is one of the only scholars to recognize the critical importance of the Levant to Lenoir. See also Poulot, *Musée, nation, patrimoine*. 335; and Dominique Poulot, "L'Egypte imaginaire d'Alexandre Lenoir," in *L'Egypte imaginaire de la Renaissance à Champollion*, ed. Chantal Grell (Paris: Presses de l'Université de Paris-Sorbonne, 2001). 127-149. Poulot touches on many of the elements contributing to Lenoir's perspective on Syria/Egypt without fully integrating the pointed arch.

[7] The origin of the pointed arch is no longer such a focus of modern inquiry. Paul Frankl's emphasis on the rib vault as the defining element of Gothic architecture, first published in 1962, led to the current approach of emphasizing the integration of the pointed arch with this vaulting system to obtain height in concert with the aesthetic qualities of linearity and lightness, both of which contribute to a veritable transparency in the wall surface. Paul Frankl, *Gothic Architecture*, rev. Paul Crossley (New Haven: Yale University Press, 2000). 41-50

[8] John Milner, *A Treatise on the Ecclesiastical Architecture of England, during the Middle Ages* (London: J. Taylor, 1811). ii-iii. For summaries of the "tree theory" see Paul Frankl, *The Gothic: Literary Sources and Interpretations through Eight Centuries* (Princeton: Princeton University Press, 1960). 273-274, 403; Jurgis Baltrušaitis, *Aberrations: An Essay on the Legend of Forms*, trans. Richard Miller

(Cambridge, MA: MIT Press, 1989). 108-135. On eighteenth-century appraisals of Gothic architecture see Robin Middleton, "The Abbé de Cordemoy and the Graeco-Gothic Ideal: A Prelude to Romantic Classicism," *Journal of the Warburg and Courtauld Institutes* 25 (1962). 278-320, esp. 303-305; and Robin Middleton, "The Abbé de Cordemoy and the Graeco-Gothic Ideal: A Prelude to Romantic Classicism," *Journal of the Warburg and Courtauld Institutes* 26 (1963). 90-123

[9] "faire germer dans l'imagination des premiers architectes gothiques le désir d'imiter dans leurs constructions ces temples vivans, ouvrages de la nature….Observez la position des premières branches; vous les verrez, sortant de leur tronc, présenter à vos yeux comme autant d'arêtes d'ogive…." J.-C. Huet, *Parallèle des temples anciens, gothiques et modernes* (Paris: Desenne, 1809). 38-39

[10] "Pourquoi…priver nos ancêtres d'une portion de gloire...?" Ibid. 42

[11] Ibid. 46, 42 respectively

[12] Sir James Hall, *Essay on the Origin, History, and Principles of Gothic Architecture* (London: W. Bulmer, 1813). 17

[13] Alexandre Lenoir, *Musée des momunens français, ou Description historique et chronologique…pour servir à l'Histoire de France et à celle de l'Art*, 8 vols. (Paris: Guilleminet-Nepreux, years IX [1800]-1821). 7: 129, 216 (hereafter Lenoir, *Description historique*); Alexandre Lenoir, "De l'architecture syrienne," Estampes, Ya2 151-8, t. 4, 114, Bibliothèque nationale de France, Paris.

[14] In the early nineteenth century, "Syria" was part of the Ottoman Empire. Historically, it encompassed lands bordering the eastern shore of the Mediterranean Sea stretching from the modern nations of Greece to Egypt. See http://ccat.sas.upenn.edu/~rs143/Resources/Pics/rels143a.jpg

[15] The Spanish connection was one Lenoir did his best to avoid, finally allowing that the appearance of the pointed arch in Iberia was a parallel manifestation, rather than any kind of direct influence. Alexandre Lenoir, "Sur l'origine de l'architecture appelée improprement gothique," *Mémoires de l'académie celtique ou mémoires d'antiquités celtiques, gauloises et françaises* 3 (1809). 352. See also Matilde Mateo, "The Making of the Saracen Style: The Crusades and Medieval Architecture in the British Imagination of the 18th and 19th Centuries," in *The Crusades: Other Experiences, Alternate Perspectives*, ed. Khalil I. Semaan (Binghamton: Center for Medieval and Early Renaissance Studies, 2003). 115-140; Matilde Mateo, "En busca del origen del Gótico: El viaje de Thomas Pitt por España en 1760," *Goya* 292 (2003). 9-22

[16] Although Lenoir's contemporary (and detractor) Quatremère de Quincy referenced Giorgio Vasari's sixteenth-century assessment of late-medieval architecture as a barbarian style associated with the German nomadic tribes, Lenoir never mentions this progenitor of the term. His focus was relentlessly literal and nationalistic. Antoine Quatremère de Quince, *Dictionnaire historique d'architecture comprenant de son plan les notions historiques, descriptives, archéologiques* (Paris: A. Le Clère, 1832). 671

[17] Jacques-François Blondel the Younger, "Architecture Françoise" in Denis Diderot, ed., *Encyclopédie; ou Dictionnaire raisonné des sciences, des arts et des*

métiers, par une société des gens des letters, ed. Denis Diderot, vol. 1 (Paris: Briasson, 1751). 617

[18] "des cintres parfaits, des pilastres et des colonnes…." Lenoir, "De l'architecture syrienne." 113

[19] "l'ogive a remplacé l'arc dans l'architecture." Ibid. 113-114. See also Lenoir, *Description historique*. 2:39; Lenoir, *Description historique*. 3:2; Jean-Baptiste Séroux d'Agincourt, *Histoire de l'art par les monuments, depuis sa décadence au IVe siècle jusqu'à son renouvellement au XVIe*, vol. 1 (Paris: Treuttel et Wurtz, 1810). 55, 66

[20] Lenoir, "De l'architecture syrienne." 114. For Lenoir's equation of the pointed arch with the ogive see Stephanie Moore Glaser, "Explorations of the Gothic Cathedral in Nineteenth-Century France" (Ph.D. diss., Indiana University, 2004). 363-364 n. 14. I am indebted to Elizabeth Emery for this reference.

[21] Lenoir, "De l'architecture syrienne." 115; François Eudes de Mézeray, *Abrégé chronologique de l'histoire de France*, vol. 5 (Amsterdam: D. Mortier, 1755). 359

[22] Alexandre Lenoir, *Description historique et chronologique des monumens de sculpture, réunis au Musée des monumens français*, 3rd ed. (Paris: au Musée, year V [1796]). 12; Lenoir, *Description historique*. 1: 193-194; 2:18 n.6

[23] André Thévet, *Les Vrais portraits et vies des homes illustres, 1584: A facsimile reproduction*, vol. 1 (Delmar: Scholar's Facsimiles & Reprints, 1973). 503-504; Robert Branner, *St. Louis and the Court Style in Gothic Architecture* (London: A. Zwemmer, 1965). 8 n. 25, 117 n.17

[24] "de retour en France, il bâtit plusieurs édifices dans le goût de ceux qu'il avait vus et copiés à Jérusalem…." Lenoir, *Description historique*. 1:193-194; 2:18 n. 6. It was not Eudes but Pierre who had traditionally been credited with designing the Sainte-Chapelle, an attribution that came under question only with the pioneering work of Robert Branner in the 1960s. See Branner, *Court Style*. 61

[25] "son architecte particulier." Lenoir, "De l'architecture syrienne." 115

[26] "La sainte Chapelle de Paris, ornée de ses vitraux magnifiques, de ses peintures et de ses dorures antiques, était une imitation parfaite des monumens arabes...." Alexandre Lenoir, *Recueil de gravures pour servir à l'histoire des arts en France prouvée par les monumens* (Paris: no publisher, 1811). 39

[27] "la belle ordonnance de ce dernier édifice, que son auteur avait étudié l'architecture syrienne sur les lieux." Lenoir, "De l'architecture syrienne." 115-116; Lenoir, *Description historique*. 2:18 n. 6

[28] "On admirait surtout l'effet magique des vitraux, qui, frappés du soleil, réfléchissaient les couleurs les plus vives et les plus variées sur les peintures et les dorures dont les colonnes et la voûte étaient ornées." Lenoir, "De l'architecture syrienne." 116

[29] "les couleurs mystiques...une physionomie étrangère." Lenoir, *Description historique*. 3:8. For Lenoir's theories on medieval stained glass see Mary B. Shepard, "Medieval Stained Glass and Alexandre Lenoir," in *The Four Modes of Seeing: Approaches to Medieval Art*, ed. Evelyn Staudinger Lane, Elizabeth Carson Pastan, and Ellen Shortell (Aldershot: Ashgate Publishers, 2008). chap. 27

[30] For example, Lenoir used thirteenth-century dado elements from the nave of Saint-Denis for his tomb for Abelard and Heloise, but maintained they originated from the time of Abbot Suger (1081–1151), so as to associate these framing elements more closely with the twelfth-century lovers. Mary B. Shepard, "A Tomb for Abelard and Heloise," *Romance Studies* 25, 1 (2007). 35

[31] Lenoir, *Description historique*. 7:117-118

[32] "la direction, le style, les formes et le goût des anciens monumens qu'ils avaient étudiés sur les lieux mêmes. C'est ce qui se pratique encore de nos jours." Ibid. 2:20

[33] Lenoir, "Sur l'origine de…gothique." 350-351; Lenoir, *Description historique*. 7:90. Louis IX returned from crusade in 1252, but Lenoir, preferring a more nebulous timeline, never cites a specific date, or even decade.

[34] "En un mot, les Anglais ne sont pas les inventeurs de l'architecture gothique…." Ibid. 7:139-140; Lenoir, "Sur l'origine de…gothique." 353-354; Lenoir, "De l'architecture syrienne." 122. For the claim of German invention see Bernard Hundeshagen, "Sur les formes générales et les principaux traits de l'architecture gothique des églises, surtout par rapport à son origine," *Mémoires de l'académie celtique* 3 (1809). 357

[35] "Lenoir, vous me transportez en Syrie." Quoted in Alexandre Lenoir, *Description historique et chronologique des monumens de sculpture, réunis au Musée des monumens français*, 6th ed. (Paris: Chez l'auteur et al., year X de la République 1801-1802). 124

[36] Paintings of Napoleon's battles in Egypt and Syria were yet to come, including Antoine-Jean Gros' epic work, *Napoleon Visiting the Plague House at Jaffa* (1804), which lionized the moral superiority of the general in the face of humiliating defeat.

[37] "en coupant un oeuf en deux parties égales, on a précisément un arc ogive…." Lenoir, "De l'architecture syrienne." 114

[38] Poulot, "L'Egypte imaginaire d'Alexandre Lenoir." 131

[39] For Adélaïde Lenoir's portrait of Dupuis (exhibited at the 1808 Salon) see Emile Bellier de La Chavignerie and Louis Auvray, *Dictionnaire général des artistes de l'école française depuis l'origine des arts du dessin jusqu'à nos jours* (Paris: Renouard, 1882-1887). 1004; Pierre Sanchez and Xavier Seydoux, *Les Catalogues des salons des Beaux-Arts*, vol. 1 (Paris: Echelle de Jacob, 1999). 154

[40] Charles-François Dupuis, *Abrégé de l'origine de tous les cultes* (Paris: H. Agasse, year VI [1797]). esp. chap. 2; Charles François Dupuis, *The Origin of All Religious Worship*, intro. and trans. Robert D. Richardson, Jr. (New York: Garland, 1984). v-vii, 6-14

[41] Dupuis, *Abrégé de l'origine de tous les cultes*. 82; Dupuis, *Origin of All Religious Worship*. 70; C.-F. Volney, *Les Ruines* (Paris: Lebigre Frères, 1833). 251, 253; C.-F. Volney, *Ruins; or, Meditation on the Revolutions of Empires* (Boston: J.P. Mendum, 1869). 111, 112, 147

[42] Dupuis, *Abrégé de l'origine de tous les cultes*. 83, 477-478; Dupuis, *Origin of All Religious Worship*. 70, 83-84

---

[43] Recent analyses regarding the reception of Gothic architecture have overlooked this mythographic dynamic, an important and vibrant vestige of the Enlightenment. See, for example, Françoise Choay, *The Invention of the Historic Monument*, trans. Lauren M. O'Connell (Cambridge: Cambridge University Press, 2001). 47-50; Tina Waldeier Bizzarro, *Romanesque Architectural Criticism: A Prehistory* (Cambridge: Cambridge University Press, 1992). 107-131, esp. 111-112

[44] "L'ogive que nous avons reçue de ces peuples est une représentation de l'oeuf sacré…." Lenoir, *Description historique*. 3:3-4; "Les peuples de l'Asie révéraient l'œuf, ils y voyaient le symbole du monde, et de l'harmonie universelle…." Lenoir, "De l'architecture syrienne." 114

[45] Lenoir, *Description historique*. 3:3; Lenoir, "De l'architecture syrienne." 114

[46] Alexandre Lenoir, "Examen historique de l'architecture saracenique, connue sous le nom d'architecture gothique," *Journal des artistes* 1 (1827). 425

[47] James Stevens Curl, *The Art and Architecture of Freemasonry* (Woodstock: Overlook Press, 1991). 22

[48] "de lier le grande oeuvre de la nature à des idées morales, afin d'en former une doctrine propre à l'instruction des peuples…une véritable religion….Je considère la Franche Maçonnerie…comme un tableau parfait des causes agissantes dans l'Univers, et comme un livre dans lequel on auroit inscrit le moral de tous les peuples." Alexandre Lenoir, *La Franche-maçonnerie rendue à sa véritable origine* (Paris: Fournier, 1814). 1, 7, 6 respectively

[49] Alain Le Bihan, *Francs-maçons et ateliers Parisiens de la Grand Loge de France au XVIIIe siècle (1760-1795)* (Paris: Bibliothèque nationale de France, 1973). 501. During the Napoleonic Empire, Lenoir was associated with the Scottish Rite Lodge of Saint-Jean d'Ecosse du Contrat Social in Paris. Alain Le Bihan, *Francs-maçons Parisiens du Grand Orient de France (fin du XVIIIe siècle)* (Paris: Bibliothèque nationale de France, 1966). 313; Geneviève Bresc-Bautier, "Denon et Lenoir, éternels rivaux, vieux complices," in *Les Vies de Domique-Vivant Denon*, ed. Daniela Gallo, vol. 2 (Paris: La documentation Française, 2001). 374-375. Two years following the closing of the Musée des monuments français (and with the restoration of the monarchy), Lenoir applied to join the Grand Maison Metropolitaine de l'Initiation. MS fr. nouv. acq. 2480, Bibliothèque nationale de France, Paris.

[50] "le trois ages de la nature." Lenoir, *Franche-maçonnerie*. 60

[51] Curl, *Art and Architecture of Freemasonry*. 118

[52] Lenoir, *Description historique*. 7:130-131. On the importance of the *Grand Architecte* in Masonic thinking see Daniel Ligou, ed., *Dictionnaire universel de la Franc-Maçonnerie* (Paris: Editions de Navarre, 1974). 77. For the role of the Temple of Solomon in early Masonic rituals and thought see Vidler, *Writing on the Walls*. 87, 90-92; and Curl, *Art and Architecture of Freemasonry*. 118. I am grateful to Daniel Monk for suggesting a possible Masonic link between Lenoir and his theories of architectural origin.

[53] "La construction des temples, chez les anciens, tout le cérémonial religieux et tout l'appareil des ornemens sacrés…étoilent symboliques et tendent à lier

l'homme à la nature, par des rapports de ressemblance entre l'appareil du culte et l'être adore." Lenoir, *La Franche-maçonnerie*. 289

[54] Ibid. Fig. 10

[55] While the illustration caption cites the trials posed by the Four Elements, Lenoir omits any discussion of earth in his text.

[56] Lenoir, *Description historique*. 3:3

[57] Edward W. Said, *Orientalism* (New York: Pantheon, 1978). 67

[58] Stewart Wolf, "French Civilization and Ethnicity in the Napoleon Empire," *Past and Present* 124 (1989). 96; Said, *Orientalism*. 86-87

[59] Lenoir, "Sur l'origine de l'architecture…gothique." 349

[60] Lenoir, "De l'architecture syrienne." 122

[61] For Lenoir's *Jardin Elysée* see Shepard, "A Tomb for Abelard and Heloise." 31-32; and Roland Recht, "L'Elysée d'Alexandre Lenoir: nature, art et histoire," *Revue Germanique Internationale* 7 (1997). 47-58

[62] "Ce lieu, quoique tout proche de la maison est tellement caché…qu'on ne l'aperçoit de nulle part." Jean-Jacques Rousseau, *La Nouvelle Héloïse*, ed. Daniel Mornet, vol. 3 (Paris: Hachette, 1925). 224; Jean-Jacques Rousseau, *Julie, or the New Heloise. Letters of Two Lovers who Live in a Small Town at the Foot of the Alps*, trans. Philip Stewart and Jean Vaché (Hanover: Dartmouth College and University Press of New England, 1997). 387

[63] In this way, the courtyards were visualized as a series of independent and sequential spaces of time, rather than formal framing devices as described in Vidler, *Writing on the Walls*. 172

[64] "Ainsi, par ce plan, l'artiste et l'amateur jouiront de la vue de trois styles différens, qui ont été successivement employés en France." Lenoir, *Description historique*. 4:58-59

[65] Alexander Lenoir, "Architecture. Enfance et perfection d'art," Estampes, Ya2 151-8, vol. 1, 129, Bibliothèque nationale de France, Paris.

[66] Ibid.

[67] Arts graphiques, RF5279/1 and RF5279/3, Musée du Louvre, Paris. The latter shows the courtyards in their historical guises, with the former *"petit cloître"* designated as "C", "cour Arabe, dit gothique." Lenoir, *Description historique*. 4: Pl. 165

[68] "sera ornée d'ogives formant arcades…."; "débris d'anciens monumens." Ibid. 58. See also a project drawing for the gateway: Arts graphiques, RF5279/37r, Musée du Louvre, Paris.

[69] Shepard, "A Tomb for Abelard and Heloise." 29-42

[70] This dado element, together with other architectural remnants from the Virgin Chapel, now languishes in the *Jardin Apollinare* adjacent to the church of Saint-Germain-des-Prés. See Mary B. Shepard, "The Thirteenth-Century Stained Glass from the Parisian Abbey of Saint-Germain-des-Prés" (Ph.D. diss., Columbia University, 1990). 21-22

[71] See, for example, *Inventaire général des richesses d'art de la France: Archives du Musée des monuments français*, 3 vols. (Paris: Plon, 1883-1897). 1:125, 279; 2:55, 59, 64 (hereafter *Archives du Musée*)

[72] Lenoir, "Architecture. Enfance et perfection d'art." 129

[73] Accession number Cl. 11656. See *Un trésor gothique: La chasse de Nivelles*, exh. cat., Cologne, Schnütgen-Museum and Paris, Musée national du Moyen Age-Thermes et hôtel de Cluny, 1995-1996 (Paris: Editions de la Réunion des musées nationaux, 1996). 284-285. With the closing of the Musée des monumens français in 1816, numerous objects for which there was no claim of reclamation were transported to Saint-Denis, where they were, more often than not, hidden away in storage. Many of these works were eventually transferred to the then Musée de Cluny (now the Musée national du Moyen Age), their provenances lost in the process. See Louis Grodecki, *Les Vitraux de Saint-Denis*, Corpus Vitrearum France, Etudes I (Paris: CNRS, 1976). 46-48, 59; Jean-Michel Leniaud, *Saint-Denis de 1760 à nos jours* (Paris: Gallimard, 1996). 94-99, 245-246

[74] "apportée alors en France par les croisés…." Lenoir, *Description historique*. 2:40, 94

[75] Reau, *Histoire du vandalisme*. 565; Shepard, "Stained Glass from Saint-Germain-des-Prés." 18-22

[76] "en me rendant acquéreur, pour le Musée des monumens français, d'une partie du portail de cet 'edifice'." *Archives du Musée*. 1:233; François Ribadeau-Dumas, *Histoire de Saint-Germain-des-Prés, Abbaye Royal* (Paris: Editions Académie Français, 1958). 199

[77] This misidentification stemmed from a longstanding belief in royal support based on the presence of castle-shaped emblems (interpreted as word-play on the name of the mother of Louis IX, Blanche of Castile) in the window borders of the refectory, also built by Pierre. Shepard, "Stained Glass from Saint-Germain-des-Prés." 8-10

[78] Bann, *Clothing of Clio*. 83-84

[79] Pierre Nora, "Between Memory and History: *Les Lieux de mémoire*," trans. Marc Roudebush, *Representations* 16 (1989). 7-24

[80] "la troisième cour du Musée des monumens Français" and "la dernière cour du Musée." Dessins, RF 5279/37 and RF 5279/107, Musée du Louvre, Paris.

[81] See Lenoir's discussion of Winckelmann in Alexandre Lenoir, *Description historique et chronologique des monumens de sculpture, réunis au Musée des monumens français*, 5th ed. (Paris: Chez l'auteur, year VIII [1799]). 351, referring to Johann Joachim Winckelmann, *Histoire de l'art chez les anciens*, trans. Gottfried Sellius, 2 vols. (Paris: Saillant, 1766).

REVIVING "THE PAST GREATNESS OF THE FLORENTINE PEOPLE": RESTORING MEDIEVAL FLORENCE IN THE NINETEENTH CENTURY

NANCY M. THOMPSON

> "The antique Palazzo del Podestà [Bargello], built by the architect Arnolfo, and currently being returned to its primitive form with a well-conceived restoration, is one of the principal monuments of the past greatness of the Florentine people."[1]
>
> —Bettino Ricasoli, 1859

Introduction

Ricasoli issued this decree on the restoration of the Palazzo del Podestà, also called the Bargello [Fig. 1], in his new capacity as the provisional head of the Florentine government following the departure of the last Habsburg Grand Duke from Florence in 1859. Habsburg control of Tuscany had begun to loosen already in the late 1840s. During the wars of 1848, many Tuscans, including the artists Luigi Mussini, Ulisse De Matteis, and Stefano Ussi, fought against the Austrians under the charge of Carl Albert of Piedmont.[2] Although initially supportive of Tuscan independence, Grand Duke Leopold II was forced to leave Florence in February of 1849.[3] However, the uprisings of 1848-1849 were ultimately unsuccessful. Austria reestablished control over the northern part of the peninsula, and Leopold returned to Tuscany with Austrian reinforcements in April of 1849.[4] Despite Austrian control, the decade from 1849-1859 in Florence was peppered with revolts against Habsburg rule. In May of 1851, Florentines had gathered in Santa Croce to pray for their fellow Tuscans, who had died fighting the Austrians in the wars of 1848-1849. During their prayers, Austrian soldiers came into the church and fired on the worshipers.[5] Events like this, in addition to the growing desire for independence, culminated in a "huge revolutionary demonstration in

Florence on April 27, 1859, which overthrew the regime and opened the way for Tuscany to join a united Italy."[6] The demonstration was orchestrated by Giuseppe Dolfi, the radical political figure and master baker, who organized the artisan class of Florence. An eyewitness to the demonstration reports that the Grand Duke's soldiers did not attack the city as had been rumored. "On the contrary, the Duke went away with a great quantity of luggage; the crowd assembled to witness his departure remained perfectly silent as his carriages rolled out of the gate; it was most impressive. The town was not bombarded or sacked."[7] Following the period of provisional government headed by Ricasoli, Tuscany voted to join the Kingdom of Italy in 1861, with Victor Emmanuel II, the son of Carl Albert, ruling from Piedmont.

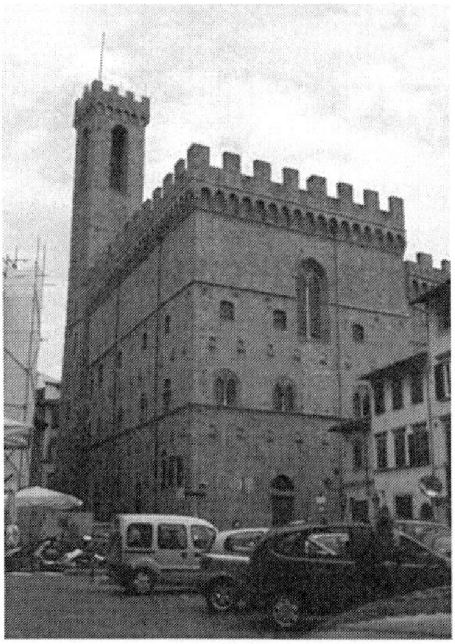

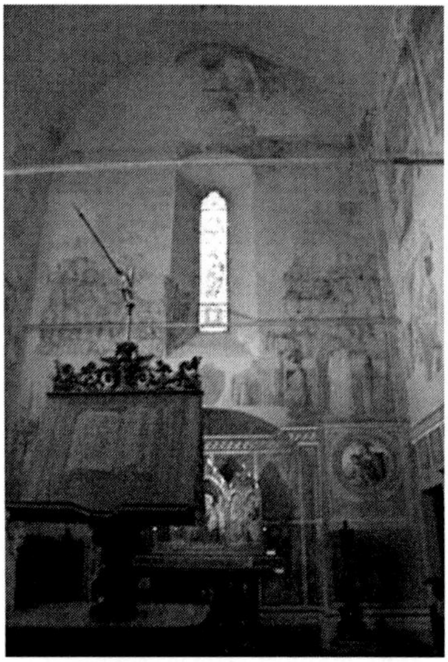

Fig. 1 (L) National Museum of the Bargello (Palazzo del Podestà), Florence, begun 1255 (Photo: Author)

Fig. 2 (R) Frescoes, including the *Portrait of Dante*, ca. 1320s, chapel, National Museum of the Bargello, Florence (Photo: Author)

Interest in restoring the Bargello first occured in 1839, almost two decades before liberation, when a group of English and American scholars living in Florence proposed to find Giotto's portrait of Dante, which Vasari describes in his *Lives of the Artists* as one of many portraits painted by Giotto in the "chapel of the Palazzo of the Podestà of Florence."[8] On 20

July 1840, Antonio Marini (1788-1861), a painter and restorer from Prato, uncovered Dante's portrait with great fanfare [Fig. 2].[9] Dante appears within a crowd of people gathered below a judging Christ and a chorus of angels and saints. The newly discovered image of Dante and the subsequent restoration of the chapel drew a great deal of attention from both Florentines and foreigners. Florentines were generally supportive of Marini's work, but the English community in Florence was critical of his restoration because they found it to be too invasive.[10] Despite the controversy, the restoration of the chapel was one of the first events to inspire a renewed interest among artists and intellectuals in the cultural, political, and artistic heritage of medieval Florence. In fact, according to Cristina Giannini, "The recovery of the Bargello and the exhaustive research on the *Portrait of Dante* signal the beginning of an out-and-out campaign to re-appropriate the art of the Primitives."[11]

Plans for the architectural restoration of the Bargello began in 1854, when the Grand Duke commissioned the architect Francesco Mazzei, who had recently restored the civic palazzo in Volterra, to complete a detailed study of the building.[12] From 1858, when Mazzei began the work, until 1865, the Bargello was radically transformed from a dilapidated prison and police headquarters into a grand medieval palazzo housing a museum of Tuscan history. Although Mazzei's specific approach to the restoration is not preserved in any textual sources, the physical evidence indicates that his restoration of the Bargello was most likely informed by the work of Giuseppe Martelli (1792-1876), the leading voice in architectural restoration in Florence in the 1850s and 60s, and of the Frenchman Eugène Emmanuel Viollet-le-Duc (1814-1879), whose theories became increasingly popular in Florence after 1860.[13] Instead of repairing the Bargello and maintaining the later additions to the building, Mazzei removed any trace of work carried out after the fourteenth century and remade the palazzo into what he and his contemporaries believed to be its original medieval state. Not only was the structure of the building completely changed, but Mazzei also called on artists working in revival styles to decorate the Bargello. Following a discussion of the restoration of medieval architecture in nineteenth-century Florence, this paper explores Mazzei's work on the Bargello and its significance in light of the politics of the Risorgimento in Tuscany. Ultimately, the attempt to restore and recreate the Bargello and other medieval buildings in Florence was driven by a desire to resurrect the political and artistic values of the medieval *comune* and excise the period of Medici and Habsburg rule from the city's memory. The newly restored monuments became symbols of the Florentine people's sovereignty over their own city and history.

Restoration and the *medioevo* in Nineteenth-Century Florence and Tuscany

Although scholars and archaeologists explored Italy's Roman heritage in various parts of the peninsula during the eighteenth century, Italians, and particularly Tuscans, did not begin to focus on their medieval heritage until the period of the Risorgimento.[14] In the 1850s, when the liberation of Tuscany from the Habsburgs was becoming a reality, scholars, artists, and critics often viewed the *medioevo*, generally spanning the thirteenth through early fifteenth centuries, as a time of political freedom. Although Jacob Burckhardt defined the period of the Renaissance in his 1860 *Civilization of the Renaissance in Italy* as beginning in 1300 and ending precisely in 1530, many nineteenth-century Italian scholars and critics used the term *medioevo*, with its political connotations, to refer to this period.[15] These scholars and critics defined the *medioevo* as the age of the *comune* in Tuscany, a time when citizens and artists lived and worked free from foreign domination and despotic rulers. The Renaissance, in contrast, was often associated with the rise of the Medici and the repressive rule of Cosimo I (1537-1574), which, through marriages and political alliances, led to the concession of Tuscany to the Habsburgs after the death of the last Medici, Gian Gastone, in 1737. Cosimo I established the Florence Academy in 1563. Under Austrian and French rule, the Academy continued, run according to the standards of colonial regimes and answering directly to the Grand Dukes and Emperor. In the 1840s and 50s, many artists, the Macchiaioli and "puristi" in particular, rejected the traditional subject matter of academic painting and the Baroque and Neoclassical styles so closely associated with foreign rule and looked instead to the period of the *comune* for artistic inspiration.[16]

Interest in the *medioevo* in Italy was in part inspired by a group of Tuscan artists called the "puristi" (purists), headed by the painter Luigi Mussini (1813-1888).[17] Influenced by the leaders of the German Nazarene movement whom he had met in Rome, Mussini and the Swiss painter Franz Adolph von Stürler, established an art school in Florence in 1844 based on the workshop model of the fourteenth and fifteenth centuries that served as an alternative to the classicism of the Academy.[18] In his 1847 essay, "On the Study of Old Masters," Mussini charged Tuscan artists to look for inspiration to the period before the Medici duchy to understand the true nature of art.[19] He lamented that, while there was a great amount of discussion of Raphael, the *trecento* and *quattrocento* churches of Florence were empty of Florentines and tourists. He also praised the removal of the "insults" that the Baroque (*il barocchismo,* a style associated with the Medici) had "thrown on the façades of ancient monuments."[20] Mussini's fellow "puristi" nominated him as the director of the Sienese Academy of Fine Arts in 1851. As a professor of painting, Mussini encouraged his students to look to Italian art of the fourteenth and fifteenth centuries for inspiration.[21] In his 1852 essay "Del purismo nell'arte: a proposito di un quadro di Luigi Mussini," Cesare Guasti, one of the purists who pressed Mussini to accept the position at the Sienese Academy, defended purism against its detractors. Guasti wrote that purists do not oppose invention, nor do they slavishly copy the work of the *trecento*. Instead, purists are inspired by the way that *trecento* artists, Giotto in particular, were directly inspired by nature and expressed emotions "semplicemente e efficacemente."[22]

While the ideas of the "puristi" inspired interest in medieval art and the restoration of medieval architecture, the architect Giuseppe Martelli formulated a specific approach to architectural restoration in mid-nineteenth-century Florence.[23] Martelli studied at the Florentine Academy in the first decade of the nineteenth century and began working as an architect in the 1810s. Following a brief stay in London, Martelli took courses in civil and military architecture and hydraulics at the Ecole Polytechnique in Paris from 1818-1819, making him the only Tuscan architect of his generation to study outside of Italy.[24] Upon his return to Florence, Martelli was named an assistant architect in the Royal Office of Public Works of Tuscany (*Scrittoio delle Regie Fabbriche*). In the 1830s, Martelli began work on the restoration of the upper half of the Palazzo Vecchio in Florence. The majority of the work on the exterior, carried out in the 1830s and 40s, consisted of a restoration of the masonry and glass of the windows, the crenellation of the upper part of the palazzo, and the stonework on the tower. According to Paolo Mazzoni, it is only in the 1840s that one can talk of a Tuscan approach to architectural restoration, an approach characterized by Martelli's work on the tower of the Palazzo Vecchio in particular.[25] The restoration of the tower, begun in 1840, consisted of "sostituzioni" and "ricostruzioni" (substitutions and reconstructions): while some damaged stone was simply repaired, much of the tower's structure, including the crenellations with their triangular indentations, was completely reconstructed to appear more medieval in style.[26]

While Martelli significantly altered the appearance of the Palazzo Vecchio tower, he did not take the same approach in restoring Donatello's Marzocco, a heraldic stone sculpture of a lion commissioned for the Palazzo Vecchio in 1418 that by Martelli's day had been greatly damaged from exposure to the elements. Martelli decided to bring the original sculpture inside the palazzo and commission a copy to be placed outside. In his 1846 report on the Marzocco's restoration, Martelli remarks that to change the sculpture in any way would be to insult the honor of the artist.[27] Even as Martelli preserved the Marzocco in its damaged state, the tower was, according to Mazzoni, made "more medieval, more like the works of Arnolfo di Cambio, than before."[28]

Little is known about the formation of Martelli's ideas on architectural restoration. Mazzoni notes that the papacy and the Kingdom of Naples both issued brief statements on the maintenance of historic monuments and that in the period of the Restoration, the Tuscan government issued a brief decree on the maintenance and improvement of decaying structures that posed a safety threat. However, the decree included no specific directive on how the buildings should be repaired, leaving these decisions to the architects in charge of individual projects.[29] While in Paris, Martelli learned geometry and the latest innovations in engineering at the Ecole Polytechnique, and he was exposed to French neo-classicism through studies with the architect Jean-Baptiste Rondelet, Soufflot's student who continued his master's work on the Parisian Pantheon.[30] There is no evidence, however, that Martelli studied architectural restoration either at the Academy in Florence or in Paris, indicating that when he began to restore buildings in Florence, Martelli was most likely inventing his own approach to restoration.

There are similarities between Mazzoni's approach to the architectural restoration of the Palazzo Vecchio and the theories of Viollet-le-Duc, which weren't published until the 1850s. Viollet-le-Duc did see the Palazzo Vecchio in 1836 on his tour of Italy. In a letter to his father, Viollet-le-Duc notes the gigantic tower, pierced by small windows, which he characterized as inspiring respect mixed with fear.[31] At that point, however, Martelli had not begun to restore the tower. In his entry on restoration in the *Dictionnaire*, Viollet-le-Duc argues that to restore a building is not to repair it or remake it, but is instead to return it to a "complete state" that may have never existed at any one moment in time.[32] Martelli was apparently acting on a similar principle when he made the Palazzo Vecchio tower appear "more medieval" and more in the style of Arnolfo di Cambio through restoration.

Following liberation from the Habsburgs, Martelli was named the director of the Department of Public Works for the provisional Tuscan government in 1860; also in this year, a commission for the protection and conservation of works of art was established in Tuscany with Martelli as its vice-president.[33] While preparations for the first National Italian Exhibition of 1861 occupied much of the commission's time in its early years, Martelli also issued a decree on the most urgent restoration projects in Florence, which encapsulated his thoughts on restoration. He wrote that:

> ...Ancient monuments must be left as they are and where they are found; if the damage done by time and by the hand of man necessitate restoration, one must study the most favorable method to complete the restoration with as little intervention as possible, changing only the most worn out and corroded parts, always taking care to conserve the primitive forms of the original building.[34]

According to Martelli, he employed this precise system when he restored the upper portion and tower of the Palazzo Vecchio. His decree strongly recommended against the removal of Orcagna's tabernacle from Orsanmichele and supported restoration of the church's interior architecture, including the removal of the walls between the church's exterior arches, which were put in place decades after the original construction of the church. The walls were to be replaced by historiated stained glass windows similar to those found in monuments from the same period in order to give the sacred place "that austere character that invites man to meditate."[35] In his specific prescription for Orsanmichele's architectural restoration, Martelli likely incorporated the new, widely published and discussed theories of Viollet-le-Duc into his own approach. As with the Palazzo Vecchio restoration, Martelli treats architecture very differently from other works of art: while buildings can be reshaped in order to recreate the original or ideal state of a building, sculpture and painting should be cleaned and preserved but should not be altered.

As Tuscany's public works director, Martelli's projects were wide-ranging and included the widening of Florence's medieval streets and improvements to the public water system; however, his specific interest in Orsanmichele, the Palazzo Vecchio, and the Bargello is indicative of a resurgence of interest in medieval architecture in mid-nineteenth-century Tuscany.[36] In his monograph, *Teoria e storia del restauro*, Carlo Ceschi argues that an increasing interest in the Middle Ages gave way to the completion and restoration of Romanesque and Gothic monuments in Tuscany in particular. Ceschi categorizes much of this work as "restorations, completions and reconstructions 'in style'," and he discusses the work carried out at Santa Croce and Florence Cathedral in this context.[37] In 1847, Gaetano Baccani completed a new belltower for Santa Croce in a Gothic style that replaced the sixteenth-century tower that fell during a storm.[38] One of the most important changes to Santa Croce in the nineteenth century was the addition of the church's current façade (1857-1862), designed by Niccola Matas.[39] And from 1876-1883, Emilio De

Fabris completed the new façade for Florence's cathedral after fifteen years and a series of three competitions, which included entries from internationally known architects.[40]

By the later half of the nineteenth century, Viollet-le-Duc's theories shaped the approach of many Tuscan architects to restoration. According to recent scholars, Bardeschi and Masetti, the restoration of Santa Trinita in Florence, a late medieval church admired by Guasti and the "puristi," perhaps best exemplifies the Florentine application of Viollet-le-Duc's concepts of a "restoration in style."[41] Bardeschi and Masetti argue that Viollet-le-Duc was quite influential in Florence in the later part of the nineteenth century: the Florentine Academy nominated Viollet as a member in 1860, and in 1864 and 1865, the mayor of Florence asked him to act as a judge in the contest to create the new cathedral façade.[42] The restoration of Santa Trinita was initiated in 1881 by the city government of Florence whose officials advocated a "complete restoration" of the church and appointed the architect Giuseppe Castellazzi to head the project in 1884.[43] Guido Carocci, the critic who published the journal *Arte e storia* in Florence, supported Castellazzi's plans. On 11 May 1884, Carocci wrote that the plans to restore Santa Trinita were finally underway and that the work was of the utmost importance because it would restore the "primitive" character of the church that had been ruined in part by the "barbaric" additions of the Baroque period.[44] Athough its thirteenth-century form was unknown, Castellazzi reshaped the nave arcade into a series of pointed Gothic arches, which must have been part of what he believed to be the "complete state," in Viollet-le-Duc's terms, of the medieval church. Members of the English community in Florence, as well as William Morris's London-based Society for the Protection of Ancient Buildings (SPAB), protested the restoration of Santa Trinita. SPAB issued a statement that deplored the "irreparable damage" that the Florentines were incurring on their city's monuments. Their protests were ignored, however, and the restoration was carried out, leaving no trace (neither physical nor photographic) of the church before the restoration.[45]

Viollet-le-Duc's ideas directly informed the Sienese architect Giuseppe Partini (1842-1895).[46] In his role as the architect of the Siena Cathedral, Partini oversaw numerous restoration projects and consistently advocated that the Baroque elements of the cathedral's interior be removed because they interfered with the original intentions of the medieval architects. Near the beginning of his 1883 report on the restoration of Siena Cathedral, Partini refers to Viollet-le-Duc's restoration of medieval churches in France, which Partini believed were carried out with "faithful scrupulousness" and "exquisite taste." In Partini's view, Viollet-le-Duc's goal was to concentrate light in upper parts of the church, in the clerestory, and leave the nave in semi-obscurity, lit only by the darkly colored light of stained glass windows.[47] As it did in the Middle Ages, Partini hoped that the celestial light of the clerestory windows, coupled with the relative darkness of the nave, would generate profound religious devotion in the heart of nineteenth-century Catholics. This desire echoes that of Martelli, when he sought to alter the interior of Orsanmichele in Florence to create a more spiritual environment. While the clerestory windows of Siena Cathedral were enlarged according to plan, Partini's goal to remove the Baroque side aisle altars and reopen the Gothic windows, outlines of which are visible on the exterior of the cathedral, was never carried out. By flooding the upper part of the church with clear light and bathing the nave in darkly colored light, Partini hoped to inspire true Catholic piety in nineteenth-century visitors to the cathedral, a piety that he believed to be in keeping with the intent of his medieval predecessors.

Later in the nineteenth century, when Partini carried out the majority of his work in Siena and Castellazzi restored Santa Trinita in Florence, Italian critics and scholars debated proper approaches to restoration. At the 1883 meeting of engineers and architects, Camillo Boito (1836-1914) proposed a theory of restoration often considered to be the first national Italian theory. Boito advocated that a building should be conserved rather than restored: that is, later additions to older structures should not be removed but should be preserved as part of the building's history.[48] Boito maintained the validity and necessity of architectural restoration for the preservation of ancient monuments.[49] Although Boito's thoughts on the subject are not preserved, Boito most likely would not have approved of Castellazzi's work in Santa Trinita or of Partini's work in Siena Cathedral because both restoration campaigns so radically altered the interior of the churches. Both Castellazzi and Partini, in Boito's terms, did not maintain or preserve the churches but instead remade them in keeping with the theories of Viollet-le-Duc. A later Italian restorer, Alfredo Melani, went so far as to declare in his 1899 *Manuale di architettura italiana antica e moderna* that Italian restorers must forget the theories of Viollet-le-Duc.[50] To restore a building, according to Melani, was to conserve and fortify it in order to preserve the building's life; to remake a structure into a new building with a cohesive style that reflected only an abstract concept was to murder it.[51] If Melani were to judge Castellazzi's work on Santa Trinita and Partini's on Siena Cathedral, he most likely would have declared that the architects had brutally murdered the churches.

The Restoration of the Bargello

Melani might have also considered Francesco Mazzei's restoration of the Bargello a brutal murder. Martelli, however, in his 1860 report on urgent restorations in Florence, wholeheartedly approves of Mazzei's work: he calls the restoration an important one and notes that the restoration consists of removing the modern additions to the palazzo, especially the dividing walls, in order to reveal the original, impressive architectural form of the structure.[52] Mazzei approached his work on the Bargello in much the same way that Martelli undertook his work on the Palazzo Vecchio's tower. Mazzei transformed the Bargello by removing later additions, restructuring the interior, and completely altering the building's façade in order to make it more medieval in style. Likely influenced by Martelli and the theories of Viollet-le-Duc, which were published just as Mazzei began his work in the late 1850s, Mazzei and his contemporaries believed that the restoration brought the Bargello back to its ideal, medieval state.

Begun in 1255, the building now called the Bargello was constructed to house the *capitano del popolo*, the official who represented the Florentine *popolo minuto* within the larger city government. By 1266, the building became the home of the Podestà, a foreigner hired by the city on a yearly basis since 1207 to enforce the laws of the city, quell the violence between Florence's ruling factions, and represent the general interests of the *popolo grasso*.[53] The palazzo was enlarged several times in the late thirteenth and fourteenth centuries: it was extended onto the Via dell'Aqua from 1260-1280, the loggia added in the courtyard in 1285, the veranda built between 1317-1320, and the Magdalene chapel constructed and decorated between 1316 and 1322.[54] A fire in 1332 and a flood in 1333 necessitated a reconstruction, which was first entrusted to Giotto and then, in 1345, to Neri di Fioravante.[55]

The structure was not substantially altered until 1502, during the short-lived republican period of 1494-1512 when the Medici were ousted from Florence, the office of the Podestà was abolished, and the Council of Justice formed in its stead. Consequently, the architects Giuliano da Sangallo and Baccio d'Agnolo reconfigured the palazzo to make office and living spaces for the new magistrates.[56] When Cosimo I (1519-1574, ruled as Duke of Florence 1537-1574, and Grand Duke of Tuscany 1569-1574) restructured the Florentine government, he harshly punished those who were disloyal to the Medici. He established the Security Commission and installed secret informers in almost every institution in the city.[57] In the last year of his reign, he moved the Council of Justice to another location and the building became the home of the Bargello, the police captain of the city.[58] Cosimo stripped the building of any populist associations and reconverted the entire building into a prison. Any Florentine accused of disloyalty to Cosimo, and subsequent Medici rulers, would have met an unlucky fate in the prison and torture cells of the Bargello.

The Bargello continued to serve as police headquarters and prison after the last Medici Duke, Gian Gastone, died childless in 1734 and Tuscany was given by political concession to the Habsburg-Lorraine dukes, who brought Enlightenment ideals to their rule.[59] In 1782, during the reign of the Grand Duke Leopold I, torture was abolished in Tuscany, and all the instruments of torture were burned in the Bargello courtyard.[60] In 1847, however, the Bargello still carried negative associations. In this year, Samuele Iesi wrote in the daily newspaper *La patria* that "this majestic building which was the residence of the Podestà, and then with the fall of the Republic took the sad name of the Bargello…, this great work of Lapo di Cambio, where Giotto painted the eternal effigy of Dante, has become now a place of torment and wailing."[61] The idea that the Bargello was a symbol of oppression in need of liberation, in addition to the growing desire for independence in Florence, pushed Leopold II to officially close the prison in 1854 and order Mazzei's study of the palazzo.[62] Only in 1858, when all the prisoners were finally moved from the Bargello, was Mazzei officially commissioned to restore the palazzo.

With the departure of the Grand Duke in 1859, the restoration of the Bargello took on a new urgency. Two of Mazzei's major tasks were to return the façade to its original medieval appearance and to reconstruct the original configuration of the rooms in the palazzo from the maze that made up the prison. Mazzei was particularly concerned with recreating the large room on the first floor, the room that now houses Donatello's *David* and other famous *quattrocento* sculpture. This great room had been broken up into four floors, which were in turn broken up into many prison cells and offices during the building's life as a prison. In an 1857 proposal for restoration, Mazzei imagines the room as a large uninterrupted space with a double lancet window in the center of the main wall and pairs of smaller windows below [Fig. 5].[63] Mazzei's drawing of the building's exterior before the restoration [Fig. 3] shows that the large double lancet had been filled in and windows were cut in seemingly random places. In this drawing, Mazzei emphasizes the cracks in the masonry and the haphazardness of the placement and shape of the windows that evolved during the palazzo's life as a prison. In his plan for the exterior restoration [Fig. 4], Mazzei organized the windows; he imagined the large central

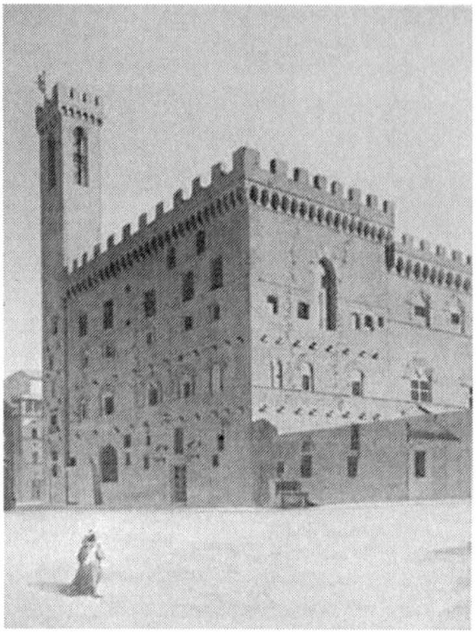

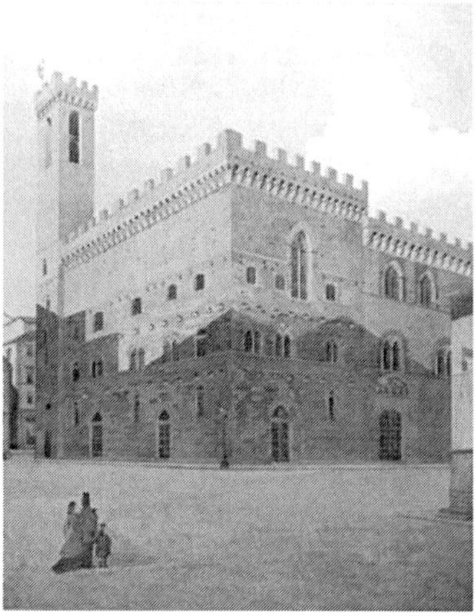

Fig. 3 (L) Francesco Mazzei, Drawing of the Bargello before restoration, 1857 (Photo: Archivio Storico Comunale di Firenze)

Fig. 4 (R) Francesco Mazzei, Proposal for the restoration of the exterior of the Bargello, 1857 (Photo: Archivio Storico Comunale di Firenze)

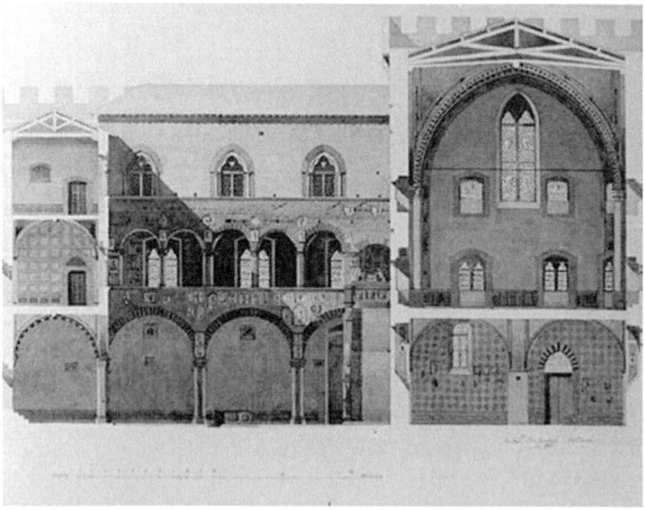

Fig. 5 Francesco Mazzei, Proposal for the restoration of the interior of the Bargello, 1857 (Photo: Archivio Storico Comunale de Firenze)

double lancet straddled by the smaller windows, with a third set of windows at the corner. Mazzei filled in the top level with masonry, and regularized the windows on the floors below. The style of the double lancet windows on the first floor was likely adopted from the windows of the newer, Gothic part of the palazzo on the Via dell'Aqua. Mazzei also opened up the arcade of the veranda [Fig. 5, left side], which had been closed off in the intervening centuries, and pierced the exterior wall with three double lancet windows.

Mazzei's restoration involved a redecoration of the interior spaces, and both the stained glass artist Ulisse De Matteis and the painter and restorer Gaetani Bianchi worked on the Bargello at the beginning of their careers. Bianchi restored the traces of fresco that were uncovered with the restructuring of the palazzo walls and painted new decoration on many of the walls and ceilings of the new spaces. Although some of Bianchi's decoration was painted over in a more recent restoration, much of the palazzo is still covered with Bianchi's signature work, consisting of gold stars, geometric patterns and coats-of-arms on vivid blue ground [Fig. 8].[64] Mazzei called on De Matteis and Natale Bruschi of the Francini company to equip almost all of the palazzo's newly created windows with glass. For the Bargello chapel, the heart of the palazzo that inspired the restoration itself, De Matteis designed a window featuring Saint John the Baptist, Florence's patron saint [Fig. 6]. In what is likely De Matteis' first large-scale figural window, the artist depicted a heavily bearded Baptist, wearing a yellow hair shirt and swathed in an elaborate, regal purple cloak decorated in typical fourteenth-century style with a band of yellow diamonds on a blue-green ground. The saint's facial features and beard are realistically modeled in grisaille, displaying De Matteis' painterly abilities in his newly chosen vitreous medium. The arcade that frames Saint John resembles those in fourteenth-century Florentine stained glass. Like the window above the Bardi chapel in the basilica of Santa Croce depicting Franciscan saints and popes [Fig. 7], De Matteis' Baptist is framed by a trefoil arch that forms the bottom of an elaborate architectural structure. Under the Bardi chapel window, and probably contemporary with it, appear frescos of the life of Saint Francis from ca. 1320 by Giotto. It was, therefore, an appropriate model for De Matteis, since the Bargello frescoes were also believed to have been painted by Giotto. In both windows, flames border the triangular top of the arch, and the space within contains geometric decoration. De Matteis' arcade, while clearly based on the Santa Croce model, is more complicated in its construction, resembling later fourteenth-century windows in the nave of Florence Cathedral.[65] De Matteis' use of a variety of period models, first seen in his work in the

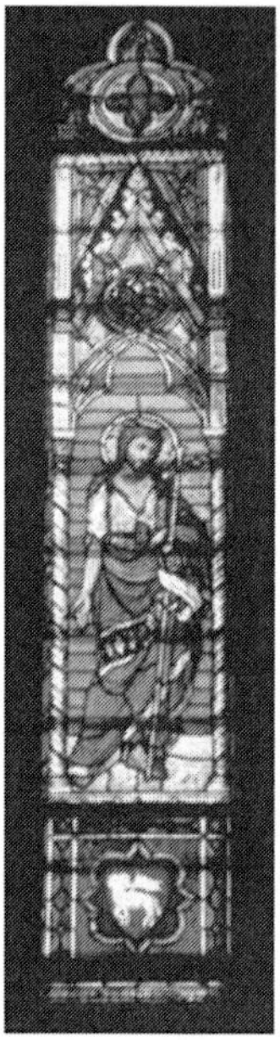

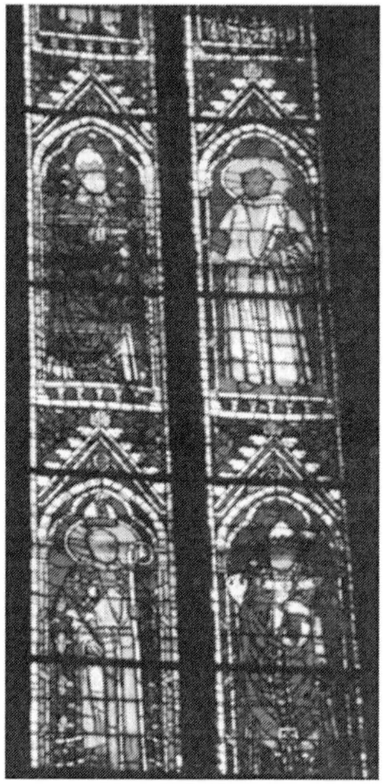

Fig. 6 (L) Ulisse De Matteis, Saint John the Baptist, stained glass window, 1869, chapel, Bargello, Florence (Photo: Author)

Fig. 7 (R) Franciscan saints and popes, stained glass window, 1320s, Santa Croce, Florence (Photo: Author)

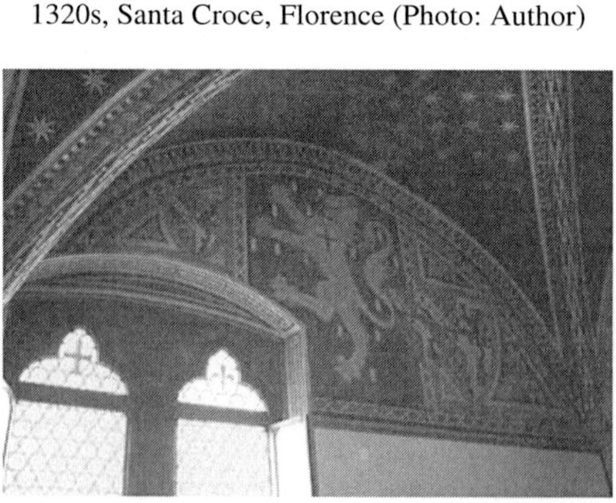

Fig. 8 Ulisse De Matteis, window; Gaetano Bianchi, wall painting, Bargello, Florence (Photo: Author)

Bargello chapel, became his standard method for the creation of stained glass windows for medieval monuments.[66]

De Matteis painted brightly colored coats-of-arms with enameled pigments in the upper portion of the Bargello's Gothic windows, made of bull's eye glass typical of the thirteenth and fourteenth centuries [Fig. 8]. These windows complement the coats-of-arms painted by Bianchi on the palazzo's walls. In his communications with the Director of Civic Works (*Direttore Generale delle Fabbriche Civili dello Stato*), Mazzei indicates that the coats-of-arms on each window were painted with enameled paints, "as the painters of church windows used to use."[67] Mazzei refers to the authenticity of De Matteis and Bruschi's technique, which was verified by a committee from the Technical Institute in Florence in 1861. The committee's report commends De Matteis and Bruschi for their perfect imitations of "ancient" stained glass, an art that had been lost in the preceding centuries, and recommends that the restoration of any deteriorated stained glass windows in Florence be entrusted to De Matteis and Bruschi.[68]

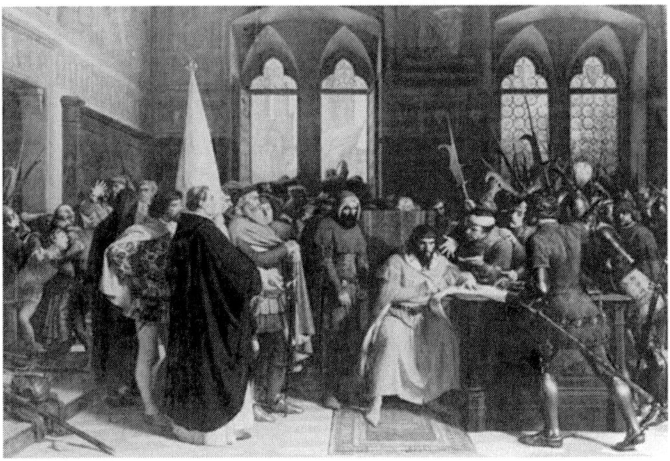

Fig. 9 Stefano Ussi, *The Expulsion of the Duke of Athens,* 1859-1861, Galleria d'arte moderna, Florence (Photo: Soprintendenza, Florence)

The new Bargello windows are exactly those represented by Stefano Ussi in his 1859-1860 painting, *The Expulsion of the Duke of Athens* [Fig. 9]. Ussi was familiar with the Bargello windows and the palazzo's restoration; he was on a committee that approved De Matteis and Bruschi's models.[69] Ussi likely referenced these authentically medieval windows and the newly restored palazzo in his painting of the *Expulsion* to reinforce its political message. Following the narrative of Giovanni Villani's 1348 *Chronica*, Ussi's painting depicts the Duke of Athens, the tyrannical Frenchman Walter de Brienne, whom the Florentines had brought to rule the city in 1342, in the moments before he surrendered to the mob of Florentines who had gathered outside the Palazzo Vecchio on 26 July 1343. In order to create an authentic period scene, Ussi placed Walter de Brienne in an interior that more closely resembles the newly restored rooms of the Bargello than the hall of the Palazzo Vecchio, which was renovated by Cosimo I in the sixteenth century. The painting was exhibited first in an unfinished state in 1860 by Ricasoli's liberal government and in its finished state in the Florence 1861 Italian National Exhibition. According to Albert Boime, the painting draws a distinct parallel between the Florence of 1859-1861, which had so recently liberated itself from Austrian control, and the Florence of 1343, which had liberated itself from a foreign dictator.[70] Ricasoli drew these parallels himself in an address to the National Guard in Florence in November 1859, just months after the Florentines drove out the Austrians in the revolution of 27 April, in which he called to the soldiers to remember the battles of the Risorgimento and to think about Florence as a monument to the glorious deeds of its citizens, a city from which "the Duke of Athens was driven ignominiously forth."[71] Ussi referenced De Matteis' windows and the newly restored Bargello in his painting to emphasize the importance of the *medioevo* in his day: not only had the Florentines ousted Walter de Brienne, as they had so recently ousted Leopold II, but they were also beginning a campaign to reclaim the medieval monuments of their city and return them to their medieval states through architectural restoration.

Conclusion: The Bargello Becomes a Museum

The reclaimed Bargello, symbolic of the medieval *comune*, became a museum of the Tuscan Middle Ages when it officially opened in 1865. Although the city declared in 1859 that the building would house a museum, the specific nature of the museum was a subject of debate. In that year, Marco Guastalla, a wealthy Florentine collector, proposed to the Minster of Public Instruction that the Bargello house a museum of the Middle Ages that would bring together important objects in many private Florentine collections.[72] Guastalla, inspired by the Cluny Museum in Paris and the South Kensington in London (later called the Victoria and Albert Museum), wanted to display Florence's grand artistic past for the visitors expected to attend the first Italian National Exhibition. In his proposal, he laments the large amount of Florentine art sold to foreign collections, and he urges the Minister to use the newly restored palazzo to "rationally display" and "scientifically classify" the history of Florentine art.[73] While the National Exhibition would showcase the new, technologically advanced nation of Italy, the Bargello exhibit would highlight the important artistic heritage of Florence in the time of the *comune* and the "regeneration" of art. The minister approved of Guastalla's idea, but he did not think that the palazzo's restoration could be completed in time for the 1861 National Exhibition.[74] Guastalla instead held the display in his private residence, and more than twelve thousand people came, many of whom were in the city for the National Exhibition.[75] In 1862, the Florentine minister of public education appointed Paolo Feroni to direct the new National Museum of the Bargello. Like Guastalla, Feroni looked to the Cluny and South Kensington museums as role models, but he favored the Cluny and decided to model the collection after the Paris museum. The minister approved of Feroni's plan and allowed him to build the collection by taking works of art from palazzi and churches around the city. This core collection was supplemented by objects from private collections in Florence, many of which had been exhibited in Guastalla's home.[76]

The restoration of the Bargello was finally finished in 1865, the same year that Florence became the capital of the new nation of Italy, when Mazzei ordered an inactive well from the street corner outside to be transferred to the courtyard of the palazzo.[77] Upon its completion, King Victor Emmanuel II issued a decree from Florence declaring the opening that same year, the 600th anniversary of Dante's birthday. The museum opened with two exhibits, one dedicated to Dante that centered on Giotto's portrait, and another dedicated to the medieval art of Florence. Like Paris and London, the new capital of Italy had a museum dedicated to its medieval past.

Just as Italians had driven out foreign occupiers and united under the Kingdom of Italy, Mazzei's restoration rid the Bargello, an early symbol of communal government, of its history as a prison under the despotic governments of the Medici and Habsburg dukes. In his attempt to return the Bargello to an ideal, medieval state, Mazzei physically excised the violence and oppression of the prison from the palazzo and transformed it into a monument that, in its architecture and function, constructed a republican medieval past for Tuscany. Not only did the newly restored Bargello embody Florence's freedom from oppression, but, in the early years of unification, it also became an important symbol that celebrated the newly formed Italian nation's political and artistic heritage.

Notes

[1] "Considerando come l'antico Palagio del Potestà architettato da Arnolfo ed oggi ridotto con ben intesi restauri alla sua forma primitiva, sia uno dei principali monumenti della passata grandezza del popolo fiorentino." Quoted in Marco Guastalla, *Progetto d'una esposizione di oggetti del Medio-evo e del rinascimento dell'arte da farsi nel Palazzo Pretorio contemporanea a quella dell'industria nazionale in Firenze* (Florence: Barbèra, 1861). 8

[2] De Matteis and Ussi were imprisoned by the Austrians at Thereisenstadt. A list of the Tuscan prisoners appears in "Toscani o aventi militato pella Toscana ritrovati dal sottoscritto in Innsbrück, Linza, Piaga," Corda 23, inserto 603, Archivio Storico Comunale di Firence (ASCF), Florence.

[3] Nicholas Doumanis, "Italy," in *Inventing the Nation*, ed. Keith Robbins (London: Oxford University Press, 2001). 69

[4] John A. Davis, *Italy in the Nineteenth Century 1796-1900* (Oxford: Oxford University Press, 2000). 71

[5] Oreste Raggi, *La chiesa di Santa Croce a la sua facciata dell'architetto Cav. Niccola Matas* (Florence: M. Cellini, 1863).

[6] Albert Boime, *The Art of the Macchia and the Risorgimento* (Chicago: University of Chicago Press, 1993). 76

[7] The eyewitness was the American painter Elihu Vedder. Ibid. 76

[8] Paola Barocchi and Giovanna Bertelà, "Alla ricerca del ritratto di Dante nella Cappella del Palazzo Pretorio 1840," in *Dal ritratto di Dante alla Mostra del Medioevo 1840-65*, ed. Paola Barocchi and Giovanna Bertelà (Florence: SPES, 1985). 3

[9] On Marini and the culture of purism in Prato see Silvestra Bietoletti, "La pittura negli anni centrali del secolo, e Cesare Guasti," in *L'Ottocento a Prato*, ed. Renzo Fantappiè (Prato: CariPrato, 2000). 69-94. On the uncovering of whitewashed frescoes and their controversial restorations see Cristina Giannini, "Sotto lo scialbo. Firenze e la tutela del patrimonio alle soglie dell'unità," *Bollettino dell'Accademia degli Euteleti della città di San Miniato* 63 (1996). 215-269, esp. 217, 221-222, 228-230

[10] Cristina Danti, Alberto Felici, and Paola Mariotti, "La Cappella del Bargello: Vicende conservative delle pitture," in *La storia del Bargello*, ed. Beatrice Strozzi (Milan: Silvana, 2004). 79-80

[11] "Il recupero del Bargello e la faticosa ricerca del Ritratto di Dante segnarono l'inizio di una vera e propria campagna di riappropriazione dell'arte primitiva." Giannini, "Sotto lo scialbo." 229; Christina Giannini, *Lessico del restauro: storia, tecniche, strument* (Florence: Nardini, 1992). 58-64 discusses the restoration workshops of mid-nineteenth-century Florence.

[12] "Il museo nazionale del Bargello," in *La città degli Uffizi: Catalogo della*

mostra, ed. Franco Borsi (Florence: Sansoni, 1982). 99
[13] For discussions of Martelli and Viollet-le-Duc, along with specific bibliography, see nn. 23 and 32.
[14] See Carlo Ceschi, *Teoria e storia del restauro* (Rome: Bulzoni, 1970). 39-48 for an overview of restoration projects carried out on Roman monuments and on the development of classical archeology in eighteenth-century Italy. Alessandro Conti, *Storia del restauro e della conservazione delle opere d'arte* (Milan: Electa, 1973). 173-177 discusses the fascination with classical sculpture and its restoration in eighteenth-century Italy; Cesare Chirici, *Il problema del restauro dal Rinascimento all'età contemporanea* (Milan: Ceschina, 1971). 79-100 examines eighteenth-century approaches to restoration and the treatment of classical monuments in the nineteenth century. In Habsburg Tuscany, there was also an interest in the restoration of classical sculpture, a phenomenon explored in depth by Roberta Roani, *Restauri in Toscana tra settecento e ottocento* (Florence: Edifir, 2005). 7-81
[15] D. Medina Lasansky, *The Renaissance Perfected: Architecture, Spectacle and Tourism in Fascist Italy* (University Park, PA: Pennsylvania State University Press, 2004). 19-25 discusses the meaning of the term *medioevo* during the Risorgimento.
[16] Boime, *The Art of the Macchia*; Norma Broude, *The Macchaioli: Italian Painters of the Nineteenth Century* (New Haven: Yale University Press, 1987). 24
[17] See *In memoria di Luigi Mussini pittore* (Siena: S. Bernardino, 1888). 1-16 for a brief biography of Mussini and a list of his major artistic and literary works. Mussini's daughter, Luisa Anzoletti, *Epistolario artistico di Luigi Mussini* (Siena: Ignazio Gati, 1893) gives a more personal biography of her father. For a discussion of Mussini's career, see Giovanna Uzzani, "Luigi Mussini: formazione purista ed esiti senesi," in *Siena tra purismo e liberty*, ed. Bernardina Sani (Milan: Mondadori, 1988). 81-86; Cesare Guasti, "Del purismo nell'arte a proposito di un quadro di Luigi Mussini," in *Scritti d'arte di Cesare Guasti* (Prato: Successori Vestri, 1897). 53-61 outlines the concepts embraced by the "puristi." This essay was originally published in Florence in 1852.
[18] For a description of Mussini and Stürler's school, which closed in 1848, see Francesco F. Mancini, "Un omaggio di Ingres a Luigi Mussini," in *Per Luigi Grassi: Disegno e disegni*, ed. Anna Forlani and Simonetta Tempesti (Rimini: Galleria Editrice, 1998). 509
[19] Luigi Mussini, "Sullo studio de' maestri antichi e sugli ostacoli che ad esso si frappongono," in *Scritti d'arte di Luigi Mussini, pittore* (Florence: Le Monnier, 1880). 3-13. The essay was originally published in the Florentine magazine *La rivista* in August, 1847.
[20] Mussini, "Sullo studio de' maestri antichi." 11
[21] Mussini was nominated by, among others, Cesare Guasti, Carlo Pini, and Gaetano Milanesi. Uzzani, "Luigi Mussini: formazione purista ed esiti senesi." 81
[22] Guasti, "Del purismo nell'arte." 58
[23] Nancy Wolfers and Paolo Mazzoni, eds. *La Firenze di Giuseppe Martelli (1792-1876): L'architettura della città fra ragione e storia. Museo di Firenze com'era 29 March-25 May 1980* (Florence: Comune di Firenze, Assessorato alla Cultura e

Belle Arti, 1980).

[24] Nancy Wolfers, "Giuseppe Martelli e la formazione dell'architetto," in *L'architettura della città fra ragione e storia. Museo di Firenze com'era 29 March-25 May 1980*, ed. Nancy Wolfers and Paolo Mazzoni (Florence: Comune di Firenze, Assessorato alla Cultura e Belle Arti, 1980). 121-131 provides an account of Martelli's early training. On Martelli's education in Paris, Nancy Wolfers, "La formazione di Giuseppe Martelli e la Francia," in *Florence et la France* (Florence: Centro Di, 1979). 437-450

[25] Paolo Mazzoni, "Giuseppe Martelli e il restauro," in *L'architettura della città fra ragione e storia. Museo di Firenze com'era 29 March-25 May 1980*, ed. Nancy Wolfers and Paolo Mazzoni (Florence: Comune di Firenze, Assessorato alla Cultura e Belle Arti, 1980). 139; Chirici, *Il problema del restauro*. 21-22 argues that the historicizing approach of nineteenth-century restorers was harmful to buildings and that restoration theory in Italy did not come to fruition until the mid-twentieth century.

[26] Mazzoni, "Giuseppe Martelli e il restauro." 139-140

[27] Giuseppe Martelli, "Rapporto del Martelli alla Direzione dello Scrittoio, 30 Marzo 1846," Fabbriche, fol. 2194, Archivio di Stato, Florence; Mazzoni, "Giuseppe Martelli e il restauro." 140 includes a transcription of the document. Martelli also states in the report that important works of art like the Marzocco must serve as symbols of national pride to instruct the public about its national heritage.

[28] The tower was made "*più medievale e arnolfiana di prima*." Mazzoni, "Giuseppe Martelli e il restauro." 140

[29] Mazzoni, "Giuseppe Martelli e il restauro." 139

[30] Wolfers, "La formazione di Giuseppe Martelli e la Francia." 442-446

[31] Mazzoni, "Giuseppe Martelli e il restauro." 139; Eugène Emmanuel Viollet-le-Duc, *Lettres d'Italie 1836-1837* (Paris: Laget, 1971).

[32] "Restaurer un édifice, ce n'est pas l'entretenir, le réparer ou le refaire, c'est le rétablir dans un état complet qui peut n'avoir jamais existé à un moment donné." Eugène Emmanuel Viollet-le-Duc, *Dictionnaire raisonné de l'architecture français du XIe au XVIe siècle*, vol. 8 (Paris: Morel, 1858-1868). 14; for more on Viollet-le-Duc see M.F. Hearn, ed. *The Architectural Theory of Viollet-le-Duc: Readings and Commentary* (Cambridge, MA: MIT Press, 1990). An English translation of Viollet-le-Duc's restoration entry appears in Eugène Emmanuel Viollet-le-Duc, *The Foundations of Architecture: Selections from the* Dictionnaire raisonné, trans. Kenneth Whitehead (New York: Braziller, 1990). 193-227

[33] Martelli's complete title was *Direttore generale del Dipartimento d'Acque e Strade e Fabbriche Civili della Toscana.*

[34] "...gli antichi monumenti debbano essere lasciati come sono, ed ove si trovano; se le lesioni fattevi dal tempo e dalla mano dell'uomo esigono dei restauri si debba studiare il mezzo più idoneo per farvi il meno possibile, cangiando solamente le parti più logore e corrose ma sempre avendo cura di scrupolosamente conservare le primitive forme della loro originaria edificazione." The decree, "Rapporto del Martelli al direttore delle Finanze e dei Lavori Pubblici. 12 novembre 1860," is preserved in the Archivio di Stato in Florence. Mazzoni, "Giuseppe Martelli e il

restauro," 143-146

[35] "...quel carattere austero che invita l'uomo alla meditazione." Mazzoni, "Giuseppe Martelli e il restauro." 143

[36] See *La Firenze di Giuseppe Martelli*. 150-155 for a list of his extensive projects.

[37] "...restauri, completamenti e ricostruzioni 'in stile'." Ceschi, *Teoria e storia del restauro*. 93-106

[38] On the belltowers of Santa Croce see Pietro Ruschi, "I campanili di Santa Croce," in *Santa Croce nell'800*, ed. Monica Maffioli (Florence: Alinari, 1986). 17-38

[39] Monica Maffioli, "La facciata di Santa Croce: Storia di un cantiere," in *Santa Croce nell'800*, ed. Monica Maffioli (Florence: Alinari, 1986). 39-78; Matas' final design for the façade was based on a drawing purportedly from the hand of Simone del Pollaiolo (1457-1508). According to Monica Maffioli, "Il neogotico purista di Niccola Matas," in *Il neogotico nel XIX e XX secolo*, vol. 2, ed. Rosanna Bossaglia (Milan: Mazzotta, 1989). 327-335 the fifteenth-century drawing never existed; only the nineteenth-century "copy" of the drawing, probably made by Matas himself, is preserved in the church archives. However, with the idea that his design was based on an authentic, "antique" source, Matas' final design for the church façade was accepted and praised by the "puristi" of mid-nineteenth-century Florence.

[40] Mauro Cozzi, "Pietro Selvatico e il progetto per la facciata di Santa Maria del Fiore," in *Il neogotico nel XIX e XX secolo*, ed. Rosanna Bossaglia, vol. 2 (Milan: Mazzotta, 1989). 307-316; and Costanza Travaglini, "La facciata di Santa Maria del Fiore: Dialogo ottocentesco tra preesistente e progetto storico," in *Il neogotico nel XIX e XX secolo*, ed. Rosanna Bossaglia, vol. 2 (Milan: Mazzotta, 1989). 317-326. See also Timothy Verdon, ed., *La facciata di Santa Maria del Fiore*, vol. 5, *Alla riscoperta di Piazza del Duomo in Firenze: Saggi per una lettura storico-artistico-religiosa dei suoi monumenti* (Florence: Centro Di, 1996).

[41] Marco Bardeschi and Maria Masetti, "La storia tradita: guida ai monumenti infedeli d'Italia. La chiesa di S. Trinita a Firenze," *L'architettura: cronache e storia* 27, 12 (1981). 720

[42] Bardeschi and Masetti, "La storia tradita." 725 n. 1

[43] Bardeschi and Masetti, "La storia tradita." 720 summarize the stages of the restoration and the controversy it raised. See also Giuseppe Marchini and Emma Micheletti, eds., *La chiesa di Santa Trinita a Firenze*, (Florence: Cassa di Risparmio di Firenze, 1987). 61-88

[44] "Il lavoro è di somma importanza perchè si deve restituire scrupolosamente il primitivo carattere a cotesto stupendo edifizio guastato in parte dalle barbariche aggiunto dei barocchi." Guido Carocci, "Sta Trinita," *Arte e storia* 19, 3 (11 May 1884). 151; on Carocci, see Gabriella Di Cagno, *Arte e storia: Guido Carocci e la tutela del patrimonio artistico in Toscana 1870-1915* (Florence: Ponte alle Grazie, 1991).

[45] Bardeschi and Masetti, "La storia tradita." 720; Monica Maffioli, "La *querelle* ottocenttesca per il restauro della chiesa: dalle teorie al contiere," in *La chiesa di Santa Trinita a Firenze*, ed. Giuseppe Marchini and Emma Micheletti (Florence:

Cassa di Risparmio di Firenze, 1987). 63; on the English approach to restoration, Roger J.P. Kain, "Gothic Revival, Restoration and Preservation of Historic Buildings in Nineteenth-Century England," in *Il neogotico nel XIX e XX secolo*, ed. Rosanna Bossaglia, vol. 1 (Milan: Mazzotta, 1989). 43-65. In the later nineteenth-century, Vernon Lee's *Associazione per la Difesa di Firenze Antica* successfully protested the modernization of the area surrounding the Palazzo della Parte Guelfa. See D. Medina Lasansky, "Reshaping Attitudes Towards the Renaissance: The Fight against 'Modern Mania' in Florence at the Turn of the Century," in *The Renaissance in the Nineteenth Century*, ed. Yanick Portebois and Nicholas Terpstra (Toronto: Centre for Reformation and Renaissance Studies, 2003). 263-295

[46] On Partini, see Cristina Buscioni, *Giuseppe Partini: Architetto del Purismo senese* (Florence: Electa, 1981); Vittorio Mariani, *L'architetto Giuseppe Partini* (Siena: S. Bernardino, 1921); and Vittorio Mariani, *In memoria di Giuseppe Partini* (Siena: Scuola Tipografica Sordomuti, 1924). For further discussion of Partini's restoration of the cathedral, Nancy Thompson, "Architectural Restoration and Stained Glass in Nineteenth-Century Siena: The Place of Light in Giuseppe Partini's *Purismo*," in *This Year's Work in Medievalism*, ed. Gwendolyn Morgan, 19 (2004). 41-53

[47] "Ed invero, nei monumenti congeneri di origine mediovale, non solo in Italia ma anche in Francia ove dal celebre Viollet-le-Duc sono stati eseguiti restauri di chiese con fedeltà scrupolosa, e con un gusto veramente squisito, si riscontra costante applicazione del sistema di raccogliere molta luce nella parte superiore, con una semi oscurità in basso, ottenuta col mezzo di finestre riccamente storiate con vetri a foschi colori. È tutto ciò, non già per intuito di mera parvenza, ma sibbene per il duplice quanto mirabile effetto, di fare apparire maggiore l'elevatezza del tempio, e di infondere nell'ambiente quel non so che di mistico e di solenne che in tempi di schietto e forte sentire aveva un eco profondo negli animi compresi di fede religiosa fervida quanto sincera…." Giuseppe Partini, "Lavori di restauro che resterebbero ad eseguirsi nella nostra cattedrale, onde ritornarla al suo antico splendore 1883/1886," Carteggio, atti e copialettere, Affari diversi, 1770-1915, Filza 159, 2, Archivio della Metropolitana di Siena.

[48] Camillo Boito, "I restauri in architettura. Dialogo primo," in *Questioni pratiche di belle arti: Restauri, concorsi, legislazione, professione, insegnamento* (Milan: Hoepli, 1893). 3-32

[49] See Francesco Bocchino, "Camillo Boito e la dialettica tra conservare e restaurare," in *La cultura del restauro*, ed. Stella Casiello (Venice: Marsilio, 1996). 145-155; Amedeo Bellini, "Boito tra Viollet-le-Duc e Ruskin?" in *Omaggio a Camillo Boito*, ed. Alberto Grimoldi (Milan: Franco Angeli, 1991). 159-167; Chirici, *Storia del restauro*. 100-111 discusses Viollet-le-Duc, Ruskin, and Boito in similar terms. Chirici deems Viollet-le-Duc's approach "absurd" and argues that Boito attempted to reconcile the approaches of Ruskin and Viollet-le-Duc to architectural restoration.

[50] Alfredo Melani, *Manuale di architettura italiana antica e moderna* (Milan: Hoepli, 1899). 405-406

---

[51] Stella Casiello, "La cultura del restauro fra ottocento e novecento," in *La cultura del restauro*, ed. Stella Casiello (Venice: Marsilio, 1996). 13-34, esp. 19-20 for the close relationship between Melani's view and the ideas of Ruskin and the SPAB.
[52] Mazzoni, "Giuseppe Martelli e il restauro." 144
[53] Beatrice Paolozzi Strozzi, "La storia del Bargello," in *La storia del Bargello*, ed. Beatrice Strozzi (Milan: Silvana, 2004). 10-78 offers a detailed history of the Bargello's structure, renovation, and life as a museum. For a history of the Bargello's construction see Walter Paatz, "Zur Baugeschichte des Palazzo del Podestà (Bargello) in Florenz," *Mitteilungen des Kunsthistorischen Institutes in Florenz* 6 (1931). 287-321
[54] Giovanna Gaeta Bertelà, "Il restauro del palazzo del Podestà," in *Studi e ricerche di collezionismo e museografia, Firenze 1820-1920* (Pisa: Scuola Normale Superiore, 1985). 188; Strozzi, "La storia del Bargello." 16; and Janis Elliot, "The Judgement of the Commune: The Frescoes of the Magdalene Chapel in Florence," *Zeitschrift für Kunstgeschichte* 61 (1998). 509-519
[55] Strozzi, "La storia del Bargello." 16
[56] Ibid. 22-23
[57] J.R. Hale, *Florence and the Medici: The Pattern of Control* (New York: Thames and Hudson, 1977). 135-136
[58] Borsi, "Il museo nazionale del Bargello." 99
[59] For a discussion of the changes brought about by the Habsburgs in Tuscany see Valentino Baldacci, ed., *Le riforme di Pietro Leopoldo e la nascita della Toscana moderna* (Florence: Mandragora, 2000).
[60] Strozzi, "La storia del Bargello." 24. Leopold I also abolished the death penalty in 1786. Aldo Schiavone, "La riforma del codice penale e l'abolizione della pena di morte," in *Le riforme di Pietro Leopoldo e la nascita della Toscana moderna*, ed. Valentino Baldacci (Florence: Mandragora, 2000). 33-43
[61] "Quel maestoso edifizio che fu residenza del Podestà, e che poi col cadere della Repubblica prese il tristo nome del Bargello…e quella grande opera di Lapo di Cambio, ove Giotto ha eternato l'effigie di Dante, divenuto poi luogo di supplizi e di gemiti." Quoted in Bertelà, "Il restauro del palazzo del Podestà." 182. Iesi goes on to propose that the building be transformed into a museum of medieval Tuscan art.
[62] Borsi, "Il museo nazionale del Bargello." 99
[63] The restoration of the great room was already envisioned by Francesco Leoni in his 1840-1845 drawings. Paola Barocchi and Giovanna Bertelà, "Il Palazzo Pretorio prima e dopo il restauro 1840-1865," in *Dal ritratto di Dante alla Mostra del Medioevo 1840-65*, eds. Paola Barocchi and Giovanna Bertelà (Florence: SPES, 1985). 9
[64] On Bianchi's work, see Nina Olsson, "Gaetano Bianchi: restoratore e decoratore 'giottesco'," *Antichità viva* 36 (1997). 44-55. See also Antonio Torresi's edition of an 1898 manuscript by the restorer Cosimo Conti: Antonio Torresi, ed., *Del restauro in generale e dei restauratori: Il manoscritto 280 della Biblioteca degli Uffizi* (Ferrara: Liberty House, 1996). In his introductory essay (11-19), Torresi discusses the restorations of the Bargello, Santa Trinita, and Santa Maria Novella

with a focus on Bianchi's work. In the treatise itself, Conti praises the restoration of the Bargello in general and Bianchi's restoration of the original frescoes.

[65] For images of the Florence Cathedral nave windows, see the Italian Corpus Vitrearum's online database: http://www.icvbc.cnr.it/bivi/.

[66] Nancy Thompson, "Stained Glass in Nineteenth-Century Florence: Medieval Reproductions by the Atelier De Matteis," in *Interpreting the Middle Ages: Essays on Medievalism*, ed. Susan Ridyard, Sewanee Medieval Studies 13 (2005). 59-81; and Nancy Thompson, "The State of Stained Glass in Nineteenth-Century Italy: Ulisse De Matteis and the *vitrail archéologique*," *Studies in Medievalism* (2009). (in press)

[67] "Messo nelle 4 centine dei suddetti finestroni n. 4 stemmi, i colori dei quali sono stati eseguiti a pittura a smalta come solevano usare i pittori di finestroni da chiesa, come ne fede il rapporto di questo R. Istituto Tecnico, iscritto nel n. 109 del Monitore Toscano." Bertelà, "Il restauro del Palazzo del Podestà." 195-196 n. 62

[68] "Appendice: R. Accademia di arti e manifatture," *Monitore Toscano* 109 (1861). 3

[69] In addition to Ussi, Mazzei reports that Profs. Pollastrini, Ciseri, Pollastrini "and other distinguished people in the arts" ("ed altre distinte persone d'arte") inspected the windows and approved them. Bertelà, "Il restauro del Palazzo del Podestà." 195-196 n. 62

[70] Boime, *The Art of the Macchia.* 188

[71] Ibid.

[72] Guastalla, *Progetto d'una esposizione.*

[73] Guastalla, *Progetto d'una esposizione.* 5-6

[74] In his final report on the Bargello restoration, Mazzei notes that, although the work was not yet completed by the time of the 1861 Exhibition, visitors to Florence were able to enjoy the severe and elegant architecture of the Bargello and to view several of the newly restored rooms. Franceso Mazzei, "Del Palazzo del Podestà in Firenze e del suo recente restauro," *Giornale del Genio Civile*, ser. 2, 1, 7 (1869). 410-411. Cited in Bertelà, "Il restauro del Palazzo del Podestà." 200

[75] Marco Guastalla, *Catalogo della esposizione di oggetti d'arte del Medio-Evo e dell'Epoca del risorgimento dell'arte fatta in Firenze in casa Guastalla in Piazza dell'Indipendenza, contemporaneamente a quella dell'Industria Nazionale* (Florence: Torelli, 1861).

[76] For the history of the museum and its collection see Paola Barocchi and Giovanna Bertelà, "Ipotesi per un museo nel Palazzo del Podestà tra il 1858 e il 1865," in *Studi e ricerche di collezionismo e museografia, Firenze 1820-1920* (Pisa: Scuola Normale Superiore, 1985). 211-377

[77] The capital was moved to Rome in 1870.

Nineteenth-Century Restoration Politics: Recrafting Monarchy in the Stained Glass Windows of the Sainte-Chapelle in Paris

Alyce A. Jordan

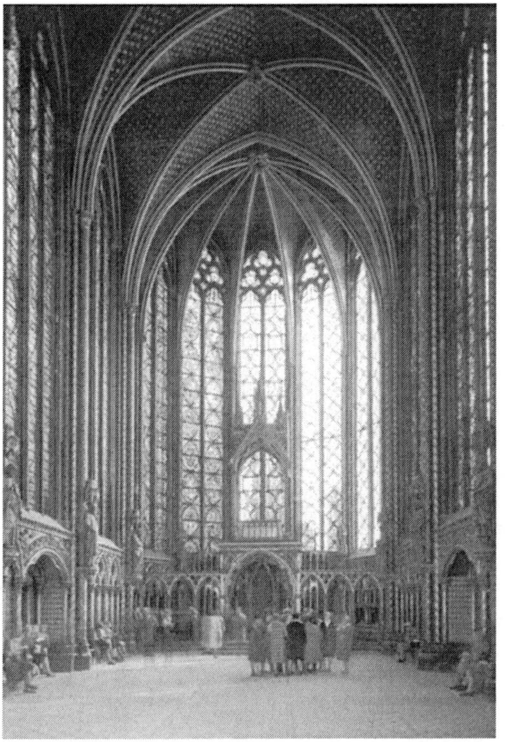

Fig. 1 Interior, Sainte-Chapelle, Paris, 1241-1248
(Photo: Courtesy of Catherine Brisac)

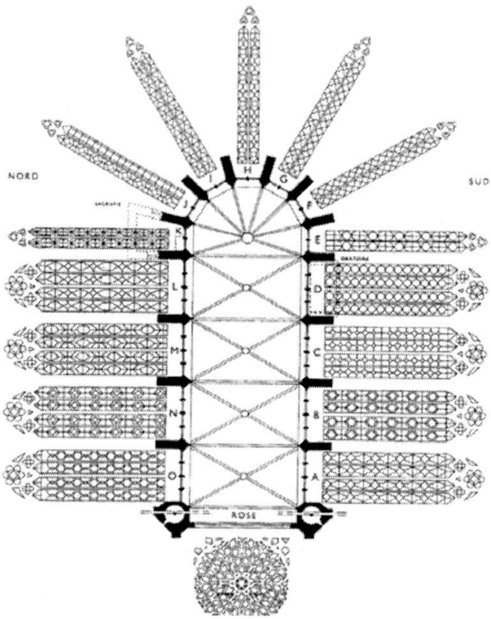

Fig. 2 Plan of the windows, Sainte-Chapelle, Paris, 1241-1248, from Louis Grodecki, Marcel Aubert, Jean Lafond, and Jean Verrier, *Les Vitraux de Notre-Dame et de la Sainte-Chapelle de Paris*, Corpus Vitrearum Medii Aevi, France, vol. 1 (Paris: Caisse Nationale de Monuments Historiques and Centre Nationale de la Recherche Scientifique, 1959). 75

The Sainte-Chapelle numbers among the most powerful statements of medieval monarchic authority espoused during the European Middle Ages.[1] Built by Louis IX between 1241 and 1248 as a private palace chapel to house the Crown of Thorns, the most sacred relic in Christendom and the nexus of the French claim to sacral kingship, the chapel's ornate interior includes expansive narrative windows devoted to exemplary Old Testament leaders [Figs. 1-2].[2] These biblical role models engage in a litany of quintessentially monarchic activities, including battles, diplomatic negotiations with their subjects, and ceremonies of coronation. Beginning in 1837, the chapel underwent a total renovation, financed and supervised by the governments of Louis-Philippe (reigned 1830-1848) and Louis Napoléon (reigned 1848-1870). In the course of this campaign, the windows were dismantled, reorganized, and completed with new scenes to replace losses suffered during the Revolution. Renovation of the windows officially began in 1848 and was completed in 1855. The medieval glass ensemble—a third of which had been destroyed in the wake of the French Revolution—was painstakingly studied, documented, and refurbished in what was widely publicized as the most scrupulous glass restoration campaign to date. In the course of this project, the scenes the windows contained were reorganized and new scenes created to replace lacunae resulting from earlier excisions and damage.[3]

These restored, reorganized and newly-completed windows, effectively proffered new stories. This is especially true of the so-called Relics window, where well-preserved medieval panels were eliminated, over thirty new panels created, and numerous old panels iconographically altered to craft a narrative devoted to the history of the relics of Christ's Passion—the True Cross and the Crown of Thorns—culminating in their acquisition by Louis IX [Fig. 2, bay A].[4] The extensive alterations made to this particular window, which several nineteenth-century scholars had identified as a history of Louis IX, suggest that its restoration comprised a purposeful "retelling" focused through the perceptual filter of contemporary governmental concerns. As such, this restored narrative, titled by its creators the "Relics" window, offers compelling evidence of the significance the Sainte-Chapelle held for the nineteenth-century French monarchy.

In contrast to the other medieval windows, all of which recounted stories drawn from the Old and New Testaments, this window depicted not a biblical story, but rather, an account of King Louis IX's acquisition of the Crown of Thorns in 1239. The details of this event comprised at least a third, or five rows, of the original thirteenth-century window [Figs. 3-5].[5] In addition to these identifiable panels, the window contained three additional rows of generic battle scenes [Fig. 6]. A final group of medieval panels depicted ambiguous subjects, including a birth scene, a scene in which kneeling figures present a king with the keys to a city, and two panels in which bedridden kings crown their successors [Figs. 8-9]. Like all the chapel's windows, the bottom four rows of the "Relics" window were empty.[6]

The window's unique historical iconography, including multiple depictions of Louis IX, his mother Blanche of Castile, brother Robert d'Artois, Archbishop Gautier Cornut of Sens, and the monks who facilitated the Crown's purchase and transport, made it especially significant from an historical perspective [Figs. 3-5]. Jean-Baptiste Lassus, the architect in charge of the restoration, and François de Guilhermy, the antiquarian-scholar who oversaw the identification of the windows' iconography and the selection of subjects for new panels, generated copious documentation and a wealth of correspondence. The quantity of

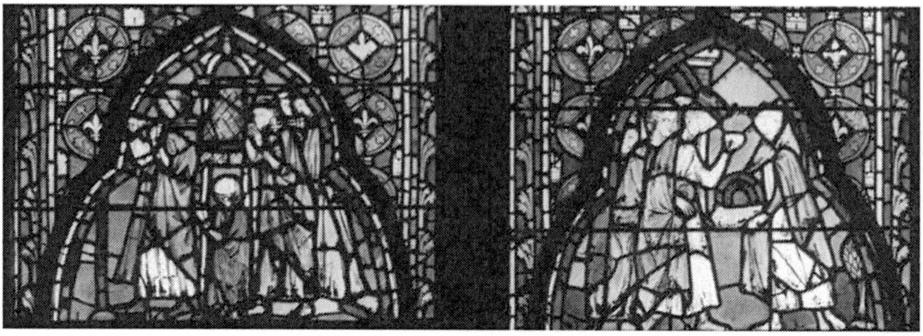

Fig. 3 Procession of the Crown of Thorns and Louis IX venerating the Crown of Thorns, medieval panels A-96 (L) and A-97 (R), ca. 1248, "Relics" Window, Sainte-Chapelle, Paris (Photo: B. Acloque/Centre des monuments nationaux, Paris)

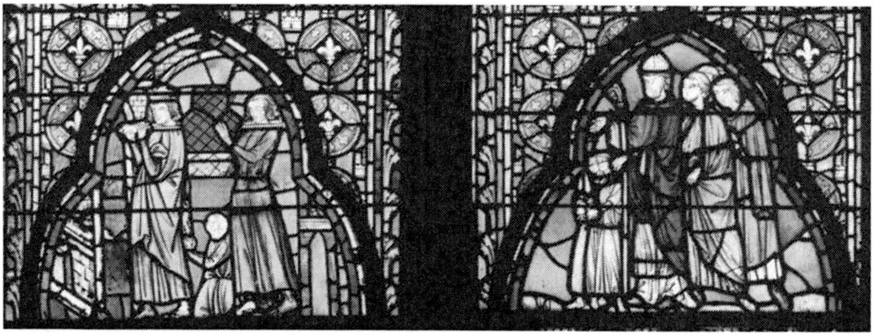

Fig. 4 Louis IX and Robert d'Artois carry the reliquary châsse containing the Crown of Thorns, medieval panel A-98 (L), ca. 1248; Clergy and laity process behind the Crown of Thorns, modern panel A-99 (R), ca. 1853-1855, "Relics" Window, Sainte-Chapelle, Paris (Photo: B. Acloque/Centre des monuments nationaux, Paris)

analyses and reports testifies to the import attached to the restoration of the glass in general and this window in particular. Guilhermy initially suggested eliminating all the panels except those that obviously related to the translation of the Crown of Thorns and subsequently proposed the establishment of a formal commission to undertake "a thorough study" of the window's imagery prior to its restoration.[7] Another antiquarian, Ferdinand de Lasteyrie, asserted the window originally depicted a biography of Louis IX.[8]

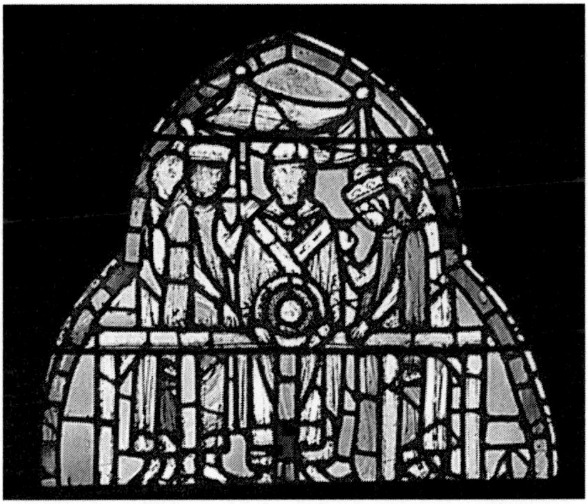

Fig. 5 Louis IX, Blanche of Castile, and Gautier Cornut, Archbishop of Sens, display the Crown of Thorns, medieval panel A-71, ca. 1248, "Relics" Window, Sainte-Chapelle, Paris (Photo: B. Acloque/Centre des monuments nationaux, Paris)

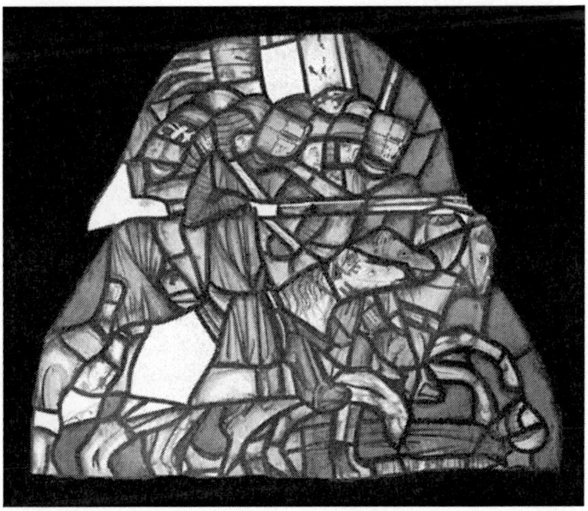

Fig. 6 Battle scene, watercolor tracing of medieval stained glass panel removed from the "Relics" window in 1853, "Relevés-calques des vitraux de la Sainte-Chapelle de Paris," vol. 15, unpaginated, Médiathèque du Patrimoine, Paris (Photo: Author)

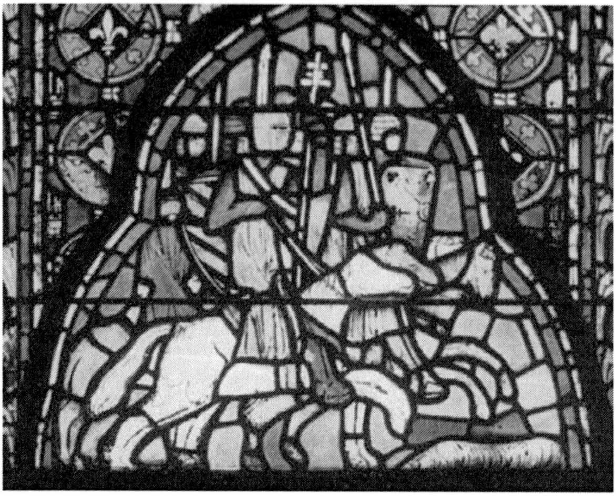

Fig. 7 Heraclius returning to Jerusalem with the True Cross, medieval panel A-125 in Fig. 6 after restoration, ca. 1853-1855, "Relics" Window, Sainte-Chapelle, Paris (Photo: B. Acloque/Centre des monuments nationaux, Paris)

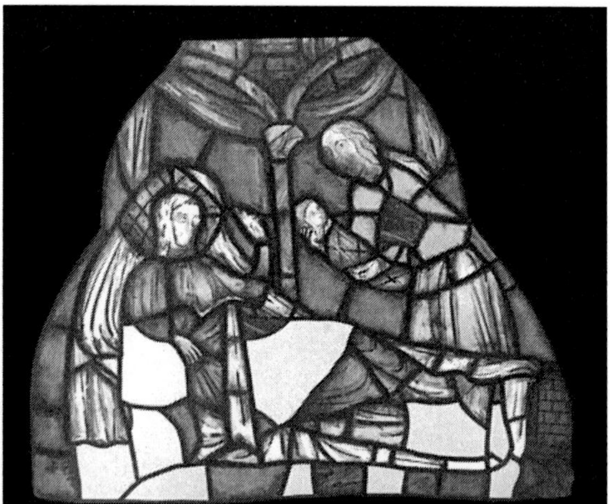

Fig. 8 Birth scene, watercolor tracing of medieval stained glass panel removed from the "Relics" window in 1853, "Relevés-calques des vitraux de la Sainte-Chapelle de Paris," vol. 15, unpaginated, Médiathèque du Patrimoine, Paris (Photo: Author)

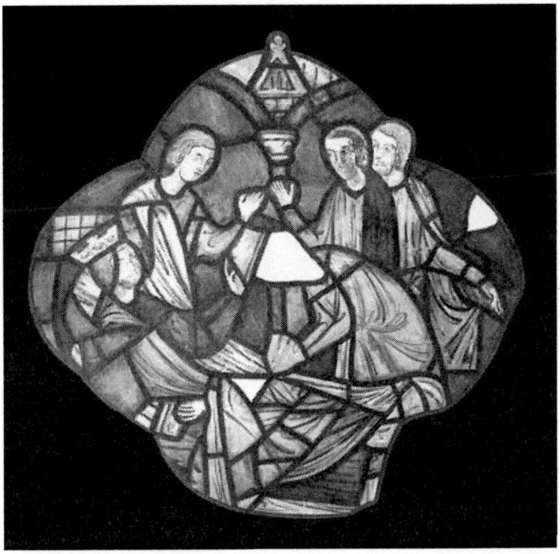

Fig. 9 Bedridden king crowning his successor, watercolor tracing of medieval stained glass panel removed from the "Relics" window in 1853, "Relevés-calques des vitraux de la Sainte-Chapelle de Paris," vol. 15, unpaginated, Médiathèque du Patrimoine, Paris (Photo: Author)

In the end the decision was made to reconstitute the window as a history of the True Cross. Using Jacobus da Voragine's *Golden Legend* as his primary textual source, Guilhermy crafted a narrative that traced the discovery and translation of the True Cross by Constantine's mother, Saint Helena, its theft by the Persian king Chosroes and recovery by the Byzantine emperor Heraclius.[9] Guilhermy continued the story with scenes of the translations of Christ's relics to Paris in the thirteenth century, which he expanded with modern panels to create two distinct narrative sequences documenting Louis IX's purchase and translation of the Crown of Thorns in 1239 and the acquisition of additional Passion relics, including a piece of the True Cross, in 1241. The restored window culminates in another sequence of modern scenes depicting the construction and dedication of the chapel itself [Figs. 3-5, 7, 10, 14-15].[10]

The medieval panels preserved in the window offered no evidence that it had ever contained scenes of the discovery of the True Cross by Saint Helena or the subsequent legends of its theft and recovery by Chosroes and Heraclius. However, the decision to situate identifiable medieval scenes of the thirteenth-century translation of the Crown of Thorns into a larger narrative dedicated to the history of the True Cross could certainly

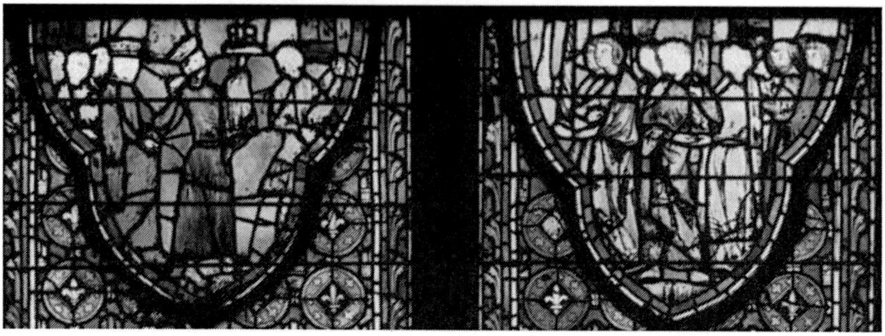

Fig. 10 Louis IX holds the True Cross (?); Procession of clergy and laity, medieval panels A-44 (L) and A-45 (R), ca. 1248, "Relics" Window, Sainte-Chapelle, Paris (Photo: B. Acloque/Centre des monuments nationaux, Paris)

be justified. The True Cross legends had been widely popular throughout the Middle Ages and Renaissance.[11] The True Cross stories also harmonized historically with the Sainte-Chapelle's liturgical emphasis on the translations of the Crown of Thorns, True Cross, and other Passion relics, feasts instituted by Louis IX and added to the Sainte-Chapelle calendar in the mid-thirteenth century.[12]

Like most medieval narrative windows, those of the Sainte-Chapelle read from bottom to top. The fourth-century discovery of the True Cross by Saint Helena occupies the bottom four rows, replacing the vacant apertures that had been filled with plaster in 1803. The emperor Constantine charges his mother Helena to travel to the Holy Land to search for the Cross of Christ. The story follows chronologically, each panel depicting a specific moment in the narrative, including Helena's interrogation of the Jews in the Holy Land and the submersion of the knowledgeable, but uncooperative, Jew (aptly named Judas) into a well until he agrees to reveal the Cross' location. The subsequent discovery of three crosses and their testing on a dead man to identify the True Cross of Christ, revealed when the corpse returns to life, transpires in five additional scenes. Judas converts to Christianity, is renamed Cyriacus, and becomes the bishop of Jerusalem. Helena then charges Cyriacus to find the nails used to affix Christ's body to the Cross, which the bishop dutifully does. The final two panels depict Helena placing a piece of the Cross into a châsse and transporting it back to Constantinople.[13] The following three registers depict the story of the Persian emperor Chosroes, who sacks Jerusalem in 615, stealing the True Cross in the process. The Byzantine emperor Heraclius leads his army to Chosroes's capital in Persia, engages his army in battle against the Persian forces, and kills their leader.

Heraclius restores the Cross to Jerusalem before returning, with additional relics, to Constantinople.[14]

These two stories comprise the lower half of the window. The vast majority of these panels are nineteenth century, although several of the medieval battle scenes that appeared in the window prior to its restoration were reinstalled as the military encounter between Chosroes and Heraclius. To further accommodate the medieval scenes to their new narrative assignment, the restorers equipped several panels with new iconographic details. Thus the military advance on horseback depicted in an unrestored panel was transformed into Heraclius' triumphant return to Jerusalem carrying the True Cross [Figs. 6-7].[15] The stories of Helena and Heraclius segue into the history of the Passion relics under Louis IX. The next five rows of scenes chronicle the acquisition of the Crown of Thorns, while the final three registers depict Louis' subsequent acquisition of the True Cross—a narrative sequence that also did not appear in the medieval window—and the newly-created scenes in which Louis oversees the construction of the Sainte Chapelle [Figs. 3-5, 10, 15].[16]

As I've suggested, the True Cross legends, while not part of the medieval ensemble, offered an effective narrative scaffold for completing the window. More importantly, the True Cross stories facilitated the semantic reorientation of a building long identified as a symbol of French monarchy. Numerous studies of the Sainte-Chapelle's medieval sculpture and glass have noted the striking emphasis on crowns and kings that pervade the ensemble.[17] I have argued elsewhere that the thirteenth-century glass designers employed popular medieval storytelling devices, predicated on rhetorical strategies of amplification and repetition, to customize the biblical narratives into a treatise on medieval kingship—a visual *Mirror of Princes* articulating the seminal responsibilities and prerogatives of French kings.[18] In the Numbers window, for example, the naming of the tribes of Israel is visualized as a series of coronations that copy the actual thirteenth-century French coronation ceremonies [Fig. 11].[19] The keystone of the chapel's emphasis on kingship was, of course, the Crown of Thorns placed upon the head of Christ, the king of kings, prior to his crucifixion. Christ's crowning appears as the centerpiece of the Passion window, the axial window of the chapel [Figs. 1-2, 12]. This scene engaged in a compositional and iconographic dialectic with the repeated scenes of coronation pervading the medieval ensemble, and resonated most strongly with those found in the pre-restoration Relics window. Here, in two separate panels employing a compositional schema comparable to the coronations found throughout the ensemble, bedridden kings crowned their successors [Fig. 9]. This same window also displayed

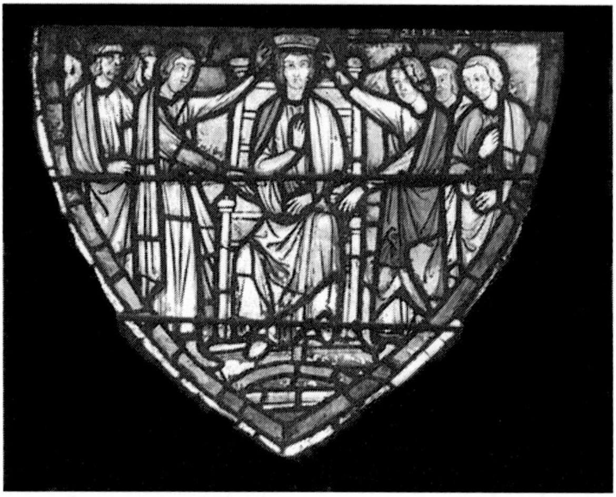

Fig. 11 Coronation of a Prince of Israel, medieval panel M-166, ca. 1248, Numbers Window, Sainte-Chapelle, Paris (Photo: B. Acloque/Centre des monuments nationaux, Paris)

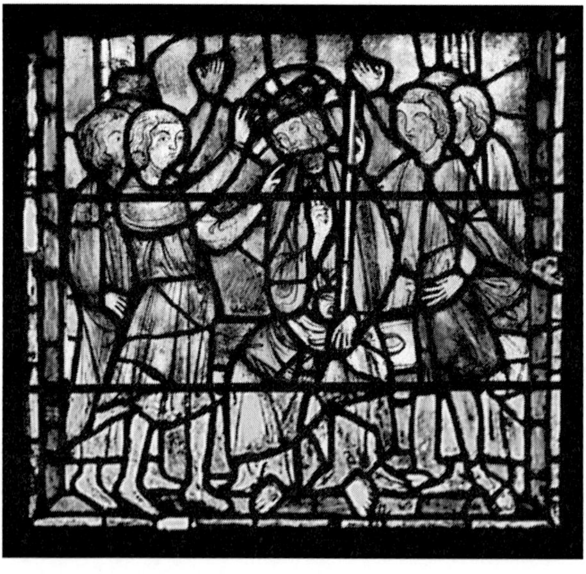

Fig. 12 Christ crowned with the Crown of Thorns, medieval panel H-81, ca. 1248, Passion Window, Sainte-Chapelle, Paris (Photo: B. Acloque/Centre des monuments nationaux, Paris)

one of the ensemble's most famous medieval scenes, the presentation of the Crown of Thorns by Gautier Cornut, flanked by Louis IX and Blanche of Castile, to the assembled populace [Fig. 5]. The juxtaposition of these deathbed coronations with the display of the Crown of Thorns gave visual form to Pope Innocent IV's pronouncement, in the charter of privileges he issued for the chapel in 1244, that "Christ has crowned you [Louis and, by extension, Louis' ancestors and descendents] with his own Crown of Thorns."[20] Louis IX's acquisition of the Crown of Thorns thus sealed the identification of France and its kings as uniquely favored by God.[21]

As a preeminent symbol of French monarchy, the Sainte-Chapelle was among those buildings singled out for destruction in the years following the revolution. From 1790 to 1792 the chapel was emptied of its furnishings, relics, and precious metalwork. In 1793, the chapel's spire was dismantled for the express purpose of removing the crown, fleur-de-lys, and royal monogram that decorated it, elements "considered dangerous, 'shameful vestiges of tyranny'."[22] The same year, an artist named Daujon was engaged to remove all the sculpted crowns, fleurs-de-lys, and other royal heraldry from the chapel.[23] The Sainte-Chapelle's restoration a half century later effectively continued this post-revolutionary program, albeit within a different political and conceptual framework. Certainly the restorers themselves were motivated by a genuine concern to save this venerable medieval building. Political support for the chapel's restoration, initiated during the July monarchy of Louis-Philippe and continued without interruption under the subsequent reign of Louis Napoléon, comprised part of a larger governmental campaign to transform problematic royal and religious buildings into *monuments historiques*—architectural exemplars of France's rich cultural (hence national) heritage.[24] Evidence of this semantic realignment is powerfully manifest in the restoration of the Sainte-Chapelle glass and is nowhere more evident than in the so-called Relics window.

The redesign of this window as a history of the Passion relics fundamentally altered its pre-restoration focus on kings, coronations, warfare, and the Crown of Thorns as a seminal emblem of French kingship. Absent the scenes of childbirth and kings crowning their successors, no one would identify this window as a history of Louis IX, as both François de Guilhermy and Ferdinand de Lasteyrie had done prior to its restoration [Figs. 8-9].[25] The elimination of specific genealogical referents facilitated the semantic reidentification of the fleurs-de-lys that blanket the window's borders and backgrounds as a French national emblem, rather than a symbol of dynasty and monarchic oppression, issues that fueled the revolutions of both 1830 and 1848.[26] The elimination of battle scenes, and the relegation of those few reinstalled to the temporally and geographically distant realm of seventh-century Persia [Figs. 6-7], diminished the emphasis on warfare clearly observable in the pre-restoration window, choices that also diminished the potential association of French kings with the military suppression of revolutions and riots that had comprised the backdrop to French life since 1789.[27]

Aligning the window with the legends of the True Cross not only shifted the emphasis away from the Crown of Thorns, but redirected it specifically *on to* the body of Christ, a focus mirrored in contemporary ultramontane ideology. Ultramontanism comprised a Catholic revival movement whose supporters, as the term implies, looked "beyond the mountains," specifically the Alps, to "the principle of authority… embodied in the person of the Pope."[28] Devotees of the ultramontane movement included many proponents of the medieval revival, including Jean-Baptist Lassus, Ferdinand de Lasteyrie, and François de Guilhermy—the same men at the center of the Sainte-Chapelle restoration.[29] Michael Driskel has deftly charted the influence of the ultramontane movement on the revival of contemporary religious painting in nineteenth-century France, and the particular iconographic and stylistic paradigms to which successful religious painting adhered. Driskel has demonstrated that the ultramontane focus on the Blessed Sacrament—the body of Christ—reached a pinnacle of liturgical significance in the mid-nineteenth century, when the Eucharist was proclaimed in religious publications as "the foundation stone upon which the Catholic religion was built" and a primary vehicle for promoting Catholic piety.[30] A parallel augmentation in the liturgical import of the Feast of Corpus Christi, together with a marked increase in contemporary religious paintings devoted to Christ, offer further evidence of ultramontane influence. Driskel credits the French painter Ingres and his 1841 depiction of *The Virgin Venerating the Host*, an iconography of the painter's own invention [Fig. 13], for imparting a defining visual form to "the importance that the ultramontane movement placed upon this sacrament."[31]

Despite the survival of crowns, crowned figures, and coronations in the restored Sainte-Chapelle glass, the new focus on the True Cross in the Relics window facilitated a reorientation of the ensemble's overall program. In theological terms, the True Cross had, since the fourth century, constituted the most important of the Passion relics, "the original agent of Christian salvation" and the "visible proof that the Crucifixion had taken place."[32] Indeed, Jacobus de Voragine's *Golden Legend*, the thirteenth-century compilation of stories devoted to the True Cross, makes no mention whatsoever of the Crown of Thorns. With its diminished

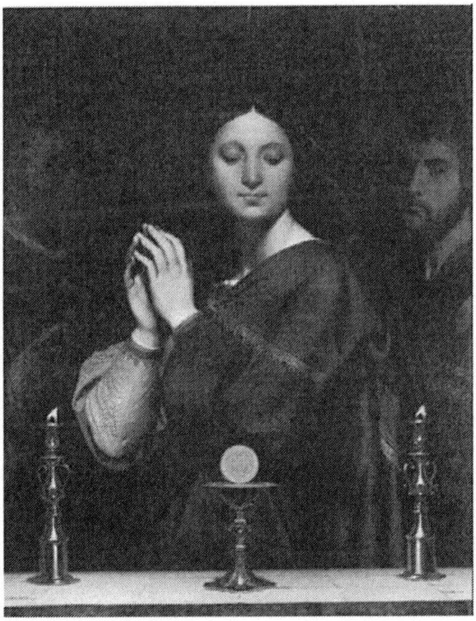

Fig. 13 Jean-Auguste-Dominique Ingres, *The Virgin Venerating the Host*, 1841 (Photo: Pushkin State Museum of Fine Arts, Moscow)

emphasis on crowns, kings, and royal prerogatives, the restored "Relics" window could now engage the Passion window in a visual conversation focused on the magnitude of Christ's sacrifice, rather than his role as the ultimate exemplar of kingship, a discourse the restorers heightened through the addition of new panels depicting angels holding instruments of Christ's Passion, and large-scale scenes of the Crucifixion and Deposition [Fig. 12].[33] The Old Testament leaders depicted in the other windows now became types of Christ, rather than model kings [Figs. 5, 11-12]. Inscribing Louis IX's acquisition of Passion relics, their translation to France, and his construction of the Sainte-Chapelle into the narrative trajectory of the Helena and Heraclius legends furthered this semantic shift, casting Louis IX not as the progenitor of the French monarchic claim to sacral kingship, but locating him, rather, within a more conventional and humble paradigm of pious leader and donor [Figs. 3-5, 10, 15].[34]

This persona appealed to a number of mid-century agendas. It underscored the popularity of Louis IX as a model king who had led France at the height of her political and artistic power, defended the Church against the infidel through the mounting of two crusades to liberate the Holy Land, and been honored with canonization. As the influential French *archéologue* Adolph Didron had said, "Louis IX is, above all, a saint."[35] Indeed, in the realm of contemporary French hagiographic painting, depictions of Louis IX numbered second only to images of Mary Magdalene.[36] Saint Louis' pictorial popularity was due in part to his status as name saint to both Louis-Philippe and Louis Napoléon, not to mention his aptitude as an exemplar of model post-revolutionary monarchic rule.[37] Louis' crusade activities may also have resonated with particular power at mid-century, given France's ongoing military engagement in Algeria. Initiated by the Bourbon king Charles X (reigned 1824-1830), inherited by Louis-Philippe and Louis Napoléon, the French occupation of Algeria enjoyed enormous popular support. Driskel notes that "[t]he French mission in North Africa was frequently dignified with the locution 'Croisade' [Crusade] in the press and from the pulpit."[38] French soldiers dispatched to Algeria were praised for their service "to Christianity," and numerous endorsements of the campaign drew parallels between France's historic leadership role in the crusades of the Middle Ages and its contemporary mission. The scholar and statesman Louis Blanc proclaimed the deliverance of Algeria "a glorious necessity" adding rhetorically, "And what people were more worthy, more capable than the people of France….France showed itself faithful to its historic role; it reprised, with more clarity and less fanaticism, the great tradition of the crusades; it once more protected civilization."[39] The Algerian campaign, then, offered a means by which France could tangibly reconnect with its medieval glory.[40] If the invocation of crusading implicitly suggested a Christian agenda, the casting of France as the defender of civilization could appeal, at once, to both religious and secular constituencies.

In the interest of clarity and, perhaps, political utility, the narrative sequences occupying the upper half of the Relics window present Louis IX *not* as crusader, but as pious public servant, and national unifier.[41] Using a combination of new and medieval panels, the restorers devoted a total of seven registers to the acquisition, translation, and veneration of the Crown of Thorns and the True Cross. The first sequence begins with Louis IX dispatching two monks to purchase the Crown. Louis meets his envoys and their precious cargo several panels later at Villeneuve-l'Archêveque. Louis and his brother, Robert d'Artois, carry the relics to Sens and on to Paris, accompanied by expansive processions of French subjects [Figs. 3-5, 14]. Louis subsequently dispatches two more monastic envoys to acquire the True Cross. While the surviving medieval panels documented only the 1239 acquisition of the Crown of Thorns, the existence of one authentic panel in which Louis IX holds a cross above his head justified, for the restorers, the creation of a separate narrative sequence devoted to Louis' 1241 purchase of additional Passion relics, which included a piece of the Cross. To create two discrete stories, the restorers produced new panels of Louis charging his envoys with their tasks and multiplied the scenes in which Louis and his subjects process with and venerate the relics [Figs. 3-5, 10, 14].[42]

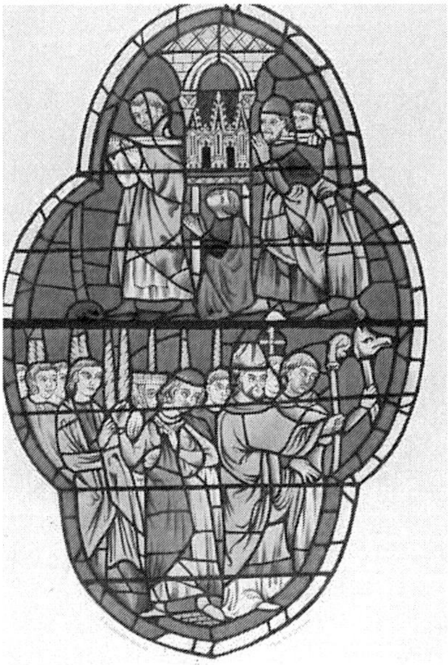

Fig. 14 Procession of the Crown of Thorns; Clergy and laity accompanying the procession of the Crown of Thorns, color lithograph of medieval stained glass panels before restoration, "Relics" window, from Ferdinand de Lasteyrie, *Histoire de la peinture sur verre*, vol. 2 (Paris: Firmin Didot Frères, 1853).

These sequences unite the king and his subjects in a paradigm of pious activity oriented around the arrival of Christ's relics on French soil, their translation to, and display in, the French capital. Numerous scholars have suggested that Louis IX perceived the acquisition of the relics, together with the carefully staged activities surrounding their arrival in France and transport to Paris, in precisely these terms, as a means of generating a collective, privileged French identity.[43] I propose that the expansion of these translation sequences through the multiplication of scenes in which "all the people of the French, without distinction of gender, rank...[or] even station,"[44] joined their king in an event that seamlessly conflated religion, culture, politics, and national identity proffered at once a nostalgic vision of French medieval history and a contemporary image of

French political aspirations.

Both Louis-Philippe and Louis Napoléon sought to unify the many factions into which post-revolutionary France had ruptured. The country's medieval past offered the foundation for a shared history when France, united by a common faith, led by a just and capable monarch was widely perceived as the political and cultural superpower of the western world. Medieval buildings, especially those executed in the Gothic style, provided the most tangible connection to this mythical common past. Under the direction of François Guizot, Louis-Philippe's Minister of Public Instruction, the first governmental agencies devoted to the study, oversight, restoration and refurbishment of medieval architecture emerged.[45] The restoration projects Guizot initiated, the Sainte-Chapelle being among the first and most high profile, continued without interruption through the Revolution of 1848, the Second Republic, the Second Empire, and beyond. The overarching agenda fueling these projects comprised nothing less than the ideological transformation of medieval architecture from debased and disreputable remnants of the *ancien régime* into treasured monuments of French history.[46] It was the Sainte-Chapelle, one of the monuments most politically "tainted," by virtue of its six-hundred-year history as a preeminent symbol of French monarchy, which would become among the most enduring exemplars of French *patrimoine*.

Meredith Cohen has described the Sainte-Chapelle's semantic metamorphosis as a form of "creative Iconoclasm" that "transformed the building into an object that projected nineteenth-century rationalist aesthetics and nationalistic values."[47] Having been subjected to strategic destruction at the hands of the post-Revolutionary government, despoiled of its royal treasures and precious relics, those of Louis IX as well as Christ,[48] the Sainte-Chapelle, newly restored, could be newly invested with meaning. No longer a private palace chapel, but a secular monument open to the public, the Sainte-Chapelle now served as a source of national pride. A transcendent gem of Gothic architecture, built by a beloved king turned national saint, the Sainte-Chapelle embodied the best of French monarchic history. Chosen as one of the first monuments to be restored according to scientific, state-of-the-art principles, and hailed as a "model restoration" that would set the standard for all subsequent renovations of medieval buildings, the Sainte-Chapelle remains to this day one of the premier tourist attractions of Paris.[49]

The most famous window in this famous building exemplifies the ways in which, as Adolph Didron proclaimed, the past could serve the present.[50] A bay filled with ambiguous scenes of kings crowning their successors and engaged in battle, together with compelling depictions of singular events from thirteenth-century French history, the chapel's final nave bay presented its restorers with multiple challenges. Working from the most specific scenes, those of the translation of the Crown of Thorns, Guilhermy and Lassus crafted an expansive epic spanning a temporal trajectory beginning in the fourth century and culminating in the 1240s. This restoration narrative downplayed monarchic claims to sacral kingship and royal prerogative in favor of monarchic piety and consensus building. The window's redirected focus on Passion relics and the defense of Christendom spoke to contemporary religious and political concerns. Its repeated scenes of French men and women, clergy and laity, in pious procession behind the reliquary châsse, carried by Louis IX and Robert d'Artois, gave visual form to a France in which all socio-economic groups, religious and secular, lived harmoniously united under a just and capable ruler [Figs. 4-10, 14]. The window's final scenes, in which Louis IX oversees the construction of the Sainte-Chapelle, offered a meta-narrative of the chapel's own re-creation and, by extension, the many other restoration campaigns undertaken by the governments of Louis-Philippe and Louis Napoléon [Figs. 1, 15].

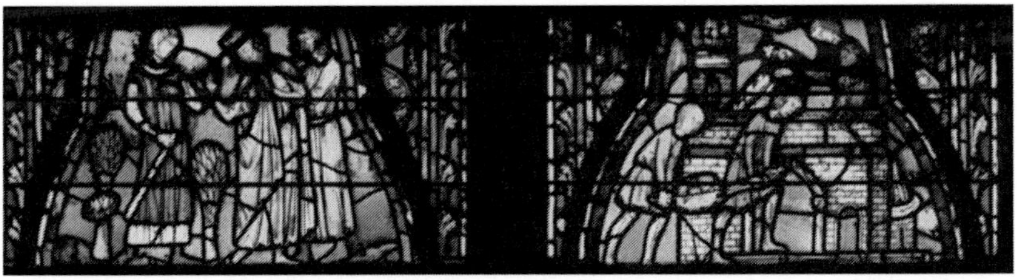

Fig. 15 Louis IX commissions the construction of the Sainte-Chapelle and the Sainte-Chapelle under construction, modern panels A-33 (L) and A-36 (R), ca. 1853-1855, "Relics" Window, Sainte-Chapelle, Paris (Photo: B. Acloque/Centre des monuments nationaux, Paris)

Like François de Guilhermy and Ferdinand de Lasteyrie, I believe this window originally contained a history of the kings of France, and I have proposed renaming it the "Royal" window to more accurately reflect its medieval narrative content.[51] The window the restorers created, however, was no longer a "Royal" window but, indeed, a "Relics" window, devoted not only to the relics of Christ's Passion, but the physical and metaphoric relics of a lost past. At the same time, the "Relics" window looked not only backwards but forwards, to a France whose new identity would be constructed in part on a medieval history crafted according to contemporary exigencies. And while it could not have been known in 1853, when this window's story was rewritten, the image of a people and their king joined in a defining act of national cohesion would prove an enduring, and elusive, leitmotif of France's own nineteenth-century narrative.

Notes

[1] The Sainte-Chapelle boasts a voluminous bibliography. See, most recently, Meredith Cohen, "An Indulgence for the Visitor: The Public at the Sainte-Chapelle of Paris," *Speculum* 83 (2008). 840-883; Meredith Marie Cohen, "The Sainte-Chapelle of Paris: Image of Authority and Locus of Identity" (Ph.D. diss., Columbia University, 2004); Daniel H. Weiss, *Art and Crusade in the Age of Saint Louis* (Cambridge: Cambridge University Press, 1998); Jean-Michel Leniaud and François Perrot, *La Sainte-Chapelle* (Paris: Nathan/CNMHS, 1991); Henri Stein, *Le Palais de justice et la Sainte-Chapelle de Paris: notice historique et archéologique* (Paris: D.A. Longuet, 1912).

[2] Recent studies of the chapel's glass include Alyce A. Jordan, *Visualizing Kingship in the Windows of the Sainte-Chapelle*, Publications of the International Center of Medieval Art, no. 5 (Turnhout: Brepols, 2002); Leniaud and Perrot, *La Sainte-Chapelle*. 120-237; Marcel Aubert, Louis Grodecki, Jean Lafond, and Jean Verrier, *Les Vitraux de Notre-Dame et de la Sainte-Chapelle de Paris*, Corpus Vitrearum Medii Aevi, France, vol. 1 (Paris: Caisse Nationale des Monuments Historiques/Centre National de la Recherche Scientifique, 1959). 71-349 (hereafter cited as *CV*)

[3] On the restoration of the Sainte-Chapelle glass see Jordan, *Visualizing Kingship*. 79-126; Alyce A. Jordan, "Rationalizing the Narrative: Theory and Practice in the Nineteenth-Century Restoration of the Windows of the Sainte-Chapelle," *Gesta* 37 (1998). 192-200; Leniaud and Perrot, *La Sainte-Chapelle*. 120-237; *CV*. 84-91. By 1848, the Sainte-Chapelle windows had already endured at least a century of relative neglect and poor-quality restorations. In 1803, approximately two meters' worth of glass was removed from the lower portion of the windows, and the iron armatures filled with plaster, to facilitate the chapel's use as a judicial archive. Some of the panels taken from the lower registers were used as stopgaps in the windows' upper registers. Most of the suppressed glass was presumably destroyed, although some panels did end up on the international art market. See Jordan, "Rationalizing the Narrative." 192

[4] The relics of Christ's Passion include, most notably, pieces of the True Cross and thorns from the Crown of Thorns. Other items subsumed under the heading of Passion relics include myriad items associated with the events between Christ's arrest in the Garden of Gethsemane and his resurrection, such as the nails employed in his crucifixion, pieces of the robe the Romans placed upon him, and the lance used to pierce his side. See Henri Leclercq, "Instruments de la Passion," in *Dictionnaire de l'archéologie chrétienne et de liturgie*, ed. Fernand Cabrol, vol.

7, pt. 1 (Paris: Letouzey, 1926). cols. 1155-1157. While the Sainte-Chapelle housed numerous Passion relics, the two most prominent were the Crown of Thorns and a fragment of the True Cross. See Stein, *Le Palais de justice et la Sainte-Chapelle*. 145-147

[5] The "Relics" window contains four panels per row. Twenty medieval panels depicting scenes associated with the translation of the Crown of Thorns survive, indicating that at least five rows of scenes were devoted to this event. See Jordan, *Visualizing Kingship*. 124-125, Pl. A

[6] Jordan, *Visualizing Kingship*. 122-126. On the suppression of glass in the windows' lower registers see n. 3.

[7] "un examen approfondi." Quoted in Jean-Michel Leniaud, *Jean-Baptiste Lassus (1807-1857) ou le temps retrouvé des cathedrales*. Bibliothèque de la Société française d'Archéologie (Paris: Arts et Métiers Graphiques, 1980). 206

[8] Ferdinand de Lasteyrie, *Histoire de la peinture sur verre*, vol. 1 (Paris: Firmin Didot Frères, 1857). 169-172. Lasteyrie described the window prior to restoration as being composed "entièrement de sujets relatifs à l'histoire de saint Louis et à la translation de la couronne d'épines."

[9] For the discovery of the True Cross and nails by Saint Helena, the theft of the Cross by King Chosroes of Persia in 615, and its recovery by Emperor Heraclius see Jacobus de Voragine, *The Golden Legend*, trans. William Granger Ryan (Princeton: Princeton University Press, 1993). 1:277-284; 2:168-173

[10] The selection of the history of the Passion relics as the orienting theme for the window appears to have been dictated entirely by Lassus. As part of a report on the restoration of the windows, Guilhermy describes this window as representing "non pas, comme on l'avait pensé, l'histoire de S. Louis, mais celle de l'acquisition, de la susception et de la translation des reliques en l'honneur desquelles ce prince fit construire la Saint Chapelle." See Jordan, *Visualizing Kingship*. 153 n. 6; for a panel-by-panel identification of the scenes see *CV*. 305-309

[11] See, for example, Richard Morris, *Legends of the Holy Rood* (London: Early English Text Society, 1871); Arthur Napier, *History of the Holy Rood-tree* (London: Early English Text Society, 1894). A verse romance of Heraclius' life was written in Old French in the late twelfth century by Gautier d'Arras, *Eracle*, ed. Guy Raynaud de Lage (Paris: Champion, 1976).

[12] On the new liturgies created to celebrate these events at the Sainte-Chapelle see Alyce A. Jordan, "Stained Glass and the Liturgy: Performing Sacral Kingship in Capetian France," in *Objects, Images and the Word: Art in the Service of the Liturgy*, Index of Christian Art Occasional Papers 6, ed. Colum Hourihane (Princeton: Princeton University Press, 2003). 274-297

[13] *CV*. 305, Pl. 86-87, panels A-171-140

[14] *CV*. 305-306, Pl. 86-87, panels A-131-112

[15] Such precise analysis of the alterations made by the restorers is possible thanks to their meticulous documentation of the restoration process, which included the identification of pre-restoration locations of panels within each window, as well as the execution of full-scale watercolor tracings of each panel's pre- and post-restoration condition. Many of the panels not reinstalled in the chapel were

ultimately lost. The scenes they depicted, however, are preserved in these watercolor tracings. "Relevés-calques des vitraux de la Sainte-Chapelle de Paris," 20 vols., 1848-1852, Médiathèque de l'Architecture et du Patrimoine, Paris. On the alteration of this panel see Jordan, *Visualizing Kingship*. 122

[16] *CV*. 306-308, Pl. 84-87, panels A-103-133

[17] Beat Brenk, "The Sainte-Chapelle as a Capetian Political Program," in *Artistic Integration in Gothic Building*, ed. Virginia Raguin, Kathryn Brush, and Peter Draper (Toronto: University of Toronto Press, 1995). 195-213; Cohen, "The Sainte-Chapelle of Paris." 80-114, 241-262; Leniaud and Perrot, *La Sainte-Chapelle*; Weiss, *Art and Crusade*.

[18] Jordan, *Visualizing Kingship*. 10-29. On the use of Old Testament leaders as monarchic exempla for medieval French kings see Donna Sadler, "The Persistence of the Royal Past on the West Façade of Reims Cathedral," in this volume.

[19] Jordan, *Visualizing Kingship*. 26-28; Jacques Le Goff, "A Coronation Program for the Age of Saint Louis: The *Ordo* of 1250," in *Coronations: Medieval and Early Modern Monarchic Ritual*, ed. Janos M. Bak (Berkeley: University of California Press, 1990). 46-57; Jacques Le Goff, *Le Sacre royal à l'époque de Saint-Louis: d'après le manuscript latin 1246 de la BNF* (Paris: Gallimard, 2001).

[20] Gautier Cornut, *Historia susceptionis corone spine*, in *Recueil des historiens des Gaules et de la France*, ed. Martin Bouquet and Leopold Delisle (1738-1904; reprint Farnborough: Gregg, 1968). 22:27, "Quod te Dominus in sua corona spinea…coronavit."

[21] Much has been written on the development of French sacral kingship. Major studies include Marc Bloch, *The Royal Touch: Sacred Monarchy and Scrofula in England and France*, trans. J. E. Anderson (1924; reprint London: Routledge and Kegan Paul, 1973); Percy Ernst Schramm, *Der König von Frankreich: Das Wesen der Monarchie vom 9. zum 16. Jahrhundert*, 2 vols. (Weimar: Nachfolger, 1960); John W. Baldwin, *The Government of Philip Augustus: Foundations of French Royal Power in the Middle Ages* (Berkeley: University of California Press, 1986); Andrew W. Lewis, *Royal Succession in Capetian France: Studies on Familial Order and the State* (Cambridge, MA: Harvard University Press, 1981); Joseph Strayer, "France: The Holy Land, the Chosen People, and the Most Christian King," in *Action and Conviction in Early Modern Europe*, ed. Theodore E. Rabb and Jerrold E. Seigel (Princeton: Princeton University Press, 1969). 3-16; and, most recently, M. Cecilia Gaposchkin, *The Making of Saint Louis: Kingship, Sanctity, and Crusade in the Later Middle Ages* (Ithaca : Cornell University Press, 2008).

[22] "réputés dangereux, 'des vestiges honteux de la tyrannie'..." Stein, *La Sainte-Chapelle*. 126-127, quoting a letter of 1793.

[23] On the systematic effacement of the Sainte-Chapelle between 1790 and the 1830s see Cohen, "The Sainte-Chapelle of Paris." 45-50

[24] That the Sainte-Chapelle's restoration comprised a conceptual and physical "makeover" that effectively reinvented the chapel as a French national monument was first articulated by Cohen, "The Sainte-Chapelle of Paris." 59-79; Meredith

Cohen, "Restoration as Re-creation at the Sainte-Chapelle," *RES* 48 (autumn, 2005). 135-154

[25] See nn. 8, 10; for potential identifications of these suppressed scenes see Jordan, *Visualizing Kingship*. 60-63

[26] The restoration of the "Relics" window did not begin until 1853, by which time Louis Napoléon's government was firmly established, although fleurs-de-lys do appear in windows restored soon after the 1848 uprising.

[27] Thirteen battle scenes appeared in the window prior to the restoration. Of these, only six were reinstalled, all in the context of the battle between Chosroes and Heraclius. Jordan, *Visualizing Kingship*. 122-126

[28] Michael Paul Driskel, *Representing Belief: Religion, Art, and Society in Nineteenth-Century France* (University Park, PA: Pennsylvania State University Press, 1992). 6

[29] Driskel, *Representing Belief*. 4-6; Michael Paul Driskel, "The Gothic, the Revolution and the Abyss: John-Philippe Schmit's Aesthetics of Authority," *Art History* 13 (1990). 200-202 provides a succinct overview of ultramontanism and its primary apologists. On the relationship of medieval architecture and the medieval revival and restoration movements to ultramontane ideology see Barry Bergdoll, "The Ideal of the Gothic Cathedral in 1852," in *A.W.N. Pugin: Master of the Gothic Revival*, ed. Megan Brewster Aldrich and Paul Atterbury (New Haven: Yale University Press, 1996). 108-109; and Catherine Brisac and Jean-Michel Leniaud, "Adolphe-Napoléon Didron ou les media au service de l'art chrétien," *Revue de l'Art* 77 (1987). 38-39

[30] Driskel, *Representing Belief*. 102-104

[31] Driskel, *Representing Belief*. 102. Ingres' iconic painting, with its strong central axis, strict symmetry, compositional stasis, and hard-edged execution offers an excellent example of the contemporary religious painting style advocated by the ultramontane movement. It also presents striking parallels to a preferred mode of medieval painting found, among other places, in the windows of the Sainte-Chapelle. See, for example, the multiple coronation scenes in the Numbers window, which employ a compositional formula very similar to Ingres' painting [Fig. 11]; and *CV*. Pl. 25, 28, panels M-160-167

[32] E. Gordon Whatley, ed. and trans., "Constantine the Great, the Empress Helena, and the Relics of the Holy Cross," in *Medieval Hagiography: An Anthology*, ed. Thomas Head (New York: Garland, 2000). 77

[33] *CV*. 198-203, Pl. 50-51, panels H-105-108, 58, 61

[34] The exceptional nature of the "Relics" window as one of the sole examples of a medieval window devoted to contemporary, secular history has been overlooked largely because of the narrative's post-restoration incarnation as a history of the Passion relics. Jordan, *Visualizing Kingship*. 58-60; Weiss, *Art and Crusade*. 77 observes that while "religious symbolism had been used to great effect in earlier imperial structures...only in the Sainte-Chapelle did the symbolism establish explicit links with the reigning monarch as part of a comprehensive thematic program."

[35] "Louis IX est saint avant tout." Adolph Didron, "Erection d'une statue à saint Louis," *Annales archéologiques* 3 (1845). 250

[36] Bruno Foucart, *Le Renouveau de la peinture religieuse en France (1800-1860)*, (Paris: Arthéna, 1987). 98. Foucart's assessment derives from the quantity of paintings devoted to Saint Louis, Mary Magdalene, and other hagiographic subjects exhibited at the annual Salons between 1800 and 1860.

[37] In his *Dictionnaire d'iconographie*, the prolific scholar J.-P. Migne described Louis IX as "un prince, le plus saint, le plus juste qui ait jamais porté la courronne." Quoted in Foucart, *Le Renouveau de la peinture religieuse*. 100. Foucart identifies Louis IX as embodying "une iconographie nationale, illustrant les valeurs civiques."

[38] Michael Paul Driskel, "Eclecticism and Ideology in the July Monarchy: Jules-Claude Ziegler's Vision of Christianity at the Madeline," *Arts Magazine* 56, 9 (May, 1982). 124

[39] "Et quel peuple était plus digne, plus capable que le peuple de France....la France se montrait fidèle à son role historique; elle reprenait, avec plus de lumières et moins de fanatisme, la grande tradition des croisades; elle abritait une fois encore la civilisation." Quoted in Driskel, "Eclecticism and Ideology." 124

[40] Driskel, "Eclecticism and Ideology." 119-129 examines the production of numerous artistic projects of the July Monarchy relative to the Algerian campaign, and the larger nationalistic agenda of Louis-Philippe and his ministers. The contemporary articulation of France's engagement in Algeria as a crusade helps account for the significance accorded Guilhermy's discovery of a panel in the Sainte-Chapelle's Isaiah window depicting the prophet Mohammad, identified by inscription, exhorting the Israelites to worship before a golden idol. François de Guilhermy, "Mahomet à la Sainte-Chapelle," *Annales archéologiques* 3 (1845). 508. In his response to a request from the mayor of Aigues-Mortes, from whose port Louis IX had embarked on crusade, requesting advice on the erection of a statue of Louis IX, Didron proposed instead the construction of "une église, une chapelle, ou tout au moins un oratoire" the design of which should copy the Sainte-Chapelle. Didron, "Erection d'une statue à saint Louis." 250-251

[41] Given the disastrous consequences of both Louis' campaigns to the Holy Land. Lasteyrie, however, described the window prior to its restoration as containing various scenes "tirés de la vie du roi saint Louis. La plupart de ces derniers ont trait aux guerres des croisades." Lasteyrie, *Histoire de la peinture sur verre*. 172

[42] *CV*. 306-308, Pl. 84-87

[43] On Louis' acquisition of the Passion relics as a vehicle for forging a collective identify see Strayer, "France: the Holy Land, the Chosen People, and the Most Christian King." 3-16; and, most recently, Weiss, *Art and Crusade*. 76, who describes the public ceremonies which attended the arrival of the Crown of Thorns and Passion relics in France as "above all a means of shaping consensus about the emergence of the Franks as the new Chosen People and that of their king as leader of the Christian world."

[44] "tota gens francorum sine differentia sexuum dignitatum ac graduum…." I quote from the liturgy written for the Translation of the Crown of Thorns, the lessons for

which derive from Archbishop Gautier Cornut's account of the translation. Jordan, "Stained Glass and the Liturgy: Performing Sacral Kinghip." 280

[45] On François Guizot and the creation of a French national heritage see Dominique Poulot, "The Birth of Heritage: 'Le Moment Guizot'," *Oxford Art Journal* 11 (1988). 40-56; Dominique Poulot, "Le Sens du patrimoine: hier et aujourd'hui," *Annales ESC* (1993). 1601-1613; Laurent Theis, "Guizot et les institutions de mémoire," in *Les Lieux de mémoire*, ed. Pierre Nora, vol. 2, 2 (Paris: Bibliothèque des Histoires, 1984). 569-592

[46] Recent studies of the ways in which this transformation was effected include Françoise Choay, *The Invention of the Historic Monument* (Cambridge: Cambridge University Press, 2001); Françoise Choay, *L'Allégorie du patrimoine* (Paris: Editions du Seuil, 1992); Elizabeth Emery, *Romancing the Cathedral: Gothic Architecture in Fin-de-Siècle French Culture* (Albany: State University of New York Press, 2001); Barry Bergdoll, "The Ideal of the Gothic Cathedral in 1852." Two important investigations of the trajectory of this process relative to specific restoration campaigns are Janet T. Marquardt, *From Martyr to Monument: The Abbey of Cluny as Cultural Patrimony* (Newcastle-upon-Tyne: Cambridge Scholars Publishing, 2007); and Kevin Murphy, *Memory and Modernity. Viollet-le-Duc at Vézelay* (University Park, PA: State University of Pennsylvania Press, 2000).

[47] Cohen, "Restoration as Re-creation." 153

[48] The Sainte-Chapelle possessed a portion of Louis IX's head, which was housed in a life-size portrait bust reliquary of the crowned king featuring the same youthful, beardless features with which he appears in the "Relics" window. The reliquary and its contents were removed from the chapel in 1791-1792 and subsequently lost. Cohen, "The Sainte-Chapelle of Paris." 46-47; Jordan, *Visualizing Kingship*. 68. On the history and artistic legacy of the reliquary see Louis Carolus-Barré, "Le Visage de Saint Louis dans les gravures du XVIIe siècle inspirèes du chef-reliquaire de la Sainte-Chapelle (1306)," *Monuments historiques de la France* 16 (1970). 22-30

[49] Cohen, "Restoration as Re-creation." 152 notes the promotion of the Sainte-Chapelle as an exemplar of "scientific" restoration and must-see tourist attraction through the publication of engravings, monographs, "even postcards." François de Guilhermy, *Description de la Sainte-Chapelle* (Paris: La Sainte Chapelle, 1857) was continually in press for over fifty years and, by 1899, and gone through no fewer than eleven new editions.

[50] Bergdoll, "The Ideal of the Gothic Cathedral in 1852." 111

[51] Jordan, *Visualizing Kingship*. 60-65

BRANNER'S "COURT STYLE" AND THE ANXIETY OF INFLUENCE

MEREDITH COHEN

Nearly half a century has passed since the publication of Robert Branner's *St Louis and the Court Style in Gothic Architecture* (1965), a book that, despite its age, remains a widely read yet controversial classic.[1] In his study, Branner examined the influence of royal patronage on art and architecture in mid-thirteenth-century France and specifically proposed that, in Paris, under the auspices of Saint Louis, there emerged a "Court Style" of architecture whose beauty and prestige inspired other patrons to imitate its forms across Europe. Branner's vivid evocation of medieval Paris and his suggestion that the king's personal involvement imparted a special aura on to Parisian art and architecture, which remains still today, made the book extremely appealing to a wide range of readers. Fascination with the concept of a "Court Style" persists and new perspectives continue to be offered with some frequency: conference sessions and university courses are dedicated to the topic; museums worldwide organize exhibitions of royal patrons and their collections; and articles on the state of the question continue to be published.[2] Such longevity is difficult to explain, particularly after the "theoretical turn" of the early 1980s. The enduring interest in the "Court Style" is especially remarkable given that many architectural historians have serious reservations about fundamental concepts in the book. Yet, as the continued engagement with it proves, there is a reluctance to dispense with its ideas altogether.

While the reception of a book or a theory is rarely unified, the ambivalence towards the *Court Style* merits some consideration, particularly because its historiography follows a classic pattern, one which finds parallels with what the literary critic Harold Bloom has described as the "Anxiety of Influence."[3] Expounded over the last thirty years, Bloom's theory addresses the issues of influence, originality, and authorship.[4] At its most general, the "Anxiety of Influence" explains the process by which younger authors overcome the work of esteemed predecessors in the process of individualization. Bloom outlines six "revisionary ratios" in this trajectory, three that delineate the reception of a predecessor's work by a younger author, and three that describe the younger author's emancipation and assumption of his or her own creative contribution.[5]

Although Bloom's theory of influence is widely disseminated within the field of literary criticism, his ideas have rarely been applied beyond that domain.[6] This may be explained in part as a function of Bloom's own efforts to curtail widespread use and to avoid subjection to the revisionary patterns he identifies in his work.[7] A cursory examination of Bloom also would lead to the conclusion that his work might only be directed to poetry, for the subtitle of *The Anxiety of Influence* was *A Theory of Poetry*. However, in the second edition of that book, he wrote that this restriction was "a false emphasis…corrected in *A Map of Misreading* and subsequent books."[8] Bloom's theory has become increasingly distinct from his literary criticism. Still, other reasons may explain why his work has not had a larger impact outside of his own field.[9] His terminology can be unnecessarily abstract, appearing sometimes as jargon, and it can be difficult to distinguish his theory from his analyses. Moreover, his ideas are polemical, and they do not invite casual applications. Often criticized for being androcentric, for privileging European white males, and for its antagonism to feminist and non-traditional/non-Western forms, Bloom's theory appears unlikely to have wide appeal or relevance to contemporary discourse.[10] Yet it is important to recognize that his theory of influence engages with a broad philosophical tradition that includes Nietzsche, Freud, Heidegger, and more recently, de Man and Derrida.[11] For this reason, it cannot be simply dismissed as external to the broader Humanities.

Although the commentary on Bloom is so extensive that a few paragraphs do not allow for an intricate explanation of the debate, a sketch of the major critiques reveals nevertheless how his theory resonates with this essay's historiographic project. Perhaps the most frequently cited criticism is that Bloom's notion of influence resembles the Freudian "family romance," wherein the youth assassinates the father in order to assert an individual identity. This drama has problematic implications: it assumes that creativity arises from self-defense, and that it is based on a single and specific relationship. Moreover, it ignores the fact that different and complex factors contribute to artistic production. For these reasons, the theory is described as reductive.[12] A second general critique is that Bloom's theory de-idealizes the author insofar as it places creativity within a relational, and more specifically, an historical framework.[13] While this problematizes the idea of originality, it resonates with historiography. Bloom's theory is particularly compelling for this study because it not only delineates the relationships between authors and texts, but also it provides a model for analysis of the process of revision, which clarifies how discourses are shaped.

This essay focuses on the reception of Branner's *Court Style*, particularly in Anglo-American scholarship, where his work had a profound impact.[14] Bloom's perspective is useful for understanding how Branner's successors received and transformed his ideas.[15] The historiography following the *Court Style* particularly resonates with the three stages of reception Bloom termed *Clinamen* or "misprision," *Tessera* or "antithesis and completion," and *Apophrades* or the "return of the dead." These descriptors serve as tools for understanding the state of the question on the *Court Style* and reveal lacunae in the revisionary process. Even though architectural historians have raised valid objections to the concept of the "Court Style," these criticisms have diverted direct engagement with some of the book's most fascinating queries, namely, the relation between Gothic architecture and the French kings, the role of Parisian architecture after the mid-thirteenth century in France and greater Europe, and more broadly, persistent questions about the iconography of style. In order to understand how these issues were overlooked, examination of the *Court Style* historiography is essential, and to begin, a review of Branner's career and his seminal book is also useful.

Robert Branner and the "Court Style"

Robert Branner was an eminent professor of medieval art and architectural history, a leader of the field.[16] He authored a monumental oeuvre, comprising some eighty-three articles and six books.[17] While his research focused on the twelfth and thirteenth centuries, he wrote about many aspects of French Gothic architecture and illuminated manuscripts, and his work remains an important reference in both fields.[18]

His premature death at the age of forty-six in 1973, at the height of his career, inspired an outpouring of praise from the academic community worldwide. Eulogies acclaimed his prolific contribution and confirmed his scholarly importance. In the 1975 volume of the *Journal of the Society of Architectural Historians* dedicated to him, Carl Barnes recalled, "Robert Branner left behind him an astonishing legacy of scholarship," and Jean Bony professed, "For historians of mediaeval art there is a pre-Branner and a post-Branner age."[19] Other colleagues and students have described him as a man remarkably inspired with an insatiable curiosity and passion for his subject, as having a formidable confidence in his own ability to solve the questions he pursued, and as a scholar who generated new directions of thought and research.[20] Bony provided additional insight on his creative powers by explaining that "he worked always with such intensity and at such a pace that he accomplished in twenty years what could be claimed with pride as the sum of a long life's work."[21] So great was Branner's reach that even scholars across the Atlantic, such as Francis Salet, followed his publications: "[he] accustomed us to the obligation of reading very attentively all that he wrote."[22] Stephen Murray provided an example of the British perception of Branner during the time when he was a doctoral student in London:

> In the 1960s, it was impossible to escape the writings of Robert Branner. When I inquired of my own teacher, Peter Kidson, why every seminar paper seemed to end up as a critique of Branner's latest book or article, he replied that this was generally the only pertinent material on the subject and the only argument worth engaging.[23]

By all accounts, Branner was an imposing figure. His productivity and commanding personality awed, and perhaps intimidated, many of those around him. The esteem in which he was held would have made any subsequent development or revision of his research a challenge.

The *Court Style* was Branner's most ambitious work in terms of the scope of its subject and its theory about artistic influence. According to Eric Fernie, the book aimed to accord the architectural style identified today as Rayonnant the prominence of High Gothic by demonstrating its wide diffusion across France and greater Europe.[24] The first chapter described a Paris at the height of cultural excellence and secular glory during the reign of Louis IX. The university, which attracted students from far and wide, thrived. The markets, too, drew people to the city for its wealth of offerings and fine wares. The honorable, pious, and wise king, loved by his people, also attracted many foreign dignitaries to the city. In Branner's Parisian utopia, the "Court Style" emerged, in large part due to the monarchy's generous patronage. The Sainte-Chapelle [Figs. 1-2] was in many ways its flagship representative: "Such was the renown of the chapel and such the prestige of the French court, that Paris rapidly became the architectural centre of Europe, for a time dominating and giving direction to the general expansion of the Gothic style throughout France and abroad."[25] The popularity of the style across Europe had less to do with the decorative forms themselves than with the Parisian glamour and royal prestige they conveyed.

The next four chapters were devoted to an exhaustive description of the "Court Style" itself. As Branner saw it, the style emerged around 1220 in the Ile-de-France, became coherent after 1240 in Paris, and reached maturity only after 1254 in and beyond Paris.[26] Branner conceived of style as an independent entity, following Focillon, who anthropomorphized artistic processes and described stylistic developments in terms of the cycle of life.[27] It is also not irrelevant that Branner lived in New York during the heyday of Modernism (which included Abstract Expressionism and the International Style), when artists and architects worked to reveal the essential qualities of artistic materials, and style itself was generally believed to be both coherent and highly expressive. This was of course before the New Criticism problematized the concept of style, fundamentally changing the practice of art history.[28]

Branner distinguished the following qualities in the "Court Style" of architecture: it had unified spaces, interchangeable parts, and thin, sharp, linear decoration; structural and decorative elements were fused so as to become indistinguishable from one another; architectonic bulk was reduced and volumes refined; walls were drawn open like curtains attached to bay responds; galleries and dados were made to appear lighter

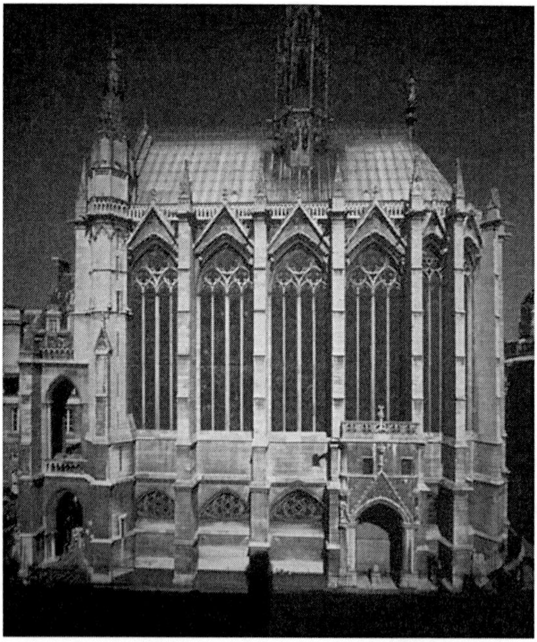

Fig. 1 Exterior, Sainte-Chapelle, Paris, 1239-1248
(Photo: David Bordes © CMN, Paris)

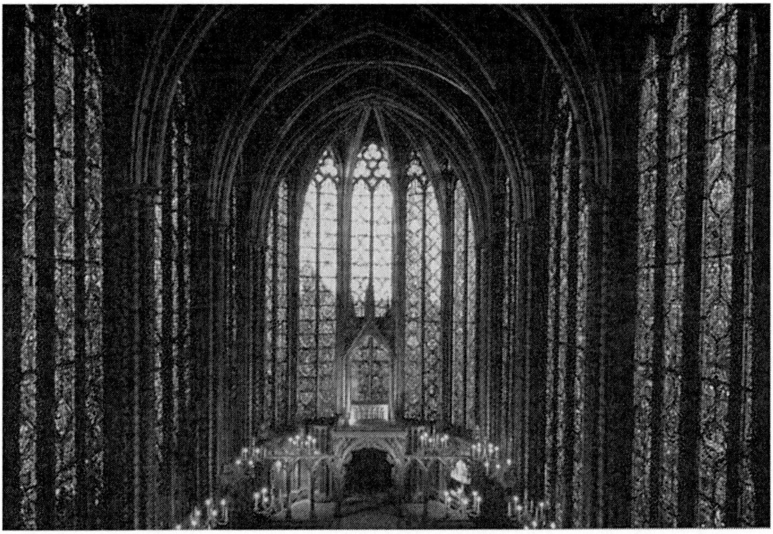

Fig. 2 Interior, Sainte-Chapelle, Paris, 1239-1248
(Photo: David Bordes © CMN, Paris)

with sheaths of fine stone decoration, and colonnettes thinned and elongated; the parts were finer and the transitions between them more fluid than in earlier High Gothic buildings; elements such as column shafts, points, arches, and finials possessed a new and distinct crispness that emphasized line and enhanced the effects of light; large windows of grisaille glass accentuated the contours of the building, generating a crystalline quality in interior spaces. The exteriors were monumental but elegant, with delicate gables adorned with crockets and pinnacles that left animated, dramatic silhouettes.[29]

Branner wrote about style as if it had a life of its own, one seemingly independent from the choices made by masons and sculptors who actually produced the forms. At the same time, he maintained that the "Court Style" was indebted to its most important patron, Louis IX. Branner attributed an extraordinary number of buildings directly to the royal purse, but not only "Court Style" buildings. The king was, among other things, a master planner, instigating the production of fortresses, hospitals, and, above all, chapels and churches.[30]

Despite the attention given to a clear definition of the "Court Style," Branner insisted that it was not immutable.[31] Acutely aware of the complexity of artistic change, he attempted to isolate the discrete stylistic strands and follow them through their course of development. With unabashed positivism, Branner seems to have aimed to identify *all* the permutations of the "Court Style," which constituted the majority of the book.

The final chapter returned to the subject of stylistic exportation. Branner explained that the implementation of the "Court Style" outside of Paris—as near as at Saint-Germer-de-Fly or Saint-Urbain at Troyes, as far away as Germany at Regensburg, Spain at Burgos, and England at Westminster—was not entirely due to the expansion of the Mendicant orders or a question of traveling master masons; it also was not related to a self-perpetuating force. Instead, the great formalist suggested that the meaningful associations of the style accounted for its widespread popularity.[32] He concluded his book with the observation that "the exportation of the Parisian style may therefore be examined from the iconographic as well as the formal point of view."[33]

Although not an entirely new idea in its time, Branner attributed the significance or meanings of style to a unique context shaped by a time, a place, and a person: the mid-thirteenth century, Paris, and Louis IX.[34] The *Court Style* aimed to identify that period when the style was encoded with meaning. The discussion of Paris and the examination of the style's development and dissemination functioned as evidence to support this theory. In short, Branner proposed a theory about the iconology of style and relied primarily on formal analysis to prove it.

In its day, the *Court Style* was heralded as a major breakthrough in the field of Gothic architecture. Even many years after its completion, on the occasion of his eulogy to Branner, Jean Bony wrote, "His book on *St Louis and the Court Style* is beautiful by the way in which he transmits his sense of the complexities of historical movements and by his ability to perceive at every moment on what points the focus of invention is poised. Its impact was immediate….Branner's *Court Style* will stand as one of the most exciting works of mediaeval scholarship."[35] Considering the number of works it inspired, this statement seems to have reflected a general consensus, until subsequent research began to cast doubts.

Clinamen or Misprision

In the mid-seventies, the first wave of *Court Style* revisions appeared in doctoral dissertations and their subsequent publications. This body of work expresses what Bloom has described as *Clinamen* or "misprision," wherein the younger author "proceeds by a misreading of the prior…[in] an act of creative correction that is actually and necessarily a misinterpretation," which enables the novice to undertake new work.[36]

Misprision is a critical turn, an intellectual trope that generates an opening for further discourse; it is not based on conceptual and factual problems in the elder author's original text that emerge from analysis over time.

There have been two ways of misreading the *Court Style*. The first has been the widespread interpretation of the book as primarily a history of style. As discussed above, stylistic analysis and the identification of sources and influences did provide the majority of material evidence in the book. However, Branner's writing on this subject functioned primarily to support the idea that mid-thirteenth-century Parisian architecture, the "Court Style," possessed an aura related to the glory of the king and the greatness of the capital city, which accounted for its wide recognition and diffusion across Europe. Misprision occurred when those inspired by Branner's ideas endeavored to prove his theory as he did himself, by analyzing the direction of stylistic development; this will be discussed further below.

The second distortion is the general perception that Branner's definition of the "Court Style" was at once too narrowly defined and too all encompassing. He went to great lengths to explain the complexity of his concept in passages such as the following from the introduction:

> Royal architectural policy, to the extent that it can be re-established, was not inflexible and several important shifts will be noted in it during the reign of Louis IX. But this policy must also have been influenced by the taste of the time, so that while certain stylistic developments appear to have originated in royal shops, others took their start outside them, in such *chantiers* as Notre-Dame. The Court Style was not the exclusive creation of the king or his architects but was broadly based and deeply rooted in the French tradition.[37]

Subsequent authors have tended to overstate Branner's understanding of the king's involvement in architecture. Assertions such as, "the importance of Paris notwithstanding, the direct association that has been created between King Louis IX and the new architectural style is misleading in many ways," simplify the complexity of Branner's vision.[38] While Branner did emphasize the importance of the royal contribution, he maintained that patronage did not determine its forms, as the above excerpt demonstrates. However, some equivocation on the subject also appears in the *Court Style* because Branner emphasized the king's involvement in architectural patronage: he wrote about the different kinds of architecture the king commissioned, and he considered whether the king had employed a Master of the Works.[39] In addition, Branner also cited chronicles, such as that by Jean de Joinville, who lauded Louis' embellishment of the capital, and Egidio Colonna (Archbishop of Bourges), who described the king's close involvement in the process of developing a new building.[40] While these examples support the idea of the king's participation in artistic choices, they also illustrate the diversity of the royal commissions within the larger field of architecture. In Chapter Five, for example, Branner distinguished the less ornate architecture of the hospitals, Mendicant buildings, convents, and university buildings made by royal workshops from "Court Style" structures. Perhaps most contradictory to his more nuanced claims, Branner wrote of a "royal architectural policy," in relation to the king's works, which suggested that Louis possessed a clearly defined program. However, Branner also affirmed that "[Louis] nonetheless did not impose his point of view on others and he did not use it as the only basis for his architectural and artistic policies."[41]

Although the king's patronage was an important impetus for the "Court Style," Branner developed the idea that the style derived from multiple sources. The second chapter discusses contributions of High Gothic architecture from northeastern France (particularly Reims and Amiens) from around 1220 to Parisian architecture a generation later. Here, Branner wrote, "The Court Style…hardly innovated at all, but rather developed to an unusually high degree certain tendencies already latent in the architecture of the early thirteenth century."[42] In the third chapter, Royaumont and Saint-Denis were considered as contributors to the "Court Style." While royal patronage at Royaumont was clearly documented, the extent of royal participation in the thirteenth-century renovation of Saint-Denis remains unknown, and Branner recognized this in his discussion of the thirteenth-century renovation of the abbey church: "Whether or not the Crown also supplied funds for the Gothic work….the abbey's relationship to the Crown may explain the presence of royal coats of arms among the ornaments of the Gothic work."[43] This subject remains debated to this day, but it is possible that Saint-Denis did not require any special financial assistance from the king, for the abbey was already extremely wealthy and received regular donations from the royal family.[44]

In his consideration of the sources and reflections of the style, Branner admitted that, "unfortunately very few buildings have survived from this time in Paris, and in order to form a picture of the Court Style we must look for reflections of it elsewhere…although we must always bear in mind that differences were likely to exist between centre and periphery."[45] The buildings he enumerated as belated reflections were thus qualified as "Courtly Works": the tribune of the Sainte-Chapelle, the Lady Chapel at Saint-Germer-de-Fly, the triforium and clerestory of Beauvais Cathedral, the priory of Chambly, the cathedral of Clermont-Ferrand, the south transept and the *Portail Rouge* of Notre-Dame, Saint-Urbain at Troyes, Saint-Nazaire at Carcassonne, and the cathedral of Orléans.[46] Despite his subtle distinctions and caveats, this list has often been seen as constitutive rather than generally representative of the "Court Style." Since Branner made the effort to describe the multiple exchanges of forms throughout the course of his book, it seems he conceived of a style in a much looser and more fluid way than scholars have assumed in more recent years.

Despite his exhaustive attempt to describe, explain, and provide nuance, the "Court Style" remains extremely difficult to distil. It is generally understood as equivalent to Rayonnant, although it is difficult to ascertain whether this is exactly what Branner intended.[47] As Brigitte Kurmann-Schwartz aptly remarked, "The reader…searches…in vain for precise formal criteria permitting the distinction of the 'Court Style' from the more general phenomenon which was the Rayonnant style."[48] While not a single building in its entirety fully exemplified the "Court Style," most structures built in Paris during the mid-thirteenth century, and many outside of the city, possessed elements of it. At the same time, it is clear that the Sainte-Chapelle held an important, almost pivotal position in the scheme. Yet Branner characterized the royal chapel only as a forerunner to the "Court Style," while the reliquary tribune, added (probably) after 1254, with its metallic, pointed, trilobe arches, was offered as an example of a "Courtly Work" [Fig. 3].[49] The dual problem of Branner's extended descriptions and lack of precise examples led to the later criticism that his concept of the style was at once too positivistic and too amorphous. While Branner did have faith in the concept of style, his constant qualifications reveal an underlying recognition of its inability to embody essential features. Today we recognize that any rigid assertion of style is problematic, yet one cannot critique Branner by the same standards; in his time, his vision of art history was entirely normative.[50]

Although Branner aspired to be comprehensive, the *Court Style* was not complete or definitive on every subject it mentioned, leaving it open to criticism. Moreover, many of the points Branner made concerning specific building chronologies were based on incomplete or unsubstantiated evidence, which provided new avenues of inquiry to young researchers. However, misprision provided a pathway for criticism of the *Court Style* based on a misinterpretation of the book as concerned primarily with style and the role of the king in the direction that the style took. The most salient and enduring contributions of the book have less to do with style than the assertion of the role of context and the associative meanings carried with its transmission.

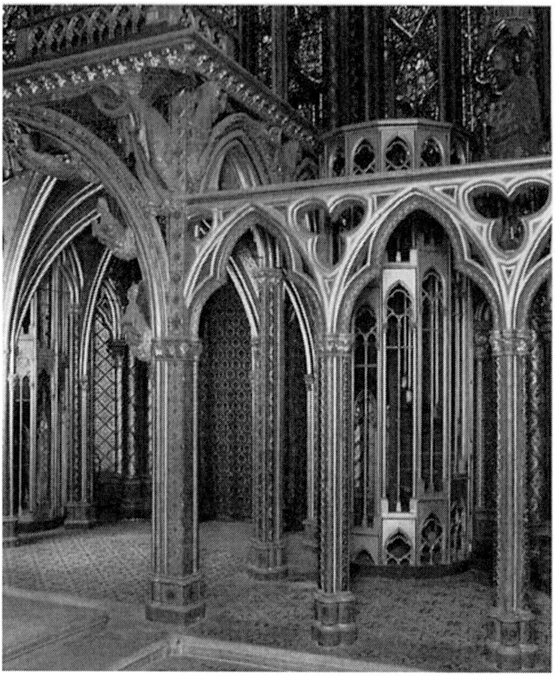

Fig. 3 Tribune, ca. 1254, Sainte-Chapelle, Paris
(Photo: Bernard Acloque © CMN, Paris)

Tessera: Completion and Antithesis

Tessera is Bloom's metaphor for the next stage in the process of revision. He describes it as a piece or token required to complete something, such as a fragment of broken pottery used to reconstruct a vase. After *Clinamen*, younger authors "complete" the work of their precursors. Bloom claims that the process is necessarily antithetical, because the precursor's concept has been made to mean something different from that which the precursor described.[51] However, the younger author's work has been defined in the first place by the precursor and must distinguish itself in some way from it.

Considered in terms of Bloom's *Anxiety of Influence*, the scholarly works following Branner, a series of detailed monographic studies of buildings mentioned in the *Court Style*, are *tesserae* in so far as they issued from, and then corrected, Branner's theory. These revisions took place within the problem that Branner defined, and appropriated his terms, monuments, and methods. His successors emphasized chronology as well as the development of style and improved on their precursor by rigorously examining building archaeologies. As a result, many of Branner's assertions about directionality have been disproved. A few examples here will serve to demonstrate the revision of the *Court Style*.

One of the first extensive reexaminations of "Court Style" architecture was Michael Davis's study of the cathedral of Clermont-Ferrand [Fig. 4].[52]

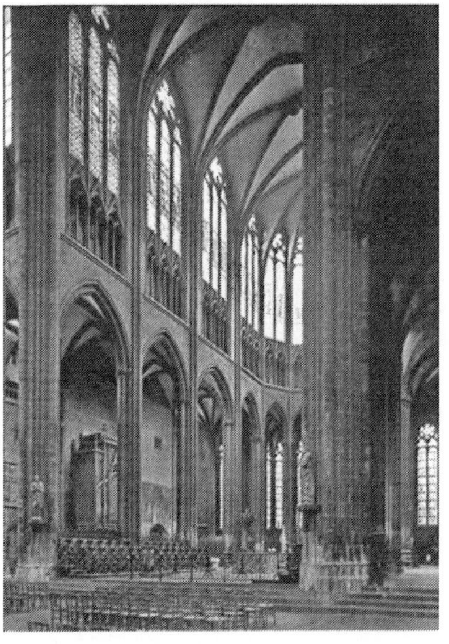

Fig. 4 Interior towards chevet, Clermont-Ferrand Cathedral, ca. 1244-1248 through 1270s (Photo: Courtesy of Michael T. Davis)

Branner ascribed this church to his group of post-1254 "Courtly Works," and more notably, he proposed a new date for the start of construction that did not correspond to the known documentation. Prior to Branner, scholars had based their knowledge of the church on a now lost inscription on the architect's tomb, which suggested that work began on the cathedral around 1248. Branner, however, argued that the archaeology of the church did not accord with this date and that construction did not begin in earnest until 1262, at which time Louis IX, who was in the city for the marriage of his son Philip to Isabella of Aragon, donated money for the project. This assertion effectively turned Clermont into a *retardataire* "monument that was geographically displaced to an area where large buildings were still needed and still desired."[53]

However, Davis found documents suggesting that fundraising for the cathedral began as early as 1244 and continued throughout the next two decades. He also discovered a document suggesting that the church was under construction in 1257, a few years prior to Branner's supposed start date.[54]

In this instance, Branner had interpreted both the written and the visual evidence in such a way that it conformed to his theory that the "Court Style" moved from Paris to the provinces. An earlier date for Clermont, one that suggested the church was planned before the completion of the Sainte-Chapelle, proved Branner wrong. Davis proposed a diplomatic revision—that Clermont reflects instead "a creative synthesis" of currents within the 1230s and 1240s, which contributed to the larger French Rayonnant style.[55] Even if Branner was incorrect about the dating, his eye did not entirely fail him: Davis maintained that the sources for Clermont lay primarily in Paris and the Ile-de-France, among other places further to the northeast in France, and this has not been challenged.[56]

A second analysis addressed the thirteenth-century reconstruction of the abbey church of Saint-Denis. Branner saw this building, with its glazed triforium and linkages, as an important precedent to the "Court Style" in Paris. However, Caroline Bruzelius's study of the monument changed conceptions about architecture in and around Paris during the 1230s. Her incisive analyses of sources and influences reversed Branner's claim that the triforium of the royal abbey church post-dated that of Troyes Cathedral [Fig. 5].[57] Bruzelius suggested instead that the upper levels of the choir at Troyes represent a reformulation of the design at Saint-Denis, and therefore it logically succeeded the Parisian abbey [Fig. 6]. This reversed Branner's discussion about Troyes, but conversely supported his larger thesis concerning the centrality of Paris. However, Troyes did not have any direct link to royal patronage, and so the style apparently was transferred by another means.

The new analysis of Saint-Denis revised Branner's identification of the location of the emergence of the "Court Style." Bruzelius dated the design of the abbey church to 1231, arguing that the alterations and changes made during the process of construction were refinements rather than revisions to the original concept or plan. Her monograph displaced the primacy of the Sainte-Chapelle and established the abbey church as the foundational monument for Rayonnant architecture as a whole, which complicated Branner's notion that the "Court Style" only reached maturity after 1254. Further destabilizing Branner's theory was Bruzelius's reiteration that the innovative qualities at Saint-Denis could not be attributed with any certainty to royal patronage.[58]

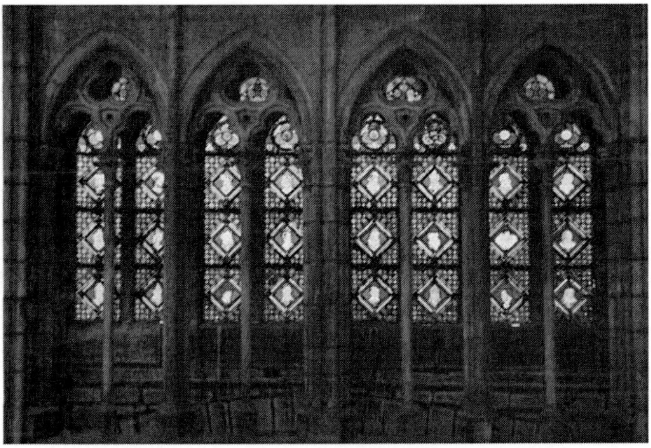

Fig. 5 Nave triforium, abbey church of Saint-Denis, reconstruction begun 1231, upper choir sections completed in the 1240s and 1250s (Photo: Author)

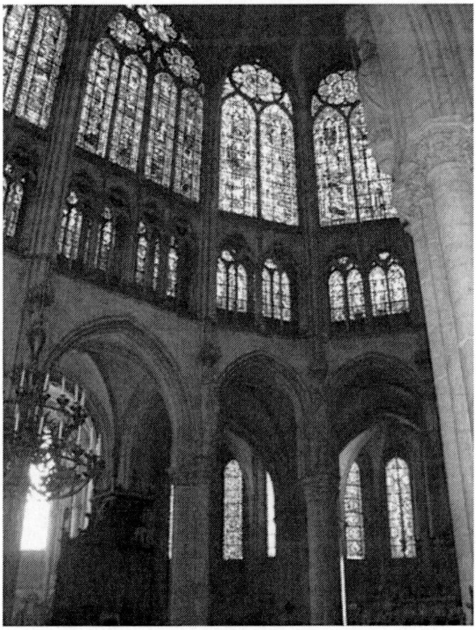

Fig. 6 Ambulatory of the chevet, Troyes Cathedral, begun ca. 1200, upper levels begun after 1228 and completed after the 1240s
(Photo: Courtesy of Stephen Murray)

Notre-Dame of Amiens has also witnessed a conceptual reversal. Branner wrote about it as a Parisian building on Picard soil, by virtue of the master mason, Robert de Luzarches, whose surname derives from a city close to Paris. Yet Stephen Murray's monograph, which confirmed Branner's sequence of master masons, placed Amiens firmly within the framework of northeastern French and particularly Picard architectural design, greatly reducing the importance of Paris in the equation. The chronology of construction outlined by Branner in an appendix to the *Court Style*, while not entirely mistaken, was also substantially revised and corrected.[59] Thus Amiens, with its stylistic resonances at the Sainte-Chapelle of Paris, emerged more firmly from this analysis as a major contributor to Parisian architecture in the 1230s and later, rather than the other way around [Fig. 7].

These monographs, the first three in Anglo-American scholarship to succeed Branner, have significantly redefined, if not completely reversed, a number of connections the *Court Style* made about buildings of this period and their relation to Paris. By dismantling Branner's chronologies, these studies have seriously weakened many of the *Court Style*'s premises. Moreover, Branner's theory has been proven inconsistent and contradictory; how, for example, could Amiens and Troyes both have been on the receiving end of Parisian style, if, even as Branner saw it, the former was a source for and the latter a derivative of the "Court Style"? Branner seemed to want to demonstrate that Paris was the center for every innovation in medieval architecture from 1200 to 1300.

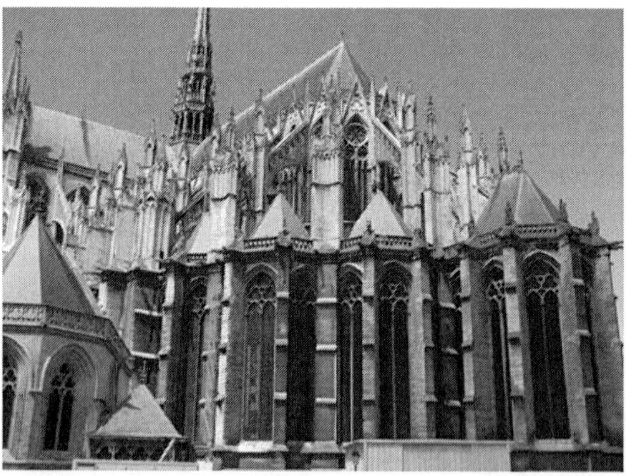

Fig. 7 Radiating chapels of the chevet, Amiens Cathedral, begun ca. 1223 (Photo: Courtesy of Stephen Murray)

Such contradictions, compounded with the conceptual problems regarding style and chronological inaccuracies, disillusioned the Anglo-American community of architectural historians. Criticisms of the "Court Style" intensified with each new publication. Caroline Bruzelius was the first to assert that the term was inappropriate and suggested that Rayonnant, which does not implicate patronage, was more accurate.[60] This alternative, a reversion to that which had been used prior to Branner's book, implies a wider chronological and geographical spectrum than the "Court Style." However, the buildings that comprise the primary monuments of Rayonnant architecture are the same that Branner considered within his "Court Style" spectrum.

Another revisionist response has been to dissociate this architecture from royal patronage by describing it as the product of a more generalized Parisian production. This is an important distinction; indeed, the cathedrals of Amiens, Paris, and Troyes, as well as Saint-Denis, the refectories of Saint-Martin-des-Champs and Saint-Germain-des-Prés (and its Lady Chapel) have no proven direct relation to royal sources. However, all of these buildings were highly decorated, privileged structures, and all of their patrons were high-ranking prelates or *seigneurs* who presumably employed the best artists of the day. Even if royal and elite patrons financed this kind of architecture, masons and sculptors created its forms. Still, the question of where new styles were generated, whether in large *chantiers* that extended to smaller ones, or vice-versa, is extremely difficult to answer with any certainty, and the lack of extant buildings in Paris renders any conclusion only tentative, although it is important to remember that styles move in both directions.

Eric Fernie has gone so far as to assert that the style between royal buildings and other metropolitan structures is indistinguishable.[61] It should be remembered that our understanding of medieval Parisian architecture is extremely limited, based primarily on a few extant buildings and some fragments. In fact, at least thirty-five buildings were under construction in Paris during the thirteenth century and more complete knowledge of them would likely generate a rather different impression. What little information remains lies deeply embedded in later reconstructions, Revolutionary history, museum reserves, and archives, and is perhaps irretrievable. Study of this material, however fragmentary, would improve our knowledge. The few examples cited below suggest that there were differences of quality, form, and function within this time period.

A fragment of the lancet tracery from the church of the Jacobins [Fig. 8], founded in 1221 and known to have received some funding from Louis IX towards its completion, suggests that certain Parisian forms, if these can be thus defined, were not reserved for royal or elite patrons, since the Jacobins were Dominican Mendicants. Illustrations of the church relay that it had a simple rectangular plan and a sparsely adorned exterior [Fig. 9]. Fragments from the excavation of the neighboring churches of Saint-Symphorien and Saint-Denis-de-la-Chartre on the Ile de la Cité illustrate a variety of styles within the Rayonnant sculptural repertoire; in addition to typical, delicately-carved crocket and foliate capitals, less elegant, more rudimentary decoration was found on thirteenth-century capitals at the site [Fig. 10].[62] The fragments from the chapel of the College of Cluny [Fig. 11] reveal carving on par with the most elegant examples of Rayonnant, although the college is not known to have received any royal funding. Of different qualities, functions, and histories, these fragments resist placement in any overarching category based on current knowledge of the art and architecture of Paris in the thirteenth century.

Fig. 8 Lancet fragment, church of the Jacobins, Paris, ca. 1230-1240, Musée Carnavalet, Paris (Photo: Courtesy of the Musée Carnavalet)

It nevertheless remains a fact that some buildings were more distinctive than others. If reception is a means of measuring influence, then the multiple copies of the forms of the Sainte-Chapelle of Paris, as well as the typological copies in the series of chapels known as the Saintes-Chapelles, indicate that this building, with its rich decoration, elaborate ceremonial, and meaningful associations, captured its audience in a way that a smaller chapel in a similar style did not.[63] It is, therefore, possible to conceive of an elite (but not exclusively royal) architecture that is both aesthetically and conceptually distinct from less privileged structures.

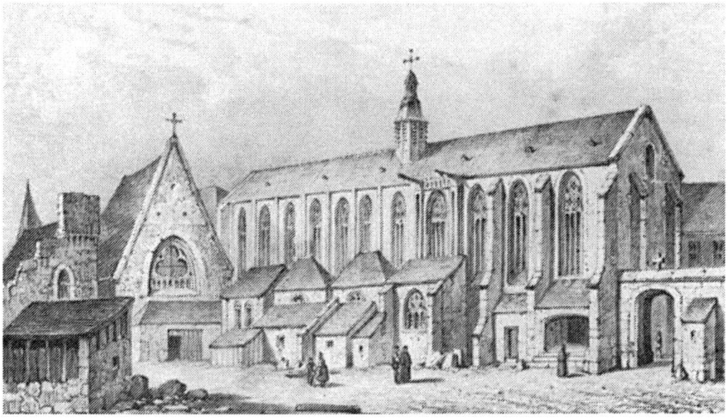

Fig. 9 Exterior, church of the Jacobins, Paris, begun after 1221, engraving, undated, Estampes, Va259i fol., Bibliothèque nationale de France, Paris (Photo: Bibliothèque nationale de France)

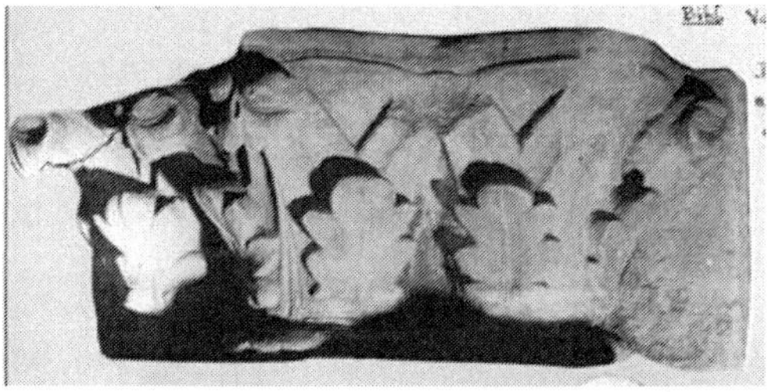

Fig. 10 Capital found at the excavation site of Saint-Symphorien/Saint-Denis-de-la-Chartre, Paris, Saint-Symphorien begun after 1206, Musée Carnavalet, Paris (Photo: Courtesy of the Musée Carnavalet)

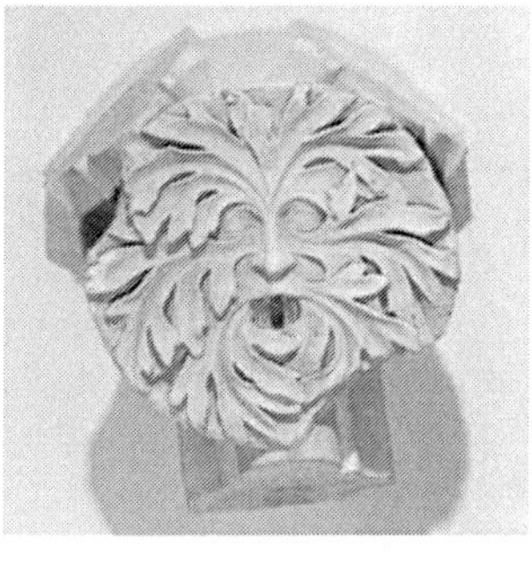

Fig. 11 Keystone, chapel begun after 1262, College de Cluny, Paris, Musée national du Moyen Age, Paris (Photo: © Réunion des musées nationaux)

In general, however, there remains a great distrust of any more specific analyses of the relationship between style, royal and elite patronage, and the meanings of thirteenth-century Parisian architecture. The "Anxiety of Influence" has arrested that avenue of inquiry, which, for all effective purposes, has never been thoroughly examined.

Apophrades: The Return of the Dead

Years have passed since researchers have directly engaged with the *Court Style*, and the field is now defined by work that has moved beyond Branner. Art and architectural history have sustained profound transformations related to the "theoretical turn" of the New Criticism. Yet, Branner's ideas persist, although in new and different guises. *Apophrades* or the "Return of the Dead," is the moment of reconciliation, an acknowledgment of the integration of the past with the future.[64] The precursor's work is acknowledged for its contribution to the discourse, but the successors' ideas transcend. As Bloom writes, "The mighty dead return, but they return in our colors, and speaking in our voices, at least in part, at least in moments, moments that testify to our persistence, and not to their own."[65]

Though the evidence supporting Branner's notion of the "Court Style" has been refuted, the theory that the prestige of Paris in the thirteenth century bestowed an aura on all things Parisian has never been entirely dismissed. Willibald Sauerländer wrote rapturously of the fame of the city, which he linked to the presence of the kings, the renowned university, the venerable abbeys, *and* its distinctive architecture.[66] Sauerländer qualified Branner in writing, "I am not sure that we should speak of a 'Court Style' in French Gothic architecture as the late Robert Branner proposed," while himself proposing a very similar idea, with an even wider scope of application: "There is, however, no doubt that the rise of Paris as an art centre in the twelfth and thirteenth centuries has been closely connected with the growing importance of the Capetian kings….The France of Saint Louis had forged the first universal style in the history of European art and architecture since the downfall of the Roman Empire."[67]

A recent volume of *Gesta* published in honor of Robert Branner with contributions by his former colleagues and students reconfirmed his position and contributions to architectural history.[68] Michael Davis's analysis of the field of medieval architecture in 1999 outlined a myriad of approaches and methods currently available, which Branner's *Court Style* presaged with its interest in class and patronage, contextual description, the dialogue between center and margins, and emphasis on the associative power of monuments.[69] The *Court Style* encouraged closer examination of artistic patronage, particularly royal and courtly patronage, which has received much attention in recent years, especially in museum exhibitions. In what seems to be a direct response to Branner's skeptics, Kimpel and Suckale affirmed in reference to the art and architecture created during the reigns of Philip Augustus and Louis IX that "it is important not to underestimate the power of the great personality."[70] Yet the focus is now on the ideological content and function of patronage, rather than the stylistic contribution.[71] Ironically, there has been no thorough analysis of Louis IX and/or Blanche of Castile as patrons. The question of whether he (or she, or perhaps, they) may have funded what we might describe as an architectural program has never been examined in any depth. Further examination of other buildings associated with Louis' generous hand may offer new evidence of a larger vision. Recent studies of the Sainte-Chapelle suggest that the building championed a much more highly sophisticated visual, liturgical, and political program than previously perceived.[72] Similarly close analysis of the patronage of other Rayonnant buildings in France will also add to the understanding of the ideology of mid-thirteenth-century architectural styles.[73]

In addition to its insistence on the contributions of patrons, the *Court Style* also emphasized the importance of social, historic, and economic factors in artistic production, previewing the new contextual emphasis in our current study.[74] The monographic format in vogue in the years following Branner's book, while not all directly related to his work, enriched such contextual studies. Indeed, no analysis of architecture is complete today without a consideration of the multiple and complex exchanges between historic and economic forces, patrons and builders, public and private interests.

If rejection of the *Court Style* has discouraged study of (primarily thirteenth-century) Paris, it has stimulated analysis of the margins or peripheries, areas that Branner had once seen in opposition, or only in relation, to the center. Caroline Bruzelius's work on Angevin Naples serves as a model example of this extension, which took patronage and the significance of style into account, but was located outside of Paris and was no longer confined to a monographic format.[75] The combination of the study of the margin and its context reveals the complexity of the different forces operating within visual culture, particularly in what can be understood by knowledge of local contributions and factors. Christian Freigang's 1992 book, with its rigorous analyses of building archaeologies and patronage patterns has also been illuminating in this respect.[76]

It is time that these new views were applied to the center that they might well redefine. In particular, the question about the relation between Gothic architecture and the French kings, and especially the confluence of the two, remains to be thoroughly examined. Essays such as Gabrielle Spiegel's still relevant "The Cult of Saint-Denis and Capetian Kingship" suggest that monastery and crown were mutually self-reinforcing, and it is difficult to see the flourishing of Gothic architecture as entirely distinct from ideological aspirations.[77] Contemporary approaches that employ these new methods and insights may be able to provide more satisfying answers than Branner was able to do with his analysis of style. This is not so much a question of the iconography of style, as Branner suggested, than a sophisticated iconology of style, informed by contemporary approaches. The question seems to be less when Gothic became royal, as whether Parisian architecture did indeed become identified with the French monarchy, especially in Paris, and what functions this could have served within and beyond the capital. Despite the *Court Style*'s downfalls, it is time to reconsider those larger trends.

The *Anxiety of Influence* serves as one model, among many, for interpreting the discourse stemming from Branner's *Court Style*. Branner's eminence appears to have contributed to an anxiety-related misreading or distortion of the *Court Style*, both by those who praised it and by those who engaged with it critically. After additional research on related topics, the generation of architectural historians following Branner rejected his conclusions to the point that further study of royal patronage and Parisian architecture in the thirteenth century was discouraged and could be justified only when claimed as unrelated to Branner's goals. Nevertheless, the subsequent turn to alternative subjects and intensified analyses of buildings and contexts has served to expand that which has never been acknowledged as his greatest but most elusive contribution: the relation between meaning and form in architecture. Further study of Paris in this direction promises compelling new outcomes.

In this study, Bloom's *Anxiety of Influence* has been instrumental in illuminating a pattern of scholarship within the process of academic revisionism. Influence, authorship, and reception are all terms that have complex patterns of production and distribution, including elements of chance. With all of its extended qualifications and explanations of anomalies, Branner's *Court Style* recognized these complexities. From this analysis, we might be reminded of both the relativity of our own interpretations and the value of those works that generate discourse in the first place.

Notes

[1] Robert Branner, *St Louis and the Court Style in Gothic Architecture* (London: Zwemmer, 1965). Hereafter the book is referred to in italics as the *Court Style* to distinguish it from conceptions of the idea indicated by quotation marks as "Court Style." Standard stylistic categories such as Gothic, High Gothic, and Rayonnant are not distinguished by quotation marks.

[2] The 92nd Annual Conference of the College Art Association in 2001 held a session organized by Caroline Bruzelius entitled "Courts and Court Styles Revisited: Studies in Memory of Harvey Stahl." Recent museum exhibitions in France dedicated to royal patrons include *Paris 1400: les arts sous Charles VI* (Louvre, 22 March-12 July 2004) and *Paris et Charles V* (Action artistique de la Ville de Paris, Bibliothèque Forney and Mairie du VIe arrondissement, 5 April-6 July 2001). For a recent reappraisal of Sainte-Chapelle historiography based on Branner's legacy, see Stefan Gasser, "L'architecture de la Sainte-Chapelle. Etat de la question concernant sa datation, son maître d'oeuvre et sa place dans l'histoire de l'architecture," in *La Sainte-Chapelle de Paris. Royaume de France ou Jérusalem céleste? Actes du Colloque* (Paris, Collège de France, 2001), ed. Christine Hediger (Turnhout: Brepols, 2007). 157-180

[3] Harold Bloom, *The Anxiety of Influence: A Theory of Poetry* (Oxford: Oxford University Press, 1973; 2nd ed., 1997). I refer to the first edition unless otherwise noted.

[4] Harold Bloom's theory was developed in four books known collectively as his "tetralogy" which comprises *The Anxiety of Influence*; *A Map of Misreading* (New York: Oxford University Press, 1975); *Kabbalah and Criticism* (New York: Seabury Press, 1975); and *Poetry and Repression: Revisionism from Blake to Stevens* (New Haven: Yale University Press, 1976). He continued to reassess and refine his theory throughout his career in other books, such as *Agon: Towards a Theory of Revisionism* (Oxford: Oxford University Press, 1982); and *Genius: A Mosaic of One Hundred Exemplary Creative Minds* (London: Fourth Estate, 2002).

[5] Summarized, the six revisionary stages are: 1) *Clinamen*, a misreading of the precursor; 2) *Tessera*, completion and antithesis of the precursor; 3) *Kenosis*, distinction and individualization from the precursor; 4) *Daemonization*, attainment of a "sublime" new theory; 5) *Askesis*, an avowal of individual achievement, with a feeling of isolation; and 6) *Apophrades*, the return to and acknowledgement of the precursor's presence in the successor's work.

[6] Bloom's earliest critics were Paul de Man, "Review of Harold Bloom's *Anxiety of Influence: A Theory of Poetry*," *Comparative Literature* 26, 3 ([first published in 1971] reprint 1974). 269-275; and Geoffrey Hartman, "War in Heaven," *Diacritics* 3, 1 (1973). 26-32. Other significant responses include Christopher Norris, "Harold Bloom: A Poetics of Reconstruction," *British Journal of Aesthetics* 20 (1980). 67-76; Elizabeth Bruss, *Beautiful Theories: The Spectacle of Discourse in Contemporary Criticism* (Baltimore: Johns Hopkins University Press, 1982); Frank Lentricchia, *After the New Criticism* (London: Methuen, 1983);

Edward Said, *The World, the Text, and the Critic* (London: Faber and Faber, 1984); Jean-Pierre Mileur, *Literary Revisionism and the Burden of Modernity* (Berkeley: University of California Press, 1985); Peter de Bolla, *Harold Bloom: Towards Historical Rhetorics* (London: Routledge, 1988); Graham Allen, *Harold Bloom: A Poetics of Conflict* (New York: Harvester Wheatsheaf, 1994).

[7] De Bolla, *Harold Bloom: Towards Historical Rhetorics.* 8 writes, "Bloom…has deliberately shunned the institutional pressure at work in a professionalized discipline which seeks to appropriate and imitate the newest and the most newsworthy as quickly as possible, and has openly pursued a mode of writing and of criticism which sets out to prevent the institution from taking it into itself and speaking in his name."

[8] Bloom, *Anxiety of Influence* (1997). xxiv

[9] In the field of art history see Norman Bryson, *Tradition and Desire: From David to Delacroix* (Cambridge: Cambridge University Press, 1984). For an examination of the possible applications of the theory to medieval manuscripts see William J. Diebold, "The Anxiety of Influence in Early Medieval Art? The *Codex aureus* of Charles the Bald in Ottonian Regensburg," in *Under the Influence: The Concept of Influence and the Study of Manuscripts*, ed. Alixe Bovey (Turnhout: Brepols, 2008). 51-64

[10] An example of a feminist critique of Bloom, which, ironically, incorporates his theory is Sandra Gilbert and Susan Gubar, *The Madwoman in the Attic: The Woman Writer and the Nineteenth-Century Literary Imagination* (New Haven: Yale University Press, 1979).

[11] For a study of Bloom's theoretical orientation see Daniel O'Hara, "The Genius of Irony: Nietzsche in Bloom," *The Yale Critics: Deconstruction in America*, ed. Jonathan Arac, Wlad Godzich, and Wallace Martin (Minneapolis: University of Minnesota Press, 1983). 109-131; see also David Fite, *Harold Bloom: The Rhetoric of Romantic Vision* (Amherst: University of Massachusetts Press, 1985), which explains how Bloom's project makes reference to contemporary issues in critical theory and provides an introduction to his work to date. For a comparative analysis of theories of influence, individuality, and authorship see William Schultz, *Genetic Codes of Culture? The Deconstruction of Tradition by Kuhn, Bloom, and Derrida* (New York: Garland, 1994).

[12] Bloom's response to this criticism is that his theory does not focus on personal relationships per se but, rather, emphasizes the connection between texts and how earlier texts must be displaced and revised before difference can be asserted. Bloom, *A Map of Misreading*. 3

[13] Bloom acknowledges and embraces this critique. See *Anxiety of Influence* (1997). 5

[14] There have been many more responses to Branner's *Court Style* than I am able to examine in this short article, and it is not my intention to discuss all of them here but, rather, to show how some early responses in the Anglo-American scholarship approached and revised the subject. An analysis of the European response, and the differences between that and Anglo-American reception, would require an independent study. For a recent assessment of the subject see Wolfgang

Brückle, "Revision der Hofkunst. Zur Frage historistischer Phänomene in der ausgehenden Kapetingerzeit und zum Problem des höfischen Pariser Stils," *Zeitschrift für Kunstgeschichte* 63 (2000). 404-434

[15] While Bloom's theory distinguishes how younger authors overcome their predecessors, examination of the way in which these authors asserted their own creative identities would require a much longer analysis than possible here.

[16] Branner completed his Ph.D. dissertation on Bourges Cathedral at Yale University in 1952. He taught as an instructor at Yale until 1954, when he joined the faculty at the University of Kansas. In 1957, he became an associate professor of Columbia University, where he was later appointed full professor and where he taught until 1973. He also taught at Johns Hopkins from 1971-1973. "Robert Branner," *Dictionary of Art Historians:* http://dictionaryofarthistorians.org.

[17] See Shirley Prager Branner, "A Bibliography and Index to the Works of Robert Branner," *Journal of the Society of Architectural Historians* 34, 3 (1975). 167-172 (hereafter cited as *JSAH*)

[18] The Department of Art History and Archaeology at Columbia University organizes an ongoing annual lecture series on medieval art and architecture in his name, "The Branner Forum."

[19] Carl F. Barnes Jr., "Guest Editor's Note," *JSAH* 34, 3 (1975). 162; and Jean Bony, "On Robert Branner," *JSAH* 34, 3 (1975). 165

[20] Paula Gerson, "Robert Branner and the Gothic: A Prologue," *Gesta* 39 (2000). 87-88

[21] Bony, "On Robert Branner." 165

[22] "Robert Branner nous a accoutumés à l'obligtion de lire très attentivement tout ce qu'il écrit." Quoted in Barnes, "Guest Editor's Note." 162

[23] Stephen Murray, "Robert Branner and the Gothic: A Prologue," *Gesta* 39 (2000). 87

[24] Eric Fernie, "Robert Branner's Treatment of Architectural Sources and Precedents," *Gesta* 39 (2000). 158-159

[25] Branner, *Court Style*. 2

[26] Branner, *Court Style*. 15-17, 67 ff., 86 ff.

[27] Henri Focillon, *Vie des Formes* (Paris: Presses universitaires de France, 1934).

[28] The concept of style came under increasing scrutiny when Branner was active. For an introduction to the theoretical aspects of style as seen in the 1960s see Thomas Munro, *Form and Style in the Arts: An Introduction to Aesthetic Morphology* (Cleveland: Case Western Reserve University Press, 1970). Revisions to the concept of style were published in the anthology edited by Berel Lang, *The Concept of Style* (Ithaca: Cornell University Press, 1979). See also Willibald Sauerländer, "From Stylus to Style: Reflections on the Fate of a Notion," *Art History* 6 (1983). 253-270; and, for an assessment of theories of style related to the Middle Ages, see Paul Crossley's introduction to Paul Frankl, *Gothic Architecture*, rev. Paul Crossley (New Haven: Yale University Press, 2000). 7-31

[29] This paragraph paraphrases Branner, *Court Style*. 85-86

[30] Ibid. 7, 11

[31] See n. 37

[32] Branner, *Court Style*. 113
[33] Ibid. 113
[34] The emphasis on the royal contribution to the Gothic style of architecture is prevalent in Eugène Emmanuel Viollet-le-Duc's *Dictionnaire raisonné de l'architecture française du XIe au XVIe siècles*, 10 vols. (Paris: B. Bance, 1858-1868). Branner might have been inspired by what in his time were recent publications on the iconography of architecture that appeared following Richard Krautheimer's "Introduction to an 'Iconography of Medieval Architecture'," *Journal of the Warburg and the Courtauld Institutes* 5 (1942). 1-33; for example, Hans Sedlmayr, *Die Entstehung der Kathedrale* (Zurich: Atlantis Verlag, 1950); and Günter Bandmann, *Mittelalterliche Architektur als Bedeutungsträger* (Berlin: Gebrüder Mann Verlag, 1951), even though Branner wrote a highly critical review of the last book.
[35] Bony, "On Robert Branner." 164-166
[36] Bloom, *Anxiety of Influence*. 30
[37] Branner, *Court Style*. 11
[38] Caroline Astrid Bruzelius, *The 13th-Century Church of Saint-Denis* (New Haven: Yale University Press, 1985). 163
[39] Branner, *Court Style*. 9; Guillaume de Saint-Pathus is given this title in the 1254 *Livre des Métiers*. René de Lespinasse et Françoise Bonnardot, *Le Livre des Métiers d'Etienne Boileau, XIIIe siècle* (Paris: Imprimerie nationale, 1879). 88-89
[40] Both cited in Branner, *Court Style*. 7
[41] Ibid. 91-92
[42] Ibid. 12
[43] Ibid. 46
[44] Ibid. 46. Concerning the patronage of the tomb program, one theory has been that the monks of Saint-Denis funded it in order to maintain their close and mutually-beneficial relationship with the French kings. See Georgia Sommers Wright, "A Royal Tomb Program in the Reign of Saint Louis," *Art Bulletin* 56 (1971). 223-243; for an alternative interpretation, see Alain Erlande-Brandenburg, *Le roi est mort: étude sur les funérailles, les sépultures, et les tombeaux des rois de France jusqu'à la fin du XIIIe siècle* (Geneva: Droz, 1975).
[45] Branner, *Court Style*. 86
[46] Ibid. 91
[47] Fernie, "Robert Branner's Treatment." 158
[48] "Le lecteur de Saint Louis and the Court Style cherche cependant en vain des critères formels précis permettant de distinguer le style de la cour du phénomène plus général que fut le style rayonnant." Brigitte Kurmann-Schwartz, "La Châsse de Sainte Gertrude et l'art de la Cour en France au XIIIe siècle. Etat de la question et problèmes," in *Un Trésor Gothique. La Châsse De Nivelles*, exh. cat., Cologne, Schnütgen-Museum, 24 novembre 1995-11 février 1996, Paris, Musée national du Moyen Age-Thermes de Cluny, 12 mars-10 juin 1996 (Paris: Réunion des musées nationaux, 1996). 238-239

[49] Branner, *Court Style*. 83, 93. The actual date of construction of the reliquary tribune is unknown, although the damaged columns behind it suggest that it was added after construction of the main frame of the building.
[50] See n. 28
[51] Bloom, *Anxiety of Influence*. 65-67
[52] Michael T. Davis, "The Choir of the Cathedral of Clermont-Ferrand: The Beginning of Construction and the Work of Jean Deschamps," *JSAH* 40, 3 (1981). 181-202. The article derived from two chapters in Davis's doctoral dissertation, one of the first post-*Court Style* architectural analyses for which the research was conducted in the years 1976-1977. See Michael T. Davis, "The Cathedral of Clermont-Ferrand: History of its Construction, 1248-1512" (Ph.D. diss., University of Michigan, Ann Arbor, 1979).
[53] Branner, *Court Style*. 100
[54] Many previously unknown documents were brought to light in this study. See Davis, "The Cathedral of Clermont-Ferrand." 182-189
[55] Davis, "The Cathedral of Clermont-Ferrand." 197
[56] Ibid. 197 n. 73
[57] See n. 38. For another early re-evaluation of Troyes, see Norbert Bongartz, *Die frühen Bauteile der Kathedrale in Troyes: architekturgeschichtliche Mongraphie*, Hochschulsammlung Philosophie, Kunstgeschichte 2 (Stuttgart: Hochschul Verlag, 1979).
[58] Bruzelius, *Saint-Denis*. 12
[59] Stephen Murray, *Notre-Dame, Cathedral of Amiens* (Cambridge: Cambridge University Press, 1996). Despite compelling evidence and argumentation, there remains some disagreement concerning the sequence of construction, most recently fuelled by the dates obtained from dendrochronological analysis of the remains of the wooden tie beams in the piers of the nave arcade. See Anne Prache, "Remarques sur les parties hautes de la cathédrale d'Amiens," *Gazette des beaux arts* 127 (1996). 55-62
[60] Bruzelius, *Saint-Denis*. 163-164
[61] Fernie, "Robert Branner's Treatment." 159
[62] On the date of Saint-Symphorien see Xavier Dectot, "Saint-Symphorien," in *Autour de Notre-Dame* (Paris: Action artistique de la ville de Paris, 2003). 138-139
[63] For the Saintes-Chapelles see Claudine Billot, *Les Saintes-Chapelles royales et princières* (Paris: Editions du Patrimoine, 1998). On the fourteenth-century iconography of the alternating gable and pinnacle pattern from the Sainte-Chapelle and buildings like it see Michael T. Davis, "Splendor and Peril: the Cathedral of Paris, 1290-1350," *Art Bulletin* 80 (1998). 34-65. The chapel at Chaâlis and the Sainte-Chapelle in the palace of Dijon employed the name "Sainte-Chapelle," although they did not reproduce the architecture, liturgy, or relics of Louis' building. For Chaâlis see Maryse Bideault and Claudine Lautier, *Ile-de-France gothique* (Paris: Picard, 1987). 133-135. This is not intended as a complete bibliographic orientation to the subject: the reception of the Parisian Sainte-Chapelle alone was profound and merits an independent study.
[64] Bloom, *Anxiety of Influence*. 140

[65] Ibid. 141
[66] Willibald Sauerländer, "Medieval Paris, Center of European Taste, Fame and Realities," in *Paris: Center of Artistic Enlightenment*, ed. George Mauner et al., Papers in Art History from the Pennsylvania State University, 4 (Pennsylvania: University of Pennsylvania, 1988). 13-45
[67] Ibid. 21
[68] See n. 20
[69] Michael Davis, "'Sic et Non': Recent Trends in the Study of Gothic Ecclesiastical Architecture," *JSAH* 58, 3 (1999). 414-423
[70] Dieter Kimpel and Robert Suckale, *L'architecture gothique en France, 1130-1270* (Paris: Flammarion, 1990). 377
[71] An exemplary study on the subject as it applies to English royal court culture is Paul Binski, *Westminster Abbey and the Plantagenets: Kingship and the Representation of Power* (New Haven: Yale University Press, 1995). See Binski's introduction for references to Branner's *Court Style.*
[72] Recent monographic studies (articles and books) that have illuminated the political ideologies of the Sainte-Chapelle include Beat Brenk, "The Sainte-Chapelle as Capetian Political Program," in *Artistic Integration in Gothic Buildings*, ed. Virginia Chieffo Raguin, et al. (Toronto: University of Toronto Press, 1995). 195-213; Daniel Weiss, *Art and Crusade in the Age of Saint Louis* (Cambridge: Cambridge University Press, 1998); and Daniel Weiss, "Architectural Symbolism and the Decoration of the Sainte-Chapelle," *Art Bulletin* 77 (1995). 308-320; Stephen Murray, "The Architectural Envelope of the Sainte-Chapelle of Paris," in *Pierre, lumière, couleur. Etudes d'histoire de l'art du Moyen Age en l'honneur d'Anne Prache,* ed. Fabienne Joubert, Dany Sandron, Cultures et Civilisations Médiévales 20 (Paris: Presses de l'Universite de Paris-Sorbonne, 1999). 223-230; Jean-Michel Leniaud and François Perrot, *La Sainte-Chapelle* (Paris: Nathan/CMNHS, 1991); Alyce A. Jordan, *Visualizing Kingship in the Windows of the Sainte-Chapelle*, Publications of the International Center of Medieval Art, no. 5 (Turnhout: Brepols, 2002); Christine Hediger, ed., *La Sainte-Chapelle de Paris: royaume de France ou Jérusalem céleste? Actes du Colloque (Paris, Collège de France 2001)* (Turnhout: Brepols, 2007). See also Meredith Cohen, "An Indulgence for the Visitor: the Public at the Sainte-Chapelle," *Speculum* 83 (2008). 840-883
[73] This subject is currently being examined by Mailan Stephanie Doquang for her dissertation tentatively titled, "Rayonnant Funerary Chapels: Architectural Additions and Changing Contexts in French Gothic," Institute of Fine Arts, New York University.
[74] Murray, *Amiens*. 4-5
[75] See Caroline Astrid Bruzelius, "*Ad modum franciae:* Charles of Anjou and Gothic Architecture in the Kingdom of Sicily," *JSAH* 50 (1991). 402-420; Caroline Astrid Bruzelius, "Charles of Anjou and the French National Style in Italy," in *Kunst im Reich Kaiser Friedrichs II. von Hohenstaufen II: Akten des zweiten Internationalen Kolloquiums zu Kunst und Geschichte der Stauferzeit*, Rheinisches Landesmuseum Bonn, 8. bis 10. Dezember 1995, ed. Alexander Knaak (Munich:

Klinkhardt and Biermann, 1997). 146-153; Caroline Astrid Bruzelius, "Charles I, Charles II, and the Development of an Angevin Style in the Kingdom of Sicily," in *L'Etat angevin: Pouvoir, culture et société entre XIIIe et XIVe siècle*, Actes du colloque international organisé par l'American Academy in Rome, l'Istituto storico italiano per il Medio Evo, l'U.M.R. Telemme et l'Université de Provence, l'Università degli studi di Napoli "Federico II," Rome-Naples, 7-11 novembre 1995, ed. André Vauchez, Nuovi studi storici, 45, 26 (Rome: Ecole française de Rome, 1998). 99-114; Caroline Astrid Bruzelius, "'Il gran rifiuto'. French Gothic in Central and Southern Italy in the Last Quarter of the Thirteenth Century," in *Architecture and Language: Constructing Identity in European Architecture c. 1000 - c. 1650*, ed. Georgia Clarke and Paul Crossley (Cambridge: Cambridge University Press, 2000). 36-45, 176-178; Caroline Astrid Bruzelius, *The Stones of Naples: Church Building in the Angevin Kingdom, 1266-1343* (New Haven: Yale University Press, 2004).

[76] Christian Freigang, *Imitare Ecclesias Nobiles: Die Kathedralen von Narbonne, Toulouse und Rodez und die Nordfranzösische Rayonnantgotik im Languedoc* (Worms: Wernersche Verlagsgesellschaft, 1992).

[77] Gabrielle Spiegel, "The Cult of Saint Denis and Medieval Kingship," *Journal of Medieval History* 1 (1975). 43-69

THE STUDY OF MEDIEVAL ILLUMINATED MANUSCRIPTS IN GERMAN SCHOLARSHIP CA. 1750–1850[1]

ANDREA WORM

In the past few decades, the afterlife of the Middle Ages in general and of medieval manuscripts in particular has attracted considerable scholarly interest.[2] Modern historiography, however, has focused on the history of medievalism and taste in the context of the Gothic Revival, rather than on the history of scholarly research, and on England and France, rather than on other European countries. The aim of this article is to explore the state of scholarship in Germany from the mid-eighteenth to the mid-nineteenth century. This material reveals important insights into changing interests and methodological approaches to the illuminated manuscript, the relationship of these changes to leading tendencies in European scholarship, as well as the part played by national agendas. In a series of case studies, continuities as well as shifts, general tendencies as well as particular features will be outlined.

Two fundamental developments must first be addressed in order to get a clearer picture of medieval manuscript scholarship at the start of the period under consideration. It was primarily the Benedictines of the congregation of Saint-Maur de Fosses near Paris (hence often referred to as Maurists) who laid the foundations later scholars built on. In 1681 Jean de Mabillon (1632–1707), one of the intellectual leaders of the Maurist congregation, published his groundbreaking six-volume study *De re diplomatica.* This work, the main concern of which was to determine the authenticity and date of charters and documents on the basis of the examination of their script, is of crucial importance for the study of medieval manuscripts. The fifth book provides several sets of alphabets from different periods as well as script samples from charters and manuscripts, reproduced in copperplate engravings of remarkable fidelity. *De re diplomatica* was the first systematic paleographical study and set the standard for all publications in the field until well into the nineteenth century.[3] At the same time, the emphasis on the form of script and initials, primarily as a way of dating documents, gradually gave way to an increasing sensitivity for the formal characteristics of medieval artifacts.[4]

The other important methodological development was the growing awareness of medieval images as pictorial sources.[5] Illuminated manuscripts played an important though often underestimated part in the scholarly interest in medieval artifacts and in the development of a general methodology for dealing with medieval art.[6] Here again, ecclesiastical scholars were crucial. Mabillon set an example in his history of the Benedictine order, published 1703–1704, by using illuminations from medieval manuscripts as visual sources for portraits of important historical figures of his order.[7] Even more marked was the use of images by another Maurist scholar, Bernard de Montfaucon (1655–1741). His monumental publication on *Les Monumens de la Monarchie Françoise*, printed 1729–1733 and dedicated to Louis XV, provided a history of the French monarchy, in which the historical account is enriched by contemporary depictions of the respective monarchs on seals and coins, in manuscripts, tomb sculpture, and other media. The interest in text and paleography on the one hand, and the miniatures as visual sources on the other, remained fundamental until well into the nineteenth century.

Gottfried Bessel, Coloman Sanftl, and Church Scholarship in the Eighteenth Century

When Gottfried Bessel (1672–1749), abbot of the Benedictine monastery of Göttweig in Austria, decided to write a chronicle of his convent, he held the opinion that only a comprehensive study of the history of the German rulers would enable his readers to fully understand the importance of his abbey. Therefore, in the first volume of this *Chronicon Gotwicense* (1732), he published examples from charters issued by the German kings and emperors, following the model provided by Mabillon.[8] Moreover, he included two plates, on which he arranged in a pastiche, specimens of script, musical notation, initials, and details taken from various illuminations from the twelfth-century antiphonal of Saint Peter in Salzburg [Fig. 1].[9] King Herod serves as an example for royal costume, Pope Gregory for ecclesiastical garments; Zacharias, the father of John the Baptist, illustrates the use of wax tablets and stylus as writing devices.[10] Bessel's publication not only demonstrates the impact of the work of Mabillon and Montfaucon, but also the framework within which Bessel and other ecclesiastical scholars operated: surviving documents prove that in order to collect the models for his reproductions, he sent out letters to other Benedictine houses asking for their assistance. To these letters, he adjoined sheets of tracing paper (paper made translucent with oil and honey) in order to attain faithful copies of the desired documents. The use of tracing paper became standard for reproductions of script and decoration in medieval manuscripts in the seventeenth and eighteenth centuries. It must be pointed out, however, that this practice alone did not yet guarantee faithful reproductions, since with images in medieval manuscripts (in contrast to their scripts!) concessions to contemporary taste can frequently be observed.

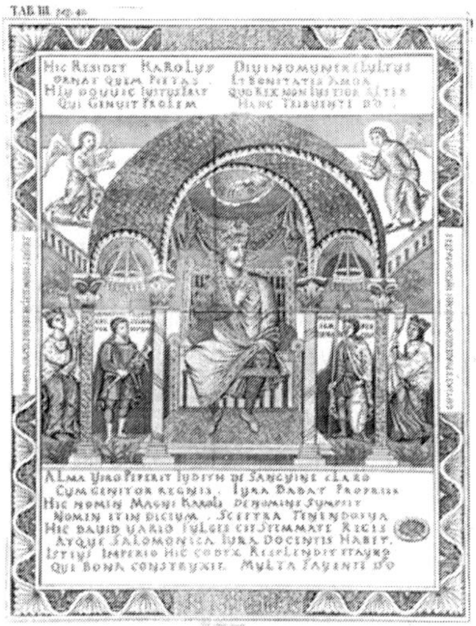

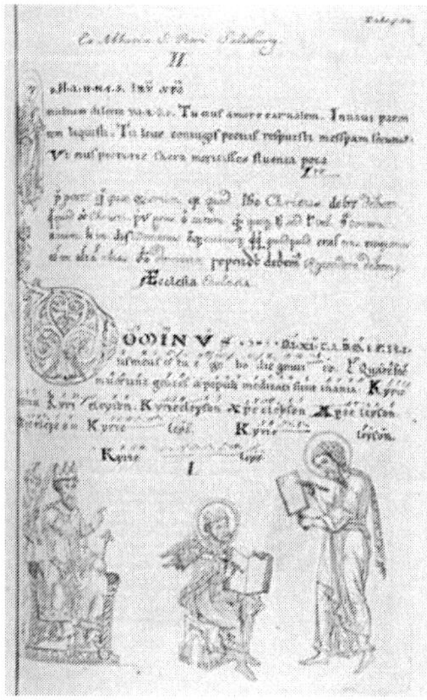

Fig. 1 (L) G. Bessel, *Chronicon Gotwicense* (1732).
(Photo: Universitätsbibliothek, Augsburg)

Fig. 2 (R) C. Sanftl, *Dissertatio in aureum* (1786). Pl. 2
(Photo: Universitätsbibliothek, Augsburg)

In 1786, around fifty years after Bessel's paleographical study appeared, Coloman Sanftl (1752–1809) published his *Dissertatio in aureum, ac pervetustum SS. Evangeliarum codicem ms. monasterii S. Emmerami Ratisbonae*,[11] which is noteworthy as one of the first monographs dedicated to a medieval manuscript. This work, better known as the *Codex Aureus*, had been written and illuminated for the Carolingian emperor Charles the Bald (823–877) and was held in high esteem in the monastery of Saint Emmeram in Regensburg, where it had been kept since 893.[12] Sanftl followed the example of Mabillon and Bessel, both of whom he quotes frequently, in method and terminology.[13] However, he not only meticulously described the manuscript's content and the script, but also devoted much attention to the artistic decoration. The engraved plates in Sanftl's publication are extraordinarily accurate, providing an apt counterpart to Sanftl's precise verbal descriptions of the manuscript. The three plates show the book cover, one of the ornamented initial pages, and the miniature of Charles the Bald [Fig. 2]. It is noteworthy that they do not single out specimens from script or from the illuminations, but always present the entire page. Moreover, they measure 42.5 by 49 cm. and thus reproduce the manuscript in its original size, which is explicitly noted by the author: "Our Codex has, in length and width, the same format as the engraved copperplates that I added to this book."[14] Regardless of his reservations about the style of the manuscript's paintings, typical for the classicizing taste of his time, Sanftl clearly appreciated its splendour, the sumptuousness of its appearance, and its venerable old age and historical importance.

Although they focused on German material, Bessel as well as Sanftl, both Benedictines like Mabillon and Montfaucon, were firmly rooted in the tradition of ecclesiastical scholarship in methodology and approach, and their affiliation also determined the international intellectual framework in which they operated. Apart from Montfaucon's history of the French kings—in which the author famously justified the inclusion of "barbarous" medieval material given the "intérêt de la nation" in its history—they did not have a national agenda.[15]

Of these four scholars, Mabillon and Montfaucon, Bessel and Sanftl, only Sanftl lived long enough to see the world shaken by the French Revolution and its aftermath. In his lifetime (he died in 1809) the abbey of Saint Emmeram fell to the newly founded principality of Regensburg. Only one year after his death, the famous *Codex Aureus* was taken to the state library in Munich, and the monastery was finally dissolved in 1812.

The Situation in Germany at the Beginning of the Nineteenth Century

Two historical and political factors seem of primary importance in explaining the preoccupation with medieval art in Germany in the nineteenth century. The first one is the dissolution of the monasteries and the secularization of church property, which also resulted in the destruction and loss of many works of art. Just as in post-Revolutionary France, this sense of loss contributed to an increasing interest in and sentimentality towards medieval art, exemplified by such important collectors as the brothers Melchior (1786–1851), Sulpiz Boisserée (1783–1854), and Ferdinand F. Wallraf (1748–1854).

The second factor is the fragmented state of Germany, in other words, the absence of "Germany" as a political entity before 1871. In contrast to England and France, where centralized monarchies had been established long before, with London and Paris as unrivaled capitals, Germany in the eighteenth and nineteenth centuries was divided into small sovereign states. In the aftermath of the French Revolution, the Holy Roman Empire was overrun in the Napoleonic Wars and finally dissolved in 1806. It fell into four parts: the region west of the Rhine and the other parts of Germany that had been ceded to France, and the states of the "Rheinbund" under Napoleon's protectorate, the most powerful of which were Bavaria, Prussia, and Austria. After the "Wars of Liberation" and the final defeat of the French troops at Leipzig in 1813, the desire for a unified and liberalized German state was strongly felt. Its realization failed, however, when, in 1815 at the Congress at Vienna, the status quo of the small autonomous states was confirmed. Only in the aftermath of the Franco-Prussian war of 1870-1871 was Germany unified as a nation state.[16] These political preconditions—the lack of a political identity and the patriotic longing for national unification—contributed to the idealized view of the Middle Ages as a period of unity and harmony.

Christian M. Engelhardt, the *Hortus Deliciarum*, and the Value of Illuminated Manuscripts for the Cultural History of the Middle Ages

To the modern art historian, the best known copies of medieval illuminations are those included in a study on the *Hortus Deliciarum* of Herrad of Landsberg, published in 1818 by Christian M. Engelhardt (1775–1858).[17] The *Hortus Deliciarum*, a richly illustrated spiritual encyclopedia, was written by Herrad of Landsberg (d. 1196), abbess of the convent of Hohenburg in Alsace, for the spiritual teaching of her nuns.[18] That the manuscript burned during the siege of Strasbourg in the Franco-Prussian war has lent a degree of familiarity to Engelhardt's reproductions that they would not have attained had the manuscript been preserved. Engelhardt's book, however, is also noteworthy as one of the earliest attempts to reproduce a manuscript's miniatures relatively comprehensively in a monographic study.

Scholarly interest in the *Hortus* resulted largely from its encyclopedic nature, but also from the high quality of its miniatures. In his outstandingly thorough study, Engelhardt first gave an account of the history of

Hohenburg and a minute description of the manuscript itself, followed by a chapter on the textual sources employed by Herrad and a chapter on the antiquarian value of the miniatures. He concluded with a transcription of all of Herrad's Latin poems and a list of the extensive German glosses in the manuscript as "a contribution to the research on the history of the early language of the Fatherland."[19] Indeed, these glosses "constitute one of the largest contemporary *corpora* of itemized lexemes still available to the student of early Middle High German."[20]

In regard to the miniatures, Engelhardt stressed their great value for the study of the cultural history of the Middle Ages:

> We offer to the friend of the Middle Ages, which have vanished in a magical fog, and to every scholar of cultural history, the first comprehensive study of the remarkable Hortus Deliciarum....The richest material unfolds in the paintings, which give manifold information about the habits, the costumes and the art of the twelfth century. These are the main focus of this study, and determine to a large extent the choice of paintings, which we append in faithful facsimiles as evidence.[21]

Of the twelve plates, the first seven present pastiches of figures and details taken from different miniatures, while the next two plates show full-page reproductions of allegorical compositions, namely a scheme of the divisions of philosophy and *artes liberales*, and the Ladder of Virtues. The tenth plate gives examples of the computistic tables, script, and musical notation, while plates eleven and twelve reproduce the manuscript's double page depiction of the legend of the convent's foundation, with "portraits" of Herrad and the nuns.[22] Engelhardt focused attention on dress and costume, especially ecclesiastical, as in the depiction of the allegorical Ladder of Virtues [Fig. 3], but also on royal garments, armor, harnesses, and carriages, as well as objects of everyday life [Fig. 4]. With his plates, Engelhardt provided the reader with a fairly comprehensive view of the content and character of the *Hortus Deliciarum*. His publication was greeted with great interest by other scholars. As the romanticist poet Achim von Arnim (1781–1831) wrote in a letter to the brothers Jacob (1786–1859) and Wilhelm (1785–1863) Grimm, "It is amazing how thoughtfully he [Engelhardt] presents the costumes from groups of figures that had not been painted for that purpose, and tools of this time, and food and drink."[23]

The numerous plates, executed as copperplate engravings (and hand-colored in many copies) make Engelhardt's study on the *Hortus Deliciarum* exceptional among the otherwise rather sparsely illustrated publications in Germany in the first half of the nineteenth century. Its relative sumptuousness was due to the financial support of the Bavarian king, Max Joseph I (1756–1825), to whom the book was dedicated. Such royal patronage of a German publication was unusual, and one reason why the king took an interest in the project may be because he had grown up in Alsace and had sentimental ties to the region.

It is thus noteworthy that Engelhardt's book has no chauvinist overtones, particularly in view of the historical circumstances and Max Joseph's support. Alsace, after its annexation by Louis XIV in 1681, had belonged to France, as it did during the years of the Revolution, when the cathedral was turned into a temple for the Cult of the Supreme Being. Even though Engelhardt characterized the Napoleonic rule as a time of suppression and grief, anti-French sentiment is entirely absent in his book. His approach to the topic is regional rather than national. He also firmly rejected nationalistic approaches to scholarship in general. With reference to Gothic art and contemporary discussions about its German origin, he remarked:

> The art of Herrad belongs to a time which, especially in regard to architecture, is usually called Gothic. To classify it, as happens nowadays, as exclusively or pre-eminently belonging to one nation, is a view that can scarcely be maintained when examined impartially, as surely the western peoples of the Middle Ages show more conformity, not only in the arts but also in their costumes and their habits, than is usually acknowledged.[24]

This is revealing since—without mentioning names—Engelhardt makes a statement against a trend in German scholarship, which was expressed most prominently three decades earlier by Johann Wolfgang von Goethe (1749–1832). In his essay "Von deutscher Baukunst" (1772), Goethe had not only attempted to rehabilitate Gothic architecture in the face of prevailing classicist taste, he had also—by employing a consciously positive adaptation of Vasari's disrespectful term "stile tedesco"—argued for the German origin and character of Gothic architecture, famously using as his example the cathedral of Strasbourg.[25] This view was shared by Friedrich Schlegel (1772–1829)[26] and universally held in Germany in the first half of the nineteenth century. Engelhardt's balanced position is therefore quite remarkable.

The *Hortus Deliciarum*, not least because it was known through Engelhardt's publication, remained one of the manuscripts to which scholars referred throughout the nineteenth century. It was also among the few manuscripts of German origin selected for inclusion in a French publication by Comte Auguste de Bastard d'Estang (1792–1883), entitled *Peintures et ornements des manuscrits, classés dans un ordre chronologique* (1832–1869).[27] This publication is of interest for our topic for two reasons. On the one hand, Bastard d'Estang's plates always represent the full page (instead of focusing on details), and clearly reproduce the illuminations for their character as works of art, not—as, for example, in Engelhardt's book—only visual sources of historical information. The *Peintures et ornements* was not only the most comprehensive publication on illuminated manuscripts that had ever appeared, but also one of the most expensive and lavishly illustrated books of all time. In fact, it was the French king, Louis-Philippe (reigned 1830–1848), who sponsored the project. This governmental interest in the illuminated manuscript, and support for its publication, stands in marked contrast to the situation in Germany.[28] Bastard's project, however, remained incomplete: not only did a disastrous fire destroy a great number of the lithographed plates in 1848, but in the same year the July monarchy collapsed, and Bastard d'Estang's project lost its financial support.

After the *Hortus Deliciarum,* Engelhardt published, in 1823, *Der Ritter von Stauffenberg, ein Altdeutsches Gedicht*, focusing on an illustrated chivalrous epic in the vernacular,[29] and on a fifteenth-century vernacular

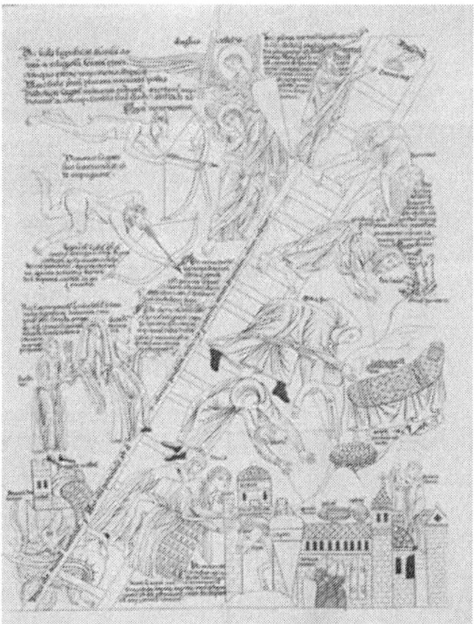

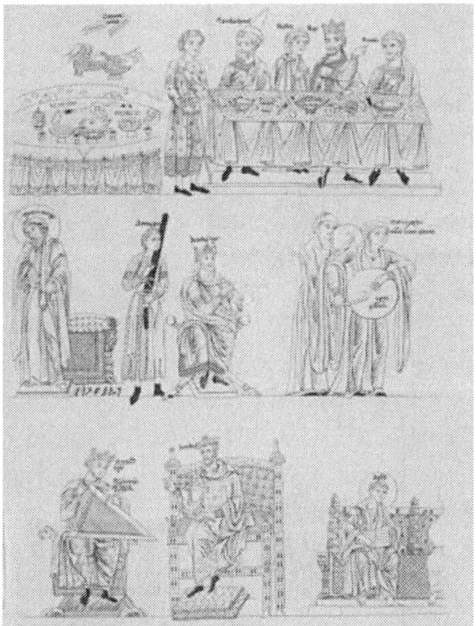

Fig. 3 (L) C. M. Engelhardt, *Hortus Deliciarum* (Stuttgart: Cotta, 1818). Pl. IX (Photo: The British Library, London)

Fig. 4 (R) C. M. Engelhardt, *Hortus Deliciarum* (Stuttgart: Cotta, 1818). Pl. IV (Photo: The British Library, London)

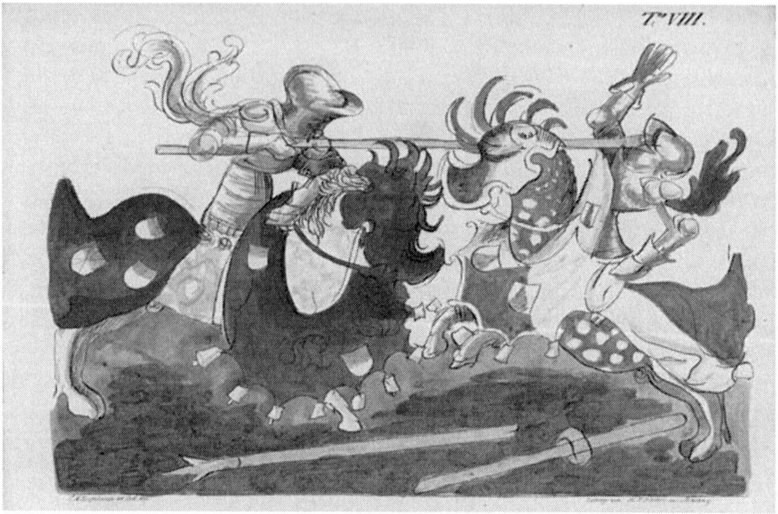

Fig. 5 C. M. Engelhardt, *Ritter von Stauffenberg* (Strasbourg: no publisher, 1823). Pl. VIII (Photo: University Library, Cambridge)

translation of the *Speculum Humanae Salvationis (Heilsspiegel)* by Heinrich of Lauffenberg. Both manuscripts, like the *Hortus Deliciarum* and many others, burned in the Strasbourg library fire of 1870. Similar in structure and approach to Engelhardt's first publication, this book was also augmented by a number of hand-colored plates based on Engelhardt's own tracings [Fig. 5]. Although highly innovative in methodology, particularly in its analysis of the images, this book did not have much of an impact, since it was only printed for a small number of subscribers.[30] In both of these books dedicated to manuscripts, Engelhardt focused on examples that were of great interest for the cultural history of the Middle Ages and for the study of German language: in the case of the *Hortus Deliciarum,* Engelhardt devoted considerable space to the publication of the German glosses, while both the *Ritter von Stauffenberg* and the German *Heilsspiegel* comprised manuscripts written in the vernacular.

The National and the Vernacular: The Study of the *Codex Manesse*

At about the same time that his monograph on the *Hortus Deliciarum* was published, Engelhardt was involved in the planned publication of a facsimile of the so-called *Codex Manesse.* This project is of considerable interest, since the *Codex* was undoubtedly the most thoroughly studied and most frequently reproduced medieval manuscript in the nineteenth century.[31] Written between 1304 and 1330, the *Codex Manesse,* a collection of poems by *Minne-Singers* from the twelfth to the fourteenth centuries, ranks among the most important vernacular manuscripts of the late Middle Ages in Germany. Over 6000 strophes long, it contains 137 portraits of poets, such as Wolfram von Eschenbach and Walter von der Vogelweide. It is a unique witness to medieval lay culture and the most comprehensive compilation of German medieval lyric that has come down to us. Kept in Paris since the mid-seventeenth century, it was only reacquired by Germany in 1888 after complicated negotiations and has been kept in Heidelberg ever since.[32]

Already in the eighteenth century, the *Codex Manesse* had attracted scholarly interest as an outstanding example of Middle High German poetry. In 1748, a preliminary study of the *Codex Manesse* was published by Johann J. Bodmer (1698–1783), the Swiss historian, classicist, and specialist in German studies, editor of Homer's works as well as the *Nibelungenlied*, in collaboration with Johann J. Breitinger (1701–1776). It consisted of a description of the manuscript and its provenance, selected biographies of the poets, an explanation of Middle High German grammar, several transcribed poems, and an extensive glossary. The book included only one plate: a tracing of a tournament scene which, in the manuscript, introduces the poems by Albrecht Marshall of Raprechtschweil [Fig. 6],[33] a noteworthy choice, given that none of Albrecht's poems were selected for the publication. Bodmer and Breitinger appear to have chosen this image for its antiquarian and heraldic interest, and also, perhaps, because Raprechtschweil (Rappertswil) is located in Bodmer and Breitinger's native Switzerland, on the Lake of Zurich. Despite their aesthetic reservations regarding the style of the images, Bodmer and Breitinger stressed the value of the manuscript for antiquarian studies:

> The splendid illuminations that introduce the poems make the codex precious and impressive. The drawings are executed very poorly according to the bad taste of the time, but the colors are extremely bright and lively....These paintings are generally very useful in respect to costume, arms, armor and the like, and make descriptions of those items in poetry or in historiography understandable, that otherwise we would not be able to interpret.[34]

Their publication was designed to raise interest in the *Codex Manesse* and solicit funds for a more comprehensive treatment, but they did not receive the anticipated response. Nevertheless, a set of twenty-two detailed tracings executed on their behalf testifies to their interest in the manuscript's images.

Another attempt at a full edition was made around 1815—under very different political circumstances—by the specialist in German studies, Friedrich H. von der Hagen (1780–1856). It was for this project that Engelhardt, who studied the manuscript in Paris in 1815, prepared several tracings.[35] However, after difficult negotiations with a number of publishing houses, this plan also failed due to the high cost projected for the publication of the plates. Apparently, interest in the text of the *Codex Manesse* exceeded interest in the images. The romanticist poet Ludwig Tieck (1773–1853), for example, stated in a letter to von der Hagen on 29 April 1818:

> Ever since I saw the manuscript in Paris I am convinced that many of the images, maybe even most of them, are of historical relevance and therefore important. Some of their features, however, seem to be just recurring phrases [*wiederkehrende Phrasen*]. The images neither show any quality of drawing nor any style [*nicht Zeichnung und Styl*]. In fact, they show no style at all, not even the style of their own time. Hence, I think, one could simply—and without doing any injustice to the matter—arrange 4 to 6 drawings on a quarto format, if finely outlined maybe even 8. This would cut down the cost [of publication] considerably.[36]

Despite all these difficulties, von der Hagen not only continued to pursue his plan for a comprehensive publication on the *Codex Manesse*, but broadened his ambitions. In 1823, he tried to negotiate with the French government to acquire the codex for Germany in exchange for several other manuscripts, but was unsuccessful. In 1830, Joseph M. C. von Laßberg (1770–1855) tried to borrow the *Codex Manesse* to have tracings made for a planned publication, but the French refused to send the manuscript to Strasbourg for copying, since they were afraid, perhaps with reason, that the Germans might not return it.[37] A general nationalistic overtone is apparent in regard to the *Codex Manesse*. On several occasions it was claimed that the publication of a manuscript of such crucial importance for German culture should not be left to "den Franzmännern" or "den Welschen" (both disrespectful terms for the French). Von der Hagen finally got to publish the numerous tracings he had gathered from various sources nearly two decades later. Between 1842 and 1853 he gave three lectures at the Royal Academy of Science and Humanities (*Königliche Akademie der Wissenschaften*) in Berlin, which subsequently appeared in the periodical *Abhandlungen der königlichen Akademie der*

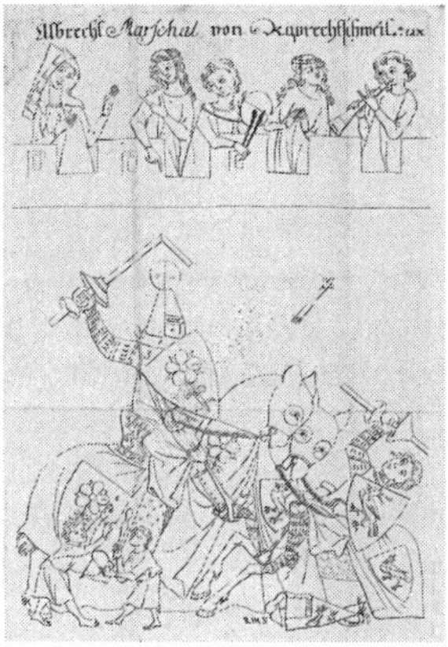

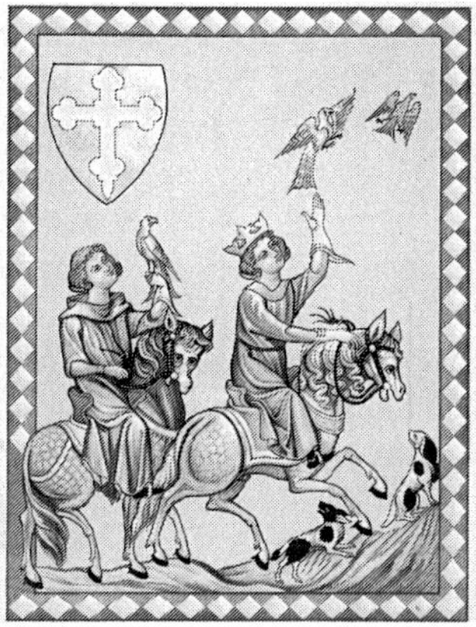

Fig. 6 (L) Scene introducing poems by Albrecht Marshall of Raprechtschweil, *Codex Manesse*, from J. J. Breitinger and J.J. Bodmer, *Proben der alten schwäbischen Poesie des 13. Jahrhunderts aus der Maneßischen Sammlung* (Zurich, 1748). (Photo: The British Library, London)

Fig. 7 (R) King Conrad the Younger, *Codex Manesse*, from F. H. von der Hagen, "Über die Gemälde in den Sammlungen der altdeutschen lyrischen Dichter...(Teil 1)," *Abhandlungen der königlichen Akademie der Wissenschaften zu Berlin*, 1842 (Berlin, 1844). Pl. 1

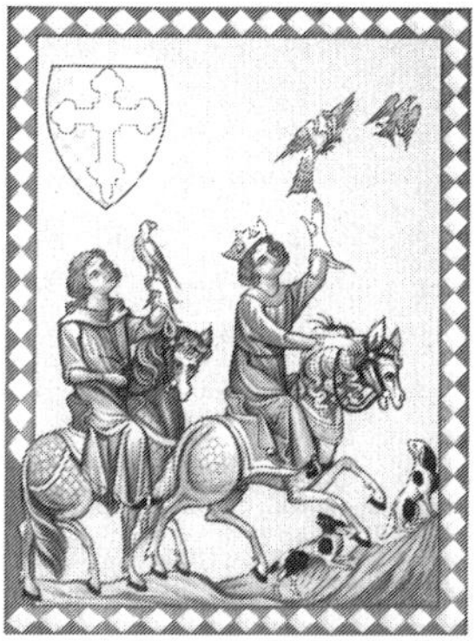

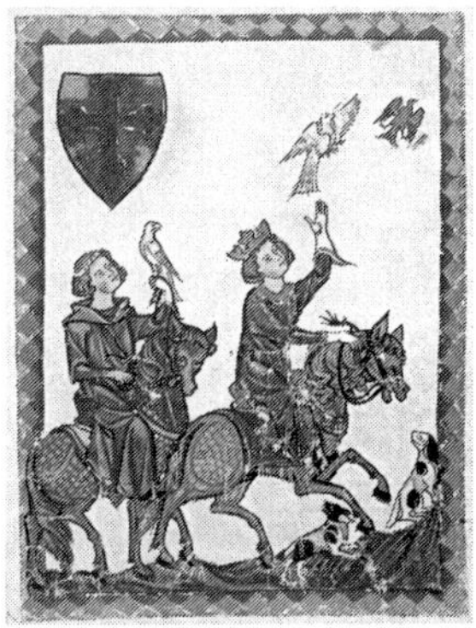

Fig. 8 (L) King Conrad the Younger, *Codex Manesse*, from F. H. von der Hagen and B.C. Mathieu, *Minnesänger aus der Zeit der Hohenstaufen* (Paris: Plon, 1850). Pl. II (Photo: The British Library, London)

Fig. 9 (R) King Conrad the Younger, *Codex Manesse*, Cod. pal. Germ. 848, fol. 7r, Universitätsbibliothek, Heidelberg (Photo: Bildarchiv Foto Marburg)

Wissenschaften zu Berlin with forty-four attendant plates.[38] They were executed as simple outline lithographs based on von der Hagen's collected tracings. Their quality, however, was for the most part rather poor [Fig. 7], and their precision left much to be desired.

A more comprehensive set of ten lithographs was published in 1850 by von der Hagen and Bernard C. Mathieu (who had previously worked for Bastard d'Estang) in a partial facsimile edition. This project also remained incomplete, with only the first installment printed. It is noteworthy that most of the plans for the publication of richly illustrated books in Germany failed specifically because, in contrast to France (as the comparison with Bastard d'Estang's publication demonstrates), no national institution existed to support these expensive projects. The plates in von der Haagen and Mathieu's publication, while visually appealing, were far from faithful reproductions. In particular, an attempt was made to give the rather linear figures in the miniatures a more three-dimensional appearance, and the character of the facial features was often fundamentally altered in adapting to the romanticized, mellow taste of the nineteenth century, as can be seen by comparing the lithograph of King Conrad the Younger with the actual miniature in the *Codex Manesse* [Figs. 8-9]. Countless copies and free adaptations of the *Codex Manesse* images that appeared in the realm of the applied arts—decorating tapestries, beer glasses, tiles, and book covers—were based upon von der Hagen and Mathieu's facsimile from 1850, thus demonstrating the manuscript's popularity as a representative of the romanticized Middle Ages.[39] That this manuscript was, more than any other, regarded as a part of German national heritage, however, continued to have more to do with its textual content and the contemporary taste for things chivalric than its artistic qualities, then still underappreciated.

That medieval manuscripts in the vernacular attracted so much attention can be explained by the importance of language and culture as a factor of unification and collective identity, most prominently expressed by Johann G. Herder (1744–1803), who defined culture as being determined by place, history, and the character of a people. The concept of these works as an expression of national character, of "German-ness," became increasingly important in the study of the material relics of the past. In Germany, the failure of political unification after the end of the Holy Roman Empire led to a definition of national identity that was mainly based on a common language and culture. Medieval German poetry was of crucial importance to scholars in the eighteenth and nineteenth centuries because it seemingly represented an ideal society.[40] As von der Haagen put it:

> This kind of poetry, even more than chivalry, was the universally uniting bond, that [from the kings and knights] down to the craftsman and traveling bard, evened out and harmonized all [social] differences in a nice and human manner through the common content of their songs, the heavenly and worldly *Minne*.[41]

The *Codex Manesse* embodied the romanticized ideal of a harmonic social structure like no other manuscript, with the different strata of society united in their common language, art, and culture. Although other texts, such as the *Nibelungenlied,* were of equal or even greater relevance to the field of German studies, the fact that the *Codex Manesse* was one of the few illustrated vernacular manuscripts made it particularly appealing to nineteenth-century romanticism. Von der Hagen explicitly pointed to the differences in medium and style between the illuminations in liturgical and vernacular manuscripts. Having remarked on the occurrence of gold-ground as a common feature in the decoration of liturgical books, he continued, "...only at a time when secular *(weltliche)* books in the vernacular were decorated with illustrations, did the paintings emancipate themselves from this rigid background, upon which until then they had adhered like cut-out silhouettes, and the figures gained more freedom and movement."[42] Scholars prior to von der Hagen had taken little interest in the formal and aesthetic qualities of the illustrations in the *Codex Manesse*, which had, overall, been judged rather negatively (hence the "improvements" in many of the reproductions). In fact, von der Hagen's sensitive description is likely to reflect the opinion of one of the most important figures in early art history, Franz Kugler (1808–1858), who had seen the plates a couple of years before their publication and given a more impartial and differentiated opinion on the formal characteristics of the *Codex Manesse* in his universal history of painting, published in 1837.[43] This also points to a fundamentally different approach in the scholarly preoccupation with manuscripts.

Manuscript Illumination and the History of Medieval Painting: Gustav F. Waagen and Franz Kugler

In the late eighteenth and first half of the nineteenth century, with the foundation of museums and the establishment of art history as an academic discipline, interest in the history of medieval painting grew. The history of art (as a collective singular) manifested itself in the presentation and arrangement of objects according to schools and chronology in newly founded museums (as opposed to the earlier arrangement of collections according to aesthetic priorities). As a result, the material presented was systematically embedded in the narrative framework of a universal (art) history. This approach to the objects and their representation reflects a tendency in scholarship towards the writing of art history as universal history that can be observed in the publications by Johann D. Fiorillo (1748–1821)[44] and Jean-Baptiste L.-G. Seroux d'Agincourt (1730–1814), both of whom incorporated illuminated manuscripts in their accounts of painting during the medieval period. Medieval miniature painting was, if only very gradually, understood and appreciated as an art form in its own right.

One of the most influential German art historians of the time was Gustav F. Waagen (1794–1868),[45] director of the newly founded Gemäldegalerie ("picture gallery"), then housed in the upper storey of the Altes Museum ("Old Museum") in Berlin from 1830 to 1864, and lecturer in art history at the university of Berlin from 1844 onwards. In 1822, he published a pioneering and methodologically innovative study on Hubert and Jan van Eyck, in which he explained their art in the context of social, political, and religious history, thus transferring an historical-critical scholarly method to the field of art history. From early on in his career, Waagen showed a keen interest in medieval miniature painting, and, in fact, planned on writing a comprehensive study of medieval illuminated manuscripts. Two factors might have increased Waagen's awareness of the importance of this medium. During his many trips to England (1835, 1850, 1851, 1862, 1865), he came in contact with many famous collectors and became more familiar with the illuminated manuscript as an artistic genre. He was certainly also well aware of contemporary English publications, such as the slightly crude but beautifully illustrated *Bibliographical Decameron*,[46] and of Séroux d'Agincourt's highly influential study of the development of the arts, *Histoire de l'art par les monuments, depuis sa décadence au IVe siècle jusqu'à son renouvellement au XVIe siècle,* published between 1810 and 1823.[47] Seroux d'Agincourt had dedicated a chapter in his book specifically to manuscript illumination, and was one of the first to explicitly stress its relevance for the understanding of medieval painting in general, because of the great losses in other media.[48] Waagen argues along similar lines when he points out that "…the history of art…at such time is solely to be traced in their miniatures. These alone furnish us with a continuous series of specimens of the pictorial art….the larger paintings of those ages…having, with rare exceptions, entirely perished."[49] Furthermore, he drew attention to the fact that manuscripts, especially the lavishly illuminated ones, could often be linked to the historic figures who had commissioned them, and thus could be dated with some degree of precision. What is most important, however, is that Waagen drew attention to the importance of manuscript illumination as an artistic genre in its own right. He also observed that:

> … the miniatures themselves considered as a portion of the history of art, the real importance of which, though first pointed out by d'Agincourt in his well-known work, has never yet been fully appreciated….miniatures possess also in themselves a very high artistic and historical significance, namely as being the only form in which the various styles of thought peculiar to the Middle Ages are fully rendered. I allude above all to the various series of symbolical and emblematical representations by which the clergy directed and ministered to the religious feelings of the people….Next to these religious subjects, I may cite that class of ideas, peculiar also to the time, which includes the chivalry, the troubadour poetry, and the fantastic and allegorical humour of that period, and which are only preserved to us in their full redundance in the pages of illuminated MSS….It is therefore my earnest desire to publish a history of the miniature painting of the Middle Ages illustrated by faithful reproductions from the finest and best authenticated MSS so as distinctly to show the development of painting in each nation from the 9th to the 15th centuries.[50]

Waagen aimed at a richly illustrated publication because, in his words, "the history of any particular department of art can be only so far satisfactorily studied as its course of development may be traceable in a series of existing specimens."[51] In the same context, he explicitly stated the superiority of illustrations over verbal descriptions. The large number of reproductions Waagen desired, however, would have made his projected publication quite expensive, and Waagen apparently never succeeded in raising money to realize it—a recurring motif with German publications.

At about the same time, Franz Kugler (1808–1858), professor at the Academy of Fine Arts in Berlin (Berliner Akademie der Künste) and author of the first survey on the history of art taking a universal approach, also dedicated his attention to medieval manuscripts.[52] Like Waagen, he emphasized the general importance of medieval book illumination, which he regarded as crucial for the understanding of the development and progress of medieval art north of the Alps: "the study of illuminations must be categorically described as utterly fundamental for medieval art in general, since from the study of their progress and development conclusions may be drawn for all other branches of art."[53] It is significant that this statement occurs in Kugler's enthusiastic review of Bastard d'Estang's great enterprise. Obviously Waagen as well as Kugler perceived the need for sufficiently illustrated publications.

Kugler's interest in illuminated manuscripts went back to 1831 when he wrote his (Latin!) dissertation on *Werners Lieder von der Magd,* an illustrated vernacular poem dedicated to the Virgin Mary from the early thirteenth century. This study, though entirely neglected by modern scholars, is of great interest, because he prefaced the actual treatment of his topic with a brief survey of illuminated manuscripts in Germany from Carolingian times up to 1300, concluding with the *Codex Manesse.*[54] In the following years, Kugler published several articles on medieval manuscripts in German libraries[55] including, in 1834, a study on the *Eneide,* a richly illuminated manuscript from around 1230 containing a vernacular adaptation of the romance of the ancient hero Aeneas, by Heinrich von Veldeke (d. before 1210). [56] Discovered in 1819 in the stock of an antiquarian bookseller, it was purchased by the Royal Library in Berlin in 1823.[57] Like Kugler's other publications, the article on the *Eneide* originally did not contain any pictures. Only in 1853, when he had his articles reprinted in *Kleine Schriften. Mit Illustrationen und anderen artistischen Beilagen,* did he succeed in having them illustrated, primarily with his own tracings and drawings. He focused his readers' attention on details that he singled out, thus creating a close interrelation between the verbal and pictorial arguments he put forward. On the one hand, these reproductions presented details of costume and armor to illustrate a section entitled *Antiquarisches,* following the traditional designation of illuminated manuscripts as sources for the material culture of the Middle Ages. Kugler's sensitivity for the artistic qualities of the miniatures, however, can be seen in the following passage, where he demonstrates the subtle ways in which emotions are represented in the *Eneide,* using as examples the scenes of Aeneas grieving the death of his friend Pallas and Aeneas taking leave of Dido [Figs. 10-11]:

> It is mainly in the movement of the hands of the depicted figures that a particular language of gestures unfolds, which can show either a calm conversation or lend expression to passionate moments. In the latter, when needing to portray lonely and painful love or the lament over deceased beloveds, pain and sorrow are expressed most appropriately in a characteristic wringing of the hands in despair.[58]

He continues and, in fact, concludes his study on the *Eneide* with the remark: "Where people kiss, the persons involved take each other by the heads in a naive manner, and since in situations of that sort, there is usually not much said, scrolls bearing text were not required."[59]

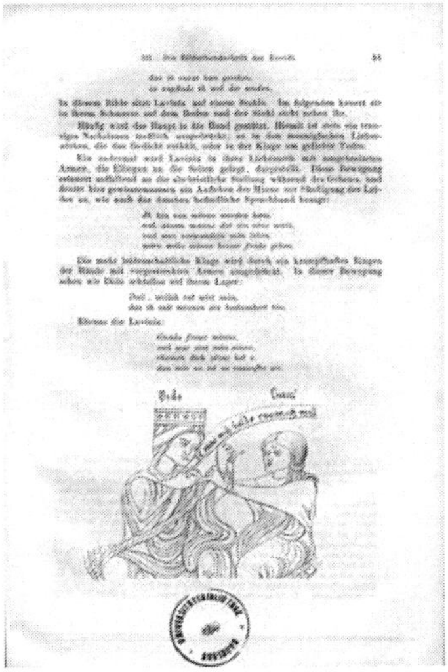

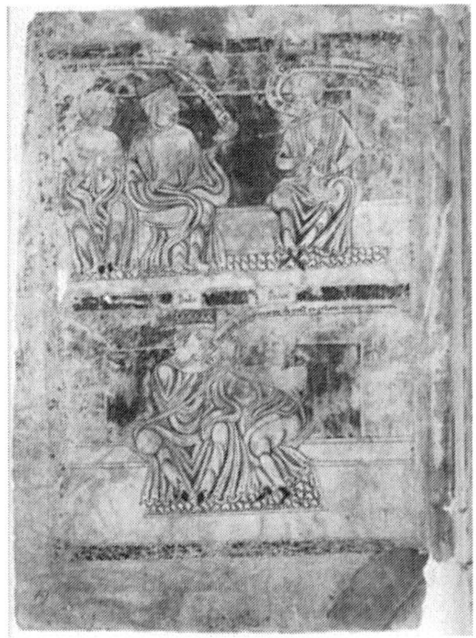

Fig. 10 (L) Franz Kugler, *Kleine Schriften und Studien zur Kunstgeschichte*, vol. 1 (Stuttgart: Ebner and Seubert, 1853). 51 (Photo: Universitätsbibliothek Augsburg)

Fig. 11 (R) Dido and Aeneas, *Eneide,* ca. 1230, MS Germ. Fol. 282, fol. 15v, Preußischer Kulturbesitz Staatsbibliothek, Berlin (Photo: from A. Boeckler, *Heinrich von Veldeke, Eneide. Die Bilder der Berliner Handschrift* [Leipzig: Harrasowitz, 1939].)

Kugler was indeed one of the first to grasp and adequately describe the artistic peculiarities of medieval art, identifying expression through gestures as one of its defining characteristics. The illustrations in his book, combined directly with the text instead of being added as separate plates, reinforced this new approach, the isolation of details emphasizing and clarifying the author's verbal arguments. It is notable that both of Kugler's monographs on illuminated manuscripts were dedicated to vernacular examples, while the passages on the development of painting in his *Handbuch,* as well as in his *Geschichte der Malerei*, included the more prominent works of book illumination from the Carolingian era to the eleventh century. For these periods, however, Kugler's primary focus was on the afterlife of the Classical and early Christian tradition (in the Carolingian manuscripts) and of Byzantine influence (in the Ottonian manuscripts). It is only in the late twelfth century, as Kugler pointed out, that the miniatures reveal a sense of the depiction of the forms of nature and the representation of feelings, passion in particular. According to his interpretation, this progress in the visual arts in Germany was brought forward by the newly emerging vernacular poetry ("nationale Poesie"), and in fact, almost all the examples that he named for illuminated manuscripts in the late twelfth and thirteenth centuries are in the vernacular.[60] This is crucial, because it emphasizes the innovative qualities of these illuminations. It is, therefore, not surprising that Kugler also stressed the relevance of the illustrated vernacular manuscripts for the formation of the "germanischer Stil" (a classification introduced by Kugler to replace the term "Gothic") in painting. Here he explicitly cites an illustrated copy of Wolfram von Eschenbach's *Parzival* in Munich and, not surprisingly, the *Codex Manesse*.[61]

Conclusion

In the period between the middle of the eighteenth and the middle of the nineteenth century, the publications devoted to medieval German illumination reveal continuities, as well as changing approaches to the medieval manuscript. These are in some ways indicative of the scholarly preoccupation with medieval art in general, in other respects specific to the medium. From Mabillon and Montfaucon to Engelhardt and Kugler there is a consistent recurrence of certain key methodological concepts, such as the perception of illuminations as visual sources analogous to written sources, and their repeated stress on the great value of such images for the study of the cultural history of the Middle Ages.

It is notable that German scholars devoted so much attention to manuscripts with vernacular texts. These were, despite their often sparse decoration (in comparison with the much more lavishly illuminated liturgical books), held in high esteem because of the crucial role of language for the concept of a German national identity. The preoccupation with the *Codex Manesse* is particularly revealing, because its images as well as its text lent themselves to the idealized interpretation of a medieval society by nineteenth-century scholars: a community united across all social and political boundaries by a common language and culture. The example of the *Codex Manesse* demonstrates how the study of the material relics of the past in some respects attained the quality of a social utopia.

Apart from the interest that scholars brought to illuminated manuscripts as witnesses of the cultural history of a distant past, their images also gained relevance as exempla for the history of painting in the Middle Ages in general. This reflects the changing approach towards the writing of a universal history of art that can be observed from the late eighteenth century onwards and particularly in the first half of the nineteenth century. In this context, manuscript illumination was particularly valued as a resource that could fill in gaps in the history of monumental painting during the early periods. Only in the course of the nineteenth century, however, did a growing sensitivity towards, and appreciation of, the stylistic aspects of medieval art develop; it was scholars like Waagen and Kugler who were pioneers in acknowledging the formal and aesthetic qualities of book illumination as a genre in its own right.

Notes

[1] I wish to express my gratitude to Janet T. Marquardt and Alyce A. Jordan for the invitation to contribute a paper to this volume and for their great kindness and patience. Also, I want to thank Gabriele Bickendorf and William Diebold for their helpful comments and suggestions. Furthermore, I am greatly indebted to Stella Panayotova, Jill Whitelock, and Michael Staunton for proofreading the manuscript at different stages. All translations in the article are mine unless otherwise stated.

[2] This holds especially true for the two most recent publications: *The Revival of Medieval Illumination: Nineteenth Century Belgium Manuscripts and Illuminations from a European Perspective,* ed. T. Coomans and J. de Maeyer (Leuven: Leuven University Press, 2007); and *Manuscript Illumination in the Modern Age: Recovery and Reconstruction,* ed. S. Hindman and N. Rowe (New Castle: Oak Knoll Press, 2001); see also A. N. L. Munby, *Connoisseurs and Medieval Miniatures, 1750-1850* (Oxford: Clarendon, 1972); C. Nordenfalk, "Notes on the History of Facsimiles of Illuminated Manuscripts," in *Color of the Middle Ages: A Survey of Book Illumination Based on Color Facsimiles of Medieval Manuscripts*, ed. C. Nordenfalk (Pittsburgh: Pittsburgh University Art Gallery, 1976). 7-28; R. Watson, "Vandals and Enthusiasts: Views of Illumination in the Nineteenth Century," catalogue (Victoria and Albert Museum, London, 1995, typescript); J.-C. Klamt, "Zur Reproduktionsgeschichte mittelalterlicher Schriftformen und Miniaturen in der Neuzeit, part I: Das 17. und 18. Jahrhundert," *Quaerendo* 29, 3 (1999). 169-207; J.-C. Klamt, "Zur Reproduktionsgeschichte mittelalterlicher Schriftformen und Miniaturen in der Neuzeit, part II: Die erste Hälfte des 19. Jahrhunderts," *Quaerendo* 29, 4 (1999). 247-274; A. Worm, "Mittelalterliche Buchmalerei im Spiegel neuzeitlicher Publikationen," in *Visualisierung und Immagination. Mittelalterliche Artefakte in bildlichen Darstellungen der Neuzeit und Moderne*, Göttinger Gespräche zur Geschichtswissenschaft, Bd. 25, ed. B. Carque et al., 2 vols. (Göttingen: Wallstein, 2006). 151-212. I am greatly indebted to Rowan Watson for bringing to my attention his "Illumination and Illuminated Manuscripts in the Nineteenth Century: A Survey of Responses in England, France and Germany to the Revival of a Medieval Art Form" (Victoria and Albert Museum, London, 1997, typescript).

[3] J. de Mabillon, *De re diplomatica VI. In quibus quidquid ad veterum instrumentorum antiquitatem, materiam, scripturam et stilum; quidquid ad sigilla,*

monogramma, subscriptiones ac notas chronologicas; quidquid inde ad antiquariam, historiam, forensemque disciplinam pertinet, explicatur et illustratur (Paris, 1681); B. Neveu, "Mabillon et l'historiographie gallicane vers 1700: Erudition ecclésiastique et recherche historique au XVIIe siècle," *Historische Forschung im 18. Jahrhundert. Organisation, Zielsetzung, Ergebnisse*, ed. K. Hammer and J. Voss, Pariser historische Studien, 13 (Bonn: Ludwig Röhrscheid, 1976). 27-81

[4] G. Bickendorf, *Die Historisierung der italienischen Kunstbetrachtung im 17. und 18. Jahrhundert*, Berliner Schriften zur Kunst, Bd. XI, (Berlin: Gebrüder Mann Verlag, 1998). 123-178

[5] I. Herklotz, "Historia Sacra und mittelalterliche Kunst während der zweiten Hälfte des 16. Jahrhunderts in Rom," in *Baronio e l'arte: Atti del Convegno Internazionale di Studi, Sora 10-13 ottobre 1984*, ed. R. de Maio et al. (Sora: Vincenzo Patriarca, 1985). 21-74; Bickendorf, *Die Historisierung der italienischen Kunstbetrachtung*. 123-178; Francis Haskell, *History and Its Images: Art and the Interpretation of the Past* (New Haven: Yale University Press, 1993); see also the influential article by A. Momigliano, "Ancient History and the Antiquarian," *Journal of the Warburg and Courtauld Institutes* 3 (1950). 285-315

[6] Bickendorf, *Die Historisierung der italienischen Kunstbetrachtung,* was the first to point out the importance of the analysis of script and written documents for the general development of methodology.

[7] Jean de Mabillon, *Annales Ordinis Sancti Benedicti occidentalum monachorum patriarchae. In quibus non modo res monasticae, sed etiam ecclesiasticae historiae non minima pars continetur* (Paris, 1703-1704).

[8] Ironically, the second volume on the history of Göttweig was never published. Gottfried Bessel, *Chronicon Gotwicense seu Annales Liberi et Exempti Monasterii Gotwicensis Ordinis S. Benedicti Inferioris Austriae, Faciem Austriae Antiquae et mediae usque ad nostra tempora, Deinde Ejusdem Monasterii fundationem, Progressum, Statumque hodiernum exhibens, Ex Codicibus antiquis, Membranis et Instrumentis tum Domesticis, tum extraneis depromptum: Pro quorum faciliori intellectu Tomus Prodomus. De Codicibus antiquis Manuscriptis, De Imperatorum ac Regum Germaniae Diplomatibus, De Eorundem Palatiis, Villis et Curtibus Regis, atque De Germaniae medii aevi Pagis. Praemittitur, Et ea Caesareorum, Regiorumque Germaniae Diplomatum antiquitatem, Materiam, Stylum, Scripturam, Monogrammata, Sigilla, Subscriptiones, notasque Chronologicas, atque ad Palatiorum et Villarum Regiarum, Pagorumque Germaniae Mediae situm pertinent, explicantur, et adjectis Speciminibus, tabulisque aeri incisis illustrantur* (Tegernsee, 1732); Klamt, "Reproduktionsgeschichte, part I." 184-191

[9] Bessel, *Chronicon Gotwicense*. 50, 52; Cod. ser. nov. 2700, fols. 167, 192, 361, Österreichische Nationalbibliothek, Vienna; on the manuscript see *Das Antiphonar von St. Peter. Vollständige Faksimile-Ausgabe des Cod. Vindob. ser. nov. 2700 der Österreichischen Nationalbibliothek,* ed. F. Unterkircher and O. Demus (Graz: Akademische Druck- und Verlagsgesellschaft, 1974).

[10] "Unde cum varia ad rem vestioriam illius aevi apprime facienta in eodem reperiantur, varias cum suis habitibus figuras aeri incidi curavimus. Comparet ibi

S. Gregorius habitu Episcopali, pennam in manibus gestans & librum, in quo consideranda venit mitra, non alta & cuspidata, sed depressa, qualem in Sigillis pluribus B. Alemanni, Udalrici & aliorum Episcoporum Pataviensum....Alia porro repraesentantur figura, tabulam in manibus gestans, quae cum cerata necessario esse videatur, ita instrumentum aliud graphium necessario est seu stylus, quamvis calamo arundineo seu pennae magis similis videatur, conspicitur etiam alia in eodem Codice figura, Regem Herodem repraesentans: cujus corona, sceptrum liligerum, et reliquus habitus regius aliquam observationem merentur." Bessel, *Chronicon Gotwicense*. 50

[11] Colomannus Sanftl, *Dissertatio in aureum, ac pervetustum SS. Evangeliarum codicem ms. monasterii S. Emmerami Ratisbonae, auctore P. Colomanno Sanftl, eiusdem monstarii presbytero Benedictino, SS. Theologiae Professore, et Bibliothecario* (Regensburg, 1786).

[12] The manuscript (Clm 14000, Bayerische Staatsbibliothek, Munich) was given to Saint Emmeram by Arnulf of Kärnten in 893. Wilhelm Köhler and F. Mütherich, *Die karolingischen Miniaturen*, vol. 5 of *Die Hofschule Karls des Kahlen* (Berlin: Verlag des Deutschen Vereins für Kunstwissenschaft, 1982). 175-198, Pl. V, Figs. 45-70

[13] Sanftl quotes Jean Mabillon, who, while visiting the convent, declared that he had never seen a more precious and elegant manuscript ("nullum pretiosiorem aut elegantiorem unquam vidisse affirmeret"). Sanftl, *Dissertatio in aureum*. Praefatio

[14] "Codex noster solii sat ampli formam habet, quam ex asse aequant tabulae, quas hic aeri incisas exhibeo." Sanftl, *Dissertatio in aureum*. 29

[15] The French tradition of national historiography did not have a counterpart in Germany at this time. The modern equivalent to Montfaucon's study is P. E. Schramm, *Die deutschen Kaiser und Könige in Bildern ihrer Zeit. Bd. I: 751–1190* (Leipzig: B.G. Teubner, 1928; second edition, ed. F. Mütherich, [Munich: Prestel, 1983]); P.E. Schramm, *Die deutschen Kaiser und Könige in Bildern ihrer Zeit. Bd. II, Ein Beitrag zur Herrschergeschichte von Rudolf I. bis Maximilian I., 1273-1519*, ed. H. Fillitz (Munich: Prestel, 1978).

[16] O. Kallscheuer and K. Leggewie, "Deutsche Kulturnation versus französische Staatsnation? Eine ideengeschichtliche Stichprobe," in *Nationales Bewußtsein und kollektive Identität*, Studien zur Entwicklung des kollektiven Bewußtseins in der Neuzeit, ed. H. Berding (Frankfurt am Main: Suhrkamp, 1996). 112-162 provide an excellent introduction to the state of scholarship.

[17] Christian M. Engelhardt, *Herrad von Landsperg, Aebtissin zu Hohenburg, oder St. Odilien im Elsaß, im zwölften Jahrhundert und ihr Werk: Hortus Deliciarum. Ein Beitrag zur Geschichte der Wissenschaften, Literatur, Kunst, Kleidung, Waffen und Sitten des Mittelalters* (Stuttgart: Cotta, 1818); L. Lapointe, "Un Strasbourgeois de l'époque romantique: Christian Moritz Engelhardt (1175-1858)," *L'Annuaire de la Société des amis du vieux Strasbourg* 9 (1977). 87-104; Rosalie Green et al., *Herrad of Hohenbourg. Hortus Deliciarum*, Studies of the Warburg Institute 36, vol. 1 (Leiden: E. J. Brill, 1979). 17-25; R. Will, "La Reconstruction des miniatures de l'Hortus Deliciarum," *Cahiers alsaciens d'archéologie d'art et d'histoire* 26 (1983). 99-116; R. Will, "La Reconstruction

des miniatures de l'Hortus Deliciarum," *Cahiers alsaciens d'archéologie d'art et d'histoire* 29 (1986). 207-210

[18] Green et al., *Herrad of Hohenbourg*; F. Griffith, *The Garden of Delights: Reform and Renaissance for Women in the Twelfth Century* (Philadelphia: University of Pennsylvania Press, 2007).

[19] "Beytrag zur altvaterländischen Sprachforschung." Engelhardt, *Herrad von Landsperg*. 177

[20] Michael Curschmann, "The German Glosses," in Green et al., *Herrad of Hohenbourg*. 63

[21] "Wir bieten dem Freunde des in einen Zaubernebel entschwebten Mittelalters, so wie jedem Forscher der Kulturgeschichte, die erste vollständige Kunde des merkwürdigen Hortus deliciarum....Den reichsten Stoff entfalten uns die Gemälde zu den manchfachsten Wahrnehmungen über Costum, Sitten und Kunst des zwölften Jahrhunderts. Diese bilden den Hauptgegenstand gegenwärthiger Beyträge, so wie sie auch größtentheils die Auswahl der Malereyen bestimmten, die wir in getreuen Facsimile's zum Belege fügen." Engelhardt, *Herrad von Landsperg*. vii

[22] Green et al., *Herrad of Hohenbourg*. Pls. 18, 124, 153-154, 159-166

[23] "Es ist wunderbar mit welchem Scharfsinn er aus den Gruppen, die gar nicht ihrer Kleider wegen gemalt sind, diese und die Geräthschaften jener Zeit, die Speisen und Getränke entwickelt." Quoted in Lapointe, "Un Strasbourgeois," 101

[24] "Herradens Kunstgebilde gehören...in die Zeit...der gewöhnlich, besonders in Anwendung auf die Baukunst, der Name Gothisch beygelegt wird. Dieselbe, wie jetzt geschieht, ganz als ausschließliches oder vorzügliches Eigenthum einer einzigen Nation gelten lassen zu wollen, dürfte doch wohl schwerlich gegen unbefangene geschichtliche Untersuchung vollkommen Stich halten, denn zuverlässig hatten die westlichen europäischen Völker des Mittelalters viel mehr Übereinstimmung und Gemeinschaft, sowohl in Kunst als auch in Sitten und Kleidung, als man wohl öfter dafür zu halten gewohnt ist." Engelhardt, *Herrad von Landsperg*. xii-xiii

[25] This article is of great importance as one of the first to reconsider and aesthetically appreciate Gothic architecture, in reaction to Johann G. Sulzer's *Allgemeiner Theorie der Bildenden Künste*, published the previous year and reviewed by Goethe himself. J. W. von Goethe, *Von Deutscher Baukunst* (Frankfurt am Main, 1772); W. D. Robinson, *The Literary Background of the Gothic Revival in Germany: A Chapter on the History of Taste* (Oxford: Clarendon Press, 1965).

[26] Friedrich Schlegel, "Grundzüge der gothischen Baukunst; auf einer Reise durch die Niederlande, Rheingegenden, die Schweiz und einen Theil von Frankreich in dem Jahre 1804 und 1805," *Friedrich Schlegels sämtliche Werke, Bd. VI* (Vienna: Jakob Mayer, 1823). 221-230

[27] Auguste de Bastard d'Estang, *Peintures et ornements des manuscrits, classés dans un ordre chronologique pour servir à l'histoire des arts du dessin depuis le quatrième siècle de l'ère chrétienne jusqu'à la fin du seizième siècle*, 4 vols. (Paris: Imprimerie impériale, 1832-1869); L. Delisle, "L'Oeuvre paléographique de M. Le

Comte de Bastard," *Bibliothèque de l'Ecole de Chartes* 43 (1882). 1-26; J. Bouquillard, "Les 'Peintures et ornements des manuscrits' du comte de Bastard. Histoire d'une entreprise de reproductions lithographiques d'enluminures sous la Monarchie de Juillet," *Bulletin du Bibliophile* 1 (1996). 108-150

[28] How greatly German scholars in the nineteenth century felt the need to reproduce illuminated manuscripts is evident in their enthusiastic response to Bastard d'Estang's project. See n. 54

[29] Christian M. Engelhardt, *Der Ritter von Stauffenberg, ein Altdeutsches Gedicht. Herausgegeben nach der Handschrift der öffentlichen Bibliothek zu Strassburg. Nebst Bemerkungen zur Geschichte, Litteratur, und Archäologie des Mittelalters, auch mit Beziehung auf mehrere andere Handschriften derselben Bibliothek, vorzüglich des Spiegels menschlichen Heils. Mit 26 lithographierten Tafeln. Auf Kosten des Verfassers* (Strasbourg: no publisher, 1823). The book contains a list of the 120 subscribers.

[30] In his analysis of the miniatures in the *Speculum Humanae Salvationis*, Engelhardt makes an interesting attempt to analyze the iconographic relationship between the images in the manuscripts and those in early printed versions of the *Speculum*. In his plates, he juxtaposes comparative scenes to advance his visual arguments, a fairly uncommon method for this time.

[31] Cod. Pal. Germ. 848, Universitätsbibliothek, Heidelberg; F. X. Kraus, *Die Miniaturen der Manesse'schen Liederhandschrift* (Strasbourg: Karl J. Trübner, 1887). 3-9; E. Grunewald, "Retuschiertes Mittelalter. Zur Rezeption und Reproduktion der *Manessischen Liederhandschrift*," in *Mittelalter-Rezeption. Ein Symposium, Germanistische Symposien, Berichtsbände VI*, ed. Rüdiger Wapnewski (Stuttgart: Metzler, 1986). 435-449; W. Werner, "Schicksale der Handschrift," in *Codex Manesse,* ed. E. Mittler and W. Werner (Heidelberg: Edition Braus, 1988). 1-21; E. M. Vetter, "Die Rezeption der Bilder," in *Codex Manesse,* ed. E. Mittler and W. Werner (Heidelberg: Edition Braus, 1988). 153-223

[32] E. Mittler, "Die Rückführung," in *Codex Manesse,* ed. E. Mittler and W. Werner (Heidelberg: Edition Braus, 1988). 22-67

[33] The forelegs of the horse entering the scene from the left were obviously forgotten in the tracing of the miniature.

[34] "Die prächtigen Mahlereien, die vor jedem Poeten stehen, machen das Werk besonders kostbar und ansehnlich. Die Zeichnung ist zwar nach dem übeln Geschmack der damahligen Zeiten sehr schlecht, aber das Colorit ist überaus hoch und lebhaft. [...] Ueberhaupt sind diese Gemählde in Absicht auf die Kleidung, die Waffen, die Krieges=Rüstungen und dergleichen sehr brauchbar, und setzen manche Beschreibung dieser Stücke, die wir in den Poeten oder Geschichtsschreibern sonst nicht verstehen könnten, in das erforderliche Licht." Johann J. Breitinger and Johann J. Bodmer, *Proben der alten schwäbischen Poesie des 13. Jahrhunderts aus der Maneßischen Sammlung.* (Zurich, 1748). vi

[35] Engelhardt had mentioned these tracings and expressed his desire for a publication on the *Codex Manesse* in Engelhardt, *Herrad von Landsperg.* xii; see also Lapointe, "Un Strasbourgois." 77

[36] "Seit ich den Codex in Paris sah, habe ich mich überzeugt, daß viele Bilder historische Beziehungen haben und wichtig sind, vielleicht die meisten sogar, manches scheint aber auch nur wiederkehrende Phrase: da sie aber nicht Zeichnung und Styl haben, gar keinen, nicht einmal den ihrer Zeit, so hätte man mit dem besten Gewissen und ohne der Sache irgend zu wehe zu thun, 4 bis 6 Zeichnungen auf ein Quartblatt bringen können, in feinen Umrissen vielleicht 8, und so die Kosten sehr vermindern." Quoted in Grunewald, "Retuschiertes Mittelalter. Zur Rezeption und Reproduktion der *Manessischen Liederhandschrift*." 437; E. H. Zeydel et al., eds., *Letters of Ludwig Tieck: Hitherto Unpublished, 1792-1853* (1937; reprint, New York: Millwood, 1973). 134

[37] Laßberg wrote in a letter to the Swiss scholar Johann Jacob Horner: "Herrn Hase's [referring to the testimonial of Karl Benedikt Hase, the librarian in charge of the manuscript in Paris] Gutachten häuft eine Menge Discrimina auf unter welchen die Furcht, die Teutschen möchten den Codex nicht zurückstellen oben ansteht." Quoted in Vetter, "Die Rezeption der Bilder." 161

[38] The German term "Wissenschaft" encompasses both sciences and humanities. Von der Hagen's lectures were published in several parts: F. H. von der Hagen, "Über die Gemälde in den Sammlungen der altdeutschen lyrischen Dichter, vornähmlich in der Manessischen Handschrift, und über andere dieselbe bezügliche Bildwerke (Teil 1)," *Abhandlungen der königlichen Akademie der Wissenschaften zu Berlin*, 1842 (Berlin, 1844). 437-460; "Über die Gemälde in den Sammlungen der altdeutschen lyrischen Dichter, vornähmlich in der Manessischen Handschrift, und über andere dieselbe bezügliche Bildwerke (Teil 2)," *Abhandlungen der königlichen Akademie der Wissenschaften zu Berlin*, 1844 (Berlin, 1846). 289-321; "Handschriftengemälde und andere bildliche Denkmale der Deutschen Liederdichter des 12. bis 14. Jahrhunderts (Teil 1)," *Abhandlungen der königlichen Akademie der Wissenschaften zu Berlin*, 1850 (Berlin, 1852). 137-158; "Handschriftengemälde und andere bildliche Denkmale der Deutschen Liederdichter des 12. bis 14. Jahrhunderts (Teil 2)," *Abhandlungen der königlichen Akademie der Wissenschaften zu Berlin*, 1852 (Berlin, 1853). 813-839; "Gemälde der Manesse'schen Handschrift von Deutschen Dichtern des 12. bis 14. Jahrhunderts," *Abhandlungen der königlichen Akademie der Wissenschaften zu Berlin,* 1853 (Berlin, 1854). 517-529

[39] F. H. von der Hagen and B. C. Mathieu, *Minnesänger aus der Zeit der Hohenstaufen* (Paris: Plon, 1850); S. Himmelheber, "Kunsthandwerkliche Reproduktionen nach Manessemotiven," in *Codex Manesse*, ed. E. Mittler and W. Werner (Heidelberg: Edition Braus, 1988). 462-466

[40] U. Meves, "Germanistik," in *Literaturwissenschaftliches Lexikon. Grundbegriffe der Germanistik*, ed. H. Brunner and R. Moritz (Berlin: Erich Schmidt Verlag, 2006). 141-146

[41] "Diese Gesangskunst war auch, wie die Ritterschaft, das allgemeine verknüpfende Band, welches noch tiefer herab, bis zum bürgerlichen Meister und fahrenden Singer, durch den gemeinsamen Hauptinhalt ihrer Gesänge, die himmlische und weltliche Minne, alle Unterschiede schön und menschlich

ausglich." Von der Hagen, "Über die Gemälde in den Sammlungen der altdeutschen lyrischen Dichter," (1844). 438

[42] "Auch haben ihn die älteren Handschriftengemälde, welche meist ebenfalls kirchliche sind, in Bibeln, Legenden, Missalen und anderen Kirchenbüchern. Erst als auch weltliche Bücher in der Volkssprache verfaßt und mit Bildern geziert wurden, löste sich die Malerei von diesem festen Grunde, auf dem sie wie ein Ausschnitt haftete, und gab auch ihren Gestalten mehr Freiheit und Bewegung." Ibid. 443

[43] Franz Kugler, *Geschichte der Malerei: von Constantin dem Grossen bis auf die neuere Zeit*, 2 vols. (Berlin: Duncker and Humblot, 1837). 1:28

[44] Johann D. Fiorillo, *Geschichte der zeichnenden Künste von ihrer Wiederauflebung bis zu den neuesten Zeiten,* 5 vols. (Göttingen: Rosenbusch, 1798-1808); Johann D. Fiorillo, *Geschichte der zeichnenen Künste in Deutschland und in den vereinigten Niederlanden,* 4 vols. (Hannover: Hahn, 1815–1820).

[45] Gabriele Bickendorf, *Der Beginn der Kunstgeschichtsschreibung unter dem Paradigma "Geschichte." Gustav Friedrich Waagens Frühschrift "Über Hubert und Johann van Eyck"* (Worms: Werner'sche Verlagsgesellschaft, 1985); on the art historians of the so-called "Berlin school" see Gabriele Bickendorf, "Die 'Berliner Schule': Carl Friedrich von Rumohr (1785–1843), Gustav Friedrich Waagen (1794–1868), Karl Schnaase (1798–1875), und Franz Kugler (1808–1858)," in *Klassiker der Kunstgeschichte*, ed. U. Pfisterer (Munich: Beck, 2007). 46-61

[46] Thomas F. Dibdin, *The Bibliographical Decameron or, Ten Days of Pleasant Discourse upon Illuminated Manuscripts and Subjects Connected with Early Engraving, Typography, and Bibliography*, 3 vols. (London: W. Bulmer and Co., Shakespeare Press, 1817).

[47] J.-B.-L.-G. Séroux d'Agincourt, *Histoire de l'art par les monuments, depuis sa décadence au IVe siècle jusqu'à son renouvellement au XVIe siècle,* 6 vols. (Paris: Treuttel et Würtz, 1823); D. Mondini, *Mittelalter im Bild. Séroux d'Agincourt und die Kunsthistoriographie um 1800* (Zurich: InterPublishers, 2005). 265-271

[48] Contemporary scholarly interest in the *Histoire de l'art par les monuments* has thus far focused almost exclusively on that part of the book dealing with architecture. An examination of Séroux's account of the history of painting in general and his use of illuminated manuscripts in the construction of that account remains a desideratum.

[49] Gustav F. Waagen, "On the Importance of Manuscripts with Miniatures in the History of Art," *Bibliographical and Historical Miscellanies, Philobiblon Society* 1 (1854). 3-11. I wish to thank Gabriele Bickendorf for bringing this reference to my attention.

[50] Waagen, "On the Importance of Manuscripts with Miniatures." 4, 9-10

[51] Ibid. 5

[52] Kugler, *Geschichte der Malerei*; Franz Kugler, *Handbuch der Kunstgeschichte* (Stuttgart: Ebner and Seubert, 1842). On Kugler see H. Karge, "Welt-Kunstgeschichte: Franz Kugler und die geographische Fundierung der Kunsthistoriographie in der Mitte des 19. Jahrhunderts," in *"Kunsttopographie":*

Theorie und Methode in der Kunstwissenschaft und Archäologie seit Winckelmann, Heft des Arbeitskreises für Theorie und Geschichte der Kunstgeschichtsschreibung (Stendal: Winckelmann Gesellschaft, 2003). 19-31

[53] "dass das Studium der Handschriftbilder für die genannte Kunstepoche mit grosser Entschiedenheit als das wichtigste bezeichnet werden muß, und dass in demselben zugleich, was das Wesentliche des Entwicklungsganges der Kunst anbetrifft, das Studium der anderen bezüglichen Werke eingeschlossen ist." Franz Kugler, "Über des Werk des Grafen August de Bastard zur Geschichte der Buchmalerei des Mittelalters," in Franz Kugler, *Kleine Schriften und Studien zur Kunstgeschichte. Mit Illustrationen und anderen artistischen Beilagen*, 3 vols. (Stuttgart: Ebner and Seubert, 1853-1854). 2:42-46 (the quote appears on 44); see also Kugler, *Handbuch der Kunstgeschichte*. 504-506

[54] Franz Kugler, *De Werinhero Saeculi XII Monacho Tegernseensi et de Picturibus Minutis, quibus Carmen suum Theotiscum de Vita B. V. Mariae ornavit* (Berlin: August Petsch, 1831). Kugler studied the history of German literature from 1826 onwards and graduated in 1831 with this dissertation. He was appointed professor in 1835.

[55] Franz Kugler, "Studien in deutschen Bibliotheken," *Museum. Blätter für die bildende Kunst* 11 (1834). 81-84; Franz Kugler, "Studien in deutschen Bibliotheken," *Museum. Blätter für die bildende Kunst* 12 (1834). 89-91; Franz Kugler, "Studien in deutschen Bibliotheken," *Museum. Blätter für die bildende Kunst* 13 (1834). 97-100; Franz Kugler, "Studien in deutschen Bibliotheken," *Museum. Blätter für die bildende Kunst* 21 (1834). 161-166; Franz Kugler, "Studien in deutschen Bibliotheken," *Museum. Blätter für die bildende Kunst* 22 (1834). 169-172; these essays are reprinted with added illustrations in Franz Kugler, *Kleine Schriften*. 1:1-12, 52-95

[56] First printed separately as Franz Kugler, *Die Bildhandschrift der Eineidt in der Königlichen Bibliothek zu Berlin befindlich. Ein Beitrag zur Kunstgeschichte des zwölften Jahrhunderts* (Berlin: J. G. Krüschke, 1834).

[57] Franz Kugler, "Die Bildhandschrift der Eineidt in der Königlichen Bibliothek zu Berlin," *Museum. Blätter für bildende Kunst,* 36-38 (1836). 286-288; F. Kugler, "Die Bildhandschrift der Eneidt in der Königlichen Bibliothek zu Berlin," *Museum. Blätter für bildende Kunst* 36-38 (1836). 293-300; reprinted with added illustrations in Kugler, *Kleine Schriften*. 2:38-52; see also A. Boeckler, *Heinrich von Veldeke, Eneide. Die Bilder der Berliner Handschrift* (Leipzig: Harrasowitz, 1939); *Heinrich von Veldeke: Eneas-Roman. Berlin, Staatsbibliothek Preußischer Kulturbesitz, Ms. Germ. Fol. 282, Facsimile,* ed. N. Henkel and A. Fingernagel (Wiesbaden: Harrasowitz, 1992). 27-34

[58] "Es entfaltet sich hier nemlich in den Handbewegungen der dargestellten Personen eine eigenthümlich durchgebildete Gebärdensprache, welche sowohl die besonderen Situationen ruhiger Gespräche vollkommen deutlich und verständlich darzulegen, als auch den leidenschaftlichen Momenten einen genügenden Ausdruck zu geben im Stande ist. In letzteren, wenn einsame Liebesnoth oder die Klage um geliebte Todte zu zeichnen war, wird Schmerz und Leiden durch ein

eigen krampfhaftes Ringen der Hände trefflich ausgedrückt." Kugler, *Kleine Schriften.* 2:52

[59] "Wo geküsset wird, fassen sich dagegen die beiden betheiligten Personen einander auf gar naive Weise bei den Köpfen, und da in solcher Situation in der Regel nicht viel gesprochen wird, so waren dabei auch keine Spruchbänder nöthig." Kugler, *Kleine Schriften.* 2:52

[60] "In all diesen Beziehungen bildet die nationale Poesie, die von jener Zeit ab sich reich und lebenvoll entwickelte, ein wichtiges Förderungsmittel. Auch ihre Erzeugnisse…wurden mit Bildern versehen, welche sich somit dem Leben uns seinen mannigfach wechselnden Verhältnissen engergischer aufschließen mußten, und wohl nicht umhin konnten, der dichterischen Stimmung…zu folgen." Kugler, *Handbuch der Kunstgeschichte.* 506

[61] Kugler, *Geschichte der Malerei.* 27-28

THE PERSISTENCE OF THE ROYAL PAST ON THE WEST FAÇADE OF REIMS CATHEDRAL

DONNA L. SADLER

The history of Reims Cathedral illustrates that the past is never really beyond the grasp of the present. Not only has the cathedral been the stage for coronation ceremonies throughout its history, but it is also the site in which the foundation of this custom lies. For it was in Reims that Saint Remigius baptized Clovis in 496 and performed countless other miracles in emulation of Christ.[1] This prototypical event is represented no less than three times on the cathedral. Further, fifth-century stories tell us that Saint Nicaise (Nicasius) was martyred on the steps of the cathedral of Reims and carried his head to the altar in a fashion similar to his Parisian counterpart, Saint Denis.[2] Saint Nicaise is depicted not only on the Saints portal of the north transept of Reims [Fig.6], but also on the inner trumeau of the verso of the west façade [Fig.1], gazing toward both the altar and the *rouelle* that commemorated the site of his decapitation by the Vandals.[3] As these historical events shaped the patrimony of Reims, so their visual memories were built into the very fabric of the thirteenth-century cathedral.

The verso of the façade is composed of moral lessons couched in biblical terms aimed at the neophyte ruler as he assumed his royal duties [Fig. 4]. Like Clovis before him, the king was anointed with the miraculous oil by the archbishop of Reims. Then, armed with the moral instruction proffered by this carved "Mirror of Princes," the king could begin his terrestrial reign.[4] Moreover, the beautiful Virgin and Child on the so-called *Porte romane* (the west portal of the north transept), coupled with the Old Testament figures on the right portal of the west façade, celebrate different stages of the cathedral's history.[5] Even the three round windows that punctuate both transepts and seem so out-of-date in their thirteenth-century context must surely allude to the Carolingian structure that occupied the site of the present building [Fig 16].[6]

According to legend, when Clovis and his 3,000 warriors returned to Reims to be baptized, Archbishop Remigius summoned the ampulla of

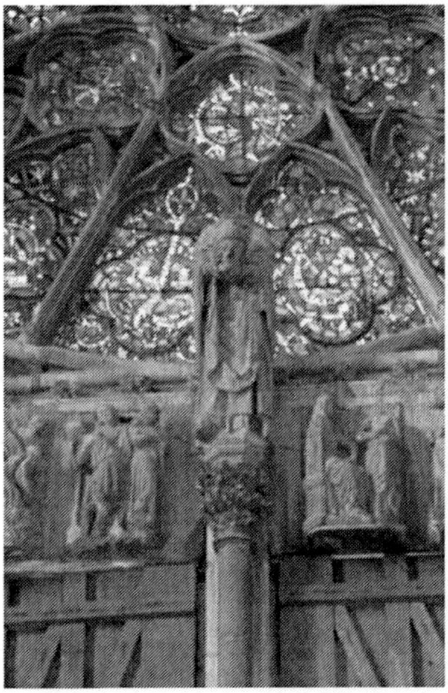

Fig. 1 Saint Nicaise, verso of central portal, ca. 1265, west façade, Reims Cathedral (Photo: Author)

holy oil housed in a neighboring church to anoint the king. However, the medieval crowds prevented the ampulla from reaching the baptismal font in time. A dove then miraculously appeared with a vial of holy oil in its beak and that divine oil was used to anoint Clovis and his soldiers. The symbolism could not be overlooked.[7] From this precious ampulla of oil stemmed the *remois* archbishops' prerogative to anoint and crown the future kings of France.

Reims remained the French coronation cathedral from Louis IX (1226) until Charles X (1825).[8] Serving as the theatre for these coronations, Reims Cathedral became a "reliquary of memory" and, as Le Goff points out, perpetuated the memory of the coronation.[9] For it was in this edifice that the monarch became a new man, the most Christian king, able to cure scrofula by the powers invested in him by the archbishop of Reims. The royal religion was enacted in the ten-bay nave, the arena of both the king's royal anointing (*sacre*) and his privilege of taking both the body and blood of Christ, the bread and wine in the sacraments; in this way, the king's stature rivaled that of the archbishop. He became Christ's vicar on earth through the holy oil bestowed on his royal forebear, Clovis, at the same site so many centuries before.[10] This legacy catapulted the entire city of Reims into the position of a theatre of memory; each *sacre* reinforced its preeminence in making kings, thus making the most Christian king a product of the ritual performed within the sacred walls of the cathedral.[11]

The purpose of this study is to consider the stylistic echoes of the past that were consciously forged by the sculptors of the seventeenth, eighteenth, and nineteenth centuries, who repaired the damage wrought by hailstorms, fire, and man [Fig. 2]. How did these successive sculptors understand the medieval program? Was their goal to achieve a stylistic unity with the past, or did the restorers wish to express the aesthetic values of their own generation? We will see that at times restorers did seek models from the thirteenth century in order to harmonize the reconstruction work with the existing sculpture.[12] However, the more common solution was to repair the battered sculpture in the style of the

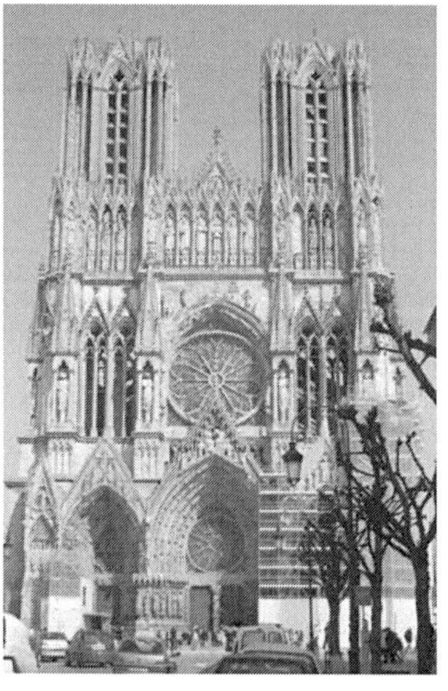

Fig. 2 West façade, ca. 1250, Reims Cathedral (Photo: Author)

restorers' day.[13] It was through the spectacles of the restorer's own historical context that he saw and realized the restoration of the damaged statues from the thirteenth-century edifice. Indeed, it is only the current generation of restorers that privileges the style of the original sculpture and consistently honors the medieval past in its efforts to reconstitute the west façade in a thirteenth-century style. After exploring the historical uses of the past deployed at Reims, from its architectural manifestations to its sculptural representations, we will turn to the restorers of Reims and their versions of the medieval past. One consistent chord that the history of restoration at Reims seems to strike is the role of prototypes in its historical makeup—personifying both physically and metaphorically the ancient exemplar that validates and characterizes the modern figure.[14] The primordial event that cemented the role of Reims in king-making was the miraculous aura that surrounded the baptism of Clovis. This event was both symbolic and forthright in its effects. Possessing both this historical memory and the holy ampulla of oil insured Reims a posterity rich in kingship. Indeed, the cathedral may be read as a biography of the monarchs of France superimposed on the west façade of Reims. By the outbreak of World War I, the identification of Reims with the heart of France was so entrenched that the cathedral had become a secular as well as religious symbol of the nation.[15] The theme of kingship underscored in each epoch of restoration only served to enhance the monument's emblematic status in French secular history.[16]

Historical Consciousness at Reims

The layers of history that underlie the cathedral's genesis resemble a palimpsest that is always visible through the Gothic cathedral, like a slip that peeks through a transparent gown. The baptism of Clovis by the archbishop Remigius in 496 was an event that garnered Reims the position of cathedral of coronations, especially after the pen of Hincmar transformed the ritual into a medieval miracle.[17] Though strikingly similar to Constantine's conversion in the fourth century, the scene acquires its own distinctive character in its depictions at Reims Cathedral.[18] The visual re-enactment of Clovis's conversion/coronation scene appears three times on the cathedral: in the local Saints portal on the north transept; the stained glass triforium of the verso of the west façade; and the center of the fourteenth-century Kings gallery on the west façade. The earliest treatment of this event, located on the first band of the tympanum of the Saints portal, assumes a narrative form in which the archbishop is poised above the shivering king in his baptismal font, while the dove descends with the holy ampulla of oil at the most dramatic moment of the story [Fig. 3]. Onlookers include Clotilde, Clovis's Christian wife, various ecclesiastics, and members of the royal retinue. The depiction does not include the 3,000 warriors baptized with Clovis that day, but rather seems to fill the space with the same number of figures used to enact the martyrdom of Saint Nicaise across from it, on the other side of the trumeau.[19]

The glazed triforium that terminates the nave and crowns the inner west wall, subdividing the lower and upper rose windows, contains a much-restored baptism of Clovis scene in which the sacrament has become an unadulterated scene of coronation [Fig. 4]. Nine figures stand beneath a continuous arcade. In the center, a crowned king wears a mantle

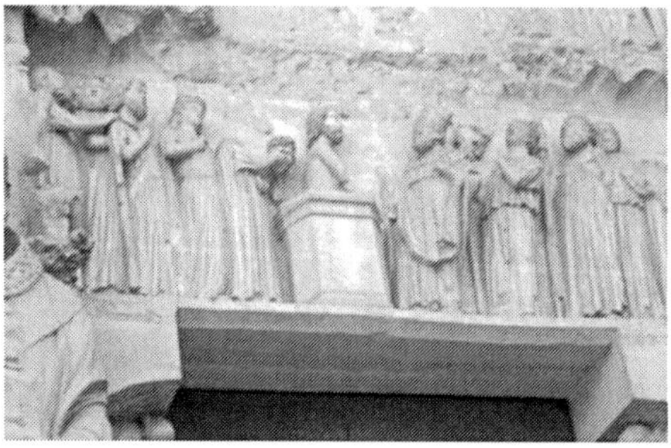

Fig. 3 Baptism of Clovis, Saints portal, ca. 1235, north transept, Reims Cathedral (Photo: Author)

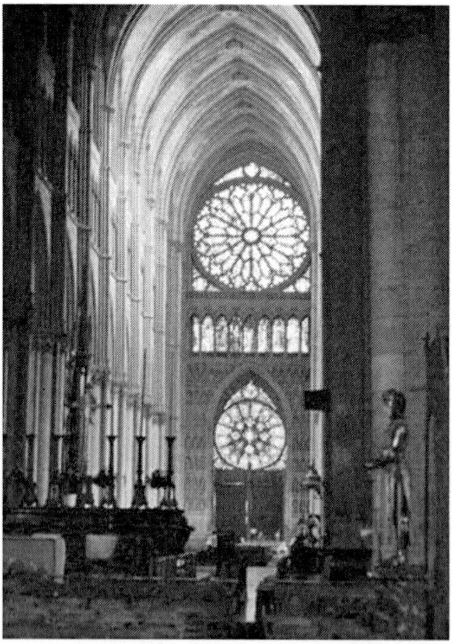

Fig. 4 Verso of central portal, ca. 1265, west façade, Reims Cathedral (Photo: Author)

decorated with fleurs-de-lys. He is flanked on either side by two prelates, two crowned women, two ecclesiastics with mitres, and two lay princes respectively. Though other kings have been proposed as the object of this *sacre,* notably Louis IX and Charles VII,[20] Clovis seems to best embody the arch-royal role model. As the miraculous prototype for the French coronation tradition, it does not seem unreasonable to read here Remigius and Clovis enshrined in the immortal act of consecration. Before turning from the glazed triforium, it is worth noting the degree of restoration work found in these panels. Only fragments remain from the thirteenth century, and the left-most lancet bears the date 1550. Many of the figures were redone by the Simon family in 1834.[21]

The baptism of Clovis also forms the centerpiece of the Kings gallery on the west façade of Reims, dating from the fourteenth century [Fig. 5]. Unlike other Kings galleries, such as that of the cathedral of Amiens, the kings that occupy the gallery at Reims culminate in a staccato narrative of Clovis's baptism. The composition conflates that of the north transept and glazed triforium so that the neophyte Christian ruler, portrayed in his waist-high baptismal font, appears between Remigius to the right and Clotilde, bearing his crown, to the left. Flanked by a figure in monastic garb and another who bears a processional cross, the group is fleshed out by the kings who proceed around the corners of the façade towers. The prototypical scene of the baptism/coronation has come home to roost in the very center of the Kings gallery. The Kings gallery is thus the ultimate sculptural reminder of the royal function fulfilled by the cathedral of Reims.

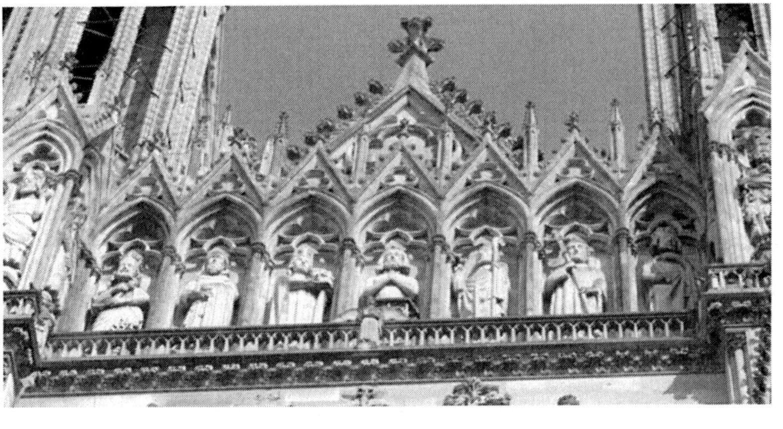

Fig. 5 Baptism of Clovis, Kings gallery, ca. 1350-1400, west façade, Reims Cathedral (Photo: Author)

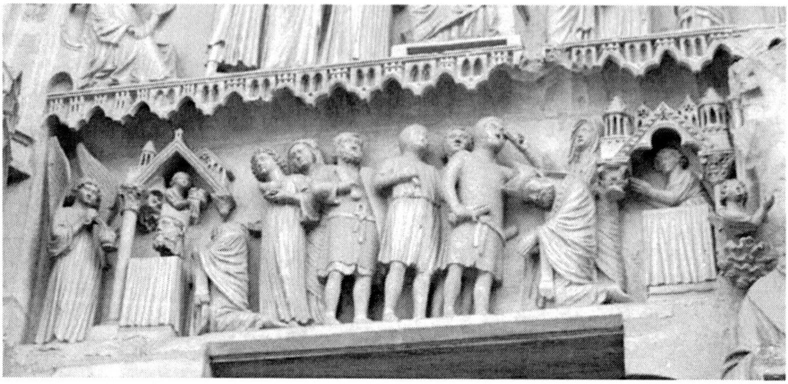

Fig. 6 Martyrdom of Saint Nicaise, Saints portal, ca. 1235, north transept, Reims Cathedral (Photo: Author)

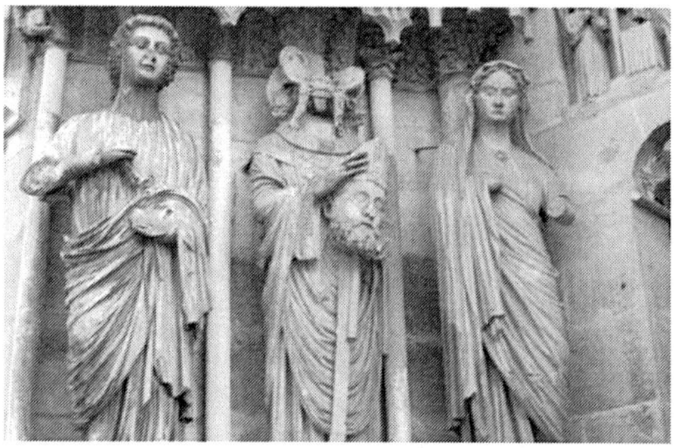

Fig. 7 Left jamb of Saints portal, ca. 1235, north transept, Reims Cathedral (Photo: Author)

A similar repetition characterizes the story of Saint Nicaise and his martyrdom on the steps of the fifth-century cathedral.[22] Represented in the tympanum of the Saints portal, Saint Nicaise meets his fate with equanimity, while his sister Eutropia, in a quintessential act of sibling loyalty, blinds one of the Vandals by poking his eyes out [Fig. 6]. To the left of this vignette the decapitated saint places his head upon the altar, where an angel hovers with a heavenly crown to reward him. Saints Nicaise and Eutropia are also commemorated on the left jamb of the Saints portal, occupying the middle and innermost positions respectively [Fig. 7].

Here, two angels extend a heavenly crown above the suggestive neckline of Nicaise.

The fate of Nicaise is further commemorated on the verso (interior wall) of the west façade in a sculptural tableau composed of the inner trumeau bearing the headless Nicaise, flanked by angels and Vandals [Figs. 1, 8]. One of the angels [Fig. 8, left] points down the nave to the altar where the saint's head once rested, while a Vandal gestures toward the *rouelle* marking the spot where the local saint was martyred [Fig. 8, right].[23] The performative aspect of this sculptural ensemble is heightened

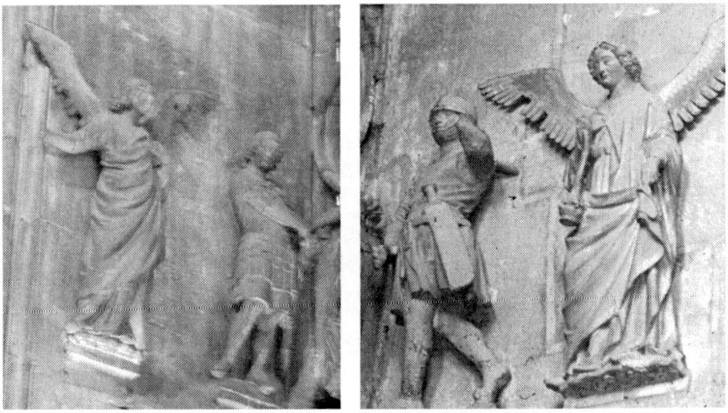

Fig. 8 Angels and Vandals, verso of west façade, ca. 1265, Reims Cathedral (Photo: Author)

by the rose window that acts as an enormous halo for Nicaise. The decapitation of John the Baptist on the lintel intersects with Nicaise's beheading on the trumeau. This juxtaposition accentuates the sanctity of the see of Reims that produced such a prodigious saint [Fig. 4].[24] Because John the Baptist was the forerunner of Christ, his presence at Reims was a sign of spiritual prestige for the cathedral. Further, the king, who was Christ's vicar on earth, stood facing the inner west wall that addressed the new ruler as he was anointed and charged with his royal ministry during his coronation.[25] That the carved figures hail from both the Old and New Testaments, together with representatives from the earlier history of Reims, underlines the ongoing nature of history. The cathedral is topographically charged with meaning, from the dedication of its altars, to the location of the *rouelle* of Saint Nicaise. Other scholars have shown that the stained glass in the choir further reasserts the power of the see of Reims and alludes to the ecclesiastical view of kingship presented by the cathedral's programmers.[26]

Restoration at Reims

What view of kingship did the restorers take when charged with the reparation of the mutilated sculpture of Reims? Let us now consider the work executed during the seventeenth century through the late twentieth century. The restoration that was begun in the 1990s was undertaken by the *Monuments historiques.*[27] The replacement of figures that occurred in the early seventeenth century through early nineteenth centuries was dictated by the French government and executed by amateurs and professionally trained sculptors.[28] As Peter Kurmann has noted, the local limestone was sensitive to extreme weather, which necessitated regular repairs, in addition to the acts of vandalism and war.[29] The earliest campaign included many archivolt figures from the central west portal refashioned in the style of Louis XIII; these figures did not adhere to the original iconographic disposition of the portal.[30] This restoration is very well-documented: it was executed by Vincent Bourgeois, who replaced nineteen out of the twenty-five figures in the first and second rows of the voussoirs of the central portal.[31] One figure in particular deserves mention, a seated, crowned figure of Moses holding the tablets of the Law, whose drapery resembles a thirteenth-century prototype from the cathedral, but who bears a facial resemblance to Henri IV [Fig.9].[32] Would the king have recognized the royal compliment implied in the association posed by Moses as a prefiguration of King Solomon? Henri IV, vacillating between Protestantism and Catholicism, finally opted for the latter and remarked that Paris was worth a Mass! Given his tumultuous reign, Henri's identification with the wise judgments of a biblical precursor would conceivably have been most welcome.[33] A similar royal salute is issued by the "Communion" enacted by Abraham and Melchisedek on the west façade verso, in which the ruler is clad in thirteenth-century armor [Fig.10]. This ensemble directs a more generic lesson to the French king: Be a good knight and defend the rights of the Church. On the left bank of archivolts of the north portal of the west façade, one encounters a protracted Entry into Jerusalem which, in turn, seems to nod to the medieval king as he enters the cathedral precinct to commence his coronation [Fig. 11]. These examples demonstrate the different degrees of royal specificity represented in the sculptural program of Reims.

In the majority of restoration campaigns that follow, the sculptors and ecclesiastics who guided them remained true to the cathedral's association with kingship and coronations. Further, the period of restoration often actually influenced the contemporary shape of this commemoration, while always retaining a resonance with the leitmotif of royalty. Indeed, why else

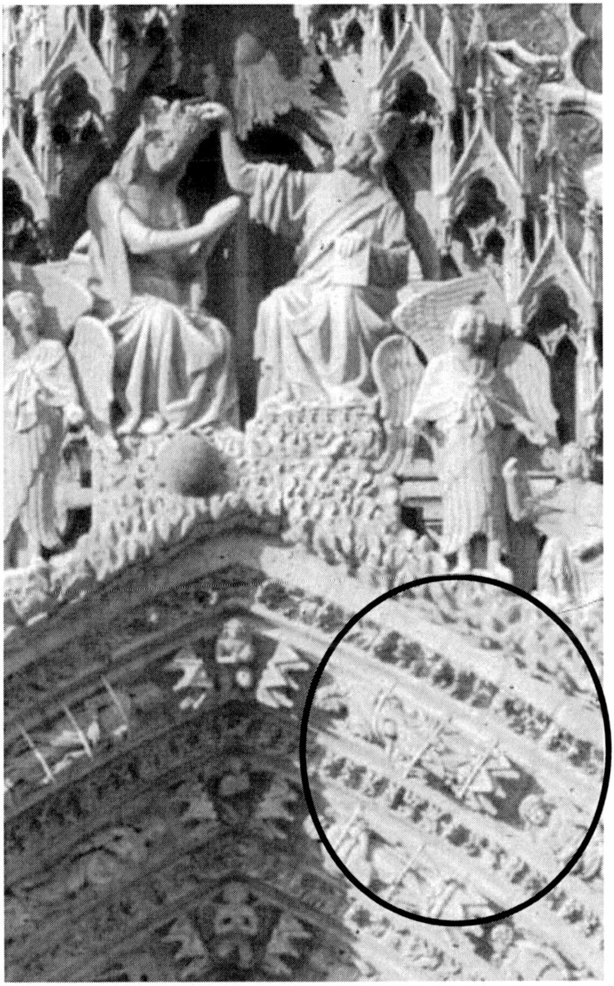

Fig. 9 Moses, voussoir, restored 1638, central portal, ca. 1250-1300, west façade, Reims Cathedral (Photo: Author)

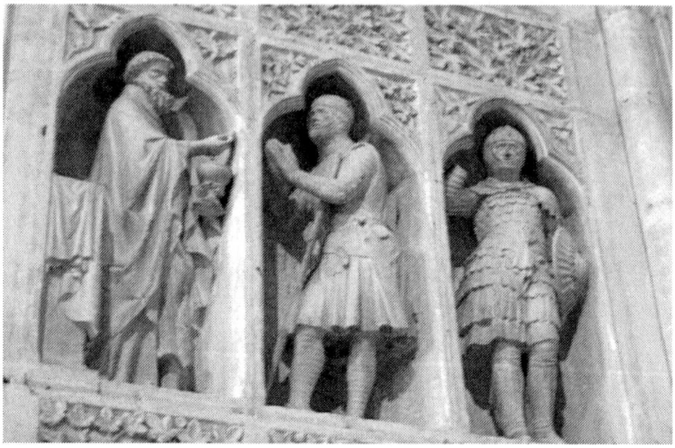

Fig. 10 Abraham and Melchisedek, verso of west façade, ca. 1265, Reims Cathedral, (Photo: Author)

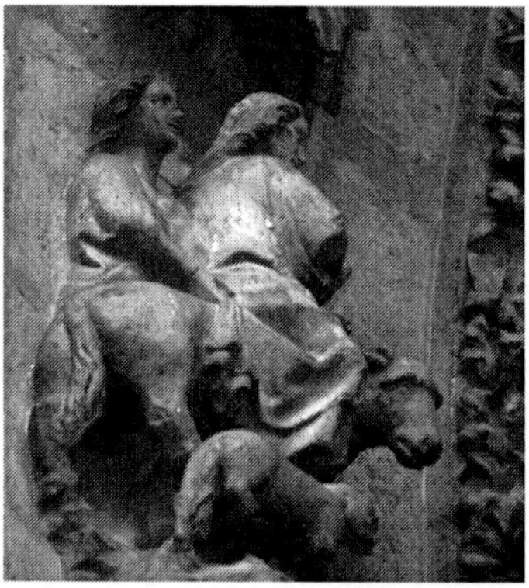

Fig. 11 Entry into Jerusalem, voussoir, north portal, ca. 1255-1300, west façade, Reims Cathedral (Photo: Author)

would the restorers substitute kings in the archivolts whenever the original figures were too damaged to discern? The next century saw restorations in 1733, 1734-1736, and again in 1737-1740. Work resumed in 1755-1760 and according to nineteenth-century records, a final campaign was waged in 1786-1792.[34] The figures fashioned during this period were of a type of local stone from Courville or another stone from either the region of Aisne or Oise; Pallot-Frossart and Decrock logically propose that the earlier campaign used one type of stone, and a later campaign, the other type.[35] Similar evidence may be gleaned from the manner in which the figures are seated in the voussoirs. Their style does not correspond to medieval precedent, but rather asserts its own Baroque personality. This restoration undertaken by the king's architect, Pierre de Vigny in 1737-1740, included the colonnettes separating the jamb statues, several of the small gables in the voussoirs, the upper tympanum containing the Crucifixion of Christ on the left portal, many extremities of the figures in the tympanum of the right portal, as well as the colossal figures of David and Goliath above the rose window, which were then restored a second time in 1906.[36] The small lateral gables on the façade may also be attributed to Vigny.[37] Louis Gillet, writing in 1938, described the disparate styles of the jamb statues of Reims' west façade as two texts bound together in one volume, whose pages were transposed and the whole somewhat muddled.[38] One could already describe the results of restoration work from as early as the eighteenth century in the same terms.

The 1755 work is identified by the use of Savonnière stone. The Magi located in the left rank of archivolts hail from this period and reveal a stylistic schizophrenia, with the upper part of the archivolts dating from 1831 and the bottom half from 1755. Other figures on the left side of the central portal may also be singled out from this period, such as four figures occupying the outer row of voussoirs and five in the second and third rows of voussoirs [Fig. 12].[39] Most of these figures have well-defined pupils, while four of the figures are distinguished by smooth, unarticulated eyes, long flat noses, and flat panels of drapery.[40] To this group may be added a figure without its head, located above Saint Roch on the left bank of archivolts of the central west portal; only one of the four restored figures in the outermost voussoir has survived the elements.[41]

The final restoration of the eighteenth century apparently took place in 1786-1792 and was financed by Louis XVI, according to various sources in the nineteenth century.[42] However, it is difficult to determine the nature of this intervention: was it to mask the hole made for the new heating system or to harmonize the color of the soiled spots between that of restored and medieval stone?[43] Reinhardt noted the minimal damage wreaked by the Revolution on the coronation cathedral of France; seemingly content to wrest the string of fleurs-de-lys from the crest of the roof and strip the central portal's lintel of its sculpture, the revolutionaries replaced the latter with an inscription.[44] This is perhaps one of the most surprising moments in the history of Reims. When one considers the damage suffered by Saint-Denis and the cathedral of Paris for its royal associations, one feels grateful that animosity against the crown focused on the capital city.[45]

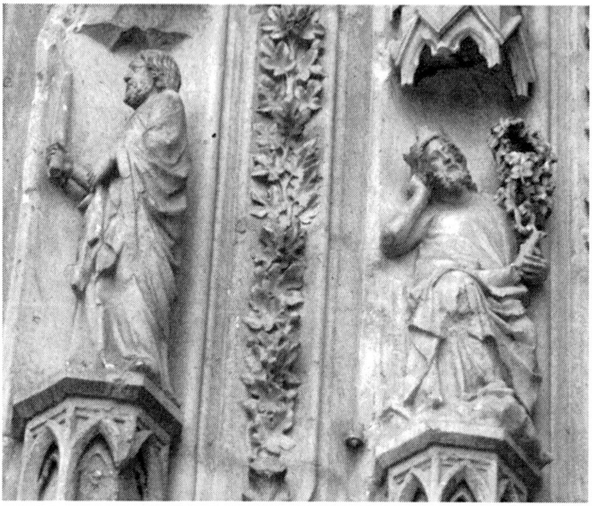

Fig. 12 Voussoirs, left figure restored 1755, central portal, ça. 1250, west façade, Reims Cathedral (Photo: Author)

But was there an eighteenth-century community of viewers implied in this restoration work? We have noted the traces of different stones and various formal distinctions, but does the style or iconography render a telling verdict? The predilection for kings, dressed in wonderfully anachronistic garb, suggests that the restorers were hitting the one note that they knew to be constant, that of kingship. Could the eighteenth century have desired to add its own typological layer to the cathedral? A wealth of models would have presented themselves to restorers who might want to add to a sculptural lineage of kings that began with Solomon and David around the rose window, culminating with the kingship of Christ embodied on the west façade, and prolonged by the reigns of Clovis, Saint Louis, and others that fill the tabernacles and converge on the baptism of Clovis. By adding more kings to the mix, the king-making power of Reims would only be further foregrounded.

Louis-Ambroise Dubut took charge of the work at Reims in 1808.[46] Although he noted the poor condition of the sculpture at this time, it was not until 1831, when the sculptor Plantar was summoned from Paris, that work on the restoration began in earnest. He turned his attention to the re-carving of the vegetation framing the voussoirs, ten apostles, the blind tympanum of the north buttress, and the outer two rows of voussoirs on the right side of the north portal [Fig. 13].[47] Plantar rather politely used models from the interior façade for the apostles on the west front [Fig. 14]; though it is tempting to read into this slavish copying of *remois* prototypes a respectful attitude towards the Middle Ages, it may also reflect upon Plantar's own artistic range.[48] Indeed, Kurmann notes a certain lack of iconograpic savvy on the part of Plantar, who, in his repair of the Church and Synagogue figures that once flanked the south transept gable, endowed the latter with a lance terminating in a fleur-de-lys.[49] Plantar's statues have sometimes been mistaken for authentic thirteenth-century works; for example, the two figures representing rivers with vases of water (and the figures that support them) were thought to be original by subsequent scholars of Reims.[50] In 1845, the architect Arveuf repaired the west façade gallery containing the baptism of Clovis [Figs. 2, 5], the north tower, part of the spire, and the gallery at the roof level along both sides of the nave in a pure neo-Gothic style.[51]

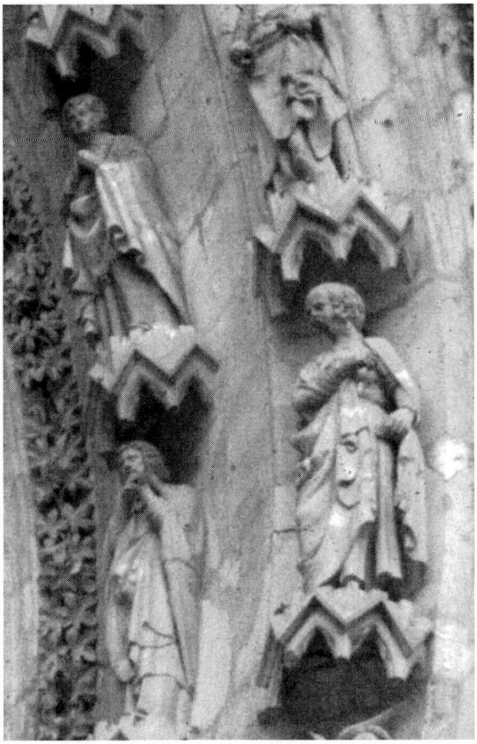

Fig. 13 Prophets, voussoirs, restored ca. 1831, north portal, ca. 1255-1300, west façade, Reims Cathedral (Photo: Author)

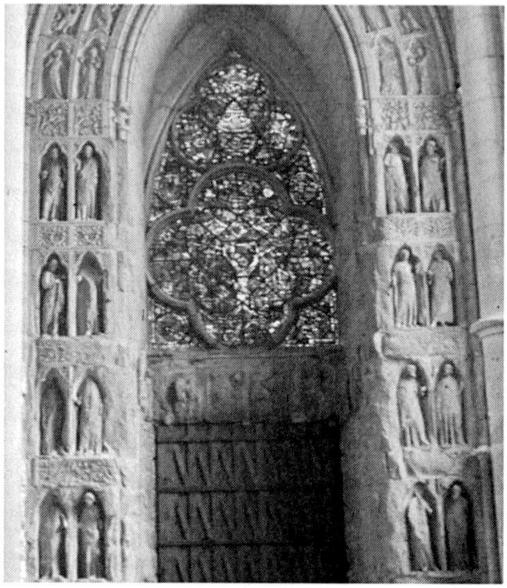

Fig. 14 Prophets, north portal, verso of west façade, ca. 1265-1300, Reims Cathedral (Photo: Author)

Before Arveuf handed the baton to Viollet-le-Duc, he completed the statues and tracery above the south transept rose window in a Flamboyant style.[52] Though detailed records are lacking for much of the eighteenth-century reconstruction, one wonders if this architectural statement is as close to emulating the thirteenth century as Arveuf could imagine it. In 1860, Viollet-le-Duc undertook the less glamorous task of clearing the blocked drains that surrounded the choir and aerating a blind arcade by creating a pierced arcade.[53] Compared to his work on other cathedrals, Viollet-le-Duc's contribution seems to have been minimal. The architects that followed, Millet, Ruprich-Robert, Darcy, and finally Gout, often added unwanted touches to the edifice, such as replacing the sixteenth-century high gallery on the south side of the nave with one in the styles "du jour."[54] So it would seem that the influence of Viollet-le-Duc did not at first inspire emulation, although the theory and practices Viollet promoted had been implemented prior to his arrival by the architect Plantar, who, already in the 1830s, sought to re-cast Reims in the style of neo-Gothic architecture.[55] That Plantar's works have been dubbed medieval by several art historians suggests that the architects of Reims were very eager to simulate the Gothic period, as well as shore up the cathedral when that was necessary. The next century will usher in a barrage of reconstruction campaigns that will not be able to fully mask the major losses of World War I.

Henri Deneux became the head architect of Reims in 1915, when the damage incurred from the shelling the year before must have been as daunting as the need to protect the cathedral from further harm.[56] Deneux's repairs to the fabric of the cathedral, both architectural and sculptural, were carried out with great fidelity to the original disposition of the building.[57] Some statues had been totally destroyed in the tabernacles surrounding the choir, as well as the figures of Ecclesia and Synagoga from the south transept gable, while many others faced future degradation because of their weakened condition.[58] When Deneux replaced figures in the tabernacles adorning the choir, transept and nave, he used his own combination of found fragments and original parts. For the jamb figures, Deneux used fragments that had been preserved during the war; if the pieces were missing, he substituted artificial stone to complete the statues.[59] Kurmann has addressed the disadvantages of this method: the original breaks in the stone were permanently effaced; the restorations are irreversible and hinder analysis of the original medieval work as well as later interventions.[60] Although we may lament our inability to trace the history of individual statuary, we can, perhaps, appreciate the complex totality of Reims' past, realized in a glorious pastiche of different hands asserting their respective silhouettes on the façade of the cathedral.

An entirely different mentality governs the approach to restoration begun in the 1990s; there is a complete respect for the previous restoration work as well as an attempt to stabilize any statues that may be at risk.[61] Restoration has become more a branch of archaeology, for example the type of metal—iron or copper—and the type of pin or bolt used to seat the statue reveal the date of the latter; similarly, analysis of the mortar and stone color allows more accurate assignment of the works to a restoration campaign.[62] Not only do thirteenth-century hooks corrode less than later models, it is also possible to uncover restoration of already restored work.[63] In the quest for stylistic or iconographic harmony in the successive campaigns of restoration on Reims' façade, Pallot-Frossard and Decrock have detected various patterns that suggest the primacy of sculptural style alternating with the precedence of iconographic veracity. [64]

For example, the voussoirs on the north side of the west façade central portal feature scenes from the Infancy of Christ, various saints, and kings, whereas the voussoirs on the south side are filled with crowned kings exuding a hyper-regal bearing. The imprint of royalty guided generations of restorers, for even Moses was crowned in the seventeenth-century restoration [Fig. 9]. In the figures of Saints Roch and Sebastian, one is confronted with both the stylistic and the iconographic signature of the eighteenth century. Both rendered in a blustery Baroque manner, the two saints were particular favorites during outbreaks of the plague [Fig. 15].[65] Because the history of restoration on the façade of Reims charts such a clear blueprint of the cathedral's past, it is possible to understand the importance this monument garnered throughout the early modern period. That history, which is still linked to the baptism/coronation of Clovis, enables us to understand how the cathedral became a secular symbol of the patrimony of France. This symbolism was only heightened during the shelling of the cathedral that occurred throughout World War I.[66]

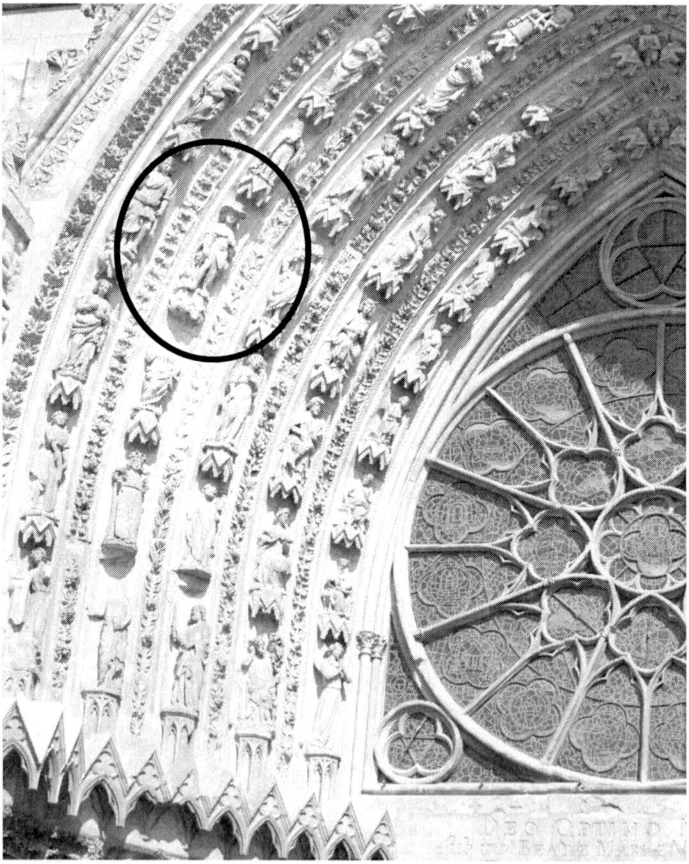

Fig. 15 Saint Roch, voussoir, restored ca. 1740, central portal, ca. 1255-1300, west façade, Reims Cathedral (Photo: Author)

Reflections on Reims Cathedral

Perhaps the words of a key theorist of the later twentieth century, whose work was fundamental in the formation of Postmodernism, will shed light on the phenomenon of Reims' position in French history. Georges Bataille (1897-1962) lamented the fate of the cathedral in the wake of World War I.[67] In "Notre Dame de Rheims," Bataille seems to conjure the medieval past and its promise of restoration in the shattered vaults. He invokes Joan of Arc and her memory of the coronation she attended, "the people exultant with pious joy and hope, the cathedral white and immense as victory, and the whole city open like the ornate portals of Notre-Dame to anyone coming in the name of the Lord."[68] In Bataille's nostalgia for the medieval cathedral of Reims, in whose shadow he grew up, scholars have seen a persistent engagement with the medieval period, its sensibilities, its material culture, its mentalities, and political history.[69] Holsinger views Bataille's ode to Reims as part of the legacy of the nineteenth century's mourning of a lost epoch, and views Bataille's subsequent theoretical trajectory as deeply immersed in the dialectic of mourning and melancholy as any rigorous example of such found in nineteenth-century philology.[70] Is it that rhetoric of loss and recovery that the restorer faces each time he wields his chisel? Indeed, could this not be the restorers' dilemma? The carvers tried to make the new (restoration) old by using the strategy of prototypes, for that was the one sure way to perpetuate the greatness of medieval Reims into the modern period. As André Vauchez points out, there was a deep connection between the development of cathedrals and the growth of monarchical power. In the case of Reims, the nation's religious and political history joined forces to establish a symbol and a model of medieval Christian France.[71] It is no accident that the restorations of Reims Cathedral were financed by the deep and royal pockets of Charles VIII and Louis XII.[72]

The same spirit of survival may be traced in the architectural history of Reims written during approximately the same period. For example, Roger Gilman published an article on the theory of Gothic architecture and the effect of shellfire at Reims and Soissons in 1920.[73] Commenting on the strength of the wall and parapet surrounding the vaults of Reims, Gilman compares the construction of the cathedral to a fortress: "It might be added that it was due also to the devotion of the French soldiers, who climbed up and built the necessary supports of masonry under bombardment when the continual shelling of the crossing vault threatened to succeed in wrecking the whole centre of the edifice."[74] Because Reims was built to be the "royal, most splendid church of France…the same lavishness shown in all these parts was carried into the construction."[75] Again, one is struck by the transformative power of Reims' history, for it has the power to seal even the gaping architectural wounds of the war and to facilitate both mourning and reconstruction of the medieval past.[76]

In an article focusing on the disparity between the French and German accounts of the war damage to the cathedral, Nicola Lambourne has traced the propagandistic tenor of each country's account of the shelling of Reims in 1914.[77] Whereas the French cast themselves as the creators of Reims and thus the ultimate victims of German brutality, the German press recalled not only the great native fathers of art history, such as Winckelmann, Vöge, and Dehio, but also the Romantic movement that reveled in art and beauty.[78] The rhetoric is as incendiary as the flames that engulfed the cathedral: pitting culture against barbarism, art against art history, and, ultimately, destroying what French culture had created.[79] As the French pondered how the Germans could obliterate the very sculpture that informed the Bamberg master, the Germans claimed to have invented Gothic art in the nationalizing vein of such works as Gerstenberg's *Deutsche Sondergotik* (1914) and especially Worringer's ideas of the northern roots of Gothic art in *Formenprobleme der Gotik* (1912). How then did the coronation cathedral, erected to transform one man into the "most Christian king," become embroiled in this contest? It would seem that the royal legacy of the cathedral continues to inscribe itself through a long line of kings, saints, and martyrs; indeed, the cathedral literally became the latest martyr in this series.[80]

Each generation of restorers has left its mark on the cathedral of Reims, yet the chisel marks do not venture far beyond the royal scope of this national monument. These restorations, coupled with a type of royal genealogy, are embedded in the sculptural program of the cathedral. For Georges Bataille, the cathedral remained God's consolation: it is in the repetitive re-dressing of the stones of the façade that one realizes the styles may be eclectic, but the royal focus of the cathedral remains both transparent and constant.

Vauchez has described the historian's task as the separation of true memory from myth.[81] Yet the beauty of Reims Cathedral is that its history is inextricably linked to its legends and myths. Saint Nicaise will continue to look down the nave towards the altar and his *rouelle*, and Clovis will be anointed three times to underscore the importance of this local and universal symbol of Reims' unique preogative to crown the kings of France. Diverse sculptural styles have characterized the history of restoration at Reims. However, the prototype of kingship that underlies the patchwork of restoration campaigns insures that the imprint of royalty reigns supreme throughout the cathedral.

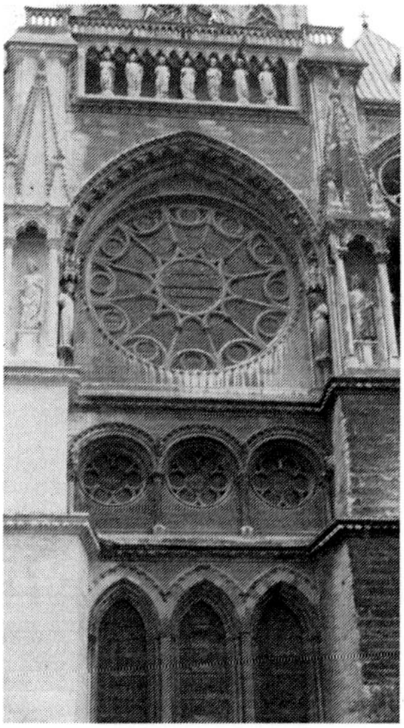

Fig. 16 North transept, ca. 1240, Reims Cathedral (Photo: Author)

Notes

[1] The miracles that parallel those of Christ are represented on the Saints portal of the north transept of Reims Cathedral. I would like to express my sincere appreciation to the reviewers for their insight and generous guidance on this paper. The errors and mixed metaphors are mine.

[2] William M. Hinkle, *The Portal of the Saints of Reims Cathedral* (New York: College Art Association of America, 1965). 39ff.

[3] Ibid. 74-75; Pierre Cocquault, *Histoire de l'église, ville et province de Reims* (MS 1609), vol. 3 (Reims, 1650). fol. 26r

[4] See Donna Sadler, "Lessons Fit for a King: The Sculptural Program of the Verso of the West Façade of Reims Cathedral," *Arte Medievale*, ser. 2, 9 (1995). 49-68

[5] The sculpture that graces the right portal of the north transept also includes angels and a small soul being lifted upward in the apex of the arch, confirming the theory that this sculpture once adorned a twelfth-century tomb. As for the six statues that occupy the right jamb of the right portal of the west façade, much ink has been spilled as to the original conception of the west façade and their role as precursors of Christ; what we can ascertain for sure is that they were carved at an earlier date and

that they seem somewhat out of place in their current context. For a summary of these issues see Willibald Sauerländer, *Gothic Sculpture in France 1140-1270,* trans. Janet Sondheimer (New York: Harry N. Abrams, 1970). 415-416, 474-488

[6] Hans Reinhardt, *La Cathédrale de Reims* (Paris: Presses Universitaires de France, 1963). 27-36

[7] Georges Tessier, *Le Baptême de Clovis* (Paris: Gallimard, 1964). 96-101; J.M. Wallace-Hadrill, *The Long-Haired Kings and Other Studies in Frankish History* (London: Methuen and Co., 1962). 163-185

[8] With some exceptions, such as Henri IV, who preferred Chartres. See Jacques Le Goff, "Reims, City of Coronation," in *Realms of Memory: The Construction of the French Past*, ed. Pierre Nora and Lawrence D. Kritzman, trans. Arthur Goldhammer, vol. 3 (New York: Columbia University Press, 1998). 208-217

[9] Ibid. 208-209

[10] Ibid. 209-217

[11] Ibid. 234-235

[12] Reinhardt, *La Cathédrale de Reims*. 205-212 provides an early overview of the restoration of the façade; the most thorough treatment of the succeeding restoration campaigns appears in Peter Kurmann, *La Façade de la cathédrale de Reims*, vol. 1 (Paris: Editions du Centre national de la recherché scientifique; Lausanne: Payot, 1987). 187ff. (hereafter Kurmann, *La Façade*); I. Pallot-Frossard and B. Decrock include a very detailed account of the voussoirs of the central portal of the west façade. *Cathédrale Notre-Dame de Reims restauration de la sculpture monumentale* (Paris: Revue scientifique et technique de la sous-direction des monuments historiques, Direction du Patrimoine, extrait n. 10/11, 1995). 66-81

[13] André Vauchez, "The Cathedral," in *Realms of Memory: The Construction of the French Past*, ed. Pierre Nora and Lawrence D. Kritzman, trans. Arthur Goldhammer, vol. 2 (New York: Columbia University Press, 1997). 53-57

[14] I would like to thank Anne F. Harris for this insight and for other helpful comments on this paper.

[15] Nicola Lambourne, "Production versus Destruction: Art, World War I, and Art History," *Art History* 22 (1999). 347-363; see also Elizabeth Emery, "The Martyred Cathedral: American Attitudes toward Notre-Dame de Reims during the First World War," in this volume.

[16] I am grateful for this wording to my anonymous reader, who so eloquently apprehended my meaning.

[17] Reinhardt, *La Cathédrale de Reims*. 27-36

[18] Gregory of Tours, *The History of the Franks,* trans. Lewis Thorpe, bk. 2 (Hammondsworth: Penguin, 1974). 30, 143

[19] Wallace-Hadrill, *The Long-Haired Kings*. 163-185; Francis Oppenheimer, *Frankish Themes and Problems* (London: Faber and Faber, 1952). 19-28, 59-69

[20] Clovis seems to best stand as royal role model. As the miraculous prototype for the French coronation tradition, it does not seem unreasonable to see here Remigius and Clovis enshrined in the immortal act of consecration. V. Tourneur, *Histoire et description des vitraux et des statues de l'intérier de la cathédrale de*

Reims (Reims: no publisher, 1857). 15-19 for a summary of the various royal candidates and the evidence offered for each. Reinhardt, *La Cathédrale de Reims*. 193 suggests that the triforium posits a type of *sacre* and not a specific coronation.

[21] Tourneur, *Histoire et description*. 15-19. For a more recent account of the stained glass and its reliance on documentary evidence see Sylvie Balcon, "Les Vitraux de la cathédrale d'après les documents du fonds Deneux conservés à la bibliothèque municipale de Reims," in Sylvie Balcon et al., *Mythes et réalités de la cathédrale de Reims de 1825 à 1975* (Paris: Somogy, 2001). 47-55. For a precise account of the west façade windows, see Meredith Parsons Lillich, "King Solomon in Bed, Archbishop Hincmar, the *Ordo* of 1250, and the Stained-Glass Program of the Nave of Reims Cathedral," *Speculum* 80 (2005). 768 nn. 6-7

[22] Nicaise's importance for the history of Reims cannot be overestimated. His cathedral bore an early dedication to the Virgin Mary. His martyrdom was spectacular in that he offered himself first to the invading Vandals as they approached the threshold of the cathedral, and they promptly murdered him. See Hinkle, *Portal of the Saints*. 69-71

[23] The "*rouelle* de Saint Nicaise" was a circular stone memorial located in the sixth bay of the nave from the west façade, a position confirmed by a 1299 charter which mentions the door in the south aisle of the present nave as being "opposite the *rouelle* of Saint Nicaise." Evidence that the *rouelle* pre-dates the Gothic edifice is provided by the tomb of Albert of Louvain (1192), which was placed near "the round marble stone on which Saint Nicaise had been beheaded." The *rouelle* at the time was situated about ten meters to the east, in front of the altar and below the crucifix of the rood screen in the nave. Jacques de Cellier's sixteenth-century plan of Reims indicates the identical location in the sixth bay as the site where Saint Nicaise was decapitated by the Vandals. See Louis Demaison, "Les Cathédrals de Reims antérieures au XIIIe siècle," *Bulletin monumental* 85 (1926). 76-77

[24] Not only is the beheading of John the Baptist depicted on the central lintel of the verso of Reims, but also the burning of his bones under the reign of Julian the Apostate, an event that occurred in the fourth century. Initiating both halves of the lintel are Herodias and Salome, even though their presence would have been rather implausible during Julian's reign. The emphasis on a bad queen and the evil she wrought was one of the lessons imparted to the neophyte ruler on the verso of the west façade; thus, the repetition of the queen and her handmaiden in this ruse was for pedagogical purposes.

[25] See Sadler, "Lessons Fit for a King." 49-68

[26] Willibald Sauerländer, "Observations sur la topographie et l'iconographie de la cathédrale du sacre," *Académie des inscriptions et belles-lettres: Comptes-rendus des séances de l'année 1992* (Paris: Eugene Piot, 1992). 463-479

[27] Pallot-Frossard and Decrock, "Cathédrale Notre-Dame." 65-81; See Françoise Choay, *L'Allegorie du patrimoine* (Paris: Seuil, 1997).

[28] Anne Prache, "Restauration des sculptures de la cathédrale de Reims," *Gazette des Beaux-Arts*, sér. 6, 66 (1965). 183-187

[29] Kurmann, *La Façade*. 30

[30] Reinhardt, *La Cathédrale de Reims*. 14; Kurmann, *La Façade*. 32-34

[31] Pallot-Frossard and Decrock, "Cathedrale Notre-Dame." 69
[32] Kurmann, *La Façade*. 38
[33] N.M. Sutherland, *Henry IV of France and the Politics of Religion 1572-1596* (Bristol: Elm Bank, 2002).
[34] Pallot-Frossart and Decrock, "Cathédrale Notre-Dame." 69
[35] Ibid.
[36] Reinhardt, *La Cathédrale de Reims*. 134. The repairs from this campaign are well-documented in "Etat des réparations à faire a l'église de Reims concernant le frontispiece," Archives départmentales de la Marne, C, 1892. Cited in J.-P. Ravaux, "Les Campagnes de construction de la cathédrale de Reims au XIIIe siècle," *Bulletin monumental* 137 (1979). 66 n. 130; Kurmann, *La Façade*. 33-34
[37] Kurmann, *La Façade*. 36
[38] "deux texts réunis sous la même relieure, non sans quelque inadvertence et quelque interversion des pages; les cahiers se sont embrouillés." Louis Gillet, "Signification de Reims et de sa renaissance," *Amour de l'Art* (1938). 148. Cited in Reinhardt, *La Cathédrale de Reims*. 134-135 n. 1
[39] Pallot-Frossard and Decrock, "Cathédrale Notre-Dame." 70
[40] Ibid.
[41] Ibid.
[42] Ibid. n. 16
[43] Ibid.
[44] Reinhardt, *La Cathédrale de Reims*. 209-210 n. 1. This inscription was replaced by that of the Concordat.
[45] David Van Zanten, "Nineteenth-Century French Government Architectural Services and the Design of the Monuments of Paris," *Art Journal* 48 (1989). 16-22; Elizabeth A. R. Brown, *The Oxford Collection of the Drawings of Roger de Gaignières and the Royal Tombs of Saint-Denis*, American Philosophical Society, new ser., 78, 5 (1988). i-viii, 1-74
[46] Ibid. 72
[47] Ibid. 37
[48] Ibid. 48 n. 174 for a delineation of models and their copies.
[49] Ibid. 38 n. 184
[50] Ibid. 39-40
[51] Kurmann, *La Façade*. 34; after 1918, when Deneux again restored this gallery, he did so in the style of the sixteenth century, which imitated the style of the fourteenth century. Venerability is clearly relative to the restorer of damaged statues on the façade of Reims.
[52] Reinhardt, *La Cathédrale de Reims*. 210
[53] Ibid. During this work, Viollet-le-Duc discovered a Merlin figure and two other small animals from the original cornice.
[54] Ibid. Other repairs included shoring up towers and consolidating the rose window.
[55] See Elizabeth Emery, *Romancing the Cathedral: Gothic Architecture in Fin-de-Siècle French Culture* (Albany: State University of New York Press, 2001); Christian

Amalvi provides an interesting discussion of the nineteenth century's love affair with medieval cathedrals. *Le Goût du Moyen Age* (Paris: Plon, 1996). 25-35

[56] Yann Harlaut, "L'Incendie de la cathédrale de Reims, 19 septembre 1914, Fait imagé…Fait imaginé…," in *Mythes et réalités de la cathédrale de Reims*. 71-79; Reinhardt, *La Cathédrale de Reims*. 210; Henri Deneux, *Dix ans de fouilles dans la cathédrale de Reims,* Conférence donnée à la Société des Amis du Vieux Reims le 1er Juin 1944 (Reims: Matot-Braine, n.d.). The heating unit housed in the north tower caught fire in 1914, causing major damage to both the sculpture and the glass.

[57] Reinhardt, *La Cathédrale de Reims*. 210-211; Kurmann, *La Façade*. 31

[58] Kurmann, *La Façade*. 31

[59] Ibid.

[60] Ibid.

[61] Pallot-Frossard and B. Decrock, "Cathédrale Notre-Dame." 73-74

[62] Ibid. 75

[63] Ibid.

[64] Ibid. 76-77

[65] Ibid.

[66] Marc Bouxin, "Le Martyre de la cathédrale: la riposte de la satire…," in *Mythes et réalités*. 81-85

[67] Denis Hollier, *Against Architecture: The Writings of Georges Bataille*, trans. Betsy Wing (Cambridge, MA: MIT Press, 1989). 162. For an incisive discussion of this piece in the context of Bataille's oeuvre see Bruce Holsinger, *The Premodern Condition, Medievalism and the Making of Theory* (Chicago: The University of Chicago Press, 2005). 28-56

[68] Quoted in Holsinger, *The Premodern Condition*. 29. The people who did not come "in the name of the Lord" were clearly the Germans invoked in the next part of the piece.

[69] Ibid. 30

[70] Ibid. Holsinger goes on to discuss the conscious organization of Bataille's three-volume *La Somme athéologique* after Thomas Aquinas' *Summa theologiae*; see also Kathleen Biddick, *The Shock of Medievalism* (Durham, NC: Duke University Press, 1998). 19-57

[71] Vauchez, "The Cathedral." 40

[72] Ibid. 54. Even Henri IV helped finance the church of Sainte-Croix in Orléans because the people of the city had been so gracious to him.

[73] Roger Gilman, "The Theory of Gothic Architecture and the Effect of Shellfire at Rheims and Soissons," *American Journal of Archaeology* 24, 1 (1920). 37-72

[74] Ibid. 68

[75] Ibid.

[76] Biddick, *The Shock of Medievalism*. 12-15

[77] Lambourne, "Production versus Destruction." 347-363

[78] Ibid.

[79] Ibid.

[80] Emery, "The Martyred Cathedral."

[81] Vauchez, "The Cathedral." 41

The Capitals from Moutiers-Saint-Jean (Harvard University Art Museums) and the Carving of Medieval Art Study in America after World War I

Kathryn Brush

This essay focuses on a group of carved capitals from twelfth-century Burgundy which have an extraordinary transatlantic history. The group is comprised of thirteen capitals from the Benedictine abbey church at Moutiers-Saint-Jean which are now in the collection of Harvard University's Fogg Art Museum.[1] The capitals' past and present contexts—the monastic complex at Moutiers-Saint-Jean (which was destroyed following the French Revolution) and the Italian Renaissance-style courtyard at the center of the Fogg Art Museum [Figs. 1-2]—could not be more different. By a strange twist of history, the architectural fragments now displayed in the ground-floor passageways of this new world art museum constitute the primary *lieu de mémoire* for a medieval church effaced from old Europe.

Like scholarly pilgrims to the Fogg before me, I am riveted by the outstanding quality and variety of these Romanesque capitals, which, since their arrival at Harvard over eighty years ago, have counted among the finest examples of their genre on this side of the Atlantic [Figs. 3-4].[2] Like others too, I have wondered how these massive, and vigorously carved capitals, when polychromed and *in situ* high atop pilasters and engaged columns, might have been perceived by their twelfth-century audiences.[3] But because my recent work has also been concerned with how we in the modern era construct knowledge about medieval art—the scholarly practice of art history being a distinctly early twentieth-century invention in the United States—I cannot help but contemplate how these medieval capitals, divorced from their original context in France and acquired by the Fogg through negotiations conducted between 1918 and 1922, might be productively studied as documents of the "carving" of medieval art study in America after the First World War. I see multiple

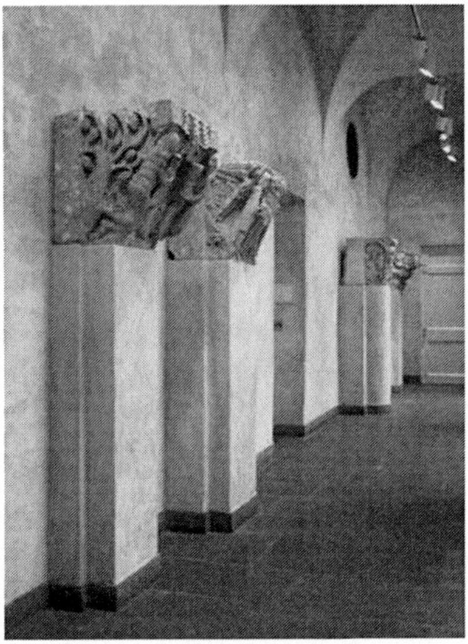

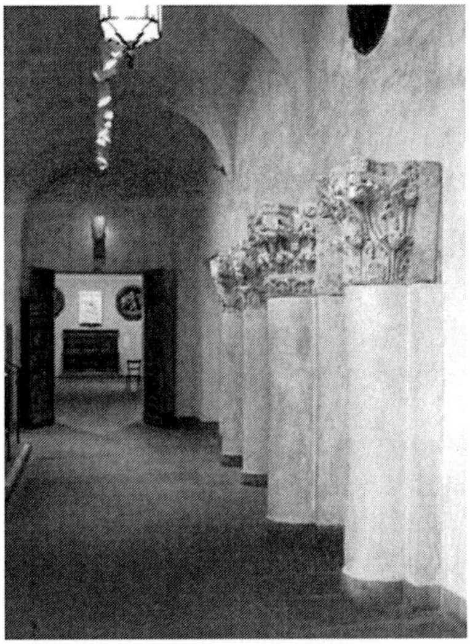

Figs. 1-2 Capitals from Moutiers-Saint-Jean, 1125-1130, installed in the north and southwest corridors, courtyard of the Fogg Art Museum, Harvard University, 2006 (Photo: Author)

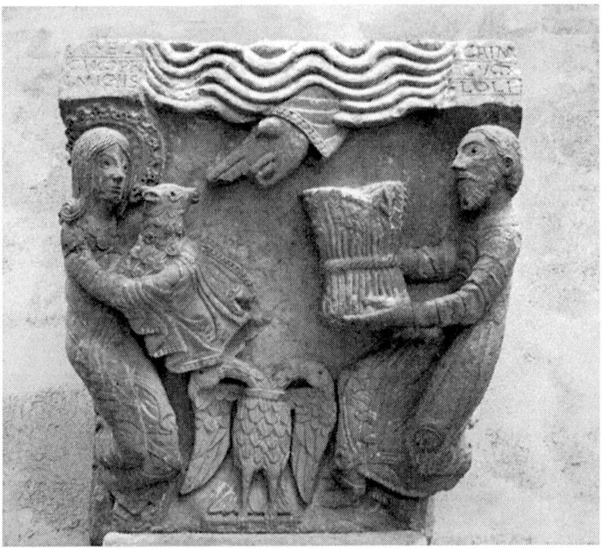

Fig. 3 Sacrifice of Abel and Cain, historiated capital of a pilaster from Moutiers-Saint-Jean, ca. 1125-1130 (Photo: Author)

concepts and histories, medieval and modern, co-existing and converging in these mute stones—complex, shifting histories that I plan to elaborate in a book.[4] This short essay aims to explore and contextualize some of the capitals' more recent, twentieth-century histories by focusing on the crucial post-World War I era. During those years these objects migrated to America and the scholarly study and collecting of medieval art gained momentum in the United States.

The Moutiers-Saint-Jean capitals were not the first works of Romanesque architecture and sculpture to arrive on American shores. Around 1900, Boston's Isabella Stewart Gardner had incorporated Romanesque carvings into the décor of her Venetian-style palazzo, while the sculptor George Grey Barnard had inaugurated his Cloisters in New York City in late 1914 to evoke the power and romance of the medieval chisel.[5] But the Moutiers capitals were the first to be acquired for an academic art museum with the intent of both stimulating the production of research-level scholarship and forming standards of historical consciousness and taste. It seems portentous in this regard that when the capitals arrived with great fanfare at the Fogg Art Museum in January 1922, they were welcomed by Edward Forbes, director of the museum, not only as outstanding medieval objects per se, but also as ones that would respond more broadly to "contemporary conditions in America."[6]

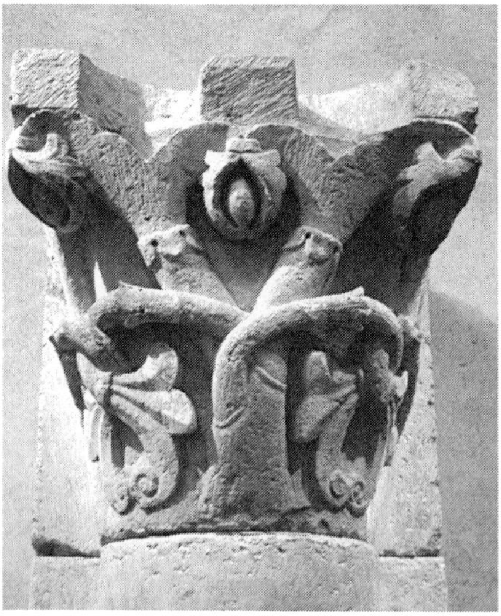

Fig. 4 Foliate capital of an engaged column from Moutiers-Saint-Jean, ca. 1125-1130 (Photo: Author)

I would contend that many of those "contemporary conditions" were present in the post-war activities of the Fogg Museum and in the scholarship of the pioneering medievalist Arthur Kingsley Porter (1883-1933) [Fig. 5]. Porter was recruited in 1919 as research professor for Harvard's Department of Fine Arts, which at that time was synonymous with the Fogg Art Museum; indeed the Museum housed Harvard's Fine Arts Department. The first North American doctoral degrees in art history were granted just prior to World War I, and, in the years immediately after the conflict, the Fogg began to be reinvented by its co-directors, Edward Forbes and Paul J. Sachs, as a national center for the training of art scholars and curators, for they recognized the need to professionalize an American branch of art study along the lines of European academic models, particularly those of the German-speaking countries.[7] The building of faculty, an art collection of original works that would stimulate hands-on learning, and a new Fogg Art Museum to house pedagogical and research activities, were vital priorities, and the projects to acquire both Porter and the Moutiers-Saint-Jean capitals figured significantly within this larger agenda.[8]

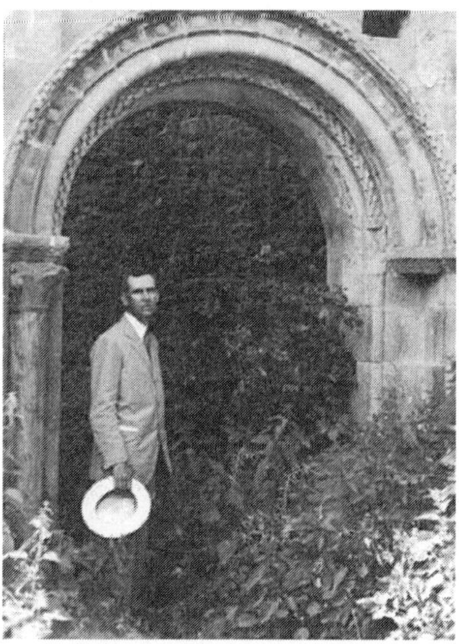

Fig. 5 Arthur Kingsley Porter at Carracedo, Léon, ca. 1920
(Photo: Harvard University Archives)

Porter was America's most prominent, internationally renowned art scholar in these years. Between 1918 and 1922, precisely when negotiations for the Moutiers capitals were underway, Porter was preparing his groundbreaking *Romanesque Sculpture of the Pilgrimage Roads*, which appeared in 1923.[9] It consisted of one volume of text and nine volumes of photographic plates, and radically revised the landscape of medieval art study by forcefully redrawing the artistic and cultural map of eleventh- and twelfth-century Europe along international rather than national lines. Porter rejected longstanding theories of French scholars, who had argued for the artistic priority of France in the development of Romanesque architecture and sculpture. The American instead hypothesized that the pilgrimage routes in France and Spain had been important channels of communication that united all of Europe. Porter's borderless vision of the transmission and simultaneity of artistic ideas made modern, nationalist-driven notions of cultural priority irrelevant and predictably provoked controversy in France (and elsewhere).[10]

I believe that Porter's foundational book remains a page-turner today, over eighty years later, not so much due to the specifics of his arguments regarding particular sites in France and Spain—what we might term the surface narrative—but because embedded in his text are concepts, values, and intellectual habits that uniquely document the conditions in which medieval art historical discourse took shape in America. More broadly, I believe that close study of the conceptual structuring of this text, along with study of Porter's unpublished correspondence and the circumstances surrounding the acquisition of the Moutiers-Saint-Jean capitals, can allow us to grasp some of the ideological complexities of the multiple versions of the Middle Ages that were fabricated and institutionalized in the United States after World War I. For example, Porter himself was involved a few years later in the founding of the Medieval Academy of America, and his Harvard colleague, the historian Charles Homer Haskins, one of the central figures in that organization's history, carved out his enduring vision of the "Renaissance of the Twelfth Century" by 1927.[11] Haskins portrayed the twelfth century as an "age of fresh and vigorous life."[12] What did the visual culture of the Middle Ages and the twelfth century in particular mean to Porter, to American society—and indeed to Europeans—in the post-war era?

Several provocative issues have emerged from my initial research into the capitals from Moutiers-Saint-Jean, which embarked upon their American lives in this highly charged post-war era. Above all perhaps, they (and their transaction records from 1918 to 1922) remind us that the genesis of academic art scholarship in America was intimately linked to the economic and commercial realms—in short, to the art market and the transatlantic trade in antiquities fueled by the war. This was quite unlike the conditions surrounding the introduction of formalized art study in European countries in the 1880s and 1890s. In America, twelfth-century carvings from Burgundy, whether historiated or foliate, became exotic commodities that could be bought and sold on Wall Street like stocks and bonds. And indeed it was a group of prominent Wall Street banker-philanthropists who made possible the purchase of the capitals for the Fogg, believing that an investment in such exemplary fragments of medieval culture would yield an enriched American pedagogy and culture.[13]

The acquisition of the Romanesque capitals also demands interpretation against the accelerated building of a culturally hybrid America after the war. It seems fruitful to explore, for example, how cross-cultural readings of the forms and designs of the medieval capitals would have been facilitated in the discursive spaces of the new Fogg Art Museum itself, an institution that was being reinvented in these very years with a view to provoking novel and unexpected relationships amongst fragments from diverse cultures, both historical and contemporary. In 1927, the capitals were installed in thc Great Hall of the new Fogg Museum (where they were located until the 1980s) in close visual and physical proximity to works not only from the Western tradition (e.g. ancient and Renaissance art), but also from Central American, Islamic, and Asian civilizations.[14] This multicultural installation was radical in a university art museum in 1920s America, as was, for example, the introduction of Asian art into the art history curriculum. Certainly this influential academic institution's internationalizing approach to the study of culture after the war was played out in Porter's own views in *Romanesque Sculpture of the Pilgrimage Roads*, in which he compared stylistic and compositional features of Romanesque sculpture to works of art from ancient China, Japan and India, the Italian *trecento*, and early twentieth-century Europe, often in a single paragraph. Moreover, Porter was collecting art from various historical eras and cultures for himself and for the Fogg at the same time.[15]

My preliminary look at the documentation for the Moutiers-Saint-Jean capitals suggests, too, that the salvaging, purchasing, and championing of French art at large in the years after 1917, when the Americans joined the war effort, was viewed as a patriotic act—indeed as a signal of support—for the continuity of *la civilisation* at an acute time of need. The Francophilia of the pre- and post-war years, manifested at Harvard in the types of exhibitions mounted by the Fogg, in the importation of the

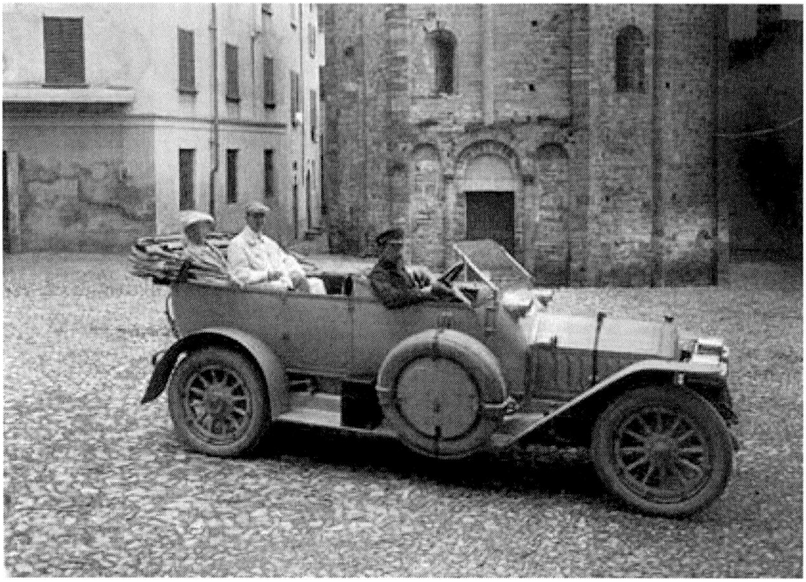

Fig. 6 Arthur Kingsley Porter and Lucy Porter in Lombardy with their chauffeur, 1912-1913 (Photo: Harvard University Archives)

Moutiers capitals, and in the scholarship of someone like Charles Homer Haskins, must of course be understood within the much longer history of American-French political and intellectual relations; we can recognize today that this early twentieth-century valorization of French culture has had a lasting impact on the study of medieval art by Americans. In 1918 and 1919 Porter himself volunteered his services to the *Commission des monuments historiques*. He and his wife Lucy collaborated with French colleagues in the devastated regions of northern France in order to draw up inventories of works of art that had been damaged or destroyed during the conflict with the German *Kaiserreich*. Porter had lived and voyaged extensively in Europe in the pre-war years, and his chauffeur-driven automobile [Fig. 6] conveyed him and his wife through the French battlefields just as it had in Lombardy and elsewhere several years earlier. During these months of fieldwork in France directly after the war, Porter refined the ideas and the technologies (most notably, photography) that would culminate in his book on sculpture of the pilgrimage roads.

One of Porter's primary theories was that Burgundy, and the abbey at Cluny specifically, together with Spain and northern Italy, had provided especially fertile ground in the eleventh century for the development of the artistic language we call Romanesque.[16] In 1920, shortly after his appointment at Harvard, Porter was asked to assess the capitals from Moutiers-Saint-Jean, which were then still in France, for the Fogg.[17] Porter's ensuing correspondence with his Harvard colleagues affords valuable insights into his developing theories. While that subject awaits further critical study, I would like to point out here that in Porter's opus of 1923, the historiated capitals from Moutiers-Saint-Jean, then newly arrived at the Fogg, were discussed and imaged early on, and positioned alongside works from such sites as Cluny, Autun, and Vézelay to illustrate his ideas regarding the pan-European impact of Burgundy—and Cluny—in the eleventh and twelfth centuries.[18] I find it striking that eight hundred years later the Moutiers capitals in the Fogg Art Museum participated in another sort of internationalizing process. This time they signaled the moment when art historical discourse was, for the first time, being globalized, largely via the scholarship of Porter.

Porter was the first American art scholar whose work generated international response because he addressed issues central to European art history—issues that focused on the study and interpretation of medieval art. While Porter's post-war work on the pilgrimage roads has necessarily been analyzed in relation to Italian, French, and Spanish scholarship, I unexpectedly discovered a few years ago that Porter had forged extensive intellectual ties with Germanic *Kunstwissenschaft*, especially from 1920 and 1921 on, when he was writing his *Romanesque Sculpture of the Pilgrimage Roads*.[19] Recently I have begun to recognize that Porter's association with German scholarship is crucial for contextualizing the production of virtually all discourse on medieval sculpture in the 1920s. I have also realized how very little we actually know about Porter's intellectual biography and the genesis of his investigative methods, although much attention has been paid to the details of his private life, which, on the surface, display the glitter and romance of a Hollywood movie. Porter was wealthy; he and his wife lived in an eighteenth-century mansion in Cambridge, Massachusetts, when they were not voyaging all over Europe; he owned a castle in Ireland; he drowned there in 1933 under mysterious circumstances; his body was never found; and so the script goes on and on. The recent discovery that Porter was increasingly consumed by homosexual desires by the mid-1920s on has only heightened scholarly and popular interest in the celebrated scholar of the pilgrimage roads. Indeed a recent novel, *The Slow Breath of Stone: A Romanesque Love Story* (2005), was inspired by the dazzling events of Porter's life.[20] But while Porter is a colorful figure, I would also argue that the prevailing tendency to study and project him as a legendary hero of

American art history has distracted scholars from arriving at a full understanding of the intellectual parameters in which he operated.

To cut a long story short, Porter entered the discursive territory of German-language scholarship when he embarked upon his intensive studies of Romanesque sculpture beginning in 1918. This post-war episode in Porter's work is especially fascinating, for until then he had focused on architecture and had relied methodologically on French scholarship. Indeed, in 1918-1919 he had collaborated with French colleagues in the battlefields of northern France. But his on-site work with buildings and artifacts convinced him that the chronologies long accepted as dogma among French scholars were faulty; *Kunstwissenschaft* became ever more attractive to him, for it shared his concern with the first-hand study of works of art and with the careful scrutiny of their formal properties. Porter's unpublished papers show that he devoured German scholarship from around 1920 on, for not only had German scholars invented the terms of discourse for the study of medieval sculpture from the 1880s and 1890s, but they had also begun the intellectual rehabilitation of Romanesque art prior to the First World War. The study of medieval art by German-speaking scholars before the war had always been universalizing in nature and agenda; it was not confined to national borders. Certainly this made Germanic scholarship sympathetic to Porter's own post-war enterprise. I therefore believe that we need to measure Porter's construction of his borderless internationalizing visions in *Romanesque Sculpture of the Pilgrimage Roads* not only in relation to his American experience, as has traditionally been suggested, but also in relation to his first-hand knowledge of German-language scholarship and scholars. For such scholars, scarred by the recent war, Porter's utopian picture of European unity in the Middle Ages offered a welcome antidote to the harsh realities of the present. Indeed Porter's correspondence demonstrates that German scholars were the ones most invigorated intellectually by Porter's work, though they also had many criticisms of it. In short, we need to work further to contextualize the book's meaning and reception within the intellectual climate of post-war Europe and to measure its success at a time when the work of the American newcomer was favored by the temporary disablement and isolation of German-speaking scholars.[21]

More specifically, it appears that Porter conceived of his work on eleventh- and twelfth-century sculpture as a dialectical pendant to the pioneering work of Wilhelm Vöge, who had written the first history of Gothic sculpture in 1894 and which still provided the standard against which an aspiring scholar like Porter could measure his own intellectual ambitions.[22] The American sent a copy of his *Romanesque Sculpture of the Pilgrimage Roads* to Vöge as soon as it appeared in 1923, but he had already sent his first article on the Moutiers-Saint-Jean capitals, written shortly after their arrival at the Fogg. Vöge's response to the article is telling. In his carefully crafted letter, Vöge marveled at how the Fogg's newly acquired capitals vividly expressed the "youth and vigor" of twelfth-century Burgundian art.[23] This reminds us of Haskins' portrayal of the twelfth century as an "age of fresh and vigorous life," a notion that must clearly be positioned within the larger international continuum of medieval scholarship in these years. The relationship between Porter and Vöge is multidimensional. Both scholars expended much ink exploring artistic volition and artistic identity in the Middle Ages, reading and interpreting medieval works like the capitals from Moutiers-Saint-Jean as three-dimensional records of the mentalities of the eras that produced them. The concept that exacting study of the carved forms of the capital could provide access to both collective and individual psyches of the Middle Ages became a form of pedagogy—and a genre of scholarship—at Harvard and elsewhere.

In sum, my initial research indicates that we need to conceive of the carving of medieval art study in America after the First World War as a dynamic process that engaged with "contemporary conditions" in both Europe and America, with Porter and the Moutiers-Saint-Jean capitals contributing vitally to that process. Many of Porter's ideas were carried forward in the work of his most productive students, including Kenneth Conant, who endeavored in the following decades to salvage and resurrect the fragments of the medieval monastic complex at Cluny in large-scale drawings.[24] As a tribute to his teacher, Conant extended his project back across the Atlantic in the mid-1930s to the courtyard of the Fogg, where, significantly, he reconstructed the apse of Cluny (in plaster cast form) a few steps from the twelfth-century capitals from Moutiers-Saint-Jean.[25] The extraordinarily lively dialogue between medievalism and modernism in these years is beyond the scope of the present essay, but it can be summed up by a photograph that is worth more than a thousand words [Fig. 7]. The image shows the Moutiers-Saint-Jean capitals in 1941 in the ritual space of the Fogg's Warburg Hall—it looks the nave of a church—with the all-male (Harvard) worshippers venerating the altar of modernism: Pablo Picasso's freshly painted *Guernica*.[26] The celebrated painting, like the fragments from the twelfth-century church in the same room, shared a history shaped by modern war and destruction.

Critical study of the post-medieval afterlives of the capitals from Moutiers-Saint-Jean thus affords a significant opportunity for understanding how Porter and others generated imaginative new concepts about medieval visual culture—new concepts that continue to provide much provocation well into the twenty-first century.

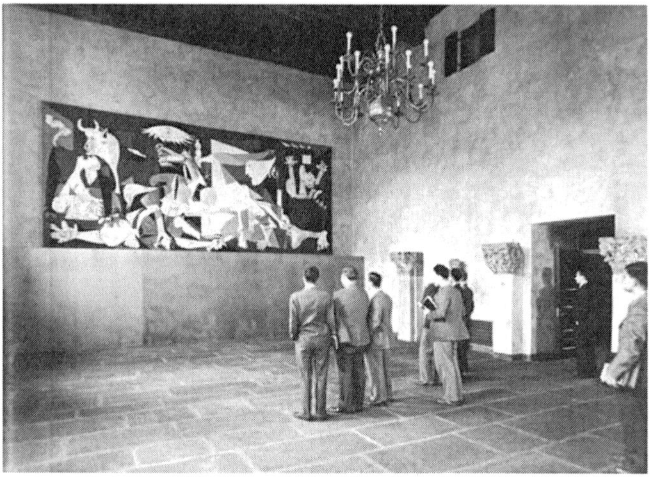

Fig. 7 Pablo Picasso's *Guernica* (1937) hanging in Warburg Hall, 1941 (Photo: Harvard University Art Museums Archives, File: Picasso's *Guernica*)

Notes

[1] Harvard University Art Museums, 1922.16-1922.27 (twelve capitals accessioned in January 1922); a thirteenth capital was acquired several years later by Paul J. Sachs from the collection of Jean Peslier, Avallon (1925.9.1). For a catalogue of the capitals, Walter Cahn and Linda Seidel, *Romanesque Sculpture in American Collections*, vol. 1, *The New England Museums* (New York: Burt Franklin, 1979). 120-141. To date, the most easily accessible on-line images of the capitals are located on the Limestone Sculpture Provenance Project website, sponsored by the International Center of Medieval Art: http://www.limestonesculptureanalysis.com.

[2] The first scholarly article on the capitals that appeared following their arrival in the United States in 1922 praised them as being "of an importance hardly equalled by any other object of mediaeval art in America"; see Arthur Kingsley Porter, "Romanesque Capitals," *Fogg Art Museum Notes* (1922). 23; for the most recent assessment of the sculptures from Moutiers-Saint-Jean and their contexts with the earlier bibliography, Neil Stratford, "La Sculpture médiévale de Moutiers-Saint-Jean (Saint-Jean-de-Réome)," *Congrès Archéologique de France, 1986 (Auxois-Châtillonnais)* (1989). 157-201; this article has been republished in Neil Stratford, *Studies in Burgundian Sculpture I* (London: Pindar Press, 1998). 175-219

[3] Most recently, Deborah Kahn, "Saint Augustin et le diable, à propos d'un chapiteau de Moutiers-Saint-Jean," *Bulletin Monumental* 162-163 (2004). 189-192

[4] In preparation; the working title is "Arthur Kingsley Porter and the Invention of Art Scholarship in America: Medievalism, Modernism, Multiculturalism." The ideas introduced in the present essay will receive detailed investigation in that book.

[5] For the larger contexts, see the essays in Elizabeth Bradford Smith, ed., *Medieval Art in America: Patterns of Collecting 1800-1940* (University Park, Pennsylvania: Palmer Museum of Art, 1996).

[6] Edward W. Forbes, quoted in *The Harvard Graduates' Magazine*, June 1924. 581. In the immediate post-war years, Forbes and Paul Sachs, the assistant director of the Fogg, regularly emphasized that the building of the collection of original works at Harvard responded to the needs of contemporary America by elevating the standard of education in the fine arts.

[7] Princeton and Harvard Universities served as focal points for the development of research-level art history in America; Princeton awarded its first doctoral degree in 1911 and Harvard in 1913. See Craig Hugh Smyth and Peter M. Lukehart, eds., *The Early Years of Art History in the United States: Notes and Essays on Departments, Teaching, and Scholars* (Princeton: Department of Art and Archaeology, Princeton University, 1993).

[8] For these initiatives and their larger contexts, Kathryn Brush, *Vastly More Than Brick and Mortar: Reinventing the Fogg Art Museum in the 1920s* (Cambridge, MA: Harvard University Art Museums; New Haven: Yale University Press, 2003).

[9] Arthur Kingsley Porter, *Romanesque Sculpture of the Pilgrimage Roads*, 10 vols. (Boston: Marshall Jones, 1923). The complex negotiations for the capitals will receive detailed analysis in the book I am preparing.

[10] The controversy that Porter's novel ideas provoked in Europe was also followed in the American press. See, for example, Nathan Haskell Dole, "A Pilgrimage to the Land of Romanesque Art. New Chronology Established for Medieval Monuments," *The New York Times*, 12 August 1923. 10, 28; James Ernest King, "Reconstructing Two Centuries of Art Hitherto Jumbled by Europe. A. Kingsley Porter of Harvard Sweeps Away the Erroneous Dates Assigned by Orthodox Scholarship to Romanesque Sculpture and Writes All Its History Anew," *Boston Evening Transcript*, 17 February 1923, sec. 4. 1, 3. The latter article compared the effects of Porter's revisionist views to the dramatic shifts in American colonial history that would result from a redating of the landing of the pilgrims at Plymouth Rock by fifty years in advance.

[11] Charles Homer Haskins, *The Renaissance of the Twelfth Century* (Cambridge, MA: Harvard University Press, 1927). The Medieval Academy of America was incorporated in Boston on 23 December 1925; at that time, Haskins was second vice-president and Porter was a councilor.

[12] Haskins, *Renaissance*. vi

[13] The primary donor to the "Romanesque Sculpture Fund" at the Fogg Art Museum in 1921-1922 was the Wall Street banker-philanthropist Felix Warburg, who gave $10,000. For Warburg's long and close ties to the Fogg, Brush, *Vastly*

More Than Brick and Mortar. John Pierpont Morgan, Jr. ($5,000) and Henry Goldman ($2,000) were among the other New York bankers who contributed to the purchase. Brush, *Vastly More Than Brick and Mortar.* 54-56, n. 25

[14] Brush, *Vastly More Than Brick and Mortar.* 114-126 with photographs

[15] To be discussed in the book I am preparing.

[16] The Benedictine monastery at Cluny, which was the motherhouse of a vast international monastic network, reached the height of its influence between the late tenth and twelfth centuries. The last and final church built at Cluny (termed Cluny III in modern scholarship; it was begun in 1088) was the largest church constructed in Europe during the Middle Ages. After the French Revolution the monastery was almost totally demolished; only a small part of the huge abbey church and fragments of its decoration have survived. Porter was among the first historians of art to recognize the impact of Cluny (and the Cluniac order) on the development of Romanesque architecture and sculpture. I will trace the genesis of Porter's thought vis-à-vis Cluny in the book I am preparing.

[17] Porter, "Romanesque Capitals," for his first published assessment of the capitals.

[18] Porter, *Romanesque Sculpture.* 1:91, 114-116; 2:62-66. Porter illustrated only the three historiated capitals.

[19] In the late nineteenth and early twentieth centuries, German-speaking scholars endeavored to transform art history into a "scientific," systematic academic discipline (*Kunstwissenschaft*), formulating such patently objective methods as stylistic analysis for the study of works of art. I first pointed to Porter's links to Germanic scholarship in Kathryn Brush, *The Shaping of Art History: Wilhelm Vöge, Adolph Goldschmidt, and the Study of Medieval Art* (Cambridge: Cambridge University Press, 1996). 145-148; for the larger contexts, Kathryn Brush, "German *Kunstwissenschaft* and the Practice of Art History in America after World War I: Interrelationships, Exchanges, Contexts," *Marburger Jahrbuch für Kunstwissenschaft* 26 (1999). 7-36

[20] Pamela Petro, *The Slow Breath of Stone: A Romanesque Love Story* (London: Fourth Estate, 2005). In this novel/travelogue/journal, which combines fact with imaginative projection, Petro meditates on the motivations underlying Porter's studies of Romanesque stone sculpture and travels around southern France and Ireland herself, visiting churches, quarries, and other sites mentioned in Lucy Porter's diaries.

[21] For a larger discussion, Kathryn Brush, "Arthur Kingsley Porter and the Transatlantic Shaping of Art History, ca. 1910-1930," in *The Shaping of Art History in Finland*, ed. Renja Suominen-Kokkonen, Taidehistoriallisia Tutkimuksia/Konsthistoriska Studier /Studies in Art History 36 (Helsinki: Taidehistorian Seura, 2007). 129-142

[22] Wilhelm Vöge, *Die Anfänge des monumentalen Stiles im Mittelalter. Eine Untersuchung über die erste Blütezeit der französischen Plastik* (Strasbourg: J. Heitz, 1894); see Brush, *The Shaping of Art History.* 146-148, for my initial discussion of the relationships between the work of Vöge and Porter.

[23] Letter of 31 July 1923 from Wilhelm Vöge to Arthur Kingsley Porter, Harvard University Archives, Arthur Kingsley Porter Papers, Letters and Papers Received,

Box 5, HUG 1706.102. Vöge was often slow to respond to correspondence; in this same letter he thanked Porter for sending him *Romanesque Sculpture of the Pilgrimage Roads*. I will analyze the exchanges between Vöge and Porter in the book I am preparing.

[24] For a comprehensive study of Conant's wide-ranging activities at Cluny see Janet T. Marquardt, *From Martyr to Monument: The Abbey of Cluny as Cultural Patrimony* (Newcastle-upon-Tyne: Cambridge Scholars Publishing, 2007). esp. chap. 5-7

[25] Discussed by Marquardt, *From Martyr to Monument.*

[26] *Guernica*, painted by Picasso in response to the savage bombing of the Basque town of Guernica by Franco's forces on 26 April 1937, came to the Fogg via the Museum of Modern Art in New York where the artist had placed the work on indefinite loan during the Second World War. Alfred H. Barr, Jr., the director of the New York museum, had conducted his graduate studies at Harvard, and he enabled the Fogg to borrow the painting in the fall of 1941 and again in 1942 for display in Warburg Hall (formerly the Great Hall). For the circumstances see Abby Smith, "Exhibiting *Guernica* at the Fogg," *Harvard University Art Museums Review* 5 (fall 1995). 5, 14-15

The Martyred Cathedral: American Attitudes toward Notre-Dame de Reims during the First World War

Elizabeth Emery

The German bombardment of Reims Cathedral in early September 1914 generated outrage from journalists, art historians, soldiers, politicians, and poets from around the world [Fig. 1]. Labeled a "barbaric" act of wanton vandalism and a "crime against humanity," the international press was unanimous in condemning the 14 September shelling, which had taken place despite flags on the towers indicating the cathedral was being used as a hospital.[1] On 19 September, more bombs set fire to the structure, burning the wooden roof of the nave and causing massive damage to statues and the incineration of much of the interior, including choir stalls and stained glass [Fig. 2].[2] The German army scrambled to justify itself, first claiming that orders had been given to protect the cathedral and that it must have been an accident. When it was shown that an accident was impossible at such close range, the Germans claimed "military necessity" because of an alleged French observation station perched on the towers sending information to a nearby battery. As the official German statement put it, "Reims was in the battle line....We regret the necessity, but the fire of the French came from that direction."[3] Despite the fact that French government, clergy, and independent observers confirmed that the cathedral served no military function and despite massive international protest, the Germans shelled Notre-Dame de Reims systematically from September 1914 until October 1918; the cathedral was estimated to have been hit by approximately 300 shells and incendiary devices, though contemporary French reports claimed as many as 700. The city was completely razed.

My goal in this essay is to examine World War I-era American images of the besieged medieval cathedral, particularly those disseminated through newly popular media such as newspaper rotogravure printing and postcards.[4] I will not depict the devastation of the bombing, which has been amply documented elsewhere, nor is it my intent to examine its causes or the national rivalries it inflamed.[5] Instead, I will argue that such widely accessible images of the cathedral served as a catalyst for encouraging Americans to support the war and for educating them about the value of medieval art.

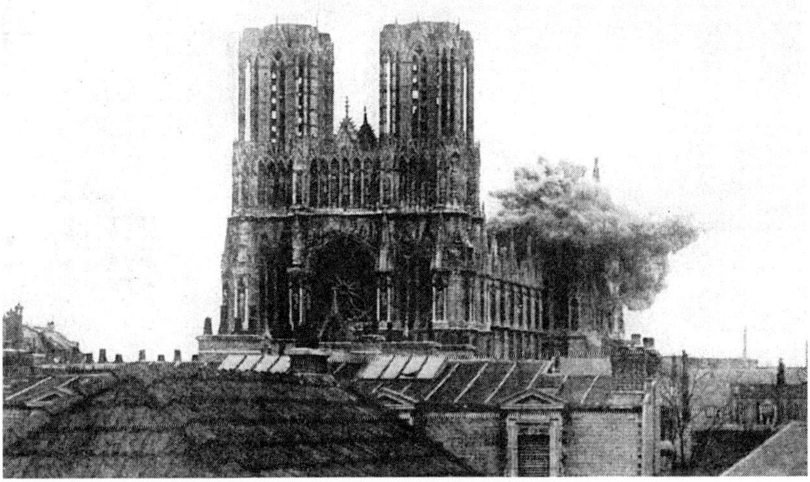

Fig. 1 Shell bursting on the cathedral at Reims, from *Collier's New Photographic History of the World's War* (New York: P.F. Collier and Son, 1918). 86

Thousands of American newspaper and periodical articles, books, posters, and postcards featured Notre-Dame de Reims from 1914 to 1918, allowing today's readers to gauge the extent to which American attitudes toward the cathedral shifted during the course of the war.[6] Surprisingly, despite a growing obsession with French art and fashion at the turn of the century, Reims Cathedral was barely mentioned in the American press until the war. When the cathedral did appear, it was as a worthwhile visit while in the "champagne city," or as one of the finest and most historic of the French cathedrals.[7] By 1918, however, Reims had become a leading American tourist attraction, infamous as a "martyred city" whose ruined cathedral symbolized the plight of the entire French nation. This essay focuses on visual representations of Notre-Dame de Reims in order to trace the pro-French sentiment generated by images of the cathedral's alleged "martyrdom."[8]

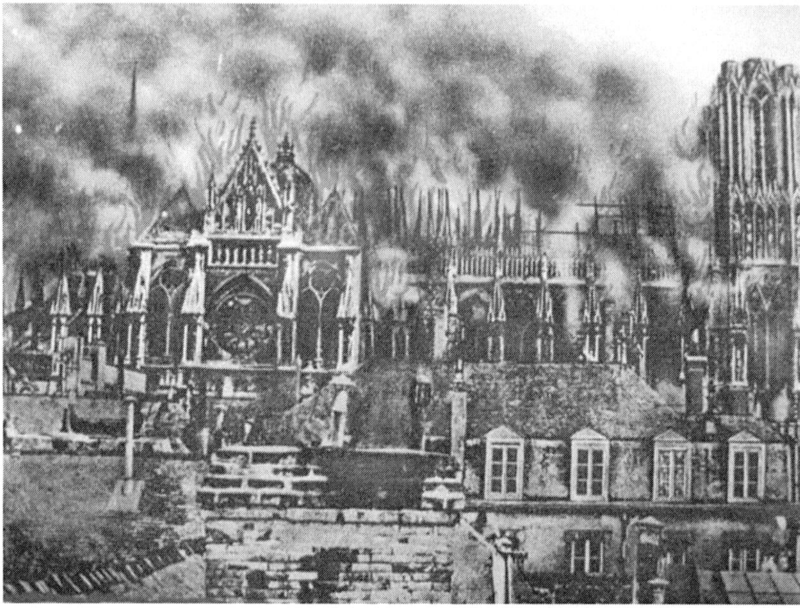

Fig. 2 "Rheims-Cathedral, during the bombardement by the german fire shells," [sic] dual-language, hand-colored postcard, 1914 (Photo: Collection of the Author)

First of all, it is important to note the American isolationism that marked the onset of World War I. Unwilling to engage in what was perceived as a European war, the United States remained resolutely neutral (despite furnishing supplies to Allied forces) until declaring war on Germany in April 1917.[9] Nonetheless, international news was avidly reported, often within hours, thanks to the speed of transatlantic cables. *The New York Times*, for example, published more than twenty-five articles related to the cathedral in the first four days following the 19 September 1914 bombing and heavily advertised a full-page rotogravure reproduction of the pre-war structure—"a prize picture for framing"—in its following Sunday pictorial section.[10] It would continue to publish photos of damage throughout the war in the mid-week and Sunday pictorials [Fig. 3].[11] Such articles create a snapshot of the world's outrage at the attack on Reims. As a local correspondent put it in a 22 September 1914 article entitled "The Great Crime of Rheims," the destruction of the cathedral would be "remembered as a critical incident of the war," in which the world first understood the "ferocity" of the modern war tactics being used by Germany: ignoring international treaties, bombing civilian

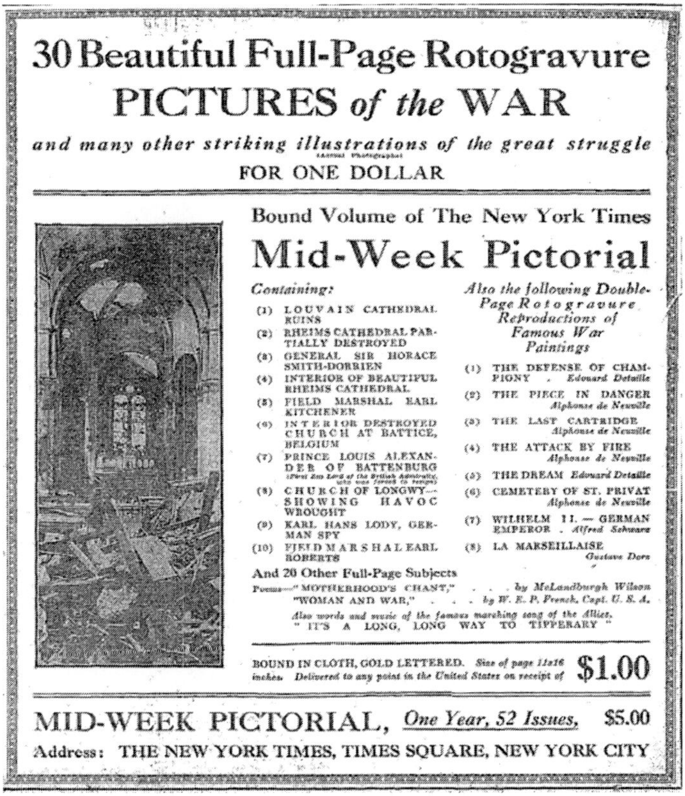

Fig. 3 "30 Beautiful Full-Page Rotogravure PICTURES of the WAR," *The New York Times*, 13 February 1916.

targets, sinking passenger ships, and extorting huge ransoms from towns such as Louvain and Reims before destroying them.[12] Reports from international correspondents confirmed such impressions, noting that violent acts did a disservice to the Germans' attempts to win neutral nations to their side. The Swiss were horrified, and "indignation" for the Reims bombing was alleged to have "transcended anything felt since the beginning of the war" in Italy.[13]

At first, Americans were curious (as the *Times*' reference to a souvenir "prize picture for framing" would suggest) and published relatively balanced reports about the event. This quickly changed, however, as eyewitness reports and photographs chronicling the "horror" of the Reims

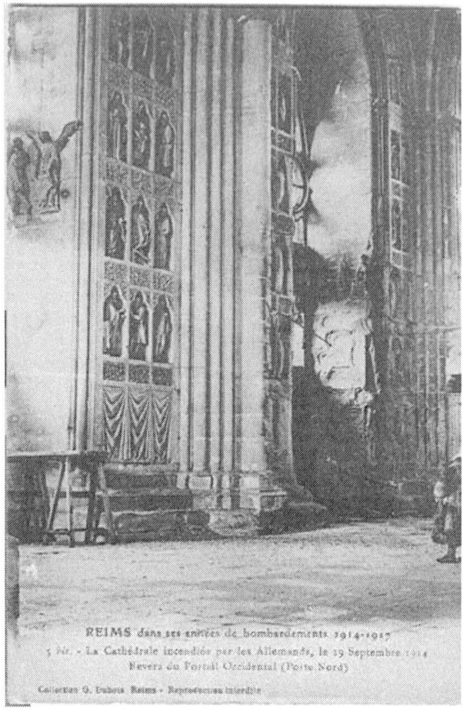

Fig. 4 Interior of the west façade of Reims Cathedral, postcard, 1914-1917
(Photo: Courtesy of Mary B. Shepard)

bombing began to appear in the daily press and such widely-read periodicals as *Newsweek*, *Century*, *Collier's*, and *Scientific American*. Even more personal were postcards of the damaged cathedral sent by acquaintances. In such images Americans could see for themselves the devastation caused by the bombing, which the German newspapers had reported as "slight" [Figs. 1-5]. They had similarly pronounced that the Louvain library's destruction (another popular photographic subject) was "exaggerated."[14] Sympathies quickly veered toward the French and Belgians as a result of such photographs, particularly when German Major General von Disfurth justified the destruction with nationalist rhetoric: "If all the glorious monuments ever created be destroyed, it is of no consequence, so that by their destruction we promote German victory. The humblest gravestone of a German grenadier is more beautiful than all the cathedrals of Europe. Let neutrals and enemies cease their empty twitter. Let them cease to talk of Rheims Cathedral. Our troops must achieve victory."[15] Although the German government claimed to have forbidden subsequent shelling, such orders (if they were given) were not respected, and the particularly fierce bombing of the cathedral in 1917 and 1918 was attributed by the French, English, and American press to revenge; if the Germans could not advance, they would "torture" the cathedral instead.[16]

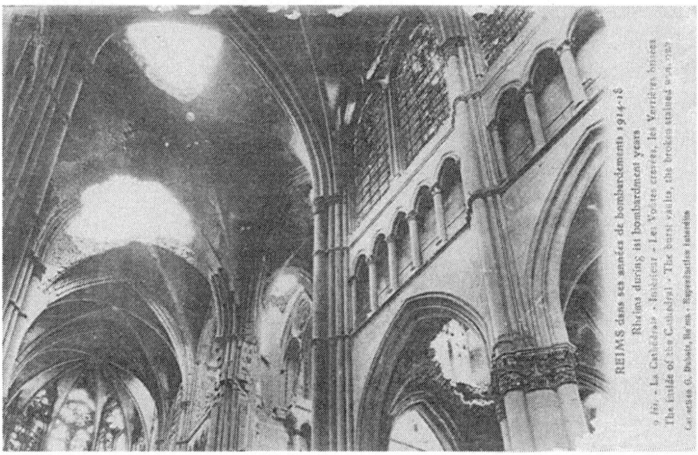

Fig. 5 Damaged vaults, Reims Cathedral, postcard, 1914-1918
(Photo: Courtesy of Mary B. Shepard)

As the attacks continued, the French furiously accused the Germans of being worse than barbarians, Attila the Hun, and Vandals.[17] Outrage turned to name-calling and virulent patriotism, as French celebrities, including Pierre Loti, Romain Rolland, and Maurice Barrès, disparaged German heritage, couching the shelling of Reims in terms of German jealousy for its lack of originality in regard to medieval art and mocking the vaunted German *Kultur*. Art historian Emile Mâle went so far as to proclaim that Germany had invented nothing, labeling Reims "a martyr who had just endured agonies that her torturers had not been able to complete."[18] Posters for benefits supporting the people of Reims featured the burning basilica in vivid colors to emphasize the brutality of the event and to provoke public outrage [Figs. 6-7].

The French hysteria concerning Reims was such that Romain Rolland wrote "He who kills this work murders more than a man, he murders the purest soul of a race," while others cited Auguste Rodin, who had proclaimed that "The country cannot perish as long as our Cathedrals are here."[19] Their words were summarized in the American press, which

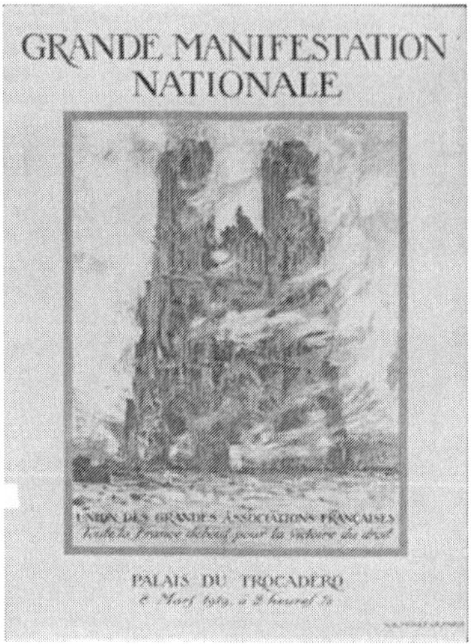

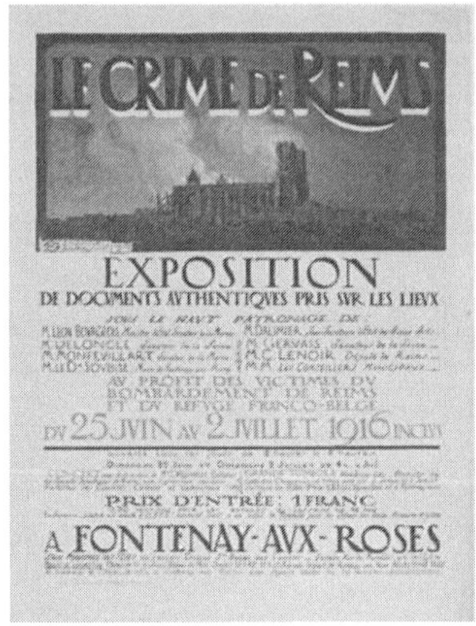

Fig. 6 (L) "Grande manifestation nationale," poster, 1919 (Photo: Library of Congress)

Fig. 7 (R) "Le Crime de Reims," poster, 1916 (Photo: Library of Congress)

featured headlines reading "Crime at Rheims," "Rheims Battered to Bits," "The Martyred Cities," or "The End of Rheims." Simultaneously, elegiac poems and texts about the cathedral by French- and English-speaking writers, including Edmond Rostand, Emile Verhaeren, Pierre Loti, Grace Walcott Hazard Conkling, McLandburgh Wilson, and Margaret Steele Anderson, were published in American magazines and reprinted throughout the war.[20] Some emphasized the national and religious character of the cathedral, stressing its victimization at the "hand of the Hun," or its perseverance and courage in the face of an unjust enemy. Others, such as a Conkling poem [Fig. 8], emphasized Reims Cathedral's resilient spirit by showing how it still stood tall, even bereft of its material components—bells, windows, and statuary. By 1915, it was common to refer to Reims as a "martyr of stone" and to describe the bombing in terms of its "gangrenous wounds," as did medievalist Ralph Adams Cram in public lectures he gave about the cathedral.[21]

Cram was one of America's best-known and most prolific architects and a specialist of medieval art; he had made his reputation by building American-inspired Gothic Revival buildings. A founding member of the Medieval Academy, he was among many American architects and art historians to criticize the German destruction from the very beginning.[22]

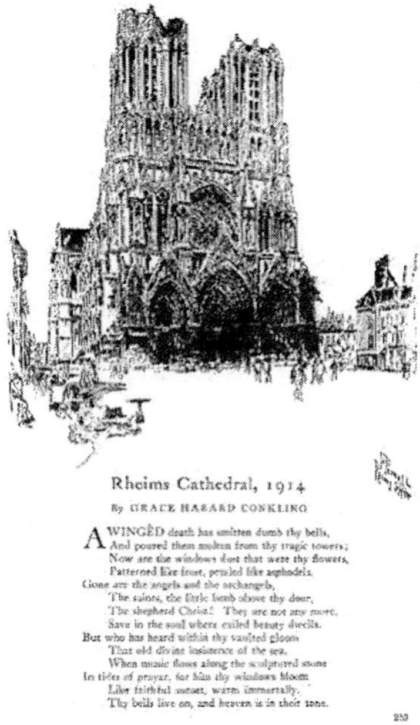

Rheims Cathedral, 1914

By GRACE HAZARD CONKLING

A WINGÈD death has smitten dumb thy bells,
And poured them molten from thy tragic towers;
Now are the windows dust that were thy flowers,
Patterned like frost, petaled like asphodels.
Gone are the angels and the archangels,
The saints, the little lamb above thy door,
The shepherd Christ! They are not any more,
Save in the soul where exiled beauty dwells.
But who has heard within thy vaulted gloom
That old divine insistence of the sea,
When music flows along the sculptured stone
In tides of prayer, for him thy windows bloom
Like faithful sunset, warm immortally.
Thy bells live on, and heaven is in their tone.

253

Fig. 8 "Rheims Cathedral, 1914," *The Century* (December 1914).

Cram himself was scheduled to speak at a 17 November 1914 meeting of the Architectural League of New York (though, ultimately, he was not able to attend) for which Thomas Hastings, a member of Cram's firm, had drafted a resolution condemning the destruction of Notre-Dame de Reims and the Louvain library. According to a *New York Times* article, the resolution requested that belligerents "hereafter respect the master-works of past generations, which belong to the whole world, and which no indemnity can replace and the ruins of which can stand only as a perpetual disgrace to their destroyers." Slides and photographs illustrated destroyed edifices at Reims, Senlis, Chantilly, Louvain, Termonde, and Liège, and although the resolution was officially neutral, off-the-cuff comments to reporters showed that the architects sympathized with the French and Belgians.[23]

Despite America's stated neutrality, it is clear that intellectuals followed their own agendas. Cram, for example, who called Reims "the crowning monument, in material form, of Christian civilization; so perfect in all its parts that it was perhaps too perfect,"[24] was tireless in his campaign to bring attention to the cathedral's plight. To encourage the

United States to join forces against the Germans, he helped found a propaganda group of intellectuals called the American Rights League, for which he traveled through nine states promoting an anti-German agenda while giving lectures ostensibly about architecture.[25] One can imagine the effect of these lectures by reading the following passage from a 1916 talk:

> The glass that rivalled Chartres is splintered in starry dust on the blood-stained pavement and its fragments made the settings in soldier's rings. Its vault is burst asunder by bombs, its interior calcined by the conflagration, the incredible sculptures of its portals blasted and burned away. Yet it stands in its infinite majesty, gaunt and scathed in a circle of ruin, still the majestic fabric of a great people, a great epoch, a consummate art.[26]

Cram's focus here on images of breakage, blood, fire, and pillage, as well as the consonance of his prose, with its emphasis on b, k, v, t sounds, poignantly evoke the damage done while imitating the sound of shell fire. His personification of the cathedral, still standing gaunt and majestic among the ruins, further emphasized its martyrdom.

His lectures followed a pattern: after describing Gothic architecture as an embodiment of spirituality (referring to the vision of Suger, the twelfth-century abbot of Saint-Denis), he would take his audience on a "pilgrimage," describing the masonry, the buttresses, the windows, the transept, and the "little sculptured heads, unmistakable portraits, any one of which would be a treasure in a museum" [Fig. 9].[27] After revealing the glories of Gothic art, he would conclude with a statement about Reims, such as: "So far as supreme art is concerned, man has never achieved anything greater."[28]

After convincing his audience of the tremendous value of medieval art, and of Reims in particular, Cram would switch tone, factually reporting the bombing itself, the number of shells that had hit the cathedral, and the damning correspondence he had received from Germans. He would then dramatically describe the damages:

> [the] incredible statues have been blasted by shell and calcined by fire, and the exquisite sculpture of all the craftsmen of France has crackled, crumbled, and fallen into indistinguishable dust. I think it was the greatest sculpture of the Middle Ages; greater than Chartres....Little by little the great windows gave up their glass that shivered down into the growing heaps of débris on the floor below, while altars and stalls crumbled under the incessant hail of shell shards and shrapnel.[29]

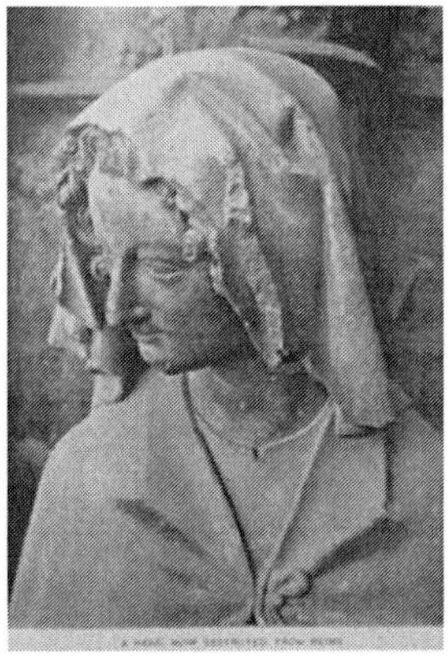

Fig. 9 "A Head now Destroyed from Reims," from Ralph Adams Cram, *Heart of Europe* (New York: Charles Scribner's Sons, 1915). facing 242

Audiences cannot have remained unmoved by such prose, especially after Cram had just shown them—with slides—that the cathedral was one of the greatest accomplishments of humankind. The comparison with Chartres, well-known in America at this time because of Henry Adams's popular *Mont-Saint-Michel and Chartres* (published in 1913 with an introduction by Cram, though previously privately printed in 1904), further allowed the public to grasp just what a masterpiece Reims had been.

Cram reached a larger audience with the publication of *Heart of Europe*, a profusely-illustrated book inspired by the "blind horror" he had felt when hearing of the Reims bombing.[30] It treats northern French and Belgian medieval architecture, specifically that area most devastated by the "indelible crime" committed by the Germans. As he and others would suggest, "martyrdom," with all its Christian resonance, was the appropriate term to apply to the victimized cathedral.[31] According to Cram, although the Germans sought to inspire terror in the hearts of the French (and the world), by showing what punishment would result from resisting German advances, they had badly miscalculated. Like the early Christian martyrs whose torture would inspire conversion, Reims' brutalization would not inspire fear, but outrage, encouraging neutral countries, such as Italy and the United States, to join France in resisting Germany.[32]

Newspapers and Cram's writings suggest the extent to which the multiplication of representations of Notre-Dame de Reims through different media brought public attention to the cathedral; such sources attested directly to the damage done. Reims—and by extension France—

was thus transformed in the United States from a subject of meager interest before the war to a wartime subject capable of eliciting the greatest hyperbole. As Cram himself noted, his 1915 writings about the devastation were met with skepticism; he received numerous American letters expressing sympathy for the Germans and their "accidental" shelling of the cathedral. Others saw nothing wrong with the destruction of such "rotten old art." This had changed by 1917, when the sheer volume of the attacks could no longer be attributed to chance, and the growing fame of the cathedral had convinced the public of its artistic value.[33]

Indeed, as a result of the many reports of the cathedral's impending demise, American art historians, architects, and tourists flooded to Reims—even during the war—to see the damage, take pictures of it, and propose ways of repairing it.[34] Interestingly, Maurice Landrieux, the archpriest of Notre-Dame de Reims from 1912-1916, complained that the public and the press, like Cram, rarely spoke of the cathedral as a house of worship.[35] Instead, both French and American reporters transformed the church into the "French Parthenon," a poignant ruin, the symbol "of the indestructible spirit of France," "the stark skeleton of its noble cathedral rais[ing] its tortured towers in eloquent agony."[36] Victor Turner has suggested that symbols flourish because of their semantic flexibility; prominent individuals are thus able to bring new associations to them.[37] This was certainly the case at Reims, where the cathedral's status in the American consciousness shifted as a result of the new rhetoric attached to its images. No longer a mere church, an important part of French national history, or even a curious work of art from the past, the cathedral became a martyr: an international symbol of innocence violated. Sympathy for Notre-Dame de Reims was then transferred to France, a country not without responsibility for the arms buildup that had provoked the war.

As we have seen, the concept of the martyrdom of Reims/France was particularly reinforced by visual media. Photographs of the devastation published in books and magazines and sold in postcards and stand-alone volumes were legion [Figs. 1-5], as were artists' renditions, which went even further in their propagandistic depiction of the German assault on Reims.[38] In North America, views of Notre-Dame de Reims incited readers to action. Occasionally it was to mobilize them, as in the case of a Liberty Bonds poster with its graphic black and white depiction of an armored Prussian hand choking the cathedral [Fig. 10]. The multiple exclamations—"Ruin, Desolation, Destruction mark the path of the Hun; Remember! Vengeance! This is Americanism!"—reinforce the violence of the Prussian act and pit America against Germany. Others, such as a Canadian poster which encouraged French-Canadians to enlist, appealed to their Catholic solidarity: "Are we waiting for ours to burn?" [Fig. 11]. Yet others represented the flaming cathedral as a pathetic backdrop for scenes of social misery, to encourage donations or the purchase of bonds.[39] In France, even after 1918, images of the martyred cathedral reminded the French to invest in France and to avoid German products, as in post-war posters where Marianne gestures to the Reims inferno [Fig. 12]. Postcards were retouched by hand to emphasize the violence done to the cathedral [Fig. 2]. Such visual rhetoric completely transformed Reims' meaning for the world. Instead of a picturesque tourist destination, an important nexus of French history, or a place of worship, it now stood as a damning commentary on German military techniques and as an international symbol of the ravages of war.

It is curious that Reims became (literally) the American poster child for a martyred France. Many other towns and cathedrals in Belgium and France had been even more devastated and were also called "martyrs," from the library in Louvain to the cathedrals at Ypres, Soissons, and Arras.[40] Examples of the monuments massacred by modern machines of war were rampant in postcards and in the illustrated press. Why then did America mobilize so notably for Reims, to the extent that—as a relief organization complained in 1922—Americans donated more to repair the cathedral after the war than to relief efforts for humans?[41]

In part, Notre-Dame de Reims was a logical symbol for Americans to choose as a representative of France because it was the French "national cathedral," known for its coronations and for its relationship to Joan of Arc, whose story Mark Twain had famously told (*Personal Recollections of Joan of Arc*, 1885). Moreover, it was one of the few theaters of war readily recognizable to American tourists. Indeed, after the cathedral's initial bombardment in 1914, the English Lord Roseberry wondered whether its destruction might prompt Americans to intervene, since they sent such a large number of tourists abroad each year to see European antiquities.[42] At the very least, news of the cathedral's scandalous treatment by the Germans was guaranteed to sell newspapers.

Another reason for American outrage may have stemmed from the fact that the shelling of Reims took place at the very moment that the United States was building its own Gothic cathedrals—Saint John the Divine in New York City and Washington National in the District of Columbia—using techniques and symbolism borrowed from the Middle Ages. Americans, particularly Easterners, would thus have been attuned to the great cost and labor involved in erecting cathedrals built in the medieval style.[43] A 22 May 1918 slide show given at Saint John the Divine by

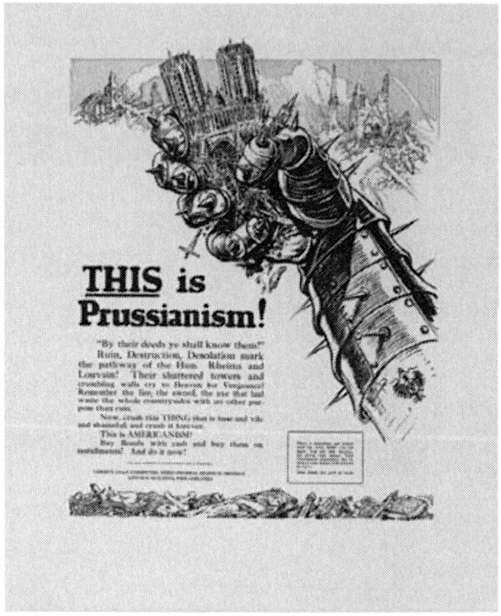

Fig. 10 "*THIS* is Pussianism!" poster
(Photo: George F. Tyler Collection, Temple University Library)

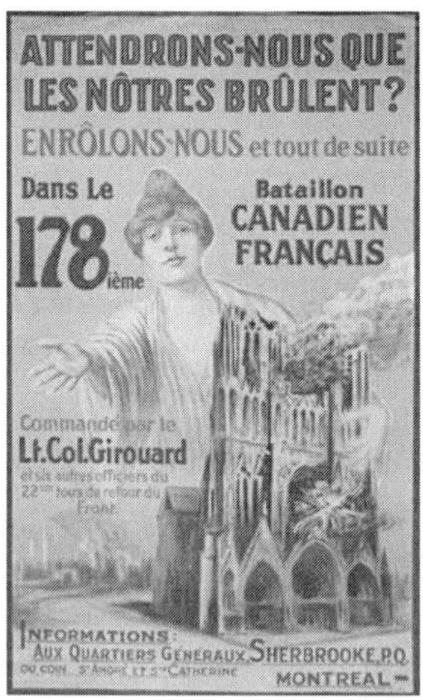

Fig. 11 "Attendrons-nous que les nôtres brûlent?" poster
(Photo: Library of Congress)

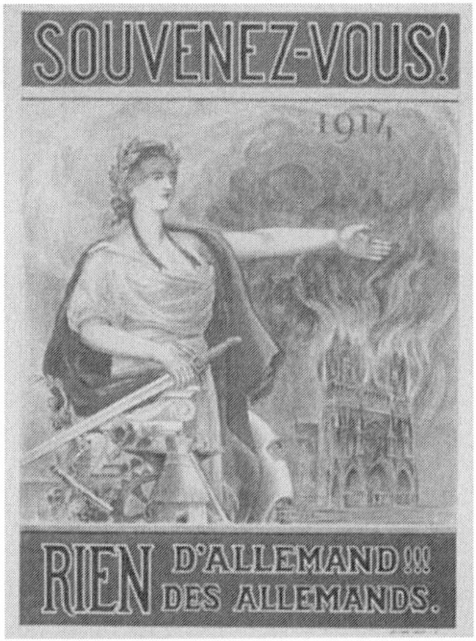

Fig. 12 "Souvenez-vous!" poster, 1914 (Photo: Library of Congress)

Edward Hagaman Hall, Secretary of the American Scenic and Historic Preservation Society, about the destruction of the European cathedrals would suggest that the public was aware of the parallels.[44] Furthermore, Cram, known as the leader of the "American Gothic" movement in architecture, would have reinforced the association of new American cathedrals with their European models in his lectures. Cram had recently been appointed architect of Saint John the Divine in a highly controversial and well-publicized decision by the cathedral's board; his mandate was to render the existing 1891 Romano-Byzantine plan of George Heins and Christopher Grant Lafarge more Gothic.[45]

Above all, however, the destruction of Reims provided Americans with a visible motive for why Germany had to be stopped. Depicting Germans as barbarians ruthlessly crushing and burning innocent victims allowed pro-war activists to appeal to an American public reluctant to intervene in what was broadly conceived as a European war. It is important to stress once more that most Americans did not want to participate; President Woodrow Wilson was re-elected in 1916 with the motto "He kept us out of war." As David M. Kennedy has pointed out, from the moment Wilson decided to declare war in 1917, his administration understood that the major battle would be to convince the American public to support him. The American government thus swiftly adopted anti-German propaganda of all sorts, including patriotic school texts and posters, which emphasized Germany's stranglehold on the world [Fig. 10]. The head of Wilson's Committee on Public Information, responsible for disseminating pro-war publicity, was former exposé journalist George Creel, a master at what we might call "spin" in today's political jargon.[46]

Even before Wilson's intervention, however, pro-war American journalists had exploited photographs as a way of influencing public opinion about the war.[47] It was Americans, working for *Collier's* in 1915, who pushed the British government to allow them access to the front lines, specifically citing their desire to build anti-German sentiment at home.[48] In the early twentieth century, photographs were considered inherently truthful documents;[49] reporters and postcard manufacturers understood that the photographs of the Reims devastation would say much more than written reports from the front.[50] Indeed, Nicola Lambourne has remarked that the French were able to garner the world's sympathy about Reims precisely because of the access they granted photographers to the damaged structure; the photographs supported their claims of German vandalism. The Germans, on the other hand, were unconvincing in their claims that the French were using the cathedral as a military facility because they had no photographic proof.[51] Allied photographs of a damaged Notre-Dame de Reims "spoke" more powerfully than any verbal rhetoric.

The Germans recognized the power of the images from 1914, complaining that the French purposefully drew fire on Reims in order to portray themselves as martyrs.[52] While it was ludicrous to propose that the French would purposefully destroy their national cathedral, often evoked as the equivalent of England's Westminster Abbey, once the damage was done, the French did milk the Reims catastrophe for all it was worth in order to raise international awareness of their plight. John Fraser has illustrated how central propaganda offices in France and Britain aligned with recognized publishers, using postcards to disseminate anti-German sentiment.[53] The bulk of postcards on sale in Reims during and immediately after the war contain captions in both French and English [Figs. 2, 5]. A wealth of illustrated books and brochures describing the cathedral before and during the war (in both French and English) also flooded the marketplace. An 8 October 1915 *New York Times* article by Jean A. Picard ("The War's Influence on French Literature") describes scores of individual works on Reims, while devoting a section to "the other victims, the silent 'Martyrs of Stone'." By 1915, the French press had already published works such as *Rheims! The Cathedral is Shelled*, while the Librairie Centrale des Beaux-Arts had published two albums of plates. *Les Allemands destructeurs de cathédrales* (Paris, 1915) is an illustrated booklet containing all the official documents covering the shelling, while the 1915 *Les Villes martyres*, by Marius Vachon, sought to expose German atrocities by publishing photographic records. Such texts would continue to be published throughout the war and afterward, notably with Paul Vitry's two-volume, *La Cathédrale de Reims* (Paris, 1915-1919)

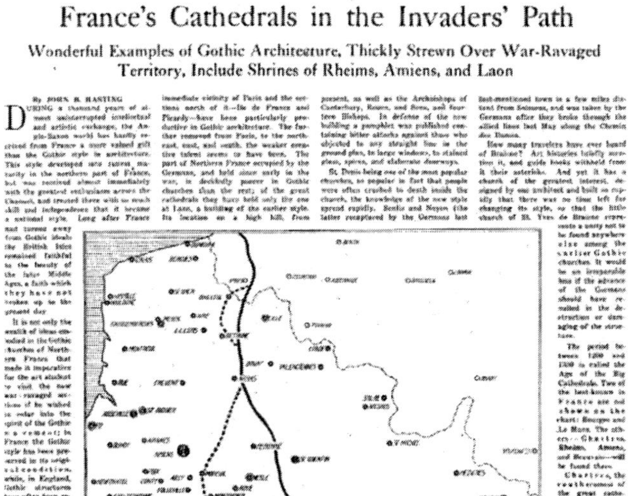

France's Cathedrals in the Invaders' Path

Wonderful Examples of Gothic Architecture, Thickly Strewn Over War-Ravaged Territory, Include Shrines of Rheims, Amiens, and Laon

DOOMED GOTHIC CHURCHES AND CATHEDRALS OF NORTHERN FRANCE.

Fig. 13 "France's Cathedrals in the Invaders' Path," *The New York Times*, 4 August 1914.

and Maurice Landrieux's *La Cathédrale de Reims. Un Crime allemand* (Paris, 1919), translated in 1920 as *The Cathedral of Reims; the story of a German crime* (London, 1920). Portraying the Germans as brutal and unrestrained vandals was effective: one of the primary reasons cited for America's entrance into the war in 1917 was Germany's aggression against neutral countries. In his 2 April 1917 special address to Congress recommending a declaration of war, President Wilson inveighed against the "irresponsible government which has thrown aside all considerations of humanity and of right" and singled out its disregard for "innocents," which the United States was compelled by its values to help.[54]

Although motivations for depicting Notre-Dame de Reims as a martyr ranged from an interest in selling newspapers to genuine outrage and a concern to incite American involvement in the war, every report cast a spotlight on the Gothic structure. The publicity given the martyred cathedral expanded American knowledge of, and interest in, medieval art. Journalists in the United States went to great lengths to explain the history of Reims, to enumerate the lost glories of its statuary and stained glass, and to show the fate of other French and Belgian national monuments [Fig. 13]. Such visual and verbal attention convinced the American public that medieval structures such as Reims were artistic treasures (and not "rotten old art").

Partially in response to the media attention given to Reims, medieval sculpture, stained glass, and textiles came back into vogue in the United States. The Metropolitan Museum opened a new tapestry gallery in 1915 and expressed interest in exhibiting the Reims tapestries then on display in Paris. The 1917 fashion season featured "cathedral gowns" of bright velvet, inspired by the lost Reims stained glass, as well as the colorful costumes worn by French cabaret singer Yvette Guilbert during an American tour featuring performances of medieval song and poetry.[55] In 1919, one of the projects proposed for a war memorial in New York was a Gothic arch inspired by Reims Cathedral.[56] Benefit concerts and movie screenings—including a Sarah Bernhardt film, *The Mothers of France*, which was shot against the backdrop of the bombarded cathedral—raised money, as did the sale of bookends, inkwells, paperweights, compacts, medals, and other memorabilia featuring the image of Reims [Fig. 14].[57] All these events drew attention to the plight of the cathedral while raising public consciousness about medieval art in general.

A 1915 Brooklyn Museum of Art exhibition, featuring enlarged photographs of Gothic churches and cathedrals, exemplifies the popular and institutional activities spawned from the destruction of Reims. The stated objective of the exhibit was architectural comparison, yet the press

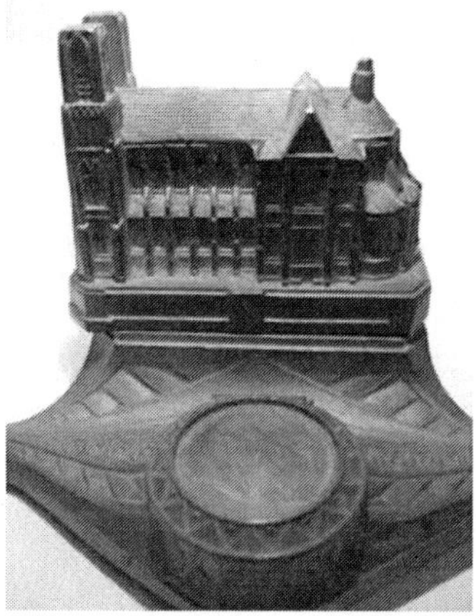

Fig. 14 Cathedral of Reims Inkwell (Photo: Collection of Author)

release suggests that curators capitalized on interest about the war-time damage and speculation about post-war restoration.[58] What would become of Reims was a hot question, debated from the first days of the attacks. The consensus was that it should remain a ruin, a testament to German vandalism. References to the "French Parthenon" were legion in this respect, suggesting that the French were eager to emulate an historical precedent: the Greek decision to leave the ruins of the Acropolis untouched for twenty years after the Persian destruction of Athens. This choice, recorded by Herodotus, would thus testify to the "barbarianism" of the Persians (i.e. Germans) while reminding future generations of what had been lost. Emulating the Greeks, the French Restoration Fund announced in 1917 that Reims would become a pantheon to the Unknown Soldier, a ruin decorated with flags of the Allied nations.[59]

Shortly thereafter, however, the German military renewed its bombing campaign, enraging international supporters of the cathedral, who argued that the Germans should not be allowed, in the words of the archbishop of Reims, to "boast of their destruction of one of the wonders of the world. The cathedral must be avenged by saving it for this vengeance."[60] Although pledges of financial assistance poured in from around the world, it was still unclear what would happen to the cathedral until Memorial Day 1924, when John D. Rockefeller pledged a million dollars to the French government of which $300,000 would go to rebuilding the roof at Reims so it could be used once again for religious services.[61] The enormous publicity generated by his gift triggered more donations, and, in 1927, when the cathedral was restored sufficiently to function as a church, Rockefeller contributed an additional 1.6 million dollars to the government to assist with other rebuilding projects in Reims, as well as Versailles, and Fontainebleau. The cathedral would not be "structurally complete" until 1938, when it was consecrated.

Even if the restoration was only partially funded by Rockefeller, American headlines consistently identified relief effort at Reims as American, thus giving the cathedral an honorary American pedigree. Had numerous public figures, including Rockefeller, not declared that the cathedral "belonged to the world"? Reims, the war darling of the United States, had become a kind of national emblem and the leading post-war tourist attraction. It was so often labeled a "Mecca" for sightseers that the Michelin Company published a special English guidebook (1920) to lead tourists on "pilgrimages" to the cathedral and nearby battlefields (*Rheims and the Battles for Its Possessions*).[62] As Americans learned more about Gothic architecture from the well-publicized martyrdom and reconstruction of Reims, and as soldiers returned bearing souvenir fragments of Gothic sculpture and stained glass from other destroyed French and Belgian monuments,[63] Americans became increasingly interested in the art of the Middle Ages.

The replica façade of Reims Cathedral on display in Wanamaker's flagship Philadelphia department store, as well as its displays of stained glass and sculpture, reveal just how far the taste for medieval art spread among the public during and after the war.[64] In 1916, Ralph Adams Cram had noted that medieval sculpture was still considered inferior to its Classical counterpart, yet by the end of the war, Americans admired the work of medieval artisans, who had built structures that could withstand such tremendous shelling.[65] Similarly, French art historian René Gimpel reported in 1923—five years after the end of the war—that it had only been in the last "two or three years" that medieval sculpture had become popular in America.[66] The Medieval Academy, the premier American association for medieval studies, took part in this post-war vogue for medieval art. Planning for the Academy began in 1920, and it was officially founded in 1925. By the inaugural issue of *Speculum*, in 1926, the organization counted 876 members, including businessmen, artists, students, and scholars.[67]

As Kathryn Brush has noted, for many of America's wealthy, salvaging French art was considered a "patriotic act" that would assure the continuation of a treasured French civilization now so violently under attack.[68] This interest in "saving" medieval sculpture by importing it led to the establishment of quixotically American displays of European medieval art, such as those at The Cloisters in New York. George Grey Barnard's curiosities—the heart of the original collection—dated from the turn of the century, even though Rockefeller's construction of these fragments into the scholarly museum we know today began only in 1935 (the museum opened in 1938). Other examples include the twelfth-century Spanish church Saint Bernard de Clairvaux in North Miami Beach, imported by William Randolph Hearst in 1925 but not assembled until the 1950s, or the twelfth-century Spanish abbey of Santa Maria de Ovila. Imported by Hearst in 1930, then given to the city of San Francisco in 1941 for a medieval museum designed by his architect Julia Morgan, the abbey's stones lay in San Francisco's Golden Gate Park until they were reassembled in 2003 as the chapter house of the Abbey of New Clairvaux in Vina, California. Many other holdings of American museums, such as the capitals of Moutiers-Saint-Jean in the Fogg Art Museum of Harvard University, had their origin in the immediate post-war period.[69] Perhaps most exemplary of Americans' fascination with war-ravaged Notre-Dame de Reims are the fragments of its stained glass hanging in the Chinese Loggia of the Isabella Stewart Gardner Museum in Boston. Presented to Gardner by an American ambulance driver in 1919, the glass pieces were given a prominent setting as a testament to Gardner's support of the war effort and her longstanding desire to preserve relics of the European past for the enjoyment and the edification of the American public.[70]

These are but a few examples that reveal the extent to which the rise of medieval studies in America was indebted to the Great War, which made the art of the European Middle Ages a topic of popular debate. While the destruction of Reims was catastrophic, the French promotion of the martyred figure of their national cathedral was a critical activity that brought American attention both to the war and to the world's medieval legacy. Medieval art and architecture began to be considered part of the "world's patrimony" and protected as such.[71] Thanks to philanthropic figures such as Rockefeller, who single-handedly jump-started the restoration at Reims, and private collectors, who salvaged fragments that Europeans did not value, America was able to build its own medieval collections and found new museums and organizations dedicated to medieval subjects. When Ralph Adams Cram famously wrote that Reims, "like the martyr in the Roman arena, has accomplished its work," little did he suspect that the cathedral would bring so many American converts to medieval studies.

Notes

[1] Much of the damage done to Notre-Dame de Reims was a result of its proximity to the western front. Germans arrived in Reims on 4 September 1914 and occupied it until 12 September when Allied forces approached, thus forcing the Germans to retreat to the hills above Reims. As the front was established, they would remain within firing range of the cathedral, essentially for the duration of the war. As soon as the French troops arrived in Reims, they attempted to protect the cathedral by using it as a hospital and flying the Red Cross flag. Several German soldiers were, in fact, killed during the bombardment. The shelling went against article 27 of the 1899 Hague Convention, an international treaty written to protect historic monuments, hospitals, and other important artistic, scientific, or charitable institutions. The facts in this paragraph have been summarized from *The New York Times* (henceforth *NYT*) articles reporting events to the American public. For a comprehensive (despite heavy anti-German bias) and liberally illustrated contemporary account of the bombing and architectural damage see Paul Vitry, *La Cathédrale de Reims* (Paris: Librairie Centrale des Beaux-Arts, 1919). Vitry was a leading art historian of the time and a conservator at the Louvre. Though there are many eyewitness accounts of the events, all are biased to one side or the other, as Nicola Lambourne has shown. "Production versus Destruction: Art, World War I, and Art History," *Art History* 22 (1999). 347-363

[2] Roger Gilman evaluates various accounts of the bombing and concludes that the incendiary bombs were the major cause of the ensuing damage. "The Theory of Gothic Architecture and the Effect of Shellfire at Rheims and Soissons," *American Journal of Archaeology* 24, 1 (1920). 37-72

[3] "Germans Regret Rheims," *NYT*, 21 September 1914. 1

[4] Rotogravure was a new printing process that allowed newspapers to print high-quality images on poor-quality newsprint paper. The *NYT* was the first to use the process in the United States (December 1912). In March 1914, shortly before the outbreak of war, the paper began printing mid-week and Sunday "pictorial" sections, thus providing a rich new forum for images of the war. Recognizing the value of these images, the Library of Congress has recently devoted a publicly accessible digital database to them. Entitled "Newspaper Pictorials: World War I Rotogravures," the collection features thousands of scanned images from the *NYT* and *New York Tribune*: http://memory.loc.gov/ammem/collections/rotogravures. Postcards, which had proliferated at the turn of the century, became, during World War I, the ultimate vehicle for propaganda. Their visual appeal, combined with free postage for soldiers and transparency for war censors, made them extraordinarily popular. See John Fraser, "Propaganda on the Picture Postcard," *Oxford Art Journal* 3, 2 (1980). 39-47

[5] For contemporary accounts see Michel Le Grand, *Reims* (Grenoble: B. Arthaud, 1932); and a Michelin guide entitled *Rheims and the Battles for its Possession: A Panoramic History and Guide* (Clermont-Ferrand: Michelin and Cie., 1920). For more reactionary, illustrated versions see Maurice Landrieux, *La Cathédrale de Reims; un crime Allemand* (Paris: Renouard, H. Laurens, 1919); and Pierre

Antony-Thouret, *Reims au lendemain de la guerre: la cathédrale mutilée, la ville dévastée* (Paris: Editions J. Budry, 1927). Lambourne, "Production versus Destruction," has deftly outlined the various arguments of the Franco-German "propaganda battle" and noted that there is no "truth" about war, arguing that all accounts of the Reims bombing were based on the national rivalries responsible for the war itself.

[6] A cursory search for "Reims" or "Rheims" and "cathedral" in the historical *Reader's Guide to Periodical Literature*, coupled with a search on ebay, gives one a sense of the pervasiveness of Notre-Dame de Reims in World War I-era America, as does browsing the "Newspaper Pictorials: World War I Rotogravures" database.

[7] For pre-war interest in Reims see, for example, "The Most Envied Town in the World," *NYT*, 26 September 1909; and "Rheims cathedral, where kings were crowned," *Century* 73 (1907). 936-945. For more about the American obsession with things French see M. H. Dunlop, *Gilded City: Scandal and Sensation in Turn-of-the-Century New York* (New York: William Morrow, 2000).

[8] Because of the abundance of material depicting the cathedral's bombardment, I will limit my discussion of the press primarily to the *NYT*, both the city's "finest and most dependable" during the war and also an important national newspaper of record. See "Newspapers" and "New York Times" in *The Encyclopedia of New York City*, ed. Kenneth T. Jackson (New Haven: Yale University Press, 1995), 809-820, 846-848. Although eastern perspectives often differed greatly from those in the rest of the country, they exerted a great deal of influence on western readers. Arkansas Senator Norris, for example, accused the eastern papers of creating war fever so that rich eastern industrialists could profit from their links to Great Britain. See David M. Kennedy, *Over Here: The First World War and American Society* (New York: Oxford University Press, 1980). 21

[9] Kennedy, *Over Here*, provides an excellent summary of American attitudes.

[10] This number is extrapolated from a word search for "cathedral and Rheims" in the *Historical Times* database, which returns thirty-four mentions, not all directly related to the cathedral.

[11] Advertisements in the *NYT* suggest the fascination that the cathedral's bombing exerted over the public.

[12] "The Great Crime at Rheims," *NYT*, 22 September 1914. This was well before the 7 May 1915 sinking of the Lusitania and the anti-German sentiment it would breed in the United States.

[13] Both countries staged protests at the German Embassy. "Special cable to the *NYT*," *NYT*, 22 September 1914.

[14] Other periodicals that quickly reported the damage included *The Nation, Catholic World*, *Living Age*, and *The Outlook*. For coverage of German reports, see "Damage Slight, Berlin Says," *NYT*, 23 September 1914; "Staff's Statement on Rheims," *NYT*, 24 September 1914; and "Charges French Outrage," *NYT*, 25 September 1914. Part of the pro-French bias on the part of American reporters may well have been due to the fact that more of them were allowed to observe from behind French lines. As Robert Lebeck has noted, press photography was highly

restricted in all countries and subject to severe censorship, especially in Germany. See the chapter "Pressefotografie im Erseten Weltgrieg 1914-1918/Press Photography in the First World War," in *Kiosk: A History of Photojournalism* (Cologne: Steidl Publishing, 2002). 92-108

[15] Quoted in "Premier Poincare [sic] Grateful," *NYT*, 30 May 1924.

[16] After Kaiser Wilhelm allowed some restorations in early 1917, deferring to Pope Benedict's request that he respect the cathedral, German troops renewed their fire in July of that year and continued to bombard the cathedral until the last month of the war. For the irony of this agreement to permit restorations only to resume bombardments see "The End of Rheims," *NYT*, 20 April 1918. The last shots were fired on 9 October 1918. For the alleged "torture" of the cathedral see, for example, "Special cable to the *NYT*"; "French's Report is Optimistic," *NYT*, 25 September 1914; "Rheims crumbling under German fire," *NYT*, 25 July 1917; and "Completing Futile Devastation," *NYT*, 26 July 1917. Torture was a commonly used analogy to refer to the cathedral's treatment, particularly because the Germans could have destroyed it quickly if they had wanted to, since they were firing at short range. See Francis W. Kelsey, "Rheims Cathedral After German Slow Torture," *NYT*, 30 November 1919.

[17] For French outrage see "French Press Aroused," *NYT*, 22 September 1914. The pages of illustrated French magazines such as *Illustration* and *Le Panorama de la Guerre* are filled with pieces about the cathedral. The French accused the Germans of purposeful destruction in accordance with the wishes of Goërres, German author of a 1914 text entitled *Christian Mysticism*: "Destroy, reduce to ashes, this Rheims basilica, where Chlodovic was consecrated, and where was born that empire of the Franks, those turncoat brothers of the noble Germans; burn the Cathedral." Quoted in *Rheims and the Battles for its Possession*. 31; Lambourne, "Production versus Destruction," analyzes the excesses of such discourse. Joëlle Prungnaud provides more such literary examples in *Figures littéraires de la cathédrale: 1880-1918* (Villeneuve d'Ascq: Presses universitaires du Septentrion, 2008). 231-242

[18] Emile Mâle, "La Cathédrale de Reims," *La Gazette des beaux-arts,* ser. 5, 63, 1 (1921). 73-88. See also Emile Mâle, *La Cathédrale de Reims* (Paris: Bloud and Gay, 1915). He denigrated German art in a three-part series of articles: Emile Mâle, "Etude sur l'art allemande," *La Revue de Paris*, 15 July 1916. 225-248; Emile Mâle, "Etude sur l'art allemande," *La Revue de Paris*, 1 August 1916. 489-520; Emile Mâle, "Etude sur l'art allemande," *La Revue de Paris*, 1 September 1916. 5-38; Lambourne, "Production versus Destruction." discusses the ways in which wartime patriotism drew him into writing such manifestly untrue things.

[19] Rodin's love of the cathedral is evident in *Les Cathédrales de France* (Paris: Librairie Armand Colin, 1914). His quotation, like that of Rolland, is cited in Elizabeth Emery, *Romancing the Cathedral: Gothic Architecture in Fin-de-Siècle French Culture* (New York: State University of New York Press, 2001). 161-171

[20] Edmond Rostand, "The Cathedral of Reims," *Literary Digest* 49 (5 December 1914). 1140; Emile Verhaeren, "Cathedral of Reims," *Catholic World* 100 (February 1915). 598-600; Pierre Loti, "At Martyred Soissons," *NYT*, 19 December 1915; Grace Walcott Hazard Conkling, "Rheims Cathedral, 1914,"

Century 89 (December 1914). 253; and Grace Walcott Hazard Conkling, "Rheims-1918," *Century* 97 (November 1918). 144; McLandburgh Wilson, "Rheims Cathedral," *Living Age* 285 (19 June 1915). 706; and Margaret Steele Anderson, "Rheims," *Current Opinion* 64 (January 1918). 54

[21] Cram described the west portal as "one vast gangrenous wound" in a lecture entitled "Reims Cathedral," later published in *Yale Review* 8 (October 1918). 40. See also Jean A. Picard, "War's Influence on French Literature," *NYT*, 8 October 1916.

[22] Douglass Shand-Tucci, *Ralph Adams Cram: Life and Architecture*, 2 vols. (Amherst: University of Massachusetts Press, 1995-2005). Architect Whitney Warren (later to be responsible for the reconstruction of Louvain library) made several visits to inspect Notre-Dame de Reims for the French and reported his horror at the devastation. Whitney Warren, "Rheims Edifice Likely to Fall," *NYT*, 15 May 1917. Thomas Hastings and Robert Tappan were among the first to inveigh against the vandalism in the New York press. See "Architects Voice Protests," *NYT*, 22 September 1914.

[23] "Stop War Vandals, is Architects' Plea," *NYT*, 18 November 1914. German citizens themselves were horrified to learn of the shelling. A notable example is that of art historian Wilhelm Vöge, a specialist of medieval art, who was so traumatized by the images of Reims—"*his* cathedral"—in flames, that the event is alleged to have contributed to his subsequent nervous breakdown. See Erwin Panofsky, "Wilhelm Vöge: A Biographical Memoir," trans. Ernest C. Hassold, *Art Journal* 28 (1968). 35

[24] Ralph Adams Cram, "The Mediaeval Synthesis," in *The Substance of Gothic* (Boston: Marshall Jones Company, 1925). 150. This book consists of published lectures given in November and December 1916 at the Lowell Institute.

[25] See Shand-Tucci, *Ralph Adams Cram*. 2:175

[26] Cram, "The Medieval Synthesis." 149-150 seemed particularly haunted by the image of stained glass as war trophy, reprising it in a 1917 lecture: "the splinters are become the settings in soldiers' rings." Ralph Adams Cram, "Reims Cathedral," *Yale Review* 8 (October 1918). 42. This article was also published in French as a free-standing booklet. Ralph Adams Cram, *La Cathédrale de Reims, Hier-Aujourd'hui-Demain* (Cambridge, MA: Marshall Jones Co., 1918).

[27] I am extrapolating primarily from lectures given in 1916 and 1917 and later published as Cram, *The Substance of Gothic*; and Cram, "Reims Cathedral." In these works, as in Ralph Adams Cram, *Heart of Europe* (New York: Charles Scribner's Sons, 1915), he follows the same rhetorical pattern of describing the value of the art before lamenting its destruction.

[28] Cram, "Reims Cathedral." 40

[29] Ibid. 44, 46

[30] Quoted in Shand-Tucci, *Ralph Adams Cram*. 2:177

[31] The term "martyr" was invoked so regularly in World War I that it became the standard adjective applied to war-damaged towns. Nicola Lambourne, *War Damage in Western Europe* (Edinburgh: Edinburgh University Press, 2001). 19

[32] Cram, *Heart of Europe*, repeats these ideas regularly throughout the book,

especially in the first chapter, "A Sanctuary Laid Waste," and the final one, "Ex Tenebris Lux." Journalists proposed that the only possible reason for the continued shelling was to serve as "a warning to the whole world of what it means to oppose Germany." See "Avenging Reverse by Shelling Reims," *NYT*, 22 April 1918; G. H. Perris makes a similar claim in "Ruin of Rheims now complete," *NYT*, 22 April 1918.

[33] Cram, "Reims Cathedral." 46-47

[34] The illustrated periodicals of the time are full of eyewitness reports describing the damages, signed by specialists of medieval art. Kathryn Brush discusses the interesting case of American art historian Arthur Kingsley Porter, who hired his own driver to take him on a tour of the devastated monuments while shelling was still taking place. Kathryn Brush, "The Capitals from Moutiers-Saint-Jean (Harvard University Art Museums) and the Carving of Medieval Art Study in America after World War I," in this volume.

[35] Maurice Landrieux, "Reims must be restored!" *NYT*, 17 October 1920. This phenomenon likely resulted from the unpopularity of Catholicism in largely Protestant turn-of-the-century America; referring to the cathedral in more universal terms was a way of building greater sympathy for it. For the history of anti-Catholicism in America see Ryan K. Smith, *Gothic Arches, Latin Crosses: Anti-Catholicism and American Church Designs in the Nineteenth Century* (Chapel Hill: The University of North Carolina Press, 2006); and Philip Jenkins, *The New Anti-Catholicism: The Last Acceptable Prejudice* (Oxford: Oxford University Press, 2004). Americans may also have simply been emulating their secular European counterparts who, as I argue in *Romancing the Cathedral*, had largely divested Gothic cathedrals of their religious signification by the turn of the century; artists and novelists had begun presenting them as rich symbolic structures capable of supporting a variety of different values.

[36] "Symbol of France—And a Glory of the World," *NYT*, 10 July 1938; "Rheims Awaits her restoration," *NYT*, 11 June 1919.

[37] Victor Turner, "Symbolic Studies," *Annual Review of Anthropology* 4 (1975). 150-151, 154

[38] Reporters' obsession with Reims may also have stemmed from a 1914 French law ("Loi du 5 août 1914") forbidding the press to comment about military activities. As a result, journalists may have projected the fate of the Allied soldiers into recognizable symbolic structures such as Reims. See Lambourne, "Production versus Destruction." 355-356

[39] See the Library of Congress database of "World War I Posters": http://lcweb2.loc.gov/pp/wwiposquery.html

[40] See "Mr. Bennett writes from the Front," *NYT*, 28 November 1915; Loti, "At Martyred Soissons," described the German devastation of Soissons Cathedral in similar terms.

[41] See the statement of Rolf William Bauhan, architect in charge of work of the American Students' reconstruction unit in the Department of the Aisne, France. "Why Rebuild War Wasted France?" *NYT*, 5 March 1922.

[42] "May Repair Rheims Wreck," *NYT*, 24 September 1914.

[43] See Elizabeth Emery, "Postcolonial Gothic: The Medievalism of America's 'National' Cathedrals," forthcoming in *Medievalisms and the (Post)Colony*, ed. Nadia Altshcul and Kathleen Davis (Baltimore: Johns Hopkins University Press).
[44] See the report about this talk in "Germans Blame Mercier," *NYT*, 23 May 1918.
[45] Janet Adams Strong provides an excellent analysis of the design competition at Saint John in "The Cathedral of St. John the Divine in New York" (Ph.D. diss., Brown University, 1990).
[46] For an overview of American reactions to the war see Kennedy, *Over Here*. He discusses Wilsonian propaganda in the chapter entitled "The War for the American Mind." 45-92
[47] Images distributed via the periodical press during wartime had been a recognized way of educating the public since the mid-nineteenth century. See Michèle Martin, *Images at War: Illustrated Periodicals and Constructed Nations* (Toronto: University of Toronto Press, 2006).
[48] Lebeck, "Pressefotografie." 92
[49] For the "truth" value of photographs at the turn of the century, see Robert Taft, *Photography and the American Scene: A Social History, 1839*-1889, 7th ed. (New York: Dover Publications, 1964).
[50] See Fraser, "Propaganda on the Picture Postcard." 42
[51] Lambourne, "Production versus Destruction." 354 discusses the French photographic advantage in this propaganda battle. A postcard in my collection shows how the French continued to emphasize German wrongdoing after the war by distributing images of the damage. Sent home by an American tourist in 1922, the correspondent discusses the cathedral, remarking how depressing it is to see the damage and commenting that it may take thirty years to rebuild.
[52] See the numerous *NYT* articles to the effect that the French had drawn fire, including "Rheims is laid in ruins," *NYT*, 21 September 1914; "Damage Slight, Berlin Says," *NYT*, 23 September 1914; and "How Germans Shift Blame," *NYT*, 27 May 1917.
[53] Fraser, "Propaganda and the Picture Postcard." 42
[54] *War Messages*, 65th Congress, 1st session, Senate Document No. 5, Serial No. 7264, Washington, D.C., 1917. 3-8
[55] They were of colored velvet, "a gown that might have been worn by one of Burne-Jones's saints or a saint in a cathedral window." "Callot Introduces Cathedral Gowns and Decollete [sic] Effects," *NYT*, 7 October 1917. For Guilbert's medieval concerts in America see Elizabeth Emery, "From Cabaret to Lecture Hall: Medieval Song as Cultural Memory in the Performances of Yvette Guilbert," *Studies in Medievalism* 15 (2006). 3-25
[56] The design was proposed by Alfred C. Bossom "in the style of the great cathedral at Rheims which underwent martyrdom at German hands." See "Keen Rivalry in War Memorial Designs," *NYT*, 14 December 1919.
[57] One way of gauging the extent of the marketing phenomenon associated with Reims is by examining the Reims-related paraphernalia from World War I available for purchase today on ebay.
[58] "Photographs of Cathedrals at the Brooklyn Museum," *NYT*, 29 September

1915. The featured churches were the cathedrals of Reims and Amiens, the abbey church of Saint-Remi and the church of Saint-Jacques at Reims, the cathedral of Châlons-sur-Marne, the collegiate church of Saint-Quentin, Rouen Cathedral, and the abbey church of Saint-Ouen at Rouen. The exhibition's overtly stated goal was to "demonstrate the existence in all the mentioned churches of constructive refinements hitherto generally unnoticed or unappreciated by antiquarians and architects."

[59] "To Use Rheims Cathedral as Pantheon for the Allies," *NYT*, 18 June 1917.

[60] "Rheims Archbishop Mourns his Exile," *NYT*, 16 April 1918.

[61] Denmark and England raised a million francs through the sales of a special stamp, while other countries, including Norway and the United States, also contributed. For a summary of contributions see articles in the *NYT*, particularly "Hospital in Memory of America's Dead," *NYT*, 11 May 1919; and "Rheims Slowly Rising from Her Ruins," *NYT*, 20 September 1925. For Rockefeller's contributions see the various articles in the *NYT*, 30 May 1924.

[62] See above, n. 4; For Reims as "Mecca" see "Rheims Awaits her restoration: Tourists find her wreckage practically as the end of the fighting left it," *NYT*, 11 June 1919.

[63] Many of these fragments were returned to Reims after the public learned that France would attempt to reconstruct the pieces instead of trying to create imitations of the originals. The moral obligation to return fragments was well-publicized. See, for example, "Premier Poincare [sic] Grateful," *NYT*; and "Ethical Problem. Finder of Rheims Glass is Puzzled About Ownership," *NYT*, 28 April 1935.

[64] See Laura Morowitz, "The Cathedral of Commerce: French Gothic Architecture and Wanamaker's Department Store," in this volume.

[65] For American admiration of the medieval builders see G. H. Perris, "Rheims Battered to Bits," *NYT*, 6 July 1917; and Cram, "Reims Cathedral."

[66] See "No Gothic Fakes here, says Expert," *NYT*, 10 June 1923. There was, of course, a great deal of pre-war interest from wealthy individual collectors such as J. P. Morgan (1870-1913) and Isabella Stewart Gardner (1840-1924), but it was not on a par with the post-war period, when the general public became interested in medieval art.

[67] Thanks to Janet T. Marquardt for supplying these figures, drawn from the Medieval Academy archives and summarized in her article on the association's site: http://www.medievalacademy.org/medacnews/news_JanMarquardt.html. See also George R. Coffman, "The Medieval Academy of America: Historical Background and Prospect," *Speculum* 1 (1926). 5-18. Interest in the Academy was international.

[68] Brush, "The Capitals of Moutiers-Saint-Jean." See also Christina Nielsen, ed., *To Inspire and Instruct: A History of Medieval Art in Midwestern Museums* (Newcastle-upon-Tyne: Cambridge Scholars Publishing, 2007).

[69] Kathryn Brush, *Vastly More than Brick and Mortar: Reinventing the Fogg Art Museum in the 1920s* (New Haven: Yale University Press, 2004).

[70] Shirin Fozi, "A Mere Patch of Color: The Stained Glass of Reims Cathedral,"

(paper presented at the International Medieval Society Symposium on Memory in Medieval France, Paris, June 2007). Her comments on a draft of this essay are much appreciated.

[71] For international laws passed after World War I to protect works of art during wartime see Lambourne, *War Damage*.

THE CATHEDRAL OF COMMERCE: FRENCH GOTHIC ARCHITECTURE AND WANAMAKER'S DEPARTMENT STORE[1]

LAURA MOROWITZ

During the Christmas season of 1928, visitors to Wanamaker's famed Philadelphia store were treated to far more than the requisite Christmas garlands and oversize tree; an entire small-scale recreation of Chartres Cathedral had been erected in the Grand Court, the great lobby of the Philadelphia store. Indeed, throughout the 1920s and 1930s, the Grand Court was repeatedly turned into a fantastic, medievalesque chamber, including recreations of fourteenth-century towers, the façade of Reims Cathedral, and a replica of the rose window at Westminster Abbey [Fig. 1]. Combining medieval-style statues, banners, and flags with precise recreations of extant medieval monuments, the displays were the joint efforts of the art and decorating department of Wanamaker's and the Voigt Company, specializing in plaster ornaments, largely pre-fabricated. For many early twentieth-century Americans, Wanamaker's recreations were the closest they got to experiencing these medieval monuments. In what way were the meanings and associations of objects from the medieval era transformed by being seen in the space of the department store? This essay examines these displays and the function they served for both the Wanamaker family and for the scores of customers who visited them year after year. These medievalesque displays played a key role in imparting the larger social vision of John Wanamaker, while helping shoppers to mediate a space fraught with the conflicts of the new Age of Consumerism.

One simply cannot overestimate John Wanamaker's role in the rise of the American department store and its modern incarnation.[2] Beginning with one dry-goods store in 1861, Wanamaker built his stores into an empire numbering sixteen, with the anchor stores in Philadelphia and on Ninth Street in New York. A master of advertising and display, Wanamaker had a keen understanding of what customers wanted, which was a luxurious shopping experience combined with a sense of fair play in pricing.[3] One of his biographers noted that Wanamaker claimed "The Golden Rule of the New Testament has become the Golden Rule of Business."[4] Born into a devout Calvinist family, Wanamaker remained deeply religious all his life, continuing to teach Sunday school until his death and refraining from advertising on Sundays. Wanamaker served as secretary and president of the YMCA, and the principles of social Christianity which he imbibed there, as we shall later see, informed all of his business decisions. His success rested on the "pioneer principles of the Wanamaker store" that carried on well beyond his death. In brief they were:

> 1. To have one absolute, fixed price, plainly marked and not changed by argument.
> 2. To sell only trustworthy goods.
> 3. To welcome people into the store without urging them to buy.
> 4. To take back purchases that proved unsatisfactory.
> 5. To establish new, fair and agreeable relations between merchant and customer.[5]

These principles created a personal relationship with the customer and served as an antidote to the anonymous, exploitative rules that seemed to govern the capitalist marketplace.

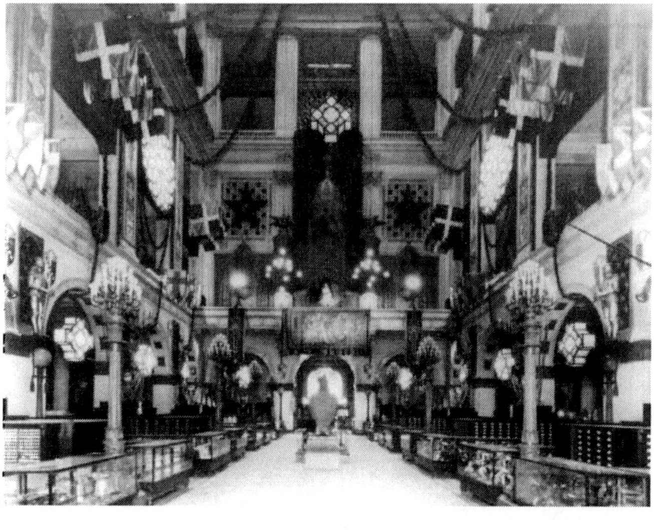

Fig. 1 Grand Lobby, December 1928, Wanamaker's Philadelphia (Photo: Wanamaker Collection, Historical Society of Philadelphia)

If customers wanted a bargain, they equally craved a glamorous and exciting shopping experience. Learning from the Bon Marché in Paris, Wanamaker turned his stores, to use Rosalind William's term, into a "dreamworld."[6] The first American store to have electric lighting, telephones and elevators, Wanamaker's was also the first store to have restaurants, waiting rooms, and attending physicians. The Grand Crystal Tea Room, The Little Gray Salons, and the French Banquet and Salons rounded out the experience of high culture. Between 1896 and 1906, Wanamaker's son and heir, Rodman, purchased over six hundred paintings from the annual Paris exhibition at the French *Salon*, many of which made their way to display in either the Philadelphia or New York stores.[7]

For many, the highlight of the shopping experience focused on the massive displays erected in the colossal lobbies and courts. At no time were these displays more grandiose than during the Christmas season, the consumer holiday *par excellence* (although they were closely rivaled at Easter).[8] The story of modern Christmas is, of course, inseparable from the history of the rise of modern consumer culture. The extravaganza of gift-giving and of eye-catching Christmas displays dates to approximately the 1880s; prior to that Christmas had been a far less expensive affair, with most gifts made by hand.[9] By the late nineteenth century, department stores in Europe and the United States marshaled their efforts to attract customers at Christmas time and to encourage them to spend lavishly on gifts. William B. Waits has written on the inherent "contradiction" that the Christmas season evoked for many marketing staff; a holiday supposedly focused on family values and religious spirit became the main premise for the selling of manufactured items, which often carried negative connotations of alienated labor and cold commercial exchange. Various strategies were invented between 1880 and 1920 to lessen this friction: "disassociating manufactured items intended for Christmas gifts from the usual manufactured items intended for purchase throughout the year"; making "manufactured items seem more like handmade items"; and using Christian emblems to "consecrate their store through holiday decorations."[10] Another strategy was to incorporate all of the displays into a kind of pre-industrial and pre-capitalist setting. These strategies were embraced by a wide variety of stores both in the U.S. and Europe, for example, through the huge mock-up of medieval London mounted at F. Parsons and Sons of Stoke, Newington in England in November 1928,[11] or the luxurious Christmas catalogues issued by leading department stores each Fall. I would argue that Wanamaker's often utilized and combined these strategies to effect this disassociation.

Beginning in 1898, many of the yearly Christmas displays in the Grand Court of Wanamaker's Philadelphia store took on a decidedly medieval flavor. Two decades later, the displays became the brainchild of the art and decoration staff, led in the 1920s and 1930s by Howard Krantz [Fig. 2]. The displays were true spectacles, incorporating murals, tapestries, reliefs, architectural features, stained glass windows, banners, flags, free-standing statues, and the famed Wanamaker organ, assembled among the glittering display cases and gleaming merchandise. While certain features were based on exact models of extant medieval works (the façade of Reims, the rose window of Westminister Abbey), the displays also included works that were far more loosely based on medieval styles or themes, for example the over-life-size identical suits of armor mounted on the buttresses of the lobby arches in 1928 [Figs. 1, 8]. In general, the designers eschewed models that pre-dated the Romanesque (except in rare reference to Byzantine objects.) British and French objects were popular, especially those signifying pageantry and courtly culture such as flags and heraldry.

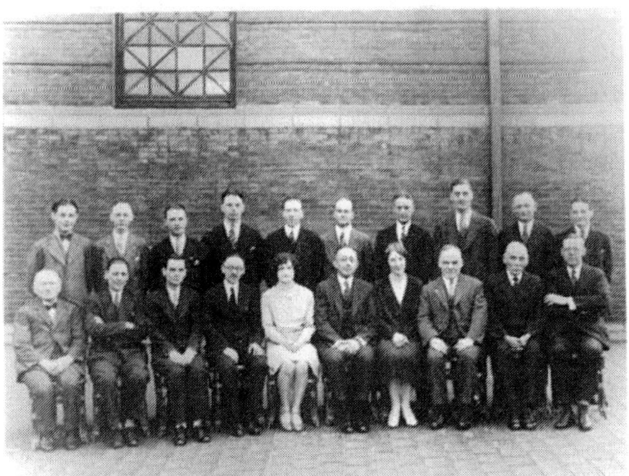

Fig. 2 Art and Decoration Staff, mid 1920s, Wanamaker's Philadelphia (Photo: Wanamaker Collection, Historical Society of Philadelphia)

The theme of the exhibits changed slightly from year to year, evoking different periods and regions. By 1924, the display brochure described a copy of a seventeenth-century Aubusson tapestry depicting the *Reges Magi*, flags and armor of the crusaders, the Greek cross, and "griffins of the ancients."[12] The centerpiece of the display was a replica of the great rose window in the south transept at Westminister Abbey. Another stained glass window ensemble from that year exemplified the eclectic mix between actual medieval stylistic features and those that more broadly signified the color and pageantry of the late medieval world [Fig. 3]. Under a rounded arch of wood were fitted three pointed panels, separated by trefoils. The two outer sections feature mirror images of a romantic-looking knight, helmet tucked beneath his arm, whose contrapposto stance and deep-eyed gaze far more closely resemble Pre-Raphaelite windows than those of the Middle Ages.[13] Nor do the letters spelling out "holiday greetings" beneath bear any resemblance to actual late medieval scripts. A similar mix of objects of dubious historical references—stained glass knights rendered in perspective, heraldic flags, and a paired "set" of rose windows—characterized other parts of the 1924 display [Fig. 4].

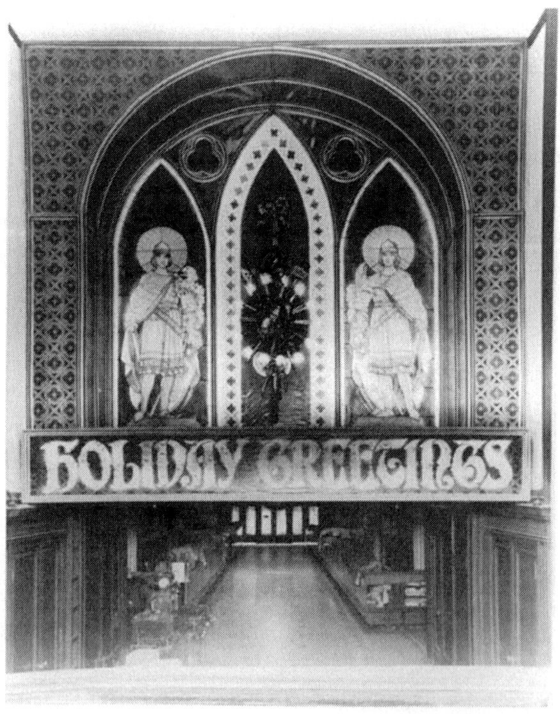

Fig. 3 "Holiday Greetings," panel, 1924, Wanamaker's Philadelphia (Photo: Wanamaker Collection, Historical Society of Philadelphia)

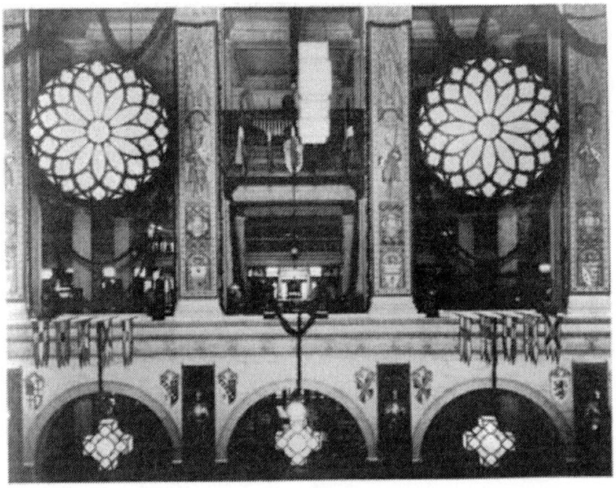

Fig. 4 Rose window display, 1924, Wanamaker's Philadelphia (Photo: Wanamaker Collection, Historical Society of Philadelphia)

Shopping at Wanamaker's in 1925 and 1926, visitors saw more historically eclectic displays focusing on ancient Rome with the inclusion of important Byzantine elements. The brochure for 1927 shows a return to the medieval period with "banners of the Middle Ages," "flags of the crusaders" (bearing a bold Greek cross), and "14th-century Gothic towers" arranged throughout the display.[14]

The lavish and monumental installations seem to have reached their highpoint in 1928, featuring newly-commissioned work of a vaguely medieval flavor, as well as several careful recreations of actual medieval objects. For the New York store, William Larkin erected a replica of the entire façade of Reims Cathedral. *Women's Wear Daily* described the "depiction of the cathedral at Reims on a scale of 60 feet for the frontage and with every one of the innumerable details of the façade faithfully reproduced."[15] The Philadelphia store also pulled out all the stops. The French artist O.D.V. Guillonet produced a "fourteenth-century Adoration of the Magi" which received a great deal of attention. The store brochure also described the "banners of the ancient kings" (flags with royal symbols relating to the ruling houses of the Middle Ages) and "banners of the crusades" (identical square flags emblazoned with bold white crosses), which were hung along with "seven allegorical plaques." Recreations of ninety stall plates from the Knights of the Order of the Garter in Saint George's Chapel at Windsor Castle were arranged together for viewing on the main floor. These plaques, and the wooden arches against which they

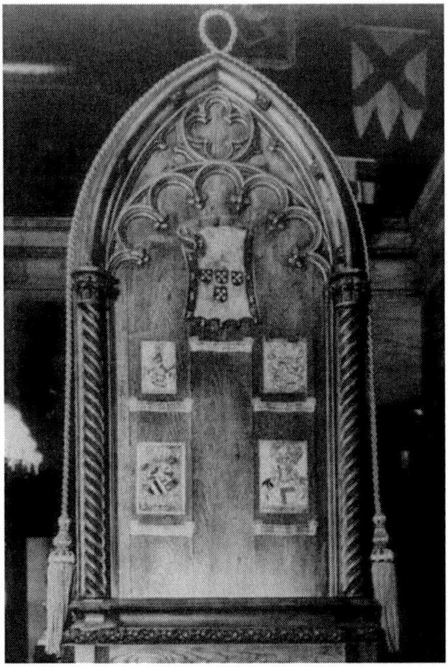

Fig. 5 Stall plates, 1928, Wanamaker's Philadelphia
(Photo: Wanamaker Collection, Historical Society of Philadelphia)

were mounted, were exact copies, showing the crests of various noble figures such as Edward King of Portugal, Sir John Talbot, and Sir Humphrey Stafford [Fig. 5]. In addition to a huge cross—the subject of several reassuring letters from the company in charge of supplying the metal bar from which it hung—was the façade of a generic Gothic French medieval cathedral, drawing features from several different monuments. The prospectus assured readers that Howard Krantz had designed the ensemble "after studious research against old documents."[16]

By 1932, the display in the Grand Court had returned to a decidedly French high Gothic flavor with a giant rose window, tall lancet windows capped by trefoils, and a gallery above the ground level arcade. A "primitive" style *Pieta* altarpiece was anachronistically mounted below the windows in a thoroughly un-thirteenth-century manner [Fig. 6].

While fine artists (many from France) were often commissioned for the paintings and murals, the majority of the work, including the recreations of stone architecture and sculpture, were carried out at the nearby studios of the Voigt Company [Figs. 7-8].[17] Taking as their motto "for better expression through the plastic arts" the firm supplied Wanamaker's with virtually all of their decorative art needs from chandeliers to "twelve identical life-size casts of the Knights Templar" (the suits of armor were actually based on sixteenth-century Italian models), to the leaded glass panels for stained-glass recreations. Located at 12th and Montgomery, the company included studios for modeling, assembly and casting, as well as a machine shop, painting shop, and inspection department. The company could supply casts for pieces in stone, wood, bronze, or iron. The materials used to recreate stone works were usually cosmopolite (a mixture of cast stone and Portland cement) or castex, a process developed for speedy and inexpensive casting. A huge variety of smaller decorative elements—from finials to shields—could be ordered directly from the catalogue, at preset prices. Many of the heraldic shields, bearing fleurs-de-lys and simplified crosses, as well as the half-life-sized Gothic angels with hands folded in prayer (available for eighteen dollars) appeared in several of the yearly displays. Krantz worked closely with the artisans of the company for the custom-made replicas. The entire decorative scheme for the Grand Court generally totaled in the neighborhood of ten thousand dollars.[18]

The careful and costly planning of these displays raises important questions about how they were intended to function, and how they were understood by audience and designers. Why did the Christmas decoration return, year after year, to medieval period designs and recreations? What functions were served by evoking these monuments and the medieval world of heraldry, chivalry, and Christian symbolism? How was the symbolism of the French and English Gothic cathedral transformed by its inclusion in the ur-modern space of mass consumption? To what extent did these displays cancel out the "nationalistic" reading of the cathedrals that prevailed throughout the nineteenth century, or contribute to a "patriotic" embrace of Christmas? The remainder of this paper will be devoted to exploring the appeal of these works for both the Wanamaker family and for the millions of customers who witnessed these displays. We can begin by understanding the appeal of these medieval displays for their originator, John Wanamaker, and then examine the multiple, and even contradictory functions of medieval reference in the context of the 1920s and 1930s. In doing so we will attempt to discover how these displays furthered John Wanamaker's original aims of uniting religion and business, as well as his notion of Social Gospel Christianity. We will also explore how the religious associations of the medieval cathedral worked within the larger context of the department store display.

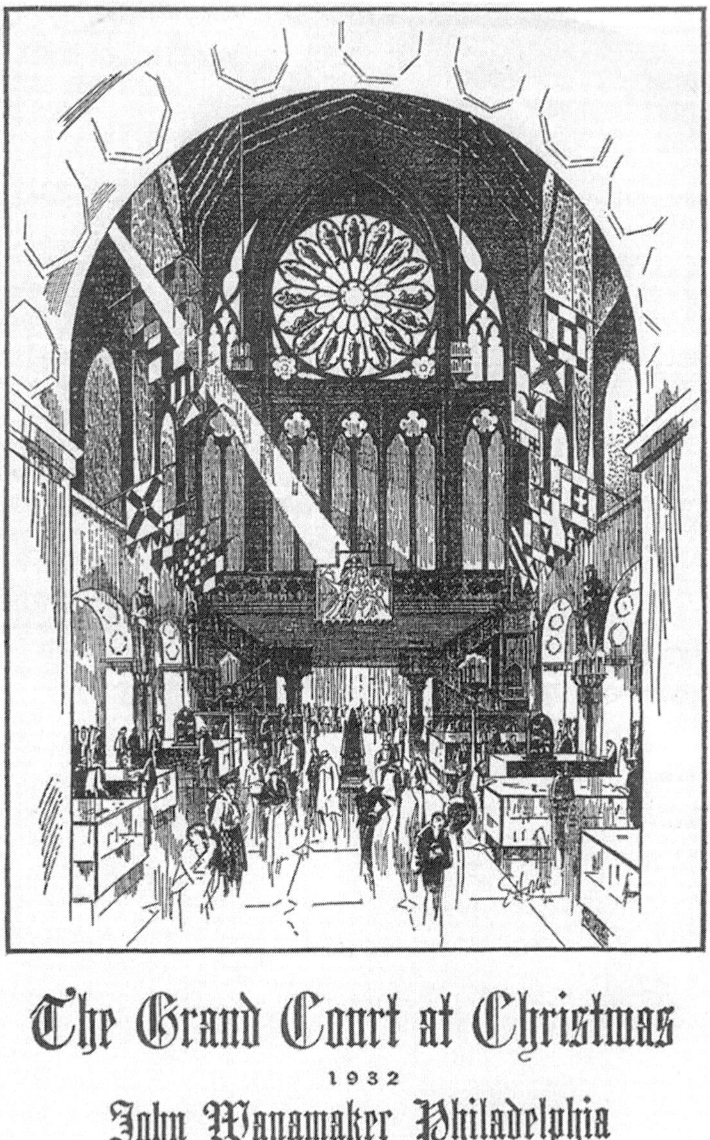

Fig. 6 "The Grand Court at Christmas, 1932, John Wanamaker, Philadelphia," cover of Wanamaker's brochure
(Photo: Wanamaker Collection, Historical Society of Philadelphia)

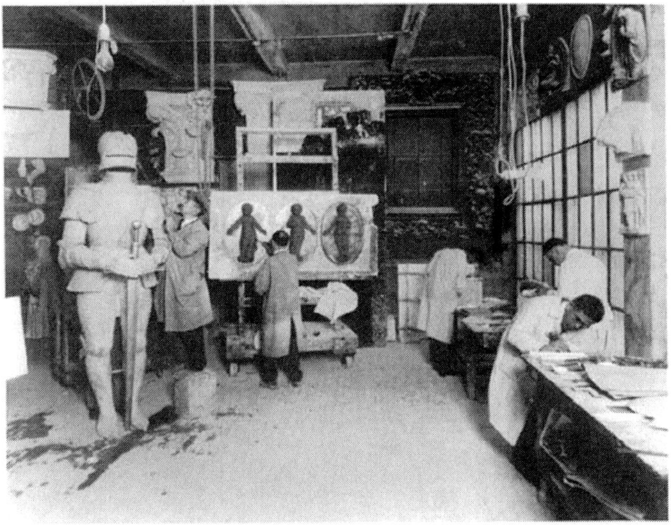

Fig. 7 Inside the Voigt Company workshops, 1924
(Photo: Wanamaker Collection, Historical Society of Philadelphia)

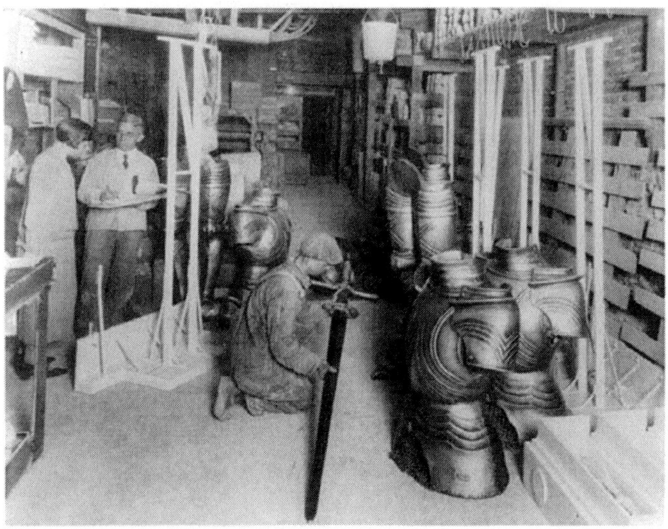

Fig. 8 Inside the Voigt Company workshops, 1924
(Photo: Wanamaker Collection, Historical Society of Philadelphia)

Although John Wanamaker had died in 1922, his social and religious philosophies guided the store under the continued direction of his son, Rodman. The elder Wanamaker, an unabashed evangelist, who once turned over his store to Dwight Moody for a religious revival, subscribed to what has been called the Social Gospel or Social Christianity.[19] For him, Christian ideals and the teaching of Jesus Christ had to benefit society at large. Rather than a Socialist revolution, the transformation of society would come about through the practice and spread of Christian ethics. Capitalism was not an evil. On the contrary, properly harnessed, capitalism could lead to increased prosperity for all. As he noted, "I am glad to stand up to say that religion is the only investment that pays the largest dividends possible to receive, both in this life and in that to come."[20] For Wanamaker, the civic and the religious were inseparably intertwined, and he was widely hailed as a leader in both domains.

This blending of the two realms was one of the central credos to which Wanamaker subscribed throughout his life; by dedicating a portion of his enormous profits to social good (like the costly public Christmas displays), a rich man *could* enter heaven. With other wealthy industrialists and businessmen of his day, Wanamaker reconciled activities in the cut-throat domain of retail and in the religious sphere through belief. Bruce Barton, author of the phenomenal best-seller of 1925, *The Man Nobody Knew*, which portrayed Jesus Christ as a successful business man and advertising agent, was himself the founder of the advertising firm of Batten, Barton, Durstine and Osborne, established in 1919.[21] Wanamaker himself made explicit the connection between the medieval cathedral and the modern sites of commerce, noting that advertisements, "…are the lesson books of the uneducated,"[22] an explicit updating of the notion of the cathedral as the "bible of the poor."[23]

A widely read man, it is logical to assume that Wanamaker would have been familiar with texts such as Barton's, and with the writings of the Reverend George Herron (1862-1925) whose *Christian Society* is a key blueprint of the Social Gospel movement. In his published sermon, "The Message of Jesus Christ to Men of Wealth," Heron claimed that:

> We are not on a vacation from God. He sends forth every man to be a guardian of his fellow man; and the businessman who fails to be a Christ to the world has made a disastrous and irreparable business failure. A man of business has no more right to make personal profit the supreme purpose of his store, his shop, his capital, his factory, his railway, than Jesus had to work miracles for personal profit.[24]

Further, Heron frankly compared the marketplace to a church and the pioneering and generous businessman to the noble crusaders of the Middle Ages:

> History has never presented to man an opportunity richer than yours. You can make the market as sacred as the church. You can make the whirl of industrial wheels like the joyous music of worship. You can be the knights of the noblest chivalry the world has ever seen….[25]

Undoubtedly, it was a similar aim to reconcile the profit-driven world of retail merchandising with a socially informed Christianity that inspired Wanamaker to exhibit, year after year, the Passion paintings of Mihály Munkácsky in the Grand Court during Easter season. John Wanamaker first purchased *Christ before Pilate* (1881) and *Christ on Golgotha* (1884) in the 1880s, paying more for them than had been spent on the works of any living artist up to that point.[26] These pieces occupied pride of place in Wanamaker's extensive art collection, which included paintings by several old masters, as well as dozens of medalled French *Salon* artists. Sent on numerous church tours with the aim of reaching a non-museum going public, *Christ before Pilate* and *Christ on Golgotha* were displayed every Easter in Wanamaker's from 1911 until the sale of the Wanamaker firm in 1988.

Wanamaker's purchase and frequent public exhibition of the Munkácsy paintings were an extension of the ideas that fueled the Christmas displays. As he saw it, the works offered great pleasure and transmitted cultural values to the audience who saw them, while relaying a crucially important religious message. A 1939 advertisement for the exhibition of the paintings in the New York store declared of Wanamaker that "it was his desire to make possible for every person in the United States to share Munkácsy's magnificent art with him! He understood the immense spiritual value that had come into his possession."[27] A letter written to friend Eugenia Bacon in 1898 reveals Wanamaker's sensitivity to charges that the paintings were simply a way of hooking people into the store:

> The fact that I have owned the two Munkácsy pictures of *Christ Before Pilate* and *Christ on Calvary* and that 8/10ths of the time they have been packed away in the dark will prove to you that I am not willing to use a masterpiece of the Christ in connection with my business.[28]

The Easter displays of the Passion scenes form a corollary to the lavish Gothic Christmas decorations [Fig. 9].

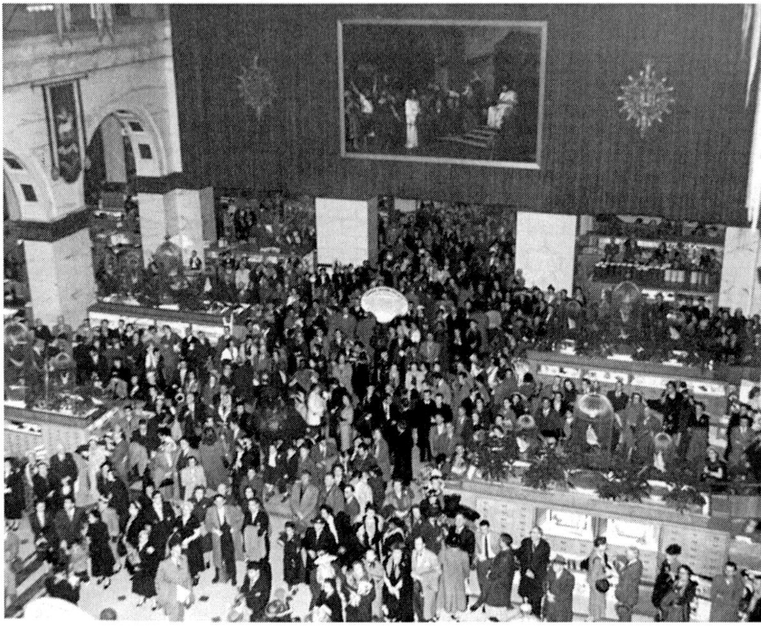

Fig. 9 Mihály de Munkácsy's *Christ before Pilate* (1881) hanging in the Great Rotunda, Wanamaker's Philadelphia, undated (Photo: Wanamaker Collection, Historical Society of Philadelphia)

While Wanamaker strove to intertwine his religious, civic, and business goals through lavish displays often focused on Christian themes, the medieval references of the ensembles mounted by Krantz could have a multiplicity of meanings and associations. Displays, interpretive guides, and quotes printed in store brochures all encouraged the public to read them in various ways. Along with the displays the department store often printed "keys" to the tableau, indicating to visitors the monument on which the work was based. Their explanation of the iconography or Christian symbolism of the work remained minimal (perhaps to avoid alienating non-Christian shoppers), focusing instead on a world of color and pageantry:

> At the head of the Court second floor, are subjects from a series of old world cathedrals that give a pulsating center to this illusion—their symbolism of figures and color, the persistence of ideals of the early centuries.[29]

It was this solid lineage and chivalric idealism that the designers hoped to evoke, beyond mere historical reference. Phrases such as "old world" and "persistence of the ideals of the early centuries" signaled a certain reactionary nostalgia. It functioned, like the Gray Salons and the Grand Crystal Tea Room, to invite the department store visitor into a world of luxury and lineage formerly reserved for the aristocracy.[30] As in his references to "old world documents" and "ancient kings," the precise periodization or citation of a motif seems to have been of far less concern to Krantz than the evocation of something timeless and noble.

While such strategies clearly appealed to the status-conscious shopper, the democratic associations of the Gothic cathedral, first fixed by writers like Victor Hugo and William Morris, were also in tune with the public image and reputation of the Wanamaker's store.[31] Although innovative formal and iconographic studies on the cathedral appeared in the writings of medieval art historians in the 1920s,[32] the displays of this period harked back to the nineteenth-century notion of the cathedral as the best possible symbol of pre-industrial life. The image of the cathedral as the product of an inspired community of workers—popularized in countless nineteenth-century novels and art-historical texts from John Ruskin to J.K. Huysmans—dovetailed with Wanamaker's vision of his own enterprise.[33] From early on, Wanamaker concerned himself with improved conditions and wages for his employees and was one of the first to offer profit-sharing, health benefits, two-week vacations, and pleasant working conditions.[34] In hundreds of published editorials, Wanamaker consistently extolled a simple pride in labor, urging that the lowliest of jobs carried no stigma if done well. Moreover, the corporate identity embodied by one's place in the medieval guild or Church could now be reified in the company itself, as in Case Gilbert's Woolworth Building, which drew explicitly on Gothic models for its silhouette, towers, and allegorical plaques on the façade.[35]

Another way in which medieval references may have functioned in the context of the department store was to counteract the image of the commodity-hungry and machine-driven modern business emporium. Through the writings of Hugo, Ruskin, and Morris, among others, the Middle Ages emerged as a model for organic craftsmanship, "joy in labor" and inspired production.[36] Setting the mass-produced objects for sale in the environment of a medieval court or cathedral lent them an "authentic" air and helped to transform the space of distribution and consumption. As in the medievalesque Christmas displays, Wanamaker's sponsored another event in the early 1920s that simultaneously engaged Christian symbolism, medieval craftsmanship, and modern selling techniques. The Grand Court became the setting for the production of handcrafted and religiously inspired works: the emporium was transformed into the medieval craftsman's shop. In 1924—the very year in which the rose window of Westminster was first displayed—Rodman Wanamaker helped to sponsor the visit of several of the key actors in the Oberammergau Passion Play, including those playing Christ, Judas, and Peter, to New York [Fig. 10].

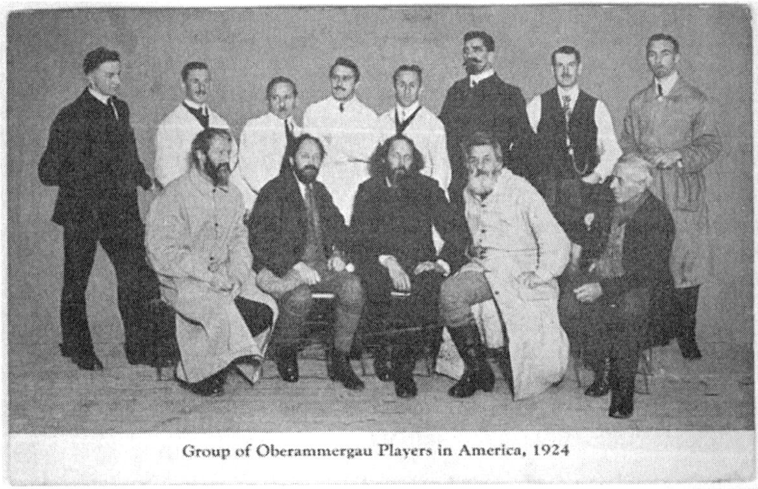

Fig. 10 Group of Oberammergau Players in America, 1924, postcard (Photo: Collection of the Author)

A result of the desperate German economic depression of the 1920s, the centuries-old play was in danger of folding due to lack of funds, when an American committee was formed to rescue the production. In addition to financing their trip, Rodman came up with a fascinating idea—he would sell the medievalesque handmade wares of this isolated Bavarian village, many explicitly religious such as carved crucifixes—in the New York Department store. The actors set up shop in Wanamaker's, where they created their wares before a live audience. As advertised in the "Store News" running in the 12 August 1924 *New York Times*, the sale was held in the "China and Pottery Gallery," which displayed "2700 Art Pieces of the Passion Player Handicraft." Customers were urged to help the poor Bavarian village:

> The constructive task of saving the village and play has been accomplished; there remains these art pieces which were so successfully

> exhibited, the proceeds from the sale of which will add to the fund to support the stricken village and enable the inhabitants to make ready for the next Passion Play in 1930....The art objects range from very small carvings to great and glorious pieces of pottery, the latter all bearing the name of Anton Lang, who is a potter by trade and has three times served as the Christus in the play.[37]

The next day's *Times* carried the text of a radiogram sent from Anton Lang to the chairman of the Oberammergau Reception Committee:

> You cannot imagine the degree of encouragement and uplifting of hope that has come to the people of this village since receiving your advices [*sic*] that Mr. Rodman Wanamaker's great store has generously consented to open up its door, receive and then offer to the public for sale the carvings and pottery handicraft of our workers, which remained in America at the end of our recent tour in quest of outside markets for our wares. A final disposition of these art objects will further insure a presentation of the Passion Play in 1930 and so we have no words to express to Mr. Wanamaker and yourself our deep and lasting gratitude since we know that a translation of our art products into cash will enable us to tide over the gap between the perplexities of today and the better conditions we all hope for in the near future.[38]

The wares "went rapidly," raising enough money to secure the 1930 production of the Passion Play along with an extra production in 1934. The modern conditions of mass production and consumption—essential to the existence of the department store—could again be obscured by embracing this pre-industrial system of production. Wanamaker's thus associated itself with a pre-industrial craft tradition and with a group of workers whose profits led directly to continuing a centuries-old Christian tradition. The workers themselves, with their long beards and smocks, were no less exotic, pre-modern, and timeless than the crafts they produced, or the statues and banners displayed each year during Christmas.

Like the village craft shop, the medieval cathedral could symbolize Wanamaker's fair contract with his workers, but could also evoke the pre-industrial social values of honesty, integrity, and face-to-face exchanges embodied in his business guarantee of a fixed price and respect for customers. This "old world" credo could serve to counteract the notion of an exploitative department store, playing on the dreams and fears of a mass audience. Along these lines, the cathedral could also play on the myth of transcending class frictions—best embodied by the "cult of the carts" at Chartres Cathedral, where legend tells that all classes of townspeople hitched themselves to carts full of building materials in a frenzy of pious industry.[39] At Wanamaker's all customers were equal; as promised "the prices are precisely the same to everybody for same quality, on same day of purchase."[40] If Hugo had fixed the notion of the cathedral as an embodiment of medieval democracy, in the twentieth century this role came to be replaced by the department store, which offered luxury and comforts fit for a king to all who were willing to patronize it. In his prospectus, Krantz incorporated Hugo's idea of the "democratic" access to beauty that these displays offered:

> After all the Decorator is a species of a super showman presenting really beautiful things—just so quickly will the public become instilled with the love of beauty; consequently it will be of benefit to everyone devoting their energies in uplifting the public educationally to the more beautiful things in life.[41]

In contrast to Wanamaker's commitment to providing a *religiously* uplifting message to his customers, Krantz—like many museum directors of the age—believed the beautiful in and of itself could be morally uplifting to the broader public. [42]

To function in these capacities—and to reach the wide audience of shoppers—these fragments of the medieval world needed to be stripped of their explicitly Catholic symbolism. Scholars such as Colleen McDannell and Leigh Eric Schmidt have noted that by the late nineteenth century, Protestant America was ready to embrace specifically Catholic symbols and art as representative of general "Christian" values. Protestant homes, for examples, often contained Catholic-style altars,[43] and, by the end of the nineteenth century, the Gothic style was used for churches of nearly every Protestant persuasion. As architectural historian Peter Williams noted of the Gothic Revival in American religious architecture, "Romanesque and Gothic revival could shelter liturgical uses thoroughly Protestant and unmedieval."[44] Like the Virgin enthroned in the Adoration or the crucified Christ by Mihály de Munkácsy, displayed in the Grand Court every Easter, the banners of the Crusaders or the Rose Window of the Gothic cathedral were not presented so much as Catholic, but as emblems of a larger Christian world of values—honesty, decency, integrity, and brotherhood.

Likewise, the explicitly nationalist or royalist tone of the English or French cathedral hardly resonated in the large Grand Court. The nationalist associations of these Gothic monuments was diffused—if not totally destroyed—by their eclectic mix. Giant Greek crosses hung over fourteenth-century French towers, beneath flags from countless nations and regions. In contrast to the nationalist appropriation of the Gothic by nineteenth-century German, French, and English proponents, such as the explicit use of medieval motifs and figures (including Jeanne d'Arc and Roland) in France following the first World War, no such "patriotic" embrace of the medieval characterized the United States. The mixing and alternating of specific medieval references—to French cathedrals, the windows of Westminster, generic angels and knights of decidedly indistinct heritage—negated any claim to contemporary American culture as the "heir" of these older nations. As such, the monuments and replicated images belonged to all shoppers equally, that is, to anyone willing to participate in the consumption of Christmas. The illusion was that the essence of the Christian world now lay neither in the great church monuments of Europe nor in the Church itself, but in the heart of the American department store, where Christmas was increasingly fetishized.[45]

The Wanamaker's displays were hardly an isolated use of the cathedral for popular spectacle and dramatic display. Numerous scholars have pointed out that the dazzling and almost surreal overabundance of department store displays shared much in common with cinemas, theater, and world's fair exhibits of the period.[46] In 1924, Norman Bel Geddes constructed a cathedral half a city block long as the set for a staging of Max Reinhardt's *The Miracle*. Studying the Gothic architecture of Mont-Saint-Michel, Saint-Malo, and several abbeys in Germany, Bel Geddes turned the Century Theater on Central Park West into an inhabitable thirteenth-century church, complete with forty-two multi-lancet windows, the largest thirty-seven feet high, and a rose window triple the diameter of ones at Notre-Dame de Paris [Fig. 11].[47] Geddes' reconstructions were so accurate, he was praised by a committee headed by Ralph Adams Cram, a prominent Boston medieval revival architect and surely one of the most important proponents of medieval architecture in his time. Geddes was subsequently nominated into the Medieval Academy of America.

As the beauty of Reims or Chartres, or even the set of *The Miracle*, transported medieval viewers to another, heavenly realm, so the department store functioned to carry its visitors to an otherworldly land of fantasy. While the conjunction of glass, color, and light immediately evokes the French Gothic cathedral, so too were these the chosen materials for transforming the spaces of capital into dream worlds. Cultural historian William Leach notes, "At the heart of the evolution of the commercial aesthetics were the visual materials of desire—color, glass and light."[48] For anyone familiar with medieval aesthetics, such materials immediately

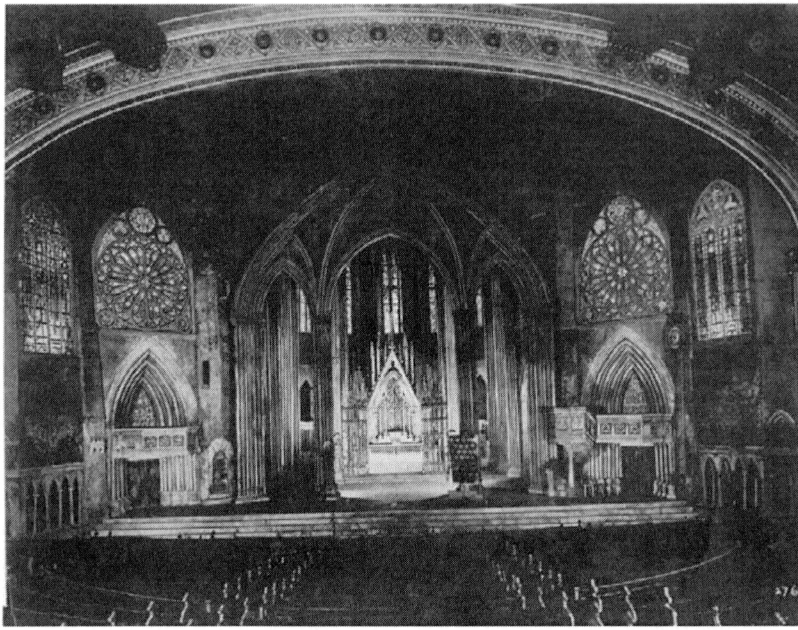

Fig. 11 Francis Brugière, Stage of the Century Theatre, New York, photograph showing medieval cathedral set for production of *The Miracle,* 1924 (Photo: Billy Rose Theatre Division, The New York Public Library for the Performing Arts, Astor, Lenox, and Tilden Foundations)

conjured the writings of Abbot Suger and other proponents of the Gothic.[49] Longing—albeit in entirely different forms—permeates both the medieval and the modern spaces of worship.

Perhaps most startling of all was the transformation of the cathedral, the symbol of an organic, inseparable totality—a medieval *Gesamtkunstwerk*—into a series of temporary, isolated parts. As such, the greatest Gothic monuments themselves seem bowed to the forces of commodification. John Wanamaker had stated:

> What is not for sale is still for sale. Whatever the possession you prize, when others see it you want to sell it to them. You may not want to be paid with money and you may not want to transfer the physical possession of the thing to another. But you do want the person to whom you show it to pay for it, in admiration and intelligent appreciation.[50]

This conjunction of worship, consumption, and the desire for transcendence, evoked through the Gothic cathedral, continued to serve as a keen marketing strategy well into the 1950s; H. and S. Pogue of Cincinnati relied on it at Easter time "…because the really beautiful reproduction of a church window is a lovely, appropriate way to show women's fashions at Easter time."[51] Even the great mountains of stone—or rather their replicas—were forced to follow the law of the commodity—fragmented, transportable, shined up like new, and paid for with the all-mighty American dollar. Now in early twenty-first century America, rather than transforming our department stores into churches, the process is well underway of transforming our churches into department stores, complete with all the razzle-dazzle of marketing, consumerism, and the ultimate reward for piety: not a place in Heaven, but the privilege, and power, of purchasing in the great cathedrals of commerce.

Notes

---

[1] I am grateful to Janet Marquardt and Alyce Jordan for inviting me to contribute to this anthology and to first present these ideas at the Medieval Academy of America in March of 2005. Janet and Alyce's careful reading of my text and suggestions are deeply appreciated as are those of the anonymous reader who provided insightful critiques. I wish to thank the helpful staff of the Wanamaker Archives at the Historical Society of Philadelphia, especially Mr. Max Moeller. My sincere thanks go also to Laurie Lico Albanese for her encouragement and assistance and for raising many interesting points in relation to Wanamaker.

[2] There are several (largely uncritical) biographies on John Wanamaker. These include Joseph H. Appel, *The Business Biography of John Wanamaker, Founder and Builder* (New York: MacMillan Co., 1930); Herbert Adams Gibbons, *John Wanamaker* (New York: Harper and Brothers, 1926); William Allen Zulker, *John Wanamaker: King of Merchants* (Wayne, PA: Eaglecrest Press, 1993).

[3] William Leach, *Land of Desire: Merchants, Power and the Rise of the New American Culture* (New York: Pantheon, 1993).

[4] Appel, *The Business Biography of John Wanamaker*. xv

[5] These principles are repeated in various forms throughout the Wanamaker's literature. See, for example, *The Golden Book of the Wanamaker Store: Jubilee Year 1861-1911* (Philadelphia: no publisher, 1911-1913).

[6] Rosalind H. Williams, *Dream Worlds: Mass Consumption in Late Nineteenth-Century France* (Berkeley: University of California Press, 1983).

[7] Gibbons, *John Wanamaker*. 77

[8] Leigh Eric Schmidt, "The Easter Parade: Piety, Fashion and Display," *Religion and American Culture* 4, no. 2 (Summer 1994). 135-164

[9] William B. Waits, *The Modern Christmas in America: A Cultural History of Gift Giving* (New York: New York University Press, 1993).

[10] Ibid. 21; Schmidt, "The Easter Parade." 233

[11] Mark Connelly, *Christmas: A Social History* (London: I.B. Tauris Publishers, 1999). See, especially, "The English Christmas and the Growth of a Shopping Culture." 189-205. The display was to have included a full-scale model of the original fifteenth-century Aldersgate.

[12] Christmas Brochure 1924, Box 127-D, Wanamaker Archives, Historical Society of Philadelphia.

[13] For example the windows in Saint Saviour's Church, Leeds, designed by Edward Burne-Jones and executed by William Morris Co. in 1897, or those designed by William Morris for Burne-Jones's home, The Grange, in Fulham in 1870.

[14] Christmas Brochure 1927, Album 127-F, Wanamaker Archives, Historical Society of Philadelphia.

[15] "Fidelity to Realism in Artistic Set in Wanamaker's Credo Display," *Women's Wear Daily*, 4 February 1928. 1

[16] Prospectus 1928, Christmas Album, 127-H, Wanamaker Archives, Historical Society of Phildadelphia.

[17] *The Catalog of Voigt Company*, 4th ed. (Philadelphia: Voight Company, 1928). A copy can be found in the Historical Society of Philadelphia.

[18] Although I do not have precise totals for each year, in 1949 the combined total was $11,000. This figure comes from a Voigt Company invoice, addressed to Philip Dengler of the Wanamaker stores. Box 199, Folder 12, Wanamaker Archives, Historical Society of Phildadelphia.

[19] Gary Scott Smith, *The Search for Social Salvation: Social Christianity and America 1880-1925* (Lanham, MD: Lexington Books, 2000).

[20] John Wanamaker, quoted in Appel, *The Business Biography of John Wanamaker*. xv

[21] Bruce Barton, *The Man Nobody Knows* (Indianapolis: Bobbs-Merrill Company, 1925). The book would go on to sell 750,000 copies. For more on Barton see Richard M. Fried, *The Man Everybody Knew: Bruce Barton and the Making of Modern America* (Chicago: Ivan R. Dee, 2005).

[22] John Wanamaker, quoted in Leach, *Land of Desire*. 44

[23] This idea was widely embraced in the late nineteenth century, appearing as a major theme in the classic text of Emile Mâle, *L'Art religieux du XIIIe siècle en France. Etude sur l'iconographie du moyen âge et sur ses sources d'inspiration* (Paris: Armand Colin, 1898).

[24] Reverend George David Heron, *The Christian Society* (Toronto: Fleming H. Revell Co., 1894). 115

[25] Heron, *The Christian Society*. 116. For an excellent discussion of medievalism and the mindset of the American industrialist see T.J. Jackson Lears, *No Place of Grace: Antimodernism and the Transformation of American Culture 1880-1920* (Chicago: Chicago University Press, 1984).

[26] Mihály Munkácsy, *Christ before Pilate* (1881) and *Christ on Golgotha* (*Christ Crucified*) (1884). Both works are currently in the possession of the Magyyar Nemzetu Galerie, Budapest. A full account of his purchase, as well as both

European and American reception of these works is given in Laura Morowitz, "A Passion for Business: Munkácsy, Wanamaker, and the Depiction of Christ in Late Nineteenth-Century America." *Art Bulletin.* (forthcoming)

[27] "John Wanamaker Presents Michael de Munkácsy's Masterpieces *Christ Before Pilate, Christ on Calvary,*" *New York Times*, 24 April 1939.

[28] Letter of John Wanamaker to Eugenia Baker, 23 November 1898, Wanamaker Archives, Historical Society of Philadelphia.

[29] Box 119, Wanamaker Archives, Historical Society of Philadelphia.

[30] This attempt to provide an aristocratic experience for the department store shopper was a key strategy from the start. See Michael Barry Miller, *The Bon Marché: Bourgeois Culture and the Department Store 1869-1880* (Princeton: Princeton University Press, 1981).

[31] In the nineteenth century, the Gothic cathedral came to embody the civic and social growth of cities and was seen to play a key role in the unification of communities. The literature on this is enormous and ever growing. For an introduction to these issues see Patricia Ward, *The Medievalism of Victor Hugo* (University Park: Pennsylvania State University Press, 1975); Kevin L. Morris, *The Image of the Middle Ages in Romantic and Victorian Literature* (Dover: Croom Helm, 1984); Paul Atterbury et al., *Pugin: A Gothic Passion* (New Haven: Yale University Press, 1994); Claire A. Simmons, *Medievalism and the Quest for the "Real" Middle Ages* (London: Frank Cass, 2000). For this argument within the largest context of medievalism see the classic study by Paul Frankl, *The Gothic* (Princeton: Princeton University Press, 1960); and Frederick S. Frank, *Guide to the Gothic: An Annotated Bibliography of Criticism* (Metuchen: Scarecrow Press, 1984).

[32] See Craig Hugh Smyth and Peter M. Lukehart, eds. *The Early Years of Art History in the United States: Notes and Essays on Departments, Teaching, and Scholars* (Princeton: Department of Art and Archaeology, Princeton University, 1993).

[33] This has been exhaustively covered in the literature. See, for example, Elizabeth Emery, *Romancing the Cathedral: Gothic Architecture in Fin-de-Siècle French Culture* (Albany: State University of New York Press, 2001). See also Susan P. Casteras, *John Ruskin and the Victorian Eye* (New York: Abrams, 1993); Elizabeth Emery, "J.-K. Huysmans, Medievalist," *Modern Language Studies* 30 (2000). 119-131

[34] See Smith, *The Search for Social Salvation.*

[35] See Margaret Heilbrun, ed., *Inventing the Skyline: The Architecture of Cass Gilbert* (New York: Columbia University Press, 2000); Barbara S. Christen and Steven Flanders, *Cass Gilbert: Life and Work* (New York: W.W. Norton and Co., 2001).

[36] See the medievalist literature cited above. The notion of "joy in labor" is found in many of John Ruskin's writings. See, for example, John Ruskin, *Time and Tide by Weare and Tyne: Twenty-five letters to a Working Man of Sunderland on the Laws of Work* (1872; reprint, London: Routledge, 1994). Letter 5. "Labour without joy is base. Labour without sorrow is base. Sorrow without labour is base. Joy

without labour is base." For the way in which the medieval artist and artisan came to function as a foil for the modern creator, Elizabeth Emery and Laura Morowitz, *Consuming the Past: The Medieval Revival in Fin-de-Siècle France* (London: Ashgate, 2003). 37-60

[37] "Final Oberammergau Sale," Advertisement, *New York Times*, 12 August 1924. 7

[38] "The John Wanamaker Store News," *New York Times*, 13 August 1924. 9

[39] See E.R. Chamberlain, *Life in Medieval France* (London: William Clowes and Sons, Ltd., 1967).

[40] This was part of the oft-printed Wanamaker Guarantee, which appeared in store literature and on numerous advertisements.

[41] Prospectus 1928, Christmas Album, 127-H, Wanamaker Archives, Historical Society of Phildadelphia.

[42] See Tony Bennett, *The Birth of the Museum: History, Theory, Politics* (London: Routledge, 1995).

[43] Colleen McDannell, *The Christian Home in Victorian America 1840-1900* (Bloomington: Indiana University Press). 43

[44] Peter Williams, "The Medieval Heritage in American Religious Architecture," in *Medievalism in American Culture,* ed. Bernard Rosenthal and Paul E. Szarmach, Medieval and Renaissance Texts and Studies, vol. 55 (Binghamton: State University of New York Press, 1989). 183

[45] J.J. Duggan, "Franco-German Conflict and the History of French Scholarship on the Song of Roland," in *Hermeneutics and Medieval Culture*, ed. Patrick J. Gallacher and Helen Damico (Albany: State University of New York Press, 1989); Michael Winock, "Joan of Arc," in *Realms of Memory: The Construction of the French Past*, ed. Pierre Nora and Lawrence D. Kritzman, trans. Arthur Goldhammer, vol. 3 (New York: Columbia University Press, 1998). 433-482

[46] See Bronner and Leach, *Consuming Visions*.

[47] There is abundant material on this colossal production at the Library of the Performing Arts, Lincoln Center, New York Public Library. Some of this material was presented by the author in a recent talk: "A Passion for Theater: Max Reinhardt's *The Miracle* and 1920s New York" (paper presented at the 21st Annual Conference in Medievalism, Ohio State University, October 2007).

[48] Leach, *Land of Desire*. 104

[49] See the classic study on Suger by Erwin Panofsky, *Gothic Architecture and Scholasticism* (Latrobe, PA: Archabbey Press, 1951).

[50] Simon J. Bronner, "Object Lessons: The Work of Ethnological Museums and Collections," in *Consuming Visions: Accumulation and Display of Goods in America 1880-1920*, ed. Simon J. Bronner (New York: W.W. Norton, 1989). 233

[51] Lester Gaba, *The Art of Window Display* (New York: Studio Publications, 1952).

THE EARLY MIDDLE AGES IN THE EXHIBITION *DEUTSCHE GRÖßE* (1940-1942)

WILLIAM J. DIEBOLD

Almost unknown in comparison to some other Nazi-sponsored museum exhibitions (e.g. *Entartete Kunst*, the 1937 show of "degenerate" art), *Deutsche Größe* (hereafter *DG*) was the largest and most important cultural-historical exhibition of the Nazi era. The show, on view from 1940 to 1942, surveyed "German greatness" from the barbarian migrations to Hitler's seizure of power. Given this chronological scope, the Middle Ages necessarily played a key role in the show. This article examines the ways in which early medieval art and history were exhibited in *DG*. The early Middle Ages was a fraught period in the Nazi understanding of the past because it was seen to involve pagan and Christian, ethnic and non-ethnic Germans, Germany and Europe. In each case, the Germanophile, neo-pagan trend of Nazi historiography that dominated during the formative years of the Party, and in the period immediately following Hitler's seizure of power in 1933, clearly favored the first term of these pairs. After the start of the Second World War, however, when the Nazi goal of German domination in Europe appeared a reality, the second term of each pair came to have at least equal importance to the first. The presentation of the early Middle Ages in *DG*, a show conceived and executed in the early years of the War, shows how these tensions in the interpretation of history were manifest in the practical space of a museum exhibition.[1]

Although an early reviewer said *DG* was "Doubtless the most innovative and impressive, the most spectacular and imposing exhibition of this sort there has ever been in Germany," it has never been the subject of a sustained study.[2] The show was organized by Alfred Rosenberg in his role as "the Führer's representative for the supervision of the entire spiritual and philosophical schooling and education of the National Socialist Party," the grandiose and expansive title Hitler gave Rosenberg, one of his earliest supporters, in 1934. Originally planned for the Nazi's Nuremberg party rally of 1940 (not held because of the war), *DG* actually opened in Munich in November of that year under the patronage of Rudolf Heß, Hitler's deputy. After being seen by 127,000 people in Munich, the show travelled to Prague, Magdeburg, Breslau, Brussels, and Strasbourg, where it closed in August of 1942. An additional 430,000 people saw it in those venues.[3]

Organized by one high Nazi Party official, sponsored by another, *DG* was granted a large budget by the Party treasurer. Given the Party's intellectual and financial sponsorship, it is not surprising that the show was deeply and frankly ideological. As the review of the exhibition in the official Nazi art journal put it: "Here, for the first time, an exhibition has been realized entirely from the political perspective."[4] This explicit ideological content makes *DG* an excellent indicator of Nazi thinking about the past. But, as I will argue, that thinking was not simple or monolithic.

In his speech opening the exhibition, Rosenberg described its aspirations:

> It is *not* the goal of the exhibition "Deutsche Größe" to bring before our eyes the *full range* of German history in *all* its highs and lows and with its *full* richness of actors; a *future time of peace may later* undertake *that* great task. *We*, instead, have given ourselves the task of choosing from the immense whole the *historically most significant* forces and the *decisive* figures of the *great* eras, lifting them up as a focus of unmediated perception so that they will have an immediate place in our consciousness. In *galleries* that do *not* (in the style of *old museums*) have a *sentimental, antiquarian* character, but rather through *architectonic* form only *refer* to and define the stylistic character of a particular era, the course of the power struggles around German land and the German Empire will rise up for those who *already* have a general understanding of these struggles (emphasis as in original).[5]

Lofty goals, but how to achieve them? As an early reviewer of the show asked: "The invisible, the abstract, thoughts, ideas, powers, forces must be made visible. But what could, what should, one exhibit?"[6] *DG*'s organizers answered this fundamental question in ways both traditional and innovative. *DG* displayed a range of historical objects: works of art, documents, artifacts, and items of material culture. Surprisingly, to modern eyes, it did this not via the original objects, but entirely through reproductions. This had not been the original intention. It was only at the end of September 1940, just over a month before the show was to open, that Rosenberg's office learned that Hitler had forbidden the display of originals because of British threats to bomb Munich.[7] Rosenberg quickly turned necessity into a virtue:

> We found ourselves forced—it turned out entirely to the good for the exhibition—to make facsimiles of all the originals so that the conception of the entire exhibition could be realized. The show thus took on a very unified and modern character and, almost unwillingly, an entirely new model for exhibition design was indeed created.[8]

In the end, an astounding 1800 reproductions were made.[9]

DG is best documented through its book-length catalogue and a larger and more lavish publication put out by its organizers in 1944.[10] This later book included photographs of the galleries as well as many of the objects from the exhibition (only a handful of these were illustrated in the original catalogue). The first edition of the original catalogue opened with a brief preface by Heß, but this had to be deleted after his embarrassing flight to England in May of 1941. It was replaced by one by Rosenberg that emphasized the importance of *DG* to the German military effort then under way: "This present struggle demands recognition about the nature and mightiness of past struggles."[11] There followed a much longer introduction by the historian Karl Alexander von Müller. This kind of collaboration between leading academics and the Nazi party was typical during the Third Reich. For example, among the professional medievalists who contributed to *DG* were Otto Brunner, Kurt Holter, Fritz Rörig, Edmund Stengel, and Franz Petri. All went on to have successful post-World War II academic careers in the Federal Republic of Germany or Austria.[12]

After these opening texts, the catalogue's organization precisely mirrors the exhibition. The exhibits occupied seventeen rooms. An entrance hall, with depictions of the German imperial eagle from different eras (the earliest a Hanseatic eagle from the fourteenth century),[13] was followed by sixteen numbered rooms: an introductory map room and fifteen rooms in chronological order, spanning German history from the migration of tribes into Germany through the "Greater German Reich of Adolf Hitler."[14] This article concentrates on the show's first two historical rooms, "Die Germanenreiche" and "Das Fränkische Reich."[15]

The period of the Germanic kingdoms was said to have begun ca. 800 BCE and reached its peak in late antiquity; at its end, Germanic rulers controlled areas across Europe. The catalogue makes clear the historical conception at work: "The entry of the Germans as a decisive historical factor into the ancient world meant the rise of a new world, the birth of Europe, and the beginning of a world history under a European sign."[16] This is a programmatic sentence. One of its core ideas, that Germans are essential to Europe, is a characteristically Nazi one, with obvious resonances to the political situation in 1940. As we shall see, this belief in Germany's central role in Europe governed the presentation of the early Middle Ages in *DG*. A second claim, that the "entry of the Germans…into the ancient world" was a mark of progress, rather than decline, while corollary to the first, is independent of it. This claim was in no way an exclusively Nazi one, but it was given a distinctively Nazi interpretation in *DG*.[17]

The founding historians of European art, from Vasari into the nineteenth century, typically saw the art and culture of the Germanic peoples as a decline from Classical antiquity. In their view, medieval art, the first European art, did not begin until the Carolingian renaissance produced images that were representational, focused on the human figure, and derived from Greco-Roman models. Germanic art was rejected because it did not represent the human figure, appeared crude in comparison to the Classical tradition, and was not made by Christians; for all these reasons, it was deemed not European.

This conception of late antiquity and the early Middle Ages as a decline from Classical antiquity underwent a severe attack in the years around 1900. The most famous critic was Alois Riegl, but the movement was a broad one; Riegl, Franz Wickhoff, Josef Strzygowski, and Heinrich Wölfflin turned the tables on the idea that the early Middle Ages was a period of decline from the Classical era and, more generally, questioned whether there were periods of art-historical decline. *DG*, by seeing the Germanic migrations as a positive development in cultural history, was very much in line with advanced historical thinking of its day. But once it was agreed that Germanic culture was not just debased Classical culture, that there were positive values in the early medieval forms of northern Europe, how to understand this art? For some, such as Strzygowski, its special value was that it was the product of a different race; for others, such as Wickhoff and Riegl, it was the product of a different intention; for Wölfflin, it was the product of a different chronological era.

It is not surprising that the Nazified presentation of this issue in *DG* did not adopt the kind of cultural relativism associated with leading art-historical and cultural-historical thinkers such as Riegl. For the Nazis, it was not enough to say that the Germans and their culture were *as* good and important as any other people or culture; their glorification of the Germans required the concomitant denigration of others. As *DG* put it, the Germans "showed themselves to be superior [to the Celts and Illyrians] not only militarily, but also culturally."[18] While the historic cultural superiority of the Germans had been trumpeted by some thinkers since the early nineteenth century, the situation in 1940 provided a rare instance when this perceived cultural superiority precisely coincided with military superiority. Thus, recent German advances into France and Eastern Europe were seen to have their exact parallel in the history of early medieval Europe.

Since this kind of typological association of past and present was a common trait of Nazi historiography and Nazi thinking in general,[19] it is not surprising that it was frequently adopted in *DG*. Thus, early Germanic life was said to be characterized by "a loyal relationship between leader and follower [*Führer und Gefolgschaft*]."[20] The reference is to the early Middle Ages, but the implication, of course, is that this is also true of contemporary German life. Likewise, the rise of the Huns is described in terms that unmistakably expressed current and obsessive German fears about domination from the East (that is, in the world of 1940, by Slavs and the Soviet Union): "While the Germanic peoples were still on the path to state formation, there rose from the Asian steppe the danger of the annihilation of emerging Europe."[21] This passage is immediately followed by an account of the heroic defeat of the Huns by the Germans, in this case in the guise of the Ostrogoths and Visigoths.

The catalogue text on this gallery ends with a frank statement of the Nazis' racial conception of history and an explanation of why the distant past of the era of migrations remains important in 1940:

> Everywhere in Europe where the Germanic peoples founded their early kingdoms, countless valuable objects of material culture remain to this day, just as do the remains of their social organization [*Volksordnung*]. Germanic blood remains alive in many peoples of our time; its role in the history and culture of these countries is immeasurable.[22]

In this statement, racial ideology meets museum design, as a grammatical and ideological parallel is drawn between the now invisible *Volksordnung* of the early Germans and their concrete and tangible material culture. This belief in the illustrative power of objects is the stock in trade of the cultural-historical exhibition, so it is not surprising that *DG* emphasized the importance of material culture to our knowledge of the Germans: "From this earliest Germanic era the German soil has preserved a large number of important finds to our day. These *irrefutable* documents show us the Germans not only as successful farmers and animal breeders, but also as technically and artistically highly gifted craftsmen (my emphasis)."[23]

So much for the verbal ideology; what about the visual? How was this conception of the history of the Germanic migrations expressed in *DG* as an exhibition? In trying to answer that question, we are aided by the catalogue, which gives a complete list of the objects displayed in each gallery (many of them were illustrated in the 1944 publication *Deutsche Grösse*) and by photographs showing the installation of the galleries. Gallery two was devoted to the early Germanic kingdoms [Figs. 1-2].[24]

DG was extremely didactic; it included works of art (in reproduction), but also maps, primary and secondary texts, models, archeological finds, and photographs. The upper walls of gallery two bore a German translation of a verse from the Eddic poem *Fafnismal* accompanied by oversized renderings of motifs from Germanic art, including swastika and eagle fibulae [Fig. 2]. Lower down, there were maps showing the situation in Europe ca. 800 BCE, when the Germanic tribes first arrived, and ca. 500 CE, at the height of their power. Not all of the works of art displayed in the gallery were made in the early Middle Ages. There was an image of the battle in the Teutoburger Forest, after a drawing by the nineteenth-century German artist Alfred Rethel. This battle of 9 CE, in which an army of Cherusci, led by Herman/Arminius, defeated the Roman imperial army under Varus, had long been represented as the founding moment of Germany's national history.[25] A monument commemorating the battle was erected in 1875, soon after the unification of Germany, in the Teutoburger Forest, the site of Varus's defeat; a model of this monument, which had the form of a column-supported cupola topped by an immense copper statue of Arminius, was freestanding on a base towards one end of the room [Figs. 1-2].

The door to the next gallery was flanked by reproductions of the Hornhausen "Reiterstein," a unique figural depiction in seventh-century German art showing an armed warrior, probably Wodan, trampling a snake; a relief with a mourning German woman; and the horn known as a *lur*. The gallery's side walls were articulated with very shallow niches formed by three Corinthian columns. In one niche appeared photographs of Theodoric's mausoleum in Ravenna and one of that ruler's coins; in the other hung photographs of two sections of the sculpted friezes from the Roman imperial columns of Marcus Aurelius and Trajan. Just to the right of this niche was the reproduction of a Roman head of a German woman.[26] The wall opposite the door was marked by a larger niche, housing vitrines with many small Germanic objects.[27]

The gallery's floor was filled with even rows of large, slightly rough, rectangular and square paving stones. In what must have been an extremely striking effect, the flat ceiling of the gallery was decorated with a room-size map showing Europe and the Mediterranean ca. 500 CE. *DG*'s most striking design feature was that each of its historical rooms mimicked an architectural monument of the era represented. Normally, the architectural source of the designs is easy to detect. But this is not the case with gallery two. According to the catalogue, "the gallery is decorated in the style of Theodoric's tomb."[28] Theodoric's tomb would, indeed, have been a fitting model; illustrated elsewhere in the room, it was centrally planned, which made it especially well suited to adaptation as gallery architecture (Charlemagne's palace chapel at Aachen provided the model for the following, Frankish gallery). Yet the gallery's flat ceiling does not obviously evoke Theodoric's mausoleum; neither do the wall niches. This restrained evocation of Theodoric's tomb reflected doubts about his status as a Nazi model.

Theodoric clearly had a lot going for him as far as *DG* was concerned. The catalogue presented Theodoric both as the most important figure of his era and a direct forerunner of the Nazis: "One is tempted to see as the goal of his diplomatic dealings a unified Germanic empire that would rule all of Europe."[29] In this exhibition devoted to German greatness, Theodoric the Great was in many ways a central figure: "For over half a century this greatest [*Größte*] of the Goths ruled; he conquered Italy and left there immortal testimonies to his greatness [*Größe*]."[30] The most important of these testimonies was the Ravenna mausoleum. While modern scholarship tends to associate Theodoric's tomb with Roman imperial mausolea and eastern Mediterranean building practices,[31] for *DG* the Ravenna structure was constructed "in the manner of old Germanic princely tombs."[32] This derivation, while not supported by most modern scholars, fit well with racialized Nazi concepts of art history.[33]

Yet the catalogue's textual insistence on the central role of Theodoric is undercut by the exhibition's design; Arminius, not Theodoric, is the visual center of gallery two. The conflict of verbal and visual here mirrors a tension in Nazi thinking about Arminius and Theodoric. Germanophile (and Nazi) historiography tended to see Arminius as an absolutely crucial figure, more important than Theodoric. The historian Karl Richard Ganzer's programmatically titled book, *Das deutsche Führergesicht* ("The Face of German Leaders"), is a chronologically arranged, thoroughly Nazified collection of over two hundred portraits of German "fighters and pioneers."[34] The book begins with Arminius and moves directly to Charlemagne, eclipsing Theodoric altogether. A similar assessment of Arminius is found in *DG*; the catalogue calls him "the first leader [*Führer*] of the Germans."[35] Although Arminius had been a favorite of German nationalists since at least the nineteenth century, he was not without his problems. One problem was historical: Arminius was not a success. The large text panel in *DG* accompanying a coin of Theodoric noted that Theodoric established the rule of his "people [*Volkes*]" on Italic soil; "in

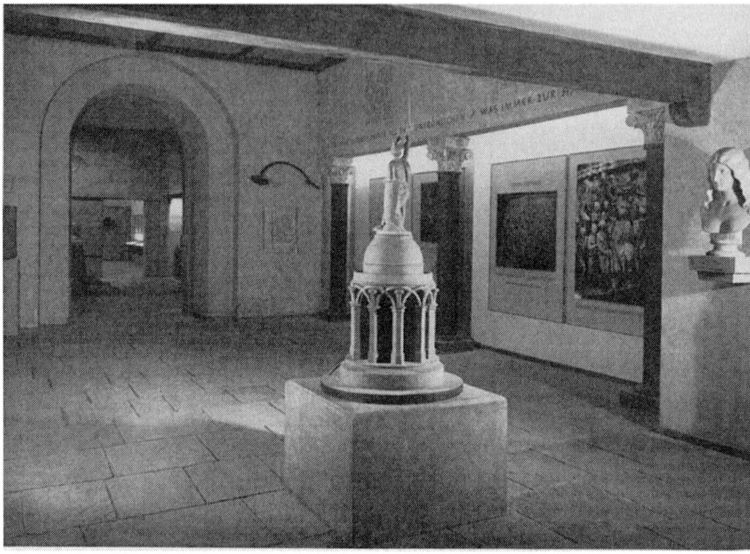

Fig. 1 "Die Germanenreiche" ("The Germanic Kingdoms"), gallery two, *Deutsche Größe,* from Karlheinz Rüdiger, "Deutsche Grösse. Ein Beispiel künstlerischer Ausstellungsgestaltung," *Die Kunst im Deutschen Reich* 5 (1941). 36

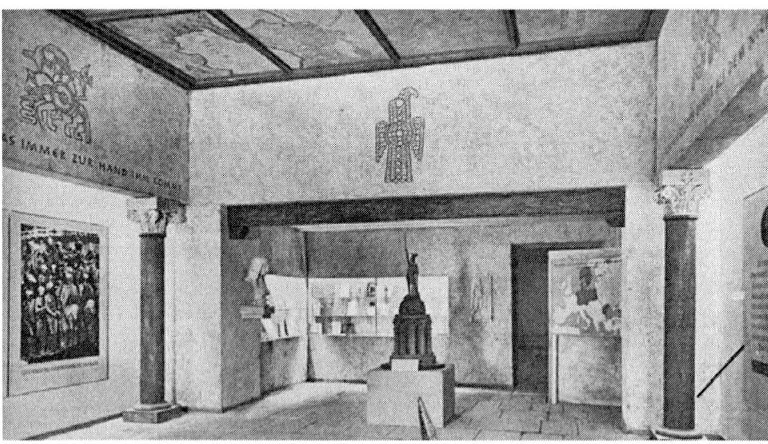

Fig. 2 "Die Germanenreiche" ("The Germanic Kingdoms"), gallery two, *Deutsche Größe,* from Karlheinz Rüdiger, "Geschichte deutscher Größe. Ansporn zur Tat des Tages," *Der Schulungsbrief* 8 (1941). unpaginated

contrast to the temporary success of Arminius, he sought to give his bold state permanence through alliances with other German kingdoms."[36] As a leader and ruler, then, Arminius was a failure in comparison to Theodoric.

A second problem with focusing too much attention on Arminius' victory in the Teutoburger Forest was that it came at the expense of the Romans. Here, politics and race came into conflict. Almost everyone agreed that the ancient Romans were not Aryans. But the Nazis were not unified on the question of what this meant for the historical status of Roman culture. For a racially-obsessed theorist such as Rosenberg, the question was easy: race trumped culture and Germans were thus always better than Romans. But Hitler, whose cultural tastes were conventional, was not willing to subvert the traditional high place accorded Classical culture, even at the expense of a certain inconsistency in Nazi racial theory. As he put it, apparently responding to colleagues such as Rosenberg and Himmler who championed the Germans: "I cannot help remembering that, while our ancestors were making these vessels of stone and clay, over which our archaeologists rave, the Greeks had already built an Acropolis."[37] Nor was this just a question of how to interpret history; it also had a significant aspect of *Realpolitik*. Especially in 1940, it would not do simply to demonize on racial grounds Mussolini, a political ally who had famously associated himself with the ancient Romans and, in particular, Augustus, who had been emperor at the time of Varus's embarrassing defeat by the Germans.[38]

DG tried to tread the line between the Rome-centric position advocated by Hitler (on cultural-historical grounds) or the foreign office (which was thinking geopolitically) and Rosenberg's Germano-centrism. Thus, Theodoric is praised for "seeking, in his empire established on Italian soil, a peaceful balance between Romans and Germans."[39] But *DG* was also committed to a racial view of history; with such a world view, the differences between Romans and Germans were, in the end, irreconcilable. In the gallery was a large-scale photographic reproduction of a small section of the frieze of the column of Marcus Aurelius showing "captured German women" [Fig. 1].[40] According to the catalogue, the Romans always represented the Germans, verbally and visually, as racially and morally admirable: "The Germans are always shown conquered, but their bearing is always heroic, their appearance noble. Through inner greatness [*Größe*] they overcome their external fate and clear the path into freedom for their successors with the sword and the power of their blood."[41] This doesn't suggest any great possibility for allegiance between Romans and Germans or Fascists and Nazis. The fact that the section of the triumphal column chosen depicted captured *women* surely does nothing to put the

Romans in a positive light (although this photograph, in a nod to foreign policy, was displayed adjacent to one showing the Roman emperor Trajan receiving, apparently on equal terms, a Germanic embassy).[42]

A different indication of the contested legacy of Germanic art and culture during this period of the Third Reich is the display of works of art and material culture in this gallery. The catalogue lists twenty-two pieces of metalwork and ceramic under a carefully constructed, but politically unambiguous rubric: "Germanic [*Germanische*] finds from various German [*deutschen*] tribal regions, in part outside the current borders of the Reich."[43] The point here is the old one: the racial borders of the German lands (where Germans live) do not correspond to the actual political ones; this is so even in 1940, when the borders of the Third Reich had recently been expanded by invasion. But this political point was partially undercut because, uniquely in *DG*, some of these objects were originals. And this is an exhibition that explicitly forbade originals because of Hitler's concern to preserve the Germanic heritage! The issue was not one of curatorial convenience; originals from Berlin collections were displayed alongside reproductions of pieces from the same museums. Nor was it one of quality. While some of the originals displayed were, indeed, objects of lower quality and less precious workmanship, the group of originals included a garnet-inlaid silver buckle (described as "especially beautiful") and an eagle fibula.[44] The point seems clear; Germanic objects were in such large supply that, in contrast to other parts of the exhibition, the loss or damage of a few originals, even a few precious, "especially beautiful" examples, wouldn't really make a difference. Here, Hitler's taste and cultural understanding have trumped Rosenberg's; Germanic objects simply aren't perceived as important enough in the scheme of world culture (or even to a history of German culture) for their potential loss to be a real concern. This appears to be a concrete manifestation of Hitler's belief that "[W]hile our ancestors were making these vessels of stone and clay…the Greeks had already built an Acropolis."

We have seen that Arminius was a conflicted figure for the designers of *DG* because he was a political failure. So too, in the end, was Theodoric. The Ostrogothic king tried to rule Italian land with Germanic blood, but Nazi *Blut und Boden* ideology made clear that such a project was destined for failure, since Theodoric's German blood was in clear and eventually disastrous conflict with the Italian land on which he found himself: "the removal [of the Ostrogoths] from their ancestral soil [*Boden*] as a result of the Hunnish invasions…led to the end of the Ostrogothic empire."[45] This turned out to be not only good Nazi thought but also good exhibition design. For it led naturally from room two, the room of promising starts but ultimate failures, to the next gallery, dedicated to the Frankish kingdoms. As the catalogue put it, immediately after describing the failure of Theodoric's empire: "The Franks were the first Germanic people who maintained the connection with their homeland and therefore did not fall apart…."[46]

Gallery three of *DG* had a central axis formed by reproductions of the thirteenth-century tomb of the eighth-century Saxon duke Widukind, in the middle of the gallery, and the small bronze equestrian statue of Charlemagne on the back wall [Figs. 3-4 show this gallery in two different configurations].[47] The representation of Widukind and Charlemagne in

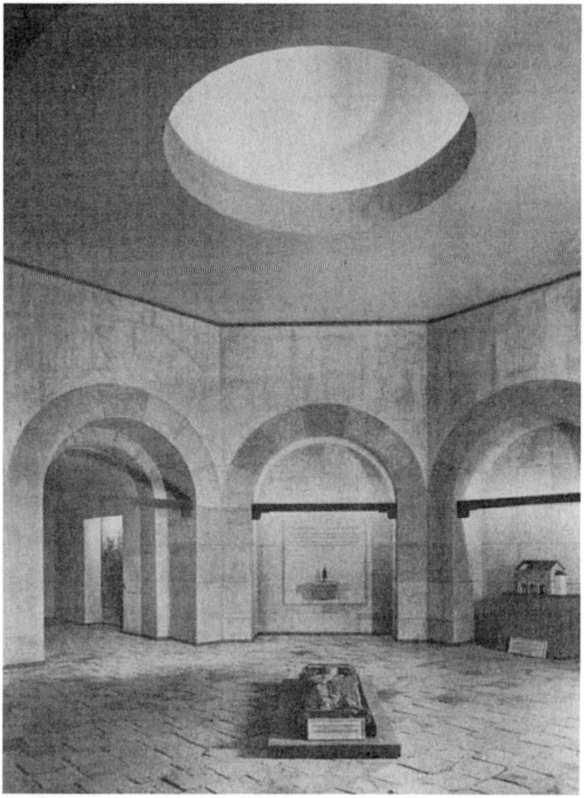

Fig. 3 "Das Fränkische Reich" ("The Frankish Empire"), gallery three (version one), *Deutsche Größe*, from *Deutsche Grösse*, ed. H. Hagemeyer (Munich: Franz Eher, 1944). 53

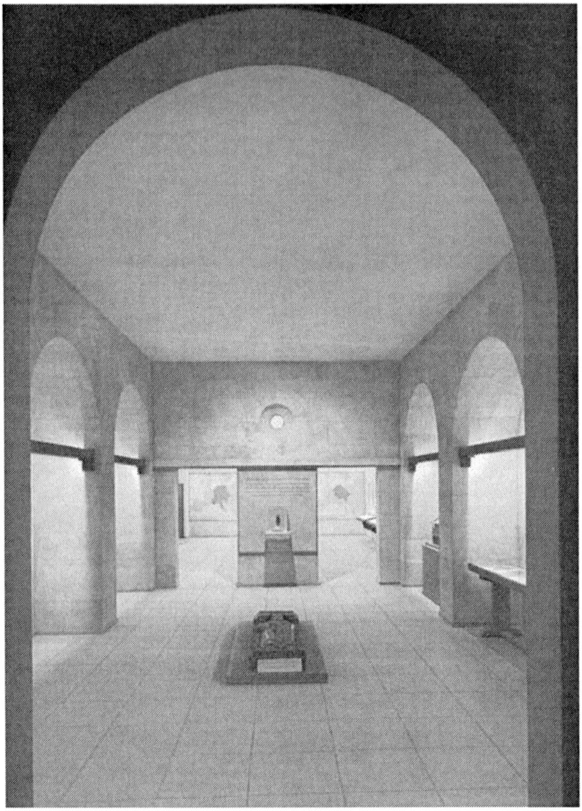

Fig. 4 "Das Fränkische Reich" ("The Frankish Empire"), gallery three (version two), *Deutsche Größe*, from Karlheinz Rüdiger, "Deutsche Grösse. Ein Beispiel künstlerischer Ausstellungsgestaltung," *Die Kunst im Deutschen Reich 5* (1941). 35

prominent places reflects a similar compromise regarding the proper representation of early medieval history to that in the previous gallery. But here the compromise was even more fraught for, unlike Arminius and Theodoric, who lived centuries apart, Widukind and Charlemagne were contemporaries and enemies; one of Charlemagne's greatest achievements (or worst crimes) was the forced Christianization of the Saxons, led by Widukind. Rosenberg had long championed Widukind's resistance to Charlemagne.[48] He favored Widukind primarily because the duke, a Saxon, was German to the core. Charlemagne, by contrast, was born in Belgium; this led some Nazis to ask if the first Carolingian emperor was better called by his French name, "Charlemagne," rather than "Karl der Grosse."[49] A second strike against Charlemagne, and a sign that his racial makeup might be suspect, was the fact that he led a brutal war against the Saxons; a favorite Nazi epithet for him was "Sachsenschlächter" ("butcher of the Saxons"). Further to Widukind's credit was his paganism. Widukind remained untainted by the Christianity that Charlemagne embraced (accepting his imperial crown from the pope, for instance) and that, for Rosenberg and the Nazi neo-pagans, was to be rejected. Rosenberg's position is clear from the title of an article about a 1934 speech he made at several Widukind cult sites in Saxony: "Duke Widukind lost in the ninth century; in the twentieth, he triumphed in Adolf Hitler."[50]

The fierce conflict over the two historical figures had been moderated in 1936, apparently through Hitler's direct intervention. Under the compromise, both Widukind and Charlemagne were to be regarded favorably. Hitler's decision again shows the triumph of politics over the purest ideology. As the Nazis consolidated and expanded their power, Widukind had to be rejected for reasons much like those that caused the ultimate rejection of Arminius and Theodoric as models—he did not convey the right message. In Widukind's case, the main problem was that, while his *Blut* and his *Boden* were good (as were his politics), he was ultimately a parochial loser. While Widukind had been an appropriate exemplar in the early days of the Nazis, as they struggled to establish themselves in Germany, his lack of success meant that, as the Nazis increased their political and military aims, the emperor Charlemagne, who ruled a united Europe that included France, Germany, the Low Countries, and Italy—all Nazi ambitions—gained favor.[51]

The catalogue to *DG* nicely resolves the debate. About Widukind's tomb we are told that the duke is represented as the "progenitor" of German kings and emperors since, through his descendants, centuries later, the Saxon emperors were able to renew Charlemagne's claims of rulership.[52] Regarding the equestrian statue, by contrast, the catalogue writes that Charlemagne "is the founder of the West," thanks to his amalgamation of the northern with the southern and his "forceful conquest" of the non-Frankish German tribes.[53] Rosenberg's earlier allegiance to Widukind is perhaps evinced in the gallery's design; the Saxon's tomb is in the center of the gallery and is much larger than the equestrian statue, which appears dwarfed. The powerful effect created by the tomb was noted by one visitor to the exhibition, who wrote that the tomb's presence caused "the viewer to walk through this room in reverent silence."[54]

Yet, while the figurative representation of Charlemagne may be minuscule in comparison to that of Widukind, the Carolingian emperor triumphs over the Saxon duke architectonically. The gallery's architectural conception is obviously derived from Charlemagne's palace chapel at Aachen, which the catalogue calls "the most important building of the era" [Fig. 3].[55] In the tension between Widukind's figurative and Charlemagne's architectural dominance, we see the tension inherent in the Widukind/Charlemagne debate.

Gallery three also contained several vitrines. One, just to the right of the equestrian statue, held a model of the Lorsch gateway, identified as the entryway to a Carolingian royal hall and said to simplify the form of a Roman city gate.[56] This derivation of the *Torhalle* from Roman architecture will surprise no contemporary medievalist, although most scholars now follow the 1942 article of the German-Jewish emigré Richard Krautheimer in seeing Roman triumphal arches, rather than city gates, as the *Torhalle*'s inspiration.[57] Important here, however, is that *DG*, just as with Theodoric's mausoleum, rejected other, ultra-Germanic Nazi treatments of the Lorsch gate. For example, in a 1936 SS periodical, Erich Kulke explicitly questioned the derivation of the *Torhalle* from Roman models and argued, instead, that the best comparison for the Lorsch gate was with the gates of two farms on the lower Rhine. He used the visual parallels to argue, in the typical Nazi art-historical manner, that there was a racial connection between the builders of these farm gateways and the *Torhalle*, and that these racial connections were manifested in the form of the two structures.[58]

One of the ideologically most telling objects to be included in the exhibition was the Tassilo chalice [Fig. 5]. Although the chalice is now one of the central monuments of early medieval art, Sibylle Ehringhaus has claimed that it is a relatively new addition to the canon.[59] Ehringhaus suggested that the chalice became especially prized only after World War II and in the Federal Republic of Germany, where it was used to argue that, from an early date, Germany had Christian rulers and so was very much part of Western Europe allied against the godless (pagan or Communist) East. According to Ehringhaus, the Nazis, by contrast, were uninterested in the Tassilo chalice because of their hostility to Christianity. But Ehringhaus misreads the Nazi era as having a single attitude toward early medieval history. She is certainly right that, for pro-Germanic, anti-Christian neo-pagans, such as Rosenberg and Himmler, the Tassilo chalice, a Eucharistic vessel, might not have constituted a treasured object. But as early as 1940, an alternative conception of the early Middle Ages was developing in official Nazi circles.

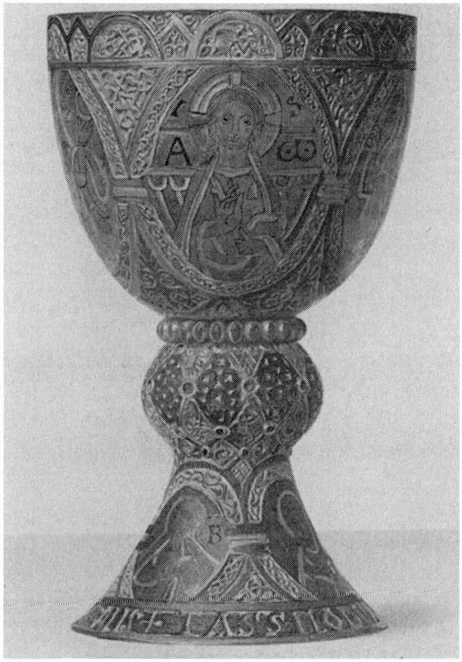

Fig. 5 Tassilo chalice, Kresmünster, Benediktinerstift, from *Kunstgewerbe des frühen Mittelalters*, ed. E. H. Zimmermann (Vienna: Österreichische Staasdruckerei, 1923). Pl. 22

One of the major themes expressed by the works on display in *DG* was that Christianity could be reconciled with Germanic paganism. The Tassilo chalice works to do this, as do other objects, including the manuscript of Otfried of Weissenburg's German translation of the gospels: "This work is an important feat; composed in German, it represents an attempt to nationalize Christianity in accord with Frankish-Christian culture."[60] The contorted vocabulary and syntax here indicate the tension between the neo-pagan and European/Christian points of view. A similar point was made by displaying a facsimile manuscript of *Heliand*, the Old Saxon poem telling the story of Christ and, even more strikingly, by the presentation of a reproduction of the purse reliquary from Enger, said in the catalogue probably to have been a gift from Charlemagne to Widukind at his baptism in 785.[61] This characterization of the Enger reliquary was a major provocation to the neo-pagan camp, which regarded the story of Widukind's reconciliation with Charlemagne, culminating in the duke's baptism, as a later and false Christian interpolation. The new power of this view of the early Middle Ages as European and Christian is clear from the inclusion of the Enger reliquary in an exhibition produced by Rosenberg's office.

But perhaps Rosenberg had the last laugh with the presentation of the Tassilo chalice at *DG*. It would have been possible, in 1940, to display the chalice as a relic of an era in which Germany, rather than being a country that insularly championed only itself, was a dominant European force, leading a unified, Christian Western Europe against an Eastern/Slavic other. (Precisely this reading of the chalice, as Ehringhaus rightly argued, was what made it so popular during the Cold War in West Germany.) Rosenberg's office took a different tack, however. The earlier battle for Widukind's supremacy at Charlemagne's expense had been lost, making it impossible to champion Widukind in the exhibit. But Rosenberg's staff found an almost perfect substitute in another Germanic duke, Tassilo of Bavaria. Thus, in *DG*, the Tassilo chalice was said to "represent in the Carolingian era the Germanic art of the brave Bavarian duke Tassilo, deposed by Charlemagne."[62] Under this reading, the Bavarian Tassilo is the double of the Saxon Widukind. Indeed, in light of the famous Bavarian parochialism of *DG*'s original Munich audience, this local hero, suppressed by the outsider Charlemagne, was perhaps an even better candidate to express Rosenberg's emphasis on German-ness than his north German counterpart.

In the 1930s, the Nazis fiercely disputed amongst themselves whether the Carolingian reconciliation of Christianity and Germanic heritage was admirable. By 1940, however, there was almost unanimous agreement that the Carolingians were usefully understood as "Germans" who ruled other countries in Europe, notably France. This point was made by another facsimile displayed in *DG*, the *Codex Aureus* of Saint Emmeram. This manuscript gospel book is primarily of interest today as one of the most spectacular objects of the early Middle Ages, made somewhere in northern France for the Carolingian emperor Charles the Bald. *DG* did not ignore this aspect of the *Codex Aureus*. Although the book's patron is not mentioned (likely because he was a fierce rival to his half-brother Louis, auspiciously cognomened, from the National Socialist point of view, "the German"), the *Codex Aureus* is said to have been made in France, probably at Saint-Denis (as was commonly thought at the time). But even more prominent in the catalogue entry is information that typically does not get much emphasis in modern treatments of the book: the story of how it got to Germany at the end of the ninth century as a gift of the east Frankish (i.e. German) emperor Arnulf to the monastery of Saint

Emmeram in Regensburg. A French object, then, but one that had come to Germany as booty secured by a German ruler; this aspect of the history of the *Codex Aureus* must have delighted Rosenberg, since another of his duties, as head of the infamous "Einsatzstab Reichsleiter Rosenberg," was to strip French libraries of their treasures and bring them back to Germany.

A fitting conclusion to this account of the various ideological strands at work in the presentation of the early Middle Ages in *DG* comes from the history of how the exhibition treated the ivory Heribert comb [Fig. 6]. In the first edition of the catalogue, the comb was included in room three, devoted to the Frankish empire. This corresponds to the typical modern stylistic assessment, which sees the comb as an example of late Carolingian ivory carving from northern France.[63] That this placement of the ivory was problematic is apparent from the catalogue text, which notes that the comb "shows how the characteristic Ottonian plastic sense differs from the classical-Carolingian tradition."[64] This perception of the comb

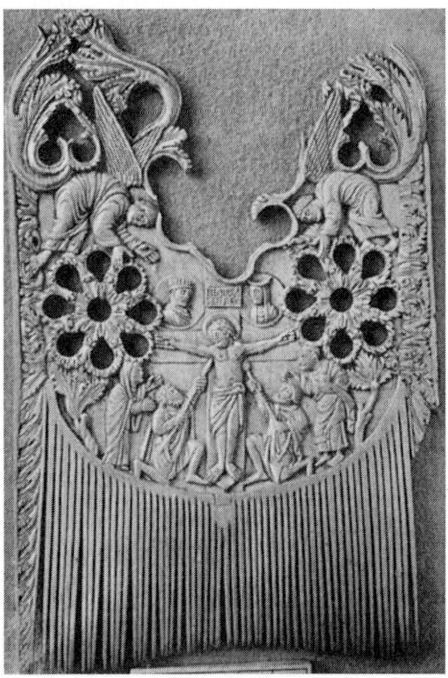

Fig. 6 Heribert comb, Schnütgen Museum, Cologne, from A. Goldschmidt, *Die Elfenbeinskulpturen aus der Zeit der karolingischen und sächsischen Kaiser, VIII-XI Jahrhundert*, vol. 1 (Berlin: Bruno Cassirer, 1914). Fig. 92a

came to dominate and, in the third edition of the catalogue, dated 1940-1941, the ivory had migrated to the next gallery, devoted to the first German emperors, the Saxons and Salians.[65] That the shift was not simply bureaucratic is made clear from a review, which says that the ivory's form "can, for the first time, be called completely German [*völlig deutsch*]."[66]

This moving of the Heribert comb in *DG* is just another example of what has now become a familiar story. The Nazis saw history as both typological (the past was a mirror to the present), and progressive and supercessionist, in that more recent eras were better than the older ones; this process culminated, of course, in the Nazi period, which was seen as the best of all. Thus, Theodoric trumped Arminius, but Charlemagne beat Theodoric. And even Charlemagne had his flaws; his imperial crown and European dominance were pluses, but he could be accused of being too cosmopolitan. The still later Heribert comb, by contrast, avoided that charge; it was "völlig deutsch." But the logic of Nazi historiography would require that it, too, be superseded by something more closely resembling the ideal Nazi present. Rosenberg's assistant Hans Hagemeyer, the intellectual and administrative force behind *DG*, summed up this philosophy of history in a lapidary phrase when he wrote that Arminius, Theodoric, and Charlemagne were all "historically decisive, but also historically conditioned."[67]

While the presentation of the early Middle Ages in *DG* was of course propagandistic and ideological, the exhibition was not predictable in the way it represented the past. Although the Nazis had available a reading of the early Middle Ages that saw the period as pagan, Germanic, and centered in the borders of Germany established after the First World War, they also had available another and very different (but equally Nazi) view of the era, one which saw it as fusing pagan and Christian, Germanic and Mediterranean, and encompassing both the post-1918 borders of Germany and those established through Hitler's military conquests of 1939 and 1940. It is the tension between these two views and their attempted reconciliation that is expressed in *DG*'s complex presentation of the early Middle Ages. It is important to recognize that the complexity of interpreting the period does not derive from the unique peculiarities of Nazi historiography. In the twentieth century, the Middle Ages were often an object of fascination; the era was represented nostalgically, as an ideal period of social, religious, and ideological harmony; reviled as thoroughly anti-modern; or, most typically, perceived as some combination of these extremes. Germany, with its rich medieval heritage and its exceptionally turbulent modern history, was the site of some of the most striking, and therefore most interesting, twentieth-century confrontations with and uses of the Middle Ages.[68] Like all modern interpretations of this distant, strange, and fascinating period, *Deutsche Größe* continually struggled to make sense of the era and to use it.

Notes

---

[1] This article forms part of a book-length project on the exhibition of early medieval art in twentieth-century Germany. It benefited greatly from critical comments by Alyce Jordan, Janet Marquardt, and an anonymous reader and was supported by Reed College in the form of Stillman Drake and Dean's Summer Scholarship Funds.

[2] "Zweifellos die eigenartigste und eindrucksstärkste, anschaulichste und imposanteste Schau dieser Art, die es jemals in Deutschland gegeben." Peter Trumm, "Deutsche Größe—Vermächtnis und Anspruch," *Münchner Abendblatt*, 8 November 1940. 3. Unless otherwise noted, all translations are my own.

The only even moderately extended discussions of *DG* known to me are: Christoph Kivelitz, *Die Propagandaausstellung in europäischen Diktaturen* (Bochum: Verlag Dr. Dieter Winkler, 1999). 205-208; Hans-Ulrich Thamer, "Geschichte und Propaganda. Kulturhistorische Ausstellungen in der NS-Zeit," *Geschichte und Gesellschaft* 24 (1998). 355-356; and Karen Schönwälder, *Historiker und Politik* (Frankfurt: Campus, 1992). 234-237. The present article is the pendant to another, more general one, "The Exhibition Deutsche Größe: Planning, Execution, Ideology" (in preparation), that lays out the organization and reception of *DG*.

[3] Data from Bundesarchiv (hereafter BA), NS8/247, Berlin. 290-293; these statistics were compiled by Rosenberg's office and so may be inflated.

[4] "Hier wurde zum erstenmal eine Ausstellung ausschließlich unter politischen Gesichtspunkten durchgeführt." Karlheinz Rüdiger, "Deutsche Grösse. Ein Beispiel künstlerischer Ausstellungsgestaltung," *Die Kunst im Deutschen Reich* 5 (1941). 41

[5] "Es ist (anderseits) *nicht* die Aufgabe der Ausstellung 'Deutsche Größe,' nun die *ganze* deutsche Geschichte in *allen* ihren Höhen und Tiefen und mit *all* ihrem Reichtum der Persönlichkeiten von unserem Auge vorüberziehen zu lassen. *Dieses* große Werk *mag später* eine *kommende Friedenszeit* gestalten. *Wir* haben uns hier aber die Aufgabe gestellt, aus der ungeheuren Fülle die *geschichtsmächtigen* Kräfte und *entscheidenden* Gestalten der *großen* Epochen herausergreifen und sie als *Blickpunkt* für die unmittelbare Anschauung in unser Bewußtsein zu erheben. In *Räumen*, die *nicht* nach dem Beispiel *alter Museen* einen *antiquarisch sentimentalen* Charakter haben, sondern nur durch eine *architektonische Andeutung* das Stilgefühl der bestimmten Epoche abgrenzen, soll die Entwicklung der Machtkämpfe um den deutschen Raum und um das Deutsche Reich vor jenen erstehen, die *schon* ein allgemeines Verstehen für diese Kämpfe mitbringen." BA, NS8/62. 201-205, which appears to be the text from which Rosenberg delivered the speech; the italicized words in the German text and the English translation

reproduce handwritten or typed underlinings in the original.

[6] "Unsichtbares, Abstraktes, Gedanken, Ideen, Mächte, Kräfte mußten sichtbar gemacht werden, aber was konnte, was sollte man zeigen?" Peter Trumm, "Vermächtnis und Anspruch," *Das Reich*, 17 November 1940. 26

[7] Memorandum of telephone call from Bormann to Amt Rosenberg, 26 September 1940, BA, NS 8/247.

[8] "So sahen wir uns gezwungen—und es ist der Ausstellung durchaus zum Guten gereicht—die Originale alle nachbilden zu lassen, damit der Plan der ganzen Ausstellung verwirklicht werden konnte. Die Ausstellung hat dadurch gerade einen sehr einheitlichen und modernen Zug bekommen, und nahezu unfreiwillig ist tatsächlich ein ganz neues Muster für die Ausstellungsform geschaffen worden." Rosenberg to Schwarz, 28 January 1941, BA, NS1/945.

[9] Bauer to Schwarz, 29 January 1941, BA, NS 1/945. The use of reproductions in *DG* needs to be understood as part of a widespread debate about authenticity in the German museum world (and, more generally, German intellectual life) during the Weimar era and the Third Reich. I discuss this complex issue more fully in "The Exhibition Deutsche Größe: Planning, Execution, Ideology."

[10] The catalogue is *Ausstellung Deutsche Größe*, 3rd ed. (Berlin: Wilhelm Limpert, 1940-1941). (hereafter *ADG*); the later publication is *Deutsche Grösse*, ed. H. Hagemeyer (Munich: Franz Eher, 1944).

[11] "Dieser Kampf der Gegenwart fordert das Bewußtein über Wesen und Mächtigkeit des Ringens der Vergangenheit." *ADG*. 3

[12] See the list of participating scholars on the last page of *ADG*; Petri's name is not on this list, but he contributed an essay to *Ausstellung Deutsche Grösse* (Brussels: no publisher, 1942), the catalogue produced to accompany the Brussels showing of *DG*.

[13] *ADG*. 38-39. For reproductions of the various eagles, see Hagemeyer, *Deutsche Grösse*. 23-24

[14] *ADG*. 5 for a list of rooms.

[15] Also relevant to the early Middle Ages, but not treated here for lack of space, were the following two rooms, both devoted to "Das Altdeutsche Kaiserreich"; one was on the Saxon and Salian rulers, the other on the Staufer.

[16] "Der Eintritt der Germanen als geschichtsgestaltende Faktoren in die Welt der Antike bedeutet den Aufstieg einer neuen Welt, die Geburt Europas und den Beginn einer Weltgeschichte unter europäischen Vorzeichen." *ADG*. 41

[17] The following paragraphs draw on the background provided by Sibylle Ehringhaus, *Germanenmythos und deutsche Identität. Die Frühmittelalter-Rezeption in Deutschland 1842-1933* (Weimar: Verlag und Datenbank für Geisteswissenschaften, 1996).

[18] "nicht nur militärisch, sondern auch kulturell als überlegen erwies." *ADG*. 41

[19] Eric Michaud, "Images of Nazi Time: Accelerations and Immobilizations," chap. 5 of *The Cult of Art in Nazi Germany*, trans. J. Lloyd (Stanford: Stanford University Press, 2004).

[20] The specifically Nazi connotations of "Führer" are well known; for the special senses of "Gefolgschaft" during the Third Reich see R. Michael and K. Doerr, *Nazi*

Deutsch/Nazi German (Westport: Greenwood Press, 2002), svv. "Gefolgschaft," "Gefolgschaftsappell," "Gefolgschaftsführer," and "Gefolgschaftssparen."

[21] "Während die germanischen Völker noch auf dem Wege zu Staatenbildungen waren, stieg aus den Steppen Asiens die Gefahr der Vernichtung des werdenden Europas." *ADG*. 45

[22] "Überall aber in Europa, wo germanische Völker ihre frühen Reiche gründeten, blieben unzählige Werte der dinglichen Kultur, blieben Reste ihrer Volksordnungen erhalten bis in die Gegenwart. Germanisches Blut blieb lebendig in vielen Völkern unserer Zeit, sein Anteil an Geschichte und Kultur dieser Länder ist nicht meßbar." *ADG*. 47; Michael and Doerr, *Nazi Deutsch/Nazi German*, define "Volksordnung" as "the only true (German) order."

[23] "Aus dieser urgermanischen Zeit hat der deutsche Boden eine große Anzahl bedeutsamer Funde für unsere Tage bewahrt. Diese *unwiderlegbaren* Dokumente beweisen uns die Germanen nicht nur als erfolgreiche Ackerbauer und Viehzüchter, sondern auch als technisch und künstlerisch hochbegabte Handwerker (my emphasis)." *ADG*. 42

[24] For an additional view of room two see Hagemeyer, *Deutsche Grösse*. 38

[25] *Arminius und die Varusschlacht. Geschichte-Mythos-Literatur*, ed. R. Wiegels and W. Woesler (Paderborn: Schöningh, 1995). esp. Volker Losemann "Nationalistische Interpretationen der römisch-germanischen Auseinandersetzung." 419-432; and M. Fansa, ed., *Varusschlacht und Germanenmythos* (Oldenburg: Isensee Verlag, 1994).

[26] For photographs of all of these objects see Hagemeyer, *Deutsche Grösse*. 41-44

[27] Each historical gallery of *DG* also displayed a series of modern books on the room's subject. The titles are listed in the catalogue. These books may have been in vitrines in this niche, although none are clearly visible in the photographs.

[28] "Der Raum ist im Stil des Grabmales von Theoderich…gehalten." *ADG*. 48. The catalogue goes on to claim that Theoderic's mausoleum is "an allegory of Theoderic's rule." ("Das Grabmal ist ein Gleichnis für Theoderichs Herrschaft.") *ADG*. 49. The logic here is not entirely clear, but seems to rest on the notion that the building, by its size and massiveness, expressed Theodoric's overwhelming force.

[29] "Man ist versucht, hinter seinem Handeln das Ziel eines einheitlichen Germanenreiches zu ahnen, das ganz Europa beherrschte." *ADG*. 46-47

[30] "Über ein halbes Jahrhundert regierte dieser Größte der Goten, eroberte Italien und hinterließ dort unsterbliche Beweise seiner Größe." *ADG*. 46

[31] R. Krautheimer, *Early Christian and Byzantine Architecture*, 2nd ed. (Harmondsworth: Penguin Books, 1975). 286

[32] "in der Art altgermanischer Fürstengräber." *ADG*. 46. The mausoleum is also compared to "a Germanic megalithic tomb" ("germanisches Hünengrab"). *ADG*. 49

[33] For a particularly strained attempt to associate Theodoric's tomb with "Germanic" trends see Hermann Phleps, "Das Theoderich-Grabmal in Ravenna vom Norden aus gesehen," *Germanen-Erbe* 1, 2 (June, 1936). 41-47; Phelps's article is discussed in Ehringhaus, *Germanenmythos und deutsche Identität*. 66

[34] Karl Richard Ganzer, *Das Deutsche Führergesicht*, 3rd ed. (Munich: J. F. Lehmanns Verlag, 1939). Ganzer's book was first published in 1935.

[35] *ADG*. 50

[36] Theodoric "sucht im Unterschied zu dem vorübergehenden Erfolg des Arminius seinen [sic] kühnen Staat durch Bündnisse mit anderen Germanenreichen Dauer zu verleihen." Hagemeyer, *Deutsche Grösse*. 43. It is telling that Arminius is not called by the German form of his name, Hermann.

[37] *Hitler's Table Talk 1941-1944*, trans. N. Cameron and R. H. Stevens (New York: Enigma Books, 2000). 566. For the German see Henry Picker, *Hitlers Tischgespräche im Führerhauptquartier*, ed. G. Ritter (Bonn: Athenäum, 1951). 315

[38] I owe this last observation to Janet Marquardt.

[39] Theodoric "hat…den friedlichen Ausgleich zwischen Römern und Germanen gesucht." *ADG*. 51

[40] "gefangene germanische Frauen." *ADG*. 42

[41] "Stets sind die Germanen als Besiegte dargestellt, stets aber ist ihre Haltung heldisch, ihre Erscheinung edel. Durch innere Größe überwinden sie ihr äußeres Schicksal und bahnen ihren Nachfahren den Weg in die Freiheit durch das Schwert und die Kraft des Blutes." *ADG*. 49

[42] *ADG*. 49; reproduced in Hagemeyer, *Deutsche Grösse*. 42

[43] "Germanische Funde aus verschiedenen deutschen Stammesgebieten, z. T. außerhalb des heutigen Reichsgebietes." *ADG*. 51

[44] *ADG*. 52

[45] "Die Loslösung vom angestammten Boden als Folge der Hunneneinfälle…hat das Ende des Ostgotenreiches (554) herbeigeführt." *ADG*. 51

[46] "Die Franken sind das erste Germanenvolk gewesen, das die Verbindung mit der Heimat aufrechterhielt und daher nicht…zerbrach." *ADG*. 51

[47] As is apparent from a comparison of Figs. 3-4, this gallery was installed in at least two different ways in the various venues of *DG*. Version one mimicked an octagon [Fig. 3]; version two was rectangular [Fig. 1 background, Fig. 4]. For additional views of version two see Hagemeyer, *Deutsche Grösse*. 38; and H. Biberger, "Deutsche Geschichte—Deutsche Größe. Zewi Wege zu deren Veranschaulichung," *Deutsche Technik* 9 (1941). 201 (I would like to thank Eve Duffy for bringing this important article to my attention.)

[48] Alfred Rosenberg, "Der erste Dreißigjährige Krieg," in his *Gestaltung der Idee. Blut und Ehre II. Band. Reden und Aufsätze von 1933-1935*, ed. T. von Trotha (Munich: Franz Eher, 1936). 107-115

[49] See *Karl der Große oder Charlemagne? Acht Antworten deutscher Geschichtsforscher* (Berlin: E. S. Mittler & Sohn, 1935).

[50] Kurt Jeserich, "Herzog Widukind unterlag im IX. Jahrhundert, im XX. hat er in Adolf Hitler gesiegt," *Völkischer Beobachter*, 26 June 1934. There is, at present, no comprehensive account of the Nazi representation of Widukind; see Wolfgang Balz, "Die Widukind-Gedächtnisstätte im Spiegel nationalsozialistischer Ideologie," *Stadt Enger—Beiträge zur Stadtgeschichte*, vol. 2 (Enger: Stadt Enger, 1983). 17-40; Justus H. Ulbricht, "'Heil Dir, Wittekinds Stamm.' Verden, der

'Sachsenhain' und die Geschichte völkischer Religiosität in Deutschland," *Heimatkalender für den Landkreis Verden*, 1995. 69-123; Justus H. Ulbricht, "'Heil Dir, Wittekinds Stamm.' Verden, der 'Sachsenhain' und die Geschichte völkischer Religiosität in Deutschland," *Heimatkalender für den Landkreis Verden*, 1996. 224-267; Walter Zöllner, *Karl oder Widukind? Martin Lintzel und die NS-"Geschichtsdeutung" in den Anfangsjahren der faschistischen Diktatur* (Halle: Martin-Luther-Universität, 1975); and esp. Rolf Köhn, "Kirchenfeindliche und antichristliche Mittelalter-Rezeption im völkisch-nationalsozialistischen Geschichtsbild: die Beispiele Widukind und Stedinger," in *Mittelalter-Rezeption. Ein Symposion*, ed. P. Wapnewski (Stuttgart: J. B. Metzler, 1986). 581-609; on the National Socialist conception of Charlemagne see Karl Ferdinand Werner, "Karl der Grosse in der Ideologie des Nationalsozialismus. Zur Verantwortung deutscher Historiker für Hitlers Erfolg," *Zeitschrift des Aachener Geschichtsvereins* 101 (1997-1998). 9-64

[51] For a strong representation of Charlemagne as the ruler of western Europe against an eastern enemy see Kurt Borries, "Die Staatsschöpfung Karls des Grossen," *Deutschland-Frankreich* 1, 2 (1942). 122-128

[52] *ADG*. 75

[53] "Er ist der Begründer des Abendlandes." *ADG*. 78

[54] "das [Grabmal] den Beschauer in ehrfurchtsvollem Schweigen diesen Raum durchwandern läßt." Biberger, "Deutsche Geschichte." 206

[55] "das bedeutendste Bauwerk der Zeit." *ADG*. 75. The dependence of the gallery's design on Aachen is much more apparent in the first version of the installation [Fig. 3], which mimics the chapel's unusual octagonal plan.

[56] *ADG*. 78

[57] Richard Krautheimer, "The Carolingian Revival of Early Christian Architecture," *Art Bulletin* 24 (1942). 1-38

[58] Erich Kulke, "Die Halle zu Lorsch, ein Werk germanischer Hoftorbaukunst," *Germanien* 5 (1936). 136-139. *Germanien*, associated in this period with the SS research institute the "Ahnenerbe," stood bureaucratically in direct opposition to the Rosenberg-supported journal *Germanen-Erbe*, although it would be difficult to find any real intellectual differences in the editorial attitudes of the two.

[59] Ehringhaus, *Germanenmythos und deutsche Identität*. 59-61

[60] "Das Werk ist eine bedeutende Tat. Es ist in deutscher Sprache gedichtet und stellt sich dar als ein Versuch, das Christentum im Sinne der fränkisch-christlichen Kultur zu nationalisieren." *ADG*. 80

[61] *ADG*. 79

[62] "vertritt der Kelch des tapferen, von Karl dem Großen abgesetzten Bayernherzogs Tassilo gemanische Kunst in karolingischer Zeit." *ADG*. 79

[63] For a survey of modern opinions on the comb, see A[nton] L[egner], "Kamm des hl. Heribert," in *Ornamenta ecclesiae*, ed. A. Legner, vol. 2 (Cologne: Schnütgen Museum, 1985). cat. no. E 92

[64] "zeigt, wie sich die ottonische Eigengestaltung von der antik-karolingischen Tradition abhebt." *Ausstellung Deutsche Größe* (Berlin: Wilhelm Limpert, 1940). 80. This quotation comes from a different catalogue than the one cited throughout

as *ADG.*
[65] *ADG.* 91
[66] "zum ersten Male als völlig deutsch anzusprechen ist." Josef Magnus Wehner, "2000 Jahre deutscher Größe. Gedanken zur Münchener Ausstellung," *Das Reich*, 1 December 1940. 19; for another attempt to define a different Ottonian ivory carver as the first true German artist see William J. Diebold, "'Except I shall see…I will not believe' (John 20:25): Typology, Theology, and Historiography in an Ottonian Ivory Diptych," in *Objects, Images, and The Word: Art in the Service of the Liturgy*, ed. C. Hourihane (Princeton: Princeton University Press, 2003). 257-273
[67] "zeitbestimmend, aber auch zeitbedingt." Hagemeyer, *Deutsche Grösse.* 354
[68] As an introduction to this topic see the stimulating essay by Otto Gerhard Oexle, "Das Mittelalter und das Unbehagen an der Moderne. Mittelalterbeschwörungen in der Weimarer Republik und danach," in *Spannungen und Widersprüche. Gedenkschrift für Frantisek Graus*, ed. S. Burghartz et al. (Sigmaringen: Jan Thorbecke, 1992). 1-29; reprinted in Otto Gerhard Oexle, *Geschichtswissenschaft im Zeichen des Historismus* (Göttingen: Vandenhoeck and Ruprecht, 1996). 137-162

CONTRIBUTORS

MARIAN BLEEKE (Ph.D., University of Chicago) is Assistant Professor of Art History at Cleveland State University. Her article "Sheelas, Sex, and Significance in Romanesque Sculpture: The Kilpeck Corbel Series" appeared in *Studies in Iconography* (2005).

KERRY BOEYE is a Ph.D. candidate in the Department of Art History at the University of Chicago, where he is completing a dissertation on illustrations of King Solomon in twelfth- and thirteenth-century manuscripts. He currently works for the University of Michigan Museum of Art and as a freelance editor.

KATHRYN BRUSH (Ph.D., Brown University) is Professor of Art History at the University of Western Ontario. Her publications include: *The Shaping of Art History: Wilhelm Vöge, Adolph Goldschmidt, and the Study of Medieval Art* (1996) and *Vastly More Than Brick and Mortar: Reinventing the Fogg Art Museum in the 1920s* (2003).

MEREDITH COHEN (Ph.D., Columbia University) is currently a Post-Doctoral Research Fellow at the Institute for Medieval Studies at the University of Leeds. She specializes in medieval French art and architecture and has published articles in the journals *Res* and *Speculum*, as well as in edited anthologies.

WILLIAM J. DIEBOLD (Ph.D., Johns Hopkins University) is Jane Neuberger Goodsell Professor of Art History and Humanities at Reed College. He is the author of *Word and Image: An Introduction to Early Medieval Art* (2000).

ELIZABETH EMERY (Ph.D., New York University) is Professor of French at Montclair State University. She is the author of *Romancing the Cathedral: Gothic Architecture in Fin-de-Siècle French Culture* (2001) and co-author of *Consuming the Past: The Medieval Revival in Fin-de-Siècle France* (2003), among other works about nineteenth-century French medievalism.

ALYCE JORDAN (Ph.D., Bryn Mawr College) is Associate Professor of Art History at Northern Arizona University. She has published articles in *Gesta* and *Word and Image*, as well as in several edited collections and is the author of *Visualizing Kingship in the Windows of the Sainte-Chapelle* (2002).

GRAŻYNA JURKOWLANIEC (Ph.D., University of Warsaw) is Assistant Professor at the Institute of Art History, University of Warsaw. Her dissertation was published as *Chrystus Umęczony. Ikonografia w Polsce od XIII do XVI wieku* [Iconography of the Man of Sorrows in Poland from the thirteenth to sixteenth century] (2001).

JANET T. MARQUARDT (Ph.D., University of California, Los Angeles) is Professor of Art History and Women's Studies at Eastern Illinois University. She is lead author of *Frames of Reference: Art, History, and the World* (2005). Her work on medieval France includes *From Martyr to Monument: The Abbey of Cluny as Cultural Patrimony* (2007).

LAURA MOROWITZ (Ph.D., Institute of Fine Arts, New York University) is Professor of Art History at Wagner College, New York. She is co-editor, with William Vaughan, of *Artistic Brotherhoods in the Nineteenth Century* (2000) and co-author of *Consuming the Past: The Medieval Revival in Fin-de-Siècle France* (2003).

ELIZABETH CARSON PASTAN (Ph.D., Brown University) is Associate Professor of Art History at Emory University and in 2006 received the Emory Williams Award for teaching excellence in the Humanities. She is the author of *Les Vitraux du choeur de la cathédrale de Troyes (XIIIe siècle)* with Sylvie Balcon, Corpus Vitrearum (2006).

DONNA L. SADLER (Ph.D., Indiana University) is Professor of Art History at Agnes Scott College. Her published works include: "Lessons Fit for a King," *Arte Medievale* (1995) and "Predictions, Prophecies, Prose, and Poetry on the Reverse Façade of Reims Cathedral," in *Perspectives for an Architecture of Silence* (2004).

MARY B. SHEPARD (Ph.D., Columbia University) has authored numerous articles on medieval art and its reception. She revised and edited *English and French Medieval Stained Glass in the Collection of The Metropolitan Museum of Art*, Corpus Vitrearum (2003), served as president of the

International Center of Medieval Art, and teaches at Friends University in Wichita, Kansas.

ANNE RUDLOFF STANTON (Ph.D., University of Texas at Austin) is Associate Professor of late medieval and Northern Renaissance art at the University of Missouri. Relevant publications include *The Queen Mary Psalter: a Study of Affect and Audience* (2001) and "Isabelle of France and her Manuscripts, 1308-1358," in *Capetian Women* (2003).

NANCY THOMPSON (Ph.D., Indiana University) is Associate Professor of Art History at Saint Olaf College. Her essays on Santa Croce appear in *The Art of the Franciscan Order in Italy* (2005) and *Gesta* (2004). She is currently examining Ulisse De Matteis and the revival of stained glass in nineteenth-century Florence.

DAVID WALSH (Ph.D., University of Minnesota) is Professor of History and Art History at the University of Rochester. Two examples of published work are: "The Iconography of the Bronze Doors of Barisanus of Trani," *Gesta* (1982) and S.M. Hirst, D.A. Walsh and S.M. Wright, *Bordesley Abbey II* (1983).

ANDREA WORM (Ph.D., University of Augsburg) is Assistant Professor at the University of Augsburg and a recent fellow at the University of Cambridge, where she also worked on the "Cambridge Illuminations Project." She has published *Das Pariser Perikopenbuch und die Anfänge der romanischen Buchmalerei an Rhein und Weser* (2008).